# 7th Global Wordnet Conference

# (GWC 2014)



## Tartu, Estonia
## 25-29 January 2014

**Editors:**

**Heili Orav**
**Christiane Fellbaum**
**Piek Vossen**

**ISBN: 978-1-63266-289-7**

**Printed from e-media with permission by:**

Curran Associates, Inc.
57 Morehouse Lane
Red Hook, NY 12571

**Some format issues inherent in the e-media version may also appear in this print version.**



Printed by Curran Associates, Inc. (2014)

For permission requests, please contact the Association for Computational Linguistics
at the address below.

Association for Computational Linguistics
209 N. Eighth Street
Stroudsburg, Pennsylvania 18360

Phone: 1-570-476-8006
Fax: 1-570-476-0860

acl@aclweb.org

**Additional copies of this publication are available from:**

Curran Associates, Inc.
57 Morehouse Lane
Red Hook, NY 12571 USA
Phone: 845-758-0400
Fax: 845-758-2634
Email: curran@proceedings.com
Web: www.proceedings.com

European Union
Regional Development Fund

Investing in your future

CLARIN
ERIC

Common Language Resources and Technology Infrastructure

Tartu
city of good thoughts

EXCS
ESTONIAN COMPUTING

Center of
Estonian Language
Resources

## ORGANIZATION

The seventh Global Wordnet Conference is organized by the University of Tartu, Institute of Computer Science in co-operation with the Global WordNet Association.
The conference homepage can be found at http://gwc2014.ut.ee/

## PROGRAMME COMMITEE

Eneko Agirre (University of the Basque Country), Francis Bond (Nanyang Technological University), Sonja Bosch (University of South Africa), Agata Cybulska (VU University Amsterdam), Christiane Fellbaum (Princeton University), Darja Fišer (University of Ljubljana), Yoshihiko Hayashi (Osaka University), Ales Horak (Masaryk University), Chu-Ren Huang (The Hong Kong Polytechnic University), Hitoshi Isahara (Toyohashi University of Technology), Kaarel Kaljurand (University of Zuerich), Kyoko Kanzaki (National Institute of Information and Communications Technology), Adam Kilgarriff (Lexical Computing Ltd), Kow Kuroda (National Institute of Information and Communications Technology), Margit Langemets (Institute of the Estonian Language), Haldur Õim (University of Tartu), Heili Orav (University of Tartu), Adam Pease (Articulate Software), Bolette Pedersen (University of Copenhagen), Ted Pedersen (University of Minnesota), Maciej Piasecki (Wroclaw University of Technology), German Rigau (IXA Group, UPV/EHU), Horacio Rodriguez (Universitat Politecnica de Catalunya), Virach Sornlertlamvanich (National Electronics and Computer Technology Center), Takenobu Tokunaga (Tokyo Institute of Technology), Gloria Vazquez (Universitat de Lleida), Zygmunt Vetulani (Adam Mickiewicz University), Kadri Vider (University of Tartu), Piek Vossen (VU University Amsterdam)

## ORGANIZING COMMITEE

Heili Orav (Chair)
Kairit Šor (Secretary)
Sven Aller (Homepage)
Sirli Parm, Kadri Vare, Katrin Alekand, Ingmar Jaska, Helen Türk, Eleri Aedma, Liisi Pool (Helpers)
Chistiane Fellbaum , Piek Vossen (Co-organisers)

## ADDITIONAL REVIEWERS

Kahusk, Neeme
Kubis, Marek
Marciniak, Jacek
Neverilova, Zuzana
Obrebski, Tomasz
Šmerk, Pavel

**Volume editors**
Heili Orav
University of Tartu
e-mail: heili.orav@ut.ee

Christiane Fellbaum
Princeton University
e-mail: fellbaum@princeton.edu

Piek Vossen
VU University Amsterdam
e-mail: piek.vossen@vu.nl

# Preface

The seventh Global WordNet Conference includes presentations about new wordnets in languages like Amharic, Kurdish and Northern Sotho. The map shows the countries where wordnets are built in the local languages; if one colored in all the regions where these languages are spoken, most of the world would be covered!

Beyond the emergence of new lexical resources, the global wordnet endeavor has generated and facilitated research in linguistics, computational linguistics, psycholinguistics, ontology, lexicology, mathematics and a wide range of practical applications. The presentations in this volume reflect the manifold activities of our thriving global wordnet community.

We are grateful to the colleagues who reviewed submissions and provided constructive criticism as well as to the local organizers who performed uncountable large and small tasks. And we thank all of you present here for making this an exciting meeting.

Tartu, January 2014

Christiane Fellbaum, Piek Vossen, Heili Orav

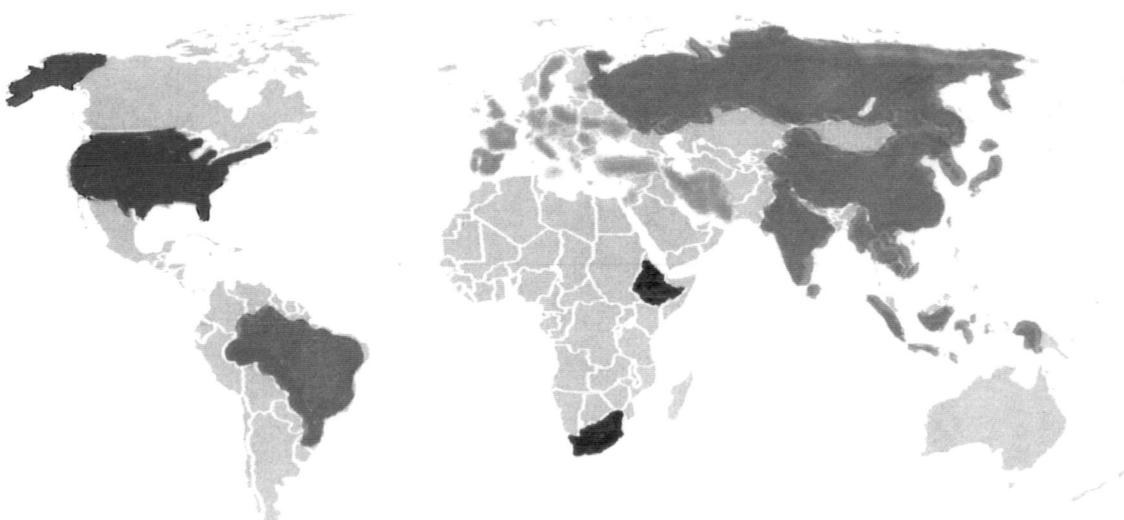

# Invited speaker: Alessandro Lenci

# Will Distributional Semantics Ever Become Semantic?

Computational Linguistics Laboratory
Dept. of Philology, Literature, and Linguistics
University of Pisa (Italy)

alessandro.lenci@ling.unipi.it

## Abstract

Distributional Semantics (DS) is a rich family of computational models that build semantic representations of lexical items from their statistical distribution in linguistic contexts. DS is currently experiencing an unprecedented fortune with a growing attention not only in computational linguistics, but also in cognitive science and theoretical linguistics. This is proved by the wide range of DS models that have appeared (e.g., vector spaces, Bayesian models, neural networks, etc.), but even more by the increased number of semantic tasks that these models have been applied to.

DS was born to address a specific issue, that is measuring the semantic similarity of lexical items to be used for thesaurus construction or synonym identification. The Distributional Hypothesis, the main theoretical foundation of DS, is in fact a statement about lexical semantic similarity, which is defined in terms of similarity of linguistic contexts. However, human semantic competence well exceeds the ability to judge lexical similarity. Polysemy, compositionality, inference, semantic creativity are only some of the main phenomena that must be part of the agenda of any full-fledged semantic theory. DS aims at becoming a general model for semantic representation and processing, and therefore it must be evaluated with respect to its ability to explain semantic facts like these. What is the current ability of DS to address these issues? To what extent semantic properties can be modeled in terms of distributional semantic similarity, or alternatively, can DS go beyond the mere notion of semantic similarity? What lies beyond its possibilities? Recently, DS has begun to address issues such as compositionality, polysemy, and semantic relations, but lots of questions remain open. The purpose of this talk is to explore the current boundaries of DS and the chances to enlarge them, in particular by finding new synergies with other types of semantic models.

# Table of Contents

# Towards Building KurdNet, the Kurdish WordNet

**Purya Aliabadi**
SRBIAU
Sanandaj, Iran
purya.it@gmail.com

**Mohammad Sina Ahmadi**
University of Kurdistan
Sanandaj, Iran
reboir.ahmadi@gmail.com

**Shahin Salavati**
University of Kurdistan
Sanandaj, Iran
shahin.salavati@ieee.org

**Kyumars Sheykh Esmaili**
Nanyang Technological University
Singapore
kyumarss@ntu.edu.sg

**Abstract**

In this paper we highlight the main challenges in building a lexical database for Kurdish, a resource-scarce and diverse language. We also report on our effort in building the first prototype of KurdNet – the Kurdish WordNet– along with a preliminary evaluation of its impact on Kurdish information retrieval.

## 1 Introduction

WordNet (Fellbaum, 1998) has been used in numerous natural language processing tasks such as word sense disambiguation and information extraction with considerable success. Motivated by this success, many projects have been undertaken to build similar lexical databases for other languages. Among the large-scale projects are EuroWordNet (Vossen, 1998) and BalkaNet (Tufis et al., 2004) for European languages and IndoWordNet (Bhattacharyya, 2010) for Indian languages.

Kurdish belongs to the Indo-European family of languages and is spoken in Kurdistan, a large geographical region spanning the intersections of Iran, Iraq, Turkey, and Syria. Kurdish is a less-resourced language for which, among other resources, no wordnet has been built yet.

We have recently launched the Kurdish language processing project (KLPP[1]), aiming at providing basic tools and techniques for Kurdish text processing. This paper reports on KLPP's first outcomes on building KurdNet, the Kurdish WordNet.

At a high level, our approach is semi-automatic and centered around building a Kurdish alignment for Base Concepts (Vossen et al., 1998), which is a core subset of major meanings in WordNet. More specifically, we use a bilingual dictionary and simple set theory operations to translate and align synsets and use a corpus to extract usage examples. The effectiveness of our prototype database is evaluated via measuring its impact on a Kurdish information retrieval task. Throughout, we have made the following contributions:

1. highlight the main challenges in building a wordnet for the Kurdish language (Section 2),
2. identify a list of available resources that can facilitate the process of constructing such a lexical database for Kurdish (Section 3),
3. build the first prototype of KurdNet, the Kurdish WordNet (Section 4), and
4. conduct a preliminary set of experiments to evaluate the impact of KurdNet on Kurdish information retrieval (Section 5).

Moreover, a manual effort to translate the glosses and refine the automatically-generated outputs is currently underway.

The latest snapshot of KurdNet's prototype is freely accessible and can be obtained from (KLPP, 2013). We hope that making this database publicly available, will bolster research on Kurdish text processing in general, and on KurdNet in particular.

## 2 Challenges

In the following, we highlight the main challenges in Kurdish text processing, with a greater focus on

[1] http://eng.uok.ac.ir/esmaili/research/klpp/en/main.htm

| | 1 | 2 | 3 | 4 | 5 | 6 | 7 | 8 | 9 | 10 | 11 | 12 | 13 | 14 | 15 | 16 | 17 | 18 | 19 | 20 | 21 | 22 | 23 | 24 |
|---|---|---|---|---|---|---|---|---|---|---|---|---|---|---|---|---|---|---|---|---|---|---|---|---|
| Arabic-based | ا | ب | ج | چ | د | ێ | ف | گ | ژ | ک | ل | م | ن | ۆ | پ | ق | ر | س | ش | ت | وو | ڤ | خ | ز |
| Latin-based | A | B | C | Ç | D | Ê | F | G | J | K | L | M | N | O | P | Q | R | S | Ş | T | Û | V | X | Z |

(a) One-to-One Mappings

| | 25 | 26 | 27 | 28 |
|---|---|---|---|---|
| Arabic-based | ئ / | و | ی | ە |
| Latin-based | I | U / W | Y / Î | E / H |

(b) One-to-Two Mappings

| | 29 | 30 | 31 | 32 | 33 |
|---|---|---|---|---|---|
| Arabic-based | ڕ | ڵ | ع | غ | ح |
| Latin-based | (RR) | - | (E) | (X) | (H) |

(c) One-to-Zero Mappings

Figure 1: The Two Standard Kurdish Alphabets (Esmaili and Salavati, 2013)

the aspects that are relevant to building a Kurdish wordnet.

### 2.1 Diversity

Diversity –in both dialects and writing systems– is the primary challenge in Kurdish language processing (Gautier, 1998; Gautier, 1996; Esmaili, 2012). In fact, Kurdish is considered a *bi-standard*[2] language (Gautier, 1998; Hassanpour et al., 2012): the **Sorani** dialect written in an Arabic-based alphabet and the **Kurmanji** dialect written in a Latin-based alphabet. Figure 1 shows both of the standard Kurdish alphabets and the mappings between them.

The linguistics features distinguishing these two dialects are phonological, lexical, and morphological. The important morphological differences that concern the construction of KurdNet are (MacKenzie, 1961; Haig and Matras, 2002): (i) in contrast to Sorani, Kurmanji has retained both gender (feminine v. masculine) and case opposition (absolute v. oblique) for nouns and pronouns, and (ii) while is Kurmanji passive voice is constructed using the helper verb "hatin", in Sorani it is created via verb morphology.

In summary, as the examples in (Gautier, 1998) show, the "same" word, when going from Sorani to Kurmanji, may at the same time go through several levels of change: writing systems, phonology, morphology, and sometimes semantics.

### 2.2 Complex Morphology

Kurdish has a complex morphology (Samvelian, 2007; Walther, 2011) and one of the main driving factors behind this complexity is the wide use of inflectional and derivational suffixes (Esmaili et al., 2013a). Moreover, as demonstrated by the example in Table 1, in the Sorani's writing system definiteness markers, possessive pronouns, enclitics, and many of the widely-used postpositions are used as suffixes (Salavati et al., 2013).

One important implication of this morphological complexity is that any corpus-based assistance or analysis (e.g., frequencies, co-occurrences, sample passages) would require a lemmatizer/morphological analyzer.

### 2.3 Resource-Scarceness

Although there exist a few resources which can be leveraged in building a wordnet for Kurdish – these are listed in Section 3– but some of the most crucial resources are yet to be built for this language. One of such resources is a collection of comprehensive monolingual and bilingual dictionaries. The main problem with the existing electronic dictionaries is that they are relatively small and have no notion of *sense*, *gender*, or *part-of-speech* labels.

Another necessary resource that is yet to be built, is a mapping system (i.e., a transliteration/translation engine) between the Sorani and Kurmanji dialects.

## 3 Available Resources

In this section we give a brief description of the linguistics resources that our team has built as well as other useful resources that are available on the Web.

### 3.1 KLPP Resources

The main Kurdish text processing resources that we have previously built are as follows:

– *the Pewan corpus* (Esmaili and Salavati, 2013): for both Sorani and Kurmanji dialects. Its basic statistics are shown in Table 2.

[2]Within KLPP, our focus has been on Sorani and Kurmanji which are the two most widely-spoken and closely-related dialects (Haig and Matras, 2002; Walther and Sagot, 2010).

| دا | + | تان | + | یش | + | ەکان | + | کتێو | = | کتێوەکانیشتاندا |
|---|---|---|---|---|---|---|---|---|---|---|
| *daa* | + | *taan* | + | *ish* | + | *akaan* | + | *ktew* | = | *ktewakaanishtaandaa* |
| postpos. | + | poss. pron. | + | conj. | + | pl. def. mark. | + | lemma | = | word |

Table 1: An Exemplary Demonstration of Kurdish's Morphological Complexity (Salavati et al., 2013)

| | Sorani | Kurmanji |
|---|---|---|
| `Articles No.` | *115,340* | *25,572* |
| `Words No. (dist.)` | *501,054* | *127,272* |
| `Words No. (all)` | *18,110,723* | *4,120,027* |

Table 2: The Pewan Corpus' Basic Statistics (Esmaili and Salavati, 2013)

– *the Pewan test collection* (Esmaili et al., 2013a; Esmaili et al., 2013b): built upon the Pewan corpus, this collection has a set of 22 queries (in Sorani and Kurmanji) and their corresponding relevance judgments.
– *the Payv lemmatizer*: it is the result of a major revision of Jedar (Salavati et al., 2013), our Kurdish *stemmer* whose outputs are stems and not lemmas. In order to return lemmas, Payv not only maintains a list of exceptions (e.g., named entities), but also takes into consideration Kurdish's inflectional rules.

### 3.2 Web Resources

To the best of our knowledge, here are the other existing readily-usable resources that can be obtain from the Web:
– *Dictio*[3]: an English-to-Sorani dictionary with more than 13,000 headwords. It employs a collaborative mechanism for enrichment.
– *Ferheng*[4]: a collection of dictionaries for the Kurmanji dialect with sizes ranging from medium (around 25,000 entries, for German and Turkish) to small (around 4,500, for English).
– *Wikipedia*: it currently has more than 12,000 Sorani[5] and 20,000 Kurmanji[6] articles. One useful application of these entries is to build a parallel collection of named entities across both dialects.

## 4 KurdNet's First Prototype

In the following, we first define the scope of our first prototype, then after justifying our choice of construction model, we describe KurdNet's individual elements.

[3] `http://dictio.kurditgroup.org/`
[4] `http://ferheng.org/?Daxistin`
[5] `http://ckb.wikipedia.org/`
[6] `http://ku.wikipedia.org/`

### 4.1 Scope

In the first prototype of KurdNet we focus only on the Sorani dialect. This is mainly due to lack of an available and reliable Kurmanji-to-English dictionary. Moreover, processing Sorani is in general more challenging than Kurmanji (Esmaili et al., 2013a). The Kurmanji version will be built later and will be closely aligned with its Sorani counterpart. To that end, we have already started building a high-quality transliterator/translator engine between the two dialects.

### 4.2 Methodology

There are two well-known models for building wordnets for a language (Vossen, 1998):

- **Expand**: in this model, the synsets are built in correspondence with the WordNet synsets and the semantic relations are directly imported. It has been used for Italian in MultiWordNet and for Spanish in EuroWordNet.

- **Merge**: in this model, the synsets and relations are first built independently and then they are aligned with WordNet's. It has been the dominant model in building BalkaNet and EuroWordNet.

The expand model seems less complex and guarantees the highest degree of compatibility across different wordnets. But it also has potential drawbacks. The most serious risk is that of forcing an excessive dependency on the lexical and conceptual structure of one of the languages involved, as pointed out in (Vossen, 1996).

In our project, we follow the Expand model, since it can be partly automated and therefore would be faster. More precisely, we aim at creating a Kurdish translation/alignment for the Base Concepts (Vossen et al., 1998) which is a set of 5,000 essential concepts (i.e. synsets) that play a major role in the wordnets. Base Concepts (BC) is available on the Global WordNet Association (GWA)'s Web page[7]. The Entity-Relationship (ER) model for the data represented in Base Concept is shown in Figure 2.

[7] `http://globalwordnet.org/`

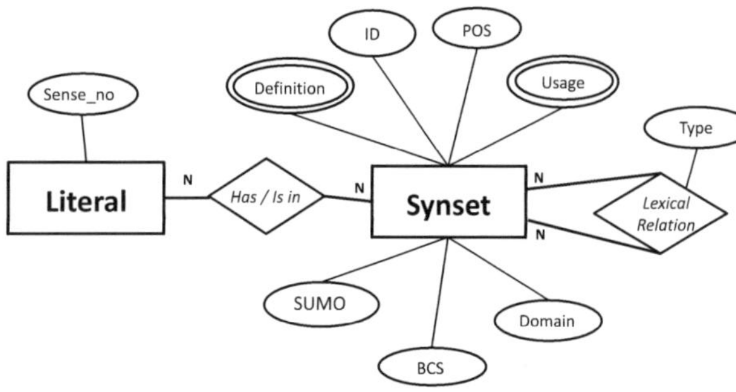


Figure 2: Base Concepts' ER Model

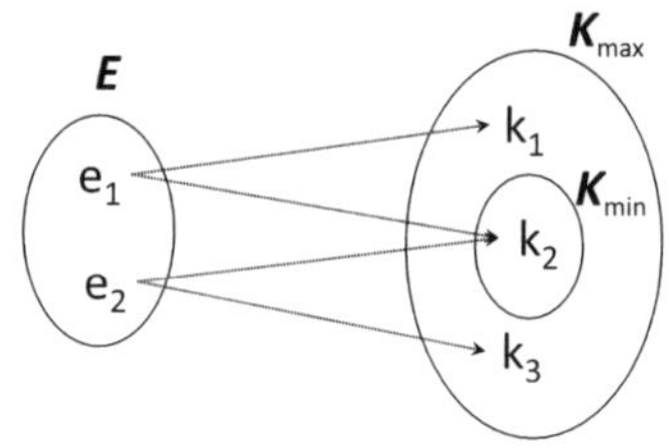


Figure 3: An Illustration of a Synset in Base Concepts and its Maximal and Minimal Alignment Variants in KurdNet

| | **Base Concepts** | **KurdNet** (max) | **KurdNet** (min) |
|---|---|---|---|
| Synset No. | *4,689* | *3,801* | *2,145* |
| Literal No. | *11,171* | *17,990* | *6,248* |
| Usage No. | *2,645* | *89,950* | *31,240* |

Table 3: The Main Statistical Properties of Base Concepts and its Alignment in KurdNet

### 4.3 Elements

Since KurdNet follows the Expand model, it inherits most of Base Concepts' structural properties, including: synsets and the lexical relations among them, POS, Domain, BCS, and SUMO. KurdNet's language-specific aspects, on the other hand, have been built using a semi-automatic approach. Below, we elaborate on the details of construction the remaining three elements.

**Synset Alignments**: for each synset in BC, its counterpart in KurdNet is defined semi-automatically. We first use Dictio to translate its literals (words). Having compiled the translation lists, we combine them in two different ways: (i) a maximal alignment (abbr. **max**) which is a *superset* of all lists, and (ii) a minimal alignment (abbr. **min**) which is a *subset* of non-empty lists. Figure 3 shows an illustration of these two combination variants. In future, we plan to apply more advanced techniques, similar to the graph algorithms described in (Flati and Navigli, 2012).

**Usage Examples**: we have taken a corpus-assisted approach to speed-up the process of providing usage examples for each aligned synset. To this end, we: (i) extract all Pewan's sentences (820,203), (ii) lemmatize the corpus to extract all the lemmas (278,873), and (iii) construct a lemma-to-sentence inverted index. In the current version of KurdNet, for each synset we build a pool of sentences by fetching the first 5 sentences of each of its literals from the inverted list. These pools will later be assessed by lexicographers to filter out non-relevant instances. In future, more sophisticated approaches can be applied (e.g., exploiting contextual information).

**Definitions**: due to lack of proper translation tools, this element must be aligned manually. The manual enrichment and assessment process is currently underway. We have built a graphical user interface to facilitate the lexicographers' task.

Table 3 shows a summary of KurdNet's statistical properties along with those of Base Concepts.

## 5 Preliminary Experiments

The most reliable way to evaluate the quality of a wordnet is to manually examine its content and structure. This is clearly very costly. In this paper we have adopted an indirect evaluation alternative in which we look at the effectiveness of using KurdNet for rewriting IR queries (i.e. query expansion).

We measure the impact of query expansion using two separate configurations: (i) **Terms**, which uses the raw version of the evaluation components (queries, corpus, and KurdNet), and (ii) **Lemmas**, which uses the lemmatized version of them. Furthermore, as depicted in Figure 4, we have considered two alternatives for expanding each query term: (i) add all of its **Synonyms**, and (ii) add all of the synonyms of its direct **Hypernym(s)**. Hence –given the *min* and *max* variants of KurdNet's synsets– there can be at least 10 different experimental scenarios.

In our experiments we have used the Pewan test collection (see Section 3.1), the **MG4J** IR engine (MG4J, 2013), and the Mean Average Precision (MAP) evaluation metric.

The results are summarized in Table 4. The notable patterns are as follows:

- since lemmatization yields additional

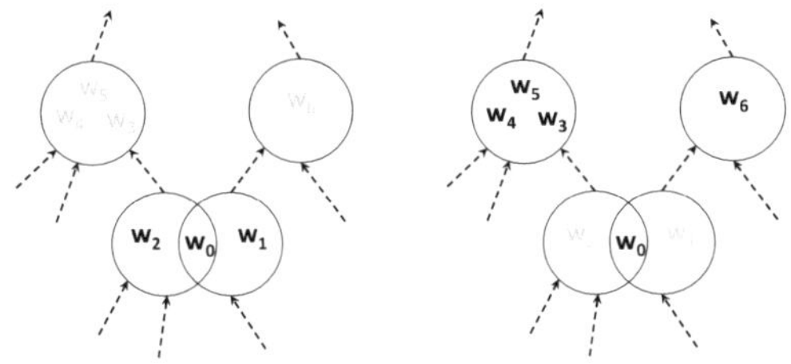


(a) By its Synonyms (b) By its Hypernyms

Figure 4: Expansion Alternatives for the Term $\mathbf{W}_0$

matches between query terms and their inflectional variants in the documents, it improves the performance (row 2 v. row 3). Expansion of the same lemmatized queries, however, degrades the performance (7-10 v. 1,4-6). This degradation can be attributed to the fact that the projection of KurdNet from terms to lemmas introduces imprecise entry merges.

- the *min* approach to align synsets outperforms its *max* counterpart overwhelmingly (1,4,7,8 v. 5,6,9,10), confirming the intuition that the *max* approach entails high-ambiguity,
- expanding query terms by their own synonyms is less effective than by their hypernyms' synonyms. This phenomena might be explained by the fact that currently for each query term, we use all of its synonyms and no sense disambiguation is applied.

Needless to say, a more detailed analysis of the outputs can provide further insights about the above results and claims.

## 6 Conclusions and Future Work

In this paper we briefly highlighted the main challenges in building a lexical database for the Kurdish language and presented the first prototype of KurdNet –the Kurdish WordNet– along with a preliminary evaluation of its impact on Kurdish IR.

We would like to note once more that the KurdNet project is a work in progress. Apart from the manual enrichment and assessment of the described prototype which is currently underway, there are many avenues to continue this work. First, we would like to extend our prototype to include the Kurmanji dialect. This would require not only using similar resources to those reported in this paper, but also building a mapping system between the Sorani and Kurmanji dialects.

Another direction for future work is to prune the current structure i.e. handling the lexical idiosyncrasies between Kurdish and English.

| # | Scenario | MAP |
|---|---|---|
| 1 | `Terms & Hypernyms` (min) | *0.4265* |
| 2 | `Lemmas` | *0.4263* |
| 3 | `Terms` | *0.4075* |
| 4 | `Terms & Synonyms` (min) | *0.3978* |
| 5 | `Terms & Hypernyms` (max) | *0.3960* |
| 6 | `Terms & Synonyms` (max) | *0.3841* |
| 7 | `Lemmas & Hypernyms` (min) | *0.3840* |
| 8 | `Lemmas & Synonyms` (min) | *0.3587* |
| 9 | `Lemmas & Hypernyms` (max) | *0.2530* |
| 10 | `Lemmas & Synonyms` (max) | *0.2215* |

Table 4: Different KurdNet-based Query Expansion Scenarios and Their Impact on Kurdish IR

## References

Pushpak Bhattacharyya. 2010. IndoWordNet. In *Proceedings of the 7th International Conference on Language Resources and Evaluation (LREC'10)*.

Kyumars Sheykh Esmaili and Shahin Salavati. 2013. Sorani Kurdish versus Kurmanji Kurdish: An Empirical Comparison. In *Proceedings of the 51st Annual Meeting of the Association for Computational Linguistics (ACL'13)*, pages 300–305.

Kyumars Sheykh Esmaili, Shahin Salavati, and Anwitaman Datta. 2013a. Towards Kurdish Information Retrieval. *ACM Transactions on Asian Language Information Processing (TALIP)*, To Appear.

Kyumars Sheykh Esmaili, Shahin Salavati, Somayeh Yosefi, Donya Eliassi, Purya Aliabadi, Shownem Hakimi, and Asrin Mohammadi. 2013b. Building a Test Collection for Sorani Kurdish. In *Proceedings of the 10th IEEE/ACS International Conference on Computer Systems and Applications (AICCSA '13)*.

Kyumars Sheykh Esmaili. 2012. Challenges in Kurdish Text Processing. *CoRR*, abs/1212.0074.

Christiane Fellbaum. 1998. *WordNet: An Electronic Lexical Database*. MIT Press.

Tiziano Flati and Roberto Navigli. 2012. The CQC Algorithm: Cycling in Graphs to Semantically Enrich and Enhance a Bilingual Dictionary. *Journal of Artificial Intelligence Research*, 43(1):135–171.

Gérard Gautier. 1996. A Lexicographic Environment for Kurdish Language using 4th Dimension. In *Proceedings of ICEMCO*.

Gérard Gautier. 1998. Building a Kurdish Language Corpus: An Overview of the Technical Problems. In *Proceedings of ICEMCO*.

Goeffrey Haig and Yaron Matras. 2002. Kurdish Linguistics: A Brief Overview. *Language Typology and Universals*, 55(1).

Amir Hassanpour, Jaffer Sheyholislami, and Tove Skutnabb-Kangas. 2012. Introduction. Kurdish: Linguicide, Resistance and Hope. *International Journal of the Sociology of Language*, 217:1–8.

KLPP. 2013. KurdNet's Download Page. Available at: `https://github.com/klpp/kurdnet`.

David N. MacKenzie. 1961. *Kurdish Dialect Studies*. Oxford University Press.

MG4J. 2013. Managing Gigabytes for Java. Available at: `http://mg4j.dsi.unimi.it/`.

Shahin Salavati, Kyumars Sheykh Esmaili, and Fardin Akhlaghian. 2013. Stemming for Kurdish Information Retrieval. In *The Proceeding (to appear) of the 9th Asian Information Retrieval Societies Conference (AIRS 2013)*.

Pollet Samvelian. 2007. A Lexical Account of Sorani Kurdish Prepositions. In *Proceedings of International Conference on Head-Driven Phrase Structure Grammar*, pages 235–249.

Dan Tufis, Dan Cristea, and Sofia Stamou. 2004. BalkaNet: Aims, Methods, Results and Perspectives. A General Overview. *Romanian Journal of Information science and technology*, 7(1-2):9–43.

Piek Vossen, Laura Bloksma, Horacio Rodriguez, Salvador Climent, Nicoletta Calzolari, Adriana Roventini, Francesca Bertagna, Antonietta Alonge, and Wim Peters. 1998. The EuroWordNet Base Concepts and Top Ontology. *Deliverable D017 D*, 34:D036.

Piek Vossen. 1996. Right or Wrong: Combining Lexical Resources in the EuroWordNet Project. In *EURALEX*, volume 96, pages 715–728.

Piek Vossen. 1998. Introduction to EuroWordNet. *Computers and the Humanities*, 32(2-3):73–89.

Géraldine Walther and Benoît Sagot. 2010. Developing a Large-scale Lexicon for a Less-Resourced Language. In *SaLTMiL's Workshop on Less-resourced Languages (LREC)*.

Géraldine Walther. 2011. Fitting into Morphological Structure: Accounting for Sorani Kurdish Endoclitics. In *The Proceedings of the Eighth Mediterranean Morphology Meeting*.

# WN-Toolkit: Automatic generation of WordNets following the expand model

**Antoni Oliver**
Universitat Oberta de Catalunya
Barcelona - Catalonia - Spain
aoliverg@uoc.edu

## Abstract

This paper presents a set of methodologies and algorithms to create WordNets following the expand model. We explore dictionary and BabelNet based strategies, as well as methodologies based on the use of parallel corpora. Evaluation results for six languages are presented: Catalan, Spanish, French, German, Italian and Portuguese. Along with the methodologies and evaluation we present an implementation of all the algorithms grouped in a set of programs or toolkit. These programs have been successfully used in the Know2 Project for the creation of Catalan and Spanish WordNet 3.0. The toolkit is published under the GNU-GPL license and can be freely downloaded from http://lpg.uoc.edu/wn-toolkit.

## 1 Introduction

WordNet (Fellbaum, 1998) is a lexical database that has become a standard resource in Natural Language Processing research and applications. The English WordNet (PWN - *Princeton WordNet*) is being updated regularly, so that its number of synsets increases with every new version. The current version of PWN is 3.1, but in our experiments we are using the 3.0 version because is the latest one available for download at the time of performing the experiments.

WordNet versions in other languages are also available. On the Global WordNet Association[1] website, a comprehensive list of WordNets available for different languages can be found. The Open Multilingual WordNet project (Bond and Kyonghee, 2012) provides free access to WordNets in several languages in a common format. We have used the WordNets from this project for Catalan (Gonzalez-Agirre et al., 2012) , Spanish (Gonzalez-Agirre et al., 2012) , French (WOLF) (Sagot and Fišer, 2008) , Italian (Multiwordnet) (Pianta et al., 2002) and Portuguese (OpenWN-PT) (de Paiva and Rademaker, 2012) . For German we have used the GermaNet 7.0 (Hamp and Feldweg, 1997), freely available for research. In Table 1, the sizes of all these WordNets are presented along with the size of the PWN.

| | Synsets | Words |
|---|---|---|
| **English** | 118.695 | 206.979 |
| **Catalan** | 45.826 | 46.531 |
| **Spanish** | 38.512 | 36.681 |
| **French** | 59.091 | 55.373 |
| **Italian** | 34.728 | 40.343 |
| **Portuguese** | 41.810 | 52.220 |
| **German** | 74.612 | 99.529 |

Table 1: Size of the WordNets

## 2 The expand model

According to (Vossen, 1998), we can distinguish two general methodologies for WordNet construction: (i) the *merge model*, where a new ontology is constructed for the target language; and (ii) the *expand model*, where variants associated with PWN synsets are translated using different strategies.

### 2.1 Dictionary-based strategies

The most commonly used strategy within the expand model is the use of bilingual dictionaries. The main difficulty faced is polysemy. If all the variants were monosemic, i.e., if they were assigned to a single synset, the problem would be simple, as we would only need to find one or more translations for the English variant. In Table 2 we can see the degree of polysemy in PWN 3.0. As we can see, 82.32% of the variants of the PWN are monosemic, as they are assigned to a single synset.

It is also worth observing the percentage of monosemic variants that are written with the first

[1] www.globalwordnet.org

| N. synsets | variants | % |
|---|---|---|
| 1 | 123.228 | 82.32 |
| 2 | 15.577 | 10.41 |
| 3 | 5.027 | 3.36 |
| 4 | 2.199 | 1.47 |
| 5+ | 3.659 | 2.44 |

Table 2: Degree of polysemy in PWN 3.0

letter in upper case (probably corresponding to proper names) and in lower case. In Table 3, we can see the figures.

| | variants | % |
|---|---|---|
| upper case | 84.714 | 68.75 |
| lower case | 38.514 | 31.25 |

Table 3: Number of monosemic variants with the first letter in uppercase or lowercase

These figures show us that a large percentage of a target WordNet can be implemented using this strategy. We must bear in mind, however, that using this methodology, we would probably not be able to obtain the most frequent variants, as common words are usually polysemic.

The Spanish WordNet (Atserias et al., 1997) in the EuroWordNet project and the Catalan WordNet (Benítez et al., 1998) were constructed using dictionaries.

With the dictionary-based strategy we will only be able to get target language variants for synsets having monosemic English variants, i.e. English words assigned to a single synset.

## 2.2 Babelnet

BabelNet (Navigli and Ponzetto, 2010) is a semantic network and ontology created by linking Wikipedia entries to WordNet synsets. These relations are multilingual through the interlingual relations in Wikipedia. For languages lacking the corresponding Wikipedia entry a statistical machine translation system is used to translate a set of English sentences containing the synset in the Semcor corpus and in sentences from Wikipedia containing a link to the English Wikipedia version. After that, the most frequent translation is detected and included as a variant for the synset in the given language.

Similarly to WordNet, BabelNet groups words in different languages into sets of synonyms, called Babel synsets. Babelnet also provides definitions or glosses collected from WordNet and Wikipedia. For cases where the sense is also available in WordNet, the WordNet synset is also provided. We can use Babelnet directly for the creation of WordNets for the languages included in Babelnet (English, Catalan, Spanish, Italian, German and French). For other languages, we can also exploit Babelnet through the Wikipedia's interlingual index.

Recently Babelnet 2.0 was released. This version includes 50 languages and uses information from the following sources: (i) Princeton WordNet, (ii) Open Multilingual WordNet, (iii) Wikipedia and (iv) OmegaWiki. a large collaborative multilingual dictionary.

Prelimiary results using this new version of Babelnet will be also shown in section 3.3.4.

With the Babelnet-based strategy we can get the target language variants for synsyets having both monosemic and polisemic English variants, that is, English words assigned to one or more synsets.

## 2.3 Parallel corpus based strategies

In some previous works we presented a methodology for the construction of WordNets based on the use of parallel bilingual corpora. These corpora need to be semantically tagged, the tags being PWN synsets, at least in the English part. As this kind of corpus is not easily available we explored two strategies for the automatic construction of these corpora: (i) by machine translation of sense-tagged corpora (Oliver and Climent, 2011), (Oliver and Climent, 2012a) and (ii) by automatic sense tagging of bilingual corpora (Oliver and Climent, 2012b).

Once we have created the parallel corpus, we need a word alignment algorithm in order to create the target WordNet. Fortunately, word alignment is a well-known task and several freely available algorithms are available. In previous works we have used Berkeley Aligner (Liang et al., 2006). In this paper we present the results using a very simple word alignment algorithm based on the most frequent translation. This algorithm is available in the WN-Toolkit.

With the parallel corpus based strategy we can get the target language variants for synsyets having both monosemic and polisemic English variants, that is, English words assigned to one or more synsets.

### 2.3.1 Machine translation of sense-tagged corpora

For the creation of the parallel corpus from a monolingual sense-tagged corpus, we use a machine translation system to get the target sentences. The machine translation system must be capable of performing a good lexical selection, that is, it should select the correct target words for the source English words. Other kinds of translation errors are less important for this strategy.

#### 2.3.2 Automatic sense-tagging of parallel corpora

The second strategy for the creation of the corpora is to use a parallel corpus between English and the target language and perform an automatic sense tagging of the English sentences. Unfortunately word sense disambiguation is a highly error-prone task. The best WSD systems for English using WordNet synsets achieve a precision score of about 60-65% (Snyder and Palmer, 2004; Palmer et al., 2001). In our experiments we have explored two options: (i) the use of Freeling and UKB (Padró et al., 2010b) and (ii) Word Sense Disambiguation of multilingual corpora based on the sense information of all the languages (Shahid and Kazakov, 2010).

We have used *Freeling* (Padró et al., 2010a) and the integrated *UKB* module (Agirre and Soroa, 2009) to add sense tags to a fragment of the DGT-TM corpus (Steinberger et al., 2012). Before using this algorithm we have evaluated its the precision by means of automatically sense tag some sense tagged corpora: Semcor, Semeval2, Semeval3 and the Princeton WordNet Gloss Corpus (PWGC). After the automatic sense-tagging is performed, the tags are compared with those in the manually sense tagged-version. In Table 4 we can see the precision figure for each corpus and pos. As we can see, there is a great difference in precision. This difference can be explained by the complimentary values given in the table: the degree of ambiguity in the corpus and the percentage of open class words that are tagged in the corpus. As we can observe, the better precision value is achieved by the PWGC, having the smaller degree of ambiguity and the smaller percentage of tagged words. By contrast, the worse precision is achieved by the Semeval3 corpus, which has the highest degree of ambiguity and the highest percentage of tagged words.

We have also explored a word sense disambiguation strategy based on the sense information provided by a multilingual corpus, following the idea of (Ide et al., 2002). We have used the DGT-TM Corpus (Steinberger et al., 2012) in six languages: English, Spanish, French, German, Italian and Portuguese. We have sense tagged all the languages with no sense disambiguation, that is, giving all the possible senses to all the words in the corpus present in the WordNet versions for these languages. With all this sense information the Word Sense Disambiguation task consists of comparing the synsets in all languages for the same sentence, and taking the sense appearing the most times. Using this strategy some degree of ambiguity is still present after disambiguation. For example, for English the average number of synsets for tagged words before disambiguation is 5.96 (16.05% of the tagged words are unambiguous), and, after disambiguation, this figure is reduced to 2.46 (55.5% of the tagged words are unambiguous).

We have manually evaluated a small portion of this disambiguation strategy for the English DTG-TM corpus, obtaining a precision of 51.25%, very similar to the worst results for the Freeling+UKB strategy. One of the problems of the practical use of the multilingual word sense disambiguation strategy is the sensitivity of the methodology on the degree of development of the target WordNets. It is very important that the target WordNets used for tagging the target language corpora have registered all the senses for a given word. If this is not the case, we will get the wrong results.

## 3 The WN-Toolkit

### 3.1 Toolkit description

The toolkit we present in this paper collects several programs written in Python. All programs must be run in a command line and several parameters must be given. All programs have the option -h to get the required and optional parameters. The toolkit also provides some free language resources. The toolkit is divided in the following parts: (i) Dictionary-based strategies; (ii) Babelnet-based strategies, (iii) Parallel corpus based strategies and (iv) Resources, such as freely available lexical resources, pre-processed corpora, etc.

The *toolkit* can be freely downloaded from `http://lpg.uoc.edu/wn-toolkit`.

In the rest of this section, each of these parts of the toolkit are presented, along with the results of the experiments of WordNet extraction for the following languages: Catalan, Spanish, French, German, Italian and Portuguese. The evaluation of the

| | Ambiguity | % tagged w. | Global | Nouns | Verbs | Adjectives | Adverbs |
|---|---|---|---|---|---|---|---|
| **Semcor** | 7.61 | 84.24 | 51.99 | 58.64 | 40.68 | 61.57 | 68.91 |
| **Senseval 2** | 5.48 | 88.88 | 59.77 | 70.55 | 31.49 | 62.82 | 66.28 |
| **Senseval 3** | 7.84 | 89.44 | 51.82 | 57.08 | 42.46 | 59.72 | 100 |
| **PWGC** | 4.72 | 65.9 | 85.56 | 84.74 | 80.09 | 89.74 | 92.16 |

Table 4: Precision figures of the Freeling's implementation of UKB algorithm for four English Corpora

results is performed automatically using the existing versions of these WordNets. We compare the variants obtained for each synset in the target languages. If the existing version of WordNet for the given languages has the same variant for this synset, the result is evaluated as correct. If the existing WordNet does not have any variant for the synset, this result is not evaluated. This evaluation method has a major drawback: as the existing WordNets for the target languages are not complete (some variants for a given synset are not registered), some correct proposals can be evaluated as incorrect. For each strategy we have manually evaluated a subset of the variants evaluated as incorrect and those not evaluated for Catalan or Spanish. Crrected precision figures are presented for these languages.

### 3.2 Dictionary-based strategies

#### 3.2.1 Introduction

Using this strategy we can obtain variants only for the synsets having monosemic English variants. We can translate the English variants using different kinds of dictionaries (general, encyclopedic and terminological dictionaries). We then assign the translations to the synset of the target language WordNet.

The WN-Toolkit provides several programs for the use of this strategy:

- **createmonosemicwordlist.py**: for the creation of the lists of monosemic words of the PWN. Alternatively, it is possible to use the monosemic word lists corresponding to the PWN version 3.0 distributed with the *toolkit*.

- **wndictionary.py**: using the monosemic word list of the PWN and a bilingual dictionary this program is able to create a list of synsets and the corresponding variants in the target language.

- **wiktionary2bildic.py**: this program creates a bilingual dictionary suitable for use with the program wndictionary.py from the xml dump files of Wiktionary[2].

- **wikipedia2bildic.py**: this program creates a bilingual dictionary suitable for the use with the program wndictionary.py from the xml dump files of the Wikipedia[3].

- **apertium2bildic.py**: this program creates a bilingual dictionary suitable for the use with the program wndictionary.py from the transfer dictionaries of the open source machine translation system Apertium[4] (Forcada et al., 2009). This resource is useful for Basque, Catalan, Esperanto, Galician, Haitian Creole, Icelandic, Macedonian, Spanish, Welsh and Icelandic, as there are available linguistic data for the translation system between English and these languages.

- **combinedictionary.py**: this program allows for the combination of several dictionaries, creating a dictionary with all the information from every dictionary, eliminating the repeated entries.

#### 3.2.2 Experimental settings

We have used this strategy for the creation of WordNets for the following 6 languages: Catalan, Spanish, French, German, Italian and Portuguese. We have used Wiktionary and Wikipedia for all these languages and we have explored the use of additional resources for Catalan and Spanish. In Table 5 we can see the number of entries of the dictionaries created with the *toolkit* for all six languages using Wiktionary and Wikipedia.

| | Wiktionary | Wikipedia |
|---|---|---|
| **cat** | 9,979 | 31,578 |
| **spa** | 26,064 | 106,665 |
| **fre** | 30,708 | 142,142 |
| **deu** | 29,808 | 164,463 |
| **ita** | 20,542 | 77,736 |
| **por** | 15,280 | 42,653 |

Table 5: Size of the dictionaries

[2] www.wiktionary.org
[3] www.wikipedia.org
[4] http://apertium.org

#### 3.2.3 Results and evaluation

In Table 6 we can see the results of the evaluation of the dictionary-based strategy using Wiktionary. The number of variants obtained depends on the Wiktionary size for each of the languages and ranges from 5,081 for Catalan to 18,092 for German. The automatic calculated precision ranges from 48.09% for German to 84.8% for French. This precision figure can be strongly influenced by the size of the reference WordNets, and more precisely on the number of variants for each synset. In the column *New variants* we can see the number of obtained variants for synsets not present in the target reference WordNet.

| | Var. | Precision | New var. |
|---|---|---|---|
| **cat** | 5,081 | 78.36 | 1,588 |
| **spa** | 14,990 | 50.93 | 8,570 |
| **fre** | 16,424 | 84.80 | 1,799 |
| **deu** | 18,092 | 48.09 | 12,405 |
| **ita** | 10,209 | 75.45 | 3,369 |
| **por** | 7,820 | 80.71 | 1,104 |

Table 6: Evaluation of the dictionary based strategy using Wiktionary

In Table 7 the results for the acquisition of WordNets from the Wikipedia as a dictionary are presented. The precision values are calculated automatically. The number of obtained variants is lower than the previous results from the Wiktionary.

| | Var. | Precision | New var. |
|---|---|---|---|
| **cat** | 290 | 63.29 | 132 |
| **spa** | 607 | 63.19 | 463 |
| **fre** | 654 | 71.49 | 177 |
| **deu** | 766 | 24.14 | 737 |
| **ita** | 361 | 52.17 | 292 |
| **por** | 315 | 72.93 | 85 |

Table 7: Evaluation of the dictionary based strategy using Wikipedia

We have extended the dictionary-based strategy for Catalan using the transfer dictionary of the open source machine translation system Apertium along with Wikipedia and Wiktionary. The resulting combined dictionary has 65,937 entries. This made it possible to create a new WordNet with 11,970 entries with an automatic calculated precision of 75.75%. We have manually revised 10% of the results for Catalan and calculated a corrected precision of 92.86% (most of the non-evaluated variants were correct and some of those evaluated as incorrect were correct too).

As we can see from Tables 6 and 7 the number of extracted variants from Wikipedia is smaller than the extracted from Wiktionary, although the dictionary extracted from Wikipedia is 3 or 4 times larger. This can be explained by the percent of encyclopedic-like variants in English WordNet, that can be calculated counting the number of noun variants starting by a upper-case letter. Roughly 30% of the nouns in WordNet are encyclopaedic variants, and this means about the 20% of the overall variants.

### 3.3 Babelnet-based strategies

#### 3.3.1 Introduction

The program babel2wordnet.py allows us to create WordNets from the Babelnet glosses file. This program needs as parameters the two-letter code of the target language and the path to the Babelnet glosses file. With these two parameters, the program is able to create WordNets only for the languages present in Babelnet (in fact the program simply changes the format of the output). The program also accepts an English-target language dictionary created from Wikipedia (using the program wikipedia2bildic.py). This parameter is mandatory for target languages not present in Babelnet, and optional for languages included in Babelnet. The program also accepts as a parameter the $data.noun$ file of PWN, useful for performing caps normalization.

#### 3.3.2 Experimental settings

For our experiments we have used the 1.1.1 version of Babelnet, along with the dictionaries extracted from Wikipedia as explained in section 3.2.2. We used the babel2wordnet.py program using the above-mentioned dictionary and the caps normalization option.

#### 3.3.3 Results and evaluation

In Table 8 we can see the results obtained for Catalan, Spanish, French, German and Italian without the use of a complementary Wikipedia dictionary. Note that no values are presented for Portuguese, as this language is not included in Babelnet. For all languages, the precision values are calculated automatically taking the existing WordNets for these languages described in Table 1 as references.

Table 9 shows the results using the optional Wikipedia dictionary. Note that now results are presented for Portuguese, although this language

|  | Var. | Precision | New var. |
|---|---|---|---|
| **cat** | 23,115 | 70.95 | 9,129 |
| **spa** | 31,351 | 76.80 | 19,107 |
| **fre** | 32,594 | 80.71 | 8,291 |
| **deu** | 32,972 | 52.10 | 27,243 |
| **ita** | 27,481 | 66.78 | 16.945 |
| **por** | - | - | - |

Table 8: Evaluation of the Babelnet-based strategy

is not present in Babelnet. These results are very similar with the results with no Wikipedia dictionary, except for Portuguese. This can be explained by the fact that Babelnet itself uses Wikipedia, so adding the same resource again (although a different version) leads to a very little improvements.

|  | Var. | Precision | New var. |
|---|---|---|---|
| **cat** | 23,307 | 70.85 | 9,244 |
| **spa** | 31,604 | 76.61 | 19,301 |
| **fre** | 32,880 | 80.60 | 8,415 |
| **deu** | 33,455 | 51.79 | 27,651 |
| **ita** | 27,695 | 66.53 | 17,069 |
| **por** | 1,392 | 75.23 | 532 |

Table 9: Evaluation of the Babelnet-based strategy with Wikipedia dictionary

We have manually evaluated 1% of the results for Catalan and we obtained a corrected precision value of 89.17%

#### 3.3.4 Preliminary results using Babelnet 2.0

In Table 10 preliminary results using the Babelnet 2.0 are shown. Please, note that precision values for Catalan, Spanish, French, Italian and Portuguese are marked with an asterisk, indicating that these values can not be considered as correct. The reason is simple, we are automatically evaluating the results with one of the resources used for constructing the Babelnet 2.0. Remember than one of the resoures for the construction of Babelnet 2.0 are the WordNet included in the Open Multilingual WordNet, the same WordNet used for automatic evaluation. Figures of new variants are comparable with the results obtained with the previous version of Babelnet.

|  | Var. | Precision | New var. |
|---|---|---|---|
| **cat** | 84,519 | *94.12 | 9,453 |
| **spa** | 81,160 | *94.58 | 20,132 |
| **fre** | 34,746 | *79,03 | 8,660 |
| **deu** | 35,905 | 49,43 | 29,522 |
| **ita** | 64,504 | *93,83 | 17.782 |
| **por** | 28,670 | *86.88 | 7,734 |

Table 10: Evaluation of the Babelnet-based strategy using Babelnet 2.0

Anyway, Babelnet 2.0 can be a good starting point for constructing WordNets for 50 languages. The algorithm for exploiting the Babelnet 2.0 for WordNet construction is also included in the WN-Toolkit. Please, note that this algorithm simply changes the format of the Babelnet file into the Open Multilingual Wordnet format.

### 3.4 Parallel corpus based strategies

#### 3.4.1 Introduction

The WN-Toolkit implements a simple word alignment algorithm useful for the creation of WordNets from parallel corpora. The program, called synset-word-alignement.py, calculates the most frequent translation found in the corpus for each synset. We must bear in mind that the parallel corpus must be tagged with PWN synsets in the English part. The target corpus must be lemmatized and tagged with very simple tags (n for nouns; v for verbs; a for adjectives; r for adverbs and any other letter for other pos).

The synset-word-alignment program uses two parameters to tune its behaviour:

- The $i$ parameter forces the first translation equivalent to have a frequency at least $i$ times greater than the frequency of the second candidate. If this condition is not achieved, the translation candidate is rejected and the program fails to give a target variant for the given synset.
- The $f$ parameter is the greater value for the ratio between the frequency of the translation candidate in the target part of the parallel corpus and the frequency of the synset in the source part of the parallel corpus.

#### 3.4.2 Experimental settings

For our experiments we have used two strategies for the creation of the parallel corpus with sense tags in the English part.

- Machine translation of sense-tagged corpora. We have used two corpora: Semcor and Princeton WordNet Gloss Corpus. We have used Google Translate to machine translate these corpora to Catalan, Spanish, French, German, Italian and Portuguese.
- Automatic sense tagging of parallel corpora, using two WSD techniques: (i) WSD using multilingual information and (ii) Freeling + UKB. We have used a 118K sentences

fragment of the DGT-TM multilingual corpus (available in English, Spanish, French, German, Italian and Portuguese, but not in Catalan). We have chosen this number of sentences to have a corpus of a similar size to the Princeton WordNet Gloss Corpus

For our experiments we have set the parameter $i$ to 2.5 and the parameter $f$ to 5.

#### 3.4.3 Results and evaluation

In Table 11 and 12 we can see the results for the use of machine translation of Semcor an PWGC. As we can see, the precision figures are very similar for both corpora, but the number of extracted variants is greater for the PWGC, due to the larger size of the corpus. We have manually evaluated 20% of the results for Catalan. In the case of Semcor we have calculated a corrected value of 94.74%, whereas for PWGC corpus we have obtained a corrected value of 96.18%.

| | Var. | Precision | New var. |
|---|---|---|---|
| **cat** | 2,001 | 87.63 | 449 |
| **spa** | 2,076 | 88.93 | 504 |
| **fre** | 1,844 | 91.83 | 142 |
| **deu** | 2,657 | 70.26 | 1,285 |
| **ita** | 858 | 93.81 | 66 |
| **por** | 2,064 | 84.14 | 324 |

Table 11: Evaluation of the parallel corpus based strategy: machine translation of Semcor corpus

| | Var. | Precision | New var. |
|---|---|---|---|
| **cat** | 4,744 | 87.87 | 1,125 |
| **spa** | 4,959 | 84.28 | 2,102 |
| **fre** | 4,598 | 91.63 | 510 |
| **deu** | 5,055 | 71.11 | 2,559 |
| **ita** | 4,870 | 88.68 | 904 |
| **por** | 4,845 | 86.26 | 871 |

Table 12: Evaluation of the parallel corpus based strategy: machine translation of PWGC corpus

In Table 13 and 14 we can see the results for the use of automatic sense tagging for the DGT-TM corpus using a multilingual strategy and Freeling+UKB. Here the precision figures are also similar for both strategies, but the number of extracted variants is greater for the Freeling+UKB strategy. The reason is that using Freeling and UKB we can disambiguate all the ambiguous words, while using the multilingual strategy we are not able to disambiguate all of them and in some cases some degree of ambiguity remains. For the extraction process we have only considered the fully disambiguated words.

| | Var. | Precision | New var. |
|---|---|---|---|
| **spa** | 313 | 75.35 | 171 |
| **fre** | 173 | 75.89 | 32 |
| **deu** | 207 | 36.54 | 155 |
| **ita** | 266 | 82.44 | 61 |
| **por** | 302 | 79.20 | 52 |

Table 13: Multilingual WSD of 118K sentences fragment of the DGT-TM corpus

| | Var. | Precision | New var. |
|---|---|---|---|
| **spa** | 1,155 | 79.71 | 386 |
| **fre** | 484 | 68.66 | 82 |
| **deu** | 609 | 24.72 | 431 |
| **ita** | 1,031 | 78.31 | 252 |
| **por** | 1,075 | 74.23 | 194 |

Table 14: Freeling + UKB of 118K sentences fragment of the DGT-TM corpus

In this case we have manually evaluated the results for Spanish as Catalan is not available in this corpus. For the multilingual strategy we have manually evaluated 100% of the results and calculated a corrected precision figure of 91.67%. For the Freeling + UKB results we have manually evaluated 25% of the results, obtaining a corrected precision of 88.94%.

If we analyse the results, we see that the extraction task has a much higher precision than the Word Sense Disambiguation strategies used to process the corpora. This may seem a little odd but we must bear in mind that we have used very restrictive values for the parameters $i$ and $f$ of the extraction program. These parameters allow us to extract only the best candidates, ensuring a good precision value for the extraction process, but a very poor recall value. It should be noted than for Spanish with the machine translation strategy we are getting 2,076 candidatesfor the Semcor Corpus and 4,959 for the Princeton Gloss Corpus, and we are now getting 313 candidates for the multilingual WSD strategy and 1,155 for the UKB WSD. If we force the extraction process to get 2,076 candidates, we obtain a precision value of 43.77% for the multilingual WSD strategy and 58.12% for UKB.

## 4 Resources

We are distributing some resources for several languages with the hope they can be useful to use the toolkit to create new WordNets or extend existing ones.

- Lexical resources: dictionaries created from Wiktionary, Wikipedia and Apertium transfer dictionaries.

- Preprocessed corpora: DGT-TM, Emea and United Nations Corpus from Opus[5] (Tiedemann, 2012). We have semantically-tagged the English part of the corpora with Freeling and UKB and lemmatized and tagged some of the target languages. We plan to preprocess other parallel corpora in the future.

## 5 Conclusions

We have presented the results of the automatic creation of WordNets for six languages using several techniques following the expand model. All these techniques are implemented in the freely available WN-Toolkit and have been successfully used for the expansion of the Catalan and Spanish WordNets under the Know2 project. The WordNets and the toolkit itself are being improved under the Skater Project. The successful use of this toolkit has also been reported for the Galician WordNet (Gómez Guinovart and Simões, 2013).

We can analyse the coincident extracted synsets and their associated precision for Catalan in Table 15. Here we have mixed the results for extended dictionary, Babelnet, translated PWGC and translated Semcor. The overall precision is 71.06% but, if we take into account the variants extracted using 2 or more methodologies, this precision rises up to 91.35%, although the number of extracted variants is drastically reduced.

| Freq. | Var. | Precision | New var. |
|---|---|---|---|
| 1+ | 35,142 | 71.06 | 13,997 |
| 2+ | 5,661 | 91.35 | 1,062 |
| 3+ | 1052 | 94.92 | 87 |
| 4+ | 135 | 96.06 | 8 |

Table 15: Evaluation of the repetition of the results for different strategies for Catalan

This combination of methodologies allows us to classify the extracted variants with an estimated precision value so we can obtain variants and give each variant a score. This score can be updated if the variant is obtained again using a different methodology or resource.

It's important to take into account the fact that the automatically-calculated precision value is very prone to errors, as, if a given synset having a variant lacks other possible variants and if those unregistered correct variants are extracted, the evaluation algorithm will consider them as incorrect. In Table 16 we can see the comparison between the automatic and corrected values of precision.

| Strategy | Lang. | % rev. | $\mathbf{P}_{auto.}$ | $\mathbf{P}_{corr.}$ |
|---|---|---|---|---|
| Dictionaries | cat | 10 | 75.75 | 92.86 |
| Babelnet | cat | 1 | 70.85 | 89.17 |
| Semcor trad. | cat | 20 | 87.63 | 94.75 |
| PWGC trad. | cat | 20 | 87.87 | 96.18 |
| DGT-TM mult. | spa | 100 | 75.35 | 91.67 |
| DGT-TM UKB | spa | 25 | 79.71 | 88.94 |

Table 16: Comparison of automatic and corrected precision figures

## 6 Future work

We plan to follow the development of the WN-Toolkit in the following directions: (i) change the script-oriented implementation of the current version to a class-oriented implementation allowing easy integration into another applications; (ii) increasing the number of integrated freely available resources and implementing a web query based use of some resources; (iii) developing a simple graphical user interface to facilitate its use and (iv) pre-processing and distributing more freely available corpora.

We also plan to use the toolkit to develop preliminary versions of WordNets for other languages.

## Acknowledgments

This research has been carried out thanks to the Project *SKATER*, (TIN2012-38548-C06-01) of the Spanish Ministry of Science and Innovation

## References

Eneko Agirre and Aitor Soroa. 2009. Personalizing pagerank for word sense disambiguation. In *Proceedings of the 12th Conference of the European Chapter of the Association for Computational Linguistics*, pages 33–41.

Jordi Atserias, Salvador Climent, Xavier Farreres, German Rigau, and Horacio Rodriguez. 1997. Combining multiple methods for the automatic construction of multi-lingual WordNets. In *Recent Advances in Natural Language Processing II. Selected papers from RANLP*, volume 97, pages 327–338.

Laura Benítez, Sergi Cervell, Gerard Escudero, Mònica López, German Rigau, and Mariona Taulé. 1998. Methods and Tools for Building the Catalan WordNet. In *In Proceedings of the ELRA Workshop on*

[5] `http://opus.lingfil.uu.se/`

*Language Resources for European Minority Languages*.

Francis Bond and Paik Kyonghee. 2012. A survey of wordnets and their licenses. In *Proceedings of the 6th International Global WordNet Conference, Matsue (Japan)*, pages 64–71.

Valeria de Paiva and Alexandre Rademaker. 2012. Revisiting a brazilian WordNet. In *Proceedings of the 6th Global Wordnet Conference*, Matsue (Japan).

Christiane Fellbaum. 1998. *WordNet: An electronic lexical database*. The MIT press.

Mikel L. Forcada, Francis M. Tyers, and Gema Ramírez-Sánchez. 2009. The apertium machine translation platform: five years on. In *Proceedings of the First International Workshop on Free/Open-Source Rule-Based Machine Translation*, pages 3–10.

Aitor Gonzalez-Agirre, Egoitz Laparra, and German Rigau. 2012. Multilingual central repository version 3.0. In *Proceedings of the 6th Global WordNet Conference*.

Xavier Gómez Guinovart and Alberto Simões. 2013. Retreading dictionaries for the 21st century. In *Proceedings of the 2nd Symposium on Languages, Applications and Technologies (SLATE'13)*, pages 115–126.

Birgit Hamp and Helmut Feldweg. 1997. GermaNet - a Lexical-Semantic net for german. In *Proceedings of the ACL Workshor on Automatic Information Extraction and Building of Lexical and Sematic Resources for NLP Applications*, pages 9—15.

Nancy Ide, Tomaz Erjavec, and Dan Tufis. 2002. Sense discrimination with parallel corpora. In *Proceedings of the ACL-02 workshop on Word sense disambiguation: recent successes and future directions-Volume 8*, pages 61–66.

Percy Liang, Ben Taskar, and Dan Klein. 2006. Alignment by agreement. In *Proceedings of the HLT-NAACL '06*.

Roberto Navigli and Simone Paolo Ponzetto. 2010. BabelNet: building a very large multilingual semantic network. In *Proceedings of the 48th Annual Meeting of the Association for Computational Linguistics*, ACL '10, pages 216–225, Stroudsburg, PA, USA. Association for Computational Linguistics. ACM ID: 1858704.

Antoni Oliver and Salvador Climent. 2011. Construcción de los wordnets 3.0 para castellano y catalán mediante traducción automática de corpus anotados semánticamente. In *Proceedings of the 27th Conference of the SEPLN, Huelva Spain*.

Antoni Oliver and Salvador Climent. 2012a. Building wordnets by machine translation of sense tagged corpora. In *Proceedings of the Global WordNet Conference, Matsue, Japan*.

Antoni Oliver and Salvador Climent. 2012b. Parallel corpora for wordnet construction. In *Proceedings of the 13th International Conference on Intelligent Text Processing and Computational Linguistics (Cicling 2012). New Delhi (India)*.

Lluís Padró, Miquel Collado, Samuel Reese, Marina Lloberes, and Irene Castellón. 2010a. FreeLing 2.1: Five years of open-source language processing tools. In *LREC*, volume 10, pages 931–936.

Lluís Padró, Samuel Reese, Eneko Agirre, and Aitor Soroa. 2010b. Semantic services in freeling 2.1: Wordnet and UKB. In *Proceedings of the 5th International Conference of the Global WordNet Association (GWC-2010)*.

Martha Palmer, Christiane Fellbaum, Scott Cotton, Lauren Delfs, and Hoa Trang Dang. 2001. English tasks: All-words and verb lexical sample. In *The Proceedings of the Second International Workshop on Evaluating Word Sense Disambiguation Systems*, pages 21–24.

Emanuele Pianta, Luisa Bentivogli, and Christian Girardi. 2002. Developing an aligned multilingual database. In *Proc. 1st Int'l Conference on Global WordNet*.

Benoît Sagot and Darja Fišer. 2008. Building a free french wordnet from multilingual resources. In *Proceedings of OntoLex 2008*, Marrackech (Morocco).

Ahmad R. Shahid and Dimitar Kazakov. 2010. Retrieving lexical semantics from multilingual corpora. *Polibits*, 41:25–28.

Benjamin Snyder and Martha Palmer. 2004. The English all-words task. In *Proceedings of the 3rd International Workshop on the Evaluation of Systems for the Semantic Analysis of Text (Senseval-3)*, pages 41–43, Barcelona (Spain).

Ralf Steinberger, Andreas Eisele, Szymon Klocek, Spyridon Pilos, and Patrick Schlüter. 2012. Dgt-tm: A freely available translation memory in 22 languages. In *Proceedings of the 8th International Conference on Language Resources and Evaluation*, pages 454–459.

Jörg Tiedemann. 2012. Parallel data, tools and interfaces in OPUS. In *In Proceedings of the 8th International Conference on Language Resources and Evaluation (LREC'2012)*, pages 2214–2218.

Piek Vossen. 1998. Introduction to Eurowordnet. *Computers and the Humanities*, 32(2):73–89.

# Onto.PT: recent developments of a large public domain Portuguese wordnet

**Hugo Gonçalo Oliveira**
CISUC, University of Coimbra
Portugal
hroliv@dei.uc.pt

**Paulo Gomes**
CISUC, University of Coimbra
Portugal
pgomes@dei.uc.pt

**Abstract**

This document describes the current state of Onto.PT, a new large wordnet for Portuguese, freely available, and created automatically after exploiting and integrating existing lexical resources in a wordnet structure. Besides an overview on Onto.PT, its creation and evaluation, we enumerate the developments of version 0.6. Moreover, we provide a quantitative view on this version, its comparison to other Portuguese wordnets, in terms of contents and size, as well as some details about its global coverage and availability.

## 1 Introduction

Onto.PT is a new wordnet-like resource for Portuguese. It is under development since 2009 in the Center for Informatics and Systems of the University of Coimbra, after we realised the limitations of existing Portuguese wordnets and related resources. Onto.PT was one of the main contributions of Hugo Gonçalo Oliveira's PhD (Gonçalo Oliveira, 2013), concluded on May 2013, under the supervision of Paulo Gomes. Since then, several developments were made and a new version (v0.6) was released.

Likewise Princeton WordNet (PWN, Fellbaum (1998)), Onto.PT is freely available but, in opposition to the previous resource and most wordnets, it is created automatically, after the exploitation of existing public lexical resources. While the latter fact led to a resource which may not be 100% reliable, it also enabled the development of a larger resource and with a wider coverage, as compared to other Portuguese wordnets. This makes Onto.PT a viable alternative for several natural language processing tasks. Having this in mind, in order to ease the integration of Onto.PT with other applications, this resource is available as a standard model for knowledge representation, namely the Resource Description Framework (RDF, Miller and Manola (2004)).

In the rest of this document, we give a brief overview on the creation of Onto.PT, where several lexical resources for Portuguese are exploited and integrated in a wordnet-like structure, across four automatic steps that combine different information extraction techniques. We then highlight the developments that lead to version 0.6. After that, we describe the contents of Onto.PT, compare it with other wordnets for Portuguese, and provide some details on its availability and global coverage. The latter reports the results of finding suitable matches between Onto.PT synsets and the so-called "core" wordnet concepts. We conclude with additional information on the utility of Onto.PT and leave ideas for future work.

## 2 Creation

The creation of Onto.PT follows ECO, an automatic approach for creating wordnets, described briefly in this section, and more extensively elsewhere (Gonçalo Oliveira and Gomes, 2013a). Also in this section, we enumerate the resources integrated in the current version of Onto.PT and how they were exploited. The section ends with a brief reference to the evaluation of Onto.PT.

### 2.1 The ECO approach

Originally, ECO consisted of three main steps, that combine different information extraction techniques, namely:

1. **Extraction:** exploitation of regularities in textual sources to extract instances of semantic relations, connecting plain words – e.g. [*vírus* causation-of *doença*] ([*virus* causation-of *disease*])

2. **Synset discovery**:

(a) Computation of graph-based similarities between the extracted synonymy instances and available synsets, as those in existing thesauri, if available. When there is enough confidence, the synonymy instances are added to suitable synsets – e.g. [*comutar* synonym-of *mutuar*] + {*trocar, permutar, mutuar*} → {*trocar, permutar, mutuar, comutar*} ([*interchange* synonym-of *exchange*] + {*change, swap, exchange*} → {*change, swap, exchange, interchange*})

(b) Cluster discovery on the remaining synonymy instances and inclusion of the identified clusters as new synsets – e.g. [*tiritante* synonym-of *trémulo*] ∧ [*trémulo* synonym-of *convulso*] ∧ [*convulso* synonym-of *tiritante*] → {*tiritante,trémulo,convulso*} ([*shivering* synonym-of *trembling*] ∧ [*trembling* synonym-of *shaking*] ∧ [*shaking* synonym-of *shivering*] → {*shivering,trembling,shaking*})

3. **Ontologisation**: Computation of graph-based similarity measures to integrate the rest of the relations, by assigning each argument to a suitable synset – e.g. [*iluminar* purpose-of *vela*] → {*iluminar, candear*} purpose-of {*vela, tocha, lume*} ([*illuminate* purpose-of *candle*] → {*illuminate, light_up*} purpose-of {*candle, torch, fire*})

Recently, a fourth step was added to ECO:

4. **Definition assignment**: selection of suitable dictionary definitions for the discovered synsets. Definitions might work as glosses, also common in wordnets – e.g. {*multidão, massa*}: *grande quantidade de pessoas* ({*crowd, mass*}: *great amount of people*)

## 2.2 Integrated resources

The current version of Onto.PT includes lexical-semantic information acquired from six public domain lexical resources of Portuguese, namely:

- The relation instances of PAPEL (Gonçalo Oliveira et al., 2009), a lexical-semantic network extracted automatically from a proprietary Portuguese dictionary. Those are represented by {<*arg1*> RELATION-TYPE <*arg2*>} with words as arguments, and a rich set of relation types that include, for instance, synonymy, hypernymy, several types of meronymy, causation, purpose-of and property-of.
- The definitions and relations instances, extracted from Dicionário Aberto (DA, Simões et al. (2012)) and from the Portuguese Wiktionary (Wikt.PT)[1], both open dictionaries;
- The antonymy instances and synsets of TeP (Maziero et al., 2008), an electronic thesaurus, created manually by experts;
- The synsets of OpenThesaurus.PT (OT.PT)[2], another electronic thesaurus, smaller than TeP, and created collaboratively;
- More recently, the synsets of OpenWordNet.PT (OWN.PT, de Paiva et al. (2012)), a Portuguese wordnet obtained after the translation of part of PWN.

In the first step of ECO, DA and Wikt.PT are exploited using the grammars developed during the creation of PAPEL, which are distributed freely[3]. The extracted relation instances are merged with those from PAPEL's network thus originating a larger lexical-semantic network where words are connected by semantic relations.

Then, the synonymy instances extracted from the dictionaries, as well as those of OT.PT, are assigned to suitable synsets, according to their similarity. Clusters are discovered in a synonymy network established by the unassigned synonymy instances, and added as new synsets.

After that, the arguments of the non-synonymy relations are assigned to the discovered synsets, thus becoming synset relations. Antonymy relations from TeP are also added in this step. Finally, when possible, the synsets have assigned suitable definitions from DA and Wikt.PT (see more in Gonçalo Oliveira and Gomes (2013b)).

## 2.3 Evaluation

Besides occasional evaluations of each step of ECO, which guided us in the selection of the appropriate parameters, a previous version of Onto.PT (v0.3.5) was the target of an extensive manual evaluation where synsets and synset relations were evaluated by two human judges[4]. We estimated that about 81% to 85% of the synsets were correct. More precisely, for the synsets with

[1]See http://pt.wiktionary.org

[2]See http://openthesaurus.caixamagica.pt/

[3]See http://www.linguateca.pt/PAPEL

[4]See additional details in section 8.3 of Hugo Gonçalo Oliveira's PhD thesis (Gonçalo Oliveira, 2013)

more than one word, 73.9% were classified as correct and 7.5% as incorrect by both judges. For the remaining 18.6% synsets, there was no agreement. As for the relations, considering only correct synsets, hypernymy relations were estimated to be about 79% accurate, with a $\kappa$ agreement of 0.47. A set containing relations of the other types got between 88% and 92% accuracy, depending on the judge, with a $\kappa$ agreement of 0.48.

The accuracy of the definition assignment step was estimated to be between 79-80% for Onto.PT v0.4.1, with 0.62 $\kappa$ agreement. This number should be similar in Onto.PT v0.6, because no big changes were made.

## 3 Developments of Onto.PT v.0.6

The most recent version of Onto.PT was released after some progress regarding, namely: improvements in the creation process, integration of the OWN.PT synsets, removal of redundant hypernymy instances, and the availability of synset definitions. This also lead to improvements on the resource evaluation.

### 3.1 Procedural improvements

Onto.PT v0.6 was created after several improvements on the previous versions, including:

- The refinement of some extraction patterns, after exploring the results of previous evaluations;
- Increasing the synonymy attachment threshold to improve synset accuracy.

### 3.2 Integration of OpenWordNet.PT

For the first time, in the creation of Onto.PT, we took advantage of OWN.PT and integrated part of its contents. More precisely, TeP and OWN.PT were merged before synset discovery, in order to create a single synset resource. For this purpose, synsets with high word intersections are clustered – e.g. {*praia, beira-mar, borda, litoral, ribamar*} + {*praia, beira-mar, litoral, costa*} $\rightarrow$ {*praia, beira-mar, borda, litoral, ribamar, costa*} ({*beach, seaside, seaboard, seashore*} + {*beach, seaside, coast*} $\rightarrow$ {*beach, seaside, seaboard, seashore, coast*})

### 3.3 Removal of redundant hypernymy

In order to move towards a better-formed taxonomic tree, redundant hypernymy relation instances in Onto.PT were removed. These instances are those that may be inferred by transitivity – e.g. ~~{*animal*} hypernym-of {*porco, suíno*}~~ $\wedge$ {*animal*} hypernym-of {*mamífero, mastozoário*} $\wedge$ {*mamífero, mastozoário*} hypernym-of {*porco, suíno*} (~~{*animal*} hypernym-of {*pig, swine*}~~ $\wedge$ {*animal*} hypernym-of {*mammal, mammalian*} $\wedge$ {*mamífero, mammalian*} hypernym-of {*pig, swine*})

### 3.4 Synset definitions

Although the first experiments on assigning definitions to the synsets of Onto.PT were done with version 0.4.1 of the resource, definitions were only made available together with the resource in version 0.6. We recall that these definitions might work as glosses.

### 3.5 New evaluation results

Given that a similar extensive evaluation effort required much time, we reused the classified synsets and synset relation instances from Onto.PT v0.3.5[5] to speculate on the current quality of Onto.PT. Depending on the judge, the new evaluation led respectively to synset accuracy between 89-93%, hypernymy accuracy between 79-100%, and accuracy of other relations between 93-96%.

These results should, nevertheless, be analysed more carefully in the future. While a substantial amount of incorrect contents were removed or corrected, a lower, but still substantial, number of contents that were previously classified as correct were also removed.

## 4 Contents and Availability

This section presents a quantitative view on the contents of Onto.PT v0.6, including the covered relations types, a comparison to other Portuguese wordnets, and its global coverage. Details about the availability of Onto.PT are provided in the end of this section.

### 4.1 Quantitative view

Onto.PT v0.6 contains almost 169k unique lexical items, organised in about 117k synsets, which are connected by almost 174k relation instances. Table 1 shows the distribution of covered lexical items, according to their part-of-speech (POS), and included synsets according both to their POS and number of words (size).

Table 2 shows the set of covered semantic relations, richer than in typical wordnets, as well as their quantities. In fact, these are relation types

[5]Datasets available at `http://ontopt.dei.uc.pt`

| POS | Lexical Items | Synsets | | |
|---|---|---|---|---|
| | | size = 1 | size > 1 | Total |
| Nouns | 97,531 | 44,495 | 23,378 | 67,873 |
| Verbs | 32,958 | 20,723 | 5,728 | 26,451 |
| Adjectives | 34,392 | 10,909 | 9,851 | 20,760 |
| Adverbs | 3,995 | 1,283 | 1,083 | 2,366 |
| **Total** | 168,876 | 77,410 | 40,040 | **117,450** |

Table 1: Onto.PT v0.6 synsets.

originally defined during the creation of PAPEL, after the analysis of frequent patterns in dictionary definitions. In this set, for each relation type, there are different subtypes, depending on the POS of the accepted arguments. For instance, [$x$ purpose-of $y$] has the following subtypes:

- $noun(x)$ *fazSeCom* $noun(y)$
  $\rightarrow x$ is performed or obtained with $y$
- $noun(x)$ *fazSeComAlgoComPropriedade* $adj(y)$
  $\rightarrow x$ is performed or obtained with something that is $y$
- $verb(x)$ *finalidadeDe* $noun(y)$
  $\rightarrow x$ is an action performed with $y$
- $verb(x)$ *finalidadeDeAlgoComPropriedade* $adj(y)$
  $\rightarrow x$ is an action performed with something that is $y$

Different types of meronymy are also covered, namely part-of, member-of, contained-in and material-of. Moreover, for each relation subtype, there is an inverse type (e.g. [$x$ causadorDe $y$] $\rightarrow$ [$y$ resultadoDe $x$]), except for antonymy, which is a symmetric relation. If we consider the inverse subtypes, Onto.PT has about 341k relation instances.

### 4.2 Comparison with Portuguese wordnets

Though it is commonly referred that there is not a wordnet for Portuguese, this is not completely true. The problem is that all wordnet projects targeting Portuguese have strong limitations. To our knowledge, besides Onto.PT, there are other four resources – Wordnet.PT (WN.PT, Marrafa et al. (2011)), Wordnet.Br (WN.Br, Dias-da-Silva (2006)), MultiWordNet.PT (MWN.PT)[6] and OpenWordnet.PT (OWN.PT, de Paiva et al. (2012)) – listed in Table 3, together with some information on their creation and availability.

¿From those, besides Onto.PT, only OWN.PT is freely available[7]. The synsets of WN.Br are free,

[6]See http://mwnpt.di.fc.ul.pt/

[7]OWN.PT is available from https://github.com/arademaker/wordnet-br and distributed in two main RDF files, one with the synsets and their PWN match, and another with PWN, including relations, glosses and other inheritable properties.

| Resource | Availability | Creation |
|---|---|---|
| **WN.PT** | web interface<br>no download | manual |
| **WN.Br** | free synsets | man. (synsets)<br>from PWN (relations) |
| **MWN.PT** | paid license | man. translation (synsets)<br>from PWN (relations) |
| **OWN-PT** | free | man. translation (synsets)<br>from PWN (relations) |
| **Onto.PT** | free | automatic |

Table 3: Portuguese WNs: availability & creation

with the name of TeP (Maziero et al., 2008), but the relations, inherited from PWN given manual synset correspondences, are not. MWN.PT is not free but it is available upon a paid license. However, this resource only covers nouns, while all the others cover verbs, adjectives and adverbs as well.

All but WN.PT and Onto.PT follow a translation approach, one of the most popular alternatives to the creation of non-English wordnets, where PWN is translated to a target language (de Melo and Weikum, 2008). This approach is followed at different levels by WN.Br, MWN.PT and OWN.PT. In WN.Br, the synsets were created specifically for Portuguese and manual correspondences to PWN were defined afterwards. On the other hand, the synsets of MWN.PT and OWN.PT are, as far as possible, the direct translation of a set of key PWN synsets. But a problem arises for this kind of approaches. Different languages represent different socio-cultural realities, they do not cover exactly the same part of the lexicon and, even where they seem to be common, several concepts are lexicalised differently (Hirst, 2004). This explains the existence of "lexical gaps" in some MWN.PT synsets. We thus believe that, whether created manually, semi-automatically or automatically, a wordnet should be developed from scratch for its target language. Only after that, it should be devised to align part of the synsets to wordnets of other languages, but having in mind that some rich meanings might be lost in the translation process.

Table 4 presents the same wordnets regarding their size, in terms of covered lexical items, included synsets, semantic relations and the presence of glosses written in Portuguese. Regarding the last property, the wordnets relying on translation do not contain glosses in Portuguese, even though the English glosses can potentially be inherited from PWN and translated. WN.PT has contained Portuguese glosses for a long time. And since the last version of Onto.PT, part of its synsets

| Relation | Args | Given name | Instances |
|---|---|---|---|
| **Hypernymy** | n, n | *hiperonimoDe* | 79,425 |
| **Part** | n, n | *parteDe* | 3,782 |
| | n, adj | *parteDeAlgoComPropriedade* | 4,922 |
| | adj, n | *propriedadeDeAlgoParteDe* | 101 |
| **Member** | n, n | *membroDe* | 5,957 |
| | n, adj | *membroDeAlgoComPropriedade* | 111 |
| | adj, n | *propriedadeDeAlgoMembroDe* | 922 |
| **Contained** | n, n | *contidoEm* | 365 |
| | n, adj | *contidoEmAlgoComPropriedade* | 272 |
| **Material** | n, n | *materialDe* | 879 |
| **Causation** | n, n | *causadorDe* | 1,396 |
| | n, adj | *causadorDeAlgoComPropriedade* | 30 |
| | adj, n | *propriedadeDeAlgoQueCausa* | 667 |
| | v, n | *accaoQueCausa* | 8,168 |
| | n, v | *causadorDaAccao* | 84 |
| **Producer** | n, n | *produtorDe* | 1,662 |
| | n, adj | *produtorDeAlgoComPropriedade* | 80 |
| | adj, n | *propriedadeDeAlgoProdutorDe* | 463 |
| **Purpose** | n, n | *fazSeCom* | 6,787 |
| | n, adj | *fazSeComAlgoComPropriedade* | 77 |
| | v, n | *finalidadeDe* | 8,507 |
| | v, adj | *finalidadeDeAlgoComPropriedade* | 338 |
| **Location** | n, n | *localOrigemDe* | 1,458 |
| **Quality** | n, n | *temQualidade* | 977 |
| | adj, n | *devidoAQualidade* | 1,118 |
| **State** | n, n | *temEstado* | 334 |
| | adj, n | *devidoAEstado* | 197 |
| **Property** | adj, n | *dizSeSobre* | 9,769 |
| | adj, v | *dizSeDoQue* | 24,131 |
| **Manner** | adv, n | *maneiraPorMeioDe* | 1,976 |
| | adv, adj | *maneiraComPropriedade* | 1,675 |
| **Manner without** | adv, n | *maneiraSem* | 231 |
| | adv, v | *maneiraSemAccao* | 20 |
| **Antonymy** | n, n | *antonimoNDe* | 2,300 |
| | adv, adv | *antonimoAdvDe* | 127 |
| | adj, adj | *antonimoAdjDe* | 2,475 |
| | v, v | *antonimoVDe* | 1,844 |
| | | **Total** | **173,627** |

Table 2: Onto.PT v0.6 relations and their quantities

also contain glosses, automatically selected from dictionaries (see section 2).

The numbers on the size of the Portuguese wordnets are put side-by-side to those of PWN, to show that they are substantially smaller, except for Onto.PT. Despite being the second youngest Portuguese wordnet (OWN.PT is the youngest), Onto.PT has a size comparable to PWN, and it covers a richer set of semantic relations. We should recall that Onto.PT integrates several public resources for Portuguese, including the synsets of WN.Br (TeP) and of OWN.PT, so it was expected to be larger than those two.

Although size is probably not the most important property of a wordnet, these numbers show the benefits of an automatic creation. Besides typically larger resources, automatic approaches provide a faster creation, an easier maintenance, and a higher growth potential, in a trade-off on the virtual 100% reliability. Therefore, in the case of Portuguese, selecting the most adequate(s) wordnet(s) to use in some project should consider, among others, the language coverage needs, the tolerance to errors and the available budget.

| Resource | Lexical items | Synsets | Relations | Glosses (in PT) |
|---|---|---|---|---|
| **WN.PT** | 11k | 13k | 40k | Yes |
| **WN.Br** | 44k | 20k | N/A | No |
| **MWN.PT** | 16k | 17k | 69k | No |
| **OWN.PT** | 48k | 39k | 83k | No |
| **Onto.PT** | 169k | 117k | 341k | Yes (40%) |
| **PWN 3.0** | 155k | 118k | 285k | Yes (EN) |

Table 4: Portuguese WNs: contents

### 4.3 Global coverage

The Global WordNet Association provides several lists of key concepts that should be present in wordnets. One of them, contains a reduced set of

164 Core Base Concepts which can be seen as the most important in the wordnets of four languages[8]. They are divided into 98 abstract and 66 concrete concepts, and are represented as PWN 1.5 synsets.

We used this set to speculate on the global coverage of Onto.PT v0.6. For this purpose, we made manual rough matches between the 164 base concepts and suitable Onto.PT synsets. We concluded that Onto.PT roughly covers most of the concepts in the list, more precisely 95 abstract and 66 concrete synsets (98%). The three uncovered concepts are the following: {*change magnitude, change size*}, {*spacing, spatial arrangement*} and {*visual property*}. As one can see, they denote abstract generic classes which are sometimes created artificially, in order to work as the hypernym of a set of more specific concepts. We should add that the global coverage increased since Onto.PT v0.3.5, where 93% base concepts were covered. The integration of OWN.PT had a positive impact on this improvement.

Looking at the other Portuguese wordnets, we can say that, given that WN.PT was created in EuroWordNet's framework, it should cover all the 164 concepts. Moreover, the website of MWN.PT refers that it covers all these concepts. However, MWN.PT only contains nouns, while 35 of the abstract concepts are verbs. So, this information is probably incorrect.

### 4.4 Availability

Onto.PT and related resources are freely available from `http://ontopt.dei.uc.pt`. There, the resource can be downloaded as a RDF model, and in two different notations, RDF/XML and the more compact N3. This model is based on the WordNet RDF/OWL basic representation (van Assem et al., 2006) that was adapted for Portuguese and to include our broader relation set. Moreover, Onto.PT may be browsed through an online interface, OntoBusca, very similar to the PWN search interface and available from the previous website.

## 5 Concluding remarks

We believe that Onto.PT is a valuable add to the Portuguese wordnets and an important contribution to Portuguese NLP, that may be useful in a broad range of tasks. So far, previous versions of Onto.PT were used in query expansion and we have shown that it can be used for word sense disambiguation[9]. And we have some preliminary results of exploiting Onto.PT and OWN.PT for answering open domain cloze question automatically – the results show that, due to its larger size, more questions are answered correctly using Onto.PT.

We should add that Portuguese was recently added to range of languages covered by the multilingual knowledge base BabelNet (Navigli and Ponzetto, 2012). This resource integrates PWN with Wikipedia and some open wordnets, in a very large ontology. Therefore, from this moment, BabelNet should also be seen as one more alternative to Portuguese wordnets. Or, perhaps, as a complement, because, despite its large size (9M synsets in all languages), BabelNet integrates both lexical and world knowledge and the Portuguese Wikipedia (about 800k articles) is still small when compared, for instance, to the English (about 4.3M) and the German (about 1.63M).

We recall that Onto.PT is created automatically and is not a static resource, but an ongoing project. Therefore, improvements are expected in the future. Among other ideas, we are devising the conversion of Onto.PT to specific representations for lexical ontologies (e.g. Lemon, Buitelaar et al. (2009)), we are considering to assign confidence values to its contents and to exploit the World Wide Web for more synset definitions, and we are studying approaches for aligning it to PWN, given that the Onto.PT synsets are not static. We are also devising the integration of the relations of OWN.PT. In fact, with ECO, we can likewise integrate knowledge from additional sources including, for instance, Wikipedia, but keeping in mind that most information in Wikipedia is out of the scope of classic wordnets.

For more information on ECO and on Onto.PT, please refer to Hugo's PhD thesis (Gonçalo Oliveira, 2013) or to our article in the Language and Resources Evaluation Journal (Gonçalo Oliveira and Gomes, 2013a).

## Acknowledgements

The development of Onto.PT v0.6 has been supported by the iCIS project (CENTRO-07-ST24-FEDER-002003), co-financed by QREN, in the scope of the Mais Centro Program and European Union's FEDER.

[8] Available from `http://w.globalwordnet.org/gwa/ewn_to_bc/corebcs.html`

[9] See section 8.4 of Hugo Gonçalo Oliveira's PhD thesis (Gonçalo Oliveira, 2013)

## References


Paul Buitelaar, Philipp Cimiano, Peter Haase, and Michael Sintek. 2009. Towards linguistically grounded ontologies. In *Proceedings of the 6th European Semantic Web Conference on The Semantic Web: Research and Applications*, ESWC 2009, Heraklion, Crete, Greece. Springer. Pages 111–125.

Gerard de Melo and Gerhard Weikum. 2008. On the utility of automatically generated wordnets. In *Proceedings of 4th Global WordNet Conference*, GWC 2008, Szeged, Hungary. University of Szeged. Pages 147–161.

Valeria de Paiva, Alexandre Rademaker, and Gerard de Melo. 2012. OpenWordNet-PT: An open brazilian wordnet for reasoning. In *Proceedings of the 24th International Conference on Computational Linguistics*, COLING (Demo Paper).

Bento C. Dias-da-Silva. 2006. Wordnet.Br: An exercise of human language technology research. In *Proceedings of the 3rd International WordNet Conference*, GWC 2006, South Jeju Island, Korea, January. Pages 301–303.

Christiane Fellbaum, editor. 1998. *WordNet: An Electronic Lexical Database (Language, Speech, and Communication)*. The MIT Press.

Hugo Gonçalo Oliveira and Paulo Gomes. 2013a. ECO and Onto.PT: A flexible approach for creating a Portuguese wordnet automatically. *Language Resources and Evaluation*, to be published.

Hugo Gonçalo Oliveira and Paulo Gomes. 2013b. On the automatic enrichment of a Portuguese wordnet with dictionary definitions. In *Advances in Artificial Intelligence, Local Proceedings of the 16th Portuguese Conference on Artificial Intelligence*, EPIA 2013, Angra do Heroísmo, Azores, Portugal. APPIA. Pages 486–497.

Hugo Gonçalo Oliveira, Diana Santos, and Paulo Gomes. 2009. Relations extracted from a portuguese dictionary: results and first evaluation. In *Proceedings of 14th Portuguese Conference on Artificial Intelligence*, EPIA 2009. APPIA, October. Pages 541–552.

Hugo Gonçalo Oliveira. 2013. *Onto.PT: Towards the Automatic Construction of a Lexical Ontology for Portuguese*. Ph.D. thesis, University of Coimbra. `http://eden.dei.uc.pt/~hroliv/pubs/GoncaloOliveira_PhdThesis2012.pdf`.

Graeme Hirst. 2004. Ontology and the lexicon. In Steffen Staab and Rudi Studer, editors, *Handbook on Ontologies*, International Handbooks on Information Systems. Springer. Pages 209–230.

Palmira Marrafa, Raquel Amaro, and Sara Mendes. 2011. WordNet.PT Global – extending WordNet.PT to Portuguese varieties. In *Proceedings of the 1st Workshop on Algorithms and Resources for Modelling of Dialects and Language Varieties*, Edinburgh, Scotland, July. ACL Press. Pages 70–74.

Erick G. Maziero, Thiago A. S. Pardo, Ariani Di Felippo, and Bento C. Dias-da-Silva. 2008. A Base de Dados Lexical e a Interface Web do TeP 2.0 - Thesaurus Eletrônico para o Português do Brasil. In *VI Workshop em Tecnologia da Informação e da Linguagem Humana (TIL)*, pages 390–392.

Eric Miller and Frank Manola. 2004. RDF primer. Published: W3C Recommendation.

Roberto Navigli and Simone Paolo Ponzetto. 2012. BabelNet: The automatic construction, evaluation and application of a wide-coverage multilingual semantic network. *Artificial Intelligence*, 193:217–250, December.

Alberto Simões, Álvaro Iriarte Sanromán, and José Jo ao Almeida. 2012. Dicionário-Aberto: A source of resources for the Portuguese language processing. In *Proceedings of Computational Processing of the Portuguese Language, 10th International Conference (PROPOR 2012), Coimbra Portugal*, volume 7243 of *LNCS*. Springer, April. Pages 121–127.

Mark van Assem, Aldo Gangemi, and Guus Schreiber. 2006. RDF/OWL representation of WordNet. W3c working draft, World Wide Web Consortium, June.

# Lexico-Semantic Annotation of *Składnica* Treebank by means of PLWN Lexical Units

**Elżbieta Hajnicz**
Institute of Computer Science, Polish Academy of Sciences
ul. Ordona 21, 01-237 Warsaw, Poland
hajnicz@ipipan.waw.pl

## Abstract

In this paper we present the principles of lexico-semantic annotation of *Składnica* Treebank using Polish WordNet lexical units. We describe different means of annotation, depending on the structure of a sentence in *Składnica* on the one hand and the availability of adequate lexical unit in PLWN on the other. Apart from "standard" annotation involving lexical units with the same lemma as the token under annotation, multi-word units, different verb lemmas including reflexive marker *się* as well as synonyms and hypernyms have also been involved. Some tokens have obtained tags explaining why they require no annotation. Additionally, we discuss the assessment of the annotation of whole sentences.

## 1 Introduction

It is widely acknowledged that linguistically annotated corpora play a crucial role in NLP. There is even a tendency towards their ever-deeper annotation. In particular, semantically annotated corpora become more and more popular, because they have several applications in word sense disambiguation (Agirre and Edmonds, 2006) or automatic construction of lexical resources (McCarthy, 2001; Schulte im Walde, 2006; Sirkayon and Kawtrakul, 2007). The important part of semantically annotated corpora are semantically annotated treebanks.

In this paper, the procedure of lexico-semantic annotation of *Składnica* Treebank (cf. section 3.1), the largest Polish treebank, is presented. Verbal, nominal and adjectival tokens forming sentences are annotated using Polish WordNet (PLWN, cf. section 3.2) lexical units. Special attention is paid to tokens for which a correct interpretation was not found in the wordnet.

The annotation is performed using a dedicated tool *Semantikon* (Hajnicz, 2013c). Each sentence is annotated by two linguists, and conflicts are resolved by a master linguist.

The procedure of lexico-semantic annotation of *Składnica* was preceded by tagging named entities with corresponding PLWN-base semantic types (Hajnicz, 2013b), by means of semi-automatic transfer of information from the NE annotation layer (Savary et al., 2010) of the National Corpus of Polish (NKJP). Unlike with common words, this information was linked to nonterminal nodes, since named entities are very often multi-word units. For NEs present in PLWN, corresponding lexical units were used, other NEs were tagged by means of synset identifiers corresponding to their semantic types.

Section 2 presents related work on semantic annotation of text corpora. Section 3 contains the description of resources used. The principles of the actual annotation of tokens are discussed in section 4, whereas the rules of the assessment of whole sentences are presented in section 5.

## 2 Semantically annotated corpora

Semantic annotation of text corpora seems to be the last phase in the process of corpus annotation, less popular than morphosyntactic and (shallow or deep) syntactic annotation. However, there exist semantically annotated subcorpora for many languages, some of them wordnet-based. They are usually substantially smaller than other types of corpora.

The most famous semantically annotated corpus is SemCor (Miller et al., 1993). It is a subcorpus of the Brown Corpus (Francis and Kucera, 1964) containing 250 000 words semantically annotated using Princeton WordNet (PWN) (Miller et al., 1990; Fellbaum, 1998; Miller and Fellbaum, 2007, http://wordnet.

princeton.edu/) synset identifiers. The annotation includes proper names and collocations (the ones present in PWN). A special tag is assigned for tokens with no available sense considered appropriate (supplemented with a corresponding comment).

For Polish, lexico-semantic annotation was performed for the sake of experiments in WSD, and was limited to small sets of highly polysemic words (Broda et al., 2009; Kobyliński, 2011; Przepiórkowski et al., 2011), first of them using PLWN lexical units.

Unlike other corpora, semantic annotation of treebanks usually are not limited to lexico-semantic annotation. Nevertheless, there exist some lexico-semantically annotated treebanks. In particular, a fragment of the Penn Treebank was lexico-semantically tagged by means of PWN senses (Palmer et al., 2000). The Portuguese Treebank *Floresta sintá(c)tica* (Alfonso et al., 2002) was annotated by means of a predefined hierarchy of semantic tags called *semantic prototypes* (Bick, 2006).

An interesting example is the Italian Syntactic-Semantic Treebank (Montemagni et al., 2003b; Montemagni et al., 2003a), which lexico-semantic annotation is based on ItalWordNet (IWN) (Roventini et al., 2000) sense repository being a part of EuroWordNet. When more than one IWN sense applies to the context being tagged, underspecification is allowed (expressed by disjunction/conjunction of senses). Special tags allow marking the lack of a corresponding sense in IWN, metaphoric or methonymic usage of words or expressions, diminutive and augmentative derivatives, and idioms. Moreover, named entities are tagged with their (rather coarse) semantic types.

## 3 Data resources

Presented work is based on two resources: the Polish Treebank *Składnica* and the Polish Wordnet called *Słowosieć* (English acronym PLWN).

### 3.1 *Składnica*

*Składnica* (Świdziński and Woliński, 2010; Woliński et al., 2011) is a bank of constituency parse trees for Polish sentences taken from selected paragraphs in the balanced manually-annotated subcorpus of the Polish National Corpus (NKJP). To attain consistency of the treebank, a semi-automatic method was applied: trees were generated by an automatic parser[1] and then selected and validated by human annotators. The resulting version 0.5 of *Składnica* contains 8241 manually validated trees.

As a consequence of the method used, some sentences do not have any correct parse tree assigned, if *Świgra* did not generate any tree for a particular sentence or no generated tree has been accepted as correct one.

Parse trees are encoded in XML, each parse being stored in a separate file. The parse tree of sentence *Taki był u nas zwyczaj od pokoleń.* ('There was such a habit among us for generations.') in *Składnica* is shown in Fig. 1.

### 3.2 Polish wordnet—*Słowosieć*

In contrast to NKJP annotation, we decided to annotate tokens with very fine-grained semantic types represented by wordnet synsets. For this goal, we used PLWN (Piasecki et al., 2009).

PLWN is a network of lexico-semantic relations, an electronic thesaurus with a structure modelled on that of the Princeton WordNet and those constructed in the EuroWordNet project. Polish WordNet describes the meaning of a lexical unit comprising one or more words by placing this unit in a network representing relations such as synonymy, hypernymy, meronymy, etc.

A lexical unit (LU) is a string which has its morphosyntactic characteristics and a meaning as a whole. Therefore, it may be an idiom or even a collocation, but not a productive syntactic structure (Derwojedowa et al., 2008). An LU is represented as a pair ⟨lemma, meaning⟩, the last being a natural number. Technically, any LU also has its unique numeric identifier. Each lexical unit belongs to a synset, which is a set of synonyms. Synsets have their unique numeric identifiers as well. A fragment of the table of triples ⟨identifier, lemma, meaning⟩ is presented in Fig. 2.

Version 2.0 of PLWN is used for the semantic annotation of tokens. It contains 106438 lemmas, namely 17486 verb lemmas, 77662 noun lemmas and 11290 adjective lemmas, 32199 of them (7234 verb, 20625 noun and 4340 adjective lemmas) being ambiguous. The number of lexical units is 160100 (31980 verb, 109967 noun and 18153 adjective units). On the other hand, named entity annotation was performed by means of PLWN 1.6.

[1] *Świgra* parser (Woliński, 2005) based on the revised version (Świdziński and Woliński, 2009) of metamorphosis grammar GFJP (Świdziński, 1992).

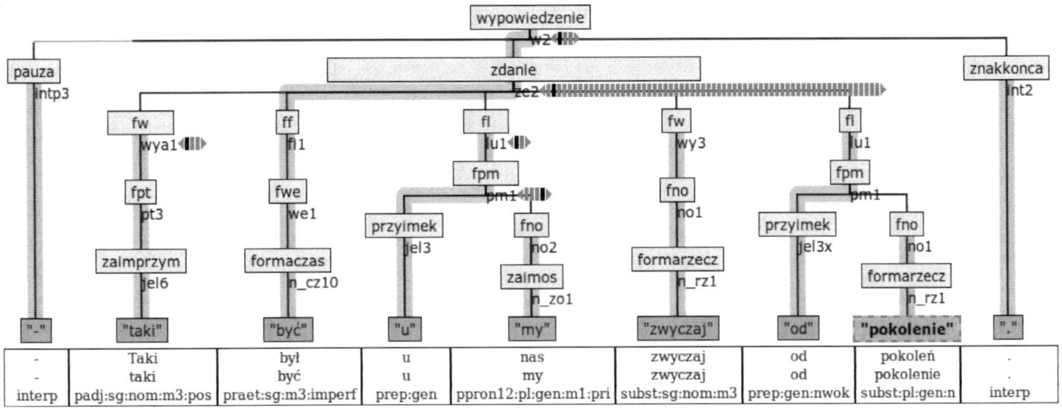


Figure 1: Exemplary parse tree from *Składnica*

| | | |
|---|---|---|
| 124 | aparycja | 1 |
| 136 | apteka | 1 |
| 139 | arbiter | 2 |
| 198 | atrybut | 3 |
| 199 | atrybut | 1 |
| 18382 | atrybut | 2 |
| 19474 | arbiter | 1 |

Figure 2: The fragment of the table of triples ⟨identifier, lemma, meaning⟩ of PLWN 1.6

### 3.2.1 Named entities in PLWN

Polish WordNet contains some number of named entities, selected rather randomly. They are represented in the same way as common words, by means of lexical units. LUs representing NEs are grouped in synsets as well, since the same object can be identified by means of several NEs (e.g., a full name and its acronym). The only difference is that they are connected by 'type' and 'instance' relations instead of 'hypernym' and 'hyponym'.

The representation of NEs in PLWN is far from satisfactory. Therefore, a table of names (a sort of a gazetteer) has been created, in which a list of semantic types represented by PLWN synset identifiers is assigned to every NE lemma. The order of synsets in a list reflects their preference.

## 4 Principles of annotation

### 4.1 The scope of annotation

PLWN contains lexical units of three open parts of speech: adjectives, nouns and verbs. Therefore, only tokens belonging to these POS are annotated. This concerns abbreviations and acronyms as well[2].

[2]Acronyms usually are named entities.

Unfortunately, it does not contain adverbs so far, hence we have no possibility of annotating them. This causes a kind of inconsistency in annotation, which we hope to correct in the future.

On the other hand, only sentences having parse trees are annotated. The reason for this is that corresponding LUs are assigned to terminal nodes representing tokens being annotated. This feature can limit applicability of the resulting resource in WSD.

In the case of tokens being elements of multi-words named entities, the human annotators were free to decide whether they should be annotated. The reason is that some NEs (mainly names of institutions) are compositional.

Semantic annotation is introduced into XML structure of a parse tree as a new type child element of the element `node`: a terminal node (element `plwn_interpretation`) for common words and a nonterminal node (element `named`) for named entities. All LUs from PLWN with the corresponding lemma (and POS) are included, the correct ones having the attribute `chosen="true"` (see Fig. 3 for the noun *pokolenie—generation*). The attribute `polysemy` is used to indicate whether the list of lemmas is a singleton or not. Storing all LUs enables to check what choices were accessible for human or automatic annotators during the process of annotation. The actual annotation is not ambiguous.

In PLWN, there are also units whose lemmas differ only in letter case (lower- vs. uppercase). If the attribute `case_agreement` has the value `true`, only LUs with the lemma identical with the token lemma are considered. Otherwise, the chosen LU lemma differs from the token lemma

```
<plwn_interpretation sem_id="sem_5">
    <plwn_units case_agreement="true"
                polysemy="true">
        <unit luid="sem_5-sv1"
              chosen="true">
            <lubase>pokolenie</lubase>
            <lusense>1</lusense>
            <luident>20791</luident>
            <synset>2418</synset>
        </unit>
        <unit luid="sem_5-sv2">
            <lubase>pokolenie</lubase>
            <lusense>2</lusense>
            <luident>5921</luident>
            <synset>7789</synset>
        </unit>
    </plwn_units>
</plwn_interpretation>
```

Figure 3: XML representation of a polysemic common word

in that aspect (and all corresponding LUs are included).

Additionally, the root element is augmented with three attributes, `name-plwn_version`, `sense-plwn_version`, `final-plwn_version` pointing out which version of PLWN was used for a particular phase of semantic annotation. Certainly, it is possible that these three parameters are equal, but since both resources are under long-lasting intensive manual development, this is highly unlikely. The procedure of updating the annotation to the current version of resources (Hajnicz, 2013a) has been elaborated (the third attribute).

The Table 1 summarises the XML elements ant their attributes used for lexico-semantic level of annotation. The element `plwn_units` is used for standard annotation, as in Fig. 3, the element `other_units` is used for synonyms, hypernyms, multi-element units etc., whereas the element `derived_units` is used for gerunds and participles (see Fig. 4). The attributes `type`, `relat`, and `chosen` are optional; the attributes `deriv_type` and `deriv_dest` appear in `plwn_units` only if the element `derived_units` is present (see section 4.2.4).

### 4.2 Non-standard annotation

Apart from the standard annotation involving lexical units of the same lemma as a token itself, some tokens are tagged in a special way, including:

- multi-word units,
- verb lemmas including reflexive marker *się*,
- synonyms and hypernyms.

For such annotations, the XML element `other_units` instead of `plwn_units` is used, having the attribute `relat` determining the type of special annotation.

If LUs having the same lemma as a token under annotation occur in PLWN, then the corresponding `plwn_units` element appears in the corresponding `plwn_interpretation`. However, no of its units are provided with the attribute `chosen="true"`, as they were not adequate interpretation of a token in a particular context. Note also that the attribute `case_agreement` is not considered for`other_units`, as the lemma of LUs is different from the lemma of a token, hence their case cannot be compared.

#### 4.2.1 Multi-word units

PLWN contains a growing number of multi-word units. In PLWN 2.0, 12% of units have multi-word lemmas: (15% nouns LUs, 5% verb LUs and only 0.2% adjective LUs). There are two kinds of such units:

- units specifying the meaning of the head of lemma, e.g., *szkoła podstawowa* ('primary school') is a school; such LUs are hyponyms of units representing the head of their lemmas;
- units changing the meaning of the head of lemma, e.g., *centrum handlowe* ('shopping centre') is not a *centre*; such LUs are not connected with any unit representing the head of their lemmas.

In the first case, the annotation of tokens using the single-word hypernym is correct, even though less precise. In the second case, using a multi-word expression is indispensable to obtain the correct annotation. In any case, the attribute `relat` gets the value `multi-unit`.

As in the standard case, multi-word LU annotation is attached to individual tokens. The reason for this is twofold. First, due to its structure, *Składnica* may not contain a single node corresponding to the relevant expression. For instance, the expression *szkoły podstawowej w Tychnowach* ('primary school in Tychnowy') from the sentence *Adam [...] chodzi do III klasy szkoły podstawowej w Tychnowach* ('Adam attends the III class of the primary school in Tychnowy'), is represented in *Składnica* by a single node, having three child

Table 1: XML representation for lexico-semantic level of annotation

| elements | attribute | values |
|---|---|---|
| plwn_interpretation | sem_id | `identifier` |
| | type | multi-element, grammatical, foreign, lack, neologism, prep-element, wrong-lemma |
| plwn_units, derived_units, other_units | polysemy | true, false |
| plwn_units, derived_units | case_agreement | true, false |
| | deriv_type | ger, pact, ppas |
| plwn_units | deriv_dest | `lemma` |
| derived_units | deriv_source | `lemma` |
| other_units | relat | refl, multi-unit, synonym, hypernym |
| unit | luid | `identifier` |
| | chosen | true, match |

nodes corresponding to *szkoły* ('school'), *podstawowej* ('primary') and *w Tychnowach* ('in Tychnowy'), and no node corresponding to *szkoły podstawowej* ('primary school'). Secondly, there are sentences in which only the heads of such expressions occur (e.g., *Lubimy zaglądać do takich dużych centrów*—'We like to visit such big [shopping] centres').

If a multi-word expression (present in PLWN) is semantically compositional, its non-head elements are annotated in the standard way. Otherwise, the element `plwn_interpretation` obtains the attribute `type="multi-element"`.

#### 4.2.2 Verb lemmas with the reflexive marker

As in other Slavic languages, in Polish, the reflexive marker *się* can form an integral part of the lemma of a verb[3]. In Polish, *się* is a separate orthographic word, not attached to a verb. Verbs with and without *się* included in their lemma have different meaning and are represented by means of separate LUs. For instance, *zalecać* means 'to recommend, to order', whereas *zalecać się* means 'to make advances (to somebody)'. 9% of LUs have lemmas with the reflexive marker (23% of verbs, 6,5% of nouns: 23% of gerunds, as could be expected).

If a verb token is annotated in such a way, its annotation contains the attribute `relat="refl"`. It is considered separately from typical multi-word expressions, since it is a linguistic feature completely different and independent from collocations. In particular, there are verbal multi-word expressions in spite of the occurrence of the reflexive marker (e.g., *podać się do dymisji*—'to demit').

[3]Some occurrences of *się*, namely impersonal, strictly reflexive and reciprocal, are not part of a verb lemma.

#### 4.2.3 Synonyms and hypernyms

It is almost impossible that there is a corresponding lexical unit in PLWN for every token in *Składnica*, since both words and their meanings exhibit Zipfian distribution, the more so as PLWN is a resource under intensive development.

SemCorr and the Italian Syntactic-Semantic Treebank apply special tags for such tokens. However, such a solution limits the information about the missing senses to informal textual comments. We decided to introduce annotation using synonyms or hypernyms. Such annotation locates the absent meaning of a word in a structure of PLWN as precisely as possible. The attribute `relat` of the corresponding `other_units` element gets the value `synonym` or `hypernym`, respectively.

Hypernyms are used if synonyms of absent LUs do not occur in PLWN. Usually, synonyms for absent noun units are proportionally easy to establish, but adjective units and verb units are approximated by their hypernyms much more often.

The annotation by means of synonyms and hypernyms is used for tokens lemmatised improperly in *Składnica* (`type="wrong-lemma"`), and for foreign-language words tagged morphosyntactically as verbs, nouns or adjectives (`type="foreign"`).

This kind of annotation allows for finding a correct interpretation of tokens by means of newly-added LUs during an update of lexico-semantic annotation of *Składnica* to the new version of PLWN (Hajnicz, 2013a).

A similar procedure is applied for spelling errors (`type="spelling"`). The difference between spelling errors and improper lemmatisations is that the latter are supposed to be corrected.

#### 4.2.4 Gerunds and participles

Gerunds and participles are lemmatised to verb lemmas in *Składnica*, hence they have obtained a verb interpretation. Nevertheless, they occur in sentences in nominal and adjectival positions, hence it would be natural to interpret them as nouns and adjectives, respectively.

PLWN 2.0 contains a lot of gerunds (27% of noun units) and a considerably smaller amount of participles (1.2% of adjective units). Each of them is connected with the verb unit it is derived from by means of inter-paradigmatic synonymy. Therefore, they obtain double interpretation, both by means of verbal and nominal/adjectival units (see Fig. 4 for the gerund *funkcjonowanie—functioning*).

### 4.3 Tokens without semantic interpretation

The procedure of annotation assumes providing as many verb, noun and adjective tokens with lexico-semantic annotation as possible. However, there are some exceptions to this rule. First, individual elements of named entities and multi-words expression need not be interpreted, having the attribute `type` equal to `name-element` or `multi-element`, respectively. For the tokens for which finding an interpretation (even by means of a hypernym) fails, this attribute equals `lack`.

Next, tokens having a grammatical function in a sentence only are not semantically interpreted and tagged as `grammatical`. This concerns mainly future forms of the verb *być (to be)* forming future tense, e.g., *Zarobki wszystkich nauczycieli* ***będą*** *rosły co rok* ('Earnings of all teachers will grow every year'), forms of the verb *być* ('to be; will') and *zostać* ('to become') forming passive voice, e.g., *Maciej R. został już dyscyplinarnie zwolniony* ('Maciej R. was already dismissed on grounds of discipline'). Non-anaphoric occurrences of pronouns are treated in the same way.

In Polish, there exist compound prepositions composed of a simple pronoun and a noun, e.g., *na temat* ('on the subject of'). Some of them were represented in *Składnica* as standard PPs, with their NP complement represented as a modifier of the noun element of the whole preposition. Such mistagged tokens have not been not semantically interpreted, obtaining instead the attribute `type="prep-element"`.

## 5 Assessment of a sentence

In spite of lexico-semantic interpretation at the level of single tokens, the assessment procedure involves annotation of a whole sentence. There are following assessment marks:

1. fully annotated sentence,
2. lack of corresponding lemma,
3. lack of corresponding LU,
4. occurrence of anaphora,
5. occurrence of ellipsis,
6. occurrence of metaphor,
7. occurrence of metonymy,
8. incorrect lemmatisation of a token,
9. incorrect sentence.

The first category requires that the annotation of all autosemantic tokens in the sentence is correct and final, the last one means that the sentence has not been annotated at all. Other marks concern particular problems and phenomena occurring in the sentence, hence several such marks can be attached to it, forming a list of assessments. In particular, the 3rd assessment means that there is no lexical unit in PLWN corresponding to a particular word meaning in context, whereas the 2nd assessment means that the whole lemma was not considered in PLWN.

We decided to attach information about metaphorical or metonymical usage to whole sentences instead of tokens, contrary to the Italian Syntactic-Semantic Treebank. The reason for this is that, in our opinion, they are expressed through the relations between the words rather than through any particular words.

The assessments can be used for several purposes. First, the user can search *Składnica* for sentences having particular features (i.e, metaphorical ones). Second, the information of lacking LUs and whole lemmas can be used for PLWN development and updating *Składnica* to new versions of PLWN (Hajnicz, 2013a). Finally, such an information can be used for WSD training and evaluating, and for determining selectional preferences of predicates, we are particularly interested in.

```
<plwn_interpretation sem_id="sem_2">
    <plwn_units case_agreement="true" polysemy="false"
                deriv_type="ger" deriv_dest="funkcjonowanie">
        <unit luid="sem_2-sv1" chosen="match">
            <lubase>funkcjonować</lubase>
            <lusense>1</lusense>
            <luident>1824</luident>
            <synset>54227</synset>
        </unit>
    </plwn_units>
    <derived_units case_agreement="true" polysemy="false"
                   deriv_type="ger" deriv_source="funkcjonować">
         <unit luid="der_2-sv1" chosen="true">
             <lubase>funkcjonowanie</lubase>
             <lusense>1</lusense>
             <luident>126208</luident>
             <synset>91200</synset>
        </unit>
    </derived_units>
</plwn_interpretation>
```

Figure 4: XML representation of a gerund semantic interpretation

## 6 Conclusions

In this paper, we have presented the principles of lexico-semantic annotation of *Składnica* Treebank by means of Polish WordNet lexical units. We have devoted the most attention to issues connected with PLWN usage.

The procedure of semantic annotation of *Składnica* is not finished yet. The 8283 sentences in *Składnica* contains 49264 nouns, verbs and adjectives for annotation, and 17410 of them belonging to 2785 (34%) sentences has been already annotated. For 2072 tokens (12%), the LU appropriate in the context has not been found in PLWN.

Applying annotation by means of (potential) synonyms or hypernyms of units absent in PLWN seems to be the main novelty of our approach, the more so as PLWN is a resource still under intensive development. Therefore, sentence assessments allow for easily finding the set of sentences containing tokens without a final interpretation, whereas synonyms and hypernyms used for their approximate annotation will facilitate their localisation in the PLWN structure.

PLWN contains a rich set of lexical and synset relations, including diminutive, augmentative, feminine derivatives, etc. Such relations could be used in the case of absence of the LU appropriate for a token, in spite of synonyms and hypernyms. However, this would further complicate the process of annotation and, as a consequence, increase the risk of errors during manual annotation. Similarly, we resigned from using interparadigmatic synonymy and hypernymy for annotating derivatives belonging to different POS.

More details about the procedure and the results of manual annotation could be found in (Hajnicz, 2013c).

**Acknowledgements** This research is supported by the POIG.01.01.02-14-013/09 project which is co-financed by the European Union under the European Regional Development Fund.

## References

Eneko Agirre and Philip Edmonds, editors. 2006. *Word Sense Disambiguation. Algorithms and Applications*, volume 33 of *Text, Speech and Language Technology*. Springer-Verlag, Dordrecht, the Netherlands.

Susana Alfonso, Eckhard Bick, Renato Haber, and Diana Santos. 2002. Floresta sintá(c)tica: a treebank of portuguese. In *Proceedings of the 3rd International Conference on Language Resources and Evaluation (LREC-2002)*, pages 1698–1703, Las Palmas, Spain.

Eckhard Bick. 2006. Noun sense tagging: Semantic prototype annotation of a portuguese treebank. In Jan Hajič and Joakim Nivre, editors, *Proceedings of the 5th Workshop on Treebanks and Linguistic Theories*, pages 127–138, Prague, Czech Republic.

Bartosz Broda, Maciej Piasecki, and Marek Maziarz. 2009. Evaluating LexCSD—a weakly-supervised method on improved semantically annotated corpus in a large scale experiment. In Mieczysław A. Kłopotek, Małgorzata Marciniak, Agnieszka Mykowiecka, Wojciech Penczek, and Sławomir T. Wierzchoń, editors, *Intelligent Information Systems*, Challenging Problems in Science: Computer Science, pages 63–76, Warsaw, Poland. Academic Publishing House Exit.

Magdalena Derwojedowa, Maciej Piasecki, Stanisław Szpakowicz, Magdalena Zawisławska, and Bartosz Broda. 2008. Words, concepts and relations in the construction of Polish WordNet. In Attila Tanacs, Dora Csendes, Veronica Vincze, Christiane Fellbaum, and Piek Vossen, editors, *Proceedings of the Global WordNet Conference*, pages 162–177, Seged, Hungary.

Christiane Fellbaum, editor. 1998. *WordNet — An Electronic Lexical Database*. MIT Press, Cambridge, MA.

W. Nelson Francis and Henry Kucera. 1964, revised and amplified 1979. Brown corpus manual. Internet.

Elżbieta Hajnicz. 2013a. Actualising lexico-semantic annotation of *Składnica* treebank to modified versions of source resources. in preparation.

Elżbieta Hajnicz. 2013b. Mapping named entities from NKJP corpus to *Składnica* treebank and polish wordnet. In Mieczysław A. Kłopotek, Jacek Koronacki, Małgorzata Marciniak, Agnieszka Mykowiecka, and Sławomir T. Wierzchoń, editors, *Proceedings of the 20th International Conference on Language Processing and Intelligent Information Systems*, volume 7912 of *LNCS*, pages 92–105, Warsaw, Poland. Springer-Verlag.

Elżbieta Hajnicz. 2013c. Procedure and results of the lexico-semantic annotation of *Składnica* treebank. in preparation.

Łukasz Kobyliński. 2011. Mining class association rules for word sense disambiguation. In Pascal Bouvry, Mieczysław A. Kłopotek, Franck Leprevost, Małgorzata Marciniak, Agnieszka Mykowiecka, and Henryk Rybiński, editors, *Proceedings of the International Joint Conference on Security and Intelligent Information Systems*, volume 7053 of *LNCS*, pages 307–317, Warsaw, Poland. Springer-Verlag.

2000. *Proceedings of the 2nd International Conference on Language Resources and Evaluation (LREC-2000)*, Athens, Greece.

Diana McCarthy. 2001. *Lexical Acquisition at the Syntax-Semantics Interface: Diathesis Alternations, Subcategorization Frames and Selectional Preferences*. PhD thesis, University of Sussex.

George A. Miller and Christiane Fellbaum. 2007. WordNet then and now. *Language Resources and Evaluation*, 41:209–214.

George A. Miller, Richard Beckwith, Christiane Fellbaum, Derek Gross, and Katherine J. Miller. 1990. Introduction to wordnet: an on-line lexical database. *International Journal of Lexicography*, 3(4):235–244.

George A. Miller, Claudia Leacock, Randee Tengi, and Ross Bunker. 1993. A semantic concordance. In *Proceedings of the ARPA Human Language Technology Workshop*, pages 303–308, Plainsboro, NJ.

Simonetta Montemagni, Francesco Barsotti, Marco Battista, Nicoletta Calzolari, Ornella Corazzari, Alessandro Lenci, Vito Pirrelli, Antonio Zampolli, Francesca Fanciulli, Maria Massetani, Remo Raffaelli, Roberto Basili, Maria Teresa Pazienza, Dario Saracino, Fabio Zanzotto, Nadia Mana, Fabio Pianesi, and Rodolfo Delmonte. 2003a. The syntactic-semantic treebank of Italian. an overview. *Linguistica Computazionale*, XVI–XVI:461–492.

Simonetta Montemagni, Francesco Barsotti, Marco Battista, Nicoletta Calzolari, Ornella Corazzari, Alessandro Lenci, Antonio Zampolli, Francesca Fanciulli, Maria Massetani, Remo Raffaelli, Roberto Basili, Maria Teresa Pazienza, Dario Saracino, Fabio Zanzotto, Nadia Mana, Fabio Pianesi, and Rodolfo Delmonte. 2003b. Building the Italian syntactic-semantic treebank. In Anne Abeillé, editor, *Treebanks: Building and Using Parsed Corpora*, Language and Speech, pages 189–210. Kluwer Academic Publishers, Dordrecht, Holland.

Martha Palmer, Hoa Trang Dang, and Joseph Rosenzweig. 2000. Semantic tagging the Penn treebank. In LREC (LRE, 2000), pages 699–704.

Maciej Piasecki, Stanisław Szpakowicz, and Bartosz Broda. 2009. *A Wordnet from the Ground Up*. Oficyna Wydawnicza Politechniki Wrocławskiej, Wrocław, Poland.

Adam Przepiórkowski, Mirosław Bańko, Rafał L. Górski, Barbara Lewandowska-Tomaszczyk, Marek Łaziński, and Piotr Pęzik. 2011. National Corpus of Polish. In Vetulani (Vetulani, 2011), pages 259–263.

Adriana Roventini, Antonietta Alonge, Nicoletta Calzolari, Bernardo Magnini, and Francesca Bertagna. 2000. ItalWordNet: a large semantic database for Italian. In LREC (LRE, 2000), pages 783–790.

Agata Savary, Jakub Waszczuk, and Adam Przepiórkowski. 2010. Towards the annotation of named entities in the National Corpus of Polish. In *Proceedings of the 7th International Conference on Language Resources and Evaluation (LREC-2010)*, Valetta, Malta. ELRA.

Sabine Schulte im Walde. 2006. Experiments on the automatic induction of German semantic verb classes. *Computational Linguistics*, 32(2):159–194.

Chaloemphon Sirkayon and Asanee Kawtrakul. 2007. Automatic lexico-semantic acquisition from syntactic parsed tree by using clustering and combining techniques. In *Proceedings of the International Workshop on Intelligent Systems and Smart Home (WISH 2007)*, volume 4743 of *LNCS*, pages 203–213. Springer-Verlag.

Marek Świdziński. 1992. *Gramatyka formalna języka polskiego*. Rozprawy Uniwersytetu Warszawskiego. Wydawnictwa Uniwersytetu Warszawskiego, Warsaw, Poland.

Marek Świdziński and Marcin Woliński. 2009. A new formal definition of Polish nominal phrases. In Małgorzata Marciniak and Agnieszka Mykowiecka, editors, *Aspects of Natural Language Processing*, volume 5070 of *LNCS*, pages 143–162. Springer-Verlag.

Marek Świdziński and Marcin Woliński. 2010. Towards a bank of constituent parse trees for Polish. In Petr Sojka, Aleš Horák, Ivan Kopeček, and Karel Pala, editors, *Proceedings of the International Conference on Text, Speech and Dialogue TSD 2010*, volume 6231 of *LNAI*, pages 197–204, Brno, Czech Republic. Springer-Verlag.

Zygmunt Vetulani, editor. 2011. *Proceedings of the 5th Language & Technology Conference*, Poznań, Poland.

Marcin Woliński, Katarzyna Głowińska, and Marek Świdziński. 2011. A preliminary version of Składnica — a treebank of Polish. In Vetulani (Vetulani, 2011), pages 299–303.

Marcin Woliński. 2005. An efficient implementation of a large grammar of Polish. In Zygmunt Vetulani, editor, *Proceedings of the 2nd Language & Technology Conference*, pages 343—-347, Poznań, Poland.

# WoNeF, an improved, expanded and evaluated automatic French translation of WordNet

**Quentin Pradet, Gaël de Chalendar** and **Jeanne Baguenier Desormeaux**
CEA, LIST, Laboratoire Vision et Ingénierie des Contenus
Gif-sur-Yvette, F-91191, France
quentin.pradet|gael.de-chalendar@cea.fr

**Abstract**

Automatic translations of WordNet have been tried to many different target languages. JAWS is such a translation for French nouns using bilingual dictionaries and a syntactic language model. We improve its precision and coverage, complete it with translations of other parts of speech and enhance its evaluation method. The result is named WoNeF. We produce three final translations balanced between precision (up to 93%) and coverage (up to 109 447 (literal, synset) pairs).

## 1 Introduction

Reproducing the lexicographic work of WordNet (Fellbaum, 1998) for other languages is costly and difficult to maintain. Even with some theoretical problems, (Fellbaum and Vossen, 2007; de Melo and Weikum, 2008) show that translating Princeton WordNet literals while keeping its structure and its synsets leads to useful linguistic resources.

WordNet automatic translations use the *expand approach*: its structure is preserved and only literals are translated. Three main techniques represent this approach in the literature. The simplest one seeds WordNet using bilingual dictionaries (Rigau and Agirre, 1995), which can be filtered manually by lexicographers (Vossen, 1998; Tufiş et al., 2004). A second translation method uses parallel corpora, which avoids the use of dictionaries that may cause lexical bias. Back-translations between Norwegian and English were first explored (Dyvik, 2002), while (Sagot and Fišer, 2008) combine a multilingual lexicon and the different BalkaNet wordnets to help disambiguation. Finally, the bilingual dictionaries extracted from the Wiktionary and the Wikipedia interlanguage links allow to create new wordnets (de Melo and Weikum, 2009; Navigli and Ponzetto, 2010) or improve existing ones (Hanoka and Sagot, 2012).

Three French WordNets exist. The French EuroWordNet (Vossen, 1998) has a limited coverage and requires significant improvements to be used (Jacquin et al., 2007). It is also neither free nor freely accessible, which prevented the community from using and improving it. WOLF is a second French translation originally built using parallel corpora (Sagot and Fišer, 2008) and since then expanded using various techniques (Apidianaki and Sagot, 2012). WOLF is distributed under a free LGPL-compatible license. Finally, JAWS (Mouton and de Chalendar, 2010) is a translation of WordNet nouns developed using bilingual dictionaries and a syntactic language model.

Our work expands and improves the techniques used in JAWS and evaluates it based on the adjudication of two annotators work. The result is called WoNeF[1] and is distributed under the LGPL-LR licence. To our knowledge, all current WordNet machine translations only exist in one version where the authors decide what metric to optimize. We provide such a version, but add two resources that can serve different needs and have been obtained using different means. The main WoNeF has an F-score of 70.9%. Another version has a precision of 93.3%, and the last one contains 109 447 (literal, synset) pairs. The main contributions of this paper are the improvement and completion of JAWS with all parts of speech (section 3) and its evaluation (sections 4 and 5). The evaluation is done through an adjudication itself validated by measuring the inter-annotator agreement, which validates the expand approach to translate WordNet.

## 2 JAWS

### 2.1 Translation process

JAWS was built with a weakly supervised algorithm that does not require any manually anno-

[1]This work was partially funded by the ANR ASFALDA ANR-12-CORD-0023 project.

tated data, only the links between the French and English Wiktionaries and a target syntactic language model. The language model was trained on a large corpus extracted from the Web (Grefenstette, 2007). The corpus was analyzed by LIMA (Besançon et al., 2010), a rule-based parser producing fine-grained syntactic dependencies. For a given relation $r$ and a word $x$, the language model indicates what are the first 100 words co-occurring most frequently with $x$ through the relation $r$. Thanks to the dictionary, JAWS does not need to select each synset literals from the entire vocabulary but only among a small number of candidates (9 on average). The translation process is done in three steps. First, an empty wordnet is created, preserving WordNet structure, but with no literal associated to synsets. Then, the easiest translations among dictionaries candidates are selected to start filling JAWS. Finally, JAWS is extended incrementally using the language model, relations between synsets and the existing JAWS.

**Initial selectors** Four algorithms called initial selectors choose correct translations among those proposed by the dictionary. First, words appearing in only one synset are not ambiguous: all their translations are added to the French wordnet. This is the monosemy selector. For example, all translations of *grumpy* are selected in the only synset where it appears. Second, the uniqueness selector identifies words with only one translation and selects this translation in all synsets where the words appear. The five synsets containing *pill* in English are thus completed with *pilule*. These two first selectors were previously used in (Atserias et al., 1997) and (Benítez et al., 1998). A third selector translates words that are not in the dictionary using the English word itself: the direct translation selector. A fourth selector uses the Levenshtein edit distance: despite some false friends, if the distance between an English word and its translation is short, it can be considered that they have the same sense. Two examples are *portion* and *university*).

**JAWS expansion** JAWS being partially filled, a new expansion phase leverages the relationships between WordNet synsets to propose new translations. For example, if a synset S1 is a meronym of a synset S2 in WordNet and there is a context where a selected literal in S1 is a meronym of a candidate literal C in S2, then the literal C is considered correct. The translation task is thus reduced to the task of comparing on the one hand the lexical relations between WordNet synsets and on the other hand the lexical relations between French lexemes.

Let's take as an example the literal *quill* which can be translated to *piquant* or *plume* (Figure 1). In WordNet, *quill* is a meronym of *porcupine* which has already been translated by *porcupine* by an initial selector. In the language model, *piquant* is a noun modifier of *porcupine* but this is not the case of *plume*. Here, the noun-complement relation implies meronymy. It is thus *piquant* that must be chosen as the correct translation of *quill*. The language model allowed to choose between the two possible translations.

A potential problem with this approach could be that the noun modifier relationship is not limited to meronymy. For example, *mémoire* in the language model comes from a book entitled *Mémoires d'un porc-épic* ("Memoirs of a porcupine"). Fortunately, *mémoire* is not in the *quill* translation candidates and thus cannot be chosen. Paradoxically, the language model cannot choose between two very different words, but is able to choose the correct translation of a polysemous word. While automatically translating WordNet only with a dictionary or a syntactic language model is impossible, combining the two resources can solve the problem.

Each such syntactic selector follows the same principle as the meronymy selector and translates new synsets by identifying relationships between lexemes through the syntactic language model. The match between the noun modifier relation and the meronymy relation is direct, but this is not the case for all relations: there is for example no syntactic relationship that directly expresses the synonymy between two literals. For these relations, JAWS uses second order syntactic relations (Lenci and Benotto, 2012). See (Mouton and de Chalendar, 2010) for more details and other selectors.

### 2.2 JAWS limits

JAWS suffers from two main limitations. Above all, it only contains nouns, which prevents its use in many applications. Also, its evaluation procedure makes it difficult to judge its quality. Indeed, JAWS was evaluated by comparing it to the French EuroWordNet and WOLF 0.1.4 (released in 2008). These two French wordnets are not gold standards:

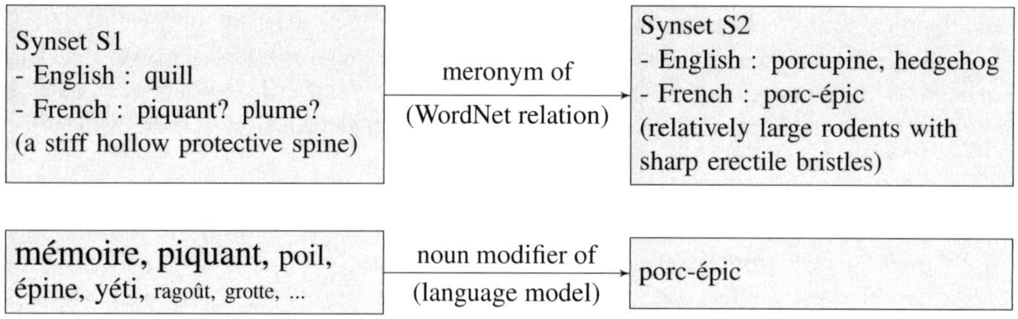


Figure 1: Translation through the part-of meronym relation.

they suffer from either limited coverage or limited accuracy. The authors decided to supplement this limited evaluation by a manual evaluation of literals that do not exist in WOLF, but it has been done on 120 (literal, synset) pairs only by a single annotator. The accuracy of JAWS is evaluated to 67.1%, which is lower than WOLF 0.1.4 and significantly lower than the accuracy of WOLF 1.0b. Furthermore this score should be taken with caution because of the size of the test sample: the confidence interval is approximately 25%.

## 3 WoNeF: JAWS improved and extended to other parts of speech

This section presents three key enhancements that have been made to JAWS and its extension to cover verbs, adjectives and adverbs. A change that is not detailed here is the one that led to a dramatically higher execution speed: JAWS built in several hours *versus* less than a minute for WoNeF, which helped to run many more experiments.

### 3.1 Initial selectors

JAWS initial selectors are not optimal. While we keep the monosemy and uniqueness selectors, we changed the other ones. The direct translation selector is deleted as its precision was very low, even for nouns. A new selector considers candidate translations coming from several different English words in a given synset: the multiple sources selector, a variant the variant criterion of (Atserias et al., 1997). For example, in the synset *line, railway line, rail line*, the French literals *ligne de chemin de fer* and *voie* are translations of both *line* and *railway line* and are therefore chosen as translations.

Finally, the Levenshtein distance selector has been improved. 28% of English vocabulary is of French origin (Finkenstaedt and Wolff, 1973) and anglicization produced predictable changes. It is possible to apply the same changes to the French candidate literal before computing the Levenshtein distance, bringing related words closer. We remove diacritics before applying several operations to word tails (Table 1). For example, reversing the "r" and "e" letter takes into account (*ordre/order*) and (*tigre/tiger*). [2] As before, false friends are not taken into account.

### 3.2 Learning thresholds

In JAWS, each English literal can only correspond to the highest scoring French translation, regardless of the scores of lower-rated translations. This rejects valid candidates and accepts wrong ones. For example, JAWS does not include *particulier* in the *human being* synset because *personne* is already included with a higher score.

In WoNeF, we learned a threshold for each part of speech and selector. We first generated scores for all (literal, synset) candidate pairs, then sorted these pairs by score. The 12 399 pairs present in the WOLF 1.0b manual evaluation (our training set) were considered to be correct, while the pairs

[2]The Damerau-Levenshtein distance which takes into account transpositions anywhere in a word (Damerau, 1964) led to poorer results.

| | | | | |
|---|---|---|---|---|
| -que | -k | banque | → | bank |
| -aire | -ary | tertiaire | → | tertiary |
| eur | er | chercheur | → | researcher |
| ie | y | cajolerie | → | cajolery |
| -té | -ty | extremité | → | extremity |
| -re | -er | tigre | → | tiger |
| ais | ese | libanais | → | lebanese |
| -ant | -ing | changeant | → | changing |

Table 1: Changes to French word tails before applying the Levenshtein distance.

outside this set were not. We then calculated the thresholds maximizing precision and F-score.

Once these thresholds are defined, the selectors choose all candidates above the new threshold. This has two positive effects: valid candidates are not rejected when only the best candidate is already selected (improving both recall and coverage) and invalid candidates which were previously accepted are now rejected thanks to a stricter threshold (increasing precision).

### 3.3 Vote

After applying all selectors, our WordNet is large but contains some noisy synsets. In WoNeF, noise comes from several factors: selectors try to infer semantic information from a syntactic analysis without taking into account the full complexity of the syntax-semantics interface; the parser itself produces some noisy results; the syntactic language model is generated from a noisy corpus extracted from the Web (poorly written text, non-text content, non French sentences); and selected translations in one step are considered valid in the following steps while this is not always the case.

For the high-precision resource, we only keep literals for which the selectors were more confident. Since multiple selectors can now choose a given translation (section 3.2), our solution is simple and effective: translations proposed by multiple selectors are kept while the others are deleted. This voting principle is inspired from ensemble learning in machine learning. It is also similar to the combination method used in (Atserias et al., 1997) but we can avoid their manual inspection of samples of each method thanks to the development of our gold standard.

This cleaning operation retains only 18% of translations (from 87 757 (literal, synset) pairs to 15 625) but the accuracy increases from 68.4% to 93.3%. This high precision resource can be used as training data for other French WordNets. A typical voting methods problem is to choose only easier and poorly interesting examples, but the resource obtained here is well balanced between synsets containing only monosemic words and other synsets containing polysemous and more difficult to disambiguate words (section 5.2).

### 3.4 Extension to verbs, adjectives and adverbs

The work on JAWS began with nouns because they represent 70% of the synsets in WordNet. We continued this work on all other parts of speech: verbs, adjectives and adverbs. Here, generic selectors have been modified, but in the future, we will develop selectors taking into account the different parts of speech characteristics in WordNet.

**Verbs** Selectors chosen for verbs are the uniqueness and monosemy selectors. Indeed, the Levenshtein distance gave poor results for verbs: only 25% of the verbs chosen by this selector were correct translations. For syntactic selectors, only the selector by synonymy gave good results, while the selector by hyponymy had the performance of a random classifier.

**Adjectives** For adjectives, all initial selectors are chosen, and the selected syntactic selector is the selector by synonymy.

**Adverbs** The configuration is the same than for adjectives. We have no gold standard for adverbs, which explains why they are not included in our evaluation. However, comparison with WOLF (section 5.4) shows that adverbs are better than other parts of speech.

## 4 WoNeF: an evaluated JAWS

### 4.1 Gold standard development

Evaluation of JAWS suffers from a number of limitations (section 2.2). We produced a gold standard for rigorous evaluation to evaluate WoNeF. For nouns, verbs and adjectives, 300 synsets have been annotated by two authors of this paper, both computational linguists, both native French speakers and respectively with a background in computer science and linguistics. For each candidate provided by our translation dictionaries, they had to decide whether or not it belonged to the synset. They used WordNet synsets to examine their neighbors, the Merriam-Webster dictionary, the French electronic dictionary TLFi and search engines to demonstrate the use of different senses of the words in question. Because dictionaries do not provide candidates for all synsets and some synsets have no suitable candidate, the actual number of non-empty synsets is less than 300 (section 4.2).

During manual annotation, we encountered difficulties arising from the attempt to translate the Princeton WordNet to French. Most problems come from verbs and adjectives appearing in a collocation. In WordNet, they can be grouped in a way that makes sense in English, but that is not reflected directly in another language. For example, the adjective *pointed* is the only element of a synset defined as *Direct and obvious in meaning or reference; often unpleasant, "a pointed critique", "a pointed allusion to what was going on", "another pointed look in their direction".* These three examples would result in three different translations in French: *une critique* ***dure***, *une allusion* ***claire*** and *un regard* ***appuyé***. There is no satisfactory solution in translating such a synset: the resulting synset contains either too many or too few translations. We view this issue as a mainly linguistic one in the way WordNet has grouped those three usages of *pointed*. We marked the concerned synsets and will handle them in a future work, either manually or with other approaches. These granularity problems concern 3% of nominal synsets, 8% of verbal synsets and 6% of adjectival synsets.

The other main difficulty stems from translations in our bilingual dictionaries. Rare meanings of a word are sometimes missing. For example, there is a WordNet synset containing the *egg* verb for its *coat with beaten egg* sense. Our dictionaries only consider *egg* as a noun: neither our gold standard nor JAWS can translate this synset. This case appeared rarely in practice, and none of these senses are in the most polysemous synsets (BCS synsets as defined in section 5.2), confirming that it doesn't affect the quality of our gold standard for the most important synsets. Yet WoNeF could be improved by using specific dictionaries for species (as in (Sagot and Fišer, 2008) with WikiSpecies), medical terms, etc. Unwanted translations are another issue. Our dictionaries translate *unkindly* to *sans aménité* (*without amenity*) which is a compositional phrase. While such a translation is expected in a bilingual dictionary, it should not be integrated in a lexical resource. The last difficulty lied in judgment adjectives: for example, there is no good translation of *weird* in French. Although most dictionaries provide *bizarre* as a translation, this one does not provide the *stupid* aspect of *weird*. There is no translation that would fit in all contexts: the synset meaning is not fully preserved after translation.

### 4.2 Inter-annotators agreement

Table 2 shows the inter-annotator agreement measured through Fleiss kappa for the three annotated parts of speech. Even if it is a discussed metric (Powers, 2012), all existing evaluation tables consider these scores as high enough to describe the inter-annotator agreement as "good" (Gwet, 2001), which allows us to say that our gold standard is good. The expand approach for the translation of WordNets is also validated : it is possible to produce useful resource in spite of the difficulties mentioned in section 4.1.

| | Nouns | Verbs | Adj. |
|---|---|---|---|
| Fleiss Kappa | 0.715 | 0.711 | 0.663 |
| Synsets | 270 | 222 | 267 |
| Candidates | 6.22 | 14.50 | 7.27 |

Table 2: Gold standard inter-annotator agreement

## 5 Results

We present in this section the results of WoNeF. We first describe the initial selectors and proceed with the full resource. Our gold standard is divided into two parts: 10% of the literals form the validation set used to choose the selectors that apply to different versions of WoNeF, while the remaining 90% form the evaluation set. No training was performed on our gold standard. Precision and recall are based on the intersection of synsets present in WoNeF and our gold standard. Precision is the fraction of correct (literal, synset) pairs in the intersection while recall is the fraction of correctly retrieved pairs.

### 5.1 Initial selectors

For nouns, verbs and adjectives, we calculated the efficiency of each initial selector on our development set, and used this data to determine which ones should be included in the high precision version, the high F-score version and the large coverage one. Scores are reported on the test set.

Table 3 shows the results of this operation. Coverage gives an idea of the size of the resource. Depending on the objectives of each resource, the selected initial selectors are different. Since different selectors can choose the same translation, the sum of coverages is greater than the coverage of the high coverage resource.

### 5.2 Global results

We now focus on the overall results which include the application of initial selectors and syntactic selectors (Table 4). The high-precision method also

| | P | R | F1 | C |
|---|---|---|---|---|
| monosemy | 71.5 | 76.6 | 74.0 | 54 499 |
| unicity | 91.7 | 63.0 | 75.3 | 9 533 |
| mult. sources | 64.5 | 45.0 | 53.0 | 27 316 |
| Levenshtein | 61.9 | 29.0 | 39.3 | 20 034 |
| high precision | **93.8** | 50.1 | 65.3 | 13 867 |
| high F-score | 71.1 | **72.7** | **71.9** | 82 730 |
| high coverage | 69.0 | 69.8 | 69.4 | **90 248** |

Table 3: Top part: Precision, Recall and F1-measure of initial selectors on all translations (nouns, verbs and adjectives). Bottom part: scores for various combinations of them. Coverage C is the total number of pairs (literal, synset).

applies a vote (section 3.3). As in the previous table, the coverage C is the number of (literal, synset) pairs. Without using structure-based nor conceptual distance-based selectors as in (Farreres et al., 2010), we obtain a coverage at 93% precision for our French wordnet (15 625) equal to their Spanish one (11 770) and larger than their Thai one (2 013).

| **All synsets** | P | R | F1 | C |
|---|---|---|---|---|
| high precision | **93.3** | 51.5 | 66.4 | 15 625 |
| high F-score | 68.9 | 73.0 | **70.9** | 88 736 |
| high coverage | 60.5 | **74.3** | 66.7 | **109 447** |
| **BCS synsets** | P | R | F1 | C |
| high precision | **90.4** | 36.5 | 52.0 | 1 877 |
| high F-score | 56.5 | 62.8 | **59.1** | 14 405 |
| high coverage | 44.5 | **66.9** | 53.5 | **23 166** |

Table 4: Global results for all synsets and BCS synsets only.

In WordNet, most words are monosemous, but a small minority of polysemous words are the most represented in texts. It is precisely on this minority that we wish to create a quality resource. To evaluate this, we use the list of **BCS** (Basic Concept Set) synsets provided by the BalkaNet project (Tufiş et al., 2004). This list contains 8 516 synsets lexicalized in six different translations of WordNet. They should represent the most frequent synsets and those with the most polysemous words. While the high F-score and the high coverage resources lose precision for BCS synsets, this is not the case for the high precision resource. In fact, the voting mechanism makes the high-precision resource very robust, even for the BCS synsets.

### 5.3 Results by part of speech

Table 5 shows the detailed results for each part of speech. Concerning nouns, the high precision mode uses two selectors, both based on the noun modifier syntactic relation: the meronymy selector described in section 2.1 and the hyponymy selector. The high precision resource for nouns is our best resource. The high F-score version has an F-score of 72.4%, which ensures that present (literal, synset) pairs have good quality and that it does not miss too many translations. The nominal version is better than JAWS by 2.8% points of F-score.

| | | P | R | F1 | C |
|---|---|---|---|---|---|
| PR | nouns | **96.8** | 56.6 | 71.4 | 11 294 |
| | verbs | **68.4** | 41.9 | 52.0 | 1 110 |
| | adj. | **90.0** | 36.7 | 52.2 | 3 221 |
| F1R | nouns | 71.7 | 73.2 | **72.4** | 59 213 |
| | **JAWS** | 70.7 | 68.5 | 69.6 | 55 416 |
| | verbs | 48.9 | **76.6** | **59.6** | 9 138 |
| | adj. | 69.8 | 71.0 | 70.4 | 20 385 |
| CR | nouns | 61.8 | **78.4** | 69.1 | **70 218** |
| | verbs | 45.4 | 61.5 | 52.2 | **18 844** |
| | adj. | 69.8 | **71.9** | **70.8** | **20 385** |

Table 5: Results by part of speech. Horizontal parts give scores for the high-precision resource (PR), the high-F1-measure one (F1R) and the high coverage one (CR). JAWS containing only nouns, it is compared with the high F-score nominal WoNeF resource.

Results for verbs are lower. The main reason is that verbs are on average more polysemous in WordNet and our dictionaries than other parts of speech: verbal synsets have twice as many candidates as nouns and adjectives synsets (Table 2). This shows the importance of the dictionary to limit the number of literals from which algorithms must choose. The synonymy selector is the only syntactic selector applied to verbs: it uses second-order syntactic relations for three types of verbal syntactic dependencies: if two verbs share the same objects, they are likely to be synonyms or near-synonyms. This is the case for *dévorer* and *manger* which both accept the object *pain*. Other syntactic selectors have not been used for verbs because of their poor results. Indeed, while the detection of hyponymy using only the inclusion of contexts was effective on the nouns, it has the performance of a random classifier for verbs. This highlights the complexity of verbal polysemy.

For adjectives and verbs, only the synonymy selector was applied. For high F-score and high coverage resources, the same selectors (initial and syntactic) are applied, which is why the results are the same. While the inter-annotator agreement was lower on adjectives than on verbs, results are much better for adjectives. This is mainly due to the number of candidates from which to select: there are twice as less candidates for adjectives. This highlights the importance of dictionaries.

### 5.4 Evaluation against WOLF

Using our gold standard to compare WOLF and WoNeF would unfairly penalize WOLF for all correct words not present in our dictionaries. Conversely, we cannot consider WOLF as a direct reference as WOLF itself is not fully validated. The last publication giving overall WOLF figures (Sagot and Fišer, 2012) indicates a number of pairs around 77 000 with 86% precision[3]. We thus compare the intersections between the high-precision WoNeF (93.3% precision) and WOLF 0.1.4 and 1.0b (Table 6). It shows that although WoNeF is still smaller than WOLF, it is a complementary resource. The comparison of the differences between WOLF 0.1.4 and WOLF 1.0b is instructive as it highlights WOLF improvements.

| **WOLF 0.1.4** | $\subset$ | $\supset$ | $\oplus$ |
|---|---|---|---|
| Nouns | 18.7 | 3.0 | 10 526 |
| Verbs | 6.5 | 0.8 | 1 743 |
| Adjectives | 26.9 | 5.8 | 3 710 |
| Adverbs | 23.8 | 5.6 | 757 |
| **WOLF 1.0b** | $\subset$ | $\supset$ | $\oplus$ |
| Nouns | 49.7 | 8.6 | 6 503 |
| Verbs | 26.5 | 2.6 | 1 338 |
| Adjectives | 36.4 | 13.3 | 2 530 |
| Adverbs | 41.2 | 12.6 | 543 |

Table 6: Intersections between the high precision WoNeF and WOLF 0.1.4 and 1.0b. $\subset$ is the percentage of WoNeF pairs included in WOLF and $\supset$ is the percentage of WOLF pairs included in WoNeF. $\oplus$ is the number of new elements contributed by WoNeF.

The $\oplus$ column gives the number of translations that are present in WoNeF but not in WOLF. For nouns, verbs and adjectives, it means that we contribute 10 914 new high precision (literal, synset) pairs by merging WoNeF and WOLF 1.0, in other words 94% of the high precision WoNeF pairs which shows how much the two approaches are complementary: different literals are selected. This produces a French wordnet 10% larger than WOLF with an improved accuracy. A merging with the high F-score resource would be slightly less precise, but it would provide 81 052 new (literal, synset) pairs comparing to WOLF 1.0b, resulting in a merge containing 73 712 non-empty synsets and 188,657 (literal, synset) pairs, increasing WOLF coverage by 75% and the WoNeF one by 63%.

[3]The detailed results for WOLF 1.0b are not currently available.

## Conclusion

In this work, we have shown that the use of a syntactic language model to identify lexical relations between lexemes is possible in a constrained environment and leads to results with a state of the art precision for the task of translating WordNet. We offer three different resources, each with a different purpose. Finally, we provide a validated high quality gold standard that has enabled us to demonstrate both the validity of the approach of translating WordNet by extension and the validity of our specific approach. This gold standard can also be used to evaluate and develop other French WordNet translations. WoNeF is freely available on `http://wonef.fr/` under the LGPL-LR licence. A web interface based on sloWTool (Fi[Pleaseinsertintopreamble]er and Novak, 2011) (initially developed for sloWNet, the Slovenian WordNet) allows to browse the resulting WordNet online. The current distribution formats are the DEBVisDic XML and WordNet-LMF formats. This allows to integrate WoNeF into the Global WordNet Grid and facilitates access and conversions into any lexical resource format.

Future work on WoNeF will focus on verbs, adjectives and adverbs, for which dedicated new selectors may be considered to improve coverage. For example, the synonymy selector can be extended to the WordNet adjectival quasi-synonymy relationship because distributional semantic techniques tend to identify quasi-synonyms rather than synonyms.

Another important source of improvement will be to enrich our syntactic language model by taking into account reflexive verbs and multi-word expressions. We would also like to move towards a continuous language model (Le et al., 2012). This will be coupled with the collection of a more recent and larger Web corpus analyzed with a recent version of our linguistic analyzer. This will allow us to measure the impact of the language model quality on the WordNet translation.

The WOLF French wordnet was built using several techniques. Merging WoNeF and WOLF will soon improve again the status of the French translation of WordNet: we are working with WOLF authors to merge WOLF and WoNeF.

## References


Marianna Apidianaki and Benoît Sagot. 2012. Applying cross-lingual WSD to wordnet development. In *LREC'12*, May.

Jordi Atserias, Salvador Climent, Xavier Farreres, German Rigau, and Horacio Rodr Guez. 1997. Combining Multiple Methods for the Automatic Construction of Multilingual WordNets. In *RANLP'97*, September.

Laura Benítez, Sergi Cervell, Gerard Escudero, Mònica López, German Rigau, and Mariona Taulé. 1998. Methods and Tools for Building the Catalan WordNet. In *ELRA Workshop on Language Resources for European Minority Languages*, May.

Romaric Besançon, Gaël de Chalendar, Olivier Ferret, Faiza Gara, and Nasredine Semmar. 2010. LIMA: A Multilingual Framework for Linguistic Analysis and Linguistic Resources Development and Evaluation. In *LREC 2010*, May.

Fred J. Damerau. 1964. A technique for computer detection and correction of spelling errors. *Communications of the ACM*, 7(3):171–176, March.

Gerard de Melo and Gerhard Weikum. 2008. On the Utility of Automatically Generated Wordnets. In *GWC 2008*, January.

Gerard de Melo and Gerhard Weikum. 2009. Towards a universal wordnet by learning from combined evidence. In *CIKM 2009*, November.

Helge Dyvik. 2002. Translations as Semantic Mirrors: From Parallel Corpus to WordNet. In *ICAME 23*, May.

Javier Farreres, Karina Gibert, Horacio Rodríguez, and Charnyote Pluempitiwiriyawej. 2010. Inference of lexical ontologies. The LeOnI methodology. *Artificial Intelligence*, 174(1):1–19, January.

Christiane Fellbaum and Piek Vossen. 2007. Connecting the Universal to the Specific: Towards the Global Grid. In *IWIC 2007*, January.

Christiane Fellbaum, editor. 1998. *WordNet: An Electronic Lexical Database*. MIT Press, Cambridge, MA, May.

Thomas Finkenstaedt and Dieter Wolff. 1973. *Ordered profusion: Studies in dictionaries and the English lexicon*, volume 13 of *Annales Universitatis Saraviensis*. C. Winter.

Darja Fišer and Jernej Novak. 2011. Visualizing slownet. In *eLex 2011*, November.

Gregory Grefenstette. 2007. Conquering language: Using NLP on a massive scale to build high dimensional language models from the web. In *CICLing 2007*, February.

Kilem L. Gwet. 2001. *Handbook of inter-rater reliability*. Advanced Analytics, LLC, September.

Valérie Hanoka and Benoît Sagot. 2012. Wordnet extension made simple: A multilingual lexicon-based approach using wiki resources. In *LREC'12*, may.

Christine Jacquin, Emmanuel Desmontils, and Laura Monceaux. 2007. French eurowordnet lexical database improvements. In *CICLing 2007*, February.

Hai-Son Le, Alexandre Allauzen, and François Yvon. 2012. Continuous Space Translation Models with Neural Networks. In *NAACL-HLT 2012*, June.

Alessandro Lenci and Giulia Benotto. 2012. Identifying hypernyms in distributional semantic spaces. In **SEM 2012*, June.

Claire Mouton and Gaël de Chalendar. 2010. JAWS: Just Another WordNet Subset. In *TALN 2010*, June.

Roberto Navigli and Simone Paolo Ponzetto. 2010. BabelNet: Building a very large multilingual semantic network. In *ACL 2010*, July.

David M W Powers. 2012. The Problem with Kappa. In *EACL 2012*, April.

German Rigau and Eneko Agirre. 1995. Disambiguating bilingual nominal entries against WordNet. In *Workshop "The Computational Lexicon". ESSLLI'95*, August.

Benoît Sagot and Darja Fišer. 2008. Building a free French wordnet from multilingual resources. In *Ontolex 2008 Workshop*, May.

Benoît Sagot and Darja Fišer. 2012. Automatic Extension of WOLF. In *GWC 2012*, January.

Dan Tufiş, Dan Cristea, and Sofia Stamou. 2004. BalkaNet: Aims, methods, results and perspectives. a general overview. *Romanian Journal of Information Science and Technology*, 7(1-2):9–43.

Piek Vossen. 1998. *EuroWordNet: a multilingual database with lexical semantic networks*. Kluwer Academic, October.

# Bringing together over- and under-represented languages: Linking Wordnet to the SIL Semantic Domains

**Muhammad Zulhelmy bin Mohd Rosman**
**Francis Bond** and **František Kratochvíl**
Linguistics and Multilingual Studies,
**Nanyang Technological University**, Singapore
muhammad20@e.ntu.edu.sg, bond@ieee.org, fkratochvil@ntu.edu.sg

**Abstract**

We have created an open-source mapping between the SIL's semantic domains (used for rapid lexicon building and organization for under-resourced languages) and WordNet, the standard resource for lexical semantics in natural language processing. We show that the resources complement each other, and suggest ways in which the mapping can be improved even further. The semantic domains give more general domain and associative links, which wordnet still has few of, while wordnet gives explicit semantic relations between senses, which the domains lack.

## 1 Introduction

In this paper we compare, and semi-automatically link using Python with NLTK (Bird et al., 2009), two very different approaches to organizing lexical knowledge. The first is the **Semantic Domains** (**SD**) from SIL International.[1] **SD** is a tool designed to aid in the rapid construction and subsequent organization of lexicons for languages which may have no dictionary at all. The second is the linked concepts from the **wordnet** (**WN**) lexical databases, largely based on the Princeton WordNet of English (Fellbaum, 1998). This lexical database was designed to be consistent with models of how human beings process language and is now widely used in natural language processing.

**SD** is a standard tool in development of dictionaries for under-resourced languages. Wordnets on the other hand, are primarily built for languages that already have many lexical resources, such as English, Japanese and Finnish (Bond and Paik, 2012).

**SD** is designed for rapid construction and intuitive organization of lexicons, not primarily for the analysis of the resulting data. As a result, many potentially interesting relationships are only implicitly realized. By linking **SD** to **WN** we can take advantage of the relationships modeled in **WN** to make more of these explicit. For example, the semantic relations in **WN** would be a useful input into **SD** while the domains hierarchy would enforce the existing **WN** relations. This will allow more quantitative computational modeling of under-resourced languages.

It is currently an exciting time for field lexicography with better tools and hardware allowing for rapid digitization of lexical resources. Typically, linguists tag text soon after they collect it. As semantic tags are integrated into the workflow, the new words are instantly linked to structured data. We will make it possible to then link them to languages with fuller descriptions and formal ontologies.

In the following sections we introduce the resources in more detail (Section 2), then describe the automatic mapping (Section 3). The results of the mapping are presented (Section 4) and discussed (Section 5). Both **SD** and **WN** are freely available under open licenses, and we release our mapping in the same way (licensed with the Creative Commons Attribution License (CC-BY).[2]

## 2 Resources

In this section we introduce the resources. As WordNet is more established in the field of computational linguistics, we will mainly describe the semantic domains.

[1] "SIL International is a [Christian] faith-based nonprofit organization committed to serving language communities worldwide as they build capacity for sustainable language development." `http://sil.org`

[2] See `http://creativecommons.org/licenses/by/3.0/`

### 2.1 Semantic Domains (SD)

**SD** is a standard tool in descriptive linguistics aiding in dictionary building and organization. It comprises of nine major headings where similar domains are placed close to each other. We show the two upper levels in Figure 2.[3] There are several versions in circulation for various regional languages, the latest version is DDP.v4, on which **SD** is built. **SD** draws on a number of thesauri developed as tools for historical linguists (enabling them to track words despite sound change or meaning shift). An excellent example of such approach is Buck (1949), which is a dictionary of synonyms in principal Indo-European languages. It contains more than 1,100 clusters of synonyms grouped into 172 domains, listing related words and reviewing their etymology and semantic history. It allows to detect changes in meaning and replacement of older forms by newer forms, of colloquial or foreign origin. **SD** are also informed by English lexicographic resources, including the 20,000 most frequent words from the Corpus of Contemporary American English (450m words).

Multilingual versions of **SD** are available, covering currently besides English also Chinese, French, Hindi, Indonesian, Khmer, Nepali, Russian, Spanish, Telugu, Thai, and Urdu.

**SD** has been built into several standard software tools for language documentation and description such as SIL Toolbox, SIL FieldWorks, and WeSay (Moe, 2013).[4]

Each domain includes:

- a number for sorting purposes
- a domain label (consisting of a word or short phrase that captures the basic idea of the domain)
- a short description of the domain
- a series of questions designed to help people think of the words that belong to the domain
- a short list of words under each question that belong to the domain.

We show examples of the domains in Figure 1. The semantic domains are released under an open source license — Creative Commons Attribution-ShareAlike license (CC-BY-SA).

There are no explicit relational links between the domains, although the most common tool used with it (FLEX[5]) allows for the addition of **hypernym/hyponym**, **meronym/holonym**, **antonym/synonym** and **calendar** relations. We show more detailed of a group of domains in Figure 1. The relations between super and sub domains is generally random. Within each domain questions are designed to elicit words associated with the domain, and these can be related in almost any way.

#### 2.1.1 Users

We took a survey among the users of SIL Toolbox and SIL Fieldworks on the respective online fora. Among the 12 respondents, DDP is mainly used to build dictionaries (72%), organize them (63%), and let native speakers enrich them (54%). The option to produce language materials is also valued. Most respondents would appreciate an increased compatibility with other systems such as WordNet (Fellbaum, 1998) and were planning to make their dictionaries available online in the future. The DDP tool has been used in several projects aimed to crowd-source the vocabulary documentation. The RapidWords project explores rapid vocabulary building where within 2 weeks a substantial dictionary can be compiled, counting up to 15,000 entries [6].

In our recent experience with Abui[7] we were able to triple the size of the corpus-based lexicon (about 2,500 entries which took around 10 years to compile) in just four days, during a workshop with just 15 Abui speakers. We expect to easily go over 15,000 words, when we continue for another ten days next year. The structured intuitive interface of **SD** is extremely easy to grasp even for native speakers of under-resourced languages who only have a basic literacy and received limited or no formal training. It is a great resource to substantially increase the amount of information on the lexicons of under-resourced languages.

The **SD** method opens up new possibilities for refining linguistic analysis. As an example of such

[3] The list of domains was developed by Ron Moe, a linguist working with SIL International, and originally called The Dictionary Development Process (DDP).

[4] See `http://www.sil.org/computing/toolbox;` `http://fieldworks.sil.org/;http://wesay.palaso.org/`

[5] FieldWorks Language Explorer (FLEx) is a tool for language documentation and analysis `http://fieldworks.sil.org/flex/`.

[6] See `http://rapidwords.net/`

[7] ISO 639-3 abz: a language spoken by approximately 16,000 speakers in the central part of the Alor Island in Eastern Indonesia.

1 **Universe, creation**

Use this domain for general words referring to the physical universe. Some languages may not have a single word for the universe and may have to use a phrase such as 'rain, soil, and things of the sky' or 'sky, land, and water' or a descriptive phrase such as 'everything you can see' or 'everything that exists'.

Q What words refer to everything we can see?

– ***universe, creation, cosmos, heaven and earth, macrocosm, everything that exists***

1.1 **Sky**

Use this domain for words related to the sky.

Q1 What words are used to refer to the sky?

– ***sky, firmament, canopy, vault***

Q2 What words refer to the air around the earth?

– ***air, atmosphere, airspace, stratosphere, ozone layer***

Q3 What words are used to refer to the place or area beyond the sky?

***heaven, space, outer space, ether, void, solar system***

...

1.1.1 **Sun**

Use this domain for words related to the sun. [...]

- Related domains: 8.3.3 Light, 8.3.3.2.1 Shadow, 8.4.1.2.3 Time of the day

Q1 What words refer to the sun?

– ***sun, solar, sol, daystar, our star***

Q2 What words refer to how the sun moves?

– ***rise, set, cross the sky, come up, go down, sink***

Q3 What words refer to the time when the sun rises?

– ***dawn, sunrise, sunup, daybreak, cockcrow***

...

1.1.1.1 **Moon**

Use this domain for words related to the Moon. [...]

1.1.1.2 **Star** [...]

1.1.1.3 **Planet** [...]

Figure 1: Depth First View of **Universe**

new step is the study of verbal semantics. Abui is a language with a complex alignment system described most recently in Kratochvíl (2011). There are multiple parameters determining the realization of arguments. **SD** method enables us to map the verbal inventory in great detail, map the **SD** for Abui onto **WN** and use computational tools to test the predictions outlined in Kratochvíl (2011). Linguistic description and the accuracy of linguistic analysis will be improved by the compatibility with **WN**, a standard resource in natural language processing.

### 2.1.2 Access to Lexical Resources

The structure of the **SD** further opens a possibility to create useful and refined lexical resources for the language community, such as dictionaries and language teaching materials.

Dictionaries using DDP have already been made available online in projects such as Webonary[8] or E-kamus2.org for languages of Eastern Indonesia.[9] There are many dictionaries in informal circulation, because there is no easy way to publish them online. By linking **SD** and **WN**, we open a possibility for small dictionaries to be published in the multilingual WN environment, which is better established and supported.

## 2.2 Wordnet (WN)

A wordnet is a semantic lexicon modeled on the Princeton WordNet (Fellbaum, 1998). Groups of similar words[10] are grouped together into synonym sets (or **synsets**) which are roughly equivalent to concepts. A combination of a word and synset defines a **sense**. Synsets are linked together by semantic relations, predominantly **hyperonymy** and **meronymy**, but including many others. Relations can also link senses to senses or synsets. Wordnets have been built for many languages, in this research we use the Princeton WordNet and the Wordnet Bahasa: a wordnet with Malay and Indonesian words linked to the Princeton WordNet structure (Nurril Hirfana at al., 2011). Over twenty wordnets have been linked together as the Open Multilingual Wordnet[11] and there is data for many, many more (Bond and Foster, 2013). Almost all wordnets have been built for established languages: building a wordnet from scratch is a considerable undertaking. The Princeton WordNet is released under an open source license that allows reuse with attribution , and most new wordnets (including the Wordnet Bahasa we use here) are released under a similar license.

The Princeton WordNet has been linked to

[8]See `http://webonary.org/`

[9]See `http://e-kamus2.org/`

[10]More properly, **lemmas**, which may be multiword expressions.

[11]See `http://compling.hss.ntu.edu.sg/omw/`

| No. | Domain |
|---|---|
| 1 | **Universe, creation** |
| 1.1 | Sky |
| 1.2 | World |
| 1.3 | Water |
| 1.4 | Living things |
| 1.5 | Plant |
| 1.6 | Animal |
| 1.7 | Nature, environment |
| 2 | **Person** |
| 2.1 | Body |
| 2.2 | Body functions |
| 2.3 | Sense, perceive |
| 2.4 | Body condition |
| 2.5 | Healthy |
| 2.6 | Life |
| 3 | **Language and thought** |
| 3.1 | Soul, spirit |
| 3.2 | Think |
| 3.3 | Want |
| 3.4 | Emotion |
| 3.5 | Communication |
| 3.6 | Teach |
| 4 | **Social behavior** |
| 4.1 | Relationships |
| 4.2 | Social activity |
| 4.3 | Behavior |
| 4.4 | Prosperity, trouble |

| No. | Domain |
|---|---|
| 4 | **Social behavior** (cont) |
| 4.5 | Authority |
| 4.6 | Government |
| 4.7 | Law |
| 4.8 | Conflict |
| 4.9 | Religion |
| 5 | **Daily life** |
| 5.1 | Household equipment |
| 5.2 | Food |
| 5.3 | Clothing |
| 5.4 | Adornment |
| 5.5 | Fire |
| 5.6 | Cleaning |
| 5.7 | Sleep |
| 5.8 | Manage a house |
| 5.9 | Live, stay |
| 6 | **Work and occupation** |
| 6.1 | Work |
| 6.2 | Agriculture |
| 6.3 | Animal husbandry |
| 6.4 | Hunt and fish |
| 6.5 | Working with buildings |
| 6.6 | Occupation |
| 6.7 | Tool |
| 6.8 | Finance |
| 6.9 | Business organization |

| No. | Domain |
|---|---|
| 7 | **Physical actions** |
| 7.1 | Posture |
| 7.2 | Move |
| 7.3 | Move something |
| 7.4 | Have, be with |
| 7.5 | Arrange |
| 7.6 | Hide |
| 7.7 | Physical impact |
| 7.8 | Divide into pieces |
| 7.9 | Break, wear out |
| 8 | **States** |
| 8.1 | Quantity |
| 8.2 | Big |
| 8.3 | Quality |
| 8.4 | Time |
| 8.5 | Location |
| 8.6 | Parts of things |
| 9 | **Grammar** |
| 9.1 | General words |
| 9.2 | Part of speech |
| 9.3 | Very |
| 9.4 | Semantic constituents related to verbs |
| 9.5 | Case |
| 9.6 | Connected with, related |
| 9.7 | Name |

Figure 2: Top two levels of the Semantic Domains

many other useful resources, including corpora (Landes et al., 1998), images (Bond et al., 2008; Deng et al., 2009), geographical locations, verb frames (Baker et al., 1998), Wiktionary and Wikipedia (de Melo and Weikum, 2010; Bond and Foster, 2013), many NLP tools (Bird et al., 2009) and ontologies (Niles and Pease, 2001; Gangemi et al., 2003). Allowing under-resourced languages to access these is an important goal for this project.

### 2.3 Comparison

As can be seen from Figures 1 and 2, the relations between domains are not as strongly typed as in WordNet, or at all uniform: for example **bodily functions** are related to **person**, but not as **synonyms, hyponyms** or **meronyms**. These somewhat looser relations are not captured well by WordNet: the so-called **tennis problem** (Wordnet does not link clearly related words such as ***racket***, ***ball***, ***net***: Fellbaum, 1998). The general associations of the **SD**s can go some way to providing these kinds of links.

## 3 Mapping

The objective of this task is to map the **SD** files to the **WN** files. Both the Indonesian and English versions of **SD** and **WN** were used. For Wordnet Bahasa, only the words tagged under Indonesian were taken. As such, mapping was done for the same language file (i.e. English **SD** to English **WN**) while across the two languages these two mappings were merged. As both files are in different formats, they were normalized first. This is to ensure that words from both the **SD** and **WN** file will be able to match each other during mapping.

To make the mappings more specific, we treat each question as a **class**: so we build for example: **1.1.s1** "What words are used to refer to the sky?" which contains the words: ***sky, firmament, canopy, vault***. We remove any meta information in brackets, part of speech information and so forth. We thus try to link both domains and classes (we will use the terms interchangeably from here on).

For both the English and Indonesian **WN** words, the underscore character was replaced with a space to harmonize with the **SD** words: ***outer_space*** becomes ***outer space***.

### 3.1 Initial Mapping

For each class in **SD**, the class name and each word was looked up in **WN**, and any matching synsets recorded (examples are given in Table 1). It was possible for **SD** classes to match to **WN** synsets through multiple paths: through more than one word (in either English or Indonesian). Of

| **SD** ID (class) | **WN** Synset | Word |
|---|---|---|
| 6.5.2.4.s3 | 01202651-v | bolt |
| 8.3.1.5.1.s2 | 00124854-v | scroll |
| 7.4.1 | 05021151-n | give |
| 2.1.2.s2 | 05578911-n | girdle |
| 1.6.4.2.s1 | 01181166-v | feed |

Table 1: **SD-WN** ID mapping

course, many of these mappings would be inappropriate, due to the ambiguity of the word used as a pivot, so we need to further constrain the mapping.

We give some examples of words that did not match in Table 2. Typically the **SD** title is more informal than the **WN** synset entries. For example **SD**'s something used to see should map to **WN**'s optical instrument "an instrument designed to aid vision". The automatic mapping is very much a lower bound on the number of possible mappings.

### 3.2 Confirming the mappings

We looked at a variety of sources of information to improve confidence in the mappings: the structure of the domains and WordNet, the degree of polysemy, and the cross-lingual reliability.

#### 3.2.1 Extracting Relations

We compared classes that were in a hierarchical relation to see if we could identify it with one of the relations used in WordNet. We used the following semantic relations from WordNet (**hypernym, part meronym, member meronym, substance meronym , part holonym, member holonym, substance holonym, entailment, attribute, cause, also see, verb group, similar to**). As the objective of **WN** and **SD** is to map semantic relationships of languages, we did not used formal relationships such as derivational links.

Some examples of classes linked in this way are given in Table 3. In general, if we could find a link, it was good evidence that the synset used in the link was the correct mapping to the domain. For example, in Wordnet, dry (**SD** ID:1.3.3.1) is a hyponym of sear (**SD** ID:1.3.3.1.s4). As the relations exist in Wordnet and these two words occurs under the same ID (1.3.3.1). We consider the Wordnet mapping to be applicable to Semantic Domains.

Table 4 shows another good example of mapping for the **SD** labels using the WordNet semantic relations. 75% of the related **SD** words were mapped to the main words (8.4.1: period of

| **SD** ID | Word |
|---|---|
| 1.3.3.1: | dry |
| Hypernym of: | |
| 1.3.3.1.s5: | sear |
| 1.3.3.1.s4: | wither |
| Cause: | |
| 1.3.3.1.s2: | thirsty |
| 1.3.3.1.s1: | dehydrated, desiccated, dried |
| 1.3.3.1.s4: | wither |
| Similar to: | |
| 1.3.3.1.s2: | thirsty |
| 1.3.3.1.s1: | dehydrated, desiccated, dried |
| 1.3.3.1.s5: | sear |

Table 3: Classes linked with Semantic Relations

time/ janka waktu). For **SD** word 8.4.1.8 (Special days/hari-hari khusus), it was unable to be mapped under 8.4.1 as the expression, for both English and Indonesian, does not exist in WordNet. While for 8.4.1.1 (Calendar/Kalender), there is no direct semantic relation between the words available WordNet synsets and the main word 8.4.1. As such, 8.4.1.8 could not be mapped using WordNet relations (2nd level mapping) even though the word was mapped with WordNet synsets (1st level mapping).

#### 3.2.2 Monosemous Words

If a word is monosemous (that is it only appears in one synset) then we can assume it links a class to a synset unambiguously. We give some examples of such mappings in Table 5. In this case, there is no ambiguity, so the mapping is good.

#### 3.2.3 Translation

Lexical ambiguity is often language specific and multiple languages can thus be used to disambiguate meanings (Bond and Ogura, 2007). If we can find matching synsets through pivots in two languages (in our case English and Indonesian) then we consider it a good mapping. We give an example in Table 6.

## 4 Results

We produced three kinds of mappings:

- **class↔ synset**: classified as related; monosemous; translated. (monosemous, e.g. 1.3.1.3↔ 09411430-n ***river***)
- **class↔ class**: classified with the WordNet relation. (hypernym↔ hyponym,

| | English | | Indonesian |
|---|---|---|---|
| 8.3.3.3.4: | colors of the spectrum | 8.3.3.3.4: | rentetan warna yang diuraikan oleh cahaya |
| 3: | language and thought | 3: | bahasa dan pikiran |
| 9.4: | semantic constituents related to verbs | 9.4: | konstituen atau unsur semantik yang berkaitan dengan |
| 1.3.5: | solutions of water | 1.3.5: | larutan air |
| 2.3.1.9: | something used to see | 2.3.1.9: | sesuatu yang digunakan untuk melihat |

Table 2: **SD** main words not mapped to **WN**

| | English | | | Indonesian | |
|---|---|---|---|---|---|
| 8.4.1 | 15113229-n | period of time | 8.4.1 | 15115926-n | jangka waktu |
| | Hyponym | | | Hyponym | |
| 8.4.1.2 | 14484516-n | day | 8.4.1.2 | 14484516-n | hari |
| 8.4.1.3 | 15135996-n | week | 8.4.1.3 | 15135996-n | minggu |
| 8.4.1.4 | 15206296-n | month | 8.4.1.4 | 09358226-n | bulan |
| 8.4.1.5 | 00294884-v | season | 8.4.1.5 | 15239292-n | musim |
| 8.4.1.6 | 15201505-n | year | 8.4.1.6 | 15201505-n | tahun |
| 8.4.1.7 | 15248564-n | era | 8.4.1.7 | 15248564-n | zaman |
| | not mapped | | | not mapped | |
| 8.4.1.1 | 08266849-n; 06487395-n; 15173479-n | Calendar | 8.4.1.1 | 15173479-n | Kalender |
| 8.4.1.8 | NIL | Special days | 8.4.1.8 | NIL | Hari-hari khusus |

Table 4: Example of a good 2nd level mapping

e.g. 8.4.1↔ 8.4.1.2)

- **sense↔ sense**: this is the direct word level, sense disambiguated mapping (class+lemma↔ synset+lemma, e.g. 7.4.1+give↔ 05021151-n+give ).

The results of the mapping in terms of **class↔ synset** are summarized in Table 7 (which also shows the numbers of **class↔ class** mappings found). Potential mappings were found for 75% the domains, but confirmations were only found for around 21%.

The results for **class+lemma↔ synset+lemma** are shown in Table 8: about 69% of the English and 60% of the Indonesian **SD** words were mapped to entries in their respective wordnets. Out of the mapped **SD** label names, 27.92% and 31.92%, for English and Indonesian respectively, were confirmed using the **WN** semantic relations. Overall, about 20% of the **SD** label names were mapped to the second level.

Thus, the **class↔ synset** mapping improved as we go towards the lower levels as there is an increase in monosemous terms. However, the opposite occured for the SD-WN Main mapping because of the difference in word usage and structures in the two dictionaries. These weaknesses will be discussed in the following section

## 5 Discussion and Further Work

This is only the first step in the **SD-WN** mapping. The work that was done focuses on linking the **SD** words to the **WN** words before the **WN** semantic relationship is used to connect the words. As **WN** categorizes its words differently than **SD**, we expect some relations not to be mapped by the program: the cover should not be 100%, and is rarely one-to-one. In most cases, a single **SD** class links to multiple **WN** synsets.

When we started this process, full **SD** files were only available for English and Indonesian. There are now versions for Chinese and French which we intend to map to Chinese and French WordNets in the same way (Xu et al., 2008; Huang et al., 2010; Wang and Bond, 2013; Sagot and Fišer, 2012). This should increase the number of monosemous and translated mappings.

| **SD** ID | Word | **WN** ID | Meaning |
|---|---|---|---|
| 4.1.9.2.s3 | intermarry | 02490090-v | marry within the same ethnic, social, or family group |
| 6.5.2.7.s4 | kantor | 08337324-n | an administrative unit of government |

Table 5: Monosemous Words

| **SD** ID | Word | **WN** ID | Meaning |
|---|---|---|---|
| 2.s2 | someone, somebody | 00007846-n | a human being |
| 2.s2 | seseorang | 00007846-n | a human being |

Table 6: Classes that are Matched through Multiple Languages

Most of the **SD** words that were not mapped to **WN** synsets were not lemmas in **WN**. As shown in Table 2, these are mainly informal multi-word expressions, consisting of 4 or more words while the multi-words expression in wordnet are rarely of more than 3 words. As that mapping was done by matching both **SD** and **WN** expressions as a whole, these **SD** expressions were unable to be matched with **WN**. Having formal and informal names for the concepts (domains/synsets) could be useful for both resources.

Error analysis found some matches due to inconsistent structures, which suggest the resources themselves may need to be revised. For example, ***contact lens*** is under **SD** "something used to see" which we hand-mapped to **WN**'s optical instrument "an instrument designed to aid vision". However in **WN** it is a hyponym of optical device "a device for producing or controlling light" which puts it in the same grouping as camera lenses, not spectacles. It is possible it should inherit from both, but it should definitely inherit from optical instrument, as it is an aid to vision. In this case **SD** reveals a missing link in **WN**. The opposite case was also common.

We intend to use the mapping to generate a wordnet for the under-resourced language Abui (Kratochvíl, 2007). As a part of this process, we will correct and refine the mapping. We can then compare, for example, verb classes in Abui with those in wordnets for English and other well described languages. Linking descriptions of under-studied languages to well-studied languages makes it easier to leverage existing linguistic knowledge.

Even though most classes do not map one-to-one to WN synsets, the combination of class and lemma/gloss is generally enough to disambiguate. For example, consider the class 1.1.1.s2 "What words refer to how the sun moves". This links to at least four WordNet classes $\text{rise}_{v:16}$ "come up, of celestial bodies", $\text{sink}_{v:6}$ "appear to move downward", $\text{cross}_{v:1}$ "travel across or pass over" and $\text{set}_{v:10}$ "disappear beyond the horizon". Linking to these suggests several other possible entries for the class: ***go under*** [the horizon], ***traverse*** [the sky]. When we want to build a wordnet for, e.g., Abui, we would look at the Abui word with the gloss "go down" ***sei*** in the class 1.1.1.s2 and we know that this links to the synset $\text{sink}_{v:6}$. Even though the mapping is not one-to-one, the combination of mapping and gloss will generally lead to a specific synset. In addition, **WN** gives the information that $\text{rise}_{v:16}$ and $\text{set}_{v:10}$ are antonyms and this is true for the Abui equivalents ***marang*** and ***sei***.

The mapping can also be used to help translate the semantic domains into new languages (assuming there is a wordnet for the language) and to add new instances of the classes from the wordnets.

Finally, there has been a recent movement within the wordnet community to make the lexical resources more open (Bond and Paik, 2012; Bond and Foster, 2013). We hope to show the advantages of openness (more usable and accessible data) with the under-resourced language community and make the data open in the same way. The Wordnet-Semantic Domain Mappings themselves are available for download at the Open Multilingual Wordnet,[12] and linked in the search interface.

## 6 Conclusion

A simple **SD-WN** mapping was done using the **WN** semantic relationships. Even though the program was unable to cover all the semantic relationships that exist in both the English and Indonesian **SD** data, it provided a basis for further work in mapping the semantic relationships that are available in the **SD** file. The mapping is freely avail-

[12]See `http://compling.hss.ntu.edu.sg/omw/`

| LVL | Example | # IDs | ID linked to WN | | ≥ 1 relation | | ≥ 2 relation | | monosemous | |
|---|---|---|---|---|---|---|---|---|---|---|
| | | | eng | ind | eng | ind | eng | ind | eng | ind |
| 1 | 1: universe | 9 | 3 | 4 | 3 | 4 | 1 | 2 | 1 | 1 |
| 2 | 1.1: sky | 68 | 54 | 46 | 27 | 27 | 6 | 13 | 7 | 7 |
| 3 | 1.1.1: sun | 419 | 252 | 237 | 73 | 74 | 16 | 32 | 33 | 29 |
| 4 | 1.1.1.1: moon | 985 | 702 | 605 | 90 | 69 | 8 | 8 | 86 | 65 |

Table 7: Summary of Mapping

| | English (eng) | | | Indonesian (ind) | | |
|---|---|---|---|---|---|---|
| | Word | Immediate (%) | Label (%) | Word | Immediate (%) | Label (%) |
| **SD** words | 1,793 | | | 1,793 | | |
| 1st level mapping | 1,243 | 69.32 | | 1,090 | 60.75 | |
| 2nd level mapping | 347 | 27.92 | 19.35 | 384 | 31.92 | 21.42 |

Table 8: Coverage of **SD-WN** Main mapping

able, and we hope that it will provide a useful link between wordnet and the semantic domains.

## Acknowledgments

This research was partially funded by the NTU SUG grant on *Documentation and Analysis of Endangered Papuan Languages of Alor-Pantar Archipleago, Southern Indonesia* (M4080390.100). We would like to thank Ronald Moe for producing and sharing with us the SIL semantic domains, as well as his constructive support.

## References

Collin F. Baker, Charles J. Fillmore, and John B. Lowe. 1998. The Berkeley FrameNet project. In *36th Annual Meeting of the Association for Computational Linguistics and 17th International Conference on Computational Linguistics: COLING/ACL-98*. Montreal, Canada.

Stephen Bird, Ewan Klein, and Edward Loper. 2009. *Natural Language Processing with Python*. O'Reilly. `www.nltk.org/book`.

Francis Bond and Ryan Foster. 2013. Linking and extending an open multilingual wordnet. In *51st Annual Meeting of the Association for Computational Linguistics: ACL-2013*, pages 1352–1362. Sofia. URL `http://aclweb.org/anthology/P13-1133`.

Francis Bond, Hitoshi Isahara, Kyoko Kanzaki, and Kiyotaka Uchimoto. 2008. Boot-strapping a WordNet using multiple existing WordNets. In *Sixth International Conference on Language Resources and Evaluation (LREC 2008)*. Marrakech.

Francis Bond and Kentaro Ogura. 2007. Combining linguistic resources to create a machine-tractable Japanese-Malay dictionary. *Language Resources and Evaluation*, 42(2):127–136. URL `http://dx.doi.org/10.1007/s10579-007-9038-4`, (Special issue on Asian language technology).

Francis Bond and Kyonghee Paik. 2012. A survey of wordnets and their licenses. In *Proceedings of the 6th Global WordNet Conference (GWC 2012)*. Matsue. 64–71.

Carl Darling Buck. 1949. *A dictionary of selected synonyms in the principal Indo-European languages : a contribution to the history of ideas*. Chicago University Press, Chicago.

Gerard de Melo and Gerhard Weikum. 2010. Towards universal multilingual knowledge bases. In Pushpak Bhattacharyya, Christiane Fellbaum, and Piek Vossen, editors, *Principles, Construction, and Applications of Multilingual Wordnets. Proceedings of the 5th Global WordNet Conference (GWC 2010)*, pages 149–156. Narosa Publishing, New Delhi, India.

J. Deng, W. Dong, R. Socher, L.-J. Li, K. Li, and L. Fei-Fei. 2009. ImageNet: A Large-Scale Hierarchical Image Database. In *IEEE Computer Vision and Pattern Recognition (CVPR09)*.

Christine Fellbaum, editor. 1998. *WordNet: An Electronic Lexical Database*. MIT Press.

A. Gangemi, N. Guarino, C. Masolo, and A. Oltramari. 2003. Sweetening WordNet with DOLCE. *AI Magazine*, 24(3):13–24.

Chu-Ren Huang, Shu-Kai Hsieh, Jia-Fei Hong, Yun-Zhu Chen, I-Li Su, Yong-Xiang Chen, and Sheng-Wei Huang. 2010. Chinese wordnet: Design and implementation of a cross-lingual knowledge processing infrastructure. *Journal of Chinese Information Processing*, 24(2):14–23. (in Chinese).

František Kratochvíl. 2007. *A Grammar of Abui: A Papuan Language of Indonesia*. LOT, Utrecht.

František Kratochvíl. 2011. Transitivity in Abui. *Studies in Language*, 35(3):588–635.

Shari Landes, Claudia Leacock, and Christiane Fellbaum. 1998. Building semantic concordances. In Fellbaum (1998), chapter 8, pages 199–216.

Ron Moe. 2013. Semantic domains. `http://semdom.org`. (Accessed 2013-04-01).

Nurril Hirfana Mohamed Noor, Suerya Sapuan, and Francis Bond. 2011. Creating the open Wordnet Bahasa. In *Proceedings of the 25th Pacific Asia Conference on Language, Information and Computation (PACLIC 25)*, pages 258–267. Singapore.

Ian Niles and Adam Pease. 2001. Towards a standard upper ontology. In Chris Welty and Barry Smith, editors, *Proceedings of the 2nd International Conference on Formal Ontology in Information Systems (FOIS-2001)*. Maine.

Benoît Sagot and Darja Fišer. 2012. Automatic Extension of WOLF. In *Proceedings of GWC2012 - 6th International Global Wordnet Conference*. Matsue, Japan.

Shan Wang and Francis Bond. 2013. Building a Chinese wordnet: Starting from core synsets. In *Proceedings of the 11th Workshop on Asian Language Resources*. Nagoya.

Renjie Xu, Zhiqiang Gao, Yuzhong Qu, and Zhisheng Huang. 2008. An integrated approach for automatic construction of bilingual Chinese-English WordNet. In *3rd Asian Semantic Web Conference (ASWC 2008)*, pages 302–341.

# Modeling Prefix and Particle Verbs in GermaNet

**Christina Hoppermann**
Department of Linguistics
University of Tübingen, Germany
christina.hoppermann@uni-tuebingen.de

**Erhard Hinrichs**
Department of Linguistics
University of Tübingen, Germany
erhard.hinrichs@uni-tuebingen.de

## Abstract

Verbal word formation processes involving prefixes and particles are highly productive in Germanic languages. The compositional semantics of such prefix and particle verbs requires an in-depth analysis of the interdependence of their constituent parts for adequately representing these types of complex verbs in lexical-semantic networks. The present paper introduces modeling principles that account for such language-specific phenomena in the German wordnet *GermaNet* (Hamp and Feldweg, 1997; Henrich and Hinrichs, 2010), considering the continuum between full semantic transparency and highly lexicalized meanings as well as the semantic contribution of the prefix or particle to the meaning of the complex verb as a whole.

## 1 Introduction

This paper addresses the question how morphologically complex words can be adequately modeled in a wordnet and focuses on two classes of such verbs in German: (i) prefix verbs such as *entladen* 'unload' and *zerstören* 'destroy', and (ii) particle verbs such as *übergehen* 'bypass someone' and *losfahren* 'start driving'. Both types of verbs consist of a word-initial element followed by a host constituent. In the case of prefix verbs, the word-initial element is a bound morpheme such as *ent-* or *zer-*, while for particle verbs it is typically a free[1] morpheme such as *über* or *los*, which can be separated from its host constituent depending on the clause type[2] that the particle verb appears in. The host constituent of a prefix or particle verb can either be a simplex (or: base verb) as in the examples above or a nominal or adjectival base as in *bedachen* 'put on a roof' or *erblassen* 'grow pale'.

A systematic treatment of prefix and particle verbs in a wordnet setting is desirable and significant for at least the following reasons:

1. The word formation processes involved in the two classes of verbs are highly productive for all Germanic languages.
2. The host constituent of a prefix or particle verb can be derived from an adjectival or nominal base. Therefore, an adequate treatment of these verbs has to include suitable morphological and semantic relations among the word classes involved. What makes such an account particularly interesting in a wordnet setting is the fact that nouns, verbs, and adjectives are the very word classes modeled in a wordnet.
3. The lexical semantics of prefix and particle verbs crucially involves a continuum between full semantic transparency on the one hand and highly lexicalized meanings on the other hand. Verbs such as *entladen* 'unload' and *losfahren* 'start driving' are fully transparent: Their semantics can be compositionally derived from the meanings of their parts, as the preverbs[3] *ent-* and *los* contribute the meanings of removal and initiation of the actions denoted by the simplex. By con-

[1] There are also occurrences of inseparable particles (e.g., *umfähren* 'bypass sth.'), which are always unstressed (Dewell, 2011) in contrast to separable particles (e.g., *úmfahren* 'run into so.').

[2] Free particles are separated in verb-first and verb-second clauses. They are only inseparable as infinitives or in subordinate clauses in clause-final position (Dewell, 2011).

[3] The term *preverb* is used as cover term for both prefixes and particles (Booij and Kemenade, 2003; Los et al., 2012).

trast, *zerstören* 'destroy' and *übergehen* 'bypass someone' are highly lexicalized, since their base verbs do not make a semantically transparent contribution to the meaning of the expression as a whole in present-day language use.

The continuum of semantic transparency and lexicalization is not restricted to the lexical semantics of German prefix and particle verbs. It has also been observed with respect to other word formation processes such as nominal compounding and is, thus, of wider interest. A case in point is the contrast between *Hauswand* 'house wall', which is compositionally derived from its parts, and *Bahnhof* 'train station', which according to a simple composition of its constituent parts should denote a yard for trains, but which actually refers to a building.

What lexicalized meanings of morphologically complex words have in common is that the meaning of the complex word is not a hyponym of the meaning of its host or head constituent: *zerstören* 'destroy' is not a hyponym of *stören* 'disturb' and *Bahnhof* 'train station' is not a hyponym of its head constituent *Hof* 'yard'. This finding also indicates that a simple account that establishes a hyponymic relation between a particle or prefix verb and its host constituent will not provide a satisfactory account of the phenomena in question.

In the remainder of this paper, we will argue that an adequate account of prefix and particle verbs has to be based on the following two main considerations: (i) the distinction between semantic transparency and lexicalization, and (ii) the way in which the word-initial element contributes to the meaning of the complex verb as a whole. These considerations will lay the foundation for defining general principles of hypernym selection for modeling complex verbs in the German wordnet GermaNet (GN).

## 2 Prefix and Particle Inventory

The inventory of prefixes considered in the present study includes all *native* (Los et al., 2012) inseparable prefixes in German: *be-*, *ent-*, *er-*, *miss-*, *ver-*, and *zer-* (Eisenberg, 1998; Fleischer and Barz, 1995; Mungan, 1986; Stiebels, 1996). Prefixes with a Latinate origin, such as *de-*, *dis-*, *re-*, or *trans-* (Fleischer and Barz, 1995), are not within the scope of this study. In contrast to the closed set of prefixes, the particle inventory is more extensive and comprises particles such as *ab*, *an*, *auf*, *aus*, *bei*, *durch*, *ein*, *los*, *nach*, *über*, *um*, *unter*, *voll*, *vor*, *wider*, *wieder*, and *zu* (Dewell, 2011; Eisenberg, 1998; Fleischer and Barz, 1995; Mungan, 1986; Stiebels, 1996).

The present analysis makes use of existing semantic classifications of preverbs (e.g., Augst, 1998; Dewell, 2011; Donalies, 2005; Fleischer and Barz, 1995; Mungan, 1986; Stiebels, 1996) and develops them further in a wordnet setting. At the time of writing the paper, GermaNet contains 94273 nouns, 12111 adjectives and 14333 verbs, of which 3040 are prefix verbs and 5171 are particle verbs. Out of the total number of prefix verbs, the frequency distribution is as follows: *ver-* (45%), *be-* (25%), *er-* (14%), *ent-* (11%), *zer-* (4%), and *miss-* (1%).

## 3 Modeling Complex Verbs in GN

Although it seems natural that the host constituent of a complex verb could be used as its hypernym, the subsequent analysis of the continuum between lexicalization and semantic transparency will demonstrate that this solution is not viable in all cases. Rather, the continuum requires a distinction between various classes, which differ in the selection and in the number of hypernyms.

### 3.1 Lexicalization

Highly lexicalized verbs are at one end of the continuum between full semantic transparency and highly lexicalized meanings. Both German prefix and particle verbs are subject to lexicalization. As pointed out in section 1, it is not possible to assign lexicalized prefix and particle verbs as hyponyms to their host constituents, since the semantics of the host constituent is no longer part of the meaning of the complex verb. As a consequence, this lack of semantic transparency requires finding an appropriate hypernym that takes account of the meaning of the lexicalized verb as a whole.

For the majority of lexicalized complex verbs, the semantic contribution of the word-initial element is not apparent so that the hypernym selection is to be conducted in the same way as for simplex verbs (Vossen, 2002). This is the case for particle verbs such as *aufnehmen* 'record', which is modeled as hyponym of the synset *aufzeichnen/mitschneiden* 'record', as it cannot be linked to its base verb *nehmen* 'take'.

Nevertheless, there are cases in which semantic classifications of the word-initial element can be used as indicator for choosing an appropriate hypernym. This mainly applies to lexicalized complex verbs such as *zerstören* 'destroy', for which the meaning of the prefix *zer-* expresses 'destroying or damaging something' (Augst, 1998; Fleischer and Barz, 1995; Mungan, 1986). Thus, the stand-alone transparent semantics expressed by *zer-* is used as indicator for finding an appropriate hypernym (*"materielle Zustandsveränderung"* 'material change of state'), as a relation to the contemporary meaning of the simplex *stören* 'disturb' is not possible.

Although there is no conceptual relation to the simplex, the information on the individual word-internal components of the complex lexicalized verb is still available in GN in the form of a morpho-syntactic analysis, which separates the preverb from its simplex.

### 3.2 Semantic Transparency

In contrast to highly lexicalized verbs, semantically transparent complex verbs form the opposite end of the continuum. What these transparent verbs have in common is that there is always either a conceptual (i.e., hypernymic/hyponymic) or lexical (e.g., antonymic) relation to the respective base verb. However, there are two interrelated factors that vary along the continuum: (i) the degree of semantic transparency, and (ii) the semantic contribution of the word-initial element to the complex verb as a whole. On the basis of these two factors, three different classes can be distinguished and will be introduced below.

**Class 1: Full Transparency, Light Contribution**
The meaning of complex verbs within this class is fully transparent and is always represented by the respective simplex as the exclusive hypernym. This can be ascribed to the interaction of the preverb with its base verb: The semantics of the complex verb can be compositionally derived from the meaning of its parts. Thus, the simplex keeps its original meaning while the semantic contribution of the preverb is light, fulfilling one of the following two core functions: (a.) indication of a direction or (b.) intensification of the meaning denoted by the simplex.

**a. Indicator of a Direction**
The majority of German particle verbs indicate a direction. Particles are typically free morphemes that are frequently used as adpositions or adverbs without being part of a complex verb (Los et al., 2012). In combination with a verbal base, they usually retain the meanings they have in isolation (Brinton and Closs Traugott, 2005), such as path expressions (Dewell, 2011). Thereby, they only add further directional information to the simplex, whose meaning remains highly transparent. As a consequence, the simplex always serves as the exclusive hypernym of the respective complex verb. This applies, e.g., to the verb *laden* 'load', which has, inter alia, the following directional hyponyms in GN: *aufladen* 'load up', *einladen* 'load into', and *umladen* 'reload'. These particle verbs all denote a specific direction by the particles *auf* ('up', i.e., upward movement), *ein* ('into', i.e., inward movement), and *um* (i.e., movement from one location to another), sharing the semantics of the corresponding adposition.

**b. Intensifier**
The second core function within class 1 refers to the use of word-initial elements as intensifiers of the meanings denoted by their host constituents. The word-initial element only has a light semantic contribution so that the entire complex verb remains highly transparent and is thus assigned as hyponym to its simplex. This is, e.g., the case for *verärgern* 'annoy', which has a hyponymic relation to its simplex *ärgern* 'tease'.

**Class 2: Full Transparency/High Contribution**
This class represents an exceptional case that is only valid for a limited number of complex verbs such as prefix verbs with *miss-* as negator of the meaning denoted by the simplex (Fleischer and Barz, 1995). Consequently, the simplex cannot function as hypernym, as shown below for the synset *missgönnen/neiden* 'begrudge'.

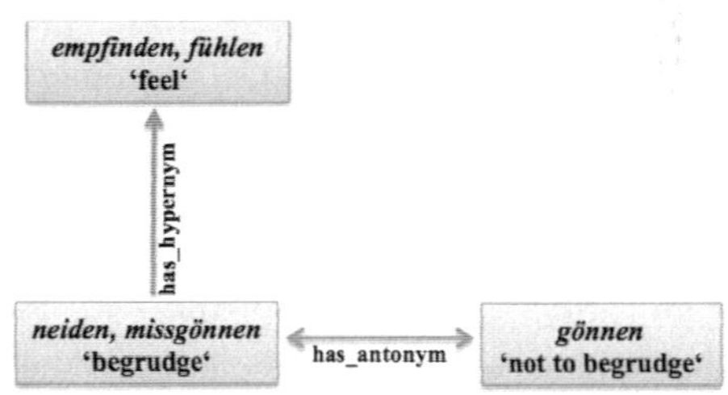

Figure 1. Conceptual and lexical relations.

Instead, another hypernym is chosen that takes account of the semantics of the complex verb (i.e., the synset *empfinden/fühlen* 'feel'). As for all transparent complex verbs, the relation to the simplex *gönnen* 'not to begrudge' is still present and is indicated by an antonymic relation.

The relation to the simplex can also be implicit, as some verbs with *ent-*, which refer to the inversion of an action denoted by the base (Fleischer and Barz, 1995), are antonyms of another complex verb sharing the same simplex. This is the case for *entladen* 'discharge', whose antonym is the particle verb *aufladen* 'charge'.

**Class 3: Low Transparency/High Contribution** The third class displays the highest semantic contribution of the word-initial element while the meaning of the complex verb as a whole still remains transparent. Accounting for this predominant semantics requires treating verbs within this class both as hyponyms of their base verbs and of an additional hypernym, which expresses the prevailing semantic contribution of the preverb. The two hypernyms thus jointly account for the semantic contributions of preverb and base verb and lead to a more precise definition of the verb classes in question (cf. Bosch et al., 2008). This is, for instance, the case for one of the meanings of the prefix *ver-* 'make a mistake' (Mungan, 1986). This meaning is contained, e.g., in the reflexive prefix verbs represented in Figure 2 as a selection of hyponyms of both the *artificial concept*[4] *"falsch machen/Fehler machen"* 'make a mistake' and of each corresponding base verb: *sich versprechen* 'make a slip of the tongue', *sich verfahren* 'get lost while driving', and *sich verrechnen* 'miscalculate'.

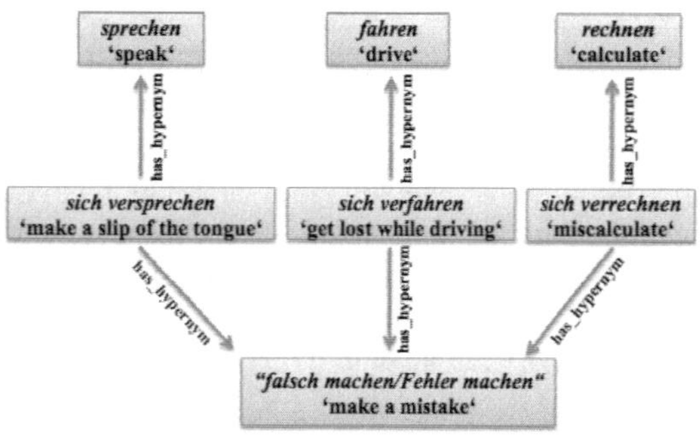


Figure 2. Selected verbs with two hypernyms.

Complex verbs in class 3 do not only include prefix but also particle verbs. Thus, the same approach can be applied to the verb *aufschrauben* 'unscrew', which has the following two hypernyms: its base verb *schrauben* 'screw' and the verb *öffnen* 'open'.

Another type of word-initial elements, which can be systematically modeled in class 3, represents preverbs indicating lexical aspect or *Aktionsart* 'manner of action'. On the one hand, this includes *ingressive* markers such as the prefix *er-* (e.g., *erklingen* 'start to sound') and the particle *los* (e.g., *loslaufen* 'start running'). On the other hand, the prefix *ver-* (e.g., *verglühen* 'burn out') as well as some word formations with the particles *auf* and *aus* characterize *egressive* verbs (e.g., *aufessen* 'eat up', *auslesen* 'finish reading'), which express the termination or accomplishment (Vendler, 1957) of an action or state denoted by the base verb (Donalies, 2005; Stiebels, 1996; Helbig and Buscha, 1987). Both types of Aktionsart markers are modeled as hyponyms of two verb forms: of their respective simplex as well as of a verb denoting the particular aspectual meaning.

### 3.3 Principles of Hypernym Selection

The decision tree in Figure 3 summarizes the principles of hypernym selection, which specify the number of hypernyms to be chosen (i.e., one versus two), the synsets to be selected as hypernyms (i.e., simplex or not), and the use of further relations. Following the decision tree from top to bottom, it first needs to be determined whether the complex verb has a verbal, nominal, or adjectival base. If the base is verbal, the left branch of the tree needs to be passed through, deciding whether the complex verb is lexicalized or transparent. While lexicalized verbs only have one hypernym that does not equal the simplex, transparent verbs always have either a conceptual or (implicit) lexical relation to the simplex and are distinguished into three classes (cf. section 3.2).

The topmost right branch of the decision tree considers verbs with a nominal or adjectival base. As there is consequently no verbal base that could be used as hypernym for the respective complex verb, another verb form is to be chosen that expresses the semantics of the complex verb as a whole. Thus, the semantic contribution of the word-initial element is of prime importance for selecting an adequate hypernym. For instance, the meaning *to equip sth. with a/an <base noun>* is expressed by the prefixes *be-* and *ver-* as well as by the particle *um*. This can be represented by the synset *versehen/ausrüsten/ausstatten/ausstaffieren*. The hyponyms for this synset include the following entries, where the base noun is indicated in angle brackets: *be<dach>en* 'equip sth. with a <roof>', *ver<glas>en* 'enclose sth. with <glass>', and *um<mantel>n* 'surround with a <sheath>'. In order to account for the relation to the host constituent, a new derivational relation needs to be introduced that creates a connection to the base noun. This way, it is possible to tighten the wordnet by establishing relations that cross the line of word classes.

[4] In GermaNet, artificial concepts are not only used for filling lexical gaps. Similar to the verb classes defined by Levin (1993), they also serve the purpose of classifying semantically related concepts together by means of co-hyponymy.

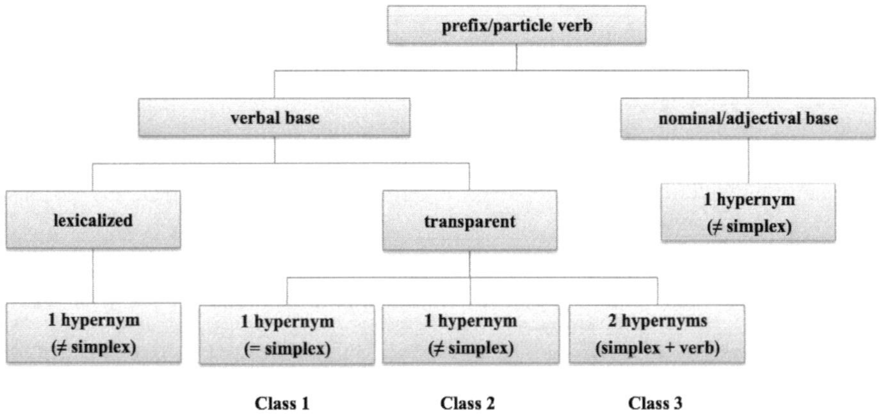


Figure 3. Principles of hypernym selection.

In the case of deadjectival verbs, the meaning *to become/to make <base adjective>* is often denoted by the preverb. An example provides the artificial concept *"materielle Zustandsveränderung"* 'material change of state', which is used as hypernym of deadjectival verbs such as *verflüssigen* 'liquefy', *verdicken* 'thicken', or *erwärmen* 'warm up'. If applicable, the causative meaning expressed by these preverbs is explicitly modeled by the *causes*[5] relation, which refers to the base adjective being the result of the process denoted by the complex verb (e.g., *<erblassen>* 'grow pale' *causes <blass>* 'pale').

## 4 Related Work

The use of multiple hypernyms for representing the compositional semantics of complex verbs can be identified in the Dutch wordnet project (Vossen et al., 1999). As in GN, the Dutch complex verb *opendraaien* 'open by turning' has two hypernyms (Vossen et al., 1999): its simplex *draaien* 'turn' and the verb *openmaken* 'open'.

In contrast, complex verbs in the Princeton WordNet (Fellbaum, 1999) only make use of one hypernym: The phrasal verb *to blow sth. up* is only a hyponym of the verb *expand.* The hypernym of its German equivalent *aufblasen* expresses the same semantics (i.e., *vergrößern* 'expand'), but the particle verb additionally has the simplex *blasen* 'blow' as second hypernym.

Regarding the different kinds of relations used in wordnets, Šojat et al. (2012) discuss the inclusion of morphosemantic relations in the Croatian WordNet (CroWN). These relations e.g. group the meanings of preverbs into the class *location*, which indicates the directions of movements (e.g., *loc_bott_up* for upward movement).

Other wordnets dealing with (morpho-) semantic or derivational relations include the Polish wordnet (Maziarz et al., 2012) and the Czech wordnet (Bosch et al., 2008). They make fine-granular distinctions between various relation types, such as *inchoativity* and *derivationality*, which have also been addressed in this paper.

## 5 Conclusion

The present paper has established criteria for modeling morphologically complex verbs in the lexical-semantic network GermaNet, focusing on German prefix and particle verbs and accounting for their compositional semantics. Two main factors have been identified that provide the basis for their representation: (i) the continuum between full semantic transparency and highly lexicalized meanings, and (ii) the semantic contribution of the word-initial element to the meaning of the complex verb as a whole.

It has been demonstrated that a compositional analysis of the word-initial element and its host constituent enables a rule-based derivation of general modeling principles, which can systematically be applied in order to achieve a consistent depiction of complex verbs in the wordnet.

**Acknowledgments**

Financial support was provided by the German Research Foundation (DFG) as part of the Collaborative Research Center 'Emergence of Meaning' (SFB 833) and by the German Ministry of Education and Technology (BMBF) as part of the research grant CLARIN-D.

[5] The use of the *causes* relation is not restricted to complex verbs with an adjectival base. It is generally used for denoting resultative states for both simplex and complex verbs complying to the pattern *<causative transitive verb> causes <resultative intransitive verb>*, thereby signifying the *causative-inchoative alternation* (Levin, 1993), e.g., *zerbrechen* 'sb. breaks sth. to pieces' *causes zerbrechen* 'sth. breaks to pieces' (Bohnemeyer, 2007).

## References


Gerhard Augst. 1998. *Wortfamilienwörterbuch der deutschen Gegenwartssprache*. Max Niemeyer Verlag, Tübingen.

Jürgen Bohnemeyer. 2007. Morphological Transparency and the argument structure of verbs of cutting and breaking. *Cognitive Linguistics*, 18(2):153-177.

Geert Booij and Ans van Kemenade. 2003. Preverbs: An Introduction. In Geert Booij and Jaap van Marle, editors, *Yearbook of Morphology 2003*. Kluwer, Dordrecht, pages 1-12.

Sonja Bosch, Christiane Fellbaum, and Karel Pala. 2008. Enhancing WordNets with Morphological Relations: A Case Study from Czech, English and Zulu. In *Proceedings of the Fourth Global WordNet Conference 2008*, Szeged, Hungary, pages 74-90.

Laurel J. Brinton and Elizabeth Closs Traugott. 2005. *Lexicalization and Language Change*. Cambridge University Press, Cambridge.

Robert D. Dewell. 2011. *The Meaning of Particle/Prefix Constructions in German*. John Benjamins Publishing Company, Amsterdam/Philadelphia.

Elke Donalies. 2005. *Die Wortbildung des Deutschen: Ein Überblick*. Gunter Narr Verlag, Tübingen.

Peter Eisenberg. 1998. *Grundriß der deutschen Grammatik: Das Wort*. Metzler, Stuttgart/Weimar.

Christiane Fellbaum. 1999. *WordNet: An Electronic Lexical Database*. MIT Press, Camebridge.

Wolfgang Fleischer and Irmhild Barz. 1995. *Wortbildung der deutschen Gegenwartssprache*. Niemeyer, Tübingen.

Birgit Hamp and Helmut Feldweg. 1997. GermaNet - a Lexical-Semantic Net for German. In *Proceedings of ACL workshop Automatic Information Extraction and Building of Lexical Semantic Resources for NLP Applications*, Madrid.

Gerhard Helbig and Joachim Buscha. 1987. *Deutsche Grammatik: Ein Handbuch für den Ausländerunterricht*. Verlag Enzyklopädie, Leipzig.

Verena Henrich and Erhard Hinrichs. 2010. GernEdit – The GermaNet Editing Tool. In *Proceedings of the Seventh International Conference on Language Resources and Evaluation (LREC 2010)*, Valletta, Malta, pages 2228-2235.

Beth Levin. 1993. *English Verb Classes and Alternations: A Preliminary Investigation*. The University of Chicago Press, Chicago.

Bettelou Los, Corrien Blom, Geert Booij, Marion Elenbaas, and Ans van Kemenade. 2012. *Morphosyntactic Change: A Comparative Study of Particles and Prefixes*. Cambridge University Press, Cambridge.

Marek Maziarz, Maciej Piasecki, and Stan Szpakowicz. 2012. An Implementation of a System of Verb Relations in plWordNet 2.0. In *Proceedings of the Sixth Global WordNet Conference 2012*, Matsue, Japan, pages 181-188.

Güler Mungan. 1986. *Die semantische Interaktion zwischen dem präfigierenden Verbzusatz und dem Simplex bei deutschen Partikel- und Präfixverben*. Peter Lang, Frankfurt am Main.

Krešimir Šojat, Matea Srebačić, and Marko Tadić. 2012. Derivational and Semantic Relations of Croation Verbs. *Journal of Language Modelling*, 0(1):111-142.

Barbara Stiebels. 1996. *Lexikalische Argumente und Adjunkte: Zum semantischen Beitrag von verbalen Präfixen und Partikeln*. Akademie Verlag, Berlin.

Zeno Vendler. 1957. Verbs and Times. *The Philosophical Review*, 66(2):143-160.

Piek Vossen, Laura Bloksma, and Paul Boersma. 1999. *The Dutch WordNet*. Version 2, Final, July 12, 1999, University of Amsterdam.

Piek Vossen. 2002. *EuroWordNet: General Document*. Version 3, Final, July 1, 2002. http://hdl.handle.net/1871/11116.

# Developing and Maintaining a WordNet: Procedures and Tools

**Miljana Mladenović**
Faculty of Mathematics
University of Belgrade
ml.miljana@gmail.com

**Jelena Mitrović**
Faculty of Philology
University of Belgrade
jmitrovic@gmail.com

**Cvetana Krstev**
Faculty of Philology
University of Belgrade
cvetana@matf.bg.ac.rs

**Abstract**

In this paper we present a set of tools that will help developers of wordnets not only to increase the number of synsets but also to ensure their quality, thus preventing it to become obsolete too soon. We discuss where the dangers lay in a WordNet production and how they were faced in the case of the Serbian WordNet. Developed tools fall in two categories: first are tools for upgrade, cleaning and validation that produce a clean, up-to-date WordNet, while second category consists of tools gathered in a Web application that enable search, development and maintenance of a WordNet. The basic functions of this application are presented: XML support and import/export facilities, creation of new synsets, connection to the Princeton WordNet, sophisticated search possibilities and navigation, production of a WordNet statistics and safety procedures. Some of presented tools were developed specifically for Serbian, while majority of them is adaptable and can be used for wordnets of other languages.

## 1 Introduction

Development of a WordNet is always a labor-intensive task for which a work of a number of professionals is needed. If produced from the scratch and mostly manually the development will necessarily take many years if aiming at comprehensiveness and accuracy. In such a setting a valuable resource, not yet fully developed, can easily become obsolete. The reasons for this are manifold. First, since WordNet is dealing with "words", its contents can become out-of-date. A straightforward example can be found in the Princeton WordNet 3.0 (PWN): it describes *Yugoslavia* as the Union of Serbia and Montenegro (which no longer exists) while *Serbia* is described as a historical region in central and northern Yugoslavia, and not as a Republic (which it is today). Moreover, new items can be added to a WordNet content, like domain information or similar. Next, the format used to represent a WordNet necessarily changes and evolves in time. The early wordnets did not use XML representation which is almost obligatory today. However, new, more powerful representations emerge. Tools used to develop and maintain wordnets have to keep pace with content enhancement and format changes. Finally, many wordnets were developed highly relying on the PWN by using a so-called *expand model* in which synsets from the PWN are translated into a target language (Fellbaum, 2010). Wordnets developed in this way are all connected through the Interlingual Index (ILI) that links similar concepts between languages, which is highly advantageous for various multilingual applications. However, in order to maintain this network a WordNet has to regularly upgrade when new versions of the Princeton WordNet emerge.

The Serbian WordNet faced all mentioned problems. The Serbian WordNet (SWN) was initially produced in the scope of the BalkaNet project (Stamou et al., 2002). At the end of the project, in 2004, the Serbian WordNet had 7,000 synsets linked to the Princeton WordNet version 2.0. In the subsequent years approximately 14,000 synsets were added to it thanks to volunteer work of numerous specialists and the WordNet editor. The addition was not done at random - as the need arose, special attention was given to certain conceptual domains - emotions - and scientific domains - biological species, biomedicine, religion, law, linguistics, literature, librarianship, computer science, and lately, culinary. Recently, a new impetus to the enhancement and upgrade of the SWN was given by the CESAR project, in the scope of which many Polish, Slovak, Hungarian, Croatian, Serbian and Bulgarian resources were thoroughly described by meta-data and made public through the META-SHARE [1] repositories (Ogrodniczuk et al., 2012). The Serbian WordNet is available for download for non-commercial use under the CC-BY-NC license.

In the meantime, many new applications based on natural language processing were being developed for Serbian and for a number of them the Serbian WordNet became a valuable resource, e.g. for document classification systems (Pavlović-Lažetić and Graovac, 2010), multilingual queries into digital libraries (Stanković et al., 2012), multiword lexica acquisition (Krstev et al., 2010), domain specific knowledge-based ontologies and systems (Mladenović and Mitrović, 2013), etc. However, in order to profit from it as much as possible it became a necessity not only to upgrade and improve it but to establish a stable environment for its development in the future. The most important steps in this process were:

1) A safe and unequivocal mapping onto the current version of the Princeton WordNet (PWN 3.0);

2) A creation of XML Schema that would enable a thorough validation of the Serbian WordNet and automatic correction of many formal inconsistencies;

3) Mapping of Serbian WordNet to SUMO;

4) A conversion from XML format to other relevant formats.

In Section 2 we will present the present environment for the development of SWN and its limitations. In order to perform afore mentioned improvement tasks we have developed a number of preparatory tools that will be described in Subsection 3.1. Our job did not end here: in order to provide for a continuous development of the Serbian WordNet a web application that enables browsing for all and updating and enhancing of its content for a chosen set of specialists is being developed. We will present this tool in Subsection 3.2. In Section 4 we will give directions for future work.

## 2 Motivation and discussion

Serbian WordNet was structurally built following the pattern of EuroWordNet (Vossen, 1998), as was the case with other wordnets that were built in the scope of BalkaNet - wordnets for Bulgarian, Czech, Greek, Romanian and Turkish. XML-like representations of the EuroWordNet data were produced with a tool named VisDic (Horák and Smrž, 2004).

For many years VisDic has proved to be a reliable, user-friendly tool for development and maintenance of the SWN. It was particularly useful for simultaneous work on multiple WordNet XML documents of identical structure. The connection between those documents was achieved in two ways - through the AutoLookUp function, which connected the synsets of different WordNet files with the same synset identification, where their side-by-side representation was the result, and through the function CopyEntryTo which allowed for copying of the contents of a certain synset from one WordNet file into another. The search functionality of this tool leaned on the representation of synsets via a tree-structure in both directions (towards the root and towards the leaves). Two operations were implemented in that regard: TopmostEntries and FullExpansion. The first one provided all synsets that presented roots of the relational hierarchy. The second operation provided all synsets that represented the parts of a subtree in the given search. VisDic allowed for a certain degree of control over the consistency of data. It could point out to some inconsistencies such as synsets with identical IDs, duplicate Literal/Sense pairs or duplicate synset links.

In the first years of the development of the Serbian WordNet, VisDic, as a free tool, significantly contributed to the development of this semantic network. Still, the fact that it was limited to the desktop surrounding made team work difficult. This was particularly inappropriate for the development of the SWN, as a number of volunteers frequently worked simultaneously on its development (Krstev et al., 2008). Merging of parts of WordNet files made by many users into one file was always susceptible to introducing errors and inconsistencies. For that reason, the accessibility and usefulness of the WordNet editing tool needed to be improved. The resource itself did not allow for automatic processing of XML documents because the XML-like files used in VisDic did not have a root element. Furthermore, VisDic did not have a function for checking whether the input XML document was well-formed and/or valid against a DTD or XSD Schema. As a result, the structure of the Serbian WordNet was diverse from one synset to another. Moreover, due to the lack of validity control users were allowed to input un-

[1] http://www.meta-share.eu

supported as well as some unexpected tag values. The limited system of morphological labeling in VisDic did not serve well to the morphologically rich language such is Serbian. That is why morphological tags were manually added later, based on Serbian morphological electronic dictionaries. This information was added manually by the chief editor of the SWN inside the element LNOTE that was not specifically intended for this type of information. This method was susceptible to errors and slowed down the process of adding entries.

The same problem was present with adding SUMO tags to the synsets that were specifically present only in the Serbian WordNet, that is, they were not transferred from the PWN, like synsets with BILI tags, that is to say, synsets that were added in the course of the BalkaNet project, or those synsets that were specific to the Serbian language and carried the tag SRP. Also, developers of the SWN often felt that some other useful and often needed checking procedures were missing in VisDic, for instance check for hanging synsets (missing the hypernym relation). Also, it often occurred that some basic statistics had to be produced (number of synsets and literals per Part-of-Speech, number of multi-word literals vs. simple literals, literals with the highest number of senses, synsets with the highest number of literals, etc.). A number of scripts were written as needed to overcome this deficiency of VisDic.

Insufficient connection of VisDic with the SUMO (Pease, 2011) and other upper level ontologies, as well as with domain ontologies, slowed down the development of tools for ontological reasoning based on the Serbian WordNet. Also, the impossibility of transformation of the XML document to other formats, especially to RDF and OWL made the development of ontology-based knowledge bases related to WordNet even more difficult. Lastly, the search system of VisDic leaned on elementary queries over the content, without the possibility of setting logical filters or the possibility of smart search, e.g. the use of XPath. Taking into account all advantages and setbacks of the existing software solution, we took on the task of designing and building a set of tools that would improve the development of the Serbian WordNet and other semantic resources for the Serbian language.

## 3 Developing the Tools and the Web application for Semantic Resources for Serbian

The entire project aimed at enhancing the tools for developing, maintaining and using SWN was split into two phases: preparatory phase and operational phase.

### 3.1 Preparatory Phase

In this phase, we defined procedures and tools that enabled the following 6 tasks:

1. In the first step we created a software tool to upgrade the current version 2.0 of the SWN onto the version 3.0 of the PWN. This tool uses the mapping files produced and made available by The Center for Language and Speech Technologies and Applications at the Technical University of Catalunya [2]. to translate SynsetID from one PWN version to SynsetID of the other version of PWN (Daudé et al., 2003). In general, our software tool was created to transform every version of SWN to any other, as long as the appropriate mapping is available. For the cases of ambiguous or nonexistent mappings, the tool produced two additional files - a file `doubled` that lists pairs (or triples) of synset IDs in the version 3.0 that corresponded to one synset in version 2.0 (there was a total of 45 such synsets in SWN, version 2.0) and a file `missing` that lists IDs of synsets from version 2.0 that could not be mapped to the new version (a total of 147 synsets with this problem were retrieved in SWN version 2.0). All these cases were resolved manually.

2. In the second step we defined the `swn.xsd` Schema for validation and control of SWN. The first introduced XSD schema used for SWN is presented in (Krstev et al., 2004). A software tool LeXimir (the old name ILReMat) that used it, was created to work as a connection between VisDic and morphological dictionaries for Serbian. Still, functions for validation of the SWN as an XML resource were not implemented. Also, when the new tags had to be introduced in SWN (such as SNOTE - a note related to a synset, or SUMO - for SUMO concepts), the corresponding XSD schema did not follow those changes. Furthermore, the problem remained to distribute and install the new schema to all the desktop applications that would use it. Now, the new version of the SWN XSD schema (given in Figure 1) can be easily changed by SWN

[2] `http://bit.ly/18Uf8kX`

administrators, uploaded to the web server, made available to all other SWN users and maintained as a part of a web tool for on-line WordNet search, development and maintenance (presented in Section 3.2).

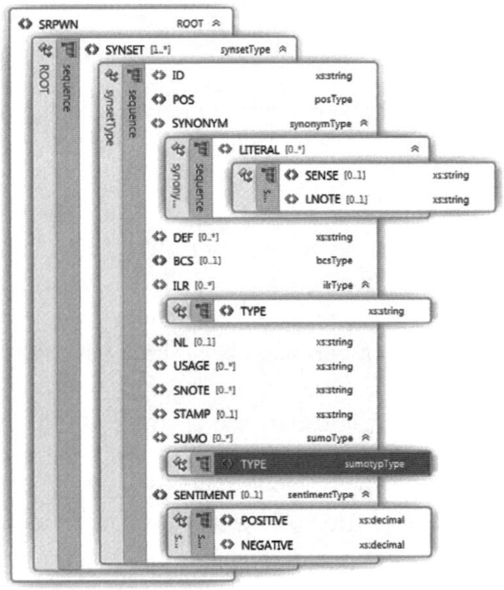


Figure 1: XSD schema for SWN XML

3. In the third step, a module was developed to validate and correct the SWN in its original VisDic XML-like representation (with the root element added) against the newly developed SWN XSD Schema. This module performed automatic correction in all unambiguous cases, such as rearrangement of elements, which represented the majority of cases. In the case of the last version of the SWN XML file a total of 17,994 POS tags, 6,110 BCS tags, 20,421 ILR tags, 130 BCS tags and 10 NL tags changed their position in the new WordNet XML document. For other types of errors, such as inappropriate or empty contents of elements an error report was issued and those errors were corrected manually. At the end, a well-formed and valid SWN was obtained.

4. This step is specific to the Serbian language. Namely, it uses two alphabets equally: Cyrillic and Latin. Translation from Cyrillic to Latin is straightforward since to each Cyrillic letter corresponds one Latin letter or digraph. The same is not valid for translation from Latin to Cyrillic because digraphs have to be distinguished from consonant groups. For instance, in *nadživeti* "outlive" dž represents a consonant group, while in *odžak* "chimney" dž is a digraph. When these two words are written in Cyrillic the problems do not exist anymore: надживети and оџак. When the development of the first Serbian language resource started back in early 80s it was still difficult to work with Cyrillic, especially if it was mixed with the Latin alphabet which normally happens in Serbian texts. For that reason a special encoding was invented that uses the ASCII character set and enables unambiguous mapping to both Serbian Cyrillic and Serbian Latin. Many valuable Serbian resources were developed using this encoding. Today, however, it is obsolete and we decided that it was time to switch to the Unicode UTF-8 for Serbian Cyrillic. This could not be done fully automatically because there are literals or parts of literals that have to remain in Latin script, e.g. names of biological species such as *породица Bovidae* "family Bovidae", chemical symbols and formulae, e.g. H2O and some acronyms, like PC for personal computer. In order to facilitate this process we have defined some simple rules that recognize instances that have to remain in the Latin alphabet. After automatic translation of SWN from ASCII to Unicode UTF-8 the SWN was checked by Serbian electronic dictionary and incorrect translations were corrected manually.

5. Serbian WordNet developed using VisDic did not contain the information about SUMO ontology. This information was indirectly available from the PWN through the alignment process. However, for one wishing to use the SWN outside the VisDic environment this information would be missing. We developed a separate module that explicitly assigns this information to synsets in the SWN. For synsets that were taken over from the PWN this was easily done. In SWN there are specific concepts: 530 Balkan specific concepts and 174 Serbian specific concepts. They were also appointed with SUMO tags. The procedure was carried out automatically, by inheriting the tag of the parent synset, if one existed and if it had a SUMO tag. After that, the rest of the mappings, that is to say the unresolved ones, were done manually.

6. In this step automatically are prepared some useful lists that help users that create new synsets by the new application to fill some elements with appropriate values. The first one is the list of all semantic relations that can be established between synsets. This list was obtained on the basis of all semantic relations that exist in PWN. The second one is the list of SUMO concepts con-

nected to the POS to which they apply. This list was obtained from existing SUMO tags in PWN (Niles and Pease, 2003). The third list is the list of all codes of inflectional paradigms for simple and multi-word units used in Serbian morphological e-dictionaries (Krstev, 2008). This list gives an example and short explanation beside each code that can help user to choose one when filling the appropriate element - LNOTE. For example (Table 1), the synset boat:1 from PWN has a corresponding synset barka:1, čamac:1, čun:1 in the SWN. The inflectional codes for these three literals are N664, N41 and N81, respectively. Entries for these three codes in the prepared list are (if these same literals were given as examples):

| | | |
|---|---|---|
| N664 | *barka* | the dative singular *barci* |
| N41 | *čamac* | fleeting a;<br>the vocative singular *čamče* |
| N81 | *čun* | the nominative plural *čunovi* |

Table 1: Examples of inflectional codes used in SWN.

These three lists are used in a form of dropdown list in the web application for WordNet search, development and maintenance presented in the next section. The first two lists are of general nature, while the third one is specific to Serbian.

### 3.2 Operational Phase

In this phase, a web application was developed and its beta version was uploaded to the address: `http://resursi.mmiljana.com` The purpose of this application was to encompass all benefits of the already existing software tool, new demands of the Serbian semantic web users and contemporary software development techniques to enable a safe, efficient, multi-user, modular and easy to expand system for development of semantic resources in Serbian. In this phase, the following procedures and tasks were carried out.

1. A very important module of the web application is the XML validator. This module is able to validate any WordNet file against any XSD scheme and to obtain validation errors and suggestions for corrections. Also, it enables a serialization into TXT, CSV, RDF or XML formats with a chosen XSL transformation of a complete file or parts of search results. RDF representation is especially interesting to us because it can be queried and processed by standard Semantic Web tools, thus facilitating the integration of the WordNet data into various Semantic Web applications.

2. The web application was built in order to facilitate changing and adding of new synsets into wordnets. The new synsets can be added one at a time (either by transferring from the PWN - see item 3 - or independently) or as a batch. The latter case is particularly useful for addition of language specific concepts. The prepared synsets have to be in a valid XML form (except for a root element) with IDs of linked synsets already filled in appropriate elements. This method was used for enhancing the SWN with Serbian specific concepts from the culinary domain (Stanković et al., 2014). For synsets that are added one at a time, a form is prepared for filling obligatory and optional elements, while a user can open new fields for repeatable ones. In the case of SWN, the drop down lists that we described in the previous subsection were used to input the ILR, LNOTE and SUMO tags which were filtered automatically according to the POS.

3. Another segment of the application is the option of forming queries over the PWN resource in the version 3.0. For that purpose, we used the WordNetEngine [3] and we enhanced it with the functionality of copying of a chosen synset from the PWN into SWN. Search over the PWN can be carried out in two ways: by entering a word (in the Word field) or by entering an ID of a synset (in the synset ID field), in which case the POS must be chosen from the drop-down list given next to the synset ID field. If we choose the ID of a synset for the POS for which it does not exist, the program will notify us, otherwise it will provide a clickable link in order to display further details about semantic relations of that synset with other synsets. The number of shown semantic relations i.e. hierarchical representations of semantic relations of a particular synset with synsets semantically connected to it, is defined by checking the type of a semantic relation which we want to represent hierarchically using the check-box lists named Noun, Verb, Adjective and Adverb which contain labels of the most common semantic relations pertaining to the given POS.

4. The implemented search functions over the SWN take into consideration all tags from a WordNet used. If a user chooses a tag SYNSET, then a full-text search over a whole wordnet is per-

[3] `http://ptl.sys.virginia.edu/msg8u/NLP/Source/ResourceAPIs/WordNet/WordNet/`

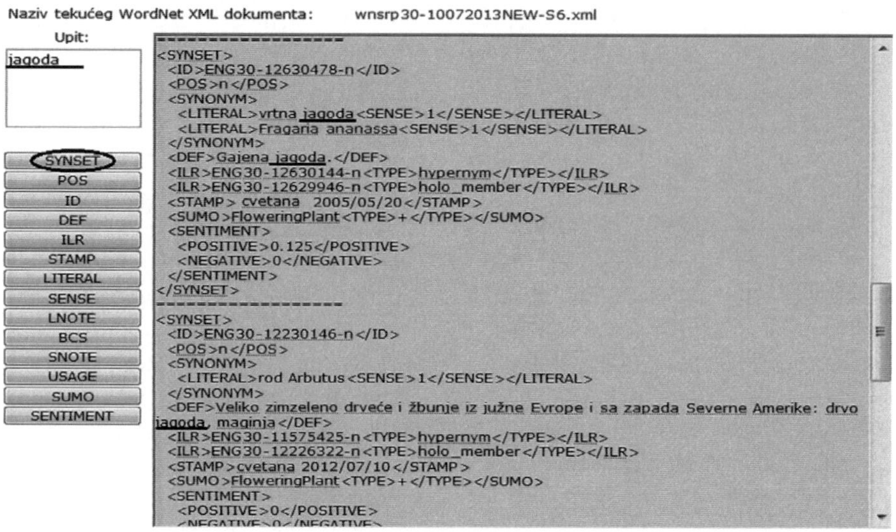


Figure 2: User-friendly XPATH queries over different SWN tags

formed. Also, they search data according to the authoring information. A search function can be either set to a simple value (Figure 2) or via a logic filter which is implemented to be user-friendly for those who are not familiar with XPath.

For example, the filter could be set to search for all synsets that have the term *jabuka* "apple" and whose SUMO tag is "PreparedFood" via an advanced logic query:

```
<SUMO> equals "PreparedFood" AND
(<LITERAL> contains "jabuka" OR
<DEF> contains "jabuka")
```

Or we could find all synsets whose part of a literal or a literal itself is also contained in the superior synset as is the case with synsets described by LITERALS *obrazovna ustanova* "educational institution", *verska ustanova* "religious institution", *medicinska ustanova* "medical institution" and their hypernym given by the LITERAL *ustanova* "institution".

Similarly, we could find: all antonym synsets for synsets which have a LITERAL tag that contains a word *ružan* "ugly". The result of an advanced logic query is a synset whose sense is *lep* "handsome".

```
(<LITERAL>contains "ružan" AND
<ILR><Type>equals "near_antonym")
```

All the query results can be displayed in textual (Figure 3) and graphical tree form. Tree representation facilitates navigation through the seman-

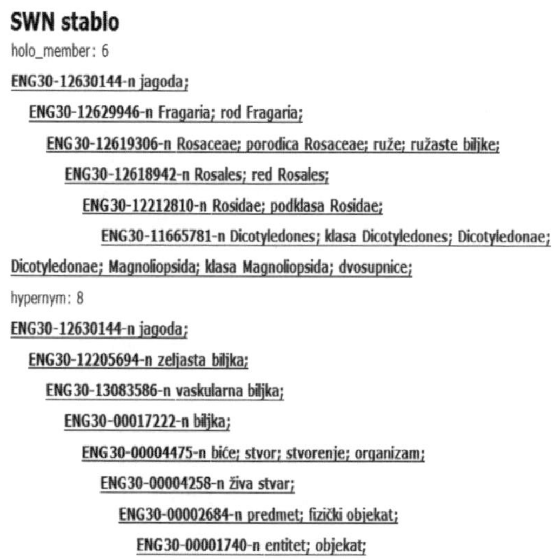


Figure 3: Semantic relations tree structure of a synset *jagoda* "strawberry"

tic relations tree structure because every synset in a tree representation is a link to the synset itself. The main purpose of textual form is its serialization as a subsegment of SWN structure to be used later as a resource in some other applications. For example: if we search for the term *osećanje* "feeling", as a result we obtain a semantic tree where the root synset has the sense of the searched term and the leaves are synsets representing emotional states. Such structure can be used as a separate XML file and mixed with other resources in the process of opinion mining tasks. A special submodule SWNengine is coded to implement all functions needed for navigation through the semantic relations tree structure of SWN.

5. Besides search functions over WordNet synsets, a separate module is created for providing statistical information about some valuable parameters of a WordNet in use that were often needed in the past. Table 2 shows some data provided by this module for the current version of SWN.

| | | | | | |
|---|---|---|---|---|---|
| **POS in Synsets** | | | | | |
| POS | Noun | Verb | Adj. | Adv. | |
| Synsets | 16978 | 2157 | 1584 | 121 | |
| **Inter Lingual Indexes in Synsets** | | | | | |
| ILI | ENG | BILI | SRB | | |
| Synsets | 20136 | 530 | 174 | | |
| **Semantic Relations in Synsets** | | | | | |
| ILR | Hyper-nym | Holo part | Holo mem | Holo portion | |
| Synsets | 19123 | 1746 | 3890 | 222 | |
| ILR | Antonym | Deri-ved | Deri-ved gen | Deri-ved pos | |
| Synsets | 783 | 665 | 38 | 45 | |
| **Number of Literals in Synsets** | | | | | |
| Literals | 1 | 2 | 3 | 4 | 5 |
| Synsets | 11356 | 6657 | 1969 | 557 | 190 |

Table 2: Examples of inflectional codes used in SWN.

6. The safety of this application was ensured via roles and levels inside those roles. Roles are granted by WordNet administrators. The following roles were defined: unauthorized users that have the right of elementary querying over the network, using complex logic filters and statistical reporting about connections and meanings inside of the network itself; WordNet users and administrators. Inside of roles, the levels are defined - ordinary users that can input and change only the synsets which they themselves have defined, and moderators who have control over the entire resource. Tag NL holds the information about status of a synset. If the moderator has not yet verified all data concerning the newly inserted synset, NL tag is set to "no", and when the new synset has been approved by the moderator, the value of NL tag switches to "yes". Also, for the information about the "hanging" semantic relations (e.g. if one of synsets in the relation doesn't exist) is presented for each synset in the visual form.

The application is developed as ASP.NET Framework 4.0 C# web site, corresponding to the relational database MS SQL Server 2005 and by using jQuery 1.8.9 library at client's side. It is available for non-commercial use under the CC-BY-NC license.

## 4 Conclusion

The Serbian WordNet has a potential to develop with more substantial speed and quality now that valuable new tools for its usage and development are available. In this new tool we wanted to keep all characteristics of the old software VisDic that proved useful in the past and to add the missing ones of which the most important are a full XML support, distributed work, and advanced search. We have achieved this goal, but it should be noted that the interface is still under construction and its development will follow users' demands in future. Also, for the time being it is given in Serbian, but we plan to enable localization for other languages in the next phase.

We hope to continue the development of SWN in several directions. In the process of further extension of this resource, domain knowledge about agroindustry, medicine, geology etc. will be added, depending on the scientific fields in which it will be used. Sentiment labels for synsets and procedures of parallelization with English resources of the same purpose are also planned in the near future. Furthermore, we plan on increasing the number of noun-adverb relations in order to enrich the system of semantic relations and semantic knowledge that would facilitate tagging of rhetorical figures in Serbian. Finally, mapping to SUMO ontologies and generating of an appropriate ontology from the existing XML resource will be taken into consideration. We believe that wordnets developed for other languages can benefit from some of our tools, namely the tool for upgrading one version of WordNet to another, as well as other tools - with minor adjustments depending on the particular needs of the administrators and users of those wordnets.

## Acknowledgments

This research was conducted through the project III 47003, financed by the Serbian Ministry of Science.

## References


Jordi Daudé, Lluís Padró and German Rigau. 2003. *Validation and Tuning of Wordnet Mapping Techniques*. In Proc. of the International Conference on Recent Advances in Natural Language Processing (RANLP'03).

Christiane Fellbaum. 2010. *WordNet*. Springer, Netherlands.

Matthew Steven Gerber. 2013. *WordNetEngine.cs, Synset.cs*. `http://ptl.sys.virginia.edu/msg8u/NLP/Source/ResourceAPIs/WordNet/WordNet/` (accessed September 2nd 2013).

Aleš Horák and Pavel Smrž. 2004. *VisDic - WordNet browsing and editing tool*. In Proc. of the 2nd International Global WordNet Conference, Brno, Czech Republic.

Cvetana Krstev, Duško Vitas, Ranka Stanković, Ivan Obradović and Gordana Pavlović-Lažetić. 2004. *Combining Heterogeneous Lexical Resources*. In Proc. of the 4th International Conference on Language Resources and Evaluation, Lisabon, Portugal, vol. 4, pp. 1103-1106.

Cvetana Krstev, Bojana Djordjević, Sanja Antonić, Nevena Ivković-Berček, Zorica Zorica, Vesna Crnogorac and Ljiljana Macura. 2008. *Cooperative Work in Further Development of Serbian WordNet*. INFOtheca 9(1-2):59a-78a.

Cvetana Krstev. 2008. *Processing of Serbian - Automata, Texts and Electronic dictionaries*. Faculty of Philology, University of Belgrade, Belgrade.

Cvetana Krstev, Ranka Stanković, Ivan Obradović, Duško Vitas and Miloš Utvić. 2010. *Automatic Construction of a Morphological Dictionary of Multi-Word Units*. LNCS 6233, Springer, pp. 226-237.

Miljana Mladenović and Jelena Mitrović. 2013. *Ontology of Rhetorical Figures for Serbian*. LNAI 8082, Springer pp. 386-393.

Ian Niles and Adam Pease. 2003. *Linking Lexicons and Ontologies: Mapping WordNet to the Suggested Upper Merged Ontology*. In Proc. of the IEEE International Conference on Information and Knowledge Engineering, pp. 412-416.

Maciej Ogrodniczuk, Radovan Garabik, Svetla Koeva, Cvetana Krstev, Piotr Pęzik, Tibor Pintér, Adam Przepiórkowski, György Szaszák, Marko Tadić, Tamás Váradi and Duško Vitas. 2012. *Central and South-European language resources in META-SHARE*. INFOtheca 13(1): 3-26.

Gordana Pavlović-Lažetić and Jelena Graovac. 2010. *Ontology-driven Conceptual Document Classification*. In KDIR, pp. 383-386.

Adam Pease. 2011. *Ontology: A Practical Guide*. Articulate Software Press, Angwin, CA.

Sofia Stamou, Kemal Oflazer, Karel Pala, Dimitris Christodoulakis, Dan Christodoulakis, Svetla Koeva, George Totkov, Dominique Totkov and Maria Grigoriadou. 2002. *BALKANET: A Multilingual Semantic Network for Balkan Languages*. In Proc. of the 1st International Global WordNet Conference, Mysore, India.

Ranka Stanković, Ivan Obradović and Aleksandra Trtovac. 2012. *An Approach to Development of Bilingual Lexical Resources*. In Proc. of the Workshop on Computational Linguistics and Natural Language Processing of Balkan Languages - CLoBL 2012, the Balkan Conference in Informatics, Novi Sad, Serbia, pp. 101-104.

Staša Vujičić Stanković, Cvetana Krstev, Duško Vitas. 2014. *Enriching Serbian WordNet and Electronic Dictionaries with Terms from the Culinary Domain*. In Proc. of the Global Wordnet Conference (in the same volume).

The Center for Language and Speech Technologies and Applications at the Technical University of Catalunya. (accessed September 2nd 2013). `http://bit.ly/18Uf8kX`

Piek Vossen. 1998. *Introduction to EuroWordNet*. Computers and the Humanities 32(2-3):73-89.

# Aligning Word Senses in GermaNet and the DWDS Dictionary of the German Language

**Verena Henrich, Erhard Hinrichs, Reinhild Barkey**
Department of Linguistics
University of Tübingen, Germany
{vhenrich,eh,rbarkey}@sfs.uni-tuebingen.de

## Abstract

A comparison and alignment of lexical resources brings about considerable mutual benefits for all resources involved. For all sense distinctions that are completely parallel in two resources, such an alignment provides supporting external evidence for the validity of sense distinction and allows enriching word senses by information contained in the other resource. By contrast, for all non-matching sense distinctions, reason for revisiting and possibly revising the lexical entries in question is provided. The purpose of this paper is to compare the German wordnet GermaNet with the Digital Dictionary of the German Language (DWDS) and to align word senses in the two resources. The paper presents issues that arise in practice when such an alignment is performed and indicates the benefits that both resources will gain.

## 1 Introduction

It has long been recognized that the identification and differentiation of word senses is one of the harder tasks that lexicographers face. As a result, lexical resources display considerable variation in the number of word senses that lexicographers assign to a given lexical entry in a dictionary. Against this background, lexicographic practice has undertaken considerable efforts to find external knowledge sources that can aid in distinguishing and identifying word senses. The external knowledge sources that are most widely used for this purpose are very large electronic corpora that can be harvested for a given word under lexicographic consideration. Another type of resource that has also been explored as an external reference point is the comparison with another semantic dictionary that has been constructed independently for the same language.

The present paper reports on an ongoing project in which the German wordnet GermaNet (Hamp and Feldweg, 1997; Henrich and Hinrichs, 2010) is compared to the word senses contained in the Digital Dictionary of the German Language (*Digitales Wörterbuch der Deutschen Sprache*[1], DWDS; Klein and Geyken, 2010). Both resources are long-term lexicographic projects aiming at a comprehensive coverage of contemporary standard German in electronic form. What makes a comparison between these resources particularly interesting and useful is the fact that they utilize two different methods for constructing word meanings.

The DWDS is based on the digital versions of three pre-existing dictionaries: the Dictionary of Contemporary German (*Wörterbuch der deutschen Gegenwartssprache*, WDG), the Grimm Dictionaries *Deutsches Wörterbuch von Jacob Grimm und Wilhelm Grimm* (1DWB) and its revised version (2DWB), as well as the Etymological German Dictionary by Wolfgang Pfeifer (EtymWb). The lexical entries inherited from these dictionaries have been revised and amended by information harvested from large electronic corpora of contemporary German (Didakowski et al., 2012). DWDS lexical entries are structured by the number of senses which may be further differentiated by an enumeration of subsenses. Senses are accompanied by examples harvested from German text corpora or by so-called *competence examples* that are manually constructed.

The conception of word meaning underlying GermaNet adheres to the idea of a network of meaningfully related words and concepts that are interlinked by a set of lexical and conceptual relations and that was first realized in the Princeton WordNet for English (Fellbaum, 1998). The set of lexical and conceptual relations include synonymy, hypernymy/hyponymy, meronymy/holonymy, causation, antonymy, and pertainymy.

The comparison of GermaNet and the DWDS dictionary will focus on the alignment of Germa-

[1] http://www.dwds.de/

Net senses (synsets and lexical units) with the senses and subsenses of DWDS lexical entries. The benefits of this GermaNet-DWDS comparison include the following:

- If the set of sense distinctions match for a given word lemma in both resources, then this provides supporting external evidence for the validity of these sense distinctions.
- If the set of sense distinctions differ between the two resources, then this provides reason for revisiting and possibly revising the lexical entries in question.

Apart from the comparison of word senses, each resource stands to gain from the GermaNet-DWDS mapping in the following ways:

- It becomes possible to implement an intelligent semantic search for the DWDS that provides users not just with the word senses of a given lexical entry but also with lexical information about related words.
- GermaNet synsets and lexical units can be enriched by suitable definitions as well as examples contained in the DWDS.

The purpose of this paper is to present the results of a pilot study that concentrates on a set of issues that arise in practice when such a mapping is performed.

## 2 Survey of the Overlapping Coverage

The total number of lemmas that have lexical entries in both resources is 48,036[2] (6,211 adjectives, 34,366 nouns, and 7,735 verbs), which covers about 53.5% of all lemmas encoded in GermaNet. At first glance, this overlap might seem low. However, on a closer look, there is an explanation for this which mainly concerns the following three points:

- The history of the two resources causes differences in coverage. The DWDS is based on the digital versions of three pre-existing dictionaries that do not include most recent contemporary language. By contrast, the terms to be included in GermaNet follow frequency lists extracted from large corpora such as newspaper texts and Wikipedia, which also contain recent contemporary language.
- Both resources have different basic decisions on what terms and senses should be included. The perspectives and guidelines that the lexicographers of both resources pursue differ. For example, the resources deviate in the inclusion of regional, obsolete, technical, and colloquial terms as well as most recent contemporary language. This further explains why the coverage of GermaNet and the DWDS differs.
- Since compounding is a highly productive phenomenon of the German language, the question of which compounds to include in a lexical resource is not trivial to answer. There are many newly created compounds that eventually – after some undefined time and depending on the frequency of general usage – might become part of the fundamental vocabulary of the German language. Thus, especially for the coverage of compounds, there is a huge deviation between the two resources.

Since senses in the DWDS might be further differentiated by an enumeration of subsenses, a survey on word senses involves more than one comparison. GermaNet distinguishes 59,495 senses for the 48,036 lemmas that the two resources share. The overall number of 61,053 main sense distinctions in the DWDS is very similar. On the contrary, the number of main senses plus subsenses on the highest level encoded in the DWDS is 74,346, which is more than in GermaNet. This suggests a mapping on the main sense level of the DWDS.

The outcome of this survey proves that there is a considerable overlap of word lemmas with a comparable amount of senses in both resources, which supports the usefulness of conducting a sense alignment.

## 3 Evaluation of the Sense Alignment

In order to be able to evaluate the alignment on the level of senses and subsenses, the lexical entries for an initial set of 470 randomly selected word lemmas (see Section 4 for the selection process) have been manually analyzed with regard to the appropriateness of matching senses from one resource onto the senses in the other resource. The variability of how good the senses can be matched leads to a division into four classes that are illustrated and described in the following four subsections – in descending order according to their alignment appropriateness.

[2] All numbers are calculated on GermaNet's current release 8.0 as of April 2013 and on the DWDS subset taken from version 0.4.17 and filtered for all lexical entries for lemmas covered by both resources. This filtered subset has been made available to us on August 9, 2013.

**Figure 1: Sense mapping using the example of *Pferd* (class 1).**

### 3.1 Class 1: Exact match of main senses

Class 1 represents the ideal case, i.e., senses in GermaNet correspond to main senses in the DWDS. The German noun *Pferd* is a case in point. As illustrated in Figure 1, this lemma has the three distinct senses in both resources representing an animal horse, a gymnastic horse, and a chess knight. All word senses that fall into this class show an identical overlapping lexical coverage and an identical granularity level of sense distinctions. For both GermaNet and the DWDS, this provides mutual supporting evidence for the validity of these sense distinctions.

For GermaNet, the obvious gain for all these senses is an enrichment by suitable definitions and examples contained in the corresponding DWDS senses. For the DWDS, it becomes possible for all these senses that an intelligent semantic search provides users not just with the word senses of a given lexical entry but also with lexical information about related words.

### 3.2 Class 2: Exact match of subsenses

There are several senses in GermaNet that do not correspond to main senses in the DWDS but which correspond to subsenses in the DWDS. These latter ones are included in class 2. Figure 2 gives an example using the word *Bogen*. In GermaNet, there are two distinct senses representing a violin bow and a bow as a weapon (see the left side of Figure 2). In the DWDS, there is a main sense described as *gebogenes Gerät* 'curved device' which is further differentiated into the two subsenses of a violin bow (*sub 1*) and a bow as a weapon (*sub 2*) – see the two entries denoted by *sub 1* and *sub 2* on the right side of Figure 2.

The overall coverage for these senses is the same. It is only the granularity level of the sense distinctions that differs. The reason for this difference results from different perspectives and guidelines of how to model word senses that the lexicographers of both resources pursue. There is an agreement between lexicographers of both resources that the two senses under consideration should be modeled separately. The question of whether to constitute two separate word senses or two subsenses of a common main sense is bound to the nature of the resources, i.e., GermaNet does not further distinguish word senses into subsenses.

The senses that fall into this class again provide support for the validity of the sense distinctions for both resources. Furthermore, the enrichment of GermaNet senses with definitions and examples as well as the enrichment of DWDS senses with information on related words is equally possible than it is described for class 1.

### 3.3 Class 3: Partly overlapping coverage and different sense distinctions

Class 3 contains senses for which a straightforward one-to-one mapping is not possible. This includes the following two cases: (i) two separate senses from one resource are jointly represented by only one sense in the other resource and (ii) the core meaning of two senses is the same, but the two senses are still not completely identical in their coverage.

The German noun *Pranke* is a case in point for case (i). The DWDS encodes a sense defined as *Vordertatze, besonders von großen Raubtieren; umgangssprachlich, scherzhaft, übertragen: große, starke Hand* 'forepaw of an animal, especially a predator; colloquial, jokingly, figurative: big, strong hand' (see the right side in Figure 3). In GermaNet, *Pranke* has the two fine-grained senses denoting the paw of an animal and the

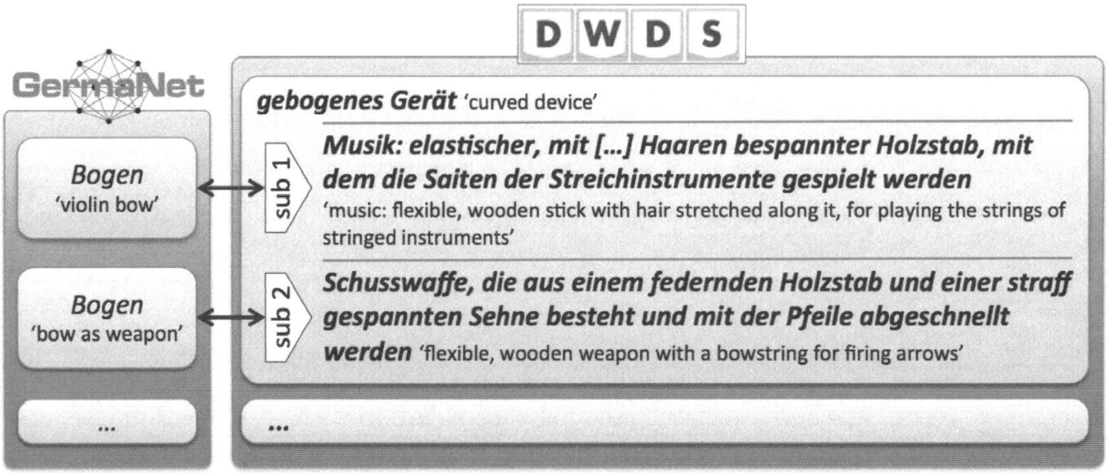


**Figure 2: Sense mapping using the example of *Bogen* (class 2).**

figurative term for the human hand (see the left side in Figure 3). In this example, both these more specific GermaNet senses are subsumed under one single DWDS sense.

In the second case (ii) that is subsumed by class 3, there is no complete coverage of the meaning of one sense in one resource with the corresponding sense in the other resource. The core sense is mostly identical, but there are meaning aspects that led the lexicographers to decide differently on whether to explicitly encode a separate sense in the dictionary or not.

An example of this type is the German noun *Sturm* 'storm'. Both GermaNet and the DWDS encode a sense referring to the weather phenomenon. Accompanying example sentences of this word sense in the DWDS include instances exemplifying a figurative usage, such as, for example, *ein Sturm der Entrüstung* 'a storm of indignation'. That means, the figurative meaning of *Sturm* is explicitly mentioned in the DWDS weather phenomenon sense – without encoding a separate sense or subsense. By contrast, the figurative meaning of *Sturm* is not present in GermaNet – neither as part of the corresponding weather phenomenon sense nor explicitly as a separate sense.

The phenomena of both cases (i) and (ii) cannot solely be explained by the lexicographic background of the two resources. They rather illustrate different lexicographic perspectives of how to distinguish senses of a word. The question at what point a meaning should be regarded as a distinct sense or subsense to be included in a dictionary is a difficult issue in lexicographic work. Aspects that affect this decision include figurative meaning, technical, colloquial, or regional usage of a term. Both in the paw and in the storm examples, the lexicographers of the two resources have made different decisions with respect to the status of the figurative meaning of a word sense.

As for the benefit from a mapping of senses in this class, it would mean that each example sentence for the DWDS senses in question has to be analyzed individually in order to decide whether it can be assigned to a GermaNet sense. Nonetheless, it is interesting to further analyze these cases since they concern the identification and differentiation of word senses which is one of the harder tasks that lexicographers face.

### 3.4 Class 4: Distinct coverage

This class comprises lemmas where there is at least one sense or subsense in one resource that does not have a corresponding entry in the other resource. An example of this kind is illustrated in Figure 4 using the example of *Maus*. For this word, GermaNet encodes the two senses of the mouse as an animal and the computer mouse (see the left side of Figure 4). The DWDS also encodes the animal sense of a mouse, but it does not include the computer mouse sense. Instead, the DWDS lists *Mäuse* (plural for *Maus*) in the sense of an informal synonym for money (see the right side of Figure 4).

As illustrated in the mouse example, both resources gain benefit from a sense alignment by mutually providing suggestions of possibly missing senses. In general, with the help of simple word comparisons, it is easy to automatically compile lists of lemmas that serve as candidates to be inserted into a dictionary. By contrast, it is much more difficult to provide (automatic) suggestions of possibly missing senses. In all cases where the sense alignment discovers different

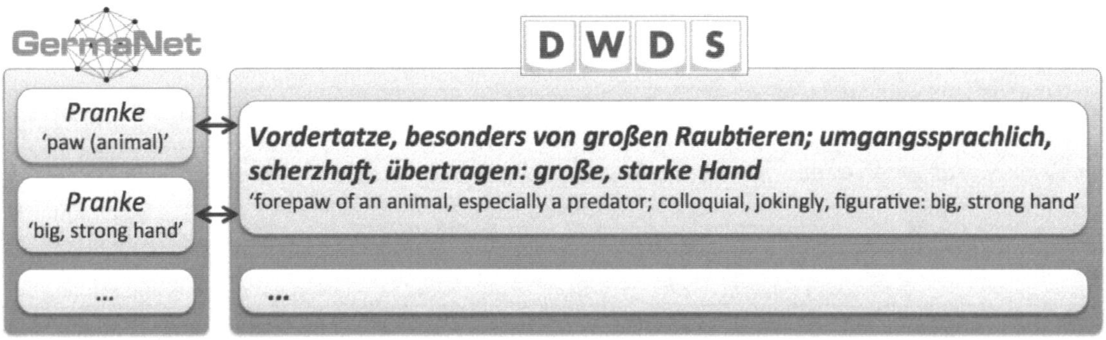


**Figure 3: Sense mapping using the example of *Pranke* (class 3).**

sets of sense distinctions between GermaNet and the DWDS, this provides reason for revisiting and possibly revising the lexical entries in question.

## 4 Evaluation Statistics

The selection of the initial set of manually aligned word lemmas is guided by the following criteria:

- The selected words include all three word classes of adjectives, nouns, and verbs.
- In order to ensure a detailed evaluation of lexical items with different degrees of polysemy, the evaluation reports results for five different polysemy classes: words having (i) one sense in GermaNet, (ii) two senses in GermaNet, (iii) three or four senses, (iv) five to ten senses, and (v) more than ten senses in GermaNet.
- The sample as a whole represents a good balance of word classes and number of distinct word senses.

That is, for adjectives and verbs, 35 lemmas were randomly selected for each of the polysemy classes (i) to (v). Since the coverage for nouns is higher compared to the coverage of the other two word classes, 50 nominal lemmas were randomly chosen for each polysemy class. Table 1 shows the total number of word lemmas and corresponding word senses (in parentheses) in each polysemy class for the three word classes[3] that were manually aligned by two experienced lexicographers. Column *All POS* contains the summed numbers for all word classes (i.e., part-of-speech, POS) separately for the polysemy classes.

| *Senses* | *Adjectives* | *Nouns* | *Verbs* | *All POS* |
|---|---|---|---|---|
| 1 | 35 (35) | 50 (50) | 35 (35) | 120 (120) |
| 2 | 35 (70) | 50 (100) | 35 (70) | 120 (240) |
| 3 – 4 | 35 (114) | 50 (161) | 35 (112) | 120 (387) |
| 5 – 10 | 8 (51) | 50 (282) | 35 (209) | 93 (542) |
| > 10 | – | 3 (36) | 14 (192) | 17 (228) |
| Total | 113 (270) | 203 (629) | 154 (618) | 470 (1,517) |

**Table 1: Aligned word lemmas (corresponding word senses in parentheses) and their sense distributions**

Note that the number of lemmas for adjectives with three or four senses and for nouns and verbs with more than ten senses is lower than mentioned above. The reason is simply because there are only few lemmas encoded both in GermaNet and the DWDS that fall into these classes, i.e., 8, 3, and 14, respectively. Adjectives with more than ten senses do not exist at all.

Altogether, 470 distinct word lemmas were manually checked by the lexicographers. These lemmas correspond to 1,517 senses (in GermaNet) of which 113 adjectives, 203 nouns, and 154 verbs. That is, the 470 words have an average of 3.2 senses (2.4 for adjectives, 3.1 for nouns, and 4.0 for verbs). With the help of the manual sense alignment, it is possible to classify senses according to their alignment appropriateness, i.e., into classes 1 to 4 described in Sections 3.1-3.4.

Table 2 lists the counts of these 1,517 GermaNet senses classified into the four alignment classes separately for the previously defined polysemy classes (columns). The rightmost column depicts the overall results without classifying words with respect to their number of different senses. The rows show the different alignment classes 1 – 4 separately for each of the three word categories of adjectives, nouns, and verbs. The last row (*All cl.*) sums all aligned senses for each word class per polysemy class. Rows marked with Σ denote results for all word categories.

[3] The information both about the number of distinct word senses as well as about the word category of the lemmas is taken from GermaNet.

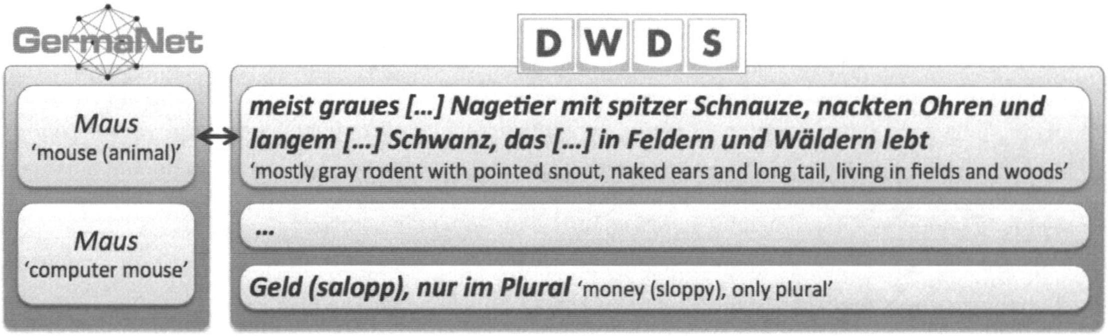


**Figure 4: Sense mapping using the example of *Maus* (class 4).**

| | | *Senses in GermaNet* | | | | | |
|---|---|---|---|---|---|---|---|
| | | 1 | 2 | 3–4 | 5–10 | > 10 | Total |
| *Class 1* | adj. | 35 | 29 | 46 | 16 | – | 126 (47%) |
| | nouns | 49 | 64 | 77 | 136 | 9 | 335 (53%) |
| | verbs | 34 | 36 | 51 | 73 | 56 | 250 (40%) |
| | Σ | 118 | 129 | 174 | 225 | 9 | **711 (47%)** |
| *Class 2* | adj. | 0 | 5 | 19 | 12 | – | 36 (13%) |
| | nouns | 0 | 2 | 11 | 43 | 4 | 60 (10%) |
| | verbs | 0 | 0 | 7 | 48 | 55 | 110 (18%) |
| | Σ | 0 | 7 | 37 | 103 | 4 | **206 (14%)** |
| *Class 3* | adj. | 0 | 35 | 38 | 19 | – | 92 (34%) |
| | nouns | 1 | 18 | 54 | 58 | 22 | 153 (24%) |
| | verbs | 0 | 32 | 46 | 71 | 71 | 220 (36%) |
| | Σ | 1 | 85 | 138 | 148 | 22 | **465 (31%)** |
| *Class 4* | adj. | 0 | 1 | 11 | 4 | – | 16 (7%) |
| | nouns | 0 | 16 | 19 | 45 | 1 | 81 (13%) |
| | verbs | 1 | 2 | 8 | 17 | 10 | 38 (6%) |
| | Σ | 1 | 19 | 38 | 66 | 1 | **135 (9%)** |
| *All Cl.* | adj. | 35 | 70 | 114 | 51 | – | 270 (100%) |
| | nouns | 50 | 100 | 161 | 282 | 36 | 629 (100%) |
| | verbs | 35 | 70 | 112 | 209 | 192 | 618 (100%) |
| | Σ | 120 | 240 | 387 | 542 | 228 | 1,517 (100%) |

**Table 2: Sense distribution of the different alignment classes**

The numbers in Table 2 count senses rather than lemmas. Note that this implies that senses of a single lemma do not necessarily all have to be classified to the same alignment class but can belong to different classes – what arises quite frequently in practice. An example of this kind is the lemma *Maus* which has already been discussed in Section 3.4 (see Figure 4). The first GermaNet sense depicting the mouse as an animal has a corresponding main sense on the DWDS side; meaning that this sense is counted for alignment class 1. On the contrary, the second GermaNet sense for this lemma, which represents the computer mouse sense, does not have a corresponding match on the DWDS side. Thus, the second sense has to be counted for class 4.

## 5 Discussion of the Results

To begin with the most prominent and important result, classes 1 (exact match of main senses) and 2 (exact match of subsenses) together arise in 61% of all cases, i.e., 47% and 14%, respectively – see Table 2. This suggests that for three out of five word senses from GermaNet there is a matching sense in the DWDS with which a GermaNet sense can be aligned. This underscores the overall feasibility of a sense alignment between the two lexical resources. The obvious gain for all these senses is the mutual enrichment by sense-specific information – such as suitable definitions, examples, and lexical relations – taken from the matching sense.

Class 1 arises in 47% of all cases and thus much more frequently than all other classes. The fact that matches between GermaNet senses and main senses in the DWDS (class 1) outnumber matches between GermaNet senses and subsenses in the DWDS (class 2) was to be expected. This confirms the conception of word senses on the same granularity level in both resources.

Both classes 3 (partly overlapping coverage and different sense distinctions) and 4 (distinct coverage) reveal differences between GermaNet and the DWDS that prevent a straight forward sense alignment. The explanation why class 3 arises in 31% of all cases, i.e., why there are differences in the distinction of senses, is due to the lexicographic background of the two resources. The lexicographers of GermaNet and the DWDS pursue different perspectives and guidelines of how to model word senses, e.g. with respect to the sense granularity. Thus, from a lexicographer's perspective, it is interesting to analyze these cases since they concern the identification and differentiation of word senses which is one of the harder tasks that lexicographers face. To gain benefit from a mapping of senses in this class, it would mean that all information for a sense has to be analyzed in order to be individually assigned to a corresponding sense.

Class 4, which indicates a distinct coverage of GermaNet and the DWDS, shows fewest occurrences. In only 9% of all GermaNet senses, there is no corresponding entry in the DWDS. It should be kept in mind that this number only applies to those 48,036 lemmas that are encoded in both resources. For all remaining lemmas, there are no lexical entries in the DWDS at all and thus these word senses would fall into class 4 as well. The evaluation for class 4 is biased towards one direction, i.e., it regards GermaNet senses with missing entries in the DWDS. Since it is also interesting to analyze and compare the other way around where there are DWDS senses lacking matches in GermaNet, these cases have also been recorded during the manual alignment. Altogether, there are 384 word senses (122 adjectival, 104 nominal, and 158 verbal senses) in the DWDS that do not have a corresponding entry in GermaNet. In all cases where the sets of sense distinctions differ between the two resources, this provides reason for revisiting and possibly revising the lexical entries in question. Of course, this also applies to all those word lemmas for which there is a lexical entry in only one of the two resources.

A comparison of the results for the three different word classes and polysemy classes yields the following tendencies:

- Words with only one GermaNet sense almost exclusively fall into class 1 – for all three word classes. This is not surprising since those words usually have one or few senses in the DWDS and thus the probability that the "same" most prominent sense of a word is encoded in both resources is significant.
- More than half of all nouns (53%) fall into class 1 – much fewer nouns (10%) fall into class 2. By contrast, there are only 40% of all verbs in class 1, but proportionally almost twice as many verbs (18%) classified to class 2 compared to nouns. This is especially remarkable for verbs with more than four senses. One reason for this difference is the variety in the granularity level of the sense distinctions in GermaNet and the DWDS which arises more often for verbs than for nouns.
- The deviation between the three word classes for polysemous words, i.e., words with more than one sense in GermaNet, is interesting to observe. Adjectives and verbs show a proportionally larger number of occurrences in class 3 (34% and 36%, respectively) compared to nouns (24%). This means that there are more words with a partly overlapping coverage and different sense distinctions for adjectives and verbs than for nouns, e.g., where two senses from one resource jointly describe one sense of the other resource.
- By contrast, this ratio is reversed for class 4, where there are proportionally nearly twice as many occurrences for nouns (13%) than for adjectives and verbs (7% and 6%, respectively). The explanation for this is that there are more nominal senses that are not encoded in one resource, but more adjectival and verbal senses that encode an overlapping coverage with a different distinction of senses.

All in all, it is worthwhile to perform a complete sense alignment between GermaNet and the DWDS. This will open up a wide range of benefits for both resources, including the harvesting of sense-specific information and the external support of sense distinctions for matching senses as well as indicators for revisiting and possibly revising the lexical entries in question for non-matching senses.

## 6 Related Work

There has been a considerable body of research for English that investigates the alignment of the Princeton WordNet with Wikipedia (including Ruiz-Casado et al., 2005; Ponzetto and Navigli, 2010; Niemann and Gurevych, 2011), with Wiktionary (including Meyer and Gurevych, 2011), with the Longman Dictionary of Contemporary English and with Roget's thesaurus (Kwong, 1998), with the Hector lexicon (Litkowski, 1999), or with the Oxford Dictionary of English (Navigli, 2006).

Previous work for German has been on the alignment of GermaNet with the German version of Wiktionary (Henrich et al., 2011) and with the German Wikipedia (Henrich et al., 2012).

However, there is no other previous research that tries to align GermaNet to the DWDS.

## 7 Conclusion and Future Work

This initial pilot study has proven the feasibility of a sense alignment between GermaNet and the DWDS both in term of quantity and appropriateness. We have learned about the differences in the distinction of senses that are due to different perspectives and guidelines of how to model word senses that the lexicographers of both resources pursue. The classification of senses according to their appropriateness to be aligned with senses from the other resource allows an individual treatment of different issues and phenomena that arise in practice when an alignment of two resources is performed.

The alignment of GermaNet with the DWDS brings about considerable mutual benefits for both resources. For all sense distinctions that are completely parallel in the two resources, the alignment provides supporting external evidence for the validity of sense distinction and allows enriching word senses by information contained in the other resource. By contrast, for all non-matching sense distinctions, reason for revisiting and possibly revising the lexical entries in question is provided.

The natural next step, which we have already started to work on, is to implement an algorithm that automatically aligns senses from the two resources. This provides a good basis for the lexicographer's work of post-correcting the automatic alignment and revising the senses in both resources, which still remains a complex and substantial task to be performed.

## Acknowledgments

We are very grateful to our student assistants Sabrina Galasso and Amit Vrubel, who helped us with the evaluation reported in Sections 4 and 5. Special thanks go to our colleagues in Berlin for making available the DWDS to us.

Financial support was provided by the German Research Foundation (DFG) as part of the Collaborative Research Center 'Emergence of Meaning' (SFB 833), by the German Ministry of Education and Technology (BMBF) as part of the research grant CLARIN-D, and by a research grant from the University of Tübingen.

## References

Jörg Didakowski, Lothar Lemnitzer, and Alexander Geyken. 2012. *Automatic example sentence extraction for a contemporary German dictionary*. Proceedings of EURALEX 2012, Oslo, pp. 343-349.

Christiane Fellbaum. (eds.). 1998. WordNet – An Electronic Lexical Database. The MIT Press.

Birgit Hamp and Helmut Feldweg. 1997. *GermaNet – a Lexical-Semantic Net for German*. Proceedings of ACL workshop Automatic Information Extraction and Building of Lexical Semantic Resources for NLP Applications, Madrid.

Verena Henrich and Erhard Hinrichs. 2010. *GernEdiT – The GermaNet Editing Tool*. Proceedings of the Seventh Conference on International Language Resources and Evaluation, pp. 2228-2235.

Verena Henrich, Erhard Hinrichs, and Klaus Suttner: *Automatically Linking GermaNet to Wikipedia for Harvesting Corpus Examples for GermaNet Senses*. Journal for Language Technology and Computational Linguistics (JLCL), Vol. 27, No. 1, 2012, pp. 1-19.

Verena Henrich, Erhard Hinrichs, and Tatiana Vodolazova. 2011. *Semi-Automatic Extension of GermaNet with Sense Definitions from Wiktionary*. Proceedings of 5th Language & Technology Conference (LTC 2011), Poznań, Poland, 2011, pp. 126-130.

Wolfgang Klein and Alexander Geyken. 2010. *Das Digitale Wörterbuch der Deutschen Sprache (DWDS)*. Heid, Ulrich/Schierholz, Stefan/Schweickard, Wolfgang/Wiegand, Herbert Ernst/Gouws, Rufus H./Wolski, Werner (Hg.): Lexikographica. Berlin/New York, pp. 79-93.

Oi Yee Kwong. 1998. *Aligning wordnet with additional lexical resources*. Proceedings of the COLING-ACL'98 Workshop on 'Usage of WordNet in Natural Language Processing Systems', Montreal, QC, Canada, pp. 73-79.

Kenneth C. Litkowski. 1999. *Towards a meaning-full comparison of lexical resources*. Proceedings of the ACL Special Interest Group on the Lexicon Workshop on Standardizing Lexical Resources, College Park, MD, USA, pp. 30-37.

Christian M. Meyer and Irina Gurevych. 2011. *What psycholinguists know about chemistry: Aligning Wiktionary and WordNet for increased domain coverage*. Proceedings of the 5th International Joint Conference on Natural Language Processing (IJCNLP 2011), pages 883–892,

Elisabeth Niemann and Iryna Gurevych. 2011. *The People's Web meets Linguistic Knowledge: Automatic Sense Alignment of Wikipedia and WordNet*. Proceedings of the Ninth International Conference on Computational Semantics, pp. 205-214.

Roberto Navigli. 2006. *Meaningful clustering of senses helps boost word sense disambiguation performance*. Proceedings of COLING 2006 and ACL 2006. Association for Computational Linguistics, pp. 105-112.

Simone P. Ponzetto and Roberto Navigli. 2010. *Knowledge-rich Word Sense Disambiguation rivaling supervised system*. Proceedings of the 48th Annual Meeting of the ACL, pp. 1522-1531.

Maria Ruiz-Casado, Enrique Alfonseca, and Pablo Castells. 2005. *Automatic Assignment of Wikipedia Encyclopedic Entries to WordNet Synsets*. Advances in Web Intelligence, Volume 3528 of LNCS, Springer Verlag, pp. 380-386.

# Building a standardized Wordnet in the ISO LMF for aeb language

**Nadia B.M. Karmani(1)**
nadia.karmani.tn@ieee.org

**Hsan Soussou(2)**
hsan.soussou@gmail.com

**Adel M. Alimi(1)**
adel.alimi@ieee.org

(1) REGIM: REsearch Groups on Intelligent Machines
University of Sfax, National Engineering School of Sfax (ENIS)
BP 1173, Sfax, 3038, Tunisia
(2) MD Soft, Tunisia

## Abstract

Internet communication plays a considerable part in economic, financial and even politic domains. It is greatly influencing the politic revolution of many Arabic countries. That allows Internet communication to take more and more scale especially in an Arabic context. In this case, we notice that Internet communication is based on textual interchange using Arabic dialects more than Arabic language. However, few efforts were made for Arabic dialect processing particularly for aeb[1] language. In this case, we suggest building a standardized aeb Wordnet, which is a basic tool for Natural Language Processing (NLP) of aeb language. In this article, we present an extended Wordnet-LMF model acquired to aeb language specificities used to represent aeb Wordnet and we describe building steps.

## 1 Introduction

Wordnet, firstly developed for English language, cover newer days many others languages and even dialects. In an Arabic case, many efforts were make to build a Wordnet for Modern standard Arabic but no real attempt has been made for Arabic dialects.

Arabic dialects represent Arabic language variations often spoken. However, they are written in some press articles, theater pieces, poetic books and Internet based communication such as email, instant messaging, forums, blogs, social networks, etc.

With the politic revolution of several Arabic countries like Tunisia (i.e. also Egypt, Syria, etc.), Arabic dialect processing takes more and more scale in Arabic countries and particularly in Tunisia.

In this case, we suggest building a powerful semantic lexicon for Tunisian dialect (aeb language): aeb Wordnet using the expand approach which is formulated according to an adapted format of Wordnet-LMF. The use of standardized Lexical Markup Framework (LMF) ISO 24613 format allows interchange between aeb Wordnet and other standardized lexicons.

## 2 Challenges

Developing an aeb wordnet faces many constraints associated to resources, language characteristics and use.

Generally, building a Wordnet needs a lot of resources. But, for aeb language few written resources are found: an electronic bilingual dictionary eng[2]-aeb, some press articles, some theater pieces, some poesy books, etc. Indeed, aeb like other Arabic dialects is sometimes written and it's not educated.

In addition to the lack of resources, we notice many language specificities: absence of standard transcription, use of six variations (i.e. Tunis, Sahel, Sfax, occidental north, occidental south and oriental south) and estrangement from English language and even from Arabic language. Indeed, aeb language is characterized by the absence of standard transcription: the same word can be represented by different transcriptions e.g. the word [إِتْوَقَّعْ /ʔitwaqqaʔˤ/[3]] "anticipate" can be transcribed as [إِتْوَقَّعْ /ʔitwaqqaʔˤ/] or [تْوَقَّعْ /twaqqaʔˤ/]. Also, it uses six variations e.g. the variations of the personal pronoun "I" are illustrated by the Table 1.

[1] aeb is the ISO 639-3 language code for Tunisian Arabic.

[2] eng is the ISO 639-3 language code for English.

[3] phonetic transcription according to International Phonetic Alphabet (IPA).

| aeb variations | | | | | |
|---|---|---|---|---|---|
| Tunis | Sahel | Sfax | Occidental north | Occidental south | oriental south |
| آنَا | آنِي | آنَا | نَا | أنَا | أنِي |

**Table 1.** Variation of the personal pronoun [آنَا/ʔa:na:/] "I"

In addition, aeb is a Semitic language like Arabic very different from English at morphological, lexical and syntactical levels and also different from Arabic seeing that its alphabet counts three consonants which aren't used in Arabic (i.e. [ڥ /v/ ],[ڨ /q'/] and [پ /P/]), its lexicon is full of foreign words (e.g. the word [دَاكُورْدُو /da:ku:rdu:/] "all right" is borrowed from Italian language) and it uses Arabic roots to express other meanings (e.g. the Arabic root [خدم/xdm/] meaning "to serve" is used in aeb language as [خْدِمْ/xdim/] to express "to work").

Also, the use of aeb language raises other constraints. Indeed, aeb use covers spoken and written forms. The last form can be diacritized, not diacritized or partially diacritized e.g. the word [إِتْوَقَّعْ] "anticipate" can be transcribed as [إِتْوَقَّعْ], [إتوقع] [ إِتْوقَّعْ]. It can be also scripted with Arabic, Latin or a mixed script e.g. the word [إِتْوَقَّعْ] "anticipate" can be transcribed as [إِتْوَقَّعْ], [etwa99a3] or [etو993].

## 3 Wordnet-LMF

Towards generation of a standard model representing lexicons, many works are made around LMF. Wordnets, seen that they are considered as semantic lexicons, can use LMF. They precisely can use Wordnet-LMF formed by the components described below. These components are not sufficient to express correctly aeb particularities such as the use of many transcriptions for the same lexical entry, the variation, the phonetic sight or the inflected and derived forms. So, we add others LMF components as extension.

### 3.1 Components

Wordnets, all over the world, share the same basic concepts (i.e. word, verb, noun, adjective, adverb, synset, etc.) and organization (i.e. sets of synonyms, each representing a lexicalized concept (Miller, 1995)) but they have different representations. Some efforts were made, thought the project Knowledge-Yielding Ontologies for Transition-Based Organization (KYOTO[4]), to propose a standardized model for Wordnets: KYOTO-LMF or Wordnet-LMF. This model is an LMF dialect. It is a Wordnet adapted version of the common standardized framework for representing natural language processing (NLP) lexicons: ISO 24613 LMF (Soria and Monachini, 2008).

This model is composed of twenty one elements (Soria et al., 2009). LexicalResource is the root element with three children representing general information (i.e GlobalInformation), the lexicon associate to a defined language (i.e. Lexicon) and a bracketing element grouping together SenseAxis (i.e. SenseAxe). The root element describes the resource that can be a monolingual or a multilingual Wordnet. The other elements can be distributed over three different packages, i.e. the morphological, the NLP semantic and the NLP multilingual notations package.

The morphological package contains five elements describing a lexeme in a given language (i.e. LexicalEntry), a word that can be a root, a stem, an inflected form or a multiword expression (i.e. Lemma), one meaning of a LexicalEntry (i.e. Sense), a link between a Sense and another resource (i.e. Monolingual-ExternalRef) and a bracketing element grouping together MonolingualExternalRef (i.e. Mono-lingualExternalRefs).

The NLP semantic package is formed by seven elements representing a set of shared meanings within the same language (i.e. Synset), the gloss associate with one synset (i.e. Definition), an example of use associate to one synset (i.e. Statement), a relation between synsets (i.e. SynsetRelation), a bracketing element grouping together RelationSynset (i.e. RelationSynsets), a link between a Synset and another resource (i.e MonolingualExternalRef) and a bracketing element grouping together MonolingualExternalRef (i.e. Monolingual-ExternalRefs).

And finally, the NLP Multilingual notations package containing four elements used only to describe multilingual Wordnets.

This model contains also an element describing administrative information (i.e. Meta) used with LexicalEntry, MonolingualExternal-Ref, Synset and SynsetRelation.

### 3.2 Wordnet-LMF vs aeb language

Wordnet-LMF is a model adopted, in the project

[4] KYOTO (project nr. 211423) FP7-ICT-2007-1

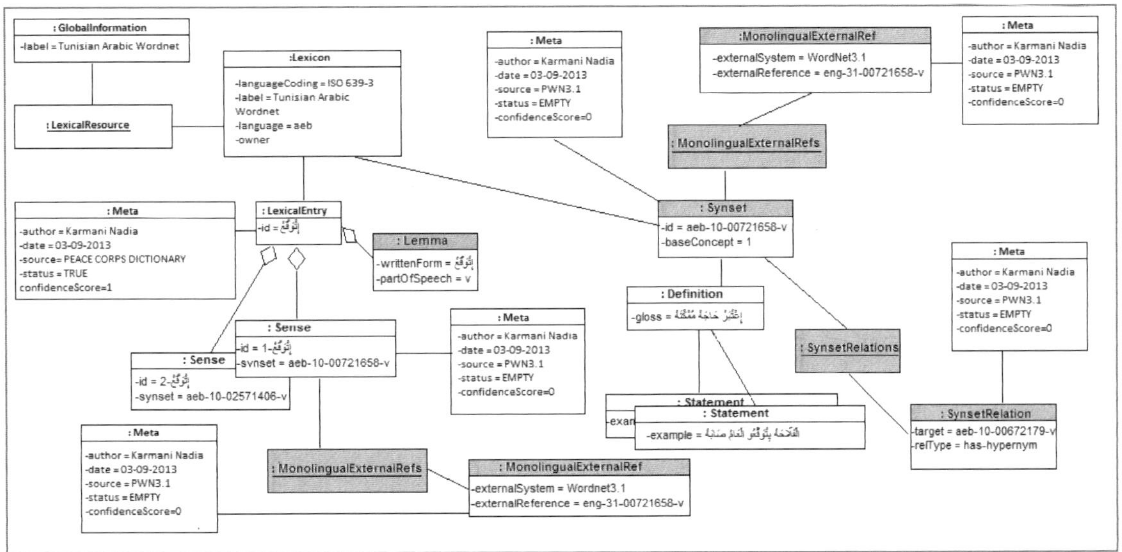


**Figure 1.** Wordnet-LMF object diagram of the word [إِتْوَقَّعْ /ʔitwaqqaʔˁ/] "anticipate"

KYOTO, to represent Wordnets of English, Dutch, Italian, Basque, Spanish, Chinese and Japanese (Soria et al., 2009). These languages are different from aeb language. So, the use of Wordnet-LMF to represent aeb language can't preserve the language specificities.

The Figure 1 represents the Unified Modeling Language (UML[5]) object diagram of Wordnet-LMF associated to the word [إِتْوَقَّعْ /ʔitwaqqaʔˁ/] "anticipate". It illustrates the limits of Wordnet-LMF for aeb language description. Indeed, Wordnet-LMF model doesn't express the use of many transcriptions for the same lexical entry, the variation, the phonetic and the inflected forms of a lexical entry and the structure of Semitic languages (i.e. derivation phenomena).

### 3.3 Extension

To express properly the aeb language specificities, we suggest extending Wordnet-LMF using ISO LMF.

In this case, we firstly propose to replace the cardinality "1..1" of the association between LexicalEntry and Lemma by the cardinality "1..*".That allows the affection of more than one Lemma to the same LexicalEntry as it is shown in Figure 3, e.g. the lexicalEntry [إِتْوَقَّعْ /ʔitwaqqaʔˁ/] "anticipate" has two lemmas illustrated by the figure below.

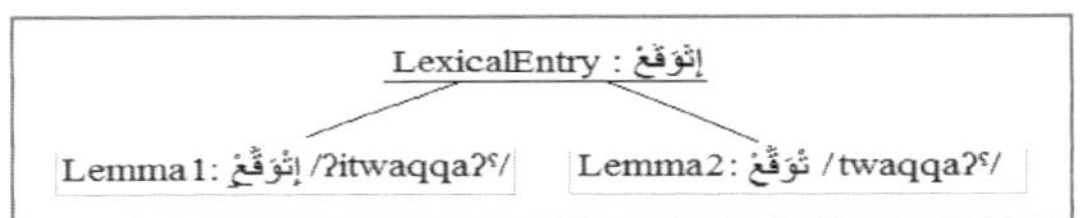


**Figure 2.** Lemmas of the word [إِتْوَقَّعْ /ʔitwaqqaʔˁ/] "anticipate"

Secondly, we propose to add two attributes for the entity Lemma: script and orthographyName, seen that aeb transcription uses Arabic or Latin script.

Finally, we suggest adding three ISO LMF elements: FormRepresentation, WordForm and RelatedForm to represent respectively the phonetic and the variation, the inflected and the derived forms of a lexical entry (ISO 24613, 2008). E.g. these elements are integrated for the word [إِتْوَقَّعْ /ʔitwaqqaʔˁ/] "anticipate" like it is shown in the Figure 3.

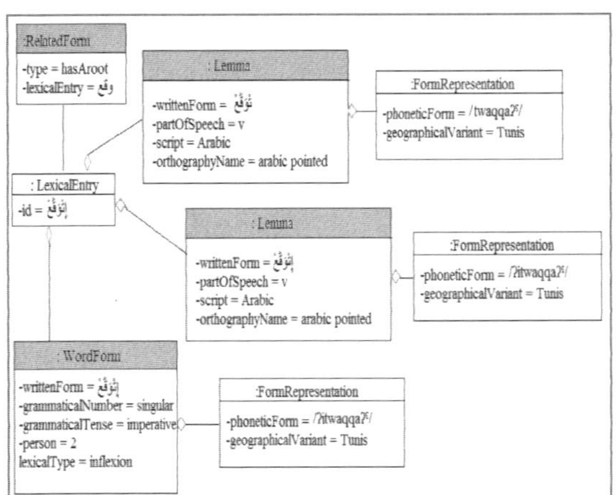


**Figure 3.** Object diagram of the word [إِتْوَقَّعْ /ʔitwaqqaʔˁ/] "anticipate"

[5] UML is a standardized (ISO/IEC 19501:2005), general-purpose modeling language in the field of software engineering (Wikipedia).

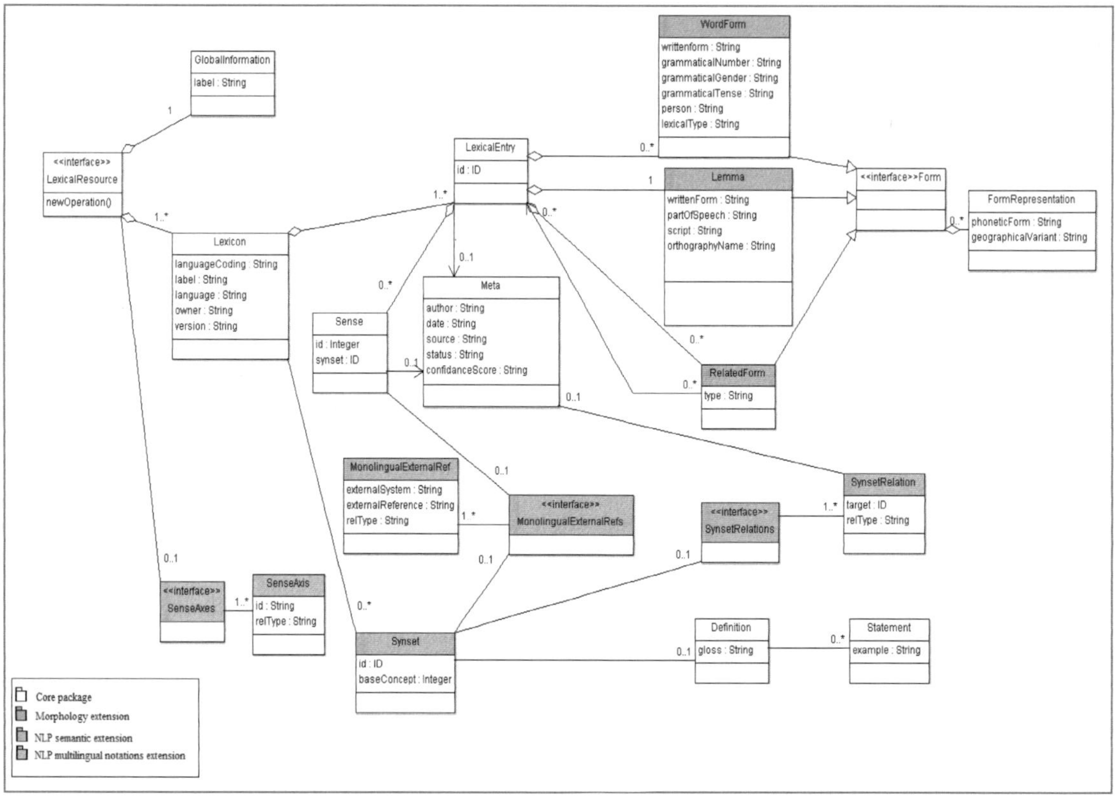


**Figure 4.** Extended Wordnet-LMF model for aeb language

Consequently, we get the Wordnet-LMF extended model accurate to aeb language shown by UML class diagram in the Figure 4.

## 4 aeb Wordnet construction

In general, building Wordnet can be done by merged or expanded approach (Vossen, 1998). The merged approach consists on the creation of synsets and synset relations using language resources. But, the expand approach generates synsets and synset relations from the widely used WordNet: Princeton WordNet (PWN) by translation.

The first approach save the language specificities but it is complex and need a lot of language resources. The second one is easy and needs only PWN and bilingual dictionaries but it generates a biased Wordnet to PWN.

In the case of aeb Wordnet development, the first approach can't be used because of the lack of aeb resources. So, we adopt the expanded approach. We use PWN 3.1 released in 2011 and the only bilingual dictionary found for English and Arabic Tunisian: Peace Corps dictionary of Rached Ben Abdelkader, Abdeljelil Ayed and Aziza Naouar edited in July 1977 listing about 6000 aeb words.

Aeb Wordnet is developed manually, with the format XML[6], throw three steps: creation, validation and extension.

### 4.1 Creation

Wordnet is a set of lexical entries L= {l} and a set of synsets S={s}. A lexical entry l is composed of one word $w \in W$ at least, which can be a Lemma or a WordForm. A synset s is composed of a subset of lexical entries L' and a set of synset relations R={r}.

To generate aeb Wordnet ($L_{aeb}$, $S_{aeb}$) we use both PWN and Peace Corps dictionary D. Indeed, for every translation $t \in D$, we generate a subset of lexical entries $L'_{aeb}$ and a subset of synsets $S'_{aeb}$.

A translation t can be monosemous (t = ($w_{eng}$, $w_{aeb}$)), divergent polysemous (t= {($w_{eng}$, $w1_{aeb}$), ($w_{eng}$, $w2_{aeb}$), {($w_{eng}$, $w3_{aeb}$) …}) or represent a lexical lacuna (t= ($w_{eng}$, ø)).

In the first case, the translation t = ($w_{eng}$, $w_{aeb}$) generates one lexical entry $l_{aeb}$ for $w_{aeb}$

[6] XML is a markup language that defines a set of rules for encoding documents in a format that is both human-readable and machine-readable (Wikipedia).

considered as a lemma and a subset of synset $S'_{aeb}$ like it is presented in the Figure 5. $S'_{aeb}$={s ($L'_{aeb}$, R)} is equivalent to $S'_{pwn}$={s ($L'_{pwn}$, R)} i.e. synsets of $w_{eng}$ in PWN and $L'_{aeb}$ is obtained from the translation of words in $L'_{pwn}$ using D.

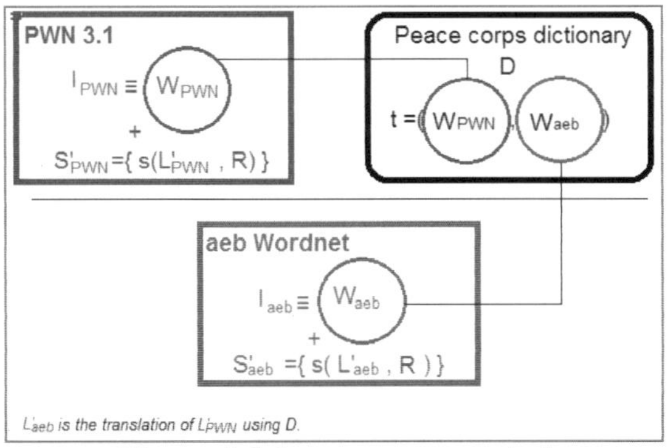


**Figure 5.** Monosemous translation

E.g. the translation t1= {("anticipate", "إِتْوَقَّعْ")} generates the lexical entry $l_{aeb}$ described by the Figure 3 with six senses (i.e. equivalent to the english word "anticipate" senses) as it is shown below.

```
<LexicalEntry id="إِتْوَقَّعْ">
  ...
  <Sense id="1_إِتْوَقَّعْ" synset="aeb-10-00721658-v">
  <Meta author="Karmani Nadia" date="2013-09-03"
source="PWN3.1" status="EMPTY"/>
  <MonolingualExternalRefs>
  <monolingualExternalRef externalSystem="WordNet 3.1"
externalReference="eng-31-00721658-v" />
  </MonolingualExternalRefs>
  </Sense>
  <Sense id="2_إِتْوَقَّعْ" synset="aeb-10-02571406-v">
  <Meta author="Karmani Nadia" date="2013-09-03"
source="PWN3.1" status="EMPTY"/>
  <MonolingualExternalRefs>
  <monolingualExternalRef externalSystem="WordNet 3.1"
externalReference="eng-31-02571406-v" />
  </MonolingualExternalRefs>
  </Sense>
  <Sense id="3_إِتْوَقَّعْ" synset="aeb-10-00722732-v">
  <Meta author="Karmani Nadia" date="2013-09-03"
source="PWN3.1" status="EMPTY"/>
  <MonolingualExternalRefs>
  <monolingualExternalRef externalSystem="WordNet 3.1"
externalReference="eng-31-00722732-v" />
  </MonolingualExternalRefs>
  </Sense>
  <Sense id="4_إِتْوَقَّعْ" synset="aeb-10-00919743-v">
  <Meta author="Karmani Nadia" date="2013-09-03"
source="PWN3.1" status="EMPTY"/>
  <MonolingualExternalRefs>
  <monolingualExternalRef externalSystem="WordNet 3.1"
externalReference="eng-31-00919743-v" />
  </MonolingualExternalRefs>
  </Sense>
  <Sense id="5_إِتْوَقَّعْ" synset="aeb-10-01808928-v">
  <Meta author="Karmani Nadia" date="2013-09-03"
source="PWN3.1" status="EMPTY"/>
  <MonolingualExternalRefs>
  <monolingualExternalRef externalSystem="WordNet 3.1"
externalReference="eng-31-01808928-v" />
  </MonolingualExternalRefs>
  </Sense>
  <Sense id="6_إِتْوَقَّعْ" synset="aeb-10-00343295-v">
  <Meta author="Karmani Nadia" date="2013-09-03"
source="PWN3.1" status="EMPTY"/>
  <MonolingualExternalRefs>
  <monolingualExternalRef externalSystem="WordNet 3.1"
externalReference="eng-31-00343295-v" />
  </MonolingualExternalRefs>
  </Sense>
</LexicalEntry>
```

Also, it creates six synsets in $S'_{aeb}$={aeb-10-00721658-v, aeb-10-02571406-v, aeb-10-00722732-v, aeb-10-00919743-v, aeb-10-01808928-v, aeb-10-00343295-v} .The synset $S_{aeb\text{-}10\text{-}00721658\text{-}v}$ is detailed below.

```
<Synset id="aeb-10-00721658-v" baseConcept="1">
<Meta author="Karmani Nadia" date="2013-09-03"
source="PWN3.1" status="EMPTY"/>
<Definition gloss="إعْتْبَرْ حَاجَةْ مُمْكْنَةْ" ><Statement example=" الْفَلَّاحَةْ
يِتْوَقْعُو الْعَامْ صَابَةْ"/></Definition>
<SynsetRelations>
  <synsetRelation target="aeb-10-00672179-v" relType="has-
hypernym"><Meta author="Karmani Nadia" date="2013-09-03"
source="PWN3.1" status="EMPTY"/>
  </synsetRelation>
  ...
  </SynsetRelations>
  <MonolingualExternalRefs>
  <monolingualExternalRef externalSystem="WordNet3.1"
externalReference="eng-31-00721658-v" />
  </MonolingualExternalRefs>
  </Synset>
```

In the second case, the translation t= {($w_{eng}$, $w1_{aeb}$), …, {($w_{eng}$, $wn_{aeb}$)} shown in Figure 6 generates a subset of lexical entries $L'_{aeb}$ (i.e. $L'_{aeb}$ = {$l1_{aeb}$, …, $ln_{aeb}$ } /$l1_{aeb}$ and $ln_{aeb}$ have respectively $w1_{aeb}$ and $wn_{aeb}$ as Lemmas) and a subset of synset $S'_{aeb}$= {s ($L'_{aeb}$, R)} equivalent to $S'_{pwn}$={s ($L'_{pwn}$, R)}.

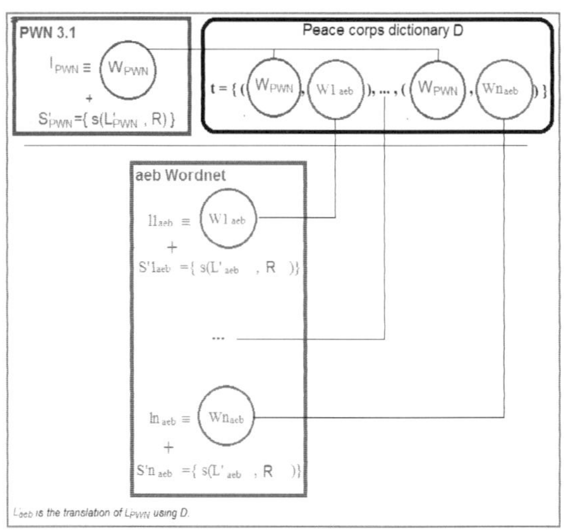


**Figure 6.** Polysemous translation

The subset of synsets $S'_{aeb}$ includes synsets of the lexical entries in L' ={ $l1_{aeb}$ , … , $ln_{aeb}$}/ $S'_{aeb}$= S'l1 $_{aeb}$ ∪ (S'l2 $_{aeb}$ − S'l1 $_{aeb}$ ∩ S'l2 $_{aeb}$) ∪ … ∪ (S'ln$_{aeb}$ -S'ln-1$_{aeb}$∩S'ln$_{aeb}$) e.g. the translation t2={("work", "خْدِمْ"), ("work"," خَدِّمْ ")} generates $L'_{aeb}$={"خْدِمْ","خَدِّمْ"} composed of two lexical entries and S'={aeb-10-02418610-v, aeb-10-02415985-v, aeb-10-02531113-v, aeb-10-01528454-v , aeb-10-02449024-v , aeb-10-00100305-v, aeb-10-02413117-v , aeb-10-02441810-v, aeb-10-02121463-v, etc} illustrated by the Figure 7.

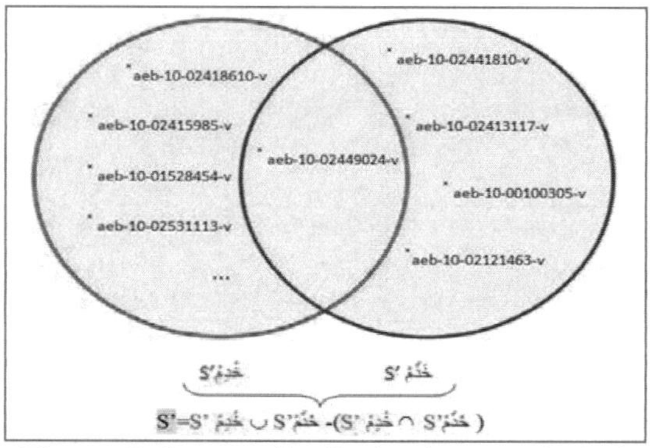


**Figure 7.** Synsets distribution between lexical entries generated from the translation t2

Finally, the third case presented in Figure 8 doesn't affect aeb Wordnet e.g. the translation t3= {("fir", ø)}.

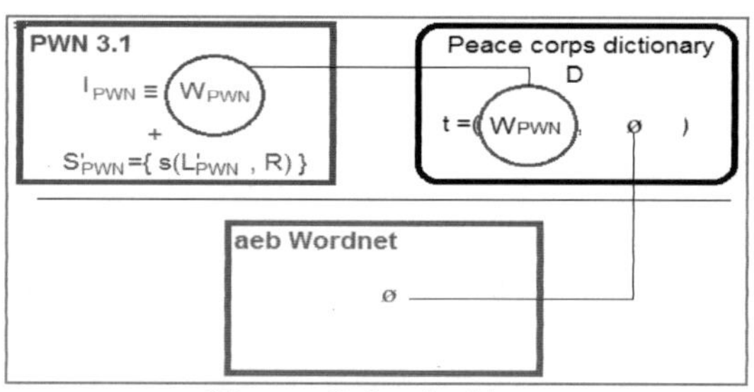


**Figure 8.** Lexical lacuna

## 4.2 Validation

Some aeb Wordnet elements need validation through or after creation. LexicalEntry is validated through creation but Sense, Synset and SynsetRelation are validated after creation. The validation consists on the affection of "True" value to the attribute status of Meta element. We validate an element when we find it in a confident resource such as dictionary, press article, theater piece, poetic book, etc.

"تراه آش حكى لك؟
قالّي ثمّه راجل مريض ... ما ينجّمش يخدم..."

(عن جريدة الصّريح الثلاثاء 21 أكتوبر 2001 "تاكسي ي ي" تحويسه معا عبد الباقي بن مسعود)

E.g. from the press article تحويسه معا عبد الباقي بن مسعود from الصّريح October 2001 at the top, we validate the Synset s $_{aeb-10-00590283-v}$ and the Sense 2_خْدِمْ of the lexicalEntry خْدِمْ as it is shown below.

```
<Synset id=" aeb-10-02415985-v" baseConcept="1">
<Meta author="Karmani Nadia" date="2013-09-03" source=" تحويسه معا عبد الباقي بن مسعود from الصّريح October 2001"
status="TRUE"/>
...
</Synset>
```

```
<LexicalEntry id="خْدِمْ ">
...
<Sense id="2_خْدِمْ" synset="aeb-10-02415985-v">
<Meta author="Karmani Nadia" date="2013-09-03"
source="PWN3.1" status="TRUE"/>
<MonolingualExternalRefs>
<monolingualExternalRef externalSystem="WordNet3.1"
externalReference="eng-31-02415985-v" />
</MonolingualExternalRefs>
</Sense>
...
<LexicalEntry>
```

## 4.3 Extension

To create aeb Wordnet, we use Peace Corps dictionary containing about 6000 aeb words used in Tunis. This potential cannot be compared to PWN 3.1 potential counting about 147278 eng words[7]. It represents 24.54% of PWN 3.1 potential.

In this case, we suggest enriching aeb Wordnet lexicon by derivation, by variation and by corpus.

The first method consists on the generation of derived forms when it is possible (i.e. when the word is derivative, not fixed or borrowed). Indeed, aeb language is a Semitic language like Arabic. So, from a root we can build many words according to defined patterns e.g. from the root [شرب /ʃrab/] "to drink" we can generate five direct derived nouns like it is shown in the Table2 (Mejri et al, 2009).

| Root [شرب / ʃrab/] | | | | |
|---|---|---|---|---|
| **Patient** | **Predicative** | **Superlative** | **Locative** | **Agent** |
| مَشْرُوبْ /maʃru:b/ | شُرْبْ /ʃurb/ | شِرِّيبْ /ʃirri:b/ | مَشْرَبْ /maʃrab/ | شَارِبْ /ʃa:rib/ |

**Table 2.** Direct derivation of the root [شرب /ʃrab/]"to drink"

[7] WordNet homepage: `wordnet.princeton.edu`

The second method is based on searching existing varied forms for the elements Lemma or wordForm created in aeb Wordnet e.g. the Lemma [قَالْ /qa:l/] "says" has a varied form [ڨَالْ /q'a:l/] used in the occidental north, the occidental south and the oriental south; the wordForm [شُوفْ /ʃu:f /] "see" of the LexicalEntry [شَافْ/ʃa:f /] "to see" has a varied form [أَرَى /ʔara:/] used only in Sfax.

The third method consists on the use of an aeb corpus composed by aeb texts collected from press articles, theater pieces, poetic books, etc to search words absent in aeb Wordnet and to add them.

With the methods presented at the top, we widely support aeb Wordnet potential.

## 5 Conclusion

In this article, we presented aeb Wordnet building using the standard ISO LMF. We adapted Wordnet-LMF to aeb specificities based on ISO-LMF and we presented aeb building steps with the expand approach.

Building aeb Wordnet consists on processing PWN by translation to instantiate wordnet-LMF extended model for aeb language. The translation is based on a bilingual dictionary seen the lack of resources. It is supported by validation and extension steps. In this way, we create easily aeb wordnet from PWN and we save aeb language specificities.

This Wordnet is basic, standard and efficient NLP tool. It is an elementary tool with the lack of aeb NLP tools. Its standard structure allows easy interchange with other Wordnets and lexicons. And its current potential i.e. 6000 aeb words is acceptable with the absence of aeb lexicons. Moreover, the extension of aeb wordnet allows its potential to attempt potential of other Wordnets even PWN potential.

Aeb Wordnet is a necessary tool. It will greatly enhance NLP of aeb and so Internet communication monitoring witch become a real challenge with the unsteadiness of economic, finance, politic, etc in Tunisia. Also, it will be very useful to wrestle against terrorism witch disrupt the democratic transition.


## Acknowledgments

This work is supported by the General Direction of Scientific Research (DGRS T), Tunisia, under the ARUB program.


## References


Sabri Elkateb, William Black, Horacio Rodriguez, Musa Alkhalifa, Piek Vossen, Adam Pease and Christiane Fellbaum. 2006. Building a WordNet for Arabic. *Proceedings of the Fifth International Conference on Language Resources and Evaluation*, Genoa, Italy.

Gil Francopoulo, Nuria Bel, Monte George, Nicoletta Calzolari, Monica Monachini, Mandy Pet, Claudia Soria. 2007. Lexical Markup Framework: an ISO Standard for Semantic Information in NLP Lexicons. *Proceedings of the Workshop on Lexical-Semantic and Ontological Resources of the GLDV Working Group on Lexicography*, Tübingen, 13-14 April 2007.

Gil Francopoulo, Monte George, Nicoletta Calzolari, Monica Monachini, Nuria Bel, Mandy Pet, Claudia Soria. 2006. Lexical Markup Framework (LMF). *Proceedings of LREC*, Genoa, Italy, 22-28 May 2006.

ISO 24613. 2008. *Language Resource Management – Lexical Markup Framework. ISO.* Geneva, 2008.

Salah Mejri, Mosbah Said, Ines Sfar. 2009. Pluringuisme et diglossie en Tunisie. *Synergies Tunisie n° 1*. pp 53–74.

George A. Miller.1995. WORDNET: a lexical database for English . *COMMUNICATIONS OF THE ACM.* November 1995/Vol. 38, No. 11.

Claudia Soria, Monica Monachini , Piek Vossen. 2009. KYOTO-LMF: fleshing out a standardized format for wordnet interoperability. *Accepted for publication at IWIC2009*. Stanford, Palo Alto, CA.

Claudia Soria and Monica Monachini. 2008. Kyoto-LMF wordnet representation format. Kyoto-LMF wordnet representation format. *KYOTO Working Paper WP02_TR002_V4_Kyoto_LMF.*

Piek Vossen (ed). 1998. EUROWORDNET a database with lexical semantic networks. (Reprinted from *Computers and the Humanities,* 32(2-3), 1998). Dordrecht: Kluwer Academic Publishers, Kluer Academic Publishers.

# Java Libraries for Accessing the Princeton Wordnet: Comparison and Evaluation

**Mark Alan Finlayson**
Computer Science and Artificial Intelligence Laboratory
Massachusetts Institute of Technology
32 Vassar Street, Room 32-258, Cambridge, Massachusetts, 02139
markaf@mit.edu

## Abstract

Java is a popular programming language for natural language processing. I compare and evaluate 12 Java libraries designed to access the information in the original Princeton Wordnet databases. From this comparison emerges a set of decision criteria that will enable a user to pick the library most suited to their purposes. I identify five deciding features: (1) availability of similarity metrics; (2) support for editing; (3) availability via Maven; (4) compatibility with retired Java versions; and (5) support for Enterprise Java. I also provide a comparison of other features of each library, the information exposed by each API, and the versions of Wordnet each library supports, and I evaluate each library for the speed of various retrieval operations. In the case that the user's application does not require one of the deciding features, I show that my library, JWI, the MIT Java Wordnet Interface, is the highest-performance, widest-coverage, easiest-to-use library available.

A Java developer seeking to access the Princeton Wordnet is faced with a bewildering array of choices: there are no fewer than 12 Java libraries that provide off-the-shelf access to Wordnet data, each with various combinations of features and performance. In addition to these 12 libraries, there are also at least 12 additional libraries[1] that, while not providing direct access to Wordnet data themselves, provide functions such as similarity metrics and deployment of Wordnet data to database servers. In this paper I compare, contrast, and evaluate each of the 12 libraries[2] that provide direct access to the Princeton Wordnet data, so as to help Java developers find the library that is right for their application. To my knowledge this is the first paper to attempt a thorough comparison of any of these libraries.

I proceed as follows. First I present the bottom line, which is a set of five deciding features most commonly encountered when using Wordnet in a Java. I then discuss other features that distinguish some libraries from the others. I present an assessment of what Wordnet data is accessible via which library, and which libraries are compatible with which Princeton Wordnet versions. I also evaluate the performance of each library on nine different retrieval metrics, as well as the time to initialize in-memory Wordnet dictionaries for those libraries that suport that function.

The code for reproducing the evaluation (including all required source code, copies of all the described libraries, and the various versions of Wordnet) is available online.[3]

While the software evaluated in this paper is exclusively for Java, and is limited to libraries available at the time of writing that are designed for accessing the original Princeton Wordnet, this work should be helpful to those who seek to evaluate other application programming interfaces (APIs) for interacting with Wordnet data. In particular the set of features identified here and the set of retrieval metrics should be of some use.

## 1 Deciding on a Library

Before discussing the feature and performance evaluation in detail I will lay out the bottom line: which library a developer should choose if your application falls into one of the common situations described below. First, I will outline which library a developer should choose if there are no particular constraints. Next, I list five deciding features that, if an application needs that feature, will de-

[1] See Table 6 for a list of all libraries and their URLs.

[2] I have made my best effort to be as complete as possible in identifying libraries that support access to Wordnet. It is possible, however, that I have missed some more obscure libraries, especially libraries whose primary purpose is not Wordnet access but some other function.

[3] Via the MIT DSpace repository as an MIT CSAIL Work Product: http://hdl.handle.net/1721.1/81949

termine which library the developer should choose (or which libraries there are to choose from).

Note that an application may have additional or alternate special requirements that are not explicitely discussed here. If this is the case the developer should examine the tables and figures in this paper, as well as the project websites (Table 6), to determine what library provides the right combination of features and performance.

### 1.1 No Special Requirements

If there have no special requirements, then the library a developer should choose is my own: JWI, the MIT Java Wordnet Interface. JWI is a mature library, nearly five years old, and has demonstrated its stability and utility, having been downloaded over 15,000 times in the past five years. It has the following nine advantages: (1) JWI supports access to the widest array of information in the widest selection of Princeton Wordnet versions (see Tables 2 and 3), plus has been tested on a number of Wordnet variants; (2) JWI uses the Wordnet files as they are distributed with no modifications; (3) JWI provides both file-based and in-memory dictionary implementations, allowing you to trade off speed and memory consumption; (4) JWI sets no limit on the number of dictionaries that may be instantiated in each JVM; (5) JWI is high-performance, with top-ranked speeds on various retrieval metrics and in-memory dictionary load time (see Tables 4 and 5 and Figure 1); (6) JWI has a small on-disk footprint and requires no additional Java libraries, no native dynamically-loaded libraries (dlls), and no configuration files; (7) JWI has extensive documentation, including Javadoc and a User's guide with code examples; (8) JWI is open-source and distributed under a license which allows it to be used for any purpose; and (9) JWI is being actively supported and developed by myself.

There are, however, at least five deciding features that, if an application requires them, will potentially lead to another library. These features are listed below (and are included in Table 1).

### 1.2 Similarity Metrics

The availability of similarity metrics is the most common deciding feature, as many developers want to use Wordnet not *per se*, but so as to measure the semantic similarity between words. JWNL has the most similarity metrics to choose from, with at least three different compatible libraries providing this function: RitaWN, WNSim, and WordnetSim.

Choosing JWNL, however, entails a few penalties: First, JWNL requires a notoriously confusing and error-prone external configuration file; second, JWNL depends on an external library, Apache Commons Logging; third, JWNL follows the singleton dictionary model, in that it only allows one dictionary to be open at a time; finally, JWNL has rather poor performance relative to other libraries. If these factors outweigh the positives of having the widest array of similarity metrics, then there are four other libraries that have some measure of similarity metric support: Javatools, Jawbone, JawJaw, and JWI.

### 1.3 Editing

If your application depends on being able to edit the Wordnet data, there is only option: extJWNL. This library is a re-implementation of JWNL for Java 1.5, copying much of the same source code, and so it suffers from the same problems as JWNL as described above, with the additional caveat that has an additional dependency: a custom Map implementation.

### 1.4 Maven

If an application's build process uses Maven, and the project absolutely requires that dependent libraries be available in the Maven repository, then extJWNL is the only choice.[4] As noted above, extJWNL suffers from a number of problems.

### 1.5 Retired Java Versions

Java is backward-compatible, meaning libraries compiled on older Java versions will still run under newer versions, but it is not forward-compatible: libraries compiled with newer compilance levels will not run in older JVMs. If an application requires libraries that will run under Java 1.4, then the developer should choose JWNL[5]. If an application requires Java 1.5, then the developer should choose JWI[6].

[4]Some versions of JWNL and JWI are available in the Maven repository. However, publishing artifacts to the repository is not currently a part of the JWI build process, and therefore there is no guarantee that future versions will be available there.

[5]JAWS will also run under 1.4, but lacks significantly in features and performance.

[6]JawJaw also will run under 1.5, but is sorely lacking in features, performance, and compatibility.

| Feature | CICWN | extJWNL | Javatools | Jawbone | JawJaw | JAWS | JWI | JWNL | URCS | WNJN | WNPojo | WordnetEJB |
|---|---|---|---|---|---|---|---|---|---|---|---|---|
| Version | 1.0 | 1.6.10 | 10-1-2012 | 2009-07-04 | 1.0.2 | 1.3 | 2.3.0 | 1.4.1rc2 | 1.0 | 1.0 | 1.0.1 | 1.0.0-beta |
| License | GPL | BSD | CC-BY | MIT | Apache | Custom[1] | CC-BY | BSD | GPL | GPL | GPL | GPL |
| Minimum Java | 1.6 | 1.6 | 1.6[2] | 1.6 | 1.5 | 1.4 | 1.5 | 1.4 | 1.6 | 1.5 | 1.6 | 1.6 |
| Binary Size | 1.25mb | 235kb | 398kb | 30kb | 40.9mb | 58kb | 148kb | 202kb | 188kb | 11kb | 119kb | 11.45mb |
| Standalone | Yes[3] | -[4] | Yes | Yes | Yes | Yes | Yes | -[5] | Yes | -[6] | -[7] | -[8] |
| Last Release | 2011 | 2013 | 2012 | 2009 | 2013 | 2009 | 2013 | 2008 | 2010 | 2006 | 2010 | 2010 |
| Active | - | Yes | - | - | Yes | - | Yes | - | - | - | - | - |
| Maven | - | Yes[9] | - | - | - | - | -[10] | Yes | - | - | - | - |
| Editing | - | Yes | -[11] | - | - | - | - | - | - | - | - | - |
| EJBs | - | - | - | - | - | - | - | - | - | - | - | Yes |
| Multiple Dicts | - | - | Yes[12] | - | -[13] | - | Yes | - | Yes | - | Yes | Yes |
| Normal Files | Yes[3] | Yes[14] | -[15] | Yes | -[16] | Yes | Yes | -[17] | Yes | Yes | -[18] | - |
| GUI | - | - | - | - | - | - | - | - | Yes | Yes | - | - |
| Similarity Metrics | - | - | Yes | Yes[19] | Yes[20] | - | Yes[21] | Yes[22] | - | - | - | - |
| File-Based Dict | - | Yes | - | Yes | Yes | Yes | Yes | Yes | Yes | Yes | - | - |
| Database Dict | - | Yes | - | - | - | - | - | Yes | - | - | Yes | Yes |
| In-Memory Dict | Yes | Yes | Yes | - | Yes | - | Yes | Yes | - | - | - | - |

Table 1: Information on and supported features of each library.

License

[1]JAWS license is similar to the MIT License.

Minimum Java

[2]Javatools requires a 64-bit JVM to load all supported pointers into memory.

Standalone

[3]CICWN requires Wordnet files to be placed in a particular sub-directory, plus a file containing a list of prepositions to use the plain Wordnet functionality; it requires additional libraries and data files to use the full stemming functionality.

[4]extJWNL requires an external properties file, Apache Commons Logging, and a custom Map implementation.

[5]JWNL requires Apache Commons Logging.

[6]WNJN requires a native library that depends on the wordnet version in use. The native library is available in for Windows and Linux 32-bit, but would have to be re-compiled using C++ for other platforms.

[7]WNPojo requires approximately 14 supporting libraries.

[8]WordnetEJB requires a Database server and a Java Application server deployed with the WordnetEJB implementation.

Maven

[9]extJWNL versions 1.5.0 to 1.5.3 and 1.6.0 to 1.6.10 are available in the Maven repository.

[10]JWI Versions 2.2.1, 2.2.2, and 2.2.3 are available in the Maven repository.

Editing

[11]Javatools allows you to remove synsets from the in-memory dictionary only.

Multiple Dictionaries

[12]Javatools allows multiple dictionaries to be instantiated, but each dictionary only captures one relation.

[13]JawJaw only allows single dictionary to be opened for the life of each JVM.

Normal Files

[14]extJWNL in-memory dictionary uses special files that must be compiled from the normal Wordnet files.

[15]Javatools uses the Prolog-formatted Wordnet files.

[16]JawJaw uses an sqlite3 file, generated from the Japanese Wordnet files.

[17]JWNL's in-memory dictionary implementation requires special files that must be compiled separately from the Wordnet files.

[18]WNPojo requires the normal Wordnet files to be processed and loaded into a relational database.

Similarity Metrics

[19]Jawbone has similarity metrics via the RitaWN library.

[20]JawJaw similarity metrics are provided by the WS4J library.

[21]JWI similarity metrics are available via the Java Wordnet::Similarity library (JWS).

[22]JWNL similarity metrics are available via the RitaWN, WNSim, and WordnetSim libraries.

### 1.6 Enterprise Java

Finally, if an application absolutely requires that Wordnet data be accessible via an Enterprise Java Bean (EJB), the only out-of-the-box choice is WordnetEJB, which provides all the tools to deploy an EJB that provides access to Wordnet onto a Java application server. Unfortunately, given WordnetEJB's dismal performance and difficulty of use, one is probably better off implementing one's own EJB by wrapping another library.

## 2 Features and Information

I expand now on other features of the libraries which, while not necessarily decisive, are worthy of consideration when other factors do not compel your choice.

### 2.1 Features

As noted, Table 1 shows the basic list of features, which was constructed by taking the union of all features[7] for all libraries. I describe in this section those not yet discussed. A dash in a particular cell means that I determined, either by reading the documentation or the code, that the library did not support that feature. It is important to understand that I consider here only out-of-the-box features and compatibility: because the source code for each library is available, an enterprising developer could certainly modify any of these libraries to provide any of the lacking features. Most developers, however, will not be willing or able to invest the time required for this, and thus are restricted to the features provided.

**Binary Size** This feature indicates the size of the binary jar file on disk. This number does not include the size of any required dependencies or external files, and does not include the size of the Wordnet data files. The size of the libraries ranges dramatically: from a mere 11kb for WNJN to 40.9mb for JawJaw. JWI clocks in at a quite modest 202kb, which is approximately the median of the range.

**Standalone** Whether or not the library requires additional Java libraries or external resources to run (other than the Wordnet files themselves). In certain cases, such as WNPojo, these external libraries are extensive: at least 14, comprising over 10mb of jar files.

[7]Note that due to space limitations I do not discuss in detail the ease of use of the various APIs.

Perhaps the most pernicious requirements are those for the JWNL/extJWNL pair and WNJN. Both JWNL and extJWNL require an external configuration file (in XML format) that sets various properites of the singleton dictionary. These parameters cannot be set programmatically, and the file is not well documented, which leads to quite a bit of consternation in the use of these libraries.

WNJN, on the other hand, is a JNI interface to a native dll. Using WNJN thus means that one looses the platform-independence so prized in Java (unfortunately for not much gain: WNJN is impoverished both in features and performance compared to other libraries).

JWI is especially easy to use: it requires no external libraries or files to run (other than the Wordnet files themselves), its out-of-the-box defaults are suitable to most applications, and any configuration required can be done programmatically.

**Last Release** The year when the most current version was released. JWI is one of only three libraries that saw an update in 2013, the year this paper was written.

**Active** Whether or not the project appears to be under active development. The last release year, along with indications of activity on the project's webpage or correspondence with the developer, were used to determine this feature.

**Multiple Dictionaries** Here *dictionary* refers to a Java object which manages access to the Wordnet data. This feature indicates whether or not multiple dictionaries can be open at the same time. This, for example, would be useful in a context where you want simultaneous access to different Wordnet versions. Many of the Wordnet libraries have, unfortunately, adopted the singleton design pattern, where only one Wordnet dictionary may be instantiated at a time. Fortunately, most of these libraries do allow the dictionary to be closed and a new dictionary to be opened.[8] JWI allows any number of dictionaries to be open simultaneously.

**Normal Files** Whether or not the library uses the normal Wordnet files as distributed. Some libraries require an unusual format (e.g., the Prolog versions of the files), or require the files to be processed in some way before the library can be used to access the data. JWI uses the Wordnet files as provided.

[8]The exception to this is JawJaw, which does not allow the dictionary to be disposed and thus only allows a single dictionary to open for the life of the JVM.

**GUI** Whether or not the library provides a graphical user interface (GUI) to interact with Wordnet data. Only two libraries, URCS and WordnetEJB, provide a GUI.

**File-based Dictionary** Whether or not the library provides a dictionary implementation that reads Wordnet information directly from the files when requested. Four libraries do not provide such an implementation: CICWN and Javatools, which provide in-memory implementations only; and WNPojo and WordnetEJB, which use a database-backed implementation.

**Database-backed Dictionary** Whether or not the library provides a dictionary implementation that retrieves Wordnet data from a database server. JWI does not provide database-backed access, but four libraries do: JWNL, extJWNL, WNPojo, and WordnetEJB.

**In-Memory Dictionary** Whether or not the library provides a dictionary implementation that loads Wordnet information completely into memory. These implementations allow for extremely fast data access speeds, at the price of initialization time (see Figure 1). JWI provides an in-memory dictionary implementation.

### 2.2 Accessible Data

Each library provides access to a different subset of the information contained in Wordnet. Information in Wordnet is stored across four different types of files: *index* files, *data* files, *exception* files, and the *sense.index* file. Each Wordnet library provides access to various subsets of the information contained in Wordnet, and this is captured in Table 2. The only library that provides complete access to all the Wordnet data is JWI, although JWNL, extJWNL, WNPojo, and WordnetEJB all come close.

### 2.3 Supported Wordnet Versions

Table 3 shows which libraries are compatible with which Wordnet versions. Most libraries support Princeton Wordnet versions 1.6 and above. No library supports Wordnet 1.5, and no library supports access to the Wordnet 1.6 cousin files or 3.1 stand-off annotations.

The final row in Table 3 indicates known compatibility with other Princeton Wordnet variants. JWI is the only library I know for sure that supports Wordnet variants, namely, the Stanford Augmented Wordnets (Snow et al. 2006). Other libraries can probably support Princeton Wordnet variants that conform to the Wordnet file specifications, and so the question mark only indicates that, to my knowledge, compatibility has not been demonstrated or documented.

## 3 Performance Evaluation

In addition to the features listed above, I also evaluated the performance of each library under nine different retrieval metrics (as applicable). I wrote a standard test harness that ran each library through its paces in exactly the same environment.[9] For those libraries that provide an in-memory dictionary implementation, I also measured how long it took for that implementation to load Wordnet into memory.

### 3.1 Retrieval Times

I measured three different types of retrieval metrics. First, I measured the speed of iteration over the four main object types (corresponding to the four file types). For index files, for example, I measured the average time for the dictionary to iterate over all index words in Wordnet. Second, I measured the speed of retrieval for individual objects of the four different types, given the minimally necessary identifying information. For index files, for example, I measured the average time to retrieve an index word given a lemma and part of speech. Third, I measured the time to iterate across all index words and retrieve the synsets listed in those index words.

Not every library supports all nine different types of retrieval: Tables 4 and 5 show which libraries support which retrieval type. The only libraries that support every type of retrieval are JWI and WNPojo. For retrieval of individual objects, JWI outperforms WnPojo by a factor of 10. For iteration over object types, JWI and WNPojo are approximately equivalent, except for iteration over synsets by index words, where JWI outperforms WNPojo by a factor of 25.

A note on CICWN: I include CICWN's retrieval times even though the library does not provide

[9] The testing machine was a Windows 7 Enterprise 64-bit server-class machine, with 2 Intel Xeon X5570 CPUs (4 cores each, running at 2.9 GHz), 24 GB of RAM, and two 15krpm high-performance Sata 3 drives in a RAID 0 configuration (The machine was state-of-the-art in approximately 2010). Tests were performed within Eclipse 3.8.0, using Sun Java 1.6 64-bit, revision 22. MySQL version 5.6 was used for the database server, and JBoss 5.1.0 was used for the Java Application Server. During testing the machine was unburdened with other tasks.

| File type | Data | CICWN | extJWNL | Javatools | Jawbone | JawJaw | JAWS | JWI | JWNL | URCS | WNJN | WNPojo | WordnetEJB |
|---|---|---|---|---|---|---|---|---|---|---|---|---|---|
| Index | Synsets | Yes | Yes | - | Yes | Yes | Yes | **Yes** | Yes | Yes | Yes | Yes | Yes[1] |
| | Synset Counts | Yes | Yes | - | Yes | Yes | Yes | **Yes** | Yes | - | Yes | Yes | Yes[1] |
| | Pointer Counts | - | - | - | Yes | - | - | **Yes** | - | - | Yes | - | - |
| | Pointer List | - | - | - | Yes | - | - | **Yes** | - | - | - | - | - |
| Data | Tag Sense Count | - | - | - | Yes | - | Yes | **Yes** | Yes | - | Yes | - | - |
| | Synonyms | Yes | Yes | Yes | Yes | Yes | Yes | **Yes** | Yes | Yes | Yes | Yes | Yes[1] |
| | Lexical Filenum | - | Yes | - | Yes | - | - | **Yes** | Yes | Yes | Yes | Yes | Yes[1] |
| | WordCount | Yes | Yes | Yes | Yes | Yes | Yes | **Yes** | Yes | Yes | Yes | Yes | Yes[1] |
| | LexicalID | - | Yes | - | Yes | Yes | - | **Yes** | - | Yes | Yes | Yes | Yes[1] |
| | Semantic Pointers | Yes | Yes | Yes[2] | Yes | Yes | Yes | **Yes** | Yes | Yes | Yes | Yes | Yes[1] |
| | Lexical Pointers | Yes | Yes | - | Yes | - | Yes | **Yes** | Yes | Yes | Yes | Yes | Yes[1] |
| | Verb Frames | - | Yes | - | Yes | - | Yes | **Yes** | Yes | Yes | Yes | Yes | Yes[1] |
| | Adjective Marker | - | Yes | - | Yes | - | Yes | **Yes** | Yes | - | Yes | Yes | Yes[1] |
| | Gloss | Yes | Yes | - | Yes | Yes | Yes | **Yes** | Yes | Yes | Yes | Yes | Yes[1] |
| Exception | Inflected Form | Yes | Yes | - | - | - | - | **Yes** | Yes | - | - | Yes | Yes[1] |
| | Base Forms | Yes | Yes | - | - | - | Yes | **Yes** | Yes | - | - | Yes | Yes[1] |
| Sense | Sense Key | - | Yes | - | - | - | - | **Yes** | Yes | Yes | - | Yes | Yes[1] |
| | Tag Counts | - | Yes | - | - | - | - | **Yes** | Yes | - | - | Yes | Yes[1] |

Table 2: Wordnet data accessible from each library.

[1]WordnetEJB returns all data as XML documents: it provides no Java API for accessing data within an index word, word, synset, sense entry, or exception entry record.
[2]Javatools only supports some semantic pointer types.

| Version | CICWN | extJWNL | Javatools | Jawbone | JawJaw | JAWS | JWI | JWNL | URCS | WNJN | WNPojo[1] | WordnetEJB[1] |
|---|---|---|---|---|---|---|---|---|---|---|---|---|
| 1.6 | Yes | Yes | - | Yes | - | Yes | **Yes** | Yes | Yes | Yes | Yes | Yes |
| 1.7 | Yes | Yes | - | Yes | - | Yes | **Yes** | Yes | Yes | Yes | Yes | Yes |
| 1.7.1 | Yes | Yes | Yes | Yes | - | Yes | **Yes** | Yes | Yes | Yes | Yes | Yes |
| 2.0 | Yes | Yes | Yes | Yes | - | Yes | **Yes** | Yes | Yes | Yes | Yes | Yes |
| 2.1 | Yes | Yes | Yes | Yes | - | Yes | **Yes** | Yes | Yes | Yes | Yes | Yes |
| 3.0 | Yes | Yes | -[2] | Yes | Yes | Yes | **Yes** | Yes | Yes | Yes | Yes | Yes |
| 3.1 | Yes | Yes | - | Yes | - | Yes | **Yes** | Yes | Yes | Yes | Yes | Yes |
| Other | ? | ? | ? | ? | - | ? | **Yes** | ? | ? | ? | ? | ? |

Table 3: Versions of the Princeton Wordnet supported by each library. No library supports version 1.5, version 1.6 cousin files, or the 3.1 stand-off files.

[1]WNPojo/WordnetEJB do not provide pre-compiled Wordnet database images other than for Wordnet 3.1 for MySQL; other Wordnet versions require the user to compile the Wordnet files into the database image (and load it into the appropriate database server) using the WNSQLBuilder project.
[2]Javatools throws an exception when loading Wordnet 3.0 prolog files.

a file-based dictionary implementation. This is not a completely direct comparison, however, as CICWN requires all of WordNet be loaded into memory (with associated memory footprint and initialization time penalties). It is interesting to note, however, that CICWN's in-memory performance is comparable to JWI's file-based performance, with retrieval times around the neighborhood of 10 microseconds. JWI's in-memory retrieval significantly outperforms CICWN (I do not show those results here for lack of space).

### 3.2 In-Memory Dictionaries

Six libraries support in-memory dictionary implementations. Of them, JawJaw supports only Wordnet 3.0. JWNL, extJWNL and JawJaw all have average load times (the time to load the Wordnet data fully into memory) in the 15-20 second range. Of the remaining three, Javatools and CICWN do not support access to the full range of Wordnet data. Only JWI has a load time of a few seconds and supplies complete access to all Wordnet data.

## 4 Conclusion

For an application without special constraints, most Java developers should use JWI to access Wordnet, for three reasons. First, it is among the easiest to use: it has extensive documention, a small disk footprint, requires no special configuration or supporting libraries, and is completely configurable programmatically. Second, it supports the most Wordnet versions and variants, and its API exposes all available Wordnet data. Third, it has top-tier performance, often outperforming other Java libraries by factors of 5 to 100.


## Acknowledgments

The preparation of this article was supported by DARPA under grant D12AP00210.


## References


Rion Snow, Daniel Jurafsky, and Andrew Y. Ng. 2006. Semantic taxonomy induction from heterogenous evidence. In *Proceedings of the 44th Annual Meeting of the Association for Computational Linguistics*, Sydney, Australia, pages 801–808.


| Retrieval of... ($\mu$s) | **WordnetEJB** | **JAWS** | **URCSWordnet** | **extJWNL** | **JWNL** | **Jawbone** | **WNJN** | **WNPojo** | **JawJaw** | **JWI** | **CICWN** |
|---|---|---|---|---|---|---|---|---|---|---|---|
| Index Word | 506ms | 4.1ms | 2662.5 | 1.5ms | 1.5ms | - | 253.3 | 184.5 | 67.4 | 12.3 | 22.9 |
| Synset | - | - | - | 3.3ms | 479.6 | 768 | 228.6 | 226.6 | 61.9 | 7.1 | 4.1 |
| Word-by-Sense-Key | - | - | - | 11.1ms | - | - | - | 176.1 | - | 17.2 | - |
| Exception Entry | - | 2.1 | - | 545.3 | 537.9 | - | - | 138.5 | - | 16.1 | 1.7 |

Table 4: Average time to retrieve an object of the named type (from Wordnet 3.0) using a file-backed dictionary, for libraries that support this functionality. Times are in microseconds ($\mu$s), unless otherwise noted (ms = milliseconds).

| Iteration Over... (ms) | **extJWNL** | **JWNL** | **Jawbone** | **WNPojo**[1] | **JWI** | **CICWN**[2] |
|---|---|---|---|---|---|---|
| Index Words | 16.4s | 16.4s | 192 | 393 | 296 | - |
| Synsets | 6.4m | 56.1s | - | 273 | 798 | 1 |
| Words via Sense Keys | - | - | - | 635 | 141 | - |
| Exception Entries | 271 | 274 | - | 10 | 4 | 1 |
| Synsets by Index Words | 15.7m | 2.1m | 5.6m | 51.0s | 1.8s | - |

Table 5: Average time to iterate over all objects of the named type (from Wordnet 3.0) using a file-backed dictionary, for libraries that support this functionality. Times are in milliseconds, unless otherwise noted (s = seconds, m = minutes).

[1]WNPojo uses a database-based dictionary implementation.
[2]CICWN only provides an in-memory dictionary implementation.

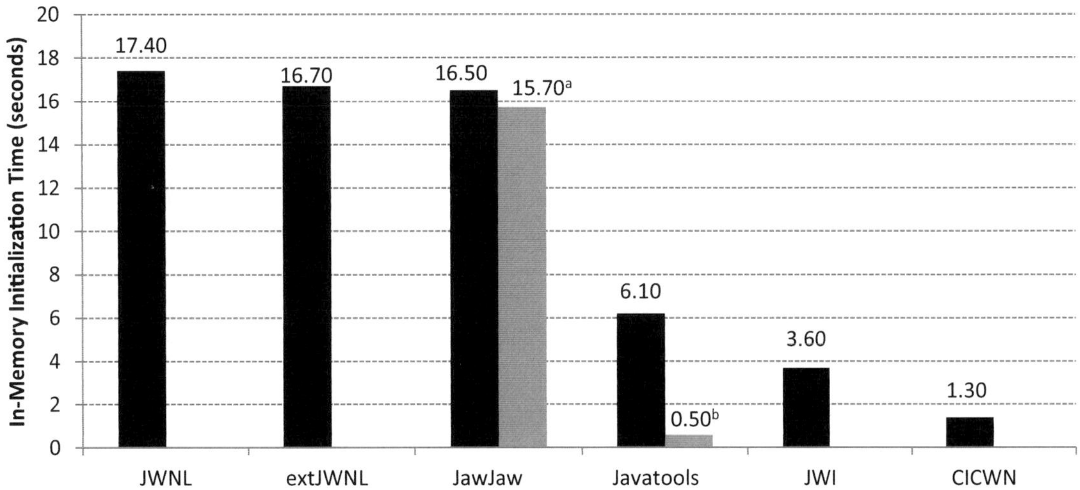


Figure 1: Times to load Wordnet into memory for the libraries that support in-memory dictionaries.
[a] JawJaw has a slightly lower load time when the data file is already present in the temporary directory.
[b] Javatools has a lower load time when loading only synsets, with no pointers.

| | Library | URL |
|---|---|---|
| **Wordnet Libraries** | CICWN | `http://fviveros.gelbukh.com/wordnet.html` |
| | extJWNL | `http://extjwnl.sourceforge.net/` |
| | Javatools | `http://www.mpi-inf.mpg.de/yago-naga/javatools/` |
| | Jawbone | `http://sites.google.com/site/mfwallace/jawbone/` |
| | JawJaw | `http://www.cs.cmu.edu/~hideki/software/jawjaw/` |
| | JAWS | `http://lyle.smu.edu/~tspell/jaws/` |
| | JWI | `http://projects.csail.mit.edu/jwi/` |
| | JWNL | `http://sourceforge.net/apps/mediawiki/jwordnet/` |
| | URCS | `http://www.cs.rochester.edu/research/cisd/wordnet/` |
| | WNJN | `http://wnjn.sourceforge.net/` |
| | WNPojo | `http://wnpojo.sourceforge.net/` |
| | WordnetEJB | `http://wnejb.sourceforge.net/` |
| **Similarity** | JWS | `http://www.sussex.ac.uk/Users/drh21/` |
| | JWordnetSim | `http://nlp.shef.ac.uk/result/software.html` |
| | Rita.WordNet | `http://rednoise.org/rita/wordnet/documentation/index.htm` |
| | WNSim | `http://cogcomp.cs.illinois.edu/page/software_view/36` |
| | WordnetSim | `http://nlp.shef.ac.uk/result/software.html` |
| | ws4j | `http://code.google.com/p/ws4j/` |
| **Other** | Lucene Wordnet | `http://mvnrepository.com/artifact/org.apache.lucene/lucene-wordnet/` |
| | WNSQL | `http://wnsql.sourceforge.net/` |
| | WNSQLBuilder | `http://wnsqlbuilder.sourceforge.net/` |
| | WNTrans | `http://wntrans.sourceforge.net/` |
| | WNWA | `http://wnwa.sourceforge.net/` |
| | XSSM | `http://code.google.com/p/xssm/` |

Table 6: URLs for each library. The libraries listed in the first section are evaluated in this paper. The similarity libraries provide similarity metrics which use the wordnet libraries. The libraries listed in the "Other" section are mentioned because they do not provide direct access to Wordnet data, but may be confused for libraries that do.

# Concept Space Synset Manager Tool

**Apurva S Nagvenkar**
DCST, Goa University
Taleigao Plateau, Goa.
apurv.nagvenkar@gmail.com

**Neha R Prabhugaonkar**
DCST, Goa University
Taleigao Plateau, Goa.
nehapgaonkar.1920@gmail.com

**Venkatesh P Prabhu**
Thyway Creation
Mapusa, Goa.
venkateshprabhu@thywayindia.com

**Ramdas N Karmali**
DCST, Goa University
Taleigao Plateau, Goa.
rnk@unigoa.ac.in

**Jyoti D Pawar**
DCST, Goa University
Taleigao Plateau, Goa.
jyotidpawar@gmail.com

## Abstract

The IndoWordNet[1] Consortium consists of member institutions developing WordNet using the expansion approach.

The WordNets developed using expansion approach are very much influenced by the source language and may not reflect the richness of the target language (Walawalikar et al., 2010). And therefore the IndoWordNet Community decided to develop concepts which were specific to their respective language viz. language-specific concepts which will help in increasing the WordNet coverage. Besides the above requirement it was also felt that it should be possible to maintain additional information about the concepts i.e. an image, document describing the concept, links to websites and other resources, etc.

In this paper, we discuss a Concept Space Synset Management Tool (CSS)[2] which was developed to assist creation of language specific concepts/synsets and manage their linkages to other Indian language WordNets.

## 1 Background and Motivation

The IndoWordNet is a multilingual WordNet which links WordNets of different Indian languages on a common identification number called as synset Id given to each concept (Bhattacharyya, 2010). WordNet is designed to capture the vocabulary of a language and can be considered as a dictionary cum thesaurus and much more (Miller, et al., 1993; Miller, 1995; Fellbaum, 1998).

Synset (Fellbaum, 1998) is composed of a gloss describing the concept, example sentences and a set of synonym words that are used for the concept. Besides synset data, WordNet maintains many lexical and semantic relations. Table1 gives the number of concepts/synsets created by the language groups of the Indradhanush WordNet Consortium which is a part of the IndoWordNet Consortium.

| Sr. No. | Language | Nouns | Adjectives | Verbs | Adverbs | Total |
|---|---|---|---|---|---|---|
| 1. | Bengali | 27178 | 5183 | 3249 | 445 | 36685 |
| 2. | Gujarati | 21659 | 5802 | 2804 | 444 | 30709 |
| 3. | Hindi | 28163 | 6056 | 3079 | 456 | 37754 |
| 4. | Kashmiri | 17959 | 6382 | 2354 | 305 | 27000 |
| 5. | Konkani | 22912 | 5648 | 2983 | 471 | 32014 |
| 6. | Odia | 27216 | 5273 | 2418 | 377 | 35284 |
| 7. | Punjabi | 18982 | 5786 | 2808 | 442 | 28018 |
| 8. | Urdu | 20816 | 5787 | 2800 | 443 | 29846 |

Table1: Synset linkage status

[1]http://www.cfilt.iitb.ac.in/indowordnet
[2]http://indradhanush.unigoa.ac.in/conceptspace

Also a sense marked newspaper corpus (sense marking is a task to tag each word of the corpus with the WordNet sense) consisting of minimum 1,00,000 words has been created by each of the members of the Indradhanush WordNet Consortium. The coverage is found to be low. In order to increase the coverage of the WordNet it was decided that a corpus will be created by all language groups and the corpus will be sense marked.
To increase the coverage it was decided to add the concepts which were specific to their respective language viz. language-specific concepts and nullify the effect of influence of the source language on the target language WordNet. The CSS Manager Tool[3] was developed to assist in creation of language-specific concepts, linking to other language WordNets, providing additional information about synsets, etc. The features and the detailed framework of the CSS Manager Tool is explained in section 3 and 4.
The rest of the paper is organized as follows – section 2 introduces the related work. The features of CSS Manager Tool are presented in section 3; section 4 presents the architecture of CSS Manager Tool. Section 5 presents the implementation details followed by the conclusion and future work.

## 2 Related Work

For many Indian languages, WordNets are constructed using the expansion model where Hindi WordNet synsets are taken as a source using the MultiDict Tool (Chatterjee, 2010) created by IIT Bombay. The tool also had feature to add comments and references but it was not an ideal tool for creation of language-specific synsets.
The limitations of the MultiDict Tool are:

- Creating and linking of language-specific synsets across languages was not possible,
- finding the overlap of synsets across languages was not possible,
- Feature to provide additional information about the synset was not present,
- Validation of synsets was not possible.
- Features to search synsets based on domain, date, category was not present.

And therefore the CSS Manager Tool was developed in order to overcome the above limitations.

[3] https://www.youtube.com/watch?v=BMhixBI7xOY&feature=youtu.be

## 3 Features of CSS Tool

CSS Manager Tool is a centralized tool meant for effective creation and management of synsets. The features supported currently by the CSS Manager Tool are as follows:

**1. Synset Creation:**

- Addition/updation/validation of synsets, linking of two or more synsets with similar gloss across languages,
- Comments- Comments can be provided in case of any issue in the synset content.
- Allows adding additional information about the synset (images, documents, links, etc.).

**2. Interactive User Interface:**

- The CSS Manager Tool is designed keeping in mind the broadest range of users and contexts of use.
- Supports both left-to-right and right-to-left text rendition.
- Allows adjustment of the layout as per direction in which content language is written through a simple setting of a flag.
- Viewing various media added for clarity on synsets, etc.

**3. Security:**

- The CSS Manager Tool stores information in a centralized database system where access control mechanisms can more easily restrict access to your content.
- User Management supports adding/ blocking/ unblocking users, and assigns privileges to the users.

**4. Use of RBAC approach**

- Role-based access control (RBAC) is an approach to restricting system access to authorized users.
- Roles are created for various functions. The permissions to perform certain operations are assigned to specific roles.
- Members or staff are assigned particular roles, and through those role assignments acquire the permissions to perform particular functions.
- Roles can be easily created, changed, or discontinued as the needs evolve, without having to individually update the privileges for every user.

## 4 Architecture of CSS Tool

Figure 1 represents the architecture of CSS Manager Tool. The CSS Manager Tool is implemented in three blocks: User block, Super Admin block, and the Database. The CSS Manager tool is developed using the Hierarchical Role Based system with Access Control (RBAC) to control the access to certain parts and features of the CSS Manager Tool across different users. Refer Figure 2 for the block diagram of RBAC.

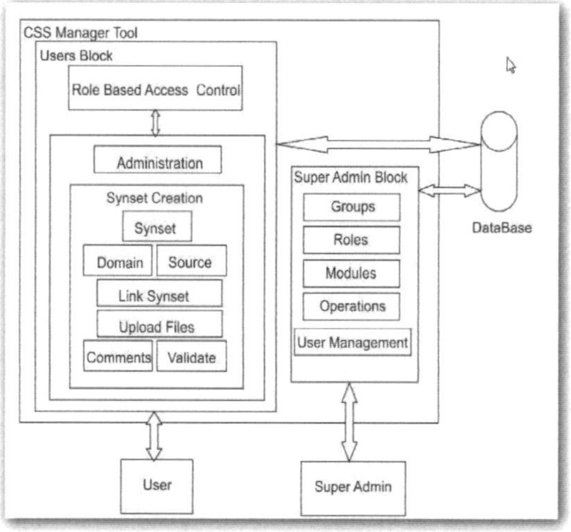


Figure1: Architecture of CSS Manager Tool

- The User block is responsible for creation/updation/validation of synsets, linking of synsets across languages, adding comments, source, and domain.
- The Super-Admin block is responsible for the creation of groups, users, roles to be assigned to the members in a group, modules and its operations, etc.
- The heart of the CSS Manager Tool is a centralized database that stores all the CSS data.

### 4.1 Modules of CSS Manager Tool

A module is an independent component which offers specific functionality. Each module is assigned different operations related to the module. The different operations are: Advance search, add/view/edit/delete/link synsets, and add/delete/change priority of example, add source, upload/delete file/add/view/reply comments, etc. Only those operations that need to be performed by members of a language group are assigned to the modules and these modules are allotted to the roles. These modules depend on CSS database. While the addition of new modules does not require any changes to the CSS database, new tables may need to be added to store data specific to module functionality.

Presently there are five modules, they are:

1. **View All Synset:** The view synset module allows the linguist to view synsets belonging to a language group/ category/ domain/source. The linguist/ lexicographer can perform the operations which are assigned for this module.
2. **Synset Creation:** Allows the linguist to create synsets. The linguist/ lexicographer can also add source/domain/images/ documents/links in order to give additional information about the synset.
3. **View Linked Synset:** Allows the linguist to view the list of synsets linked across languages.
4. **User Management:** Allows the administrator of a group to create new users, to block/unblock user, to assign privileges to the users, etc.
5. **Synset Validation:** Allows validation of synsets.

### 4.2 Role-Based system used in CSS Manager Tool

A role hierarchy is a way of organizing roles to reflect authority, responsibility, and competency. Some general operations may be performed by all the group members such as adding, viewing, searching synsets. In this situation, it would be inefficient and administratively cumbersome to specify repeatedly these general operations for each role that gets created. Therefore role hierarchy is used in order to avoid repetitive tasks. Also when a user is associated with a role, the user can be given additional privileges.

Currently, the CSS Manager Tool has four roles: Super admin, Admin, senior linguist and junior linguist.

- The super admin is responsible for creation of groups, users of a group, creation of roles to be assigned to the members in a group, addition of new modules and operations, and various other administrative operations such as adding source, domain, etc. which other roles cannot perform.

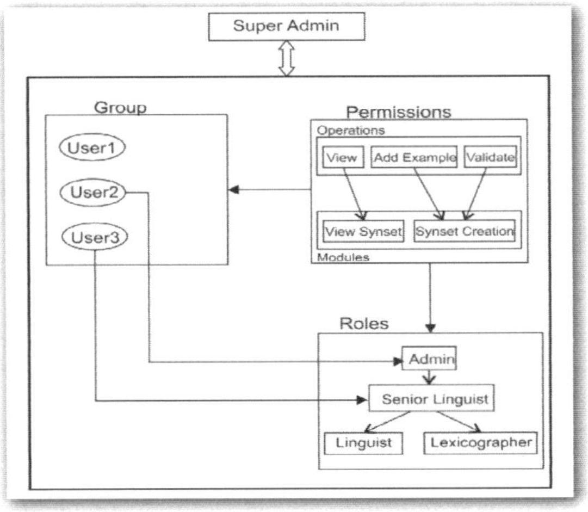

Figure2: Role Based system with Access Control

- The Admin is responsible for managing his/her language group created by the Super admin. The admin of a group can add/block users to his group. And can use all the modules which are assigned to the Admin by the Superadmin.
- The linguists are part of a language group. The operations (such as creating/ validating/ linking of synsets) performed by the junior linguists are further validated and approved by the senior linguists of the group.

## 5 Implementation Details

The CSS Manager Tool is developed using PHP scripting language and is hosted on a Web Server supporting PHP version 5.3.15. Currently MySQL version 5.5.21 is used as database. The CSS Manager Tool was developed using XAMPP on 32 bit Microsoft Windows platform. It has been deployed on Fedora 16 Linux Platform using Apache version 2.2.22 and MySQL version 5.5.21 which come bundled with Fedora 16 Linux Platform. The screenshots of the tool are shown at the end of the paper.

## 6 Conclusion and Future Work

The advantages of CSS Manager Tool can be summarized as follows:

- **Ease in accessing synsets:** The synset is represented by an identification number called as synset id. Remembering id's is difficult for user, than remembering the concept of the synset. Earlier, the linguists had to remember synset id in order to perform any operation on synset in future. In CSS Manager Tool, the user need not remember the synset ids, all the operations can be performed with the help of concept and synonymous set of the words.
- **Decentralized maintenance:** Need of specialized software or any specific kind of technological environment to access the tool is not required. Any browser device connected to the Internet would be sufficient for the job.
- **WordNet Enhancement:** Creation of language specific concepts/synsets, adding additional information about the synset and their linkages to other Indian language WordNets is possible. The tool is being enhanced to support validation of WordNets.

## Acknowledgement

This work has been carried out as a part of the Indradhanush WordNet Project (11(13)/2010-HCC(TDIL), dated 3-8-2010) jointly carried out by nine institutions. We wish to express our gratitude to the funding agency DeitY, Govt. of India and also all the members of the Indradhanush Consortium.

## References

Pushpak Bhattacharyya. 2010. *IndoWordNet,* Lexical Resources Engineering Conference 2010 (LREC2010), Malta.

Arindam Chatterjee, Salil Joshi, Mitesh Khapra, Pushpak Bhattacharyya. 2010. *Introduction to Tools for IndoWordNet and Word Sense Disambiguation.* 3rd IndoWordNet workshop, International Conference on Natural Language Procesing.

Christiane Fellbaum (ed). 1998. *WordNet: An Electronic Lexical Database.* Cambridge, MA: MIT Press.

George A. Miller, Richard Beckwith, Christiane Fellbaum, Derek Gross, and Katherine Miller. 1993. *Introduction to WordNet: An On-line Lexical Database.*

George A. Miller. 1995. *WordNet: A Lexical Database for English.* Communications of the ACM Vol. 38, No. 11: 39-41.

Shantaram Walawalikar, Shilpa Desai, Ramdas Ka rmali, Sushant Naik, Damodar Ghanekar, Chandrekha D'souza and Jyoti Pawar. 2010. *Experiences in Building the Konkani Word Net using the expansion Approach.* In Proceedings of the 5th GlobalWordNet Conference on Principles, Construction and Application of Multilingual WordNets (Mumbai-India).

Konkani WordNet: WordNet For Konkani Language: http://konkaniwordnet.unigoa.ac.in

IndoWordNet Website: Multilingual WordNet which links WordNets of eighteen Indian languages: http://www.cfilt.iitb.ac.in/indowordnet/

Indradhanush Website: WordNets for seven Indian Languages: http://indradhanush.unigoa.ac.in

Concept Space Synset Manager Tool (CSS Manager Tool) : http://indradhanush.unigoa.ac.in/conceptspace/

Concept Space Manager Tool Tutorial link: https://www.youtube.com/watch?v=BMhixBI7xOY&feature=youtu.be

## Snapshots

1. **Login Page:** The login page of the CSS Manager Tool is shown below.

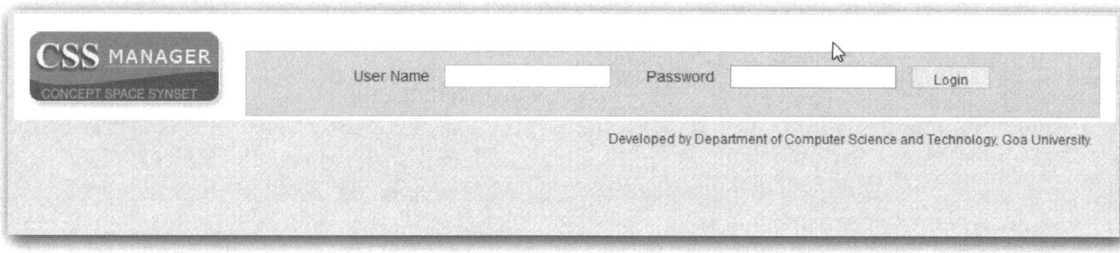


2. **SuperAdmin:** The super admin is the highest role in the role hierarchy. The super admin owns all the privileges which the admin, linguist or lexicographer have. The super admin is accountable for creation of groups, users of a group, creation of roles to be assigned to the members in a group, addition of new modules and operations, and various other administrative operations such as adding source, domain, etc. which other roles cannot perform. The snapshot of the super admin interface is shown below.

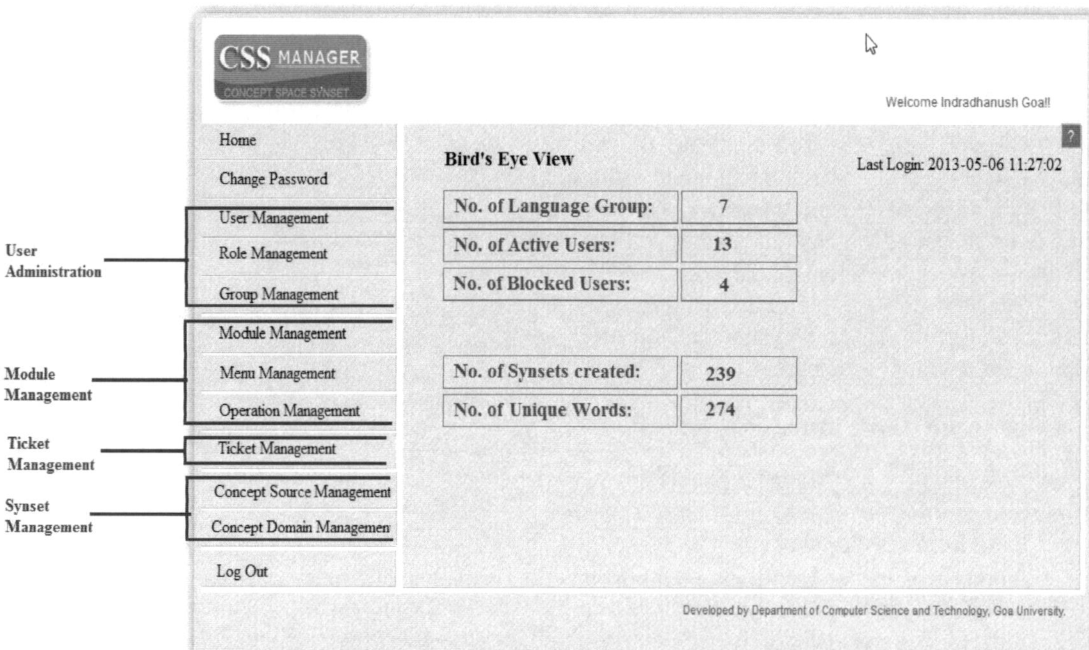

3. **User Management:** This module allows the administrator to view the users in a group, to add new users, to block or unblock user, to assign privileges to the users, etc. The User Management module is only available to the administrator of the group and not the linguist/ lexicographer.

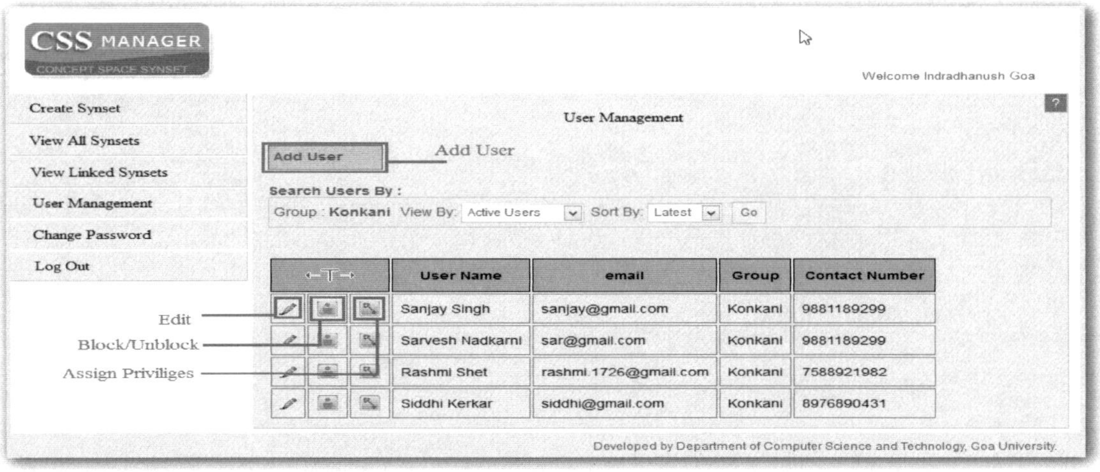


To add a new User,

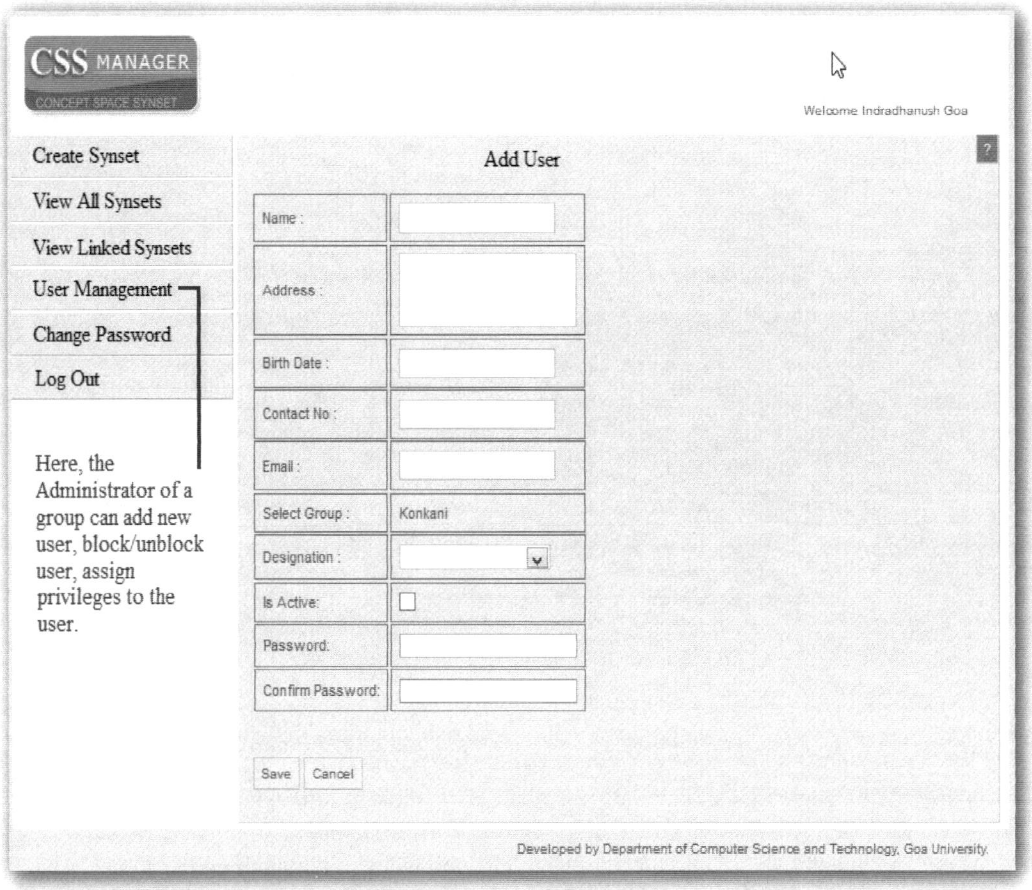


The Modules which are available to the linguist and lexicographers are as follows:

- **Create Synset:** This module allows the user to create a new synset.

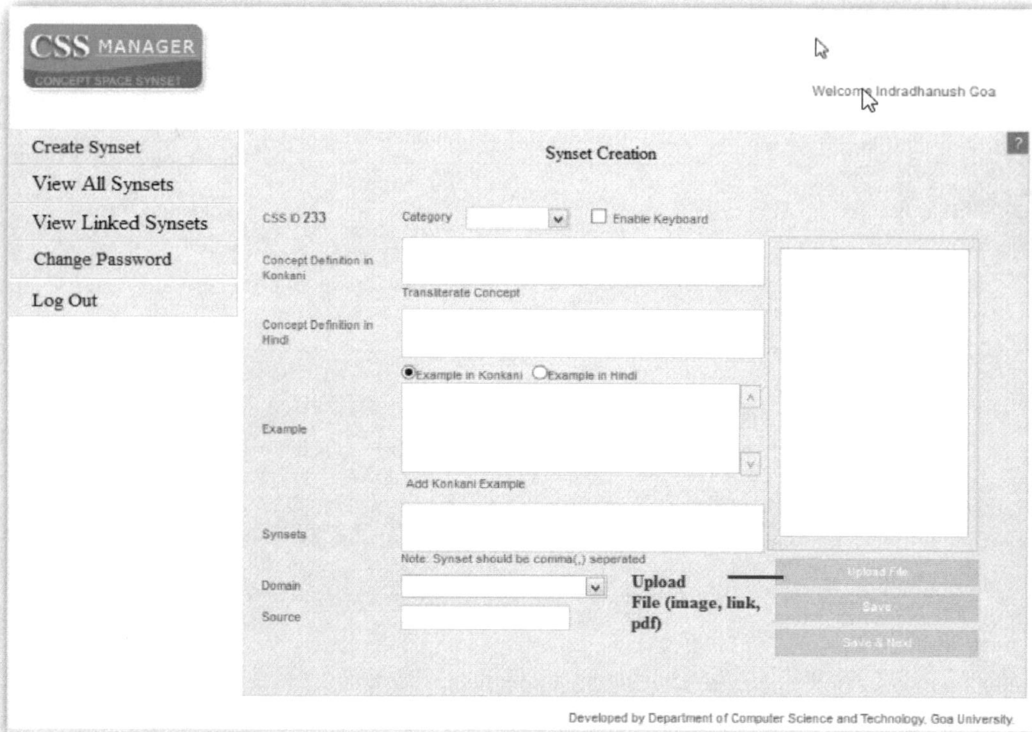


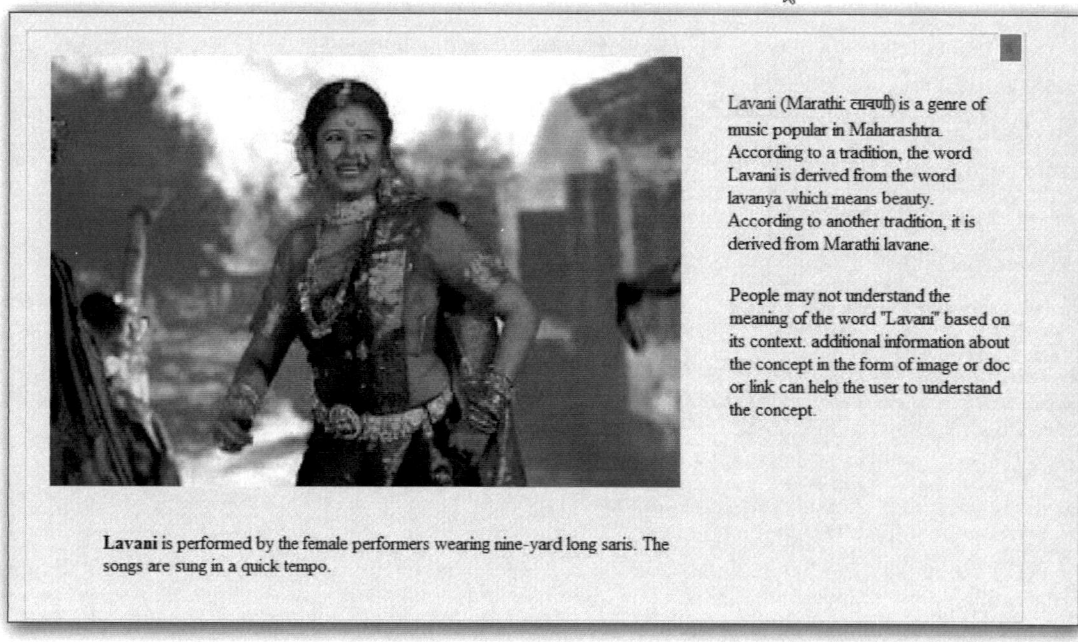


- **View All Synset:** This module allows the user to view all the synsets created so far. On selecting 'View All Synset' menu link, the user can view synsets belonging to a language. It also allows the user to select the number of synsets to be displayed per page, to view synsets based on the date of creation. Each module provides the user with the help files to assist in tool usage.

  The 'Advance search' option allows the user to view synsets belonging to a particular grammatical category i.e Noun, Verb, Adverb, Adjective, a domain, a source and also to view the synsets created by a user of a group.

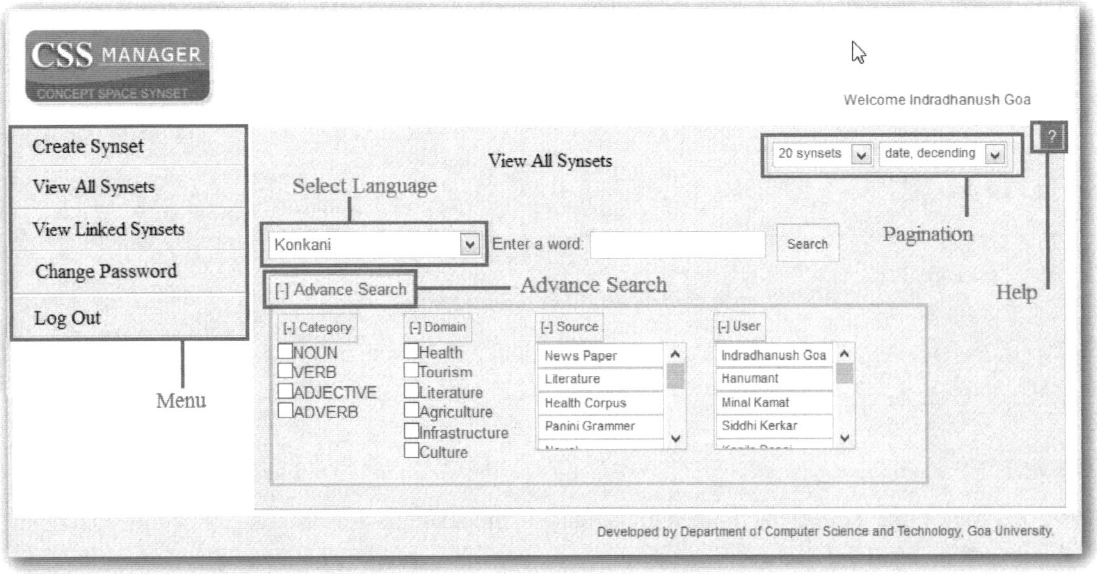


Based on the operations assigned to the modules and roles, the user can edit, view or validate the synsets.

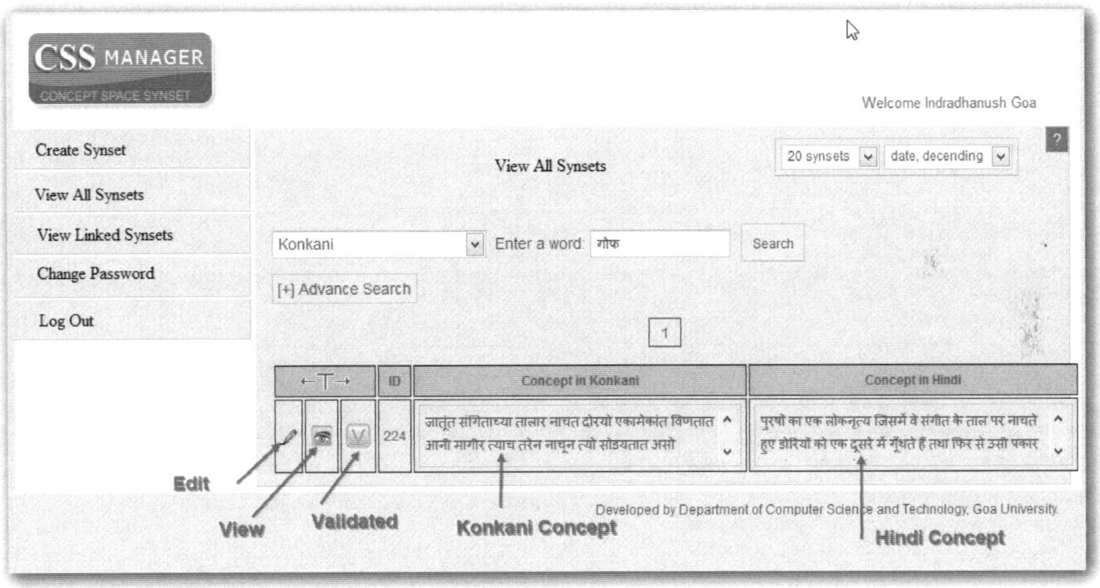


- **View Linked Synsets:** This module is similar to the View All synset module, but it only allows the users to view the synsets which are linked across languages.
- **Change Password:** This module allows the user to change the password.

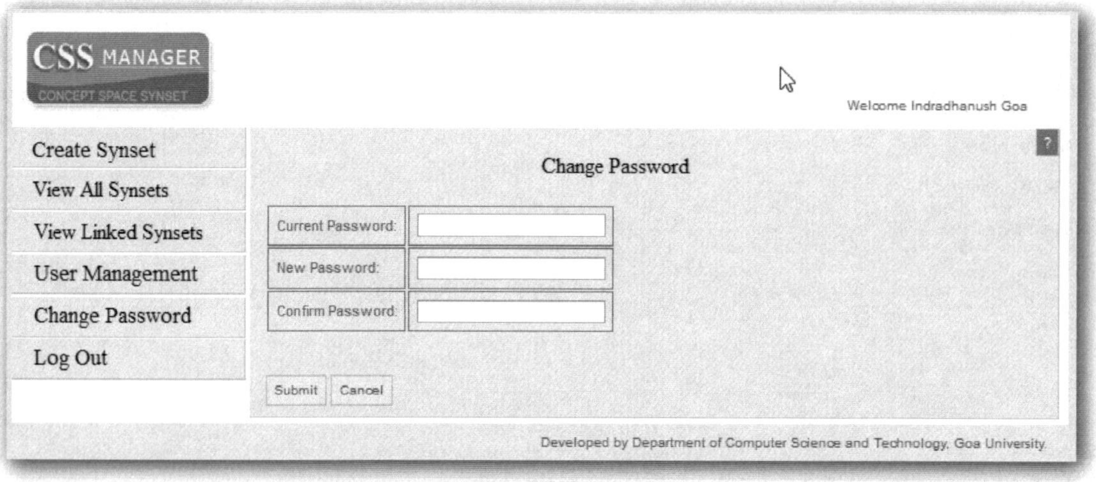


- **Log Out:** To log out from the CSS Manager Tool, the user needs to click on 'Log Out' from the menu list.

# Use of Sense Marking for Improving WordNet Coverage

**Neha R Prabhugaonkar**
DCST, Goa University
Taleigao Plateau, Goa.
nehapgaonkar.1920@gmail.com

**Jyoti D Pawar**
DCST, Goa University
Taleigao Plateau, Goa.
jyotidpawar@gmail.com

## Abstract

WordNet is a crucial resource that aids in several Natural Language Processing (NLP) tasks. The WordNet development activity for 18 Indian languages has been initiated in INDIA by the IndoWordNet[1] consortium using the expansion approach with the Hindi WordNet developed by IIT Bombay, as the source. After linking 20K synsets, it was decided that each of these languages should find the coverage of their respective language WordNets by using sense marker tool released by IIT Bombay.

The sense marking activity mainly helped in validation of WordNet and improving the WordNet coverage. In this paper, the various effects that sense marking activity had on the Konkani[2] language WordNet development are presented.

**Keywords:** sense marking, IndoWordNet, word sense disambiguation, annotation, coverage, challenges in sense marking.

## 1 Introduction

The IndoWordNet consortium in India is working towards the development of a multilingual WordNet which includes 18 Indian languages using the expansion approach with Hindi as source language. The IndoWordNet is a multilingual WordNet which links WordNets of different Indian languages on a common identication number called as synset Id given to each concept (Bhattacharyya, 2010).

Synset (Fellbaum, 1998) is composed of a gloss describing a concept, example sentences and a set of synonym words that are used for the concept. Besides synset data, WordNet maintains many lexical and semantic relations. Currently, 11 language WordNets out of 18 of the IndoWordNet have created more than 20K concepts. As of now this covers around 40-50 percent of the day to day vocabulary of the respective languages. Currently, the Konkani WordNet contains 32063 concepts and more than 43200 unique words representing these concepts.

Sense marking is a task to tag each word of the corpus accurately with the WordNet sense or lexicon. In order to train machine understand the written language and thus to ensure speedy and high quality translation, a huge amount of data needs to be sense tagged precisely by humans using a standard lexicon. A word may have multiple senses and to identify which particular sense has been used in the given context, word sense disambiguation becomes a critical inevitability (Sarawati et al., 2010). In a given text, the occurrence of a particular word will correspond to only one sense and the nearby words provide strong and consistent evidence to the sense of a target word.

| Language | No. of Files used | Total No. of words | Total No. of tagged words | Percentage |
|---|---|---|---|---|
| Bengali | 11 | 163360 | 32952 | 20.17 |
| Gujarati | 101 | 337094 | 112884 | 33.49 |
| Konkani | 625 | 213415 | 103456 | 48.48 |
| Kashmiri | 350 | 98350 | 42290 | 43.00 |
| Punjabi | 45 | 138735 | 60182 | 43.38 |
| Odiya | 120 | 236125 | 100285 | 42.27 |
| Urdu | 10 | 100000 | 68689 | 68.69 |

Table 1: Sense marking status

One of the tasks in the first phase of WordNet

[1] http://www.cfilt.iitb.ac.in/indowordnet/

[2] Konkani is an Indo-Aryan language and is spoken on the west coast of India. It is one of the 22 scheduled languages mentioned in 8th schedule of the Indian Constitution and the state language of the Indian state of Goa and minority language in Maharashtra, Karnataka, Kerala

development was to sense mark a minimum 100K words. The source of the corpus used for sense tagging was local newspaper. The Sense Marker Tool developed by IIT Bombay was used for the sense marking activity. The table 1 shows the sense marking statistics.

The rest of the paper is organized as follows section 2 describes the Sense Marker Tool usage and the procedure used for sense-marking. The experiences of sense marking and the challenges faced are discussed in section 3. Section 4 gives the details about how the challenges were overcome and the results obtained. Section 5 gives the details about how sense marking activity helped in improving the quality of the WordNet, followed by the conclusion and future work.

## 2 Procedure Used for Sense Marking

The Sense Marker Tool developed by IIT Bombay was used in the sense marking task. It helps the lexicographer to efficiently tag the words. Since WordNet contains only open-class words, Sense Marker Tool is used to tag only nouns, verbs, adjectives, and adverbs; that is to say, only about 50 percent of the words in the corpus are semantically tagged. The following procedure was followed while sense marking the corpus -

- Examine each word of the text in its context of use and decide which WordNet sense was intended. In order to facilitate this task, the tool displays the word to be tagged in its context, along with the WordNet synsets for all of the senses of that word.
- Indicate the appropriate sense to the word by selecting the correct sense from the list of possible senses.

While sense marking there were situations when either the sense of the word was not found or the existing sense was not sufficient to provide the correct sense.

The main cases encountered by the lexicographers while sense marking, are listed below -

1. **Marking the word with exact sense:** The ideal situation is when the exact sense is available for the corpus word. Here, the lexicographer applying his/her language knowledge has to select the correct sense from the list of possible senses displayed by the tool.

2. **Marking the word using hypernymy:** When the exact sense is not found, the word can be tagged with its hypernymy depending on the context of the word.

3. **Marking the word with closest sense:** Sometimes the exact sense of a word is not present in the WordNet. If closest sense is available and if the lexicographer has knowledge about its existence, then he/she can assign the tag for the word with the closest sense.

4. **Creating a new sense for the word:** There are two situations when the lexicographer needs to create new sense for the word
   - If the sense of the word is not present in the WordNet. This is obvious in cases of language specific, culture specific words, species names or multiwords. Therefore it was decided that a new sense should be created for them.
   - If the sense of the word is not appropriate in the context.

5. **Marking the corpus word with the exact sense even if the sense/concept does not have the word in its synonyms set:** The word is tagged with the appropriate synset and later the word is added to the synset.

The coverage C of language vocabulary by the WordNet is measured by the following formula -

- ***Equation 1:*** *C = M*100/N, where M is the total number of words tagged and N is the total number of words in the corpus*
- ***Equation 2:*** *c = m * 100/n, where m is the total number of unique words tagged and n is the total No. of unique words in the corpus*

Equation 1 measures the coverage of more frequent words. If a frequently occurring word is covered in the WordNet then the count will increase. For Konkani language, this percentage was 48.48 percent.

Equation 2 measures the coverage of the vocabulary. If the number of words in the WordNet is high then the count will increase. For Konkani language, this percentage was 53.2 percent.

## 3 Challenges faced while sense marking

The main challenges faced were handling of compound words, multi-word expressions, language specific words, word with affixes, etc. They can be grouped under following heads -

### 3.1 Tool related challenges:

The challenges faced due to the limitations of the Sense Marker Tool are as follows:

1. There is no feature in the Sense Marker Tool to add a new synset directly to the synset file.

2. If two lexicographers are involved in the sense marking activity and both come across a same synset which is not found in the WordNet then both may end up creating a new sense. This may result in duplication of work.

3. Though the sense distinctions in the WordNet are quite fine-grained, there have been cases when the senses provided there have been inadequate or may contain some errors.

4. There is no feature in the tool to update the synset content in case of any issues like ambiguity, POS mismatch, false positive or false negative in the synonymous set, spelling mistakes, etc.

The only solution was to keep track of the information about the synsets to be created and words to be added to the existing synsets and then modify the WordNet accordingly at one place by the lexicographers. But this was a tedious and time consuming task.

### 3.2 Culture-Specific words

For sense marking we used corpus from the Konkani newspaper, Sunaparant. It is more likely that culture specific words occur more frequently in the corpus and these are not found in the WordNet. Examples of the frequently occurring concept specific words in Konkani newspaper corpus are:

- taraMgAM- noun, decorated pole with symbol of tutelary divinity on its top.

- huddameWI- noun, special kind of curry made with black grams and fenu-greek.

- Sigamo- noun, festival celebrated to welcome the spring which starts Holy festival.

Similarly, we have come across many such words belonging to domains such as cuisines, dance, festivals, culture and traditions, household items, etc. For the purpose of marking such words with a proper sense, it is of utmost important that the senses are to be created for them.

### 3.3 Named Entity Issue

It is more natural to come across many named entities such as places, companies, organizations, persons, locations, school names, personalities, etc. since the newspaper corpus was used for sense marking and news often contains such information which is not available in the WordNet.

### 3.4 Multi-words in the corpus

The newspaper corpus contains news on politics and critics, description on places, environment, health topics, and hence one can come across many multi-word expressions of the type compound verbs, compound nouns, idioms, echo-words, reduplication, etc. Currently, the WordNet does not store multi-word expressions. Creation of synsets for such words was also a challenging task for the lexicographers.

### 3.5 Words with affixes

In Konkani, one can come across a suffix like (kAr- suffix used for male), (kaAn suffix used for female) which gives different meaning to the words it is attached to. For example, (BAjI vegetable) when (kAr) is attached to it, it conveys the sense - the man selling vegetables. Similarly, when (kaAn) is attached to it, it conveys the sense the woman selling vegetables which results in the new word obtained from (BAjI). Such occurrences are quite huge in number in the corpus. However, these kinds of words are not found in the respective WordNets for the reason that all the words with the suffixes have not been incorporated.

### 3.6 Other challenges

Other situations where sense marking was difficult are listed below -

- The newspaper also contains many words belonging to Hindi and Marathi vocabulary. This is because Hindi and Marathi are sister languages of Konkani.

- Sometimes the newspaper articles describe information about a movie or a play, which often use Hindi or Marathi terms. This may be because of the influence of these languages on the people. Tagging such words was also a challenge.

- Similarly we came across many foreign words in the corpus. Foreign words are those words written in a script other than our own script.
- Sense marking abbreviations and acronyms was also a difficult task as WordNet does not cover all the acronyms and abbreviations.

## 4 Methodologies used and Results Obtained

To overcome the challenges discussed above the following two methods were used

- **Method 1:** For each polysemous word, extract all sentences from the corpus in which that word occurs, categorize the instances and write definitions for each sense, and create a pointer between each instance of the word and its appropriate sense in the lexicon (Miller et. al, 1993). The advantage of this method was that concentrating on a single word should produce better definitions (Miller et al., 1993).
- **Method 2:** The alternative method is the sequential approach that starts with the corpus and proceeds through it word by word. This procedure has the advantage of immediately identifying deficiencies in the lexicon: not only missing words but also missing senses and inadequate senses, identifying the false positives and false negatives, etc.

The results obtained by using the combination of the above two approaches are given below -

1. Around 130 synsets were linked to Hindi WordNet and 86 new synsets having high frequency of occurrence in the corpus including concept/language specific synsets were created as a result an additional 1952 words were sense tagged.
2. Similarly, there were some synonyms which were found relevant to the context and were regarded as false negatives i.e. words which should have been present in the synset. Such words were added to the existing synsets. Additional 134 words were added which resulted in tagging of additional 380 words.
3. After analyzing the untagged words, we came across 11774 named entities in the corpus which were not available in the WordNet. It was decided that the proper noun part of the word would not be tagged, but the common noun part would be tagged. This decision helped in tagging additional 180 words.

The above methods helped in improving the WordNet coverage of Konkani language from 48.48 percent to 51.5 percent.

## 5 Role of Sense marking to improve WordNet Quality

The sense marking activity played a vital role in improving the quality of the WordNet in the following ways:

- Spelling errors, category mismatch were corrected and also the synsets with incomplete concept definition were improved.
- Words which had variations in spellings were added to the synsets.
- The synsets belonging to a language or language-specific synsets which covers a wide range of day-to-day language were added to the WordNet.
- Missed words (false negatives) which should have been present in the synset were added to the existing synsets.
- During sense-marking, false positives i.e. the words which were found to be irrelevant to the synsets were identified and deleted from the respective synsets.

## 6 Conclusion

In this paper we have discussed the importance of Sense marking activity in the WordNet development cycle. The various challenges faced, methods adopted and results obtained while sense marking have been presented. The sense marked data will act as a resource to aid in speedy and efficient machine translation, for developing and testing procedures for the automatic sense resolution in context. Our future work will be to sense mark domain specific data and to attempt to further improve the WordNet coverage and quality.

## Acknowledgments

This work has been carried out as a part of the Indradhanush WordNet Project (11(13)/2010-HCC(TDIL), dated 3-8-2010) jointly carried out by nine institutions. We wish to express our gratitude to the funding agency DeitY, Govt. of India and also all the members of the Indradhanush Consortium.

## References

Christiane Fellbaum. 1998. *WordNet: An Electronic Lexical Database. The MIT Press.*

George A. Miller, Claudia Leacock, Randee Tengi, Ross T. Bunker. 1993. *A Semantic Concordance, Pro-ceedings of the workshop on Human Language Technology, page 303–308. Stroudsburg, PA, USA, Association for Computational Linguistics.*

Jaya Sarawati, Rajita Shukla, Sonal Pathade, Tina Solanki, Pushpak Bhattacharyya. 2010. *Challenges in Multilingual Domain-Specific Sense-marking, Principles, Construction and Application of MultilingualWordNets, Proceedings of the 5th Global-WordNet Conference,* Mumbai- India.

Pushpak Bhattacharyya. 2010. *IndoWordNet. Lexical Resources Engineering Conference 2010 (LREC2010),* Malta.

# Building a WordNet for Sinhala

**Indeewari Wijesiri**
University of Moratuwa
Moratuwa, Sri Lanka
indeewari.wijesiri.09@cse.mrt.ac.lk

**Malaka Gallage**
University of Moratuwa
Moratuwa, Sri Lanka
malaka.gallage.09@cse.mrt.ac.lk

**Buddhika Gunathilaka**
University of Moratuwa
Moratuwa, Sri Lanka
buddhika.09@cse.mrt.ac.lk

**Madhuranga Lakjeewa**
University of Moratuwa
Moratuwa, Sri Lanka
lakjeewa.09@cse.mrt.ac.lk

**Daya C. Wimalasuriya**
University of Moratuwa
Moratuwa, Sri Lanka
chinthana@cse.mrt.ac.lk

**Gihan Dias**
University of Moratuwa
Moratuwa, Sri Lanka
gihan@uom.lk

**Rohini Paranavithana**
University of Colombo
Colombo, Sri Lanka

**Nisansa de Silva**
University of Moratuwa
Moratuwa, Sri Lanka
nisansadds@cse.mrt.ac.lk

## Abstract

Sinhala is one of the official languages of Sri Lanka and is used by over 19 million people. It belongs to the Indo-Aryan branch of the Indo-European languages and its origins date back to at least 2000 years. It has developed into its current form over a long period of time with influences from a wide variety of languages including Tamil, Portuguese and English. As for any other language, a WordNet is extremely important for Sinhala to take it into the digital era. This paper is based on the project to develop a WordNet for Sinhala based on the English (Princeton) WordNet. It describes how we overcame the challenges in adding Sinhala specific characteristics which were deemed important by Sinhala language experts to the WordNet while keeping the structure of the original English WordNet. It also presents the details of the crowdsourcing system we developed as a part of the project - consisting of a NoSQL database in the backend and a web-based frontend. We conclude by discussing the possibility of adapting this architecture for other languages and the road ahead for the Sinhala WordNet and Sinhala NLP.

## 1 Introduction

Despite being used by over 19 million people and being one of the official languages of Sri Lanka, there has not been much progress in developing natural language processing (NLP) applications for the Sinhala language. This is partly due to the lack of commercial interest on developing Sinhala NLP applications on a global scale. For instance, as of now, neither Google Translate[1] nor Google News[2] is available for Sinhala while both are available in Hindi and Tamil – two other regional languages spoken by a much larger population and thus with a higher business value.

Within this backdrop, we believe that developing a fully functional WordNet for Sinhala would provide a much needed boost for the Sinahla NLP work. This is because it is well recognized that a WordNet is a very important tool in performing natural language processing tasks for any language. A WordNet will be helpful to Sinhala NLP application developers in tasks ranging from word sense disambiguation and information retrieval to translation. Moreover a Sinhala WordNet will be a valuable resource to linguists

[1] http://translate.google.com/
[2] https://support.google.com/news/answer/40237

studying the Sinhala language. We paid special attention to the interests and concerns of the latter group as described later in the paper.

The project team, mainly consisting of personnel from the Knowledge and Language Engineering Lab of University of Moratuwa, started the task of developing a WordNet for Sinhala with several brainstorming sessions which involved Sinhala language experts, computer science specialists and people who had previously made some contributions in digitizing the Sinhala language (for example in developing Sinhala Unicode characters). Although we were biased towards using the expansion approach, which develops a WordNet based on an existing WordNet for another language, we discussed the possibility of adopting the merge approach, which develops a WordNet using the first principles by leveraging existing dictionaries and other resources (Bhattacharyya, 2010). We settled on the expansion approach because it was evident that we do not have the resources to successfully pursue the merge approach.

We came up with basic design for the WordNet through the above mentioned brainstorming sessions and then proceeded to develop the technical infrastructure needed. This consists of developing Sinhala WordNet APIs and a web interface as well as a crowdsourcing system to add synsets and relationships. The latter is needed because coming up with Sinhala synsets and relationships based on the synsets of another language requires a lot of manual work. Initially we were planning to use the Hindi WordNet as the source WordNet but switched to the English WordNet a couple of months into the project. The reasons for this change are discussed in Section 2.2. Apart from this the development effort proceeded fairly smoothly and we have completed the implementation of the WordNet API and the crowdsourcing system. Currently we are in the process of adding synsets using this system.

The rest of the paper is organized as follows. In Section 2, we present the details of the discussions we had with Sinhala language experts and the effects these discussions had in the structure of the Sinhala WordNet. In Section 3 we discuss the technical details of the project. Here, we describe the use of a NoSQL database to facilitate modification to a WordNet, which has not been done before to the best of our knowledge. In Section 4, we describe how the crowdsourcing system works including how it gives suggestions to the contributors simplifying their task. We reflect on some important aspects of the project including the possibility of adopting the entire system to other languages in Section 5. We present the details of some related work in Section 6 and provide concluding remarks in Section 7.

## 2 Developing the Linguistic Infrastructure

Development of linguistic infrastructure was carried out as the first phase of the project. Several discussions with Sinhala language experts were conducted to better understand the key features of the Sinhala language.

### 2.1 Discussions with Sinhala Linguists

From the beginning of the project the development team was collaborating with some prominent experts on Sinhala language. The basic idea of this collaboration was to acquire the necessary knowledge of the Sinhala language to get to know the linguistic requirements of a Sinhala WordNet and to form an expert evaluator panel to help with the crowdsourcing effort in developing the WordNet.

One important topic discussed with the experts was that Sinhala has a significant difference in written and spoken usage. These differences include differences in word usage and differences in grammar. We were particularly interested in differences in word usage in spoken and written forms as grammar rules fall outside the scope of a WordNet. It was observed that words with subtle but important differences are used in the written and spoken forms of Sinhala. For instance, for the sense "man", මිනිසා (*minisa*) is the most frequent word used in written Sinhalese while මිනිහා (*miniha*) is the most frequent word used in spoken Sinhalese. While the difference is subtle (a single phoneme in this case) its implications are significant for a natural speaker of Sinhala. In this case, using මිනිසා in normal conversations appears extremely odd. Moreover such differences are very common and combining words used in spoken and written Sinhala results in very odd phrases.

The problem faced by us was whether to include this difference in the Sinhala WordNet. Doing so would go against the main objective of a WordNet which is organizing words by their meanings; clearly there is no difference in the meanings of මිනිසා and මිනිහා as it is simply a matter of language usage. Despite this concern, we decided to include this difference as a *flag* for each word due to the following reasons.

1. Not including these in the WordNet would result in the loss of a valuable opportunity to encode these differences in a machine readable manner; the contributors of the crowdsourcing system can do this with little extra effort but doing it as a separate project would require a lot more effort. The importance of this factor is magnified by the lack of commercial interest in Sinhala NLP.
2. Since one of the primary reasons for developing a Sinhala WordNet was to serve the needs of Sinhala linguists we wanted to accommodate their requirements. We suspected that eliminating this type of information would make the WordNet less useful to them. Janssen (2002) has made a similar argument with regards to eliminating gender information from WordNets. Hence, adding this information to the WordNet was seen as a pragmatic move.
3. Different words being used in spoken and written Sinhala is an extremely common phenomenon that cannot simply be ignored or left for later consideration.

By the same reasoning, we decided to add few more features of the Sinhala language to the WordNet. One of them is the gender difference. The genders in Sinhala are masculine and feminine but none are specified for some words (typically for things that are not alive). The gender of a noun is important as it decides which morphological form of a verb is used with it. Thus the Sinhala WordNet will contain the gender of each noun, if exists.

The Sinhala words can be divided into three main categories called native words, words directly borrowed from another language which are being used without any change (තත්සම - *tatsama*) and the words borrowed from another language and have been modified (තත්භව - *tatbawa*). The words have been mainly borrowed from Sanskrit, Pali, Hindi, Portuguese, English, Tamil and Dutch. In constructing phrases in Sinhala, the origin of the word should be considered similar to how the spoken/written differentiation is used. As an example 'mathru'(මාතෘ) and 'maw'(මව්) are two forms to express the meaning "mother's" in Sinhala but 'mathru' is a tatsama while 'maw' is a tatbawa. 'snehaya'(ස්නේහය) and 'senehasa'(සෙනෙහස) means 'affection' which again are tatsama and tatbawa. To express "mother's affection", people use either 'mathru snehaya'(මාතෘ ස්නේහය) or 'maw senehasa'(මව් සෙනෙහස) while the other two combinations appear odd. This is despite the fact that all four words are acceptable in written Sinhala. Thus details of the origin of a word are also included in the Sinhala WordNet. Both the source language and the derivation type (tatsama/tatbawa) are kept on this regard.

Each noun in Sinhala can be in 9 morphological forms called 'vibhakthi'(විභක්ති). Furthermore there are fairly complicated rules in forming compound words called 'sandi'(සන්ධි) and 'samasa'(සමාස). The formation of these forms and rules as well as the inflectional forms of a verb are based on the *root* of the word, which may not be the *most commonly used form* of the word. Therefore, it was decided to keep the *word root* as well as the *most common morphological form* in storing a word in the WordNet.

In summary, we decided to include the following features for each word.

- Written/ Spoken usage
- Gender
- Origin of the word
- Word root
- The most common morphological form

It is interesting to relate these features, which are deemed important in representing Sinhala words in a machine-processable format, to a standard lexical-encoding framework. Our discussion on this regards is based on the lemon (Lexicon Model for Ontologies) framework (McCrae et al., 2012). Our view is that the written/spoken usage and the origin of the word are properties under the *linguistic description module* of lemon outside its *core*. These will be used by the *phrase-structure module* in identifying well-formed phrases. The word root is related to the *morphology module* and is used in inflection while the most common morphological form is the main lexical entry in the *core* for the word in concern. The gender information is useful for inflection in the *morphology module* and in recognizing words that do not have certain morphological forms. (e.g., රජිණ - rajina - the queen does not have a masculine form).

### 2.2 Selecting the Source WordNet

As mentioned earlier we decided to develop the Sinhala WordNet following the expansion approach due to practical considerations. Then the question was which WordNet to use as the source WordNet. We first decided to use the Hindi WordNet (Jha et al., 2001) for this purpose due to the following reasons.

1. The Sinhala language belongs to the Indo-Aryan branch of the Indo-European languages and is heavily influenced by the classical Indian languages of Sanskrit and Pali. Since Hindi is close to Sanskrit and the Hindi WordNet is fairly sophisticated - it serves as the hub of the Indo WordNet initiative (Bhattacharyya, 2010) - we assumed that the Hindi WordNet would provide a good basis for developing the Sinhala WordNet. We even considered using the Sankrit WordNet as the source WordNet but realized that it is still in an early stage.
2. The success of the Indo WordNet initiative in creating WordNets for many languages in India (Bhattacharyya, 2010) was one of the main motivations for us in embarking on this project. It was assumed that using the Hindi WordNet as the source WordNet would help us leverage the success of the Indo WordNet.

However, as we proceeded with the development work, it was apparent that using the Hindi WordNet as the source WordNet was not a viable option. The following are the main reasons for this.

1. Despite the perceived similarity in the origins of the languages, Hindi and Sinhala are very different languages in many aspects related to WordNet construction: One difficulty associated with this is that Hindi is written in Devanagari script, which is not familiar to most Sinhala speakers. (Sinhala has its own alphabet). Moreover, for many Hindi words it was difficult to identify Sinhala words with the same meaning, even after knowing how the word is pronounced. It was thought that translating Hindi words to Sinhala would be easier once the pronunciation is known because words of the languages are often pronounced similarly – e.g., Sinhala බෑයා (*baaya*) vs. Hindi भाई (*bhai*) meaning brother. It was seen that such similarities are not very common. As a result, we found ourselves frequently translating words from Hindi to English to understand the relevant Sinhala words.
2. It was seen that adopting the technical infrastructure of the Indo WordNet project to develop the Sinhala WordNet was difficult. Part of this is due the communication difficulties – all other WordNets of the Indo WordNet have been developed within India itself. In addition, our requirement to add *flags to words* in addition to *flags for synsets* as described in Section 2.1 created additional complexities and we found that accommodating these changes in the Indo WordNet text database stricture was very difficult. The Princeton English WordNet (Fellbaum, 1998), with its extensive documentation and the support network was seen as a much better alternative in this context.
3. A significant percentage of native Sinhala speakers have a working knowledge in English and it was seen that this will be very useful for a crowdsourcing system. In contrast, familiarity with the Hindi language is not widespread and this combined with the fact that most Hindi words are apparently unfamiliar to Sinhala speakers as described in (1), means that it is very difficult to use the Hindi WordNet in a crowdsourcing system.

Based mainly on the above factors, we switched the source WordNet from Hindi to English early in the development stage. The fact that the WordNets for Arabic (Rodrıguez et al., 2008) and Japanese (Isahara et al., 2008), which have very little in common with English, have also been developed with the English WordNet as the source, also weighed in on our decision.

We were mindful of the consequences of using the English WordNet as the source WordNet in developing the Sinhala WordNet. It has been stated that the source WordNet can have a distracting influence on the new WordNet being created especially when the two languages exist in different regions and cultural settings (Bhattacharyya, 2010). It is clear that this concern is applicable here. As such we decided to aggressively remove existing synsets in the English WordNet and add new synsets as necessary when developing the Sinhala WordNet.

## 3 Developing the Technical Infrastructure

After developing the linguistic infrastructure, we focused on developing the technical infrastructure according to the requirements identified. The main challenges we faced here were resolving the complications arising when extending the Princeton WordNet API, dealing with different data structures, and selecting tools and technologies. In this section, we describe the salient features of the architecture of the system and how we approached the above mentioned challenges.

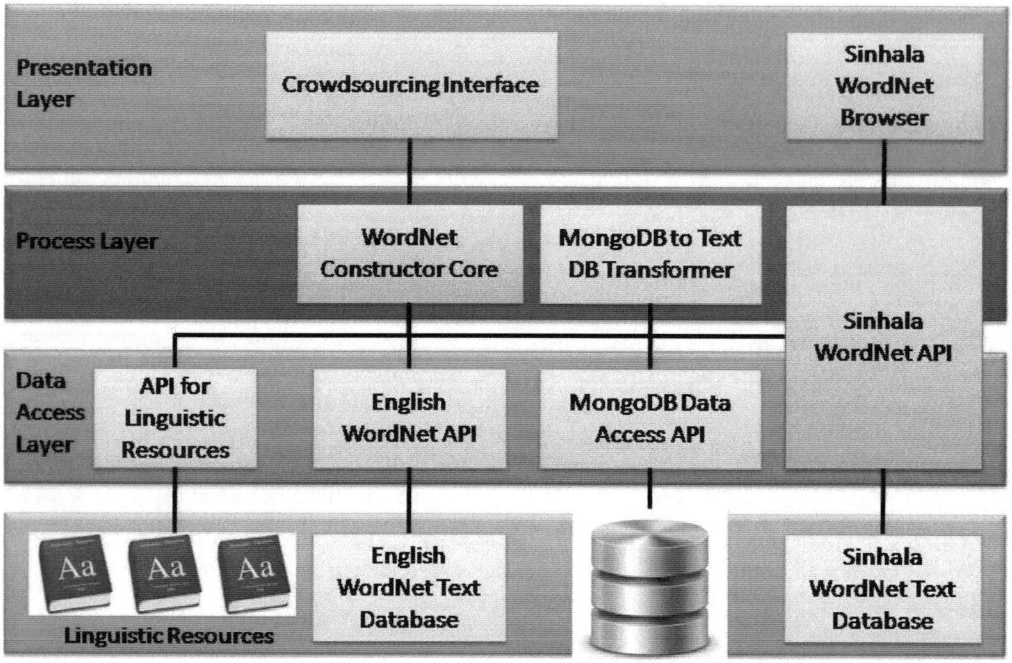


**Figure 1:** System Architecture

### 3.1 The WordNet API

The Sinhala WordNet API is implemented on the Java platform extending the English WordNet API (JWNL)[3]. The basic idea of developing this API is to provide general WordNet functionalities as well as the specific functionalities of the Sinhala WordNet discussed above. We defined new classes for synset, word, noun, verb, adjective and adverb extending the JWNL classes. The JWNL documentation and mailing lists were extremely helpful to us in this exercise. Incorporating Sinhala characters in the API was based on the Sinhala Unicode characters.

### 3.2 System Architecture

Figure 1 shows the architecture of the entire system, consisting of the API and the crowdsourcing system. For the non-technical users, the main outputs of the system are the online and offline Sinhala WordNet browsers and the web-based interface for the crowdsourcing system. Developers will have access to these components as well as the source code of the Sinhala WordNet API, WordNet Constructor Core - which governs how the crowdsourcing system operates -, the MongoDBToTextDB Transformer and the schemata of the underlying databases.

The components in the presentation layer get the data they need from three sources.

1. The English WordNet: The data contained in the English WordNet text database in terms of synsets and relationships are used.
2. The NoSQL Database: The modifications made by contributors of the crowdsourcing system to the data of the English WordNet are stored in this database.
3. Linguistic Resources: Several linguistic resources such as available machine readable dictionaries for Sinhala are used in providing suggestions for the collaborators.

Components in the Data Access Layer are used by the two components in the Process Layer to access the necessary data.

The MongoDBToTextDB transformer gets the data from the NoSQL database as well as the text database of the English WordNet because the NoSQL database *only* contains the modifications made by collaborators. It combines the data from the two sources into the text database of the Sinhala WordNet API. This step is carried out when releasing a new version of the Sinhala WordNet.

### 3.3 Use of a NoSQL Database

According to the system architecture described above, we need a database to store the modifications performed by the contributors of the crowdsourcing system. The modifications include adding Sinhala words to a synset, adding features to words and synsets, adding relation-

[3] `http://jwordnet.sourceforge.net/handbook.html`

ships between words/synsets and adding and removing synsets.

Until recently, the standard solution for this type of a data storage need has been to use a relational database system. However, the use of NoSQL databases has increased in the recent past partly due to the flexibility it offers to the schema designer. Instead of being restricted to a relational schema, which often requires multiple tuples spread across several relations for the same logical data unit, NoSQL databases allows the designers to store data according to the semantics behind them. We realized that these advantages will be important in our system since a synset consists of an unlimited number of words, each with several distinct features.

Another advantage of using NoSQL databases is that they provide better scalability than relational database systems especially in setting up multiple servers connected to a web-based front-end. This too will be helpful in using a crowsourcing approach for WordNet creation as the system will provide better performance for the contributors.

| Noun | | |
|---|---|---|
| _id | | |
| _class | | |
| userName | | |
| EWNID | | |
| Words | | |
| | _id | |
| | Lemma | |
| | wordID | |
| | wordPointerList | |
| | | pointerType |
| | | synsetType |
| | | synsetId |
| | | wordId |
| sensePointers | | |
| | pointerType | |
| | synsetType | |
| | synsetId | |
| gloss | | |

**Table 1:** Schema for Nouns

However, it was noted that NoSQL solutions *do not* guarantee consistency of the database although they provide *eventual consistency*. Therefore, it is possible, in rare conditions, for two contributors to make contradictory updates in the database. In the context of our system, these inconsistencies can be resolved later, generally in evaluation. Moreover any inconsistencies do not affect the releases of the Sinhala WordNet as they use the text database, assuming that any contradictions are resolved before a release.

We concluded that the advantages of NoSQL databases outweigh their disadvantages and decided to use one. We selected the MongoDB NoSQL (Plugge et al, 2010) system. Table 1 shows the schema we used for nouns. To the best of our knowledge, this is the first time a NoSQL database has been used in developing a WordNet.

Currently, the source repository is maintained as a private GitHub project. We will make it public in the near future.

## 4 The Crowdsourcing System

### 4.1 Overview

As mentioned earlier, a crowdsourcing system to facilitate the development of the Sinhala WordNet was designed and implemented as a part of the project. As illustrated in Figure 1, the WordNet Constructor Core component contains the major functionalities of this system. It obtains different types of data through the components of the Data Access Layer and provides an interface to be used by the web-based interface of the crowdsourcing system. The following are the different types of data used by this component through the Data Access Layer.

1. Information contained in the English WordNet through the EWN API (JWNL).
2. Information obtained from several linguistic resources for the Sinhala language including machine readable dictionaries and thesauri. These are used to specify suggestions to contributors to simplify their task as described in Section 4.2.
3. Information contained in the mongoDB database, which contains the modifications made by the contributors as mentioned earlier.

The web-based user interface allows contributors to browse through the English WordNet hierarchy and perform modifications as necessary. If no work has been done on a particular synset of the English WordNet, they will be shown the data contained in the English WordNet and are expected to replace them with Sinhala words. These changes include adding words to synsets, specifying flags for the words (e.g., whether the word is used in written/spoken Sinhala) and adding relationships. All the modifications are saved in the MongoDB database.

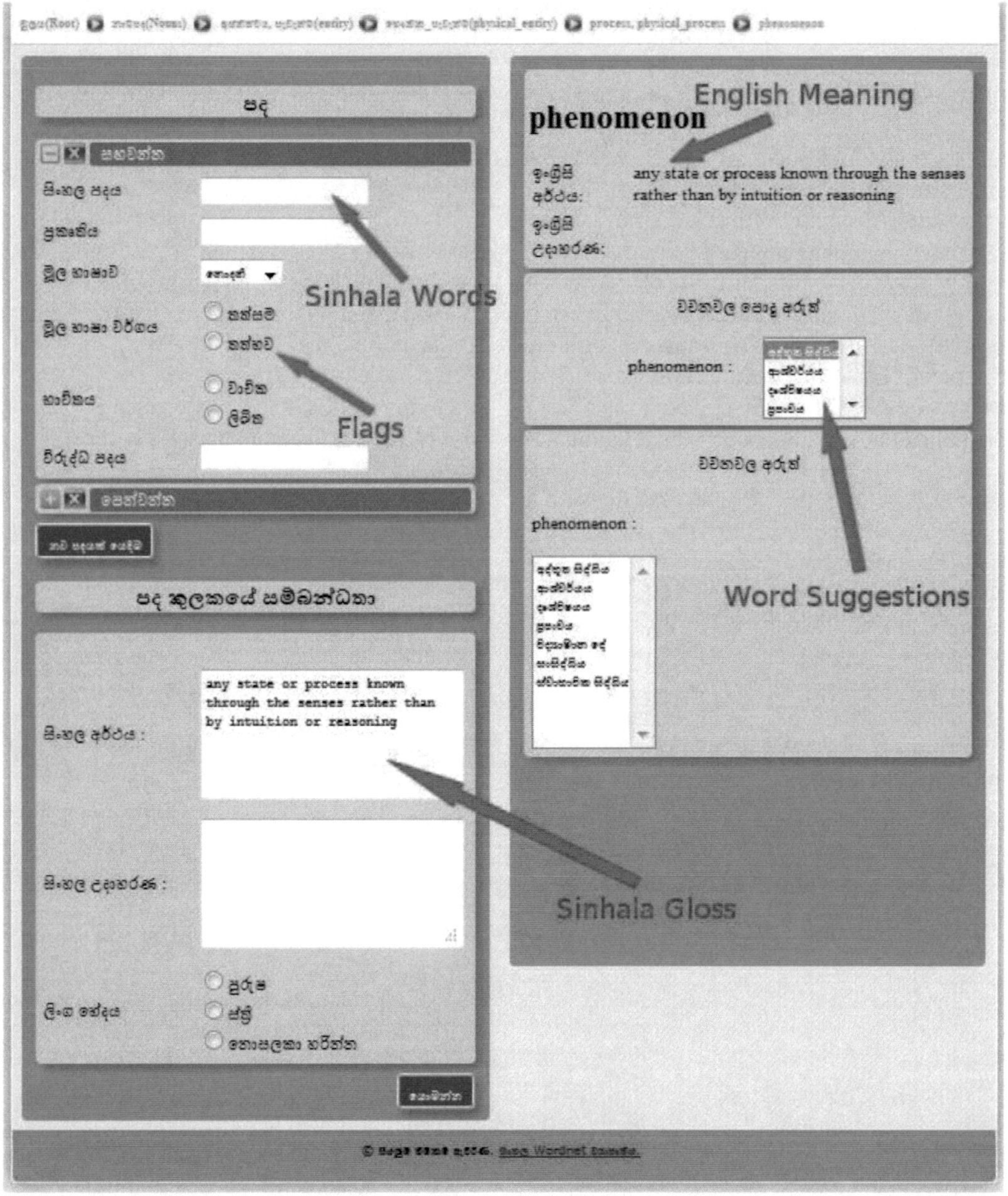


**Figure 2:** The UI of the Crowdsourcing System

Figure 2 shows the web interface when adding Sinhala words/relationships for the English synset for one sense of the word "phenomenon". Since Sinhala words have not been added to this synset, it shows the available information in the English WordNet. In addition, it shows suggested Sinhala words obtained from linguistic resources as described in Section 4.2.

The web-based user interface is operational and can be accessed from `http://www.wordnet.lk`. The modifications made by the contributors have to be approved by an evaluator before being included in a release.

How to effectively use a crowdsourcing technique to get a particular task done with acceptable quality is an open research question. Dow et al. (2012) have found that assessment of work produced, whether it is external assessment or self-assessment, if very helpful on this regard. As such, we expect the feedback provided by evaluators to help our effort.

### 4.2 Providing Suggestions

The purpose of providing suggestions for contributors is simplifying their task so that they do not have to rely entirely on their knowledge and available printed material. Currently, we provide suggestions for English words based on machine readable English to Sinhala and Sinhala to Sinhala dictionaries and thesauri. Out of the available resources, we found the Madura English-Sinhala dictionary (Kulatunga, undefined) particularly helpful. We are currently in the process of improving this component by incorporating the thesauri developed by the Department of Official Languages of Sri Lanka and a text corpus compiled by ourselves.

# 5 Discussion

## 5.1 The Morphology of the Language

Sinhala is an inflectional language where many verbs and nouns have a fairly large number of morphological forms. Verbs and nouns frequently have more than 10 morphological forms when considering both spoken and written forms. This has implications for the WordNet as a person or a software system searching for a word may use a different morphological form from what is contained in the WordNet. We decided against storing all morphological forms of a word in the WordNet since that increases the number of words for a synset to an unmanageable level. As such a good morphological analyzer, which is external to the WordNet is necessary to obtain the full benefits of the WordNet. There have been previous attempts to develop a morphological analyzer for Sinhala which have produced satisfactory results (Hettiage, 2006; Fernando and Weerasinghe 2013).

## 5.2 Extending to Other Languages

While we did not develop our system with the objective of developing WordNets for languages other than Sinhala, we recognize that it has the potential to be used in this manner. The architecture of the system has to be changed in some places, for example in using linguistic resources of other languages for providing suggestions for contributors. But the overall design of displaying the information of the English WordNet, allowing the contributors to modify them with words from the target language and storing the modifications in the NoSQL database can be easily applied in developing a WordNet for another language based on the English WordNet following the expansion approach. It is possible to reuse the schema of the MongoDB database and the source code of the crowdsourcing interface, the WordNet Constructor Core and the MongoDBToTextDB Transformer in such an exercise. We plan to separate out these parts from our codebase as a future work.

## 5.3 Current Status

The crowdsourcing system is currently operational and the number of synsets in the Sinhala WordNet is approaching 2000. This number is significant since this has been used as a marker by the Indo WordNet project in developing WordNets for languages in India (Bhattacharyya, 2010). Our goal is to release the first complete version early next year.

The Knowledge and Language Engineering Lab of the Department of Computer Science and Engineering at University of Moratuwa is coordinating this effort.

# 6 Related Work

The Hindi WordNet and the Indo WordNet initiative provided a lot of inspiration to us in attempting to develop a WordNet for Sinhala following the expansion approach. We followed their work in several aspects of the project such as the use of crowdsourcing to generate synsets.

There has been a previous work on developing a WordNet for Sinhla by Welgama et al. (2011), which is basically an exploration on developing a WordNet for Sinhala by extracting some common words from a corpus and getting the help of Sinhala language experts to come up with synsets based on them. It can be seen that this work is related to the merge approach. Our work differs from this effort in our use of the expansion approach and the objective of developing a complete WordNet.

# 7 Conclusion

Developing a fully functional Sinhala WordNet can be considered a landmark in NLP for Sinhala and we believe that we are well set to achieve this in the near future. This will provide a tremendous boost for developing Sinhala NLP applications such as information retrieval systems, text classifiers and summarizers and translators. The availability of a platform in terms of a WordNet may even attract some commercial interest for Sinhala NLP.

It should also be recognized that our work has the potential to be generalized into a system that can be used to bootstrap WordNet creation for a language. If this goal can be achieved, it will be extremely helpful in developing WordNets for minority languages such as Sinhala.

# Acknowledgements

We thank Prof. J.B. Disanayaka, Dr. Sandagomi Coperahewa and Mr. Achinthya Bandara of the Department of Sinhala of University of Colombo and Mr. Anushke Guneratne of the LK Domain Registry for their help in this project.

## References

Pushpak Bhattacharyya. 2010. IndoWordNet, *Proceedings of the Lexical Resources Engineering Conference.*

Steven P. Dow, Anand Kulkarni, Scott R. Klemmer and Björn Hartmann. 2012. Shepherding the Crowd Yields Better Work, *Proceedings of the ACM 2012 conference on Computer Supported Cooperative Work*: 1013-1022.

Christiane Fellbaum (ed.), 1998. *WordNet: An Electronic Lexical Database.* MIT Press.

Niroshinie Fernando and Ruwan Weerasinghe. 2013. A Morphological Parser for Sinhala Verbs. *Proceedings of the International Conference on Advances in ICT for Emerging Regions.*

Buddhita Hettige. 2006. A Morphological Analyzer to Enable English to Sinhala Machine Translation, *Proceeding of the 2nd International Conference on Information and Automation*: 21-26.

Hitoshi Isahara, Fransis Bond, Kiyotaka Uchimoto, Masao Utiyama and Kyoko Kanzaki. 2008. Development of the Japanese WordNet. *Proceedings of the Sixth International Conference on Language Resources and Evaluation.*

Maarten Janssen. 2002, Differentiae Specificae in EuroWordNet and SIMuLLDA. *Proceedings of the Ontologies and Lexical Knowledge Bases Workshop.*

Madura Kulatunga. (undefined). Madura English-Sinhala Dictionary. Retrieved September 6, 2013, from `http://maduraonline.com/`.

John McCrae, Guadalupe Aguado-de-Cea, Paul Buitelaar, Philipp Cimiano, Thierry Declerck, Asunción Gómez-Pérez, Jorge Gracia, Laura A Hollink, Elena Montiel-Ponsoda, Dennis Spohr and Tobias Wunner. 2012. *Interchanging lexical resources on the Semantic Web, Language Resources and Evaluation, 46(4)*: 701-719.

S. Jha, Dipak Narayan, Prabhakar Pande and Pushpak Bhattacharyya. 2001. A WordNet for Hindi, *Proceedings of the International Workshop on Lexical Resources in Natural Language Processing.*

Eelco Plugge, Tim Hawkins and Peter Membrey. 2010. *The Definitive Guide to MongoDB: The NoSQL Database for Cloud and Desktop Computing.* Apress.

Horacio Rodríguez, David Farwell, Javi Farreres, Manuel Bertran, Antonia Martí, William Black, Sabri Elkateb , James Kirk, Piek Vossen and Christiane Fellbaum. 2008. Arabic WordNet: Current state and future extensions. *Proceedings of the Fourth Global WordNet Conference.*

Viraj Welgama, Dulip Lakmal Herath, Chamila Liyanage, Namal Udalamatta, Ruvan Weerasinghe and Tissa Jayawardana. 2011. Towards a Sinhala WordNet, *Proceedings of the Conference on Human Language Technology for Development.*

# Coping with Derivation in the Bulgarian Wordnet

**Tsvetana Dimitrova**
Institute for Bulgarian Language
Bulgarian Academy of Sciences
cvetana@dcl.bas.bg

**Ekaterina Tarpomanova**
Faculty of Slavic Studies
Sofia University
katja@dcl.bas.bg

**Borislav Rizov**
Institute for Bulgarian Language
Bulgarian Academy of Sciences
boby@dcl.bas.bg

## Abstract

The paper motivates a strategy for identification and annotation of derivational relations in the Bulgarian wordnet that aims at coping with the complex morphology of the language in an elegant way. Our method involves transfer of the Princeton WordNet (morpho)semantic relations into the Bulgarian wordnet, at the level of the synset, and further detection of derivational relations between literals in Bulgarian. Derivational relations have been annotated to reflect the complexity of Bulgarian morphology. Introduced literal relations improve the consistency and employability of the wordnet.

## 1 Introduction

Bulgarian is a language with rich derivational morphology but derivational relations in the Bulgarian wordnet (BulNet) have been marked so far only at the level of the synset (Koeva, 2008). This paper outlines our strategy for representing the derivational relations at the level of the literal. We advocate for an approach with a twofold aim – to reflect the language specificity and to keep the overall structure of the Princeton WordNet (PWN) while modifying the representation of derivational and morphosemantic information (Fellbaum et al., 2009). We focus on noun-verb pairs (for encoding of other derivational patterns, cf. Koeva, 2008; Stoyanova et al., 2013). The derivational relations are to be further exploited for a prediction of (morpho)semantic relations between synsets that are not part of BulNet yet (hence, they are not found in PWN as they have no morphological realisation in English). As morphosemantic relations in PWN are transferred into BulNet, we have used them to find prospective derivationally related pairs and derivational models in Bulgarian. Thus, the introduction of derivational relations improves connectivity in BulNet by explicitly linking morphological and semantic information through encoding links between literals in synsets connected via (morpho)semantic relations.

While encoding this information on different levels to reflect different phenomena, we enrich BulNet with information about derivational patterns that can be used in NLP tasks such as information retrieval and question answering (cf. Hathout and Tanguy, 2002; Ligozat et al., 2012).

In the next section, we briefly present the Bulgarian wordnet with some remarks on the specific conventions adopted for its development. Section 3 discusses other attempts at encoding derivational relations in wordnets of languages with rich morphology. The complexity of Bulgarian derivational morphology is outlined in Section 4. In Section 5, we brush on the first step of our method for automatic identification and annotation of derivational relations. Section 6 presents the set of conventions followed in the annotation of derivational relations that have been specified, along with the manual validation and correction of the results of the method applied (as introduced in Section 5). In Section 7, we outline directions for future work.

## 2 Bulgarian Wordnet – an Overview

The Bulgarian wordnet was launched as part of the BalkaNet project that aimed at creating a multilingual lexical database of wordnets for

Bulgarian, Greek, Romanian, Serbian, Turkish, and Czech (Stamou et al., 2002). BulNet aims to preserve the original structure of the Princeton WordNet and EuroWordNet (Vossen, 2004). Non-lexicalized synsets from PWN are kept in the overall structure and marked with the label *no lexicalization*. Language-specific concepts are included in the appropriate place of the lexical hierarchy.

Currently, BulNet comprises over 50,000 synsets. Unlike PWN which contains only open-class words, BulNet is enriched with function words (in synsets) added for the development of the Bulgarian Sense-Annotated Corpus, where every word is linked to a corresponding sense (synset) (Koeva et al., 2011). Words in BulNet are distributed into nine parts-of-speech: noun, verb, adjective, adverb, pronoun, preposition, conjunction, particle, and interjection – see the numbers in Table 1.

| Part-of-speech | Count |
|---|---|
| Nouns | 33,825 |
| Verbs | 6,199 |
| Adjectives | 8,114 |
| Adverbs | 1,395 |
| Pronouns | 94 |
| Prepositions | 423 |
| Conjunctions | 108 |
| Particles | 57 |
| Interjections | 11 |
| Total | 50,226 |

Table 1: Parts-of-speech distribution in BulNet

The main part of the relations in BulNet are semantic: *also_see, causes, holo_member, holo_part, holo_portion, hypernym, near_antonym, similar_to, subevent, verb_group*. The list of semantic relations is based on the PWN lexical and conceptual relations (Koeva et al., 2004). BulNet encodes several morphosemantic – *be_in_state, bg_derivative,* and morphological (derivational) relations – *derived, participle*. *Be_in_state* is a relation between an adjective and a noun considered as state of the respective adjective: *{амбициозност:1, амбиция:1}*[1] – *{ambition:2, ambitiousness:1}* is a state of *{амбициозен:1}* – *{ambitious:1}*. *Bg_derivative* links a verb and a noun derived from it that are semantically related, as in: *{дирижирам:1}* – *{conduct:3}* and *{диригент:1, музикален ръководител:1}* – *{conductor:2, music director:1, director:1}*. The relation *bg_derivative* is transferred from PWN. *Derived* is a relation between a noun and an adjective derived from it, as in *{каменен:1}* 'made of, characteristic of or related to stone' derived from *{камък:1}* – *{stone:4}*. *Participle* is a relation between a verb and its participle – *{пулверизиран:1}* – *{spray-dried:1}* is a participle of *{пулверизирам:1}* – *{spray-dry:1}*.

[1] Curly brackets mark a synset, and square brackets mark a literal.

### 3 Previous Work

Derivational relations in the Princeton WordNet 3.0 have been extracted through automatic identification of base-derived and semantically related noun-verb pairs (Fellbaum et al., 2009). A set of semantic relations across a number of morphologically derived noun-verb classes was determined, and morphological relations were added. The identified morphosemantic links connect word pairs where one of the literals is derived from another. They are marked as related both derivationally (relations *derived/derivative*) and semantically (relations *event, state, result, agent, undergoer, property, instrument, location, means, uses, destination, material, body part, vehicle*). Derivational pairs are available in a morphosemantic database through: `http://wordnet.princeton.edu/wordnet/download/standoff/`.

Other approaches involve automatic or semi-automatic adding of new synsets to wordnet by automatically deriving new words from already existing ones and adding morphological relations. Attempts at annotation of derivational relations are mostly made for wordnets of languages with rich morphology such as Romanian, Turkish, Estonian, and Slavic languages. Some approaches involve semi-automatic and automatic identification of derived word forms and pairs. The morphological analyser *Ajka* used for the Czech wordnet, works with a list of stems from which word forms are generated. A set of words is defined by identifying prefix, suffix, and a morphological tag, and a derivational rule is applied using a substitution of morphemes (affixes), with manual modification (deleting and correcting) of the generated word forms (Pala and Hlaváčková, 2007). The analyser *Derywator* is used for semi-automated expansion of the Polish wordnet through a combination of prefix and suffix modules in two transducers trained to work in the opposite direction on pairs already described in the wordnet and extended with automated construction of mappings representing internal stem alternations (Piasecki et al. 2012). For adding morphosemantic relations to the Romanian wordnet, simple literals were extracted (Mititelu, 2012). A list of prefixes and a list of suffixes were used to form combinations, and resulting forms are matched against a list of literals in the wordnet. Estonian wordnet was also enriched with synsets that are automatically generated using derivational suffixes (Kahusk et al., 2010).

Wordnets of other languages use language-specific labels and relations. Czech and Turkish wordnets adopt a set of labels that is different from the PWN ones. The Czech wordnet uses labels referring to part-of-speech: *deriv-na*, *deriv-dvrb*, *deriv-an*, *deriv-pos*, *deriv-pas*, *deriv-aad*, *deriv-an*, *deriv-g*, *deriv-ag*, *deriv-dem* (Pala and Hlaváčková, 2007). Labels in the Turkish wordnet are more general such as *become*, *acquire*, *be-in-state*, *something-with*, *someone-with*, *someone-from*, *someone-without*, *something-without*, *pertains-to*, *with*, *reciprocal*, *causes*, *is-caused-by*, *cat-of*, *manner* (Bilgin et al., 2004). The work on the Croatian wordnet (Katunar and Šojat, 2011) plans to follow the morphosemantic field model (Raffaelli and Kerovec, 2008).

Previous attempts at adding derivational relations to BulNet are outlined in (Koeva, 2008), (Koeva et al., 2008) and (Stoyanova et al., 2013). The derivational relations in PWN are transferred into and aligned to BulNet. They are marked at the level of the synset with *bg_derivative* relation, or in *snote* when the transferred relation does not hold. Koeva (2008) proposes an approach for enlargement of BulNet that involves splitting verb synsets that contain both perfective and imperfective verbs.

The approach outlined in our paper involves automatic detection of candidate pairs and manual validation following language-specific conventions without straining too far from PWN. Morphosemantic relations hold among semantically related words sharing a stem with a close meaning. Semantic labels have been specified following PWN. After automatic detection of candidate pairs using the PWN morphosemantic database, we assign derivational relations to the identified literals. Next section gives a brief overview of some features of Bulgarian morphology to motivate our decisions for the annotation conventions adopted.

## 4 Bulgarian Derivational Morphology

Due to historical and cultural factors, Bulgarian language has preserved many Slavic features and acquired others that are common for the Balkan Sprachbund. Bulgarian is the only Slavic language with analytic nominal system, compensated by complex verb forms marked for aspect, mood, tense, voice, and evidentiality. Bulgarian derivational morphology combines inherited and borrowed word formants and shows great diversity of patterns.

### 4.1 Derivation Means

As in other Indo-European languages, there are two main morphological processes for formation of new words in Bulgarian – affixation and composition. Affixation consists in adding affixes to the root or the stem. Root is the central morpheme of a word that carries the main part of its semantic content, while stem is the root plus all derivational affixes, e.g., in *discounted* the root is *-count-* and the stem is *discount-*. Composition is defined as word formation by linking two or more stems. In Bulgarian, stems are often attached to each other by a linking morpheme – interfix, as in *вод-**О**-пад* 'waterfall'.

A relatively rare word formation means is paradigmatic derivation – a term used to denote a derivation where the derivative keeps the same stem, but differs from the source word by its paradigm (Radeva, 1991: 51), as in *работя* 'to work' – *работа* 'work'. Paradigmatic derivation may occur in different directions: noun-to-noun, noun-to-verb, verb-to-noun, adjective-to-verb, etc. Inflection markers and/or thematic vowels may be added, removed, or replaced, as in: *десет* 'ten' – *десети* 'tenth'; *нижe* 'to string' – *низ* 'a string'; *тъга* 'a grief' – *тъжи* 'to grieve'. In this paper, we will use the term *conversion* to designate such instances of zero-suffixation.

### 4.2 Derivation Formants

Suffixation is the most productive derivational process in Bulgarian, and the most complicated one. Suffixes are polysemic, i.e., one suffix usually has more than one meaning. For instance, the suffix *-ник* is used to form nouns for agent (*проповядвам* 'preach' – проповедник 'preacher'), instrument (*подема* 'lift up' – *подемник* 'gig'), location (*багаж* 'luggage' – *багажник* 'luggage-carrier'), etc. The same meaning may be expressed by different suffixes such as the agentive *-ач, -ар, -ец, -ник, -тел, -ко, -льо, -ент/-ант, -атор, -джия/-чия*, etc.

In terms of origin, suffixes are domestic or borrowed from different languages – Turkish (-*джия*), Latin, directly or more often through intermediate language (-*ция*), Russian (-*чик*), English (-*инг*), etc. Some of the borrowed suffixes become productive and may be attached to domestic stems or even to stems borrowed from other languages, as the Turkish -*джия*/-*чия* in *таксиджия* 'taxi driver' and *интересчия* 'someone who is looking after his own interests'.

New words are formed by attaching one or more suffixes to the root or the stem. Suffixes may be added to the stem by agglutination to form a derivation chain, as in: *меля* 'to mill'; *мелница* 'a mill', where the suffix for location -*ниц*- is added to the verb stem; *мелничар* 'miller', with the suffix for agent -*ар* added to the noun stem; *мелничарски* 'characteristic or belonging to a miller', with the suffix for property -*ск*-.

Apart from agglutination, suffixation involves diachronic changes in the root or the stem, decomposition of the morphological structure, fusion between suffixes, between the suffix and the stem or between the suffix and the inflection, so that morpheme boundaries may become unclear. We will illustrate this process by two examples.

1) There are two possible analyses of the morpheme structure of imperfective verbs formed with the imperfectivating suffix -*ва*-, such as *гребвам* 'to scoop': *греб-ва-м* (root – imperfectivating suffix – inflection marker), or *греб-в-а-м* (root – imperfectivating suffix – thematic vowel – inflection marker). Both interpretations are possible (Ganeva, 2010: 135).

2) The words *летища* 'airports' and *сънища* 'dreams' seem to have the same derivational model. In fact, they have different morpheme structure: *лет-ищ-а* (root – suffix for location – inflection marker for plural) and *сън-ища* (root – inflection marker for plural). The paradigm of the second word is formed by analogy and was subjected to stem decomposition.

Unlike suffixes, prefixes do not cause any changes in the stem. Derivatives formed by prefixation do not change their part-of-speech. Prefixation is a typical means for verbal derivation that involves change of verbal aspect, namely perfectivation: *пиша* 'to write-impf[2]' – *на-пиша* 'to write-pf'. Polyprefixation is characteristic for Bulgarian, where every prefix modifies the semantics of the word: *пиша* 'to write' - *пре-пиша* 'to copy out' - *до-пре-пиша* 'to copy out the rest'.

Both a prefix and a suffix can be attached to a stem to form a derivative, as in *вод-а* 'water' – *под-вод-ен* 'under-water'.

### 4.3 Phonetic Alternations

Derivation in Bulgarian is sometimes accompanied by phonetic changes that impede automatic detection of derivatives. Phonetic alternations are inherited from Old Bulgarian, and some of them are regular and still functional in Modern Bulgarian. Ablaut is a vowel alternation in the root that reflects word class or grammatical category, as in: *из-б**И**р-а-м* 'to choose' – verb, imperfective; *из-б**Е**р-а* 'to choose' – verb, perfective; *из-бр-ан* 'chosen' – participle; *из-б**О**р* – noun. Umlaut is a vowel alternation ['a]/[e] depending on the stress and the vowel in the next syllable. It can express number, as in: *б**Я**л* 'white-m,sg', *б**Я**л-а* 'white-f,sg', *б**Я**л-о* 'white-n,sg' vs. *б**Е**л-и* 'white-pl'. Consonant alternations are due to historical palatalization and other phonetic laws. Some typical consonant alternations are: *k (к)/ts (ц)/tch (ч)* – *чове**К*** 'man', *чове**Че*** 'man-vocative', *чове**Ци*** 'men'; *t (т)/sht (щ)* – *све**Тя*** 'shine', *све**Щ*** 'candle'; *d (д)/zhd (жд)* – *огра**Д**а* 'enclosure', *огра**ЖД**ам* 'enclose'.

Some of the phonetic alternations have a grammatical value, but they are not considered derivational means.

### 4.4 Derivation vs. Inflection

In Bulgarian, inflection marks verbs for person, number, tense, voice, and mood, and nominal word classes – for gender and person (and case for pronouns). Inflection markers usually stand at the end of the word, after the derivational suffix(es), with the exception of some old word forms where an inflection may appear within the word (*т-**О**-ва* 'this-n,sg'), and before the definite article in nominal word forms (*жен-**И**-те* 'the women'). In our work, inflection markers are not taken into account as they affect only word forms and have grammatical meaning, in contrast to derivational affixes. Still, there are several grammatical suffixes in Bulgarian that have a contradictory interpretation.

Thematic vowels in Bulgarian are inherited from Proto-Slavic, and were further subjected to complex diachronic modifications. In Modern Bulgarian, thematic vowels are considered classificatory suffixes showing a verb conjugation and/or tense. Unlike derivational suffixes, they

---

[2] The following abbreviations are used in the paper: 'impf' - imperfective verb; 'pf' - perfective verb; 'impf. t.' - imperfectivum tantum; pf. t. - perfectivum tantum; 'f,' - feminine; 'm' - masculine; 'n' - neuter; 1p, 2p, 3p - first, second and third person, respectively; sg - singular; pl – plural.

do not have any semantic content, but are involved in the derivation of verbs from nouns or adjectives, e.g., *мъка* 'pain' – *мъч**И**ш* 'to torment-2p,sg'3, *червен* 'red' – *червен**Е**е* 'to redden-3p,sg'. Bulgarian linguistic literature defines this mode of derivation as paradigmatic (see Section 4.1.).

Verbal aspect in Bulgarian has two opposed interpretations: 1) aspectual pairs are grammatical forms of the same word; or 2) they are separate words as they show difference in meaning, verb frame, inflection type, and usage (Koeva, 2008: 363). We follow the second interpretation, i.e., to define aspect suffixes as derivational.

Participles are not explicitly classified for part-of-speech. As non-finite verb forms, they are traditionally considered a part of the verb paradigm, but their morphological formants are defined as derivational and not inflectional suffixes, as in *ходи-**Л*** 'walked' where *-л* is a derivation suffix for aorist active participle with a zero inflection for masculine (for details on the grammar of the contemporary Bulgarian literary language, cf. Gramatika na savremenniya balgarski knizhoven ezik. T. 2 Morfologiya., 1982).

## 5 Automatic Identification of Derivational Relations in BulNet

For automatic detection of derivational relations in BulNet, we employ the applicable information encoded in PWN. The method applied does not require any additional language resources, such as dictionaries or lists of affixes. The first step is to query for pairs of synsets linked via a morphosemantic relation in PWN. If a given pair of synsets has a corresponding pair in BulNet, we search for a pair of literals in the corresponding synsets with similar representation, and add a derivational relation to the literals found.

Two literals are similar if at least one of the following conditions holds:

1. One of the literals is included into the other, i.e., is substring of it. They are similar by inclusion.
2. The two literals in a pair have a long enough common prefix (as a string of symbols in the beginning of the word form). Its length has to be at least half the length of the shorter literal. Therefore, they are defined as similar by prefix.
3. The two literals have a Levenshtein distance smaller than a given value. The value is calculated as the minimum number of: the length of the first literal, the length of the second literal; the absolute value of difference of the lengths of the two literals + a constant tolerance (2).

After calculating the similarity, we identify the differences between the words (literals) defined as relations: *prefix*, *suffix,* and *conversion.* If the literals match, the pair receives the relation *conversion*. If the two literals in the pair have the same beginning (defined as a string of symbols in the beginning of the word), the relation *prefix* cannot be attached. If the two literals have the same ending, the label *suffix* is excluded. If a relation of the type *prefix*, *suffix,* and *conversion* is not found, we compare the lengths of the common strings at the beginning and at the end. If the beginning is greater, we assign a *suffix* relation. A *prefix* relation is assigned if the ending is greater.

After the automatic assignment of derivational relations, manual validation was performed on all pairs found and annotation conventions were adopted in order to assure uniform and consistent approach to the morphological patterns in Bulgarian. We introduced two additional derivational relations – *deriv* (unspecified derivation) and *noun_suffix/verb_suffix* (substitution) to reflect specific processes and patterns (see section 6). Derivational relations were automatically assigned to literals denoting both members of the aspectual verb pairs, e.g., [*премахване:3*] 'disposal' received *without_suffix* relation to both [*премахвам:3*] 'to dispose-impf' and [*премахна:3*] 'to dispose-pf'. However, the direct derivational relation links it only to the imperfective verb (*премахва-м* > *премахва-не*), so we remove the automatically assigned relation to the perfective verb. In the next section, we discuss the annotation conventions adopted.

## 6 Conventions for Annotation of Derivational Relations in BulNet

Literals pertaining to different synsets are derivationally linked via three asymmetrical (*suffix/without_suffix*, *prefix/without_prefix*, *noun_suffix/verb_suffix*) and two symmetrical (*conversion*, *deriv*) derivational relations attached to the literals. Synsets which contain these literals are linked via (morpho)semantic relations transferred from PWN. Numbers about the annotated literals are given in Table 2.

[3] Thematic vowels are not visible in 1p, sg, present tense of verbs, so examples are in 2p and 3p.

| Derivational relation | Count |
|---|---|
| suffix/without_suffix | 2,352 |
| noun_suffix/verb_suffix | 296 |
| prefix/without_prefix | 241 |
| conversion | 177 |
| deriv | 21 |

Table 2: Number of literals with a derivational relation assigned

Literals in BulNet can be linked via more than one derivational relations reflecting different patterns. Our aim is to find and represent the highly productive derivational patterns in order to trace other words that exhibit them and can be linked through respective (morpho)semantic relations (and assigned semantic labels). The noun literals are derivationally linked to one of the verb literals in a synset that contains both members of an aspect verb pair. If two literals in a synset are linked via a direct derivational relation, we do not assign an indirect one (although it may be a member of the corresponding synset). For instance, the noun [*връщане:6*] 'return' is linked to the verb [*връщам се:1*] 'to return', and the noun with the prefix *за-* – [*завръщане:3*] 'return' is linked to the verb [*завръщам се:1*] 'to return' (respective literals are members of the same synsets – a noun and a verb one, respectively). However, there may be not a direct link, and we may link the two literals via an indirect derivational relation – we can observe further which pattern is more productive. The labels of derivational relations assigned do not reflect the real direction of the derivation. In the subsections, we will discuss the types of derivational relations assigned to verb-noun pairs.

### 6.1 Suffixation: suffix/without suffix

The derivational relation *suffix/without_suffix* is asymmetrical and marks suffixation (when a suffix or a combination of suffixes are used to generate new words) and suffix removal, respectively, as in [*плувам:1*] 'to swim' / [*плуване:1*] 'swimming' where the deverbal noun suffix *-не* is attached to the stem of the verb *плува-* (*-м* is the inflection marker for 1p, sg, present form of the verb).

In BulNet, verbs are classified as imperfective, perfective, bi-aspectual, imperfectiva tantum, and perfectiva tantum (Koeva, 2008). Though verbs in aspect pairs are members of one synset, they express difference in meaning, and form different derivatives[4]. Deverbal nouns with suffix *-не* are derived from the imperfective stem and usually denote a process. Nouns ending in *-не* are derivationally linked to the literals of imperfective verbs. Deverbal nouns formed with the suffix *-ние* are derived from the aorist stem, usually denote a result of an action, and can be derivationally linked to perfective or imperfective verbs. The synset *{миграция:1, мигриране:1, преселване:1, преселение:1}* – *{migration:1}* 'the movement of persons from one country or locality to another' is linked as *event* to the synset *{преселвам се:2, преселя се:2, мигрирам:1, разселвам се:1}* – *{migrate:1, transmigrate:1}* 'move from one country or region to another and settle there'. Literals are derivationally linked as follows:

*{преселвам се:2, преселя се:2, мигрирам:1, разселвам се:1}*
has_event: *{миграция:1, мигриране:1, преселване:1, преселение:1}*
[*преселвам се:2*]
lnote: impf.
suffix: [*преселване:1*]
[*преселя се:2*]
lnote: pf.
suffix: [*преселение:1*]
[*мигрирам:1*]
lnote: impf. and pf.
suffix: [*мигриране:1*]
noun_suffix: [*миграция:1*]

A *-ние* noun can be derivationally linked to imperfectiva tantum verbs, such as: [*тълкувам:2*] – [*interpret:3*] 'give an interpretation or explanation to' and [***тълкувание:1***] and [*тълкуване:2*] (belonging to the same synset) – [*interpretation:3*] 'a mental representation of the meaning or significance of something'.

In Bulgarian, participles can have both verbal interpretation (as in passive voice) and nominal one. If a participle is substantivised, i.e., is a member of a noun synset, and this synset is linked via a (morpho)semantic relation to a verb synset, the participle may receive a derivational relation. *Разлято* and *разляно* 'spilled' are both passive participles of the verb *разлея* 'to spill'. Thus, *{разлято:1, разляно:1}* – *{spill:1}* 'liquid that is spilled' is an *event* of *{разливам:1,*

[4] The aspect pairs are introduced in one and the same synset (the aspect is mentioned in an lnote) to keep the symmetry with PWN. However, as this representation is not sufficient, they are to be split into separate synsets subordinate to the same immediate hypernym (Koeva, 2008: 363).

*разлея:1, изливам:4, излея:4, разсипвам:4, разсипя:4, изсипвам:1, изсипя:1}* – *{spill:7, slop:2, splatter:2}* 'cause or allow (a liquid substance) to run or flow from a container' that have the following derivational relations:

[*разлея:1*]
    lnote: pf.
    suffix: [*разляно:1*]
    suffix: [*разлято:1*]

The *-не* and *-ние* patterns are among the most productive. Most *-не* and *-ние* nouns in BulNet are members of synsets linked to the verbs via an *event* (morpho)semantic relation (1,207 of the synsets with *-не* nouns, and 448 with *-ние* nouns). 57 of the synsets containing *-ние* nouns and 43 of the *-не* nouns are linked to the verbs via *result* semantic relation. The *state* relation connects 42 of the synsets with *-не* nouns and 67 of the synsets of *-ние* nouns.

In order to find productive derivational patterns in Bulgarian, we mark derivational relations on literals that are indirectly related to the derivative (derived by another member of the chain) and show a pattern containing more than one suffix. The noun [*ковачница:1*] 'forge' is linked as *location* and via *suffix* to [*кова:2*] 'to forge' although *ковачница* is derived via *ковач* 'blacksmith' (PWN shows no derivational or (morpho)semantic relation between [*forge:5*] and [*blacksmith:1*]). The semantic relation between *кова* and *ковачница* is derivationally motivated – *forge* is a *location* where a blacksmith forges. The derivation path (verb + suffix for agent + suffix for location) may be applied to find other pairs with similar morphosemantic relation, as in *тъка* 'to weave' – *тъкач* 'weaver' – *тъкачница* 'weaving workshop'.

### 6.2 Substitution: *noun_suffix/verb_suffix*

The relation *noun_suffix/verb_suffix* is asymmetrical and marks a suffix on both members of the pair, as in [*акомпанирам:1*] 'to accompany' and [*акомпанимент:1*] 'accompaniment' – the suffix on the verb is *-ира-* and the noun suffix is *-(и)мент*. The derivation process involves two operations – removing a verb suffix and adding a noun suffix to form a noun and vice versa.

A literal can have several derivatives pertaining to the same or different synsets, as in [*епилирам:1*] – [*epilate:1*] 'remove body hair' linked via *suffix* relation to [*епилиране:1*] – [*epilation:1*], and via *noun_suffix* relation to [*епилация:1*] – both are *event* members of the synset {*епилиране:1, епилация:1, депилиране:1, депилация:1, обезкосмяване:1*} – {*epilation:1, depilation:1*} 'the act of removing hair (as from an animal skin)'; and via *noun_suffix* relation to material [*епилатор:1*] – [*epilator:1*] of the synset {*депилатор:1, депилатоар:1, епилатор:1*} – {*depilatory:2, depilator:1, epilator:1*} 'a cosmetic for temporary removal of undesired hair'.

### 6.3 Prefixation: *prefix/without_prefix*

Another asymmetrical relation marks prefixation and prefix removal. In Bulgarian, prefixation does not change the part-of-speech, so adding or removing a prefix in noun-verb pairs is always accompanied by attachment of a thematic vowel to form a verb and its removal to form a noun, e.g., [*завинтя:1*] 'to screw' *without_prefix* [*винт:1*] 'screw'. As thematic vowels do not have any semantic content, their attachment or removal is not explicitly annotated.

The relation *prefix/without_prefix* can be combined with *suffix/without_suffix* or *noun_suffix/verb_suffix* when the suffix has a lexical content as in *въоръжа* 'to arm' vs. *оръжие* 'armament' where the verb is derived via prefixation (prefix *въ-*) and the noun is derived via suffixation (suffix *-ие*). Thus, the synset *{въоръжа:1, въоръжавам:1}* – {*arm:2*} is related via the (morpho)semantic relation *uses* with the synset *{оръжие:1, въоръжение:1}* – *{armament:2}*, and the the literal [*оръжие:1*] is derivationally related to [*въоръжа:1*] via the relations *prefix* and *without_suffix*.

{*оръжие:1, въоръжение:1*}
is_used_to: *{въоръжа:1, въоръжавам:1}*
[*оръжие:1*]
    prefix: [*въоръжа:1*]
    without_suffix: [*въоръжа:1*]

Derivationally related verb-noun pairs via prefixation are much rarer – 241 instances (2,352 of suffixation).

### 6.4 Conversion

The symmetrical relation *conversion* (marked on both literals of the pair) annotates zero-suffixation, as in [*викам:1*] 'to cry' and [*вик:1*] 'a cry' – the thematic vowel *-а-* and the inflectional suffix for 1p, sg, present tense *-м* are removed and no derivational suffix is added to generate the noun. The reverse process of adding a thematic vowel and an inflection marker to form a verb, is also marked as *conversion*, e.g., [*посредничa:1*] 'to mediate' is derived by conversion from [*посредник:1*] 'mediator'.

Derivational relations may link literals of the same synset to literal from different synsets:

*{тъжа:1, тъгувам:2, жаля:1} – {sorrow:1, grieve:1}* 'feel grief'

has_state: *{тъга:1, печал:2, униние:1} – {sorrow:5, sadness:3, sorrowfulness:2}* 'the state of being sad'

has_event: *{жал:1, мъка:3, печал:1} – {sorrow:3}* 'an emotion of great sadness associated with loss or bereavement'

[*тъжа:1*]
  lnote: impf. t.
  conversion: [*тъга:1*]

[*жаля:1*]
  lnote: impf. t.
  conversion: [*жал:1*]

### 6.5 Not Otherwise Specified: *deriv*

The symmetrical relation *deriv* (derivative) marks both members of the pair if a derivational pattern is unclear, as in [*помогна:1*] 'to help-pf' / [*помагам:1*] 'to help-impf' and [*помощ:1*] 'help' – historically, *помощ* is a deverbal noun but the derivation is not transparent in modern Bulgarian.

We do not expect literals with a *deriv* relation to show evidence for any productive pattern.

## 7 Conclusion and Future Work

In this paper, we presented the first results of an approach for introduction of derivational relations into the Bulgarian wordnet. We discussed the specifics of the Bulgarian morphology to support the conventions adopted for annotation of derivational patterns in Bulgarian. We identified (automatically) and annotated (through automatic identification and assignment of derivational labels with manual validation and modification afterwards) a set of noun-verb pairs in the Bulgarian wordnet.

The work on annotation allows for an observation on derivational patterns that can be used to improve the process of automatic identification and assignment of relations (derivational and (morpho)semantic ones). For instance, the nouns with suffix *-(а/и)ция* denote: *event* (312 instances), *result* (46), *means* (28), *state* (17), *undergoer* (17), *uses* (16), *agent* (5).

The annotation will allow us to enrich the Bulgarian wordnet with new relations. In addition, we can easily identify synsets that have not been created yet.

In the next stages of the experiment, we plan to rerun the automatic identification of derivational relations exploiting the newly specified relations/conventions. We can automatically detect derivational pairs using the patterns identified and link them with semantic relations. Automatic assignment of (morpho)semantic relations is also a potential direction to be exploited.

## Acknowledgments

The present paper was prepared within the project Integrating New Practices and Knowledge in Undergraduate and Graduate Courses in Computational Linguistics (BG051PO001-3.3.06-0022) implemented with the financial support of the Human Resources Development Operational Programme 2007-2013 co-financed by the European Social Fund of the European Union. The authors take full responsibility for the content of the present paper and under no conditions can the conclusions made in it be considered an official position of the European Union or the Ministry of Education, Youth and Science of the Republic of Bulgaria.

## References

Orhan Bilgin, *Özlem Çetinoğlu*, and Kemal Oflazer. 2004. Morphosemantic Relations In and Across Wordnets – A Study Based on Turkish. In *Proceedings of the Second Global Wordnet Conference*, pages 60–66.

Christine Fellbaum, Anne Osherson, and Peter E. Clark. 2009. Putting Semantics into WordNet's "Morphosemantic" Links. In *Proceedings of the Third Language and Technology Conference, Poznan, Poland.* Reprinted in: *Responding to Information Society Challenges: New Advances in Human Language Technologies*, Springer Lecture Notes in Informatics, vol. 5603, pages 350–358.

Gergana Ganeva. 2010. Kam istoriyata na sufiksite za imperfektivacija v balgarskite dialekti. / On the History of the Imperfectivating Suffixes in Bulgarian Dialects. *Eslavística Complutense* 10. Madrid, pages 135–145.

*Gramatika na savremenniya balagrski knizhoven ezik. T. 2 Morfologiya.* Sofia: Izdatelstvo na Balagarskata akademiya na naukite. 1982. / Grammar of Contemporary Bulgarian Literary Language. Vol. 2, Morphology. Sofia: Bulgarian Academy of Sciences Publishing House. 1982.

Nabil Hathout and Ludovic Tanguy. 2002. Webaffix: Discovering Morphological Links on the WWW.

In *Proceedings of the Third International Conference on Language Resources and Evaluation.* Las Palmas de Gran Canaria, Espagne, pages 1799–1804.

Neeme Kahusk, Kadri Kerner, and Kadri Vider. 2010. Enriching Estonian Wordnet with Derivations and Semantic Relations. In *Human Language Technologies – the Baltic Perspective. Proceedings of the Fourth International Conference Baltic HLT 2010.* IOS Press, pages 195–200.

Daniela Katunar and Krešimir Šojat. 2011 Morphosemantic fields in the building of the Croatian WordNet: the verbs of movement. In *Space in Time and Language.* Frankfurt am Main, Berlin, Bern, Bruxelles, New York, Oxford, Wien: Peter Lang GmbH, pages 79–89.

Svetla Koeva, Tinko Tinchev, and Stoyan Mihov. 2004. Bulgarian Wordnet – Structure and Validation. *Romanian Journal of Information Science and Technology*, Vol. 7, No. 1-2, pages 61–78.

Svetla Koeva. 2008. Derivational and Morphosemantic Relations in Bulgarian Wordnet. *Intelligent Information Systems*, XVI, Warsaw, Academic Publishing House, pages 359–389.

Svetla Koeva, Cvetana Krstev, and *Duško* Vitas. 2008. Morpho-Semantic Relations in Wordnet - a Case Study for Two Slavic Languages. In *Proceedings of the Fourth Global WordNet Conference*, Szeged, pages 239–254.

Svetla Koeva, Svetlozara Leseva, Borislav Rizov, Ekaterina Tarpomanova, Tsvetana Dimitrova, Hristina Kukova, and Maria Todorova. 2011. Design and Development of the Bulgarian Sense-Annotated Corpus. In *Las tecnologías de la información y las comunicaciones: Presente y futuro en el análisis de córpora. Actas del III Congreso Internacional de Lingüística de Corpus.* Valencia: Universitat Politècnica de València, pages 143–150.

Anne-Laure Ligozat, Birgitte Grau, and Delphine Tribout. 2012. Morphological Resources for Precise Information Retrieval. In *Text, Speech and Dialogue. Proceedings of the 15th International Conference, TSD 2012, Brno, Czech Republic, September 3-7, 2012.* Lecture Notes in Computer Science, Volume 7499, pages 689–696.

Verginica Barbu Mititelu. 2012. Adding Morpho-Semantic Relations to the Romanian Wordnet. In *Proceedings of the Eight International Conference on Language Resources and Evaluation (LREC'12)*, pages 2596–2601.

Karel Pala and Dana Hlaváčková. 2007. Derivational relations in Czech Wordnet. In *Proceedings of the Workshop on Balto-Slavonic Natural Language Processing*, pages 75–81.

Macieji Piasecki, Radosław Ramocki, and Marek Maziarz. 2012. Recognition of Polish Derivational Relations Based on Supervised Learning Scheme. In *Proceedings of the Eight International Conference on Language Resources and Evaluation (LREC'12)*, Istanbul, European Language Resources Association (ELRA), pages 916–922.

Vasilka Radeva. 1991. *Sloobrazuvaneto v balgarskiya knizhoven ezik.* Sofia: Universitetsko izdatelstvo Sv. Kliment Ohridski. / Word Formation in Bulgarian Language. Sofia: Sofia University Press.

Ida Raffaelli and Barbara Kerovec. 2008. Morphosemantic fields in the analysis of Croatian vocabulary. *Jezikoslovlje* 9.1–2: 141–169.

Sofia Stamou, Kemal Oflazer, Karel Pala, Dimitris Christoudoulakis, Dan Cristea, Dan Tufis, Svetla Koeva, George Totkov, Dominique Dutoit, and Maria Grigoriadou. 2002. BALKANET: A Multilingual Semantic Network for the Balkan Languages. In *Proceedings of the International Wordnet Conference, Mysore, India*, pages 21–25.

Ivelina Stoyanova, Svetla Koeva, and Svetlozara Leseva. 2013. Wordnet-based Cross-Language Identification of Semantic Relations. In *Proceedings of the 4th Biennial International Workshop on Balto-Slavic Natural Language Processing*, Sofia, Bulgaria, 8-9 August 2013, pages 119–128.

Piek Vossen. 2004. EuroWordNet: A Multilingual Database of Autonomous and Language-Specific Wordnets Connected via an Inter-Lingual Index. *International Journal of Lexicography*, 17(1): 161– 173.

# Non-Lexicalized Concepts in Wordnets: A Case Study of English and Hungarian

**Veronika Vincze**[1,2]
[1]MTA-SZTE Research Group on Artificial Intelligence
[2]University of Szeged
vinczev@inf.u-szeged.hu

**Attila Almási**
University of Szeged
almasia@inf.u-szeged.hu

**Abstract**

Here, we investigate non-lexicalized synsets found in the Hungarian wordnet, and compare them to the English one, in the context of wordnet building principles. We propose some strategies that may be used to overcome difficulties concerning non-lexicalized synsets in wordnets constructed using the expand method. It is shown that the merge model could also have been applied to Hungarian, and with the help of the above-mentioned strategies, a wordnet based on the expand model can be transformed into a wordnet similar to that constructed with the merge model.

## 1 Introduction

Wordnets are lexical databases in which words are organized into clusters based on their meanings, and they are linked to each other through different semantic and lexical relations, yielding a conceptual hierarchy (i.e. lexical ontology) of words. Originally, they were designed to show how linguistic knowledge is organized within the human mind (Miller et al., 1990). Multilinguality is also an important aspect in the creation of wordnets: builders of new wordnets usually map their synsets to those representing the same concept in Princeton WordNet (PWN).

However, there is no perfect mapping between two languages at the conceptual level and the lexical level. In this article, we would like to compare the wordnets built for Hungarian and English and we will discuss problems and possible solutions concerning discrepancies in the way the two languages name certain concepts in the context of wordnet-building methods and principles. First, the wordnets we study are briefly presented, then the notions of non-lexicalized and technical non-lexicalized synsets are illustrated with concrete examples. We suggest some ways of eliminating non-lexicalized synsets from wordnets, and we also show how a Hungarian tree can be built without relying on the English tree. Lastly, we argue that although a wordnet that seeks to represent the hierarchy of the given language should not contain non-lexicalized elements, they can prove useful in fields of research such as psycholinguistics, ethnography and contrastive linguistics.

## 2 Related Work

The first wordnet was created for the English language at Princeton University, so it is called the Princeton WordNet (Fellbaum, 1998). It is now the largest lexical database of the English language, and it can be readily adapted to various computational applications. Princeton WordNet 3.0 contains about 155,000 words in approximately 117,000 synsets.

Since then, other wordnets have been created and developed for different languages. EuroWordNet is a multilingual project, where synsets for Dutch, Italian, Spanish, German, French, Czech and Estonian are included in the database (Alonge et al., 1998). The BalkaNet project sought to extend EuroWordNet with lexical databases created for languages of the Balkan Peninsula, namely Bulgarian, Greek, Turkish, Serbian and Romanian (Tufiş, 2004; Tufiş et al., 2004). Other languages for which wordnets have been developed include Arabic, Croatian, Chinese, Danish, Slovene, Polish, Russian, Persian, Hindi, Tulu, Dravidian, Tamil, Telugu, Sanskrit, Assamese, Filipino, Gujarati, Nepali (Tanács et al., 2008; Bhattacharyya et al., 2010; Fellbaum and Vossen, 2012).

Typically, there are two major approaches to wordnet construction (Vossen, 1998). The first approach (merge model) starts by constructing a wordnet from scratch (or by using dictionaries and other resources developed for the language) and then the newly created synsets are linked to synsets of another language (most typically English). The second approach (expand model) starts by selecting a subset of the PWN synsets and then they are transformed into synsets of the target language, preserving relations between synsets. Wordnets created in this way inevitably reflect lexicalization of the given language to a lesser degree; however, it is known that the nodes in PWN form a network, the rendering of which into the given language may be unnatural, forced and this may result in further difficulties concerning multilingual applications (Raffaelli et al., 2008). The merge model was used for most languages in the EuroWordNet project (Alonge et al., 1998), whereas the expand model was used for Spanish, Hungarian and some other languages.

Now, languages do not overlap completely: due to the differences in culture, traditions and lifestyle, languages have concepts, words characteristic of the given language alone. They can only have approximate equivalents and cannot be translated using a single word (Derwojedowa et al., 2008), i.e. they cannot be lexicalized.

Lexicalization is defined in the following way (Lipka, 1992: 107): "the process by which complex lexemes tend to become a single unit with a specific content, through frequent use. In this process, they lose their nature as a syntagma, or combination, to a greater or lesser extent." Thus, lexicalization can be regarded as a process that is gradual, similar to the scalar view of productivity (Jackendoff, 2010). Thus, there are lexicalized items in the language, there are non-lexicalized ones and there are borderline cases in between.

For non-lexicalized concepts, artificial nodes may be introduced in wordnets so as to have a better organized structure (Fellbaum, 1998). The original PWN also contains a few such items, e.g. *bad person*. However, there are wordnets which contain only lexicalized concepts of a language and no non-lexicalized synsets are included. For instance, the Dutch wordnet does not include artificial synsets, producing a much flatter hierarchy (Vossen, 1998). Despite this, the creators of the Basque wordnet tried to include as many non-lexicalized multiword expressions as possible (Agirre et al., 2006). They differentiate between conceptual level imbalances and expression level imbalances, similar to Vossen (1999), who distinguishes cultural gaps and pragmatic gaps. The Basque wordnet, which was also built following the expand model, explicitly codes these non-lexicalized synsets (Pociello et al., 2011).

The Hungarian WordNet (HuWN) was developed by the Research Institute for Linguistics of the Hungarian Academy of Sciences, the Department of Informatics of the University of Szeged, and MorphoLogic Ltd. in a 3-year project (Alexin et al., 2006; Miháltz et al., 2008). As a result, HuWN now contains over 40,000 synsets, out of which 2,000 synsets form part of a business subontology. Here, Princeton WordNet 2.0 served as a basis for the construction of HuWN, i.e. the expand model was adhered to. More precisely, synsets belonging to the BalkaNet Concept Set were selected from PWN 2.0 and then translated into Hungarian. These were then manually edited, corrected and extended with other synonyms using the VisDic editor. The set of concepts to be included in HuWN were expanded concentrically later on. That is, descendants of the existing synsets were treated as synset candidates. The final decision on their status (whether they should be included or excluded) was influenced by several factors such as the frequency of the concept and its presence in other WordNets (Miháltz et al., 2008).

In this paper, we examine what the effects of the expand model are on the quality of the Hungarian WordNet. We investigate the types of non-lexicalized synsets and we propose some strategies that may be used to overcome difficulties concerning non-lexicalized synsets in wordnets constructed using the expand method.

## 3 Non-Lexicalized Synsets

At its inception, developers of the Hungarian wordnet decided that the so-called expand method should be used. This implies that HuWN inherited the hierarchy of PWN. The nominal and adjectival parts[1] of HuWN were built according to the following method: nodes in PWN were automatically correlated with Hungarian synsets and their relations were adopted; the basic strategy was to attach Hungarian entries of a bilingual English-Hungarian dictionary to the nominal/adjectival synsets of PrincetonWordNet.

In order not to have "holes" in the constructed tree (that is, in order for the English and Hungarian wordnets to overlap as much as possible), developers had to find a good way of handling such synsets. To indicate that such synsets do not exist (at the word level) in the lexicon of the given language, i.e. they have not become lexicalized, the *non-lex* label was introduced. Now, we will give the criteria for a synset to be non-lexicalized. First, it may be that no such concept exists in the given language (especially due to cultural differences). Second, the concept may be

[1] The verbal part of HuWN was constructed in a different way (cf. Kuti et al., 2008), so we did not consider verbs in our study.

expressed by productive and compositional constructions (e.g. with adjective + noun combinations), i.e. there is no way of expressing it using a single word or a multiword expression. Third, the concept may be an umbrella term for several single-word concepts, thus, in the other language it may only be expressed by a list. Fourth, there seemed to be inconsistencies or erroneous definitions and hypernym relations in PWN, which the builders of the Hungarian wordnet did not want to follow and they marked the problematic synset with the *non-lex* label.

Some statistics on non-lex synsets in HuWN are presented in Table 1. It can be seen that for the whole body of HuWN every twentieth synset is non-lexicalized and for the basic concept set (BCSHu) it is every twelfth synset. Hence, the problem is not negligible and it is worth examining in detail what types of nonlex synsets exist and how they can be eliminated.

| | **HuWN** | **BCSHu** |
|---|---|---|
| Synsets | 42,292 | 8446 |
| Non-lexicalized | 1,999 | 463 |
| Technical non-lexicalized | 454 | 271 |
| % of (t)non-lex synsets | 5.799 | 8.69 |

Table 1: (Technical) non-lex synsets in HuWN.

### 3.1 Types of Non-Lex Synsets

Non-lex synsets found in HuWN can be classified into six main groups, which are presented below.

**Culturally Determined Concepts.** Culturally determined concepts are related to differences in culture, lifestyle or geographical background. Since the American and Hungarian cultures, (folk) traditions and backgrounds are quite different, there are concepts which not always have verbatim equivalents in the other language. In case they have, they may not reflect the feelings and moods they evoke, that is, what comes to a person's mind when he hears them may differ in the two cultures (cf. Zidoum, 2008). Here we provide two examples:

*máglyarakás* 'stake' (in Hungarian, it refers to a kind of confectionery, which is not associated with the English word *stake*).

*Sassenach* – a Scot's term for an English person, where connotations of the original word cannot be mirrored in Hungarian.

Culturally determined concepts are called conceptual level imbalances in the Basque wordnet (Pociello et al., 2011).

Geographical background mostly determines the named entities included in wordnets. For instance, most Hungarian speakers are not familiar with **Milk River:1** or **White River:1**, thus their inclusion would be questionable in the Hungarian wordnet. However, some of them are included in HuWN due to the expand method applied, but they are classed as *non-lex*.

**Split Concepts.** Another group of non-lex synsets includes elements that simply have no counterpart in the given language. Very often, certain umbrella terms belonging to this category can only be expressed in the other language by using a paraphrase or supplying a list. For instance, **cycling:1** is used for both riding bicycles and motorcycles, which are separate lexical units in Hungarian.

**Words with a Negative Prefix.** Another basic example of non-lex synsets is that of adjectives/nouns formed with negative prefixes such as *non-*, *in-* and *un-*. Apart from a couple of cases, in Hungarian, the negated version of such lexical units is produced with a negative adverb and they together do not constitute a lexicalized synset. Examples of non-lex synsets in HuWN formed with negative prefixes in PWN include **unattractive** – *nem vonzó*, **ill-timed** – *rosszul időzített* and **incongruity** – *meg nem egyezés*, where the HuWn synsets are marked as non-lexicalized.

**Adjective + Noun Constructions.** Some concepts in PWN are expressed with adjective + noun constructions in Hungarian, which cannot be regarded as lexicalized units since they are productive and their meaning is totally compositional. For instance, words denoting nationalities (*skót* 'Scottish', *angol* 'English', *magyar* 'Hungarian' etc.) in Hungarian have a peculiar feature that although there is no distinction of gender in the nominal and pronominal system at the morphological and syntactic levels, when using these words we first and foremost mean a male person of a nation: e.g. **Scotsman:1** was annotated *skót* (a Scottish male person). Their female counterpart is usually formed by adding an extra noun, *nő* 'woman'. The two words *skót nő* 'Scottish woman' when combined, however, are regarded as a productive construction (of adjective + noun) and not as a multiword expression, which is a prerequisite for Hungarian adjective + noun constructions to be admitted into HuWN as valid synsets, and hence *skót nő* is a non-lexicalized synset paired with **Scotswoman:1, Scotchwoman:1**.

**Linguistic Differences.** Sometimes non-lexicalized synsets arise due to the ways a concept can be expressed. In the case of **people:1** – (embercsoport), it can be expressed by a suffix in Hungarian: the English phrase *200 people* can translated as *kétszázan* two.hundred-ESSIVE into Hungarian, which means that a suffix denoting the essive grammatical case is attached to the number, and the suffix corresponds to the English noun.

**Technical Terms.** Over the course of time, some non-lexicalized concepts may become lexicalized. One typical domain is technology, where such concepts are spreading worldwide at an ever accelerating rate. A few years ago, when HuWN was being constructed, *RV* (recreational vehicle) for instance was tagged *non-lex*, which, now, could be accepted as a fully acknowledged lexicalized synset.

### 3.2 Technical Non-Lexicalized Synsets

During the construction, it frequently happened that two English synsets in hierarchical relation had a single Hungarian equivalent; the two concepts are distinct at the conceptual level only. At the lexical level, however, it is impossible to find two distinct words for them. In other cases, it was not possible to find an equivalent for the word with the same part of speech. Technical non-lexicalized (t non-lex) tags are applied in the following cases: (1) identical literals in hypernym-hyponym relation; (2) identical literal in a *similar_to* relation; (3) POS difference, which are all illustrated below.

**Identical Literals in Hypernymy Relation.** The first case of technically non-lexicalized tagging in HuWN is when there are two identical literals in synsets in hypernym relation. This phenomenon is called autohyponimy in Cruse (2000). The developers of HuWN wanted to avoid such redundancies in the trees and, as a convention, they eliminated the overlapping literal from one of the synsets.

Due to entailment, a concept can be replaced by its hypernym: if a greyhound barks, then it entails that a dog barks. So it seemed reasonable to apply this axiom in HuWN building, i.e. to not repeat the hypernym in the hyponym synset. Here is an example (the numbers denoting levels of hierarchy):

| | |
|---|---|
| 1 **cube:5** | **kocka:3** |
| 2 **dice:1** | **dobókocka:1** |

In this case, due to the above-mentioned convention of having to delete the identical literal in the hyponym synset, *kocka* has been excluded, leaving only *dobókocka* as a hyponym. Thus, there is no need to mark the hyponym synset as technically non-lexicalized since there is another literal which does not coincide with the hypernym.

In cases where the hyponym synset consists of only one literal, coinciding with its hypernym, the hyponym synset is marked t non-lex:

| | |
|---|---|
| 1 **safety:1** | **biztonság:1** |
| 2 **security:1** | **biztonság:0** |

In Hungarian, there is no separate lexical item for *safety* and *security*, these being roughly equivalent to *biztonság*. In this way, the hyponym synset should be marked as t non-lex.

**Identical Literals in Focal-Satellite Synsets.** In the case of the adjectival part of the ontology, the *t non-lex* label was also employed. Since its construction is based on antonym-pairs and the associated, synonymous "satellite" synsets, it may well be that while distinct words in English are used to express the concept belonging to the focal and the satellite synsets, in Hungarian, the same word occurs in both positions. Yet, the conventions of wordnet building require that the focal and the satellite synsets should contain no identical literals (cf. identity of hypernym and hyponym). Consequently, again, the course to be followed is that the focal synset remains lexicalized and the more specific, satellite synset gets the *t non-lex* label. For example, {**wide:1**; **broad:1**}'s "satellite" synset is {**heavy:5**; **thick:5**}, but in Hungarian *széles* corresponds to both, therefore the focal synset will be {**széles:2**}, and the satellite synset {**széles:0**}.

**Different Parts of Speech.** Sometimes the target language equivalent of a synset does not share its part of speech with the source language word although it can be classified as one of the four parts of speech used in wordnets. For instance, the English word *afraid* is an adjective, but its Hungarian counterpart *fél* is a verb. In such cases, we made use of the relation *eq_xpos_synonym*, which designates synonymy among different parts of speech: here it relates *fél* and the Hungarian adjectival synset corresponding to *afraid*, which is marked as *t non-lex*.

## 4 Wordnet Errors Related to Non-Lexicalized Synsets

Now we present some of the problematic synsets from PWN and HuWN along with their solutions.

### 4.1 Problems in the Tree

In certain cases, there is an incongruence between a synset and its hypernym. For instance, **location:1** in PWN is defined as *a point or extent in space*; one of its hyponyms is **bilocation:1** with the definition of *the ability (said of certain Roman Catholic saints) to exist simultaneously in two locations* (unique beginner synset: **entity:1**). To our mind, this relation is invalid as their definitions are incompatible and only seem to make a formal hyper-hyponym pair. Instead, *bilocation* should be linked to **ability:2, power:3/képesség:2** on the basis of the definition given in PWN, or it could be also linked to **phenomenon:1/jelenség:1**. If the structure of PWN is to be preserved in HuWN, this synset should be marked as *non-lex* and a new synset should be created under the correct hypernym (**képesség:2** or **jelenség:1**).

### 4.2 Lexicalized Synsets Marked as Non-Lex

In our opinion, in certain cases the annotators of HuWN made some mistakes. For instance, **labor:1** is now a non-lex synset but it should have been classed as a full-fledged lexicalized synset, a multiword expression *fizikai munka* 'physical work'. Similarly, we think that **seating:1, area:1** should have been included as *ülőhely* 'seat'.

### 4.3 Non-Lexicalized Synsets Marked as Lexicalized

An interesting example of non-lex synsets is **bow and arrow:1/íj és nyílvessző:1**. In our view, the synset was incorrectly tagged lexicalized as – though the two parts make up a single weapon – the projector (bow) and the projectile (arrow) do not form a lexicalized phrase in Hungarian.

Attempts to find a Hungarian equivalent for PWN synsets sometimes led to such completely non-existent (although possible) synsets in Hungarian as **fúvóeszköz:1 (blower:1)**.

## 5 Eliminating Non-Lex Problems

The large number of non-lexicalized synsets in the Hungarian wordnet raises questions concerning the (organizing) principles of the Hungarian wordnet. Non-lex synsets – strictly speaking – are not part of the given language, and wordnets including many non-lexicalized items can hardly be regarded as reflecting the concepts of the given language. In order to overcome these problems, we propose to minimize the number of non-lexicalized synsets with the help of four strategies, which are presented below.

### 5.1 Shortening the Tree

We suggest that non-lex synsets without any hyponym should be deleted from the tree. As hypernyms can substitute hyponyms in every context (see Section 3.2.1), this strategy does not undermine the expressibility of certain concepts. This might be useful in the following trees:

| | | |
|---|---|---|
| 1 | **freedom:1** | **szabadság:1** |
| 2 | **liberty:1** | (szabadság) |

There is no distinction made between the senses of the PWN concepts in Hungarian, thus, the lower non-lex synset should be deleted. This solution may be applied to certain culture- or geography-specific synsets as well. For instance, it proved sufficient to include only the major rivers of the United States in HuWN, as there was no need to adapt all the rivers listed in PWN.

### 5.2 Flattening the Tree

Split concepts that can be paraphrased by giving a list should simply be deleted from the tree and all of their hyponyms can be attached to the hypernym of the deleted synset. For instance, there are two non-lex synsets in the following tree:

| | | |
|---|---|---|
| 1 | **occupation:1, business:6, job:1, line of work:1, line:19** | **foglalkozás:1, munka:3, hivatás:2, pálya:6** |
| 2 | **profession:2** | (foglalkozás) |
| 3 | **learned profession:1** | (jog, orvostan és hittudomány) |
| 4 | **law:5, practice of law:1** | **jog:2, jogtudomány:1** |
| | **medicine:3, practice of medicine:1** | **orvostudomány:1** |
| | **theology:3** | **hittudomány:1** |

The first non-lex synset corresponds to the same lexical item as its hypernym in Hungarian, so it is unnecessary to include the non-lex synset in the Hungarian wordnet. The second non-lex synset corresponds to an umbrella term in English, which has no proper Hungarian counterpart. Instead, the following tree should reflect the real conceptual hierarchy in Hungarian:

| | |
|---|---|
| 1 | **foglalkozás:1,munka:3, hivatás:2, pálya:6** |
| 2 | **jog:2, jogtudomány:1** |
| | **orvostudomány:1** |
| | **hittudomány:1** |

### 5.3 Restructuring the Tree

In certain cases, the reconstruction of the tree may be the most effective. First of all, let us illustrate the problem with two charts representing the corresponding PWN and HuWN tree-sections (Hungarian paraphrases are equivalent to PWN definitions):

| | | |
|---|---|---|
| 1 | **building:1** | **épület:1** |
| 2 | **place of worship:1** | (istentisztelet helye "place of worship") |
| 3 | **church:2** | (keresztény templom "Christian church") |
| | **temple:1** | (nem keresztény templom "non-Christian church") |

In PWN, **church:2** and **temple:1** are hyponym synsets of **place of worship:1** at the same level while, at present, they have no lexicalized counterparts in the Hungarian wordnet. In order to eliminate the three non-lexicalized synsets in HuWN and to have lexicalized items there, we propose a solution in which *templom* (meaning a building for the worship of any deity or any religion in Hungarian, without distinguishing between a Christian or non-Christian place of worship) is placed in the hypernym position in parallel with **place of worship:1** and the two hyponym synsets in PWN have no counterparts in the Hungarian tree. All the original hyponyms of **church** and **temple** can be linked under **templom** in Hungarian now.

| | | |
|---|---|---|
| 1 | **building:1** | **épület:1** |
| 2 | **place of worship:1** | **templom:1** |
| 3 | **church:2** | (-) |
| | **temple:1** | (-) |

### 5.4 Lexicalizing the Concept

In some cases, it happened that wordnet builders had made an error and marked lexicalized concepts as non-lex (see Section 4.2). In other cases (see Section 3.1.6), certain concepts (mostly from the technological domain) became lexicalized over time and now they are genuine members of the Hungarian language. The non-lex label of these synsets should be deleted and the synset should be treated as lexicalized, i.e. providing the definition, usage and literals for it.

## 6 Building Independent Hungarian Trees

At the outset of the project, wordnet builders decided to follow the expand model, which meant that HuWN was largely built by simply translating PWN synsets and taking over its relations. To test the validity of this decision, we experimented with the merge model and we also built trees that are truly representative of the structure of the Hungarian language so as to compare Hungarian and English trees.

Hence, we decided to build an independent Hungarian tree from scratch and to examine if we could find matches in HuWN and PWN. First, we took a brand of the famous Hungarian wine called Tokay aszu. The following chart illustrates the newly constructed Hungarian and the corresponding English tree from the top down. [m*X*] denotes synsets that make perfect matches in the independent Hungarian tree, HuWn and PWN. At level 8, there are two relevant concepts that are hyponyms of *fehérbor*. *Tokaji aszú* at level 10 is a hyponym of both *aszúbor* and *tokaji*.

| | | |
|---|---|---|
| 1 | entitás:1 | [m7] *entity* |
| 2 | anyag:1 | [m6] *substance* |
| 3 | folyadék:2 \| táp-anyag:1 | [m5] *liquid* \| *food* |
| 4 | ital:1 | [m4] *beverage* |
| 5 | szeszes ital:1 | [m3] *alcohol* |
| 6 | bor:1 | [m2] *wine* |
| 7 | fehérbor:1 | [m1] *white wine* |
| 8 | desszertbor \| tokaji | *dessert wine* \| *Tokaji* |
| 9 | aszúbor | *aszu wine (botrytized wine)* |
| 10 | tokaji aszú (hyponym of *tokaji* too) | *aszu wine from Tokaj* |
| 11 | hatputtonyos tokaji aszú | *six-puttonyos Tokay aszu* |
| 12 | Oremus hatputtonyos tokaji aszú | *six-puttonyos Tokay aszu from Oremus winery* |

Concepts at levels 9-12 cannot be found in HuWN at all and have no corresponding synsets in PWN either. The concepts at level 8 have no corresponding synsets in HuWN, however, *desszertbor* has a lexical and conceptual counterpart in PWN.

There seems to be a problem regarding the concept *tokaji* in the above chart and the synset *Tokay* in PWN. *Tokaji* in Hungarian (and in English language sources as well[2]) refers to all the wines produced in the Tokaj district of North-eastern Hungary. This concept does not seem to have an equivalent in PWN: it certainly has no formal equivalent and it cannot be decided what the definition of the synset **Tokay:1** (PWN definition: Hungarian wine made from Tokay grapes) refers to exactly. To our mind, it seems closer in meaning to Tokay aszu, which was formerly known throughout the English-speaking world as Tokay (Webster's 1913). Thus, it seems that the Hungarian concept, *tokaji* – which was not included in HuWN – has no equivalent in PWN.

*Fehérbor* (*white wine*) splits into *desszertbor* (*dessert wine*) and *tokaji* (*Tokaji*) at level 8, only to merge again at *tokaji aszú* (*Tokay* (*aszu*)), at level 10. *Aszúbor* (*botrytized wine*) at level 9 is a non-existent synset in PWN.

The tree was built from scratch but it is quite evident that – apart from the levels below 7 – it matches perfectly the Hungarian wordnet: synset numbers are actual sense numbers found in HuWN. **Ital:1** has two hypernyms, both merging into the same hypernym at level 2. These facts suggest that a merge model would also have been applied in the construction of HuWN.

## 7 Discussion

Since languages and cultures differ from each other, there are necessarily concepts that may be lexicalized in one but not in the other and vice versa. Non-lexicalized elements reflect either conceptual or cultural differences between languages and hence can be used for checking the similarities among languages. The Hungarian wordnet – having been constructed according to the expand model – in its present form contains a relatively high number of non-lexicalized synsets but should there be a revision, they might be deleted from the tree (either by shortening or flattening the tree), the tree might be restructured, or they might be lexicalized (if erroneously annotated as *non-lex*). In this way, the Hungarian wordnet would really reflect the hierarchy of the Hungarian language.

Our experiments with building independent Hungarian trees showed that it would also have been viable to apply the merge model for wordnet building. Most of the synsets within the trees can be linked to a corresponding English synset, thus, interlinguality can also be assured as well.

The results of our experiments also led us to ask whether it was justifiable to include non-lexicalized items in PWN. From a purely lexical point of view, these concepts do not exist in the language and so may be deleted from the hierarchy. The argument that should there be no *good person* and *bad person* synsets in PWN, *offender* and *lover* would be sisters, being the hyponyms of *person* (Fellbaum 1998) can be refuted by stating that this would not cause much difficulty given that among the children of *person*, we can already find synsets denoting positive concepts (*enjoyer*), negative concepts (*killer*) and neutral concepts (*candidate*). A second issue concerning PWN is that although it was intended to model the human mind, there are concepts that cannot be found there: see the example of elder and younger brothers and sisters, which are separate lexical items in Hungarian, so they denote different concepts and if the original plan had been followed, they should occur in PWN too – at least as non-lexicalized synsets. A third issue with PWN is that no distinction is made between lexicalized and non-lexicalized ones, i.e. no labels like *non-lex* are used, which somewhat undermines its usage as a dictionary. Although PWN was intended to reflect the hierarchy of concepts thought to be universal, it is very often used as a traditional dictionary of lexical units and hence it should be the case that lexicalized and non-lexicalized concepts are distinguished.

In spite of this, we argue that the marking of non-lex synsets can be profitable as well, especially in an interlingual context. Researchers from different fields can exploit the benefits of non-lex synsets. Psycholinguists might want to compare the hierarchy of mental concepts of speakers of different languages – with the help of non-lex labels since differences are explicitly marked in wordnets built using the expand method. Culture-specific non-lex synsets might be used in ethnographic research. Non-lex synsets associated with linguistic differences (e.g. negative prefixes) can contribute to theoretical linguistic research and contrastive linguistics.

Based on the above points, we may conclude that the usability of wordnets is greatly influenced by the way they were constructed. Wordnets based on the merge model match the lexical hierarchy of the given language, so they can be used as dictionaries as well and they do not include marked non-lexicalized synsets. Due to the absence of non-lex synsets, matching them to other languages is quite difficult and they can be used for psycholinguistic comparative studies

[2] http://en.wikipedia.org/wiki/Tokaji

only in a limited way. Wordnets based on the expand model – such as HuWN – mainly follow the conceptual hierarchy defined in PWN, and contain a lot of non-lexicalized synsets. They can be used for making interlingual or psycholinguistic comparisons, but they reflect the structure of the given language to a lesser degree. However, with the strategies of deleting unnecessary non-lex synsets and restructuring the tree, it is possible to eliminate some of the non-lexicalized items and the wordnet based on the expand model may gradually converge to the one based on the merge model, without involving the effort of building a new wordnet from scratch.

## 8 Summary

In this study, we examined the precise effects of the expand model on the quality of the Hungarian WordNet. We investigated the types of non-lexicalized synsets and we proposed some strategies – including deleting superfluous synsets and reorganizing the trees – that may be used to overcome difficulties concerning non-lexicalized synsets in wordnets constructed with the expand method. We also presented an independent Hungarian tree – built to reflect Hungarian hierarchy and concepts – to see whether we could find matches with HuWN and PWN. It was shown that the merge model could also have been applied to Hungarian, and with the help of the above-mentioned strategies, a wordnet based on the expand model can be transformed to a wordnet similar to the one constructed with the merge model, which would reflect the conceptual hierarchy of Hungarian better. As the way of construction strongly influences the usability of wordnets, this latter version can be primarily used in intralingual research that focuses on Hungarian. Still, marked non-lexicalized elements could prove useful in different fields of research such as psycholinguistics, ethnography and contrastive linguistics. Hence, the originally published version based on the expand model can be also utilized in different fields of research.

In the future, we would like to modify the Hungarian wordnet and by eliminating superfluous non-lexicalized items, we would like to develop a wordnet that really takes into account the Hungarian way of lexicalizing mental concepts.

## Acknowledgments

This work was in part supported by the European Union and co-funded by the European Social Fund through the project Telemedicine-focused research activities in the fields of mathematics, informatics and medical sciences (grant no.: TÁMOP-4.2.2.A-11/1/KONV-2012-0073).

## References

Zoltán Alexin, János Csirik, András Kocsor, Márton Miháltz, and György Szarvas. 2006. Construction of the Hungarian EuroWordNet Ontology and its Application to Information Extraction. In *Proceedings of GWC 2006*, South Jeju Island, Korea, pages 291–292.

Eneko Agirre, Izaskun Aldezabal, and Elisabete Pociello. 2006. Lexicalization and multiword expressions in the Basque WordNet. In *Proceedings of the Third International WordNet Conference (GWC2006)*, Jeju Island, Korea, pages 131–138.

Antonietta Alonge, Nicoletta Calzolari, Piek Vossen, Laura Bloksma, Irene Castellon, Maria Antonia Marti, and Wim Peters. 1998. The Linguistic Design of the EuroWordNet Database. *Computers and the Humanities. Special Issue on EuroWordNet*, 32(2–3): 91–115.

Pushpak Bhattacharyya, Christiane Fellbaum, and Piek Vossen, editors. 2010. *Principles, Construction and Application of Multilingual Wordnets. Proceedings of GWC 2010*. Mumbai, India, Narosa Publishing House.

Alan Cruse. 2000. *Meaning in language: An introduction to semantics and pragmatics*. London, Oxford University Press.

Magdalena Derwojedowa, Maciej Piasecki, Stanisław Szpakowicz, Magdalena Zawisławska, and Bartosz Broda. 2008. Words, Concepts and Relations in the Construction of Polish WordNet. In *Proceedings of GWC 2008*, Szeged, University of Szeged, Department of Informatics, pages 167–68.

Christiane Fellbaum, editor. 1998. WordNet: An Electronic Lexical Database. MIT Press.

Christiane Fellbaum, and Piek Vossen, editors. 2012. *Proceedings of GWC 2012*. Matsue, Japan.

Ray Jackendoff. 2010. *Meaning and the Lexicon: The Parallel Architecture 1975–2010*. Oxford University Press, Oxford.

Judit Kuti, Károly Varasdi, Ágnes Gyarmati, and Péter Vajda. 2008. Language Independent and Language Dependent Innovations in the Hungarian WordNet. In *Proceedings of GWC 2008*, Szeged, University of Szeged, Department of Informatics, pages 254–268.

Leonhard Lipka. 1992. Lexicalization and institutionalization in English and German. Or: Piefke, Wendehals, smog, perestroika, AIDS etc. *Zeitschrift für Anglistik und Amerikanistik* 40:101–111.

Márton Miháltz, Csaba Hatvani, Judit Kuti, György Szarvas, János Csirik, Gábor Prószéky, and Tamás Váradi. 2008. Methods and Results of the Hungarian WordNet Project. In *Proceedings of GWC 2008*, Szeged, University of Szeged, Department of Informatics, pages 311–320.

George A. Miller, Richard Beckwith, Christiane Fellbaum, Derek Gross, and Katherine Miller. 1990. Introduction to WordNet: an On-line Lexical Database. *International Journal of Lexicography*, 3(4):235–244.

Elisabete Pociello, Eneko Agirre, and Izaskun Aldezabal. 2011. Methodology and construction of the Basque WordNet. *Language Resources and Evaluation*, 45:121–142.

Ida Raffaelli, Marko Tadić, Božo Bekavac, and Željko Agić. 2008. Building Croatian WordNet. In *Proceedings of GWC 2008*, Szeged, University of Szeged, Department of Informatics, pages 349–359.

Attila Tanács, Dóra Csendes, Veronika Vincze, Christiane Fellbaum, and Piek Vossen, editors. 2008. *Proceedings of GWC 2008*. Szeged, University of Szeged, Department of Informatics.

Dan Tufiş, editor. 2004. *Romanian Journal of Information Science and Technology. Special Issue on BalkaNet*, 7(1–2).

Dan Tufiş, Dan Cristea, and Sofia Stamou. 2004. BalkaNet: Aims, Methods, Results and Perspectives. A General Overview. *Romanian Journal of Information Science and Technology. Special Issue on BalkaNet*, 7(1–2):9–43.

Piek Vossen, editor. 1998. *EuroWordNet: a multilingual database with lexical semantic networks for European Languages*. Dordrecht, Kluwer.

Piek Vossen. 1999. *EuroWordNet general document*. EuroWordNet (LE2-4003, LE4-8328), part A, final document deliverable D032D033/2D014.

*Webster's New International Dictionary of the English Language*. 1913. Springfield, Mass.: G.&C. Merriam.

Hamza Zidoum. 2008. Towards the Construction of a Comprehensive Arabic WordNet. In *Proceedings of GWC 2008*, Szeged, University of Szeged, Department of Informatics, pages 531–544.

# Enriching Serbian WordNet and Electronic Dictionaries with Terms from the Culinary Domain


**Staša Vujičić Stanković**
Faculty of Mathematics
University of Belgrade
Serbia
stasa@matf.bg.ac.rs

**Cvetana Krstev**
Faculty of Philology
University of Belgrade
Serbia
cvetana@matf.bg.ac.rs

**Duško Vitas**
Faculty of Mathematics
University of Belgrade
Serbia
vitas@matf.bg.ac.rs



## Abstract

In this paper we present three lexical resources for Serbian that are crucial for the development of applications in the culinary domain based on natural language processing. The first two of them — Serbian WordNet and morphological e-dictionaries — have already been in development for some time, while the third one – a corpus of culinary recipes -- has been developed specifically for this purpose. In this paper, we present how we use each of these resources to correct and enlarge the other two. We use various automatic procedures, but manually check all the results.


## 1 Introduction and Motivation

In recent years, linguistic processing of culinary content has become increasingly popular. One of the main reasons for this is the emergence of a large amount of content related to the culinary domain on the Internet. Culinary linguistics (Gerhardt et al., 2013) emerged from the fact that both food and language are present in everyday life. From the perspective of natural language processing, in addition to knowledge representation, culinary linguistics comprises different types of reasoning. Providing these types of processing for the Serbian written texts was the motivation for our research.

WordNet (WN) has been recognized as one of the most important resources for the development of natural language processing applications (information extraction, information retrieval, question answering applications etc.). Accordingly, enriching and enhancing WN using different lexical resources, and vice versa, has become one of the central tasks (Agirre et al., 2000; Agirre et al., 2001; Nimb et al., 2013). Nowadays, with the increasing popularity of the Semantic Web to which WN is closely associated, a lot is being done on enhancing its expressiveness by introducing new relations between concepts (Ruiz-Casado et al., 2007) or new categories (Montoyo et al., 2001).

For the development of any kind of natural language processing application for Serbian written texts from the culinary domain, it was essential to enrich both the Serbian WordNet (SWN) and electronic dictionaries with the appropriate terms from the domain. There were similar efforts taken for other languages where authors addressed the problem of enriching WN related to some specific domains (Vintar and Fišer, 2011; Navigli and Velardi, 2002), but the suggested approaches were different from the one proposed in this paper. Additionally, to the best of our knowledge there is no research dealing with these problems related to Serbian WordNet, although some research related to culinary domain were proposed in (Milićević, 2013), but for different purposes.

Our motivation for WN and electronic dictionaries domain-specific enrichment was to provide a basis for the development of language resources and more complex natural language processing applications in the culinary domain. Language resources of particular interest for this specific domain are recipe, food, meal and other ontologies. Related applications should provide extraction of the relevant concepts, attributes and relations from the recipe corpus in order to overcome standard querying by keywords, and provide advanced search, based on criteria and queries.

The goal of our (informal) culinary project is to develop application where user could query recipes in Serbian; for example, by number of calories according to some diet, even though this information is not explicitly stated in the recipes themselves, but in specially developed ontology. Other search criteria could be related to some special condition of the user health and nutritional information related to the food contained in recipes, in which case it is necessary to include food nutritional information or substitutions in ontologies, etc.

To that end, our first task was to enhance and upgrade the existing lexical resources for Serbian – SWN and morphological electronic dictionaries, and to build a corpus that we can use for terminology extraction. The organization of this paper is as follows: The details of the corpus of culinary recipes in Serbian that we created for the purposes of this research are presented in Section 2. In Section 3 and Section 4 we provide an overview of the current versions of the SWN and electronic dictionaries for Serbian, respectively, with special emphases on the terms related to the culinary domain, as well as, on the newly introduced concepts and domain-specific semantic markers. WN and electronic dictionaries enrichment process and the results obtained are presented in Section 5. Finally, some conclusions and thoughts on future work are given in Section 6.

## 2 Details of the Culinary Text Corpus

For the purpose of harvesting domain-specific terminology, we created corpus of Serbian written culinary recipes in the Latin script. Due to the growing amount of culinary content, such as recipes, various tips and descriptions, the corpus was formed from web texts.

There are numerous free programs for downloading text from web pages, that give satisfactory results — like BootCaT.[1] But besides the text that is displayed to users, we were interested in maintaining the original structure of web pages, as well. Therefore, for the purposes of our research, we decided to develop programs adjusted to particular web pages, their content and also the meta-data that could be used in our ongoing work. These individually tailored programs were implemented in the Java programming language that provides support for text processing using regular expressions.

The texts have been collected from several leading national websites from the culinary domain like Recepti[2], Kuhinjica[3] etc. The created text corpus contains approximately 14,000 recipes, which consist of approximately 1,600.000 simple word forms. However, since much of the culinary content on the Web is user-generated we discovered that we could not use everything that was collected for our purpose. Namely, when using the Latin script users sometimes tend to ignore diacritics which renders the produced texts unusable for linguistic processing. Such omissions cannot be corrected automatically, because they increase the homography of forms – e.g. *vece* itself can represent a word of the language (colloquial for WC), but we may also presume that it is missing one of two possible diacritics: *veće* 'bigger' or *veče* 'evening'. Therefore, we discarded all recipes that did not contain any Serbian-specific letters with diacritics. Since the resulting corpus still contained quite a number of errors, due to careless typing, we corrected some of the frequently occurring ones, like the use of the digraph *dj* instead of the letter *đ*, and the digraph *dz* instead of *dž*. As we did not want to introduce new errors by applying simple find/replace, we corrected only unknown words that became known Serbian words after correction (according to Serbian e-dictionaries, see Section 4).

## 3 Serbian WordNet

The production of the SWN was initiated together with the Bulgarian, Greek, Romanian, and Turkish versions by the BalkaNet project. The structure of all these WNs corresponded to the structure established by the EuroWordNet project and they were all linked to the Princeton WordNet (PWN), through the so-called Interlingual Index (version 2.1 at the end of the project). Besides, all BalkaNet WNs were developed following the *expand model* (Fellbaum, 2010), which means that synsets from the PWN were translated into target languages, and the relations between synsets were transferred as well (a hypernym/hyponym as a rule, other if applicable). At the end of the BalkaNet project, the SWN had 7,000 synsets, covering basic concept sets 1 and 2, and most of the concepts from the subset 3 (Tufis et al., 2004).

After the end of the BalkaNet project, the development of the SWN continued, but at a much slower pace, since there was no project to support it. The development mostly relied on volunteer work of its chief editor and numerous Masters and PhD students who followed the same expand model in their work. Due to such circumstances, the choice of the synsets to be transferred was not concept-dependent, but rather domain-dependent, because chief editor wanted to make the most of

[1]http://www.bootcat.sslmit.unibo.it
[2]http://www.recepti.com
[3]http://www.kuhinjica.rs

the specific knowledge and interests of her volunteers. As a result, the Serbian WordNet was enlarged to almost 20,000 synsets.

Before the beginning of the (informal) culinary project, concepts belonging to the culinary domain were not given special attention. However, 393 such concepts were already present in the SWN, 99 of which belong to basic concept sets and 91 to Balkan- or Serbian-specific concepts.

## 4 Electronic Dictionaries for Serbian

The development of Serbian e-dictionaries follows the methodology and format known as DELA presented for French in (Courtois et al., 1990). The role of electronic dictionaries, covering both simple words and multi-word units (MWUs), and dictionary finite-state transducers (FSTs), is text tagging as part of various natural language applications. Each such e-dictionary of forms consists of a list of entries supplied with their lemmas, morphosyntactic, semantic, and other information. The forms are, as a rule, automatically generated from the dictionaries of lemmas containing the information that enables the production of forms. The system of Serbian e-dictionaries covers both general lexica and proper names and all inflected forms are generated from 130,500 simple forms and 10,500 MWU lemmas (Krstev, 2008). Approximately 28.5% of these lemmas represent proper names: personal, geopolitical, organizational, etc.

Most of the word forms in the Serbian morphological e-dictionaries are supplied not only with the values of the grammatical categories, but also with the additional markers that are inherited from the lemmas from which they are generated. These markers can be grammatical (the marker +MG for the natural masculine gender, as opposed to the grammatical gender, e.g. in *muškarčina* 'macho'), derivational (+Pos for possessive adjectives, e.g. *bikov* 'belonging to a bull, taurine'), dialectic (+Ek for the Ekavian pronunciation, e.g. *devojka* 'girl'), domain specifying (+Math for mathematics, e.g. *mnogougao* 'polygon'), and semantic (+Hum for humans, e.g. *drug* 'friend'). Some of the semantic markers are redundant, e.g. the marker +Top (for geographic names) is superfluous if the marker +Gr (for settlements) is present. However, we keep them all for processing purposes – if a geographic name is needed, we do not have to list all their types.

Some of these markers were systematically added to the dictionary entries to which they apply, while others were conceived later and added systematically only to the entries included in the dictionaries at some later stage. The latter was the case for words from the culinary domain. Before starting the enrichment process, there were 218 simple word entries with the semantic marker +Food, and 217 multi-word entries. All entries with the +Food marker should also have been assigned the +Conc marker (for *concrete object*, as a more general category), but this was not the case either: 32 simple entries and 20 multi-word entries were missing it. Naturally, at this moment we still do not know how many entries in e-dictionaries are missing the +Food marker, because supplying as many entries as possible with it is one of the goals of our project.

### 4.1 Domain Specific Semantic Markers for Serbian Electronic Dictionaries

The concepts and the terminology specific to the culinary domain required introduction of a new domain marker and more refined semantic markers. Table 1 provides an overview of the newly proposed semantic markers, that could be used individually or in combination. Naturally, the domain marker +Culinary is assigned to all the lemmas from the culinary domain. All other markers are used in combination with the +Conc marker, except the +MesApp marker for approximate measures often used in cooking, like *prstohvat* 'an amount between fingers, a pinch'. Similarly, the +Food marker is assigned with all other markers except +MesApp and +Uten, that is asigned to utensils used in food preparation and serving. The +Erg marker is assigned to the names of man-created items that have the status of trademarks. It can be assigned to both food *tabasko* 'Tabasco' and utensils *teflon* 'Teflon'. It goes without saying that in the culinary domain these names are used loosely and because of that often with the lowercase initial in Serbian. Namely, if recipe states that *campari* 'Campari' should be used, it is understood that if not available, it can be replaced by some similar liqueur. The marker +Erg is used outside the culinary domain, as well, e.g. *rols-rojs* 'Rolls Royce'.

In addition to these semantic markers that are already added to the Serbian e-dictionary, in further research, we intend to address the terminology related to food condition, food taste, as well as the way of food preparation, for which we have dedicated new semantic markers – +Cond, +Taste, and +WoP, respectively, that are related mainly to adjectives and verbs. At this point, they are not included in the dictionary (except for some newly added entities), and their systematic adding would be an objective of our future work.

| Semantic marker | Description |
|---|---|
| +Culinary | culinary domain |
| +Food | food (e.g. *senf* 'mustard') |
| +Alim | aliment (e.g. *mleko* 'milk |
| +Prod | product (e.g. *sirće* 'vinegar') |
| +Meal | meal (e.g. *doručak* 'breakfast') |
| +Course | course (e.g. *puding* 'pudding') |
| +Uten | utensil (e.g. *šolja* 'cup') |
| +Erg | ergonym (e.g. *rokfor* 'Roquefort') |
| +MesApp | approximate measures (e.g. *kašičica* 'spoonful') |
| +Taste | taste (e.g. *slatkokiseo* 'sweet-sour') |
| +WoP | way of preparation (e.g. *dinstati* 'to stew'; *dinstanje* 'stewing') |
| +Cond | condition (e.g. *bajat* 'stale') |

Table 1: The overview of newly proposed semantic markers.

## 5 Enrichment Process

The process of enriching both the Serbian WordNet and Serbian e-dictionaries proceeded in several steps:

1. Manual translation of as many synsets from the culinary domain as possible belonging to the PWN.

2. Inspection of unknown words resulting from the application of Serbian e-dictionaries to the corpus of recipes in search of new entries.

3. (Semi-)automatic production of new simple word and multi-word entries for e-dictionaries with all applicable markers, derived from the synsets, in the SWN, belonging to the culinary domain.

4. (Semi-)automatic addition of all missing markers in e-dictionaries, based on the synsets in the SWN belonging to the culinary domain.

5. (Semi-)automatic addition of new culinary and/or Serbian-specific concepts to the SWN and manual correction.

Steps one and two were performed by three graduate Library and Information Science students well-educated in the field of information search. Their role in step one was to investigate specific branches in the PWN and transfer into the SWN all concepts recognized in Serbian. The branches of interest were *'food, nutrient'* related to aliments, products, drinks, meals and courses, and *'kitchen utensil'* and *'tableware'* related to utensils. The role was not very precise, but students took their job seriously and translated everything for which they could find evidence. As a result, the SWN now has all concepts related to fruits, as the PWN, although hardly anybody in Serbia has ever heard of some of them (e.g. *durian* 'durian' and *žabotikana* 'jaboticana'), let alone tasted them. The same principle could not always be applied -- for instance, quite a number of fish species represented in the PWN are completely unknown in Serbia (e.g. *scup*, *sailfish*, *sucker*, etc.). It should be stressed that the students supplied a definition for each introduced sysnet, which is in line with the strategy applied for the development of the SWN from the beginning – practically all its synets have a definition. Everything produced by the students was double checked by chief SWN editor.

Step two was equally imprecise. The students' task was to recognize, in the long list of unknown words in the corpus of recipes comprising of 9,100 word forms, all those for which they knew the meaning without further consultation. All chosen entries were assigned the appropriate markers, as well as, codes for inflectional paradigms, which was done manually for simple words and automatically for MWUs.

Step three consisted of two tasks. First, we produced new candidates for e-dictionaries of simple and MWUs automatically by inspecting the synsets belonging to the already mentioned hierarchies, choosing those that were not in e-dictionaries already. These new candidates were all supplied with the appropriate markers which were derived from the position of a synset in a hierarchy. For instance, the new candidate *fondi* 'fondue' belongs to the hierarchy {dish:2}, {nutriment:1,...}, {food:1, nutrient:1}, {substance:1, matter:1}, and therefore the suggested markers for it were +Conc, +Food, +Course (and +Culinary, as a domain marker). The second task consisted of manual checking of all new candidates and their markers. A good number of candidates were rejected for several reasons. There were duplicates (a literal belonging to several synsets, e.g. *brizle* is connected to {neck sweetbread:1, throat sweetbread:1} and to {sweetbread:1, sweetbreads:1}) for which there should be only one entry in the e-dictionaries. There were literals irrelevant to e-dictionaries, because they were of a descriptive nature and not really lexicalized (e.g. *grožđe sa glatkom kožom* corresponding to {fox grape:1, slip-skin grape:1}. In a few cases, a literal from the chosen hierarchies did not actually belong to the culinary domain (e.g. *Poslednja večera* corresponding to {Last Supper:1, Lord's Supper:2} that belongs to the branch {food:1, nutrient:1}). The markers themselves have also to be checked and if necessary corrected. For instance, *pomfrit* 'french fries' has as a hypernym {vegetable:1}, and thus it obtained the marker +Alim; however, we believed that +Prod was more appropriate.

The fourth step was performed in a similar way as the previous one, except that we considered now only the entries already in e-dictionaries missing some or all appropriate markers. The produced list of enhanced entries had also to be considered carefully in order not to add markers to wrong entries. For instance, suggested new markers for the entry *baba* 'baba' were +Conc, +Food, +Course, while the entry already in the dictionary corresponded to *baba* 'grandmother'. Similarly, the entry *luk* 'bow' obtained markers +Food+Conc+Alim intended only for the entry *luk* 'onion'.

In step five, we used new entries for e-dictionaries, produced in step two, to create new synsets in the SWN. These entries include either the concepts specific to Serbia, like *afusali*, a type of grapes very popular in Serbia, or too specific concepts that were missing in the PWN, like *friteza* 'deep fryer'. Since they were already assigned semantic markers, we used them to find the right place for the appropriate synsets. In the case of MWUs, we could do even more, because many of them contained as a unit a literal from a hypernym synset: *vatrostalna činija* 'fireproof bowl' i *zdenka sir* 'zdenka cheese, a popular cheese' are a kind of a bowl and a kind of cheese, respectively, and they could be pushed further down the hierarchy. The position of every newly added synset was checked manually and corrected if necessary.

At the end of this phase we obtained the following results:

- The SWN was enlarged by translating 1,404 synsets from the culinary domain from the PWN to the SWN, to contain a total of 1,797 such synsets;
- Serbian e-dictionaries of simple words were enlarged by 636 entries, 246 of which were obtained from the SWN and 390 from the culinary corpus.
- Serbian e-dictionaries of MWU were enlarged by 612 simple entries, 514 of which were obtained from the SWN and 98 from the culinary corpus.
- The full set of the appropriate markers was assigned to 735 simple word and 125 multiword entries.
- 450 specific concepts from the culinary domain were added to the SWN.

## 6 Conclusion and Future Work

We have completed the first phase of enrichment of the SWN and Serbian e-dictionaries. The next phase will consist of the following steps:

1. (Semi-)automatic detection in the corpus of all words belonging to the culinary domain and e-dictionaries that are still not assigned all applicable markers and manual marker selection and assignment.
2. (Semi-)automatic detection in the corpus of other MWU terms belonging to the culinary domain.
3. Extension of our approach to other PoS synsets and dictionary enties.

In order to complete this phase, we will rely on various local grammars, some of which were already developed for Serbian for different purposes (Krstev et al., 2011).

### Acknowledgements

We would like to thank the following PhD students at the Faculty of Philology, University of Belgrade for their help in enhancing the SWN with synsets from the culinary domain: Biljana Đorđević, Jelena Andonovska and Katarina Stanišić. This research was conducted through the project 178006, financed by the Serbian Ministry of Science.

## References


Eneko Agirre, Olatz Ansa, Eduard Hovy, and David Martínez. 2000. Enriching very large ontologies using the WWW. *arXiv preprint cs/0010026*.

Eneko Agirre, Olatz Ansa, Eduard Hovy, and David Martinez. 2001. Enriching WordNet concepts with topic signatures. *arXiv preprint cs/0109031*.

Blandine Courtois, Max Silberztein Ladl, et al. 1990. Dictionnaires électroniques du français. *Langue française*, 87(1):3–4.

Christiane Fellbaum. 2010. *WordNet*. Springer.

Cornelia Gerhardt, Maximiliane Frobenius, and Susanne Ley. 2013. *Culinary Linguistics: The chef's special*, volume 10. John Benjamins Publishing.

Cvetana Krstev, Duško Vitas, and Aleksandra Trtovac. 2011. Orwells 1984 — the Case of Serbian Revisited. In *Proc. of 5th Language & Technology Conference*, pages 25–27.

Cvetana Krstev. 2008. *Processing of Serbian – Automata, Texts and Electronic Dictionaries*. Faculty of Philology, University of Belgrade.

Maja Milićević. 2013. Genre-based BootCaT corpora for morphologically rich languages. *BOTWU - BootCaTters of the world unite! A workkshop on the BootCaT toolkit, Forli, 24 June 2013*. http://botwu.sslmit.unibo.it/download/milicevic.pdf.

Andrés Montoyo, Manuel Palomar, and German Rigau. 2001. WordNet Enrichment with Classification Systems. In *Proc. of WN and Other LRs: Applications, Extensions and Customisations Workshop.(NAACL-01) The 2nd Meeting of the North American Chapter of the ACL*, pages 101–106.

Roberto Navigli and Paola Velardi. 2002. Automatic Adaptation of WordNet to Domains. In *3rd International Conference LREC, Las Palmas, Canary Islands, 29-31 May 2002*, pages 1023–1027.

Sanni Nimb, Bolette S Pedersen, Anna Braasch, Nicolai H Sørensen, and Thomas Troelsgård. 2013. Enriching a wordnet from a thesaurus. *Lexical Semantic Resources for NLP*, page 36.

Maria Ruiz-Casado, Enrique Alfonseca, and Pablo Castells. 2007. Automatising the Learning of Lexical Patterns: an Application to the Enrichment of WordNet by Extracting Semantic Relationships from Wikipedia. *Data & Knowledge Engineering*, 61(3):484–499.

Dan Tufis, Dan Cristea, and Sofia Stamou. 2004. BalkaNet: Aims, Methods, Results and Perspectives. A General Overview. *Romanian Journal of Information science and technology*, 7(1-2):9–43.

Špela Vintar and Darja Fišer. 2011. Enriching Slovene WordNet with domain-specific terms. *Translation: Computation, Corpora, Cognition*, 1(1):29–44.

# What implementation and translation teach us: the case of semantic similarity measures in wordnets

**Marten Postma**
Utrecht University
Utrecht, Netherlands.
martenp@gmail.com

**Piek Vossen**
VU University Amsterdam
Amsterdam, Netherlands
piek.vossen@vu.nl

**Abstract**

Wordnet::Similarity is an important instrument used for many applications. It has been available for a while as a toolkit for English and it has been frequently tested on English gold standards. In this paper, we describe how we constructed a Dutch gold standard that matches the English gold standard as closely as possible. We also re-implemented the WordNet::Similarity package to be able to deal with any wordnet that is specified in Wordnet-LMF format independent of the language. This opens up the possibility to compare the similarity measures across wordnets and across languages. It also provides a new way of comparing wordnet structures across languages through one of its core aspects: the synonymy and hyponymy structure. In this paper, we report on the comparison between Dutch and English wordnets and gold standards. This comparison shows that the gold standards, and therefore the intuitions of English and Dutch native speakers, appear to be highly compatible. We also show that our package generates similar results for English as reported earlier and good results for Dutch. To the contrary of what we expected, some measures even perform better in Dutch than English.

## 1 Introduction

Various methods have been proposed in the past for measuring similarity between words using Princeton WordNet (Fellbaum, 1998). Some of these methods (*path* (Rada et al., 1989), *lch* (Leacock and Chodorow, 1998), *wup* (Wu and Palmer, 1994), *res* (Resnik, 1995), *lin* (Lin, 1998), *jcn* (Jiang and Conrath, 1997), among others) were implemented in the WordNet::Similarity package (Pedersen et al., 2004). WordNet::Similarity [1] has become an important instrument for measuring similarity between any set of words in a language but also for testing the performance of wordnet as a database of synonymy and semantic relations. The toolkit was used to evaluate the different measures against a gold standard of English words created by Rubenstein and Goodenough (1965) and Miller and Charles (1991). The evaluation results tell us something about the capacity of WordNet to mimic human judgements of similarity but also about the different methods in relation to each other.

Unfortunately, WordNet::Similarity only works for the Princeton WordNet released in its proprietary format and not wordnets in other languages in other formats, such as Wordnet-LMF (Vossen, Soria and Monachini, 2013). Furthermore, no gold standard exists for Dutch, the language that we study. In this paper, we describe a re-implementation of the WordNet::Similarity toolkit that can read any wordnet in Wordnet-LMF format to apply the 6 wordnet similarity algorithms. This toolkit makes it possible to carry out similarity measures across different wordnets within the same language and across different languages. This is especially useful if the wordnets were created independently using their own semantic hierarchy. We also created a gold standard in Dutch that is comparable with the gold standard in English. We tried to recreate the process through which the English gold standard was created as much as possible. Since it was not clear what instructions were given exactly to the human scorers, we decided to create a number of additional gold standards that are more explicit about the difference between relatedness, similarity and the assumed meaning of the words to be com-

[1] see http://wn-similarity.sourceforge.net/

pared. In total 6 different gold standards have been created. Using these gold standards, we first show that the 6 Dutch gold standards are very similar and that the English and Dutch gold standards are highly compatible. Secondly, we demonstrate that the performance of the Dutch wordnet is higher than the reported performance for English. There are also some differences in the results which can be explained to some well-known differences in the hierarchical organization of the Dutch and English wordnets.

The paper is structured as follows. In the next section, we describe related work. Section 3 explains how we created the Dutch gold standard and section 4 the WordnetTools implementation of the similarity functions. In section 5, we report the results using the Dutch wordnet Cornetto 2.1 (Vossen et al., 2013).

## 2 Related work

The notion of similarity is central to WordNet through the relations synonymy and hyponymy. Synsets group words that can be exchanged in contexts and thus have more or less the same denotational domain. Hyponymy groups these synsets according to a shared semantic aspect and thus defines another type of similarity. Words that do not share a synonymy relation and synsets that do not share a hyponymy relation are not necessarily disjoint but the things they can refer to are less likely to be considered similar. Words and synsets that have other relations than synonymy and hyponymy respectively, e.g. part-whole or causal relations, are most likely not similar but strongly related. This difference is dubbed the 'tennis-phenomenon' in Fellbaum (1998) : where *tennis ball*, *player*, *racket* and *game* are closely related but all very different things. Since WordNet dominantly consists of synonymy and hyponymy relations, it more naturally reflects similarity than relatedness.

Since the first release of WordNet, researchers have tried to use it to simulate similarity. Except for the *lesk* (Lesk, 1986), *vector* (Patwardhan and Pedersen, 2006), and *vector pairs* (Patwardhan and Pedersen, 2006) algorithms, these measures are all based on synonymy and hyponymy.

Another approach to measure similarity across different languages is described by Joubarne and Inkpen (2011). The aim of their paper is to show that it might be possible to use the scores from the English gold standards in other languages, hence making it unnecessary to create gold standards with human-assigned judgements in every single language. In order to show this, they used an existing gold standard for German, which is a translation of the gold standard by Rubenstein & Goodenough with human-assigned scores. For French, they used an existing French translation of the English gold standard by Rubenstein & Goodenough, and asked French native speakers to rate the similarity of meaning for each word pair in the dataset. Moreover, they used two measures of similarity to also rate the similarity of meaning of the translation of the original dataset, which are Point-wise mutual information and second order co-occurence Point-wise mutual information for which the Google n-gram corpus was used. They then compared the output from the similarity measures to the language specific gold standards and to the original scores collected by Rubenstein & Goodenough. The difference between these correlations was relatively small, which is why they claim that it is possible to use the original scores from the English gold standard in other languages.

Besides Joubarne and Inkpen (2011), other studies have made an effort to translate the original datasets by Rubenstein & Goodenough and by Miller & Charles. Hassan and Mihalcea (2009) translated these datasets into Spanish, Arabic, and Romanian. For Spanish, native speakers, who were highly proficient in English, were asked to translate the datasets. They were asked not to use multi-word expressions. They were asked to take into account the relatedness within a word pair for disambiguation. In addition, they were allowed to use so-called replacement words to overcome slang or if words were culturally dependent. They then asked 5 participants to rate the Spanish word pairs. A sixth person evaluated the translation. Because of the fact that the Pearson correlation with the original datasets was 0.86, only one translator translated the datasets into Arabic and Romanian. Finally, Gurevych (2005) translated the datasets into German. However, no instructions, as to how it was done, were provided.

## 3 Dutch gold standard

We would like to see whether the similarity intuitions of Dutch speakers are the same as the English speakers. We also want to known if the Dutch wordnet Cornetto, which was built independently of the English WordNet, would perform in the same way as the English WordNet using the same similarity measures and against a comparable gold standard. For that, we need to create a Dutch gold standard. We opted to translate the gold standards by Rubenstein & Goodenough (65 word pairs) and by Miller & Charles (30 word pairs). Because the words used by Miller & Charles are a subset of the words used by Rubenstein & Goodenough, and because words are used more than once in both experiments, there are only 49 unique words used in both experiments. In addition, Miller & Charles made one change to the dataset by Rubenstein & Goodenough. Whenever Rubenstein & Goodenough used the word *cord*, Miller & Charles uses the word *chord*.

Inspired by Hassan and Mihalcea (2009), the following general procedure is followed in the translation of the 49 words: [2]

1. The first step is to disambiguate the English word forms. The English experiments present a word form and not a specific concept the word refers to. The results from human judgement provide a good indication as to which concept in WordNet is meant.

2. Following the results in 1, a Dutch translation is chosen for each word.

3. In addition, it is checked whether the relative frequency of the Dutch and English words are in the same class of relative frequency. This is done in order to make sure that there are no outliers. A translation is an outlier when its relative frequency deviates significantly from the original word.

We will now discuss each step of the general procedure in more detail. The first step consists of disambiguating the 49 English words. For example, WordNet lists two senses for the word *asylum*:

1. 'a shelter from danger or hardship'

2. 'a hospital for mentally incompetent or unbalanced person'

[2]We made an effort to compare the polysemy of the English word and its translation. However, English words in WordNet tend to have many more meanings than words in Cornetto. In addition, Dutch words often only refer to one specific part-of-speech, whereas English words often have noun and verb meanings. Because of these differences, we decided not to use this means of comparison in our translation procedure.

In the results of Miller & Charles and Rubenstein & Goodenough, we observe that the correlation with *madhouse* is very high. Hence, the second sense as listed in WordNet is chosen for *asylum*. The same procedure is applied to all other words.

The next step is to translate all English words into Dutch. One of the difficulties we encountered was the case in which two synonyms were used in English, but no two contemporary Dutch synonyms were available. When we encountered such a problem, we opted to replace the English synonyms with two Dutch synonyms that were closely related to the English synonyms. For example, due to the fact that there is only one common Dutch word *haan* "male chicken" for the English synonyms *cock* and *rooster*, we opted to replace these two words by *kip* "female chicken" and *hen* "female chicken", the two Dutch words for female chickens.

In addition, the relative frequencies of the English word and its translation were checked. In order to calculate relative frequencies of the English words, the English sense-tagged corpus SemCor (Miller et al., 1993) was used. For Dutch, such a resource was not available. We are aware of the fact that the Dutch sense-tagged corpus DutchSemCor (Vossen et al., 2012) exists. However, an effort was made to provide an equal number of examples for each meaning in this corpus. Although this is very useful for WSD-experiments, this makes this corpus less useful for Information Content calculations. Therefore the frequencies of the lemmas in the Dutch corpus called SoNaR (Oostdijk et al., 2008) were used. It was checked whether or not the English word and its Dutch counterpart were located in the same class of relative frequency. A word is placed in the category **high** if its relative frequency is higher than 0.05%, **middle** if its relative frequency is between 0.015% and 0.05% and **low** if its relative frequency is lower than 0.015%. If two words are located in the same relative frequency class, the pair receives the value True, else False. If no frequency data was available for a word, the value of the pair was set to True. Eight word pairs received the value False. Since this step was performed to remove outliers, we claim this to be acceptable.

The Dutch translation was then used to reproduce the English experiments by Miller & Charles and Rubenstein & Goodenough. Since the instructions concerning *Similarity of meaning* are unclear in the original experiments, we reproduced each experiment with three different kinds of instructions, which are *stressing similarity aspects*, *stressing relatedness aspects*, and *no instructions*. These instructions were explained to the participants by an example of each value that could be assigned to a word pair and a general description. The WordSimilarity-353 Test Collection (Finkelstein et al., 2002) was used to obtain example word pairs for each value that could be assigned to a word pair. This dataset contains two sets of English word pairs with similarity scores assigned by humans. The first set of this collection contains 153 word pairs, with their scores, from 0 to 10, assigned by 13 subjects. In addition, participants were asked to rate the word pairs on similarity. From this set, examples were chosen *stressing similarity aspects*. The second set contains 200 word pairs, with human-assigned scores, from 0 to 10, by 16 subjects. In this case, participants were asked to rate the word pairs based on relatedness. From this set, examples were chosen *stressing relatedness aspects*. Each word pair that was chosen to serve as an example word pair was translated into Dutch. For *stressing similarity*, participants were asked to indicate to what degree two words could replace each other. For example, if two words were interchangeable, they were told to assign the highest value. They were instructed to assign a lower value to a word pair like *aardappelmesje* 'potato peeler' & *mes* 'knife', because *mes* 'knife' can be used instead of *aardappelmesje* 'potato peeler', but not the other way around. For stressing *relatedness aspects*, participants were asked to focus on how likely it is that words occur in the same situation. For example, it is very likely that *computer* 'computer' & *internet* 'internet' occur in the same situation together, whereas this is less likely the case for *komkommer* 'cucumber' & *professor* 'professor'. Finally for the *no instructions* case, the interpretation was left to the participant, except that we indicated that synonyms resulted in the highest score. Combining the two English experiments with the three different kinds of instructions thus yielded six different sets. For convenience, we will use abbreviations to refer to the six experiments. The abbreviation *Mc* will be used for the translation of the dataset by Miller & Charles. *Rg* will be used for the translation of the dataset by Rubenstein & Goodenough. In addition, the three kinds of instructions will be abbreviated in the following way: *No* for no instruction, *Sim* for similarity, and *Rel* for relatedness. By combining the abbreviations, we can refer to each of the six experiments. For example, *McSim* means that the translation of the dataset by Miller & Charles is meant with the instruction *similarity*. Pupils from five Dutch high schools participated. The pupils's age ranged from 16 to 18 years. Their level of education was one the two highest levels of Dutch secondary education, called *HAVO* and *VWO*. Numbers of participants per experiment were: 40 for *McNo*, 40 for *McRel*, 52 for *McSim*, 26 for *RgNo*, 42 for *RgSim*, and 40 for *RgRel*. The difference between the results of the different instructions turned out to be neither significant, nor systematic. We thus assume that the instructions have not been effective to override the basic intuition of the participants.

## 4 WordnetTools

WordnetTools is a reimplementation of the WordNet::Similarity package in Java1.6 that can read any wordnet in WordNet-LMF format to apply the major similarity functions: Path, Jiang & Conrath, Leacock & Chodorow, Lin, Resnik, Wu & Palmer (see above). The similarity functions can be tuned using various parameters:

**–lmf-file** Path to the wordnet file in LMF format. A few other formats are also supported.

**–pos** (optional) part-of-speech filter, values: n, v, a.

**–relations** (optional) file with relations used for the hierarchy, if not selected a standard set of relations is used: hypernym, has_hypernym, has_hyperonym, near_synonym, eng_derivative, xpos_near_synonym, xpos_near_hyperonym, xpos_near_hypernym.

**–input** File with pairs to be compared on single lines, separated with backward slash.

**–pairs** The type of input values: "words" or "synsets" or "word-synsets pairs"

**–method** leacock-chodorow, resnik, path, wu-palmer, jiang-conrath, lin or all.

**–depth** Optional: a fixed value for average depth can be given.

**–subsumers** Path to a file with subsumer frequencies, required for resnik, lin, jiang-conrath or all.

**–separator** Token for separating input and output fields, default is TAB.

The above options can be used to configure the experiments and the way similarity is calculated. The graph through which words and synsets are compared can be restricted by selecting the part-of-speech or specifying a certain set of relations. The internal data structure treats the result as a graph without further distinguishing the type of relations. It is for example possible to accept strict hypernym relations and looser relations such as near_synonym, xpos_hyperonym and xpos_near_synonym relations for all parts of speech. The toolkit will then build a graph in which synsets are connected through any of these relations.[3] Against such a graph, words such as *transport* as a verb and *transportation* and *transport* as nouns will get scores similar to cohyponyms. The more relations are included, such as role and causal relations, the more the graph will measure relatedness instead of similarity. For the purpose of this paper, we configured the settings so that graph is most similar to the hierarchical structure of the English WordNet. We thus only used the has_hypernym and has_hyperonym relations.

The toolkit can handle tangled structure as a result of e.g. multiple hypernyms. In case of multiple hypernyms, all possible paths are calculated and given back as the set of paths through the graph. Similarly, if a word has multiple senses, we generate all possible paths for each sense. When comparing two words, we compare all paths of one word with all paths of another word and calculate the similarity score to the specified metrics using each pair of paths. In the end, we keep the paths with the best result. Note that for measures that use information content this is not always the shortest path.

In addition to the similarity API, the toolkit also provides a number of auxiliary functions, for example to determine the average or maximum depth for a wordnet per part-of-speech. WordnetTools is freely available under the GPLv3 license and can be downloaded from: http://wordpress.let.vupr.nl/software/wordnettools/. The package includes the Dutch and English gold standards, as well as the English WordNet in Wordnet-LMF format and the English SemCor frequencies in the proper import format. It also includes the results of the Dutch and English evaluation. The Cornetto wordnet is not included since it is restricted by license. A free research license can be obtained from the Dutch centre for language technology (TST-centrale[4]). However, we will release an open-source version of the Dutch wordnet, which will be included in the package when released. Also the SoNaR word frequencies can be obtained from the TST-centrale. The SoNaR word frequencies have been converted to the hypernym frequencies as described by Resnik, by averaging frequencies over the senses of a word and transferring these to the hypernyms (and further up the hierarchy). These derived hypernym frequencies are also included in the package.

## 5 Results

Three evaluations have been run to compare the similarity measures across wordnets and across languages. We start by comparing the Dutch to the English gold standards, followed by an evaluation of the comparison between the Dutch gold standards and the similarity measures. Finally, we try to replicate the English experiment by Pedersen (2010) using English Wordnet-LMF and Wordnet-Tools. [5]

### 5.1 The Dutch gold standard with the English gold standard

The first evaluation that we carried out is the comparison between the English gold standards and their Dutch translations. Since we have an equivalence relation between most of the words, we can compare the rankings of the Dutch and English native speakers. In the evaluation, we left out the word pairs in which a word had not been directly translated, which was the case for word pairs like *cock* and *rooster*. Table 1 presents the evaluation:

| Dutch Gold standard | Spearman $\rho$ original dataset |
|---|---|
| McNo | 0.88 |
| McSim | 0.86 |
| McRel | 0.89 |
| RgNo | 0.93 |
| RgSim | 0.93 |
| RgRel | 0.93 |

Table 1: Evaluation of the comparison between the English gold standards and their Dutch translations.

[3]If bi-directional relations are used in the wordnet, only one of these should be chosen. If not, the path-construction can be terminated by direct circularity of the bi-directional relations.

[4]see `http://tst-centrale.org/`

[5]A github has been created to make it possible to replicate the results in this section. The url to this github is `https://github.com/MartenPostma/PostmaVossenGWC2014`

The results show that the English and Dutch intuitions concerning *Similarity of meaning* are very similar. The range of the Spearman $\rho$ correlation is between 0.86 and 0.93. It also shows that there is little difference across the different Dutch gold standards. The gold standard with similarity instructions (Sim) performs a bit lower on the Miller & Charles set but this difference disappears on the Rubenstein & Goodenough set.

### 5.2 Comparing Cornetto with the Dutch gold standard

The second evaluation consists of comparing the Dutch gold standards to the output of the similarity measures as calculated in Cornetto using the WordNetTools. We used the following settings to run WordNetTools:[6]

**–lmf-file** Path to Cornetto in LMF format

**–pos** no pos-filter was used

**–relations** has_hypernym, has_hyperonym,

**–input** path to Dutch gold standards

**–pairs** "words"

**–method** all.

**–depth** 15

**–subsumers** path to subsumers from the SoNaR word-frequencies

Table 2 presents the results for the different measures on the Dutch gold standard.

| SM | McNo | McRel | McSim | RgNo | RgRel | RgSim |
|---|---|---|---|---|---|---|
| path | 0.840 | 0.796 | 0.856 | **0.783** | **0.720** | **0.777** |
| lch | 0.840 | 0.796 | 0.856 | **0.783** | **0.720** | **0.777** |
| wup | 0.806 | 0.766 | 0.831 | 0.770 | 0.704 | 0.769 |
| res | 0.765 | 0.737 | 0.785 | 0.720 | 0.669 | 0.719 |
| jcn | **0.852** | **0.797** | **0.891** | 0.525 | 0.488 | 0.512 |
| lin | 0.838 | 0.779 | 0.880 | 0.531 | 0.495 | 0.520 |

Table 2: The Spearman $\rho$ is shown by comparing all six similarity measures to all six gold standards.

In general, the results show that all six semantic similarity measures correlate well with the gold standards. *Jcn* correlates best with the translation of the Miller & Charles' gold standards, whereas this is true for *path* and *lch* for the Rubenstein & Goodenough' gold standards. Finally, there is a significant difference between the performance of the measures *lin* and *jcn* when compared to the Miller & Charles' gold standards or the Rubenstein & Goodenough' gold standards. The gold standards are however too small to derive any conclusions from these differences. Larger more representative experiments are needed for that.

### 5.3 Replication English with Wordnet-LMF and WordnetToolkit

The final evaluation consists of comparing the WordNet::Similarity package to the Wordnet-Tools. This is mainly done to verify if the implementations of the semantic similarity measures are compatible across the packages, i.e. can we reproduce the results of WordNet::Similarity with the original WordNet database with WordnetTools with the WordnetLMF version of the English WordNet. In order to do this, we compare the correlations that Pedersen (2010) reports when calculating the correlations between the original gold standards and the scores from the six similarity measures using WordNet::Similarity to the same procedure but using the WordNetTools to compute the similarity scores.

We used the following settings for WordNet-Tools:[7]

**–lmf-file** Path to WordNet in LMF format

**–pos** no pos-filter was used

**–relations** has_hypernym, has_hyperonym,

**–input** path to English gold standards

**–pairs** "words"

**–method** all.

**–depth** 19

**–subsumers** path to subsumers using SemCor

Table 3 presents the results. The second and third column present the correlation as reported by Pedersen and by our package, respectively, for the gold standard by Miller & Charles, followed by the difference between the two correlations. The other columns presents the same scores for the gold standard by Rubenstein & Goodenough.

| SM | McPed | McWT | diff | RgPed | RgWT | diff |
|---|---|---|---|---|---|---|
| path | 0.68 | 0.72 | -0.04 | 0.69 | 0.78 | -0.09 |
| lch | 0.71 | 0.72 | -0.01 | 0.70 | 0.78 | -0.08 |
| wup | 0.74 | 0.74 | 0.00 | 0.69 | 0.78 | -0.09 |
| res | 0.74 | 0.75 | -0.01 | 0.69 | 0.76 | -0.07 |
| jcn | 0.72 | 0.65 | 0.07 | 0.51 | 0.56 | -0.05 |
| lin | 0.73 | 0.67 | 0.06 | 0.58 | 0.60 | -0.02 |

Table 3: Comparison of the results by Pedersen (2010) and the replication of these results using Wordnet-LMF and the WordnetToolkit

[6]The depth parameter is set to 15, which is mainly relevant for the measure *lch*, which requires the maximum depth of the taxonomy in which the synsets are located. In the case for nouns in Cornetto, this value is 15. For more information, we refer to section 6.

[7]The depth parameter is set to 19, For more information, we refer to section 6.

The results show that for both gold standards, we approach the correlations that are reported by Pedersen (2010), but that there are probably still differences in the implementation of the measures that lead to different output values.

## 6 Discussion

Three main points stand out in the results. Firstly, the correlations between the English and Dutch gold standards are very high. Given the fact that this was also the case for the Spanish and English intuitions, as discussed by Hassan and Mihalcea (2009), it might be the case the people with different mother tongues have a shared sense of *similarity of meaning*. It should be noted that all speakers from the different languages share a similar Western background. Secondly, the results for Dutch are generally higher than for English. We have no clear explanation for this difference. We know that the Dutch hypernym structure for nouns is more shallow than the English hierarchy. Evidence for this claim can be found in table 4, which shows the noun synset depth distribution for both Cornetto and Princeton WordNet:

| | Cornetto | | Princeton WordNet | |
|---|---|---|---|---|
| D | NoS | P | NoS | P |
| 0 | 833 | 1,26% | 1 | 0,00% |
| 1 | 8 | 0,01% | 59 | 0,06% |
| 2 | 2138 | 3,23% | 3286 | 3,45% |
| 3 | 2748 | 4,16% | 3943 | 4,14% |
| 4 | 7476 | 11,31% | 3222 | 3,38% |
| 5 | 15896 | 24,04% | 3186 | 3,34% |
| 6 | 15304 | 23,15% | 5951 | 6,24% |
| 7 | 8902 | 13,46% | 10474 | 10,99% |
| 8 | 4441 | 6,72% | 18071 | 18,96% |
| 9 | 2603 | 3,94% | 16049 | 16,84% |
| 10 | 2211 | 3,34% | 12313 | 12,92% |
| 11 | 1858 | 2,81% | 7984 | 8,38% |
| 12 | 1228 | 1,86% | 4714 | 4,95% |
| 13 | 406 | 0,61% | 2634 | 2,76% |
| 14 | 66 | 0,10% | 1511 | 1,59% |
| 15 | 3 | 0,00% | 917 | 0,96% |
| 16 | 0 | 0,00% | 468 | 0,49% |
| 17 | 0 | 0,00% | 345 | 0,36% |
| 18 | 0 | 0,00% | 165 | 0,17% |
| 19 | 0 | 0,00% | 30 | 0,03% |
| Total | 66121 | 100% | 95323 | 100% |

Table 4: Synset frequency and percentage of total number of synsets is shown for every depth value in Cornetto as well as WordNet. **D** abbreviates 'depth', **NoS** 'number of synsets' and **P** 'percentage of total number of synsets'.

Table 4 shows that the most frequent depth in Cornetto is 5, whereas this is 8 for Princeton WordNet. In addition, if we calculate the average noun depth in both lexical semantic databases based on the numbers in table 4, we observe that the average noun synset depth in Cornetto is 6.03 and 8.38 for Princeton WordNet. A flatter hiearchy may lead to a more rough but more uniform measure across different parts of the hiearchy. Neverthless, it does not explain the higher correlation with human intuitions. We also know that the Dutch wordnet has more multiple hypernyms. Table 5 provides evidence for this claim:

| | Cornetto | | Princeton WordNet | |
|---|---|---|---|---|
| H | NoS | P | NoS | P |
| 0 | 833 | 1,26% | 1 | 0,00% |
| 1 | 62847 | 95,05% | 93078 | 97,64% |
| 2 | 2330 | 3,52% | 2165 | 2,27% |
| 3 | 98 | 0,15% | 63 | 0,07% |
| 4 | 11 | 0,02% | 12 | 0,01% |
| 5 | 2 | 0,00% | 3 | 0,00% |
| 6 | 0 | 0,00% | 1 | 0,00% |
| Total | 66121 | 100% | 95323 | 100% |

Table 5: Synset frequency and percentage of total number of synsets is shown for every number of hypernyms value in Cornetto as well as WordNet. **H** abbreviates 'number of hypernyms', **NoS** 'number of synsets' and **P** 'percentage of total number of synsets'.

Table 5 shows that Cornetto contains relatively more synsets with multiple hypernyms than Princeton WordNet. Multiple hypernyms may lead to more options to connect synsets that can be classified according to different perspectives, e.g. being both a mammal and a pet. Nevertheless, more research is needed to find a direct explanation. If these multiple hypernyms occur at the higher levels, which is often the case, they apply to large proportions of the synsets. Besides this difference, we also observe similar patterns in the correlations. In both cases, we see a significant drop in the performance of the Information Content-based measures *jcn* and *lin*. This drop in performance emphasizes the strength and weakness of these measures. Their strength is found in the fact that if the Information Content of the words is available, the correlation with human judgement can be high. However, if the Information Content is not available, which is more often the case for the larger Rubenstein & Goodenough' gold standards, the correlation drops significantly. We do not observe this drop for the measure *res*, because this measure uses the Information Content of the least common subsumer, which is more robust than the measures *jcn* and *lin*, which are based on the Information Content of the words themselves. Finally, the differences between the scores from the WordNet::Similarity package and the WordNetTools show that we did not reproduce the results exactly. This in itself is not surprising, given the fact that Fokkens et al. (2013) showed that even replicating the results that Pedersen (2010) reports can be challenging. They showed that even if the main properties are kept stable, such as software and versions of software, variations in minor properties can lead to completely different outcomes. In addition, the reproduction learned us an interesting fact about the occassional inability of corpus statistics to distinguish between synsets. In order to use Information Content, cumulative synset frequencies are used. This creates the possibilty that a hyponym and its hypernym can have the same cumulative frequency. During our experiments, the similarity score was calculated between the synsets 'cushion#n#3' and 'pillow#n#1', where 'pillow#n#1' is a hyponym of 'cushion#n#3'. Neverthless, the cumulative frequency for both synsets is the same, which is 9. When the similarity score between these synsets was calculated for the Information Content measures, they are represented as synonyms according to these measures, which is in fact not the case in WordNet.

## 7 Conclusion

In this paper we described the results of reimplementing the similarity measures in a toolkit that can handle a wordnet in any language in Wordnet-LMF and the creation of a Dutch gold standard for similarity experiments similar to the English experiments. The toolkit can be tuned to handle any type of relation and thus can be used for various similarity and relatedness experiments, possibly adapted to the way the specific wordnet was built. We used these options to achieve a compatible structure to the English WordNet. We also created different variants of the Dutch gold standard to measure possible differences of interpretations of the task by the native speakers. We have shown that the Dutch gold standard is highly compatible to the English but that the Dutch wordnet performs better than the English WordNet to the same task. In the future, we will extend the toolkit to perform more operations and we will try to extend the experiment to other languages. We also want to experiment with different graphs to see the impact on the task. These graphs could reflect different degrees of relatedness depending on the relations that are selected. Such relations could also be derived from distributional properties of words and inserted into the graph, where they can be combined with wordnet relations or used separatedly.

## Acknowledgements

The authors wish to thank prof dr. Jan Odijk for his help in setting up the Dutch semantic similarity experiments. Moreover, we would like to thank the members of the Computational Lexicology and Terminology Web (CLTL) @ VU University Amsterdam for their feedback. Finally, we would like to thank the participants, which were: Katelijn van Knippenberg and her students from the high school *'t Atrium* in Amersfoort, Channah van 't Wout and her students from the high school *'t Hooghe Landt* in Amersfoort, Paul Vleer and his students from the high school *Maurick College* in Vught, Renny van der Sleen and her students from the high school *RSG Trompmeesters* in Steenwijkerland, and Ina van der Wekken and her students from the high school *Jacob-Roelandslyceum* in Boxtel.

## References

Christiane Fellbaum, editor (1998). *WordNet: An Electronic Lexical Database*. MIT Press, Cambridge, MA, USA.

Lev Finkelstein, Evgeniy Gabrilovich, Yossi Matias, Ehud Rivlin, Zach Solan, Gadi Wolfman and Eyran Ruppin (2002). *Placing search in context: The concept revisited.* In: Proceedings of the 10th international conference on World Wide Web, pages 406–414.

Antske Fokkens, Marieke van Erp, Marten Postma, Ted Pedersen, Piek Vossen, and Nuno Freire (2013). *Offspring from Reproduction Problems: What Replication Failure Teaches Us.* In: Proceedings of the 51st Annual Meeting of the Association for Computational Linguistics.

Iryna Gurevych (2005). *Using the structure of a conceptual network in computing semantic relatedness.* In: Proceedings of the 2nd International Joint Conference on Natural Language Processing, Jeju Island, South Korea, pages 767–778.

Samer Hassan and Rada Mihalcea (2009). *Cross-lingual semantic relatedness using encyclopedic knowledge.* In Proceedings of the 2009 Conference on Empirical Methods in Natural Language Processing: Volume 3, Singapore, pages 1192–1201.

Jay J. Jiang and David W. Conrath (1997). *Semantic similarity based on corpus statistics and lexical taxonomy.* In: Proceedings of the International Conference on Research in Computational Linguistics (ROCLING X), pages 19–33.

Colette Joubarne and Diana Inkpen (2011). *Comparison of semantic similarity for different languages using the Google n-gram corpus and second- order co-occurrence measures,* Proceedings of the 24th Canadian conference on Advances in artificial intelligence, Canadian AI'11,isbn 978-3-642-21042-6 Springer-Verlag, Berlin, Heidelberg, pages 216–22.

Claudia Leacock and Martin Chodorow (1998). *Combining local context and WordNet similarity for word sense identification.* In Fellbaum, C., editor, WordNet: An electronic lexical database, MIT Press, pages 265–283.

Michael Lesk (1986). *Automatic sense disambiguation using machine readable dictionaries: how to tell a pine cone from an ice cream cone.* In: Proceedings of the 5th annual international conference on Systems documentation, ACM, 1986.

Dekang Lin (1998). *An information-theoretic definition of similarity.* In: Proceedings of the 15th International Conference on Machine Learning, Madison, USA, pages 296–304.

George A. Miller and Walter G. Charles (1991). *Contextual correlates of semantic similarity.* Language and Cognitive Processes, 6(1):1–28.

George A. Miller, Claudia Leacock, Randee Tengi, and Ross T. Bunker (1993). *A semantic concordance.* In: Proceedings of the workshop on Human Language Technology, pages 303–308.

Nelleke Oostdijk, Martin Reynaert, Paola Monachesi, Gert-Jan Van Noord, Roeland Ordelman, Ineke Schuurman, and Vincent Vandeghinste (2008). *From D-Coi to SoNaR: a reference corpus for Dutch.* In: LREC.

Siddharth Patwardhan and Ted Pedersen (2006). *Using WordNet-based context vectors to estimate the semantic relatedness of concepts.* In: Proceedings of the EACL 2006 Workshop Making Sense of Sense-Bringing Computational Linguistics and Psycholinguistics Together, Trento, Italy, pages 1–8.

Ted Pedersen, Siddharth Patwardhan, and Jason Michelizzi (2004). *WordNet::Similarity: measuring the relatedness of concepts.* In: Demonstration Papers at HLT-NAACL 2004, Association for Computational Linguistics, pages 38–41.

Ted Pedersen (2010). *Information content measures of semantic similarity perform better without sense-tagged text.* In: Proceedings of the 11th Annual Conference of the North American Chapter of the Association for Computational Linguistics (NAACL-HLT 2010), Los Angeles, USA, pages 329–332.

Roy Rada, Hafedh Mili, Ellen Bicknell, and Maria Blettner (1989). *Development and application of a metric on semantic nets.* IEEE Transaction on Systems, Man, and Cybernetics, 19(1):17–30.

Philip Resnik (1995). *Using information content to evaluate semantic similarity in a taxonomy.* In: Proceedings of the 14th International Joint Conference on Artificial Intelligence (IJCAI), Montreal, Canada, pages 448–453.

Herbert Rubenstein and John B. Goodenough (1965). *Contextual correlates of synonymy.* Communications of the ACM, 8(10):627–633.

Piek Vossen, Attila Görög, Rubén Izquierdo, Antal van den Bosch. (2012) *DutchSemCor: Targeting the ideal sense-tagged corpus.* LREC, 584–589.

Piek Vossen, Claudia Soria, and Monica Monachini (2013). *Wordnet-LMF: a standard representation for multilingual wordnets* G. Francopoulo (ed.) LMF: Lexical Markup Framework, theory and practice, Hermes / Lavoisier / ISTE

Piek Vossen , Isa Maks, Roxane Segers, Hennie Van der Vliet, Marie-Francine Moens, Katja Hofmann, Erik Tjong Kim Sang, and Maarten De Rijke (2013). *Cornetto: a lexical semantic database for Dutch,* P. Spyns and J. Odijk (eds): Essential Speech and Language Technology for Dutch, Results by the STEVIN-programme, Publ. Springer series Theory and Applications of Natural Language Processing, ISBN 978-3-642-30909-0.

Zhibiao Wu and Martha Palmer (1994). *Verbs semantics and lexical selection.* In: Proceedings of the 32nd annual meeting on Association for Computational Linguistics, pages 133–138.

# Hydra: A Software System for Wordnet

**Borislav Rizov**
Department of Computational Linguistics
Institute for Bulgarian
Bulgarian Academy of Sciencies
Sofia, Bulgaria
boby@dcl.bas.bg

**Abstract**

This paper presents an overview of the software for wordnet processing Hydra. The system has fully-fledged GUI and API, both working with powerful modal query language. Hydra has been used for the development of the Bulgarian WordNet for the last 7 years and recently was improved, became open source and is distributed as part of the Meta-Share platform.

## 1 Introduction

During the development of Bulgarian WordNet (BulNet (Koeva et al., 2004)) at IBL[1] the need for a convenient and powerful tool for creating and processing wordnet arose. Multiple applications of wordnet in various computational linguistics tasks suggested definition and implementation of API (Application Programing Interface) to work with Wordnet as well. The presented system, Hydra, solved these problems, and provided additional benefits such as abstract mathematical query language, concurrent user access, undo / redo of user operations, synchronization between languages. As part of the project CESAR[2] Hydra was improved, the range of the supported linguistic databases that it can work with was increased, configurability and use by end users was greatly facilitated. Hydra's code was opened and is currently used by several teams working with wordnets for various languages like Croatian and Romanian.

## 2 Overview

Hydra is a system for dealing with lexical-semantic networks such as wordnet. It is open source under the GPL v3 license and it is available at: http://dcl.bas.bg/en/hydra.html. The program has a convenient and rich user interface. Hydra provides an API for access to the semantic networks of this type, which provides an abstract and easy access to such linguistic databases. It was used in the last several years for the development of BulNet. The relational model that Hydra uses is generic enough and allowed the archive of the Department of Bulgarian Dialectology and Linguistic Geography at IBL[3] to be imported and the user interface and API of Hydra used for its processing.

Hydra supports all the operations necessary for the creation of electronic linguistic databases similar to wordnet (definable in terms of a relational structure). The main features include editing of existing synsets and relations adding, editing and deleting a synonym set, reverting a single action (undo) or group of actions (cancel), returning a canceled operation (redo). The second type of features includes two operations (i) creation of synsets and relations which do not have analog in another Wordnet (e.g. language-specific concepts), and (ii) cloning synsets, an operation where synset is copied from one language wordnet to another.

Hydra is implemented in Python[4], using the platform independent GUI library Tkinter. The data is managed by a MySQL server, which remains hidden from the end users after the initial installation. The system has been successfully used on Windows and Linux.

Hydra has the following important features:

- The program allows users to edit or query any number of wordnets simultaneously. Individual wordnets can be synchronized, allowing

[1] http://dcl.bas.bg/

[2] http://cesar.nytud.hu/

[3] http://ibl.bas.bg/en/departments_en4.htm

[4] http://python.org/

simultaneous visualization of the equivalent synsets in different languages.

- Allows concurrent access by multiple users.
- The changes in the database are available to all users right after they are made.
- Powerful modal language for searching in linguistic data (Rizov, 2008), as well as an user interface with variety of predefined query utilities:
  - simple queries on words and combinations of words
  - search with regular expressions using MySQL syntax
  - search formulas - complex searches based on the Modal Language for WordNet.
- Enables checks for completeness and consistency, some of which are built into the program.

## 3 Wordnet as a Relational Structure

This paper does not aim to describe the properties and applications of wordnet. Let us just recall the main features to focus on the proposed solution. Words of the language are divided into synonym sets (synsets) and their relationships expressed in relations such as hyperonymy, antonymy, etc (semantic, morpho-semantic and other). (Vossen, 2004) The modal approach to logical representation of this formalism in Hydra suggests that wordnet is encoded as a relational structure: a set of objects and a set of binary relations between them. Consider the data in Wordnet. We have synsets provided with:

1. Identifier that is common to the equivalent meanings (synsets) in different languages (ili)
2. part-of-speech (pos)
3. encyclopedic definition (definition)

These data will be designated as *single type* because they have just one instance in one synset. We also have those of *multiple type* such as usage examples, the synsets notes (snotes) and others. Synsets comprise several words. They have, in the Bulgarian WordNet, the form of the word/compound word (word), basic form (lemma), and a unique number to identify the word sense (sense). These are the data of *single type*. The members of a synset often are provided with notes that are of *multiple type* – we may have any number of them. The following convention is adopted for encoding the data as a relational structure. Objects contain all *single type* data. Any object of multiple type is a separate object and its belonging to the original object is expressed by a relation. Thus the following 3 types of objects are defined ( we call them *linguistic units*). **Synset** contains the data: pos, ili, definition and other single type data. **Literal** represents a word in a synset and contains the data: word, form, sense. Membership of a literal to synset is expressed by the relation *literal*, so every literal in a synset is associated with a single synset with this relation. The third type of object is formally called **Note** and presents text information such as examples and notes. Several provisional relations such as *literal* are responsible to assign objects to their 'owners'. For example, usage examples are associated with synsets with the relation *usage*. An important assumption is that each object is associated to exactly one synset. Each synset is associated to itself, each literal to the synset it belongs to and each note is 'part of' exactly one synset or literal and thus inherits its synset association. This association is not explicit but it is important and is true in the other wordnet representations. It allows to synchronize linguistic units from different languages. This is achieved by synchronizing their synsets. Here it is appropriate to mention that synsets in different languages, which have the same meaning, are connected by the relation *ili*.

## 4 Modal Language for Wordnet

The main task of the modal language is to provide a clear formalism for queries with sufficient expressive power with which to address the major problems in dealing with Wordnet. This includes search, validation, synchronization of languages, etc. This modal language is easy to learn and use for the average user and does not require specialized knowledge of databases and programming which is common for other approaches. Another advantage of this abstraction is that it hides the data presentation from the user and allows its various implementations and modifications. Thus, it is extremely easy to add new relations or data (single type) in the already defined types.

Modal language in Hydra is based on that given in (Koeva et al., 2004).

### 4.1 Syntax and Semantics

Detailed syntax and semantics of The Modal Language for Wordnet is given in (Rizov, 2008). We will present how the syntax looks in Hydra and also its informal interpretation. Note that for a given formula the system returns all objects that are a model for it (the formula is true in them). Also, we will use the term query, together with a formula which is natural in the context of the system Hydra.

**Atomic Queries:**

- Each object in the database has a primary key and it is a nominal (constant) in our language. They are natural numbers divided into 3 disjoint sets, and thus their type is identifiable. Examples: 1 – Literal, 12111003 – Note, 1231100311 – The synset nominals are encoded to be portable and depend only on ili, pos and the language of the synsets they denote.

- constants $s – all synsets, $l – all literals, and $n – all text objects (of type Note) at the linguistic database.

- constants for fields of objects, $type('value')$, such as word('person'). Returns items that have a field $type$ with value $value$. To use a regular expression, add # before the first quote – word(#'c[au]t').

**Queries:**

- Atomic queries are queries.

  Let q and r be queries (formulae), then the following queries are true in the objects where:

- !q – q is not true;

- q & r – q and r are true;

- q | r – q is true or r is true;

- q => r – q is not true or r is true;

- q <=> r – q and r have the same thruth value.

  Let also R be a relation:

- In x the query <R> q is true if there is an object y, xRy and q is true in y. In other words, find those objects, for whose neighbours by the relation R the query q is true. For example, to find hypernyms of synset with number 10140069453, we need the query <~hypernym>10140069453 (~ R is the reversed relation of R) or <hyponym>10140069453.

- <R,n> q is true in the object x iff $|\{y \mid xRy \wedge y \Vdash \varphi\}| > n.$ So to find the synsets with more than one hypernym we can use the query <hypernym, 1>$s

- In x is true <R,n:m> q iff $|\{y \mid xRy \wedge y \Vdash \varphi\}|m > n|\{y \mid xRy\}|$

### 4.2 Example Queries

Here are some example queries and how they are expressed in the defined language:

- Find all literals that have word with value *game*: **word('game')**, then all of its meanings (synsets): **<literal>word('game')** and their meanings in bulgarian (bg): **<ili><literal>word('game')&lang('bg')**

- **ili('eng-30-01815628-v')** - returns the synset with the ILI eng-30-01815628-v in every wordnet in the wordnet database in which it is found

- **<snote>$n** - retrieves all the synsets that have at least one Snote

- **<literal><lnote>note('pl. t.')** – synsets that contain literals having an lnote pl. t. D. Searching in synset-to-synset relations

- **<hypernym>ili('eng-30-02396716-v')** – matches all the synsets that share a hypernym

## 5 Graphical User Interface

The user interface consists of a search window and a window with dictionaries. The search window provides the entry point to the data in the linguistic database. It also provides for opening dictionaries for the languages. A very useful innovation is the loading of results from external sources. File / Open menu command loads the file, assuming that the first word of each non-empty line is an identifier (nominal) of an object in the database. The same result is achieved by entering the path to the file in the search box prefixed with 'file:', e.g. 'file:/home/boby/biology.txt'. This functionality provides an easy way for using results from external scripts (for example, those who use API of Hydra). It is very important for some data extractions that cannot be expressed with the modal language, such as some transitive closures of relations. For example, we can find all the hyponyms of a given synset (not only immediate one) with this simple script:

```
from wordnet import wn

def hyponyms(synset):
    for h in wn.relations['hyponym'].neighbours(synset):
        print h.ID()
        hyponyms(h)

hyponyms(wn.ling(1231100311))
```

Then we can start it, store the output in file hyponyms.txt and open it in the searcher.

```
$ python hyponyms.py > hyponyms.txt
```

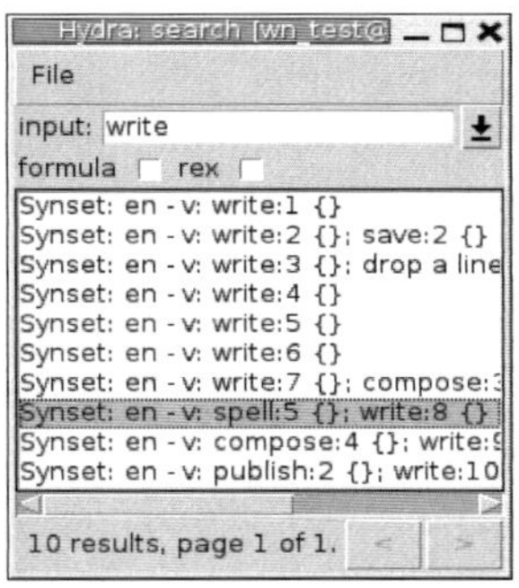


Figure 1: Search Window

Each dictionary in the second window contains multiple views for visualization of a synset. The dictionary is tied to a single language and displays the clone (see API) of the current object in this language. Dictionaries can be synchronized according to the users will.

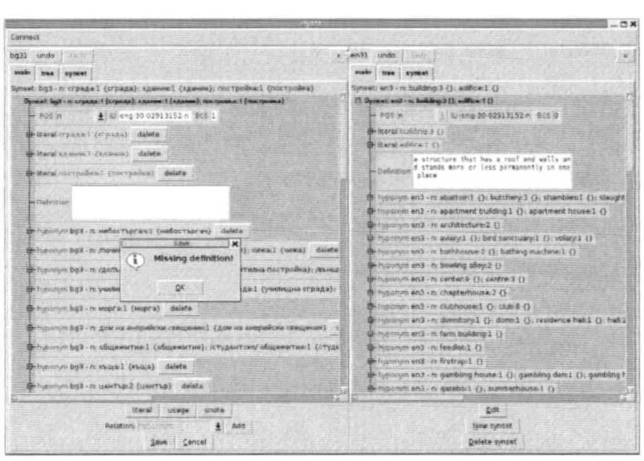

Figure 2: The Dictionaries Window

Editing and adding new linguistic units is done directly in the main view of the dictionary. Data consistency during concurrent access is provided by locking of the edited units and their neighbours. User actions in navigation and editing can be canceled one by one (undo), in groups (cancel) and redone (redo).

A detailed overview of the user interface and other features of the Hydra system is available in the user guide:

`http://dcl.bas.bg/Tools/Hydra/Hydra-UserManual.pdf`

## 6 Data Representation

When developing a solution how to store and manage the data, the choice fell to relational DBMS and specifically to MySQL. Hydra instances work directly with the MySQL server and take care for consistency of the data during the concurrent access. Modal formulas of the Language for Wordnet are translated directly to SQL queries, each returning those object where the formula is true. The main data types are stored in the tables corresponding to their names: Synset, Literal and Note. The relation pair are in table Rel. Also the table Relation keeps the definitions of the relations in Wordnet. Hydra is designed to work in a very general case(Gamma et al., 1995). The data in an object type is not strictly fixed. Its structure is configured in module descriptor.py. Consider the structure of Synset.

```
class SynsetId(Table):
    table = 'Synset'
    fields = ('id', 'ili', 'pos', 'definition',
      'stamp', 'bcs', 'lang',
      'frequency','domain')
    foreign = {'pos':  POSId,
      'lang': LangId, 'domain': DomainId}
```

In any such definition there are two mandatory fields: table – specifies the name of the database tables and fields – list of fields in that table. As is shown in the example, there is a third field, which is optional, foreign. It specifies the foreign key fields. Values in the dictionary are the descriptors of the tables whose keys are stored in the respective fields. Here, such field is pos, the part of speech of the synset. The 'Synset' table stores only keys from the table 'POS'. Its descriptor is:

```
class POSId(Table):
    table = "POS"
    fields = ('id', 'name')
```

The use of foreign keys has several advantages. Usually their values are small fixed set. This set is easily accessible and its values can be easily modified without affecting other tables in the database. For example, we can change the name of a part of speech, and that will not change any record in the table Synset. However, users will see the new name in the synsets. Another place where the changes need to be specified in the structure of the data is dbfeeder.py, which is responsible for database creation and feed with data.

## 7 API

The entry point of the Hydra API is the object *wn* in the *wordnet* module. Search by a formula is carried out with its *get* method. The method receives one argument, formula of the modal language, and returns a list of all the objects in which the formula is true. Objects in the result are in three types of objects, which build wordnet – Synset, Literal and Note. They are defined in the *linguistic_units* module.

To get all the synsets from language 'bg':

```
>>> from wordnet import wn
>>> synsets = wordnet.get("lang('bg')")
```

*wn.ling* constructs an object by its nominal (its ID in the database).

*wn.relations* is dictionary of the type 'relation name': object of type Relation (defined in module relations.py)

### 7.1 Objects

The main wordnet object types inherit the class Ling. Here are its main methods.

1. to_string(field=None) – return the string representation of the object. Can be called with an optional field name argument, in which case it returns its string value.

```
>>> literals = wn.get("word('name')")
>>> print literals[0].to_string()
name:1 {}
>>> print literals[0].to_string('word')
name
```

   More convenient way to access the field is:

```
>>> print literals[0]['word']
name
```

2. edit() – turns the object in edit mode
3. from_string(value, field) – when in edit mode, the field receives the value
4. save() – save the changes and turns the object in non-edit mode.

```
>>> print literal['word']
name
>>> literal.edit()
>>> literal.from_string('NAME', 'word')
>>> literal.save()
>>> print literal['word']
NAME
```

5. check() – Used for data consistency checks of the object and its relations. The inherited object provides implementations to maintain the invariants in the Wordnet structure. It is used by the user interface. For example, when saving a Synset it is mandatory to have at least one Literal. Literals are checked to have non-empty field word.
6. clonning(lang) – returns the corresponding object in the language lang. If lang is equal to the object language, the object itself is returned, otherwise the synset with the same ili as the synset associated with our object, but in language lang is returned.

Synset
literals() – returns the list of the literals in the synonym set.

### 7.2 Relations

Another type is that of the relations – Relation. It provides methods to add and remove elements of relation, use the reverse relation etc. Access to objects for each of the relations in the database is provided by the wn.relations dictionary, the values being of type Relation or its inheritants, such as ReverseRelation.

```
>>> relation = wn.relations['hypernym']
>>> relation['name']
u'hypernym'
>>> relation['rname']
u'hyponym'
>>> synset = wn.get("<literal>word('game')")[0]
>>> print relation.neighbours(synset)[0].to_string()
en - n: activity:2 {}
```

The example demonstrated the method *neighbours*, which returns the immediate neighbours of the given linguistic object.

### 7.3 Applications

The API is used in many products of DCL like the DCL Search Engine[5], Bulgarian WordNet–web access[6] (RESTful webservice) etc. The GUI classes were used for the open source corpora annotation tool Chooser[7] but their use is beyond the scope of this paper.


## Acknowledgments

This paper was prepared within the project Integrating New Practices and Knowledge in Un-


[5]http://search.dcl.bas.bg
[6]http://metashare.ibl.bas.bg/
[7]http://dcl.bas.bg/en/Chooser.html. Also available at Meta-Share

dergraduate and Graduate Courses in Computational Linguistics (BG051PO001-3.3.06-0022) implemented with the financial support of the Human Resources Development OP 2007-2013 co-financed by the European Social Fund of the EU. The author takes full responsibility for the content and under no conditions can the conclusions be considered a position of the European Union or the Ministry of Education, Youth and Science of the Republic of Bulgaria.

## References

Erich Gamma, R. Helm, R. Johnson and J. Vlissides. 1995. *Design Patterns: Elements of Reusable Object-Oriented Software*. Addison-Wesley.

Svetla Koeva, S. Mihov and T. Tinchev. 2004. *Bulgarian Wordnet - Structure and Validation* volume 7, No. 1-2: 61–78. Journal: Romanian Journal of Information Science and Technology.

Svetla Koeva 2010. *Bulgarian Wordnet - current state, applications and prospects*. Bulgarian-American Dialogues, Prof. M. Drinov Academic Publishing House. Sofia. 120–132

Borislav Rizov. 2008. *Processing Wordnet with Modal Logic*: 93–100. Proceedings of the 6th International Conference on Formal Approaches to South Slavic and Balkan Languages.

Piek Vossen. 2004. *EuroWordNet: A Multilingual Database of Autonomous and Language-Specific Wordnets Connected via an Inter-Lingual Index*. International Journal of Lexicography, 17(1): 161–173, June.

# Taking stock of the African Wordnets project: 5 years of development

**Marissa Griesel**
University of South Africa (UNISA)
Pretoria, South Africa
griesel.marissa@gmail.com

**Sonja Bosch**
University of South Africa (UNISA)
Pretoria, South Africa
boschse@unisa.ac.za

## Abstract

This paper reports on the development of the prototype African Wordnet (AWN) which currently includes four languages. The resource has been developed by translating Common Base Concepts from English, and currently holds roughly 42 000 synsets. We describe here how some language specific and technical challenges have been overcome and discuss efforts to localise the content of the wordnet and quality assurance methods. A comparison of the number of synsets per language is given before concluding with plans to fast-track the development and for dissemination of the resource.

## 1 Introduction

Wordnets for African languages were introduced with a training workshop for linguists, lexicographers and computer scientists facilitated by international experts in 2007. The development of wordnet prototypes for four official South African languages started in 2008 as the African Wordnet Project. This project was based on collaboration between the Department of African Languages at the University of South Africa (UNISA) and the Centre for Text Technology (CTexT) at the North-West University (NWU), as well as support from the developers of the DEBVisDic tools at the Masaryk University[1]. The initiative resulted in first versions of wordnets for isiZulu [zul], isiXhosa [xho], Setswana [tsn] and Sesotho sa Leboa (Sepedi) [nso][2], all members of the Bantu language family. An expansion of the African Wordnet followed in 2011, and currently the development has entered a third phase that aims at solidifying the African Wordnets as a valued resource with formal quality assurance, as well as further expansion of the synsets, definitions and usage examples. Figure 1 gives an overview of the development, as well as the deliverables in each phase.

In this paper, we reflect critically on the previous phases in development including challenges faced and solutions to some common problems. Section 3 gives a brief report on the current standing of the African wordnets and sections 4 and 5 give details regarding future work.

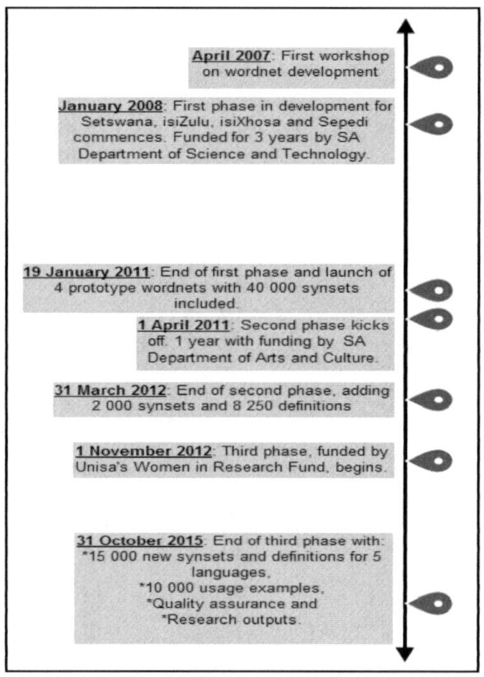


Figure. 1. Timeline of development in the African Wordnet Project.

## 2 Status quo after the first 2 phases

During the first phase (2008-2010), linguists who had participated in the introductory workshop were invited to partake in the project. Linguists representing the four languages mentioned above, volunteered and since then, the development has been constant with two phases completed. Table 1 gives a

[1] See http://deb.fi.muni.cz/clients-debvisdic.php

[2] Each language is followed by its ISO 639-3 code (ISO 2012) in order to distinguish one language from other languages with the same or similar names and to identify the names of cross-border languages.

summary of the total number of synsets and definitions that have been developed thus far.

| Language | Synsets | Definitions |
|---|---|---|
| isiZulu | 10 000 | 2563 |
| isiXhosa | 10 000 | 2370 |
| Setswana | 15 000 | 1755 |
| Sesotho sa Leboa (Sepedi) | 7005 | 2062 |
| Total | 42005 | 8250 |

Table 1. Total number of synsets and definitions developed for four African languages.

As will be mentioned in section 3, the team faced many challenges and had to apply some creative problem solving at times. During the first two phases, important fundamental training and development had to be done, for instance a second workshop, again facilitated by international wordnet experts was held at the beginning of 2011, followed by training on more technical aspects of wordnet development such as automated quality control, in 2012. The core project team has stayed largely unchanged and renewed funding for a third phase of development contributed to the continued growth of the African Wordnets.

## 3 Challenges to the development of African Wordnets

### 3.1 Availability of resources

The languages in this project are considered resource scarce compared to most other languages listed in The Global WordNet Organization[3] in the sense that lexical resources are relatively limited. The four languages included in the project so far, however, each have at least one or two paper dictionaries available, ranging from monolingual to bilingual general purpose or learners' dictionaries. Apart from a basic on-line dictionary for Sesotho sa Leboa[4] and isiZulu.net[5], which is an online isiZulu-English dictionary that anyone can contribute to, containing bidirectional lookups as well as basic morphological decomposition, there are no online or machine-readable lexicons available for any of the languages.

Currently only relatively restricted unannotated and not freely accessible corpora are available. For example, the University of Pretoria Corpora (Prinsloo & de Schryver, 2005:101) range from approximately two to nine million tokens for the various South African languages. Three types of corpora have been collected, viz. general purpose (LGP) corpora, special-purpose (LSP) corpora and true parallel corpora. The main characteristics of the eleven South African LGP corpora, which are the biggest of the three types built, are shown in Table 2.

| Corpus Name | Acronym | Tokens | Types |
|---|---|---|---|
| Pretoria isiNdebele Corpus | PNC | 1,959,482 | 250,990 |
| Pretoria siSwati Corpus | PSwC | 4,442,666 | 293,156 |
| Pretoria isiXhosa Corpus | PXhC | 8,065,349 | 846,162 |
| Pretoria isiZulu Corpus | PZC | 5,783,634 | 674,380 |
| Pretoria Xitsonga Corpus | PXiC | 4,556,959 | 115,848 |
| Pretoria Tshivenda Corpus | PTC | 4,117,176 | 118,771 |
| Pretoria Setswana Corpus | PSTC | 6,130,557 | 157,274 |
| Pretoria Sesotho sa Leboa Corpus | PSC | 8,749,597 | 165,209 |
| Pretoria Sesotho Corpus | PSSC | 4,513,287 | 107,102 |

Table 2. Pretoria LPG corpora.

Smaller, unannotated parallel corpora are freely available from the newly established Resource Management Agency (RMA). Recently the NLP Group of the University of Leipzig has also made corpora for most of the languages in the African Wordnet project, freely available (Wortschatz Universität Leipzig, 2013). Although these corpora are unannotated and still relatively small, the development work seems promising.

The agglutinating nature of the African languages belonging to the Bantu language family, particularly for those with a conjunctive orthography e.g. isiZulu and isiXhosa, call for morphological annotation for the purposes of accurate corpus searches. Although prototypes of rule-based morphological analysers have been developed for the mentioned two languages, these are not freely available yet (cf. Bosch et al., 2008).

[3] See http://globalwordnet.org/?page_id=38

[4] See http://africanlanguages.com/sdp/

[5] See http://isizulu.net/

Due to the limited availability of lexicographic and basic language resources for the African languages, wordnet construction thus presents a challenging and time-consuming task for the linguists.

### 3.2 Language specific challenges

A number of language specific challenges anticipated at the beginning of the project are discussed in Le Roux et al. (2007) and will not be repeated here. However, a number of additional challenges were encountered, some of which are dealt with in more detail in a parallel paper (cf. Mojapelo, 2014). For example, consider the following synset for “breaststroke”[6]:

> {00572097} <noun.act>[04] S: (n) breaststroke#1 (a swimming stroke; the arms are extended together in front of the head and swept back on either side accompanied by a frog kick)

A whole discussion arose around the isiZulu version of the above synset since a dictionary entry of the verb *-gwedla* (swim by breaststroke OR paddle/row) was found in a bilingual dictionary (Doke & Vilakazi, 1964:285). The debate among linguists was whether *-gwedla* in the infinitive, i.e. *ukugwedla* (lit. to swim by breaststroke) would be a suitable representation in isiZulu. Some felt that *-gwedla* is more commonly used in the context of ‘rowing an actual boat’. To complicate matters, no equivalents for other swimming strokes such as butterfly, backstroke, freestyle etc. are lexicalised in isiZulu, or for that matter, any of the languages in the project.

### 3.3 Technical challenges

One of the major worries for the African Wordnets team, was securing continual funding for the very important base work. Not only was funding needed to provide technical assistance and project management, but also to reimburse linguists for the linguistic development of the wordnets. All of the linguists involved with this project are employed full time at academic institutions and are not able to devote much of their workday to development of the wordnets, slowing progress almost to a standstill. The BalkaNet project, for instance, also incentivised or contracted the initial development of wordnets for Bulgarian, Greek, Romanian, Serbian and Turkish. The core wordnets delivered at the end of the 3 year project contained roughly 8000 synsets, developed in 3 years – comparative to our 10 000 synsets in each of our African wordnets. The Serbian team then continued development on a voluntary basis and in the next 2 years (2006 – 2008) could only add another 2240 synsets (Krstev et al., 2008). This supports our decision to apply for further funding and continue incentivising the development in order to speed up the process to a point that the wordnets are a truly useful tool for the creation of other NLP applications (where an excess of 200 000 synsets have proven to make a considerable difference in the quality those applications can deliver).

A number of problems with the connection to the server were reported by the linguists. These problems related mainly to the high level of network security and restricted access at the universities involved. The project team was dependent on collaboration of IT-departments from three universities, as we had no direct control over security policies, firewalls, etc. The distance between the linguists (mostly at UNISA in Pretoria, South Africa) and the support team (NWU in Potchefstroom, some 160 km away) also posed a threat to project progress. This risk was managed through an intent focus on regular communication between the sites, and the implementation of a backup plan, namely reverting to working on Microsoft® Excel spreadsheets during ‘down-time’, and then importing them to the database and online DEBVisDic environment afterwards. Some linguists also experienced regular interruptions in internet connectivity due to a weaker infrastructure in the whole of South Africa. Being able to revert to this offline method, meant that they could continue working from home without needing a constant internet connection.

Human capital development also took time and since this is the first project of its kind for African languages, new technical skills, like working with the DEBVisDic tools, had to be learnt. Because of the slow progress in the first project, the project team had to include more

[6] See `http://wordnetweb.princeton.edu/perl/webwn?c=6&sub=Change&o2=1&o0=1&o8=1&o1=1&o7=1&o5=1&o9=&o6=1&o3=1&o4=1&i=0&h=10000&s=breaststroke`

linguists in the development of synsets and definitions than initially planned. The advantages of this were twofold. Not only did the progress speed up significantly and were we able to deliver the contracted number of new synsets and definitions on time, but more South African linguists were trained in development of wordnets.

## 4 Current development

### 4.1 Introducing the third phase

The aim of the current third project is an extended scope of the African Wordnet Project which gained considerable momentum over the past 4 years. Our primary aim is to develop at least 15 000 new synsets and definitions, to add usage examples to existing synsets and to do continual quality assurance on the wordnets. Most importantly, a 5th African language, Tshivenda [ven], is being added to the project. From the previous phases, it became clear that a stronger emphasis needs to be placed on localisation of the wordnet. It was found that many synsets in the English wordnet are not concepts that belong in the African environment (lexicalised items). During this phase, greater care will be taken to ensure that truly African synsets are included.

### 4.2 Quality assessment and semi-automatic assistance

As mentioned earlier, very few core technologies exist for the resource scarce African languages. For this reason, many of the internationally proven methods to do quality assessment on wordnets could not be applied (cf. Smrz, 2004 and Kotzé, 2008). The team did have access to proprietary spelling checkers developed for Microsoft® Office. These spelling checkers can be seen as so called first generation technologies, since very little language analysis like with grammar or morphological analysers is available and they rely strongly on lexicon lookup.

The Excel sheets and online versions of the wordnets were consolidated in a single XML file per language before three categories of possible errors were identified automatically. Cells with potential problems were indicated with coloured formatting and linguists were asked to pay special attention while doing quality assessment to these cells. The error categories are:

- Possible spelling errors,
- Empty (critical) fields, and
- Formatting errors (i.e. missing or invalid sense numbers, English IDs and SUMO/MILO relations, recognised with a simple Perl script).

### 4.3 Localisation of the base concepts

Most of the initial decisions made regarding the design of the African wordnets, were based on the experiences of 2 international projects, namely the BalkaNet project and the EuroNet Project. In both these successful endeavours, the project teams drew up an initial list of the most important concepts to use as seed terms to start building wordnets. These so-called Base Concepts are regarded as "the fundamental building blocks for establishing the relations in a wordnet and give information about the dominant lexicalization patterns in languages" (GWA, 2013). The list of Common Base Concepts created in the EuroNet project contains roughly 1024 synsets. These Common Base Concepts were extended to 5000 synsets and mapped to the Princeton WordNet 2.0 in the BalkaNet project, using a similar approach, but applied to other (mostly European) languages.

During the first 2 phases, we followed the guidance given in the extended Common Base Concepts lists. It soon became clear that a more localised approach was needed, as this and the Princeton Core Concepts list[7] contain concepts that do not accurately describe the African context. Linguists were spending too much time on foreign concepts and especially the less experienced linguists did not have the confidence to venture off this list too far. Table 3 gives some examples of nouns that are not lexicalised in the African languages.

| Princeton core set | EuroNet base concepts |
|---|---|
| abbey | abnegator |
| apparatus | bellyacher |
| aquarium | calligrapher |
| baseball | gasbag |
| bishop | mesomorph |
| buffet | scaremonger |
| kit | slowcoach |
| mars | tiger |
| mosaic | twerp |
| soprano | urchin |

Table 3. Unfamiliar words in international standards.

[7] See `http://wordnet.princeton.edu/`

When adding the new Tshivenda wordnet to this project, we decided to take a careful look at the concepts we use as the seed terms. Our premise was that more localised terms might be extracted from real-world parallel corpora. To examine the difference, a multilingual parallel corpus, including English, Setswana, isiZulu, isiXhosa, Sesotho sa Leboa and Tshivenda equivalents was acquired from the RMA. The English version of the parallel corpus contained 50 000 tokens and was used to compare the African languages data to the Princeton core concepts.

From the multilingual corpus, we extracted a frequency list for Tshivenda and Setswana. The next step was to compare the 5000 most frequent Tshivenda and Setswana words in the multilingual African wordlist to the list of (English) base and core concepts mentioned above. Table 4 below shows some of the concepts unique to the African language list. The frequency of the word is given in brackets.

| Noun | Frequency |
|---|---|
| benefit | 2042 |
| basket | 71 |
| conflict | 419 |
| lodge | 177 |
| malaria | 355 |
| mandate | 838 |
| mine | 321 |
| money | 1592 |
| soil | 104 |
| water | 2964 |

Table 4. Frequent nouns from a large multilingual African language corpus.

It is clear that our frequency list includes concepts that reflect unique African language usage. The Princeton and EuroNets lists both include concepts that might not be completely unknown in an African context, but that certainly are less commonly used.

The new approach proposed in this third phase of the African Wordnets project entails extracting a subset of concepts that were present in this list. We now have a list of concepts that are both internationally regarded and frequent in African corpora. This new list of roughly 1000 concepts was shared with the linguists as a starting point for Tshivenda. For the other four languages, we extracted the list of concepts that were not added in the previous projects to use as a starting point for new development in this phase.

## 5 Conclusion and future work

### 5.1 Comparing development in the 4 languages

Figures 2 and 3 represent the total number of synsets and definitions for each language combination. This comparative review gives a clear indication of fast-tracking possibilities for each language by using the synsets/definitions of its closely related counterpart language. For example, synsets or definitions developed for isiZulu and not for isiXhosa, can be fast-tracked for the latter since both languages belong to the Nguni language group, and vice versa. On the other hand, synsets or definitions developed for Setswana and not for Sesotho sa Leboa (Sepedi), can be fast-tracked for the latter since both languages belong to the Sotho language group, and vice versa.

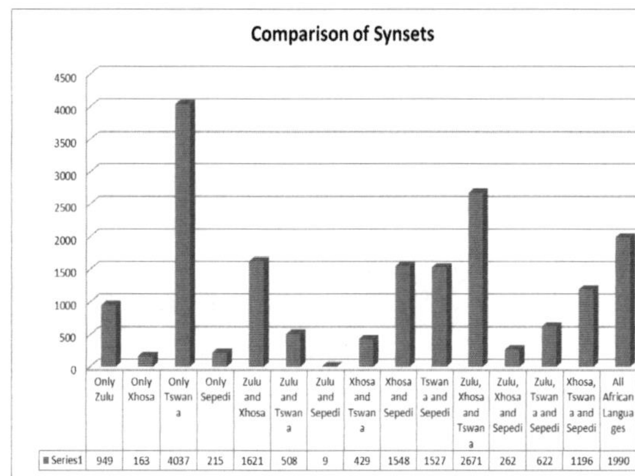


Figure 2. Comparison of synsets completed for each language.

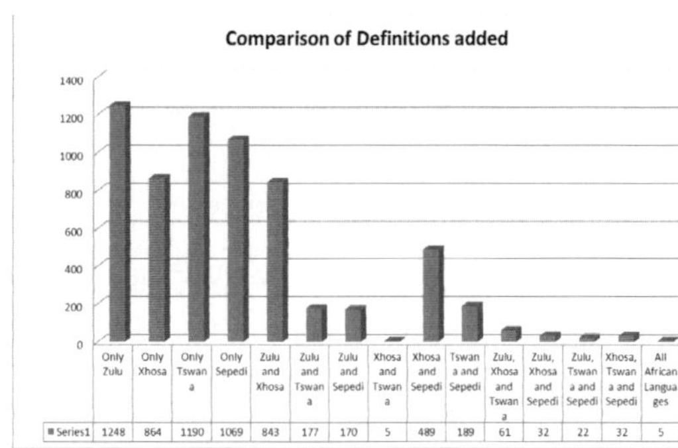


Figure 3. Comparison of definitions completed for each language.

### 5.2 Dissemination of the information

Since the resource that will be further developed in this project is vital to so many linguistic and language technology endeavours, it is essential that it be accessible to all researchers in the field. After quality assurance (see section 4.2) the wordnets will be included in the repository of the RMA, who will advertise and make available the wordnets for others to use. The appropriate licensing options and usage rights (most probably under one of the Creative Commons licenses[8]), will also be determined in conjunction with the RMA.

### 5.3 Conclusion

The African Wordnet project is unique in its approach to create wordnets for several languages in parallel, resulting in a very important language resource. This approach allows team members to share experiences during the process and thus build the lexicon more effectively. It also allows for a multilingual resource that can be applied in various other technologies, such as for machine translation, extracting content for learner's dictionaries and other teaching material, but also as a reference for linguists. There is still much work to be done, but by learning from previous projects and keeping the ultimate goal of a rich linguistc resource in mind, we trust that this work will fill many gaps in NLP in South Africa and Africa as a whole.

## Acknowledgements

The authors would like to thank the UNISA Women in Research Fund for financial support in this third project, as well as Christiane Fellbaum, Karel Pala, Piek Vossen and Adam Rambousek for their invaluable advice. Without the vast linguistic knowledge and dedication of the linguists working on the development of the African Wordnet, this project would also not be as successful. Comments of two anonymous reviewers are also appreciated.

## References

Sonja Bosch, Laurette Pretorius and Axel Fleisch. 2008. Experimental Bootstrapping of Morphological Analysers for Nguni Languages. *Nordic Journal of African Studies,* 17(2):66-88. http://www.njas.helsinki.fi/

Clement Doke and Benedict Vilakazi. 1964. *Zulu–English Dictionary*. Witwatersrand University Press, Johannesburg.

Global Wordnet Association. 2013. GWA Base Concepts.

ISO 639-3.http://www.sil.org/iso639-3

Cvetana Krstev, Bojana Đorđević, Sanja Antonić, Nevena Ivković-Berček, Zorica Zorica, Vesna Crnogorac and Ljiljana Macura. 2008. Cooperative work in further development of Serbian Wordnet. *INFOTHECA – Journal of Informatics and Librarianship.* 1(2):59-78. http://infoteka.bg.ac.rs/PDF/Eng/2008/INFOTHECA_IX_1-2_May2008_59a-78a.pdf

Gideon Kotzé. 2008. Ontwikkeling van 'n Afrikaanse woordnet : metodologie en integrasie. *Literator : Journal of Literary Criticism, Comparative Linguistics and Literary Studies : Human language technology for South African languages,* 29(1):168 – 184.

Jurie le Roux, Koliswa Moropa, Sonja Bosch & Christiane Fellbaum. 2007. Introducing the African Languages Wordnet, in Attila Tanács, Dóra Csendes, Veronika Vincze, Christiane Fellbaum, Piek Vossen (eds.) *Proceedings of The Fourth Global WordNet Conference*, Szeged, Hungary, January 22-25, 2008, pp 269-280. Szeged: University of Szeged, Department of Informatics (ISBN 978-963-482-854-9).

Mampaka Mojapelo. 2013. Morphological considerations for encoding the qualificative in African Wordnet with reference to Northern Sotho. *To be presented* at the Global Wordnet Conference 2014. Tartu, Estonia. 25 – 29 January 2014.

Princeton Wordnet. 2013. http://wordnetweb.princeton.edu

Danie Prinsloo & Gilles-Maurice de Schryver. 2005. Managing eleven parallel corpora and the extraction of data in all official South African languages. In W. Daelemans, T. du Plessis, C. Snyman & L. Teck (eds.) *Multilingualism and Electronic Language Management. Proceedings of the 4th International MIDP Colloquium*, Bloemfontein, South Africa, 22-23 September 2003. pp 100–122. Pretoria: Van Schaik Publishers.

Resource Management Agency (RMA). 2013. http://rma.nwu.ac.za/

Pavel Smrz. 2008. Quality Control and Checking for Wordnet Development: A Case Study of BalkaNet. *Romanian Journal of Information Science and Technology*, 7(1):173-181.

Wortschatz Universität Leipzig. 2013. http://corpora.informatik.uni-leipzig.de/

[8] See http://creativecommons.org/licenses/

# RuThes Linguistic Ontology vs. Russian Wordnets

**Natalia Loukachevitch**
Research Computing Center
of Lomonosov Moscow State
University
louk_nat@mail.ru

**Boris Dobrov**
Research Computing Center
of Lomonosov Moscow State
University
dobrov_bv@mail.ru

## Abstract

The paper describes the structure and current state of RuThes – thesaurus of Russian language, constructed as a linguistic ontology. We compare RuThes structure with the WordNet structure, describe principles for inclusion of multiword expressions, types of relations, experiments and applications based on RuThes. For a long time RuThes has been developed within various NLP and information-retrieval projects, and now it became available for public use.

## 1 Introduction

Since its appearance Princeton WordNet has attracted a lot of attention of researchers and other specialists in natural language processing and information retrieval (Fellbaum, 1998). National wordnets for many languages in the world were initiated.

For developing a wordnet for a new language, several approaches can be applied. The first approach is based on automated or manual translation of Princeton WordNet (Balkova et al., 2008; Linden and Carlson, 2010). The second approach consists in creating of a wordnet from scratch using language-specific dictionaries and corpora (Climent et al., 1996; Azarowa, 2008; Kunze and Lemnitzer, 2010). This approach often implies the modification of the initial set of Princeton WordNet lexical relationships, introduction and justification of new relations, which usually requires additional time-consuming efforts (Maziarz et al., 2013; Pedersen et al., 2012).

At least three attempts to create a Russian wordnet are known. RussNet (Azarowa, 2008) began to be developed from scratch and at this moment continues to be quite small (not more than 20 thousand synsets). Two other Russian wordnets were generated using automated translation (Gelfenbeyn et al., 2003; Balkova et al., 2008). The former one is publicly available (`http://wordnet.ru/`) but represents the direct translation from Princeton Wordnet without any manual revision. The webpage of the latter one ceased to exist.

The structure of Princeton WordNet (and other wordnets) is based on sets of partial synonyms – synsets, organized in hierarchical part-of-speech-based lexical nets according mainly to hyponymy-hypernymy relations. Every part-of-speech net has its own system of relations.

Wordnets are often referred as linguistic or lexical ontologies (Magnini and Speranza, 2002; Veale and Hao, 2007), synsets of WordNet are often considered as lexicalized concepts. However, wordnets are mainly intended to describe lexical relations, what is quite different from the primary aim of ontologies to describe knowledge about the world, not about the language (Buitelaar et al., 2009; Nirenburg and Raskin, 2004). This difference reveals, for example, in the above mentioned division of wordnets to different part-of-speech subnets, because a part of speech cannot be a divisive feature in construction of ontologies.

In this paper we will consider the structure and current state of Thesaurus of Russian language (linguistic ontology) RuThes, which for a long time has been developed within various NLP and information-retrieval projects (Loukachevitch and Dobrov, 2002), and now it is prepared to become available for public use. In this resource we attempted to create a linguistically motivated ontology (not a lexical net), based on the denotational part of lexical senses and concept-based (not lexical) relations. At present, RuThes comprises more than 158 thousand unique words and expressions, which are structured into 53.5 thousand concepts.

The structure of this paper is as follows. Section 2 is devoted to the comparison of units in ontologies, wordnets and information-retrieval thesauri. In Section 3 main components of RuThes are considered. In Section 4 we describe several applications and the evaluation of RuThes. At last in Section 5 we describe our licensing policy for RuThes distribution.

## 2 Units in Ontologies, Wordnets and Information-Retrieval Thesauri

Ontologies are often considered as logical theories, which should be independent of natural language (Buitelaar et al., 2009; Smith, 2004). The general recommendations on the ontology concepts (classes) are usually described as follows (Noy and McGuinness, 2001; Nirenburg and Raskin, 2004):

- one needs to distinguish the concept and its name, i.e. synonyms do not represent different classes, synonyms are just different names of the concepts
- a concept should be distinctly different from its parent and from the concepts at the same level (sibling concepts).

However, to use ontologies in natural language processing, concepts of ontologies should be associated with language expressions and structures. In (Maedche and Zacharias, 2002; Buitelaar et al., 2006; Buitelaar et al., 2009) special models for linking natural language expressions and ontological entities are proposed.

From another point of view, an ontology cannot be fully independent of natural language. Ch. Brewster and colleagues (Brewster et al., 2005) stress that people manipulate concepts through words. In all known ontologies the words are used to represent concepts. Therefore, phenomena that are not verbalized, cannot be modeled. Y. Wilks (Wilks, 2008) asserts that the symbols in representation languages are fundamentally based on the natural language.

WordNet was created as a lexical rather than ontological resource (Fellbaum, 1998). However, over time, the growing importance of the ontological research, as well as the similarity of the WordNet noun hierarchy with an ontology became apparent (Miller and Hristea, 2006).

At the same time there exist a lot of deficiencies of WordNet descriptions from the ontological point of view (Guarino, 1998). Numerous examples of confusion between a concept and its names can be found in WordNet (Loukachevitch, 2009). Separate synsets are introduced for different ways of naming the same entities including the support of specific hierarchies for different parts of speech, for description of old and new names of the same entities, specific word usage in different dialects of the language or text genres (*moke - donkey*, *nose - nozzle*) etc. This is due to the fact that the basic relation in WordNet is the synonymy, based on the principle of substitution of one for another in sentences (Fellbaum, 1998). Some of new wordnets enhance the diversity of lexical relations between words to describe mainly their derivational links (Azarowa, 2008; Derwojedowa et al., 2008; Maziarz et al., 2013; Bosch et al., 2008).

However, it was supposed in (Edmonds and Hirst, 2002; Hirst, 2009) that a fine-grained hierarchy is inappropriate as a model for the relationship between the senses of near-synonyms in a lexicon for any practical use in tasks such as machine translation and other applications. They assert that, "what is required is a very coarse-grained conceptual hierarchy so that whole clusters of near-synonyms are mapped to a single node: their core meaning".

If to look at information-retrieval thesauri as representative sources of the terminology and domain knowledge one can see that most standards and guidelines for information-retrieval thesauri construction highlight the connection between the terms and concepts of a subject field (ISO 2788-1986, 1986; Z39.19, 2005). So the American standard Z39.19 points out that a term is one or more words referring to a concept (Z39.19, 2005). A concept is considered as a unit of a thought, regardless of the terms that express them.

Creating RuThes as an ontology with concept-based (not lexical) relations, we assumed that the concept-oriented approach to the lexical knowledge representation gives the possibility of better matching between languages (Edmonds and Hirst, 2002), more natural connection with domain terminologies, which are inherently concept-based (Z39.19, 2005); and more reliable logical inference based on current ontological research (Masolo et al., 2003; Guarino, 2009; Guizzardi, 2011).

## 3 RuThes linguistic ontology

RuThes Thesaurus of Russian language can be called a linguistic ontology for natural language processing, i.e. an ontology, where the majority of concepts are introduced on the basis of actual language expressions.

In construction of RuThes we combined three different methodologies:

- methods of construction of information-retrieval thesauri (concept-based units, a small set of relation types, rules of multi-word expression inclusion)
- development of wordnets for various languages (language-motivated units, detailed sets of synonyms, description of ambiguous expressions)
- ontology research (concepts as main units, strictness of relation description, necessity of many-step inference).

RuThes is a hierarchical network of concepts. Each concept has a name, relations with other concepts, a set of language expressions (words, phrases, terms) whose meanings correspond to the concept.

### 3.1 RuThes units

In RuThes, a unit is presented not by a set of similar words or terms, as it is done in the WordNet thesaurus, but by a concept – as a unit of thought, which can be associated with several synonymic language expressions. Every concept should have distinctions from related concepts, which are independent from context and should be expressed in specific set of relations or associated language expressions – text entries.

Words and phrases, which meanings are represented as references to the same concepts of the thesaurus, are called ontological synonyms. Ontological synonyms can comprise:

- words belonging to different parts of speech (*stabilization, stabilize, stabilized*) – therefore the number of RuThes concepts is approximately 2.5 times less than in a wordnet-like resource of the same size. Text entries are provided with part-of speech information;
- language expressions relating to different linguistic styles, genres;
- idioms and even free multiword expressions (for example, synonymous to single words).

Each concept should have a clear, univocal and concise name. Such names often help to express, delimit the denotational scope of the concept. Besides, such names facilitate the analysis of the results of natural language processing.

Name of a concept can be:

- one of unambiguous text entries;
- an unambiguous multiword expression;
- a pair of synonyms that uniquely identifies the concept;
- an ambiguous word with a relator similar to those used in traditional information retrieval thesauri (Z39.19, 2005).

If necessary, a concept may have a gloss, which is not a part of the concept name.

Language expressions that may give rise to a separate concept in RuThes belong not only to the general vocabulary, but also can be terms of specific subject domains within the broad scope of social life (economy, law, international relations, politics, transport, banks, etc.), so-called *socio-political domain* (Loukachevitch and Dobrov, 2004).

This is due to the fact that many professional concepts, terms, and slang of these domains penetrate easily into the general language, and can be widely discussed in mass media. Besides, such a scope of concepts facilitates the application of RuThes in specialized subdomains of the broad socio-political domain. Examples of such concepts in RuThes include: *EMERGENCY LOAN, TAX EXEMPTION, IMPORT TAX, DEMOGRAPHIC INDICATOR* etc.

In fact, we subdivide the whole scope of RuThes concepts to:

- **General Lexicon** comprising concepts that can be met in various specific domains. In this, General Lexicon approximately corresponds to the Factotum domain in the Wordnet domain set (Gonzalez et al., 2012; Bentivogli et al., 2004),
- and **Socio-political Thesaurus** containing thematically oriented lexemes and multiword expressions as well as domain-specific terms of the broad sociopolitical domain.

After a concept has been introduced, an expert searches for all possible synonyms or derivative synonyms (that is derivates preserving the sense of an initial word), single words and phrases that can be associated with this concept. For example, a concept *ДУШЕВНОЕ СТРАДАНИЕ (wound in the soul)* has more than 20 text entries including such as: *боль, боль в душе, в душе на-*

*болело, душа болит, душа саднит, душевная пытка, душевная рана, душевный недуг, наболеть, рана в душе, рана в сердце, рана души, саднить (*several English translations may be as follows: *wound, emotional wound, pain in the soul* etc.).

At present RuThes includes 53.5 thousand concepts, 158 thousand unique text entries (75 thousand single words), 178 thousand concept-text entry relations, more than 215 thousand conceptual relations.

### 3.2 Multiword expressions in RuThes

One of difficult issues in wordnet development is inclusion of synsets based on senses of multiword expressions, for example noun compounds (Bentivogli and Pianta, 2004; Agirre et al., 2006; Kunze and Lemnitzer, 2010). Two main questions are usually discussed here: what are the principles of inclusion of multiword expressions (especially compositional or semi-compositional ones) and what types of relations should connect a multiword expression and its components in the wordnet structure.

In RuThes introduction of concepts based on multiword expressions is not restricted and even encouraged if (and only if) this concept adds some new information to knowledge described in RuThes.

Such additional information may be subdivided into several types.

*A concept denotes an important entity.* So in our Russia-oriented resource *ПРЕЗИДЕНТ РОССИЙСКОЙ ФЕДЕРАЦИИ* (*Russian President*) is an example of such a concept. Another variant of the same issue is the existence of important parts or participants for an entity or event. So, for *АРЕНДА* (lease) concept, such additional concepts as *АРЕНДНАЯ ПЛАТА* (*lease payment*), *АРЕНДНЫЙ ДОГОВОР* (*lease agreement*), *АРЕНДНОЕ ИМУЩЕСТВО* (*leasehold property*) are introduced, because they present important issues of lease services. At the same time concept *АРЕНДНЫЙ ДОГОВОР* (lease agreement) is an important subtype of concept *ГРАЖДАНСКО-ПРАВОВОЙ ДОГОВОР* (*legal agreement*).

*A new concept has relations that do not follow from the component structure of an underlying multiword expression.* This is a reason to introduce concept *ИЗБРАНИЕ ПАПЫ РИМСКОГО (papal election)* - it has a relation to concept *КОНКЛАВ (papal conclave).* Another example is concept *ТЮНИНГ АВТОМОБИЛЯ (car tuning)* having relations to concepts *АВТОСЕРВИС (auto service).*

*A new multiword-based concept has a text entry that is not motivated by the component structure* of a basic expression, for example, concept *ЗАСНУТЬ ЗА РУЛЕМ* describes also an "interesting" synonym *заснуть во время движения (*compare English expressions *falling asleep at the wheel and falling asleep while driving).* Also this concept has an "interesting" relation to concept *ДОРОЖНО-ТРАНСПОРТНОЕ ПРОИСШЕСТВИЕ (road accident).*

At last, an important additional factor, which can stimulate inclusion of a concept to the thesaurus, is the ambiguity of components of an unambiguous phrase, such as *положение дел (state of affairs).*

### 3.3 RuThes relations

RuThes relations are of conceptual nature, not lexical ones. It is not a simple task to choose an appropriate set of relations for such a broad and diverse scope of concepts. RuThes has a small set of conceptual relations consisting of three main relations that are also applicable to a lot of various domains (Dobrov and Loukachevitch, 2006) and describe the most important links of a concept.

The first relation is the traditional hyponymic (taxonomic) relation. To establish such relations we apply additional tests similar to ones used in ontology development. The tests are directed to avoid incorrect use of taxonomic relations and not to mix them up with other types of relations, because errors in relation types degrade logical inference Gangemi et al., 2001).

We consider role-type relations as especially dangerous ones when a role concept (such as *EMPLOYEE*) is located as a parent concept for a type (as *PERSON*) (see discussion about roles and related problems in (Guarino, 1998; Gangemi et al., 2001; Fellbaum, 2002)). Therefore establishing the taxonomic relationship we also check the fulfillment of the following principle: every instance of a child concept should be at the same time the instance of a parent concept (*not every person is an employee*).

The second conceptual relation used in RuThes is the part-whole relation. The part-whole relations can be applied in various domains, exist in diverse forms. Therefore in computer resources different approaches representing these relations can be taken (Winston et al., 1987; Guarino, 2009; Sowa,

2000). So, for example, the tradition to describe part-whole relations in wordnets differs considerably from the guidelines of information-retrieval thesauri construction (Z39.19, 2005; Fellbaum, 1998).

In RuThes we use the generalized part-whole relation, which means that besides traditional types of part-whole relations (physical parts, process parts), relations between the following types of entities can be considered as part-whole relations:

- an attribute and its bearer,
- a role or a participant of a situation and the situation: *investor - investing, player - playing* (compare (Loebe, 2007)),
- entities and situations in the encompassing sphere of activity: *industrial plant - industry, tennis racket - tennis, tennis player - tennis.* So these subtypes of part-whole relations in RuThes play the role of so-called WordNet domains, which were introduced to alleviate "tennis problem" – the lack of relations between synsets involved to the same situation or domain (Bentivogli et al., 2004; Gonzalez et al., 2012)

and several others.

In such a broad scope RuThes part-whole relations are close to so called *internal relations* (parthood, constitution, quality inherence, and participation) as described in (Guarino, 2009).

At the same time RuThes part-whole relations have a very important restriction: a concept-part should be related to its whole during normal existence of its instances: so called *inseparable parts* or *mandatary wholes* (Guizzardi, 2011). From this point of view, *TREE* concept is not described as part of *FOREST* concept, because trees can grow in many places, not only in forests.

Thus, the inference mechanism can rely on the chain of part-whole relations so we use the transitivity of such restricted part-whole relations (Guizzardi, 2011).

Let us see examples of the transitivity chain of part-whole relations:

- *(whole (**ACCUSED PERSON**, PUBLIC PROSECUTION),*
- *whole (PUBLIC PROSECUTION , JUDICIAL TRIAL ),*
- *whole (JUDICIAL TRIAL, **JUDICIAL PROCEEDINGS**))*
- → *whole (**ACCUSED PERSON**, **JUDICIAL PROCEEDINGS**)*

The next relation in RuThes ontology is unsymmetrical association $asc_1$-$asc_2$, which represents *external dependence* in ontological terms (Gangemi et al., 2001; Guarino, 2009).

This relation is established between two concepts $C_1$ and $C_2$ when two requirements are fulfilled:

- neither taxonomic nor part-whole relations can be established between $C_1$ and $C_2$ in RuThes linguistic ontology,
- the following assertion is true: $C_2$ exists means $C_1$ exists (necessarily existent entities are excluded from consideration).

These two conditions mean that concept $C_2$ (dependent concept) externally depends on $C_1$:

$asc_1 (C_2, C_1) = asc_2 (C_1, C_2)$

Examples of dependent concepts for *AUTOMOBILE* concepts are as follows:

- $asc_2$ *(AUTOMOBILE, AUTOMOTIVE INDUSTRY)*: concept *AUTOMOTIVE INDUSTRY* exists only if concept *AUTOMOBILE* exists;
- $asc_2$ *(FOREST, TREE)* concept *FOREST* exists only if concept *TREE* exists.

Relations of ontological dependence are applicable in various domains, therefore they are usually used in top-level ontologies (Sowa, 2000; Masolo et al., 2003; Grenon, 2003). Besides in (Kumar and Smith, 2004) authors discuss the importance of such a relation for the biology domain: cell movement cannot exist without cells. It is the first time when such relations are basic relations for a linguistic ontology.

An additional advantage of using this relation in linguistic ontologies consists in its usefulness for description of links between a concept based on the sense of a compositional multiword expression and concepts corresponding to the components of this multiword expression.

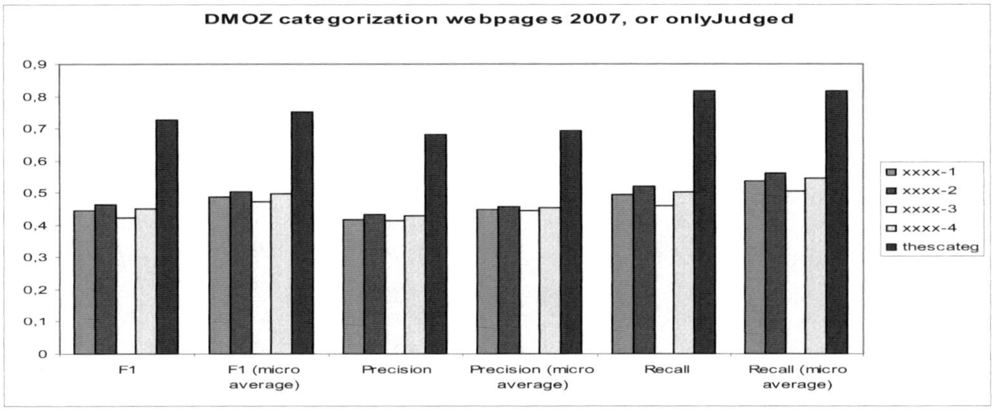


Fig 1. F1-measure, precision and recall of text categorization systems at ROMIP 2007.

So a multiword-based concept (for example, *AUTOMOBILE RACING*) is described as a dependent concept and its component concept (*AUTOMOBILE*) as a main concept. This allows us to introduce concepts based on various types of multiword expressions as described in section 3.2 and establish their necessary relations.

To conclude this section, we would like to stress there exists the similarity between all above-mentioned relations, which determines their considerable importance in concept description. These relations are established when concept instances or concepts themselves should coexist, what means that using these relations, we describe the most inherent (and, therefore, reliable) relations of concepts.

## 4 Testing RuThes in Automatic Document Processing

RuThes lingustic ontology provides the detailed coverage of single words, expressions and senses of contemporary written Russian (mainly, news articles, laws and official documents). The quality of descriptions originates from several sources.

First, since 1996 RuThes was used in various projects with governmental bodies and commercial organizations (in such applications as conceptual indexing in information-retrieval systems, knowledge-based text categorization, automatic summarization of single and multiple documents, question-answering etc.) and every project gave us the possibility to improve descriptions of lexical senses, to reveal useful expressions.

Second, 200 thousand words in a dictionary form (so called lemmas) ordered in decreasing frequency were extracted from the document frequency list of information-retrieval system RUSSIA (`www.uisrussia.msu.ru/`), in which contemporary Russian legal documents and newspaper materials are stored (2 million documents). The contemporary usage of these lemmas (distinct from proper names) was checked out during ten years of work mainly in news collections of online news services.

In combination with other techniques we applied RuThes in tasks of Russian Information Retrieval Evaluation Seminar (ROMIP) (Dobrov et al., 2004). So in 2007 we tested our knowledge-based text categorization system in ROMIP text categorization evaluation (Ageev et al., 2008a). The task was to automatically classify documents of 1.5 mln. webpages using 247 categories (Russian part of DMOZ categories `www.dmoz.org`). The training collection included 300 thousand documents with DMOZ category labels.

For every category, we created a Boolean expression over a relative small number of "supporting" concepts of the thesaurus. After that initial Boolean expressions were expanded on the basis of properties of the thesaurus relations. Final Boolean expressions usually include much more disjunctive and conjunctive components, sometimes in hundreds times more. Thus, these expanded Boolean descriptions of categories were used in automatic categorization of documents.

For example, Music category was described with single concept *MUSICAL ART*$_Y$, where Y means full expansion to lower levels of the hierarchy including hyponyms, parts and dependent concepts. So the full Boolean expression for this category looks like a disjunction of more than

400 concepts: *ADAGIO* ∨ *ACCORDION* ∨ ... ∨ *ORCHESTRA* ∨ ...).

The aim of our experiment was to obtain the best results of text categorization by minimal human efforts. The given system of 247 categories was described during eight hours by two knowledge engineers (overall time) (Ageev et al. 2008a). Fig. 1 demonstrates the performance of the created categorization system (*thescateg*) in comparison to machine learning approaches (SVM-based runs).

It is possible to see that the results of the knowledge-based system are considerably better. In our opinion, the achievement of such results is due to large volumes of knowledge described in RuThes and its consistent representation. Besides, in this evaluation machine learning approaches should process a highly inconsistent training collection because DMOZ manual labels were provided for the whole websites, but the contents of specific pages from these sites could be quite different from title pages.

In fact, more than twenty knowledge-based text categorization systems were implemented on the RuThes basis.

At last, Socio-political thesaurus (see section 3.1) is used as a search and visualization tool in several information-retrieval systems. Also in experiments the usefullness of Socio-political thesaurus for processing of long information-retrieval queries and as a basis for text clustering was proved (Ageev et al., 2008b; Dobrov and Pavlov, 2010).

## 5 Publication of RuThes

At present, RuThes thesaurus is partially involved in several commercial projects with other organizations and therefore it cannot be published as a whole. But the interest in a large thesaurus of Russian language is considerably growing therefore we decided to publish RuThes partially.

The first publicly available version of RuThes (RuThes-lite) contains around 50 thousand words and expressions and is available from `http://www.labinform.ru/ruthes/index.htm`. The next version including 100 thousand text entries will be published in the beginning of 2014. We distribute RuThes-lite as free for non-commercial use (Attribution-NonCommercial-ShareAlike 3.0 Unported license).

## 6 Conclusion

In this paper we presented RuThes linguistic ontology. This resource has been developed for a long time (more than fifteen years) and was used as a resource in various applications of NLP and information retrieval such as conceptual indexing, semantic search, query expansion, automatic text categorization and clustering, automatic summarization of a single document and multiple documents.

Now we decided to provide public access to RuThes and in this paper we described its structure and current state. We hope that this resource, having the broad and detailed lexical and terminological coverage of contemporary Russian news articles and official documents, will facilitate development of NLP techniques and research for Russian language.

## 7 Acknowledgements

The work is partially supported by Dmitrii Zimin Dynastia Foundation with financial support of Yandex founders.

## References

Mikhail Ageev, Boris Dobrov, Pavel Krasilnikov, Natalia Loukachevitch, Andrey Pavlov, Alexey Sidorov, and Sergey Shternov. 2008a. UIS RUSSIA at ROMIP-2007: Search and classification. *In Proceedings of Russian Seminar on Information-Retrieval Methods ROMIP 2007-2008* (In Russian).

Mikhail Ageev, Boris Dobrov, Natalia Loukachevitch, and Sergey Shternov. 2008b. UIS RUSSIA at ROMIP-2008: Search and classification of legal documents. *In Proceedings of Russian Seminar on Information-Retrieval Methods ROMIP 2007-2008* (In Russian).

Eneko Agirre, Izaskun Aldezabal, and Eli Pociello. 2006. Lexicalization and multiword expressions in the Basque WordNet. In *Proceedings of Third International WordNet Conference*, Jeju Island (Korea):131-138.

Irina Azarowa. 2008. RussNet as a Computer Lexicon for Russian. *In Proceedings of the Intelligent Information systems IIS-2008*: 341-350.

Valentina Balkova, Andrey Suhonogov, and Sergey Yablonsky. 2008. Some Issues in the Construction of a Russian WordNet Grid. *In Proceedings of the Forth International WordNet Conference*, Szeged, Hungary:44-55.

Luisa Bentivogli and Emanuele Pianta. 2004. Extending wordnet with syntagmatic information. *In Pro-*

*ceedings of Second Global WordNet Conference*:47-53.

Luisa Bentivogli, Pamela Forner, Bernardo Magnini, and Emanuele Pianta. 2004. Revising WordNet domains hierarchy: semantics, coverage, and balancing. *In Proceedings of COLING 2004*, Geneva, Switzerland:101-108.

Sonya Bosch, Christiane Fellbaum, and Karel Pala. 2008. Enhancing WordNets with Morphological Relations: A Case Study from Czech, English and Zulu. *In Proceedings of the Fourth Global WordNet Conference*:74-90.

Christopher A. Brewster, Jose Iria, Fabio Ciravegna, and Yorick Wilks. 2005. The Ontology: Chimaera or Pegasus. *In Proceedings Dagstuhl Seminar Machine Learning for the Semantic Web*: 89-101.

Paul Buitelaar, Philipp Cimiano, Peter Haase, and Michael Sintek. 2009. Towards Linguistically Grounded Ontologies. The Semantic Web: Research and Applications. *In Proceedings of the European Semantic Web Conference*. Springer Verlag, LNCS 5554:111-125.

Paul Buitelaar, Michael Sintek, and Malte Kiesel. 2006. A lexicon model for multilingual/multimedia ontologies. *In Proceedings of the 3rd European Semantic Web Conference (ESWC06).*

Salvador Climent, Horacio Rodriguez, and Julio Gonzalo. 1996. Definitions of the links and subsets for nouns of the EuroWordNet project. Deliverable D005, EuroWordNet, LE2-4003, Computer Centrum Letteren, University of Amsterdam.

Magdalena Derwojedowa, Maciej Piasecki, Stanisław Szpakowicz, Magdalena Zawisawska, and Bartosz Broda. 2008. Words, Concepts and Relations in the Construction of Polish WordNet. *In Proceedings of GWC-2008*:162-177.

Boris Dobrov, Igor Kuralenok, Natalia Loukachevitch, Igor Nekrestyanov, and Ilya Segalovich. 2004. Russian Information Retrieval Evaluation Seminar. In *Proceedings of LREC-2004*:1359-1362.

Boris Dobrov and Batalia Loukachevitch. 2006. In Development of Linguistic Ontology on Natural Sciences and Technology." In *Proceedings of LREC-2006.*

Boris Dobrov and Andrey Pavlov. 2010. Basic line for news clusterization methods evaluation. *In Proceedings of Russian Conference on Digital Libraries RCDL-2010:* 287-295 (in Russian).

Philip Edmonds and Graeme Hirst. 2002. Near-synonymy and lexical choice. *Computational linguistics,* 28 (2):105-144.

Christiane Fellbaum. 1998. WordNet: An Electronic Lexical Database. Cambridge, MA: MIT Press.

Christiane Fellbaum. 2002. Parallel Hierarchies in the Verb Lexicon. *In Proceedings of 'The Ontologies and Lexical Knowledge bases' workshop*. Las Palmas, Spain:27-31.

Aldo Gangemi, Nikola Guarino, Claudio Masolo, and Alessandro Oltramari. 2001. Understanding Top-Level Ontological Distinctions. *In Proceedings of IJCAI 2001 workshop on Ontologies and Information Sharing*:26-33.

Ilia Gelfenbeyn, Artem Goncharuk, Vlad Lehelt, Anton Lipatov, and Viktor Shilo. 2003. Automatic translation of WordNet semantic network to Russian language. *In Proceedings of International Conference on Computational Linguistics and Intellectual Technologies Dialog-2003.*

Aitor Gonzalez, German Rigau, and Mauro Castillo. 2012. A graph-based method to improve wordnet domains. *Computational Linguistics and Intelligent Text Processing*, Springer, LNCS-7181: 17-28.

Pierre Grenon. 2003. Spatio-temporality in Basic Formal Ontology: SNAP and SPAN, upper-level ontology, and framework for formalization. PART I. *IFOMIS Report 05/2003.*

Nicola Guarino. 1998. Some ontological principles for designing upper level lexical resources. *In Proceedings of First International Conference on Language Resources and Evaluation*: 527-534.

Nicola Guarino. 2009. The ontological Level: Revisiting 30 years of Knowledge Representation. *Conceptual Modeling: Foundations and Applications*. Springer-Verlag Berlin, Heidelberg: 52-67.

Giancarlo Guizzardi. 2011. Ontological foundations for conceptual part-wholes relation: the case of collectives and their parts. *Advanced Information Systems Engineering*, Springer CAiSE, LNCS 6741:138–153.

Graeme Hirst. 2009. Ontology and the Lexicon. In: Staab S., Studer R. (eds.) *Handbook on Ontologies in Information Systems*: 269-292.

ISO 2788-1986. 1986. Guidelines for the establishment and development of monolingual thesauri.

Anand Kumar and Barry Smith. 2004. The ontology of blood pressure: a case study in creating ontological partitions in biomedicine.

Claudia Kunze and Lothar Lemnitzer. 2010. Lexical-Semantic and Conceptual relations in GermaNet. *In Storjohann P (ed) Lexical-semantic relations: Theoretical and practical perspectives,* 28:163-183.

Krister Linden and Lauri Carlson. 2010. Finnwordnet — wordnet på finska via översättning. *LexicoNordica — Nordic Journal of Lexicography*, 17:119–140.

Frank Loebe. 2007. Abstract vs. Social Roles: Towards a general theoretical account of roles. *Applied Ontology*, v2 (2):127-158.

Natalia Loukachevitch and Boris Dobrov. 2002. Development and Use of Thesaurus of Russian Language RuThes. *In Proceedings of workshop on WordNet Structures and Standartisation, and How These Affect WordNet Applications and Evaluation.* LREC-2002:65-70.

Natalia Loukachevitch and Boris Dobrov. 2004. Sociopolitical Domain as a Bridge from General Words to Terms of Specific Domains. *In Proceedings of Second International WordNet Conference GWC-2004*:163-168.

Natalia Loukachevitch. 2009. Concept Formation in Linguistic Ontologies. Conceptual Structures: Leveraging Semantic Technologies. *In Proceedings of ICCS-2009.* Springer Verlag, LNAI-5662:2-22.

Claudio Masolo, Stefano Borgo, Aldo Gangemi, Nicola Guarino, and Alessandro Oltramari. 2003. WonderWeb Deliverable D18: Ontology library (final). *Technical report*, Laboratory for Applied Ontology, ISTC-CNR, Trento, Italy.

Alexander Maedche and Valentine Zacharias. 2002. Clustering Ontology-based Metadata in the Semantic Web. *In Proceedings PKKD-2002*:342-360.

Bernardo Magnini and Manuela Speranza M. 2002. Merging Global and Specialized Linguistic Ontologies. *In Proceedings of OntoLex*:43-48.

Marek Maziarz, Maciej Piasecki, and Stanisław Szpakowicz. 2013. The chicken-and-egg problem in wordnet design: synonymy, synsets and costitutive relations. *Language Resources & Evaluation* .

George Miller and Florentina Hristea. 2006. WordNet Nouns: Classes and Instances. *Journal of Computational linguistics*, 32(1):1-3.

Sergey Nirenburg and Viktor Raskin. 2004. Ontological Semantics. Cambridge, MIT Press.

Natalia F.Noy and Deborah McGuinness. 2001. Ontology Development 101: A Guide to Creating Your First Ontology. *Stanford Knowledge Systems Laboratory Technical Report KSL-01-05 and Stanford Medical Informatics Technical Report SMI-2001-0880.*

Bolette Pedersen, Lars Borin, Markus Forsberg, Krister Linden K., Heili Orav, and E´ırikur Rognvaldsson. 2012. Linking and Validating Nordic and Baltic Wordnets. A Multilingual Action in META-NORD. *In Proceedings of GWC-2012*: 254-259.

Barry Smith. 2004. Beyond Concepts: Ontology as Reality Representation. *Proceedings of International Conference on Formal Ontology and Information Systems FOIS-2004.*

John Sowa. 2000. Knowledge Representation: Logical, Philosophical, and Computational Foundations. Brooks Cole Publishing Co., Pacific Grove, CA.

Tony Veale and Yanfen Hao. 2007. A context-sensitive framework for lexical ontologies. *Knowledge Engineering Review*, 23(1):101-115.

Yorick Wilks. 2008. The Semantic Web: Apotheosis of annotation, but what are its semantics? *IEEE Intelligent Systems*, 23(3):41-49.

Morton Winston, Roger Chaffin, and Douglas Herrmann. 1987. A taxonomy of part-whole relations. Cognitive science, 11(4):417-444.

Z39.19. 2005. Guidelines for the Construction, Format and Management of Monolingual Thesauri. NISO.

# One Lexicon, Two Structures: So What Gives?

**Nabil Gader**
MVS Publishing Solutions
Sainte-Marguerite, F-88100, France
nabil.gader@mvs.fr

**Sandrine Ollinger**
CNRS, ATILF, UMR 7118
Nancy, F-54063, France
sandrine.ollinger@atilf.fr

**Alain Polguère**
Université de Lorraine, ATILF, UMR 7118
Nancy, F-54063, France
alain.polguere@univ-lorraine.fr

## Abstract

We present a reinterpretation of lexical information embedded in the English WordNet in an alternate type of structure called *lexical system*. First, we characterize lexical systems as graphs of lexical units (word senses) connected mainly by Meaning-Text lexical function relations, then introduce a hand-built lexical system: the French Lexical Network or fr-LN, a lexical resource that implements a new lexicography of virtual dictionaries. We later explain how a corresponding en-LN has been generated from the English WordNet. Finally, we propose a topological contrastive analysis of the two graphs showing that both structures can be characterized as being Hierarchical Small World Networks.

## 1 Introduction

### 1.1 Context: the French Lexical Network

The RELIEF project (Lux-Pogodalla and Polguère, 2011) is the first stage of a long-term lexicographic enterprise that aims at developing a broad-coverage French lexical resource: the *French Lexical Network*, hereafter fr-LN. This resource possesses two main characteristics.

Firstly, it is the product of actual lexicographic work but does not involve the writing of dictionary articles. Rather, textual dictionary-like descriptions can be automatically generated from linguistic information contained in the fr-LN, which can thus be considered as having embedded in it *virtual dictionaries*. For comparable approaches to the design of lexical resources, see for instance Atkins (1996) and Spohr (2012).

Secondly, it possesses a very specific type of graph structure called *lexical system*, conceptualized in Polguère (2009). While WordNets are before of all **graphs of synsets**, lexical systems are **graphs of specific word senses**—i.e. *lexical units*, in our terminology—, connected by a rich set of lexical relations based on Meaning-Text *lexical functions* (Mel'čuk, 1996; Mel'čuk, 2006). For instance, below is a typical synset relation taken from WordNet:

{army#1,regular army#1,ground forces#1} $\xrightarrow{\text{member meronym}}$ {corps#1, army corps#1}

whereas only lexical function relations holding between specific word senses such as:

ARMY **1** $\xrightarrow{\textsf{Sing}}$ CORPS **1**

exist in a lexical system.[1]

In addition, each piece of information in a lexical system (mainly, lexical nodes and lexical function arcs connecting nodes) is supplied with a *trust value*, that is a measure of the validity of lexical information. For instance, information directly entered by lexicographers receive high or, even, maximal trust values, while information automatically generated by analogy-based algorithms should receive a low trust value. This allows for the implementation of "fuzzy" reasoning on lexical information.

At the time of writing, the fr-LN's wordlist contains 14,311 vocable entries—the term *vocable* designates a (potentially) polysemic word—, and 20,791 *lexical units*—actual word senses. Complete statistical data on the fr-LN are provided in

[1] **Sing** is the singulative lexical function.

section 3, including data on lexical function relations that weave the lexical network. Notice that these relations are not the only lexical connections encoded in the fr-LN. Each idiom, i.e. phrasal lexical unit, is connected to the lexemes it formally contains. For instance, the noun POMME DE TERRE 'potato' is connected to the corresponding lexemes POMME 'apple', DE 'of' and TERRE 'soil', via the description of its internal syntactic structure. Additionally, we have just started to encode *copolysemy links*: i.e. metonymy, metaphor, etc. links that connect senses belonging to the same vocable and form its polysemic structure.

### 1.2 Going English

The goal of this paper is to present an experiment that we have conducted in order to automatically generate an *English Lexical Network*, hereafter en-LN, from the English WordNet. Such task presents some similarity with previous attempts at compiling WordNet into specific data structures—see for instance Graves & Gutierrez (2005) and Huang & Zhou (2007). However, in our case, we "transmute" WordNet data into an informational content that is fundamentally different in nature.

One consequence is that information embedded in WordNet that is "deeper" (more conceptual) than strict linguistic knowledge is lost. This loss of information is compensated by a very important gain: a data structure that allows us to perform lexicographic work on the English lexicon using exactly the same advanced lexicographic tools we are using in our fr-LN project (Gader et al., 2012). In other words, we can perform a lexicographic "graph weaving" activity on both French and English networks (cf. section 4).

The remainder of the paper is organized as follows. Section 2 describes how the task of compiling the English WordNet into an en-LN has been performed. Section 3 presents a contrastive topological analysis of the graph structure of both networks. Section 4 concludes on the practical interest of our experiment.

## 2 From WordNets to lexical systems

### 2.1 General characterization of the task

The extraction of an English lexical system out of WordNet's data is a process of bridging the gap between two non-equivalent information structures. The structure of lexical systems has been introduced in section 1.1. The structure of WordNet is well-known (Kamps, 2002) and a presentation in the present context would be overkill. It is however useful to summarize the main formal differences that exist between our source and target structures, i.e. to recapitulate our "one lexicon, two structures" problematics: see Table 1 below.

| English WordNet | en-LN |
|---|---|
| **Synsets** as structural units of description | **Lexical units** as structural units of description |
| Global partition based on parts of speech (N, V, Adj, Adv) | No part of speech partition |
| Top-down hierarchical organization | Multidimensional organization |
| Chiefly based on the hyper-/hyponymy relation between **synsets** | Based on a set of lexical function relations between **lexical units** |

Table 1: One lexicon, two structures.

Computationally, our source dataset was the ANSI Prolog version of Princeton WordNet 3.0.

This Prolog version of WordNet is made up of 21 files, each containing a Prolog database that is a set of Prolog "fact" clauses for a given predicate. For instance, the `wn_s.pl` file contains 212,558 clauses for the `s/6` Prolog predicate (the 6-place s(ense) predicate), each clause encoding the description of one WordNet sense. The structure of the `s/6` predicate is described as follows in the `prologdb.5.pdf` documentation file:

s(*synset_id*,*w_num*,*'word'*,
*ss_type*,*sense_number*,*tag_count*).

For example, the following Prolog clause:

```
s(107544351,4,
    'infatuation',n,2,0).
```

asserts that there exists a WordNet nominal sense `infatuation#2`, that is the fourth sense in the synset whose id is `107544351` and that was not semantically tagged in WordNet's Semantic Concordances (Miller et al., 1993).

Out of the 21 Prolog files, 18 have been identified as containing information that could indeed be translated into lexical system data.[2] Such data belong to three main categories: (i) lexical entities (mainly, lexical units and vocables), (ii) individual properties of lexical units (parts of speech, semantic gloses, etc.) and (iii) lexical function relations between lexical units.

[2]The three unused files are: `wn_cls.pl` (class relations between synsets), `wn_sa.pl` (rather heterogeneous relations between verbal or adjectival senses) and `wn_vgp.pl` (similarity relations between verbal synsets).

Next section explains how this information has been generated from WordNet's Prolog files.

### 2.2 Generation of lexical data

For lack of space, we cannot account for all aspects of the compilation process. We focus on the insertion of pieces of information into the en-LN that are central to the characterization of this database as a lexical system.

#### 2.2.1 Lexical entities

As shown earlier in Table 1 (section 2.1, above), there are no lexical entities corresponding to synsets in a lexical system. The nodes of such lexical networks are mainly lexical units, i.e. words taken in a well-specified meaning.

Our first task was to compile the en-LN's wordlist, i.e. the set of all its lexical units, grouped under poly- or monosemic vocables. In order to do so, we implemented the three following operations, using information from the `wn_s.pl` sense file (presented in 2.1 above).

**Operation 1** We had to perform a preliminary clean-up of Prolog data, as we found a significant number (5,580) of duplicated clauses in the `s/6` predicate database.[3]

**Operation 2** We then created one vocable (new entry in the en-LN wordlist) for each distinct pair: ⟨ word form, synset grammatical type ⟩.

If there were two vocables with identical form but different synset grammatical types, we added the appropriate subscript to vocable names. For instance, from the two pairs:

⟨ `'package'`, `n` ⟩ and ⟨ `'package'`, `v` ⟩,

we generated two distinct vocables: $\text{PACKAGE}_{\text{N}}$ and $\text{PACKAGE}_{\text{V}}$.

**Operation 3** For each sense in the `s/6` Prolog database, we created one lexical unit and connected it to the corresponding vocable—based on the ⟨ word form, synset grammatical type ⟩ pair found in the Prolog clause for the WordNet sense.

- If only one lexical unit was attached to a given vocable, its WordNet sense number[4] was ignored—e.g., we generated the BACKGAMMON lexical unit in the corresponding monosemic vocable.
- If several lexical units were attached to a vocable, each one received the number of the corresponding WordNet sense—e.g., we generated two lexical units, GEEK **1** and GEEK **2**, in the GEEK polysemic vocable.

The process of lexical entity generation resulted in a huge fully disconnected graph (a cloud of nodes without connecting arcs) comprising 206,976 lexical units—nodes in the graph— associated to 156,584 vocables,[5] which gives a polysemy rate of around 1.322.

To conclude on the topic of the generation of lexical entities, it is important to recall that not all WordNet senses are indeed lexical units. There is a very significant quantity of phrasal entities[6] in WordNet's synsets, and only a small proportion of those phrases are actual idioms, i.e. lexical units (Osherson and Fellbaum, 2010). The automatic processing of WordNet data cannot separate true idioms from compositional phrases, and a manual post-processing of the en-LN will be necessary in order to validate the en-LN wordlist.

**Important remark** Our data structure allows us to specify a probability—understood as a measure of trust value—for each piece of lexicographic information entered into the en-LN (cf. properties of lexical systems, section 1.1 above). We have decided that information that is automatically generated will receive a 0.5 probably. This is true for the validity of vocables and lexical units, but also for lexical links and individual properties of lexical units that we have computed from WordNet. This strategy boils down to considering the current en-LN as being a "hypothesized lexical database."

#### 2.2.2 Individual properties of lexical units

Five different types of individual properties have been assigned to lexical units in the en-LN: so-called WordNet "sense keys," parts of speech, syntactic features, semantic glosses and syntactic government patterns (subcategorization frames).

**WordNet sense keys** We found it essential to encode in the en-LN the correspondence between lexical units and WordNet senses, using WordNet

[3]We actually discovered other errors in the Prolog files (mainly, but not only duplicates) that we had to circumvent in order to avoid the generation of inconsistent data in the resulting en-LN. The list of errors can be provided on request.

[4]WordNet sense number is necessarily `1` in such cases.

[5]Cf. section 1.1 above: vocables are considered as more abstract lexical entities and are not counted as actual nodes of the lexical graph.

[6]Phrasal senses are called *collocations* in WordNet terminology. This is a different notion from that of collocation understood as semi-phraseological expression—e.g. support verb constructions such as *take a nap* (Benson, 1989).

IDs called *sense keys*. These IDs were extracted from the wn_sk.pl Prolog file and encoded as *WordNet source* features in the Grammatical Characteristics zone of the en-LN lexicographic articles. For instance, the lexeme INFATUATION **2** has received the value 'infatuation%1:12:02::' as WordNet source feature.

**Semantic glosses** In WordNet, semantic glosses are associated to synsets and not to individual senses. ⟨ Synset, gloss ⟩ pairs were extracted from the wn_g.pl file and the en-LN article of each member of a given synset received the same gloss attribute. Computationally, glosses are simply stored as strings of characters in the Definition lexicographic zone, more precisely in its Comments section.

**Parts of speech (POS)** WordNet 'synset types' have been retrieved from the wn_s.pl Prolog file and encoded as Part of speech features in the Grammatical Characteristics zone. The correspondence between WordNet synset type codes—SType—and en-LN's parts of speech—POS—is given in Table 2 below.

| SType | POS |
|---|---|
| v | 'verb' |
| n | 'proper noun' if name starts with a capital letter, 'common noun' otherwise (of course, a very approximate rule of thumb) |
| a and s | 'adjective'—we used only one part of speech for adjectives as we consider that WordNet's class of satellite adjectives (s type) pertains to WordNet internal organization rather than to the identification of grammatical behavior |
| r | 'adverb' |

Table 2: en-LN interpretation of synset types.

**Syntactic features** Features corresponding to information on syntactic behavior of adjectives (syntactic role and linear positioning) were retrieved from the wn_syntax.pl Prolog file, where they are associated to individual senses. Table 3 below describes how this information has been encoded as features in the Grammatical Characteristics zone of the en-LN.

| WordNet feature | en-LN gram. charac. |
|---|---|
| a | 'attributive' |
| p | 'predicative' |
| ip | 'postposed' |

Table 3: en-LN interpretation of syntactic features.

**Syntactic government patterns** We retrieved associations between synsets and WordNet's syntactic frame codes in the wn_syntax.pl Prolog file. The definitions of syntactic frames themselves where taken from WordNet's documentation (wninput.5.pdf file). Then, for each sense member of a given verbal synset, we entered the associated frame description into the Government Pattern zone (Comments section) of the corresponding lexical unit.

Now that the generation of lexical properties has been explained, let us move to the crucial topic of weaving lexical function relations, that give the en-LN its connected graph structure.

### 2.2.3 Lexical function relations

In total, 12 Meaning-Text lexical functions (Mel'čuk, 1996) have been used to encode lexical relations extracted from WordNet. They can be grouped into three different classes:

- 7 standard lexical functions: **Syn**$_\cap$, **Anti**$_\cap$, **Gener**, **Mult**, **Sing**, **A**$_2$ and **Caus**;
- 4 that have been "standardized" (Polguère, 2007) in the context of previous projects: **Cf**, **Hypo**, **Holo** and **Mero**;
- 1 non-standard: **Unspecified derivative**.

Table 4 below gives statistics on the distribution of lexical links pulled in the en-LN for each of those twelve lexical functions.

| Number of links | Lexical function |
|---|---|
| 315,984 | **Syn**$_\cap$ |
| 145,880 | **Gener** |
| 145,880 | **Hypo** |
| 89,107 | **Unspecified derivative** |
| 59,981 | **Mult** |
| 59,981 | **Sing** |
| 50,746 | **Cf** |
| 35,663 | **Mero** |
| 33,684 | **Holo** |
| 7,979 | **Anti**$_\cap$ |
| 1,250 | **Caus** |
| 73 | **A**$_2$ |

Table 4: Lexical function links in the en-LN.

For lack of space, we focus below on the generation of only three lexical links, that are the most significant statistically: **Syn**$_\cap$, **Gener** and **Hypo**.

**Extraction of Syn$_\cap$ relations** The **Syn**$_\cap$ lexical function stands for 'intersecting synonym'; its extraction from WordNet was done as follows:

**If** sense 's' belongs to synset S
  **And** $L_{\text{'s'}}$ is the lexicalization of 's' in the en-LN
**Then** the lexicalizations of all other senses belonging to S are targets of **Syn**$_\cap$ links originating from $L_{\text{'s'}}$
  **And** the same principle applies recursively to all other senses of S.

This principle entails the "saturation" of all possible **Syn**$_\cap$ links among all elements of all synsets in WordNets. And each application of this principle on a synset generates a saturated subgraph.

Figure 1 below shows the **Syn**$_\cap$ saturated subgraph generated from synset (1).

(1) `{puppy love,calf love, crush#3-n,infatuation#2}`

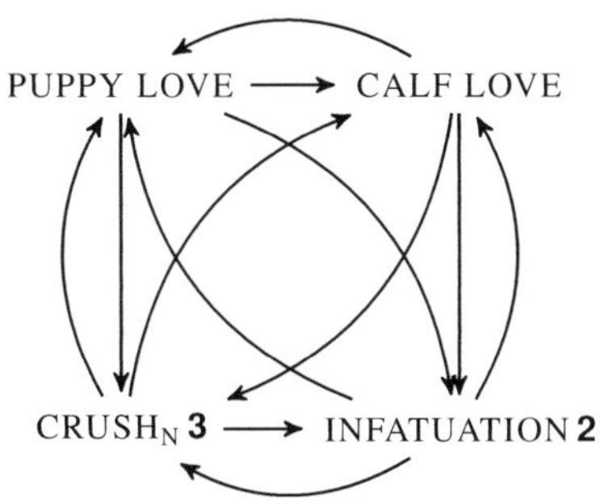


Figure 1: **Syn**$_\cap$ saturated subgraph for synset (1)

We made the hypothesis that most synset members in WordNet are connected by the intersecting approximate synonymy relation **Syn**$_\cap$, rather than by exact synonymy **Syn**. We expect that our strategy will entail less manual corrections when the en-LN will be used for lexicographic purposes (section 4). Synset (1) is a clear illustration of the potential relevance of our hypothesis, as senses in (1) are indeed not **exact** synonyms.

**Extraction of Gener $\sim$ Hypo relations** **Gener** is a Meaning-Text standard lexical function and stands for 'generic term'. Though it is close to WordNet's hypernymy, it was not possible to systematically extract **Gener** relations from WordNet's hierarchical organization, for two reasons.

Firstly, the hypernymy relation holds between synsets, whereas **Gener** connects lexical units.

Secondly, **Gener** is more specific than WordNet's hypernymy. It holds between two lexical units in only two specific cases, illustrated below.

**A.** FRUIT is a **Gener** of BANANA because it is possible to say (2).

(2) ***bananas**, apples, oranges and other **fruits***

**B.** SUBSTANCE is a **Gener** of GAS because (3a) can be paraphrased as (3b) using GASEOUS, the adjectival counterpart of GAS.

(3) a. *gas*
  b. *gaseous substance*

**Gener** is thus before all a lexical, rather than conceptual or denotational relation. In the context of our lexical projects, **Gener** is paired with a symmetrical lexical function called **Hypo**, for 'hyponym'. Notice that this latter lexical function does not belong to the original set of Meaning-Text standard lexical functions.

**Gener** $\sim$ **Hypo** relations were mainly extracted from hypernym relations between synsets (`wn_hyp.pl` file) as follows:

**If** synset $S_1$ is a hypernym of synset $S_2$
  **And** $S_1$ is the hypernym of more than 15 synsets
**Then** all senses of $S_1$ are targets of **Gener** links originating from of all senses of $S_2$
  **And** all senses of $S_2$ are targets of **Hypo** links originating from of all senses of $S_1$.

This ensures that there is no explosion of the number of invalid **Gener** and **Hypo** links. After doing some testing with different thresholds, we reached the conclusion that a synset that happened to be the hypernym of more than 15 other synsets had the greatest chance to contain true generic terms (in our sense).[7]

With this strategy, we caught in our nets "only" 111,032 **Gener** relations and the same number of **Hypo** relations. Without the ">15" constraint, numbers would have been much higher and en-LN data much less accurate.

[7]For instance, the WordNet sense `car#1` belongs to a synset that is the hypernym of 31 other synsets. It has thus been identified as good candidate for generic term; as a result, the corresponding lexical unit is the **Gener** of 66 other lexical units in the en-LN. In contrast, `desk#1` belongs to a (singleton) synset that is the hypernym of only 3 other synsets; no **Gener** link has been pulled from the DESK lexical unit.

A smaller set of **Gener** and **Hypo** relations (69,696) has been extracted from instance→type relations between nominal synsets (`wn_ins.pl` file) based on the following principle:

**If** synset $S_1$ is a type of synset $S_2$ (that is its instance)
**Then** all senses of $S_1$ are **Gener** of all senses of $S_2$
**And** all senses of $S_2$ are **Hypo** of all senses of $S_1$.

To conclude this section, notice that the strategies applied for extracting **Syn**$_\cap$, **Gener** and **Hypo** relations—which implies symetric relations—are chiefly responsible for the very high proportion of "mutual arcs" in the graph—see section 3.1 below, that presents a topological comparison of the fr- and en-LNs.

### 2.3 Accessing the resulting en-LN

Once the interpretation of WordNet information into a lexical system structure is performed, we are able to access and navigate through the en-LN with the *Dicet* lexicographic editor, designed for lexicographic work on the fr-LN. In actual fact, we are now able to edit and transform the newly generated en-LF using our lexicographic approach.

In order help the reader have a more concrete grasp of how different the English lexical system is from WordNet, we provide in Figure 2 below a lexicographic view of the first sense of the GEEK vocable. For a presentation of the specificity of lexicographic editing by means of the Dicet editor, see (Gader et al., 2012).

## 3 Graph properties

The aim of this section is three-fold:

1. to determine to what extent the fr-LN and the en-LN differ in terms of mathematical organization;
2. to formally characterize the structure of both networks as so-called *Hierarchical Small World Networks*, which is the expected graph type for lexical systems;
3. to use the full-scale nature of the en-LN, inherited from WordNet, to anticipate future formal properties of our "adolescent" fr-LN.

Section 3.1 presents a formal characterization of the fr-/en-LNs from the viewpoint of their graph structure. Topological analyses of both graphs allow us to mathematically compare their formal structure. Section 3.2 summarizes this comparison in layman terms and draws conclusions from formal differences that have emerged.

### 3.1 Formal topological analysis

Structural properties of our lexical systems were studied using *pedigree.py*, a Python script developed by Emmanuel Navarro (Gaillard et al., 2011). This script performs topological analyses—called *graph pedigrees*—, that allow for rigorous graph characterization and comparison. More specifically, we seek to determine if the fr-/en-LNs are *Hierarchical Small World Networks* (Watts and Strogatz, 1998; Newman, 2003; Gaume, 2004).

Hierarchical Small World Networks, hereafter HSWN, exhibit four properties:

1. low density, i.e. small number of arcs compared to the number of nodes;
2. high global clustering coefficient, i.e. high number of connected neighbor nodes;
3. distribution of degrees (probability distribution of number of arcs associated to a node) that follows a power law;
4. low average path length, i.e. small average minimal number of arcs between two nodes for each possible pairs.

Table 5 below shows the pedigree of our two lexical systems.

The current fr-LN comprises 9.9 times less nodes (*n*) than the English network—straight from the oven—, for 27.1 times less arcs (*m*). To determine if these densities are low, we compare *m* to $n^2$ and $nlog(n)$. $n^2$ is the maximum amount of arcs that can exist for a given number of nodes and a unique relation type.[8] It is about $432 \times 10^6$ for the fr-LN and $43 \times 10^9$ for the en-LN. From this point of view, their densities are low. $nlog(n)$ represents the order of magnitude of HSWN's density (Gaume, 2004). It is about 89,773 for the fr-LN, which is twice the current amount. For the en-LN, it is about 1,100,267, which is close to what we measured.

[8] In our case, there are 662 different relations involved in the fr-LN and 12 in the en-LN. The maximum amount of arcs increases proportionaly.

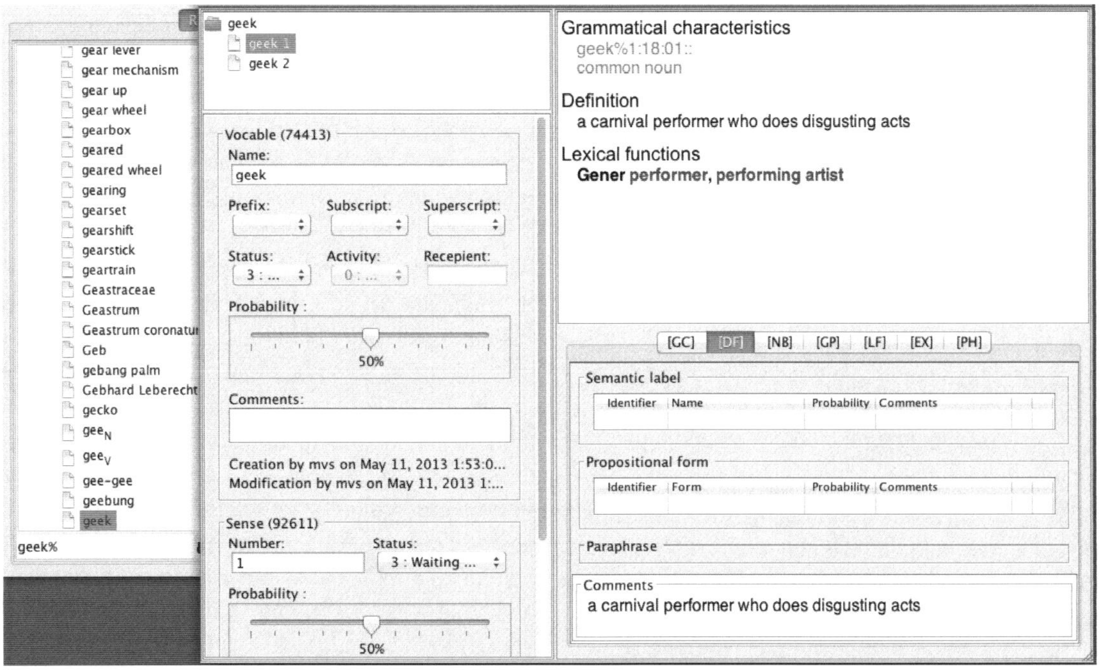


Figure 2: (Partial) lexicographic view of GEEK **1**.

| | fr-LN | en-LN |
|---|---|---|
| n | 20,791 | 206,976 |
| m | 34,920 | 946,208 |
| <k> | 3.3406 | 5.9029 |
| Directed | true | true |
| Mutuals | 15,576 | 942,795 |
| Loops | 46 | 1 |
| Single | 3,540 | 19,756 |
| Multiples | 432 | 124 |
| ncc | 14,295 | 34,342 |
| C | 0.1058 | 0.1031 |
| Out degree distribution | | |
| a | -2.0243 | -1.8479 |
| $r^2$ | 0.9572 | 0.8453 |
| LCC | | |
| n_lcc | 1,788 | 144,294 |
| m_lcc | 5,973 | 851,748 |
| C_lcc | 0.2816 | 0.0980 |
| L_lcc | 13.0861 | 10.1479 |

Table 5: Pedigree of the fr-/en-LNs.

The fr-LN is a work in progress. It includes a high proportion of single nodes (17%), which implies a high number of strongly connected components (*ncc*)[9] and explains its small largest connected component (*LCC*). The network increases in arcs more quickly than in nodes, due to the organization of the lexicographic work. In addition, the amount of single nodes decreases. Table 6 shows this evolution over five months.

| | June 2013 | Oct. 2013 | Evolution |
|---|---|---|---|
| Arcs | 25,932 | 34,920 | +35% |
| Nodes | 18,057 | 20,791 | +15% |
| Single | 3,614 | 3,540 | -2% |

Table 6: Evolution of the fr-LN.

The en-LN has not undergone any evolution yet. However, it will be manually transformed in the future. Some arcs will be added and its proportion of single nodes (2%) will decrease. Some arcs will also be modified or deleted. For example, its unique loop is a WordNet error and will be eliminated from the en-LN (as it should be from WordNet).[10]

The French network, which contains a wide variety of links (662), has 44.6% of mutual arcs—i.e. arcs $a \to b$ for which a reverse arc $b \to a$ exists. They are many more in the en-LN (99.5%), due to the nature of the 12 lexical links encoded.

To estimate how nodes and arcs are locally or-

[9]Single nodes are considered to be strongly connected components.

[10]This is a `derivationally related form` arc connecting `unicyle`$_{\text{N}}$ to itself, that is present in both the on-line WordNet 3.1 and the Prolog database we used.

ganized in networks, one needs to examine their global clustering coefficients ($C$).

| Nodes | Arcs | $C$ Lexical | $C$ Random |
|---|---|---|---|
| 20,791 | 34,920 | 0.1058 | 0.00016 |
| 206,976 | 946,208 | 0.1031 | 0.00004 |

Table 7: Global clustering coefficients.

For our networks, $C$ may seem small. However, as Table 7 shows, they are higher than for similar classical random graphs (Newman, 2003). In other words, these networks hold sets of highly connected lexical units.

To assess the structure of these lexical agregates in the network, we need to examine the distribution of degrees and the average path length ($L$).

As our networks are oriented, we focus only on their out distribution of degrees. Both networks follow a power law with a good correlation coefficient ($r^2$). In Table 5 above, $a$ stands for the coefficient of the best fitting power law of these distributions. Such a distribution is in the same range as for typical HSWNs. This means that a few number of lexical units are highly connected to a slightly higher number of other lexical units, themselves connected to a slightly higher number of other lexical units. To put it differently, our networks contain lexical hubs and are hierarchically structured.

Bollobás and Riordan (2004) have shown that the $L$ of HSWNs does not exceed $\log n / \log \log n$. Such a value for $L$ means that it is possible to move rapidly from a node of the network to another.

As our networks have more than one component, measure of their $L$ is problematic (Newman, 2003). In fact, it is difficult to define a path length between two non-connected nodes. A possible alternative can be to consider the $L$ of *LCC* (*L_lcc*).

| | n_lcc | log$n$/ log log$n$ | L_lcc |
|---|---|---|---|
| fr-LN | 1,788 | 6.350 | 13.0861 |
| en-LN | 144,294 | 7.240 | 10.1479 |

Table 8: Average path lengths.

Table 8 shows that *L_lcc* of our networks are higher than expected. For the French network, *LCC* is very small and probably not representative of the whole network. For the English network, the problem is different. The original structure of WordNet keeps separate the synsets of the four major parts of speech (with marginal transversal connections). It is reasonable to believe that some structuring lexical relations between agregates belonging to different parts of speech are missing.

To conclude, our fr- and en-LNs seem to be both structured as HSWNs, but have an average path length higher than they should have.

### 3.2 In layman terms

As indicated in section 3.1 above, the en-LN is substantially larger than the current fr-LN. In contrast, lexical relations are more diverse in the latter.

Despite such differences, the global structure of both networks appear to be similar. They seem to represent the same type of lexical organization. In both cases, senses are organized in highly connected subsets and some lexical units assume a pivotal role. These characteristics appear consistent with a semantic field structure. Further investigation is required to learn more about highly connected components, like the nature of links and lexical units involved. Some new similarities might then emerge.

The question of a fast and easy access between lexical agregates remains. More detailed observation would be required to determine why such an access is not possible in the LNs. The en-LN is made up mostly of paradigmatic links. Maybe this characteristic is the cause of our trouble. But this explanation does not hold in the case of the fr-LN. In a study of WordNet, where the different parts of speech are structured together, Sigman and Cecchi (2002) propose to introduce polysemous links to improve access between lexical units. We are currently implementing the weaving of such links in the fr-LN and more will be known soon about their incidence on the global structuring of LNs.

## 4 So what gives?

In form of conclusion, we summarize the practical interests of performing the WordNet $\rightarrow$ en-LN compilation. Two main points should highlighted.

First and foremost, as stated in section 2.3, we are able to wade through the en-LN and edit it using our "graph weaver:" the Dicet lexicographic editor. This is essential to us as we believe that the lexical system model ought to be extensively tested as an alternative to more ontological approaches to lexical knowledge structuring, such as WordNets.

Second, thanks to WordNet, we now have at our disposal a lexical unit-based access to the English lexicon that can be used to explore structural behavior of full-scale lexical systems, in anticipation of the fr-LN reaching lexicographic maturity.

## Acknowledgments

Work on the fr-LN is supported by a grant from the Agence de Mobilisation Économique de Lorraine (AMEL) and Fonds Européen de Développement Régional (FEDER). We are grateful to Veronika Lux-Pogodalla and two GWC2014 reviewers for their comments on the first version of this paper. Emmanuel Navaro has been very helpful in providing feedback on the use of Pedigree.py.

## References

B. T. Sue Atkins. 1996. Bilingual Dictionaries: Past, Present and Future. *Proc. of Euralex'96*, Martin Gellerstam, Jerker Järborg, Sven-Göran Malmgren, Kerstin Norén, Lena Rogström, Catalina Röjder Papmehl (Eds.), Gothenburg University, Department of Swedish, 2006, 515–590.

Morton Benson. 1989. The Structure of the Collocational Dictionary. *International Journal of Lexicography*, 2(1):1–14.

Béla Bollobás and Oliver Riordan. 2004. The Diameter of a Scale-Free Random Graph. *Combinatorica*, 24(1):5–34.

Nabil Gader, Veronika Lux-Pogodalla and Alain Polguère. 2012. Hand-Crafting a Lexical Network With a Knowledge-Based Graph Editor. *Proc. of the Third Workshop on Cognitive Aspects of the Lexicon (CogALex III)*, The COLING 2012 Organizing Committee, Mumbai, 109–125.

Benoit Gaillard, Bruno Gaume, and Emmanuel Navarro. 2011. Invariants and Variability of Synonymy Networks: Self Mediated Agreement by Confluence. *Proc. of TextGraphs-6: Graph-based Methods for NLP*, ACL, Portland, 15–23.

Bruno Gaume. 2004. Balades Aléatoires dans les petits mondes lexicaux. *I3 Information Interaction Intelligence*, 4(2):39–96.

Alvaro Graves and Claudio Gutierrez. 2005. Data Representations for WordNet: A Case for RDF. *Proc. of Global WordNet Conference 2006*, Petr Sojka, Key-Sun Choi, Christiane Fellbaum, Piek Vossen (Eds.), Jeju Island, 2006, 165–169.

Huang Xiao and Zhou Chang-le. 2007. An OWL-based WordNet lexical ontology. *Journal of Zhejiang University SCIENCE A*, 8(6):864–870.

Jaap Kamps. 2002. Visualizing WordNet structure. *Proc. of Global WordNet Conference 2002*, Central Institute of Indian Languages , Mysore, 2002, 182–186.

Veronika Lux-Pogodalla and Alain Polguère. 2011. Construction of a French Lexical Network: Methodological Issues. *Proc. of the First International Workshop on Lexical Resources, WoLeR 2011. An ESSLLI 2011 Workshop*, Ljubljana, 2011, 54–61.

Igor Mel'čuk. 1996. Lexical Functions: A Tool for the Description of Lexical Relations in the Lexicon. *Lexical Functions in Lexicography and Natural Language Processing*, Leo Wanner (Ed.), Language Companion Series 31, John Benjamins, Amsterdam/Philadelphia, 37–102.

Igor Mel'čuk. 2006. Explanatory Combinatorial Dictionary. *Open Problems in Linguistics and Lexicography*, Giandomenico Sica (Ed.), Polimetrica, Monza, 225–355.

George A. Miller, Claudia Leacock, Randee Tengi and Ross T. Bunker. 1993. A semantic concordance. *Proc. of the ARPA Human Language Technology Workshop*, Princeton, 303–308.

Mark E.J. Newman. 2003. The structure and function of complex networks. *SIAM REVIEW*, 45:167–256.

Anne Osherson and Christiane Fellbaum. 2010. The Representation of Idioms in WordNet. *Proc. of Global WordNet Conference 2002*, CFILT, IIT Bombay, Mumbai, 2010.

Alain Polguère. 2007. Lexical function standardness. *Selected Lexical and Grammatical Issues in the Meaning-Text Theory. In Honour of Igor Mel'čuk*, Leo Wanner (Ed.), Language Companion Series 84, John Benjamins, Amsterdam/Philadelphia, 43–95.

Alain Polguère. 2009. Lexical systems: graph models of natural language lexicons. *Language Resources and Evaluation*, 43(1):41–55.

Mariano Sigman and Guillermo A. Cecchi. 2002. Global organization of the Wordnet lexicon. *Proc. Natl. Acad. Sci.*, 99(3):1742–1747.

Dennis Spohr. 2012. *Towards a Multifunctional Lexical Resource. Design and Implementation of a Graph-based Lexicon Model*, De Gruyter, Berlin/Boston.

Duncan J. Watts and Steven H. Strogatz. 1998. Collective dynamics of 'small-world' networks. *Nature*, 393:440–442.

# Automatic Construction of Amharic Semantic Networks From Unstructured Text Using Amharic WordNet

**Alelgn Tefera**
Department of Computer Science
Jigjiga University, Ethiopia
alelgn.tefera@gmail.com

**Yaregal Assabie**
Department of Computer Science
Addis Ababa University, Ethiopia
yaregal.assabie@aau.edu.et

## Abstract

Semantic networks have become key components in many natural language processing applications. This paper presents an automatic construction of Amharic semantic networks using Amharic WordNet as initial knowledge base where intervening word patterns between pairs of concepts in the WordNet are extracted for a specific relation from a given text. For each pair of concepts which we know the relationship contained in Amharic WordNet, we search the corpus for some text snapshot between these concepts. The returned text snapshot is processed to extract all the patterns having *n*-gram words between the two concepts. We use the WordSpace model for extraction of semantically related concepts and relation identification among these concepts utilizes the extracted text patterns. The system is designed to extract "part-of" and "type-of" relations between concepts which are very popular and frequently found between concepts in any corpus. The system was tested in three phases with text corpus collected from news outlets, and experimental results are reported.

## 1 Introduction

A semantic network is a network which represents semantic relations among concepts and it is often used to represent knowledge. A semantic network is used when one has knowledge that is best understood as a set of concepts that are related to one another. Concepts are the abstract representations of the meaning of terms. A term can be physically represented by a word, phrase, sentence, paragraph, or document. The relations between concepts that are most commonly used in semantic networks are *synonym* (similar concepts), *antonym* (opposite concepts), *meronym/holonym* ("part-of" relation between concepts), and *hyponym/hypernym* ("type-of" relation between concepts). Knowledge stored as semantic networks can be represented in the form of graphs (directed or undirected) using concepts as nodes and semantic relations as labeled edges (Fellbaum, 1998; Steyvers and Tenenbaum, 2005). Semantic networks are becoming popular issues these days. Even though this popularity is mostly related to the idea of semantic web, it is also related to the natural language processing (NLP) applications. Semantic networks allow search engines to search not only for the key words given by the user but also for the related concepts, and show how this relation is made. Knowledge stored as semantic networks can be used by programs that generate text from structured data. Semantic networks are also used for document summarization by compressing the data semantically and for document classification using the knowledge stored in it (Berners-Lee, 2001; Sahlgren, 2006; Smith, 2003).

Approaches commonly used to automatically construct semantic networks are knowledge-based, corpus-based and hybrid approaches. In the knowledge-based approach, relations between two concepts are extracted using a thesaurus in a supervised manner whereas corpus-based approach extracts concepts from a large amount of text in a semi-supervised method. Hybrid approach combines both the hierarchy of the thesaurus and statistical information for concepts measured in large corpora (Dominic and Trevor, 2010; George *et al*, 2010; Sahlgren, 2006). Over the past years, several attempts have been made to develop semantic networks. Among the widely known are ASKNet (Harrington and Clark, 2007), MindNet (Richardson *et al*, 1998), and Leximancer (Smith, 2003). Most of the semantic networks constructed so far assume English text as corpus. However, to our best knowledge, there is no system that automatically constructs semantic networks from unstructured Amharic text.

This paper presents an automatic construction of semantic networks from unconstrained and unstructured Amharic text. The remaining part of this paper is organized as follows. Section 2 presents Amharic language with emphasis to its morphological features. The design of Amharic semantic network construction is discussed in Section 3. Experimental results are presented in Section 4, and conclusion and future works are highlighted in Section 5. References are provided at the end.

## 2 Amharic Language

Amharic is a Semitic language spoken predominantly in Ethiopia. It is the working language of the country having a population of over 90 million at present. The language is spoken as a monther tongue by a large segment of the population in the northern and central regions of Ethiopia and as a second language by many others. It is the second most spoken Semitic language in the world next to Arabic and the most commonly learned second language throughout Ethiopia (Lewis *et al*, 2013). Amharic is written using a script known as *fidel* having 33 consonants (basic characters) out of which six other characters representing combinations of vowels and consonants are derived for each character.

Derivation and inflection of words in Amharic is a very complex process (Amare, 2010; Yimam, 2000). Amharic nouns and adjectives are inflected for number, gender, definitnesss, and cases. On the other hand, Amharic nouns can be derived from:

- *verbal roots* by infixing various patterns of vowels between consonants, e.g. መልስ (*mäls*/answer) from ምልስ (*mls*);
- *adjectives* by suffixing various types of bound morphemes, e.g. ደግነት (*dägĭnät*/kindness) from ደግ (*däg*/kind);
- *stems* by prefixing or suffixing various bound morphemes, e.g. ውጤት (*wĭṭet*/result) from ውጥ- (*wĭṭ*-); and
- *nouns* by suffixing various bound morphemes, e.g. ልጅነት (*lĭjĭnät*/childhood) from ልጅ (*lĭj*/child).

Adjectives are also derived from:

- *verbal roots* by infixing vowels between consonants, e.g. ጥቁር (*ṭĭqur*/black) from ጥቅር (*ṭqr*);
- *nouns* by suffixing bound morphemes, e.g. ጥቁር (*ṭĭqur*/black) from ጥቅር (*ṭqr*); and
- *stems* by suffixing bound morphemes, e.g. ደካማ (*däkama*/weak) from ደካም- (*dekam*-).

In addition, nouns and adjectives can be derived from compound words of various lexical categories. Amharic verb inflection is even more complex than that of nouns and adjectives as verbs are marked for any combination of person, gender, number, case, tense/aspect, and mood resulting in the synthesis of thousands of words from a single verbal root. With respect to the derivation process, several verbs in their surface forms are derived from a single verbal stem, and several stems are derived from a single verbal root. For example, from the verbal root ስብር (*sbr*/to break), we can derive verbal stems such as ሰብር (*säbr*), ሰበር (*säbär*), ሳብር (*sabr*), ሰባብር (*säbabr*), ተሰባብር (*täsäbabr*), etc. and we can derive words such as ሰበረው (*säbäräw*), ሰበርኩ (*säbärku*), ሰበረች (*säbäräč*), ሰበርን (*säbärn*), አሰበረ (*assäbärä*), ተሰበረ (*täsäbärä*), አልሰበረም (*alsäbäräm*), ሲሰበር (*sisäbär*), ሳይሰበር (*saysäbär*), ካልተሰበረ (*kaltäsäbärä*), የሚሰበር (*yämisäbär*), etc. This leads a single word to represent a complete sentence constructed with subject, verb and object. Because of such morphological complexities, many Amharic natural language processing applications require stemmer or morphological analyser as a key component.

## 3 The Proposed Semantic Network Model

The model proposed to construct Amharic semantic networks has the following major components: *Amharic WordNet*, *text analysis and indexing*, *computing term vectors*, *concept extraction*, and *relation extraction*. First, index terms representing text corpus are extracted. Term vectors are then computed from the index file and stored using WordSpace model. By searching the WordSpace, semantically related concepts are extracted for a given synset in the Amharic WordNet. Finally, relations between those concepts in the intervening word patterns are extracted from the corpus using pairs of concepts from Amharic WordNet. Process relatioships between these components are shown in Figure 1.

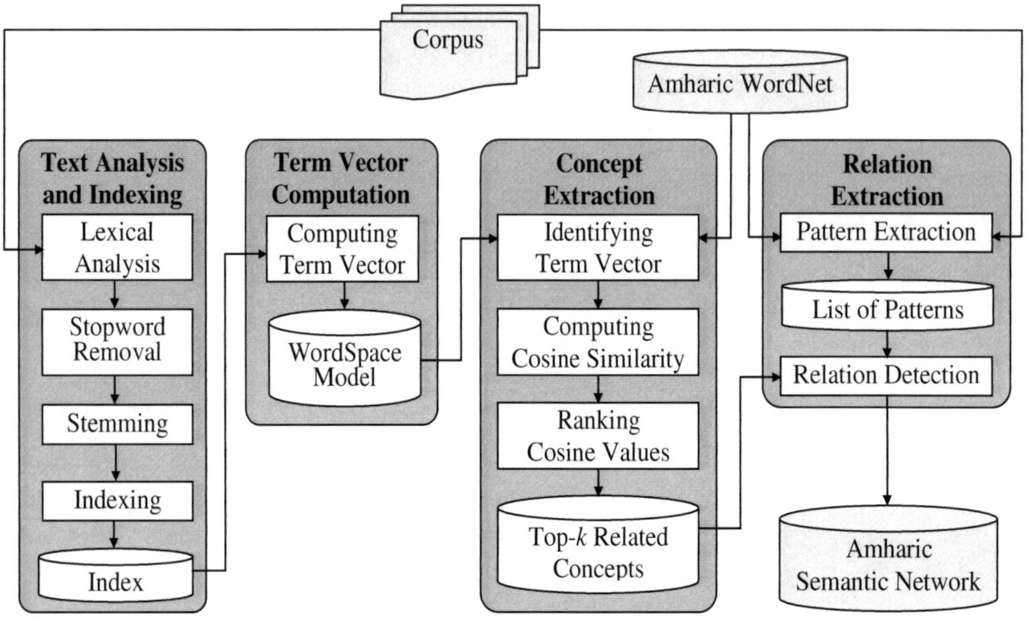


Figure 1. System architecture of the proposed Amharic semantic network.

### 3.1 Amharic WordNet

To automatically construct semantic networks from free text corpus, we need some initial knowledge for the system so that other unknown relation instances can be extracted. Accordingly, we constructed Amharic WordNet manually as a small knowledge base in which the basic relation between terms is "synonymy". Amharic WordNet is composed of 890 single word terms (all are nouns) grouped into 296 synsets (synonym groups) and these synsets are representations of the concepts of terms in the group. We chose noun concepts because most relation types are detected between nouns. Verbs and adverbs are relation indicators which are used to show relations between nouns. Synsets are further related with each other by other three relations called "type-of", "part-of" and "antonym". The Amharic WordNet is then used to set different seeds for a specific relation. Once we prepare sets of seeds from the WordNet, we can extract the patterns which indicate how these pairs of seeds exist in the corpus. The way these pairs of concepts exist in the corpus can tell us more about other concept pairs in the corpus. For example, the way the pair of terms {ኢትዮጵያ/Ethiopia, አፍሪካ/Africa} exists in the corpus can tell us that the pair of terms {ኬንያ/Kenya, አፍሪካ/Africa} can exist in same way as the former pairs. The patterns extracted between a pair of terms {ኢትዮጵያ/Ethiopia, አፍሪካ/Africa} can be used to extract the relation between other countries like ኬንያ/Kenya with that of አፍሪካ/Africa.

### 3.2 Text Analysis and Indexing

The process of text analysis starts with removal of non-letter tokens and stopwords from the corpus. This is followed by stemming of words where several words derived from the same morpheme are considered in further steps as the same token. Since Amharic is morphologically complex language, the process of finding the stem which is the last unchangeable morpheme of the word is a difficult task. We used a modified version of the stemmer algorithm developed by Alemayehu and Willet (2002) which removes suffixes and prefixes iteratively by employing minimum stem length and context sensitive rules. The stem is used as a term for indexing which is performed by applying term frequency-inverse document frequency weighting algorithm.

### 3.3 Computing Term Vectors

A term vector is a sequence of term-weight pairs. The weight of the term in our case is the co-occurrence frequency of the term with other terms in a document. Term vectors are computed from the index file where we extract the co-occurred terms and compute the term vectors in the WordSpace model. From the index file, it is possible to map the index to term-context (term-document) matrix where the values of the cells of the matrix are the weighted frequency of terms in the context (document). The WordSpace model is used to create term vectors semantically from this matrix by reducing the dimension of the matrix using random projection algorithm (Fern and Brodley, 2003). At the end, the WordSpace contains the list of term vectors found from the corpus along with co-occurrence frequencies of each term. The algorithm used to compute term vetcors is shown in Figure 2.

**Input**:
    **INDEX**=folder containing index files
    **DIM**=dimension of each term vector
**Output**:
    **TERMVECTORS**=set of term vectors
**Initialize**:
    **TERMVECTORS**={}

1. Open **INDEX**
2. Create term-document matrix **MATRIX** from **INDEX**
3. For each document **DOC** in **MATRIX**:
   - Create basic random vector **RANDVEC**
   - For each term **T** in **DOC** and dimension<=**DIM**:
     - **FREQ**= frequency of **T** within **DOC**
     - **TV**= {} //term vector
     - **TV**= **TV** + (**FEQ*****RANDVEC**)
     - Normalize **TV**
     - Add **TV** to **TERMVECTORS**
4. Return **TERMVECTORS**

Figure 2. Algorithm for computing term vectors.

### 3.4 Concept Extraction

Semantically related concepts for a seed term of Amharic WordNet are extracted from the WordSpace model which is used to create a collection of term vectors. Each term vector contains different related words along with their co-occurrence frequencies. For a concept from Amharic WordNet as input to WordSpace, related concepts are extracted by computing the cosine similarity between the term vector containing this concept and the remaining term vectors of the WordSpace model. For each term vector $TV_i$ in the WordSpace model and a term vector $TVx$ that corresponds to the synset, the cosine similarity $C$ is computed as:

$$C = \frac{\sum_{i=1}^{n} TVx * TV_i}{\sqrt{\sum_{i=1}^{n} TVx^2 * TV_i^2}} \quad (1)$$

where $n$ is the number of term vectors in the WordSpace model. Since the collection of the term vectors in the WordSpace is many in number, we rank related terms using the cosine values in decreasing order for selection of top-$k$ number of related concepts for the given synset where $k$ is our threshold used to determine the number of related concepts to be extracted.

### 3.5 Relation Extraction

The relations among concepts considered in this work are "part-of" and "type-of". We use semi-supervised approach to extract relations where a very small number of seed instances or patterns from Amharic WordNet are used to do bootstrap learning. These seeds are used with a large corpus to extract a new set of patterns, which in turn are used to extract more instances in an iterative fashion. In general, using Amharic WordNet entries, intervening word patterns for a specific relation are extracted from the corpus. For each pair of concepts ($C_1$, $C_2$) of which we know the relationship contained in Amharic WordNet, we send the query "$C_1$" + "$C_2$" to the corpus. The returned text snapshot is processed to extract all $n$-grams (where $n$ is set empirically to be $2 \leq n \leq 7$) that match the pattern "$C_1X^*C_2$", where X can be any combination of up to five space-separated word or punctuation tokens. Thus, "$C_1X^*C_2$" is a pattern extracted from the corpus using concept pair ($C_1$, $C_2$) from Amharic WordNet of specific relation. For instance, assume the Amharic WordNet contains the concepts "ኢትዮጵያ (*ityoPya*/Ethiopia)" and "አማራ (*amara*/Amhara)" with "ኢትዮጵያ/Ethiopia" being a hypernym of "አማራ/Amhara". The method would query the corpus with the string "ኢትዮጵያ/Ethiopia" + "አማራ/Amhara". Let us assume that one of the returned text snapshot is "...በኢትዮጵያ ከሚገኙ ክልሎች መካከል አማራ አንዱ ሲሆን... (*...bä'ityoPya kämigäñu kĭlĭloč mäkakäl amara andu sihon...*) ". In this case, the method would extract the pattern "...በኢትዮጵያ ከሚገኙ ክልሎች መካከል አማራ... (*...bä'ityoPya kämigäñu kĭlĭloč mäkakäl amara...*)". This pattern would be added to the list of potential hypernymy patterns list with "ኢትዮጵያ/Ethiopia" and "አማራ/Amhara" substituted with matching placeholders, like "**var1** ከሚገኙ ክልሎች መካከል (*kämigäñu kĭlĭloč mäkakäl*) **var2**". Once the patterns are extracted, the final step is to detect if there is a relation between every pair of concepts extracted from the WordSpace. If a relation between a pair of concepts are detected, the concept pair will be added to the network in which each concept is a node and the link is the relation between the concepts. Figure 3 shows the algorithm used to extract relations between concepts.

```
Input:
    CONPAIR = set of pair of concepts from
              Amharic WordNet
    CORPUS  = corpus
    PATLIST = list of patterns extracted
Output:
    SEMNET  = list containing pairs of concepts
              with relation R as a form of
              R(C1,C2)
Initialize:
    MODPAT= {}    //list of modified patterns

1. For each pair (A,B) in CONPAIR:
       For each pattern PAT in PATLIST:
           NEWPAT=A + PAT + B
           MODPAT= MODPAT + NEWPAT
2. For each phrase PHRASE in MODPAT:
       COUNT =0
       A= PHRASE [0]
       B= PHRASE [size(PHRASE)-1]
       For each file FILE in CORPUS:
           For each sentence SENTENCE in FILE
               If PHRASE exists in SENTENCE
                   COUNT=COUNT+1
               If COUNT>=TRESHOLD
                   Add pair (A,B) to SEMNET
                   Break
3. Return SEMNET
```

Figure 3. Algorithm for Relation Extraction.

# 4 Experiment

## 4.1 Corpus Collection

The corpus is composed of domain independent, unconstrained and unstructured text data. It contains two groups of text. The first group is a collection of news text documents gathered by Walta Information Center (1064 news items) and all news items are tagged with part-of-speech categries.This group of the dataset was used for the extraction of concepts in the corpus. The second group was collected from Ethiopian National News Agency (3261 news items). This dataset group was used for computing the frequency of concepts that are extracted from the first tagged dataset. Thus, a total of 4325 Amharic news documents were collected to build the corpus.

## 4.2 Implementation

The proposed model was implemented by creating the WordSpace from the index file which is mapped to term-document matrix. We used Apache Lucene and Semantic Vectors APIs for indexing and development of the WordSpace model, respectively. Concept and relation extraction processes were also implemented using Java.

## 4.3 AMSNet

We coined the name AMSNet to semantic networks automatically constructed using our system from Amharic text. AMSNet consists of a set of concepts and a set of important relationships called "synonym", "part-of" and "type-of". It holds entries as a form of first order predicate calculus in which the predicate is the relation and the arguments are concepts. AMSNet acquires new concepts over time and connects each new concept to a subset of the concepts within an existing neighborhood whenever new text document is processed by the system. The growing network is not intended to be a complete model of semantic development, but contains specific relations that can be extracted and connected between concepts of the given corpus. Semantic networks not only represent information but also facilitate the retrieval of relevant facts. For instance, all the facts related to the concept "ኢትዮጵያ/Ethiopia" are stored with pointers directed to the node representing "ኢትዮጵያ/ Ethiopia". Another example concerns the inheritance of properties. Given a fact such as "አገር ሁሉ መንግስት አለው (*agär hulu mängĭst aläw*/each country has a government)", the system would automatically conclude that "ኢትዮጵያ መንግስት አላት (*ityoPya mängĭst alat*/Ethiopia has a government)" given that ኢትዮጵያ አገር ናት (*ityoPya agär nat*/Ethiopia is a country).

## 4.4 Test Results

There is no gold standard to evaluate the result of semantic network construction. Our result is validated manually by linguists, and based on their evaluations the average accuracy of the system to extract the "type-of" and "part-of" relations between concepts (synsets) from free text corpus is 68.5% and 71.7%, respectively. Sample result generated from the our system is shown in Figure 4.

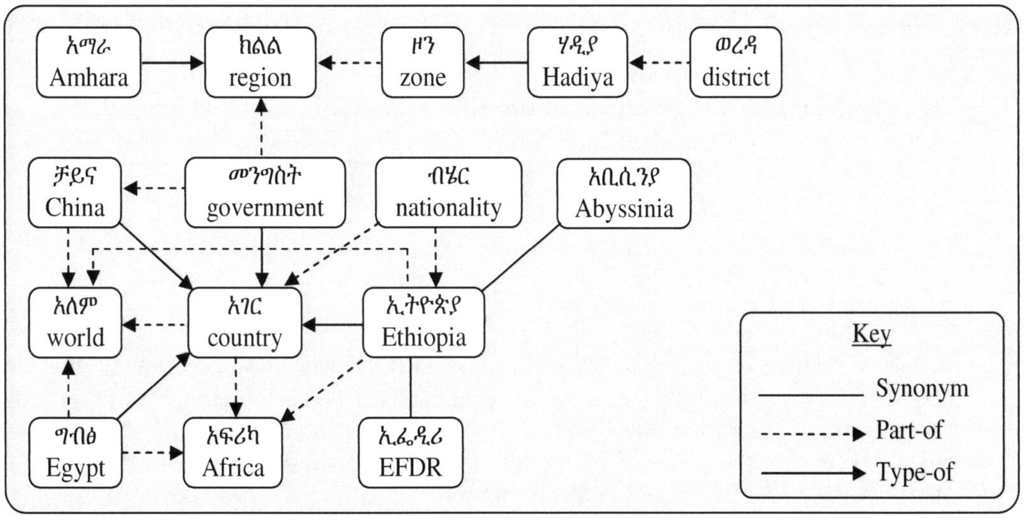


Figure 4. Part of the Amharic semantic network automatically constructed by the proposed system.

## 5 Conclusion and Future Works

A major effort was made in identifying and defining a formal set of steps for automatic construction of semantic network of Amharic noun concepts from free text corpus. The construction model of our semantic network involves the creation of index file for the collected news text corpus, development of WordSpace based on the index file, searching the WordSpace to generate semantically related concepts for a given Amharic WordNet term, generate patterns for a specific relation using entries of Amharic WordNet and detect relations between each pair of concepts among the related concepts using those patterns. The availability of Amharic semantic networks helps other Amharic NLP applications such as information retrieval, document classification, machine translation, etc. improve their performance. Future works include deep morphological analyis on Amharic and the use of hybrid approches to improve the performance of the system.

## References


Nega Alemayehu and Peter Willet. 2002. Stemming of Amharic Words for Information Retrieval, In *Literary and Linguistic Computing*, Vol 17, Issue 1, pp. 1-17.

Getahun Amare. 2010. ዘመናዊ የአማርኛ ሰዋሰው በቀላል አቀራረብ (Modern Amharic Grammar in a Simple Approach). Addis Ababa, Ethiopia.

Tim Berners-Lee. 2001. The Semantic Web, *Scientific American* , Vol 284, Issue 5, pp. 34-43.

Widdows Dominic and Cohen Trevor. 2010. The Semantic Vectors Package: New Algorithms and Public Tools for Distributional Semantics, In *Fourth IEEE International Conference on Semantic Computing (IEEE ICSC2010).* Carnegie Mellon University, Pittsburgh, PA, USA.

Christiane Fellbaum. 1998. *WordNet: An Electronic Lexical Database*. Cambridge, MIT Press.

Tsatsaronis George, Iraklis Varlamis and Michalis Vazirgiannis. 2010. Text Relatedness Based on a Word Thesaurus, *Journal of Artificial Intelligence Research*, vol. 37, pp. 1-39.

Brian Harrington and Stephen Clark. 2007. ASKNet: Automated Semantic Knowledge Network, In *Proc. 22nd National Conf. on Artificial Intelligence*, Vancouver, Canada. pp. 889-884.

Paul Lewis, Gary Simons and Charles Fennig 2013; *Ethnologue: Languages of the World, Seventeenth edition.* Dallas, Texas: SIL International.

Stephen Richardson, William Dolan and Lucy Vanderwende. 1998. MindNet: Acquiring and structuring semantic information from text, In *Proceedings of the 17th COLING*, Montreal, Canada. pp. 1098-1102.

Magnus Sahlgren. 2006. The Word-Space Model: Using distributional analysis to represent syntagmatic and paradigmatic relations between words in high-dimensional vector space. *PhD Thesis*, Stockholm University, Sweden.

Andrew Smith. 2003. Automatic Extraction of Semantic Networks from Text using Leximancer, In *Proceedings of HLT-NAACL*, Edmonton.

Mark Steyvers and Joshua Tenenbaum. 2005. The Large-Scale Structure of Semantic Networks: Statistical Analyses and a Model of Semantic Growth, *Cognitive Science,* Vol 29, Issue 1, pp. 41–78.

Xiaoli Fern and Carla Brodley. 2003. Random Projection for High Dimensional Data Clustering: A Cluster Ensemble Approach, In *Proc. of the 20th Int. Conf. on Machine Learning (ICML-2003)*, Washington, DC.

Baye Yimam. 2000. የአማርኛ ሰዋሰው (Amharic Grammar). Addis Ababa, Ethiopia.

# Graph Based Algorithm for Automatic Domain Segmentation of WordNet

**Brijesh Bhatt  Subhash Kunnath  Pushpak Bhattacharyya**
Center for Indian Language Technology
Indian Institute of Technology Bombay
Mumbai, India
{ brijesh, subhash, pb } @cse.iitb.ac.in

## Abstract

We present a graph based algorithm for automatic domain segmentation of Wordnet. We pose the problem as a Markov Random Field Classification problem and show how existing graph based algorithms for Image Processing can be used to solve the problem. Our approach is unsupervised and can be easily adopted for any language. We conduct our experiments for two domains, health and tourism. We achieve F-Score more than .70 in both domains. This work can be useful for many critical problems like *word sense disambiguation, domain specific ontology extraction etc.*

## 1 Introduction

Over the years, Wordnet has served as an important lexical resource for many Natural Language Processing (NLP) applications. Picking up a right sense of a word from the fine grained sense repository of Wordnet is at the heart of many NLP problems. Many researchers have used Wordnet for domain specific applications like *word sense disambiguation* (Magnini et al., 2002a; Khapra et al., 2010), *domain specific taxonomy/ontology extraction* (Cimiano and Vlker, 2005; Yanna and Zili, 2009) etc. These applications rely on 'One sense per discourse' (Gale et al., 1992) hypothesis to identify domain specific sense of a word. 'Dividing Wordnet's lexical and conceptual space into various domain specific subspace can significantly reduce search space and thus help many domain specific applications' (Xiaojuan and Fellbaum, 2012).

With the purpose of categorizing Wordnet senses for different domain specific applications, Magnini and Cavagli (2000) constructed a domain hierarchy of 164 domain labels and annotated Wordnet synsets with one or more label from the hierarchy. The categories were further refined by linking domain labels to subject codes of Dewey Decimal Classification system (Bentivogli et al., 2004). Beginning with Wordnet 2.0, Domain category pointers were introduced to link domain specific synsets across part of speech. However, the manual determination of a set of domain labels and assigning them to Wordnet synsets is a time consuming task. Also, the senses of words evolves over a period of time and accordingly Wordnet synsets also undergo changes. This makes the static assignment of domain label a costly exercise.

With the intention to reduce manual labor of domain categorization and to facilitate use of Wordnet in domain specific applications, there has been efforts to (semi) automatically assign domain labels to Wordnet synsets. Most of these efforts rely on Wordnet concept hierarchy and use label propagation schemes to propagate domain labels through the hierarchy. However, the heterogeneous level of generality poses a key challenge to such approaches. For example, 'Under Animal (subsumed by Life_Form) we find out specific concepts, such as Work_Animal, Domestic_Animal, kept together with general classes such as Chordate, Fictional_Animal, etc.'(Gangemi et al., 2003). Another key challenge in assigning the domain labels is the quality of domain hierarchy and semantic distance between domain labels (Xiaojuan and Fellbaum, 2012).

In this paper, we present a corpus based approach for automatic domain segmentation of Wordnet. The aim of our work is to provide a general solution that can be used across languages to construct domain specific conceptualization from Wordnet. The proposed system works in two steps,

1. We construct domain specific conceptualiza-

tion from the corpus.

2. The domain specific conceptualization is then disambiguated and linked to Wordnet synsets to generate domain labels.

We pose Wordnet domain segmentation as an image labeling problem and use existing techniques in the field of image processing system to solve Wordnet domain labeling problem. The proposed method is completely unsupervised and requires only Part Of Speech tagged corpus. Hence, it can be easily adopted across languages. Our method also does not require any predefined set of domain category labels, however if such labels are available it can be incorporated into system to generate better labeling.

The remaining of the paper is organized as follows, section 2 describes related work. Section 3 describes the proposed graph based algorithm for Wordnet domain labeling. Section 4 and 5 discuss the experiments and conclusion.

## 2 Related Work

Two major attempts to categorize Wordnet synsets are Wordnet Domain (Magnini and Cavagli, 2000) and Wordnet Domain Category pointers. In this section we first present a brief overview of these efforts and then describe some efforts to automate the task of domain labeling of Wordnet synsets. We also mention the attempts made for other languages apart from English.

### 2.1 Wordnet Domain Hierarchy and Domain Category Pointers

Domain categorization of Wordnet synset has been an active area of research for more than a decade now. Magnini and Cavagli (2000) have developed Wordnet Domain Hierarchy (WDH) by annotating Wordnet1.6 using 250 Subject Field Codes (SFC). They used semi-automated approach in which the top level concepts are manually marked with SFC and then the labels are automatically propagated through the hierarchy. Finally, the labeling is again evaluated and refined manually. The semantic structure of WDH was further refined by Bentivogli et al. (2004).

Starting from Wordnet 2.0, *domain category pointers* were introduced in the Wordnet. 'Unlike the original Wordnet Domain, the domain category pointers use Wordnet synsets as domain labels and synsets across part of speech are linked through domain pointers' (Xiaojuan and Fellbaum, 2012). However, 'only 5% of Wordnet 3.0 synsets are linked to 438 domain categories and out of these linked synsets only 30% synsets have same label in both Wordnet Domain and Domain Category'.

### 2.2 Automated Approaches

Considering the growing size of Wordnet and the amount of efforts required to construct domain categories, it is apparent to develop semi-automated or automated methods for domain categorization of Wordnets. One of the earlier efforts in this direction was by Buitelaar and Sacaleanu (2001). They extracted domain specific terms using tf*idf measure and then disambiguated these terms using GermaNet synsets. The disambiguation was performed based on the assumption that the hypernymy and hyponymy terms are more likely to have same domain label. Magnini et al. (2002b) have performed a comparative study of corpus based and ontology based domain annotation. They have used frequency of words in the synonym set as a measure to identify domain of a synset.

Gonzalez-Agirre et al. (2012) have proposed a semi-automatic method to align the original Wordnet 1.6 based domains to Wordnet 3.0. They have used domain labels already assigned to some top level synsets and then propagated the domain label across Wordnet hierarchy using UKB algorithm (Agirre and Soroa, 2009). Their approach is based on an assumption that 'A synset directly related to several synsets labeled with a particular domain (i.e biology) would itself possibly be also related somehow to that domain (i.e. biology)'(Gonzalez-Agirre et al., 2012).

Fukumoto and Suzuki (2011) have adopted a corpus based approach to assign domain labels to Wordnet synsets. They first disambiguate the corpus words with Wordnet senses and then use Markov Random Walk based Page Rank Algorithm to rank domain relevance of Wordnet senses. Zhu et al. (2011) have proposed gloss based disambiguation technique for domain assignment to Wordnet synset. They used existing domain labels of Wordnet 3.0 and predicted domains based on words in the gloss of the synsets.

There have also been efforts to adopt English Wordnet domain labels for other languages. Lee et al. (2009) have used English-Chinese Wordnet mapping to domain tag Chinese Wordnet.

### 2.3 Proposed Approach

Like Buitelaar and Sacaleanu (2001), Magnini et al. (2002b) and Fukumoto and Suzuki (2011), we also follow corpus based approach for Wordnet Domain Labeling. Key points of difference among these approaches can be summerized as follows,

1. Both Buitelaar and Sacaleanu (2001) and Magnini et al. (2002b) used word frequency to detect domain specificity of a term. They do not consider the label of neighbor terms to determine the label for a term.

2. Fukumoto and Suzuki (2011) have modeled domain labeling as a Markov Random Walk problem, but they run their algorithm on entire Wordnet graph. This is costly in terms of time and space required for the processing. In addition to that, Wordnet hypernymy-hyponymy graph may not be a true representative of domain specific conceptualization.

In contrast to the above mentioned approaches, our approach is based on the hypothesis that, 'Domain specificity of a term depends on the spatial property of the term'. So it is important to construct a domain specific conceptualization to identify domain of a term. The domain for a concept/term depends not only on the occurence of the term in the domain but also on the neighbors of the concept/term. Hence, we follow two step process in which first we construct a domain conceptualization from the corpus and then we align this conceptualization with Wordnet.

## 3 Algorithm

The proposed algorithm carves out a domain specific subgraph from the Wordnet. For that, we first construct concept graph from the corpus and then associate concepts with Wordnet senses. Figure 1 shows the overall system architecture. As shown in the figure 1 after preprocessing, the similarity graph is constructed from the corpus. Using a graph based algorithm similarity graph is converted into domain conceptualization and then it is linked with Wordnet synsets to assign domain labels to Wordnet synsets. The detailed description of each component is as follows.

### 3.1 Preprocessing

The text corpus is first POS tagged using Stanford POS tagger [1] and Morph Analyzer [2]. Then term frequency of each term is calculated using weirdness measure (Ahmad et al., 1999). Context vector for each term is constructed using Point Wise Mutual Information (Church and Hanks, 1990) measure. We used a sentence as a boundary to calculate context vector. Output of the preprocessing step is a list of domain specific terms and their context vector.

### 3.2 Constructing Document Graph

Using the term list and context vector generated from the preprocessing step, a graph G(V, E) is constructed in which each $v_i \in V$ is term and each edge $e(v_i, v_j)$ is semantic relatedness between terms $v_i$ and $v_j$. Semantic relatedness between two terms $v_i$ and $v_j$ is calculated by taking cosine of terms vectors of $v_i$ and $v_j$, as shown in fig 2.

$$\text{similarity} = \cos(\theta) = \frac{A \cdot B}{\|A\|\|B\|} = \frac{\sum_{i=1}^{n} A_i \times B_i}{\sqrt{\sum_{i=1}^{n}(A_i)^2} \times \sqrt{\sum_{i=1}^{n}(B_i)^2}}$$

Figure 2: Cosine Similarity

### 3.3 Constructing Domain Specific Conceptualization

**Algorithm 1** Graph Cut Based Energy Minimization

Input: set of labels $L$, undirected graph $G(V, E)$ where, $V$ is set of random variables, $E$ is penalty cost, $f(v_l)$ is cost of assigning label $l \in L$ to $v \in V$, A set of initial labeling $\{(v, l)$, for all $v \in V$ and $l \in L\}$ and Energy Function $\theta$

**for** $v_i$ and $v_j \in V$ **do**
  Source $\leftarrow v_i$
  Target $\leftarrow v_j$
  Perform Graph Cut
  Re-assign labels
  Calculate $\theta$
  Repeat until $\theta$ is minimized
**end for**

[1] `http://nlp.stanford.edu/software/tagger.shtml`

[2] `http://www.sussex.ac.uk/Users/johnca/morph.html`

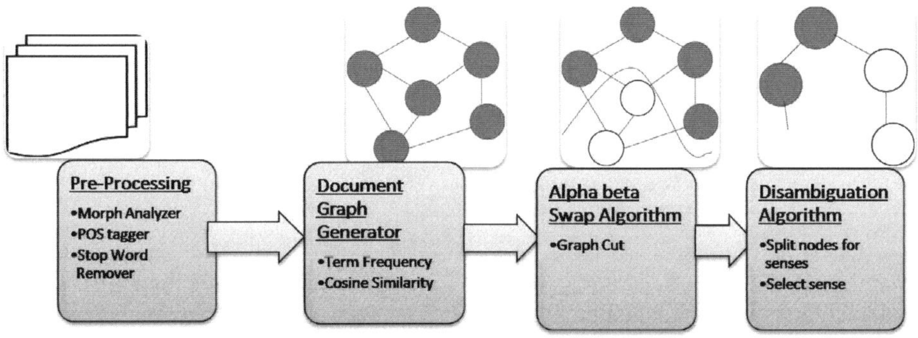


Figure 1: System Architecture

This module takes document graphs as an input and constructs a cohesive domain specific conceptual structure. In order to do this, we need to classify each node in the corpus graph into various domains. Assignment of a domain label to a node depends on two parameters,

- Term Cost: This measures how strongly a term belongs to the domain. It is measured by frequency of occurrence of a term within domain. This is formulated as a cost function as shown in equation 1.

$$tcost = \sum_{i \in V} E_i(X_i) \qquad (1)$$

  where, $X_i$ is the label assigned to term $i$ and $E_i$ is the cost of assigning label $X_i$ to node $i$.

  We use term frequency based measure to calculate cost of assigning label to a term. A term should be assigned to a domain in which it occurs more frequently. Hence, high *tf* indicates less cost to assign the term to domain. Thus,

$$E_i(X_i) = 1 - tf_i \qquad (2)$$

  where, $tf_i$ is the term frequency of the term $i$ in domain $X$.

- Edge Cost: This measures the cost of assigning separate labels to the two adjacent nodes of an edge. This is formulated as a cost function as shown in equation 3.

$$ecost = \sum_{(i,j) \in E} E_{ij}(x_i, x_j) \qquad (3)$$

  where $E_{ij}(x_i, x_j)$ = cost of assigning different label to neighboring nodes $i$ and $j$. $E_{ij}(x_i, x_j)$ is equal to semantic similarity between nodes $x_i$ and $x_j$. Higher the similarity between nodes $x_i$ and $x_j$ more is the penalty to assign different labels to $x_i$ and $x_j$.

This can be formulated as an energy minimization over a Markov Random Field (Kleinberg and Tardos, 2002). Finding optimal solution is equal to minimizing equation 4.

$$minimze\theta = \sum_{i \in V} E_i(X_i) + \sum_{(i,j) \in E} E_{ij}(x_i, x_j) \qquad (4)$$

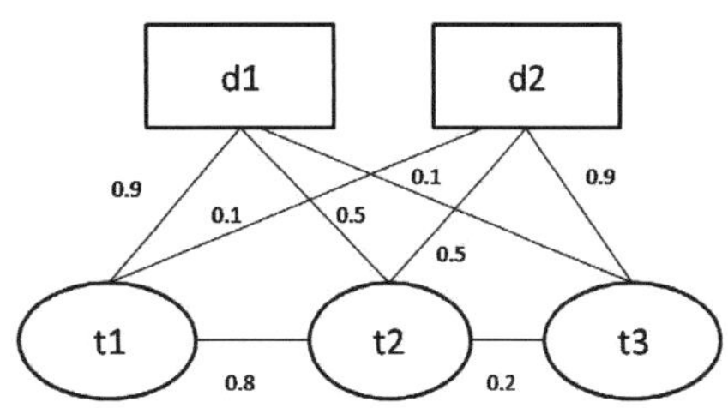


Figure 3: Domain Labeling

Figure 3 shows an example configuration of the concept graph with three nodes $t_1$, $t_2$ and $t_3$ and two domains $d_1$ and $d_2$. Edges from the nodes $t_i$ to $d_j$ indicates value of cost function $c(p, d)$ of equation 2. and edges between nodes $t_i$ and $t_j$ indicates cost for assigning different labels to node $t_i$

and $t_j$. As can be seen in the figure to minimize $\theta$ of equation 4, node $t_1$ will be assign to domain $d_2$ and node $t_3$ will be assign to domain $d_1$. Choice is to be made for $t_2$, since it has equal cost to be in $d_1$ or $d_2$. If $t_2$ is assigned label $d_1$, then $ecost$ of equation 2 is 0.8, since label for node $t_1$ and $t_2$ will be different. In the same way $ecost$ will be 0.2 if $t_2$ is assigned $d_2$. So to minimize $\theta$, Final labeling is $t_1$ and $t_2$ are assigned $d_2$ and $t_3$ is assigned $d_1$.

In other words, to minimize the cost of assignment $\theta$ we cut the edge $(t_2, t_3)$. Thus the energy minimization problem can be solved by performing 'Min-Cut' on graph. For two labels the problem is solvable in polynomial time. However, for more than 2 labels, solving this optimization problem is NP hard (Kolmogorov and Zabih, 2002).

In the field of image processing, many problems, *e.g. image forground-background detection, image segmentation etc.* are formulated as energy minimization in Markov Random Filed. Some of the graph-cut based algorithms to perform the task are, $\alpha$-expansion, $\alpha - \beta$ swap (Schmidt and Alahari, 2011) and $\alpha$ swap $\beta$ shrink algorithm . For our experiment we use $\alpha$ swap $\beta$ shrink algorithm proposed in Schmidt and Alahari (2011). We are briefly describing the basic idea of the algorithms here. Readers are directed to Kolmogorov and Zabih (2002) and Szeliski et al. (2008) for further details.

For more than two labels (domains), a suboptimal solution can be derived by iteratively performing graph cut for a pair of labels. This problem is usually solved using iterative descent technique. As shown in algorithm 1, the algorithm start with an initial assignment. In each iteration the algorithm selects a pair of labels and performs the graph cut. Based on the graph cut the labels will be reassigned to the nodes. The energy function $\theta$ is calculated at the end of each iteration and the value of $\theta$ is minimized after every iteration to guarantee the convergence.

### 3.4 Split-Merge algorithm to Link concept to Wordnet

This module takes domain specific concept graph generated from previous step as an input and assigns wordnet sense to each term. A term can have more than one sense in the Wordnet and two terms can refer to same Wordnet synset. So the basic approach for the disambiguation is 'Split for Polysemy and Merge for Synonymy'.

**Algorithm 2** *Link with Wordnet*

```
G(V, E)
V := vertices arranged in breadth first order
E := set of edges
|V| := m |E| := n
for v_i ∈ V do
  create node v'_i for each sense of v_i
  distribute edges across senses
end for
v' := new sense vertex set; k := |v'|
for i := 0 → k do
  if Edge set v'_i == 0 then
    delete v'_i
  end if
  for j := 0 → k do
    if Edge set v'_i == Edge set v'_j then
      merge v'_i and v'_j
    end if
  end for
end for
```

As shown in Algorithm 2, the algorithm iterates through the nodes of the concept graph in a breadth first manner. For each vertex in the graph, all possible senses are found from the Wordnet. If a vertex $v$ has $n$ senses then new nodes $v_1$, $v_2$, ..., $v_n$ are created. Then the sense nodes are linked with each other using Wordnet semantic relation, e.g. if two senses $s_i$ and $s_j$ are hypernym-hyponym in wordnet then and edge is created between them.

Figure 4 shows an example of vertex split. The left side of the fig. 4 shows concept graph for term node *cancer*. The term *cancer* has five different senses. Hence the algorithm creates five nodes for the term, one for each Wordnet sense. Then the edges are distributed across vertices depending upon the participating sense. Node *sign* is assigned to sense 1977832, and nodes *leukemia, lymphoma and Ailment* are assigned to sense 14239981. Other sense nodes do not have neighbors in the domain. Hence, sense 14239981 becomes winner sense in Health domain and it is tagged in the domain. Right side of the fig. 4 shows resulting wordnet sense graph.

Once new vertices are created for all vertices in the graph, the vertices with no edge are deleted and vertices for which the sense ids are same are merged as synonymy. Thus, at the end of the process we get a Wordnet sense graph specific to the domain. We label each sense with the specific do-

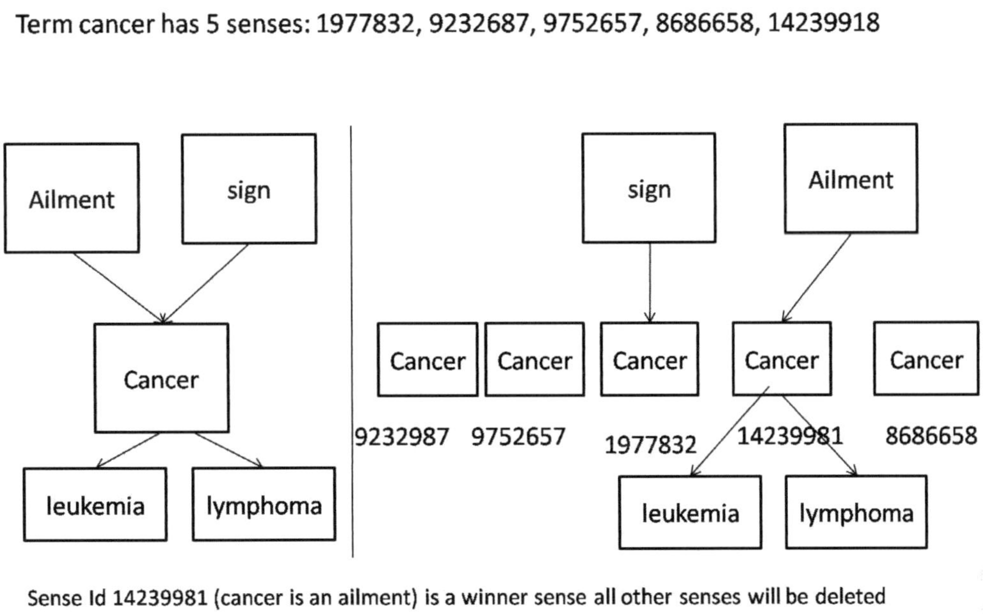


Figure 4: Sense Splitting

| | Health | Tourism |
|---|---|---|
| #terms | 25056 | 56325 |
| #terms after thresholding | 4567 | 5968 |

Table 1: Corpus Statistics

| Domain | Precision | Recall | F-Score |
|---|---|---|---|
| Health | 0.69 | 0.82 | 0.74 |
| Tourism | 0.65 | 0.80 | 0.71 |

Table 2: Precision and Recall of domain labeling

main tag.

## 4 Experiments

We have conducted our experiments on publicly available Heath and Tourism Corpus [3] (Khapra et al., 2010). As shown in Table 1 the total number of unique terms after preprocessing and stop word removal are 25056 in health domain and 56325 in tourism domain. We applied further thresholding and remove low frequency terms (Frequency less than 10) to reduce the size of the graph.

For preprocessing we have used Stanford POS tagger and morpha morph analyzer. We have used Matlab UGM package [4] which is publicly available for researchers. UGM package provides implementation of $\alpha$-expand, $\alpha - \beta$ swap and $\alpha$-expansion-$\beta$-Shrink algorithms. The graph based disambiguation algorithm is written using JGraphT library [5].

The overall performance of the system is calculated against manually labeled domain tags. Table 2 shows overall precision, recall and f-score for both the domains.

As shown in Table 2 the recall value is found to be higher than the precision in both the domains. Reason for high value of recall is the initial labels and high number of edges. Initial labels are assigned based on the term frequency, then based on the labels of the neighboring nodes, node labels are changed. We observe that in case of two domains this leads to add more false positives. In order to reduce recall value and increase precision, we need to run experiments for more domains and with higher edge weights.

[3] http://www.cfilt.iitb.ac.in/wsd/annotated_corpus

[4] http://www.di.ens.fr/~mschmidt/Software/alphaBeta.html

[5] http://jgrapht.org/

## 5 Conclusion

We have proposed a novel graph based approach for automatic domain tagging of WordNet synsets. We pose domain labeling as an energy minization problem and show how the existing image labeling algorithms can be used for the task of WordNet domain tagging. Our approach is completely unsupervised and can be easily adopted across languages. For our experiments we used term frequency based assignment of initial labels, however other existing label can be used to enhance the labeling. In future we aim to construct domain labels for more domains and compare our system with existing labeling. We are also aiming to test our system for multiple languages.

## References


Eneko Agirre and Aitor Soroa. 2009. Personalizing pagerank for word sense disambiguation. In *Proceedings of the 12th Conference of the European Chapter of the Association for Computational Linguistics*, EACL '09, pages 33–41.

Khurshid Ahmad, Lee Gillam, Lena Tostevin, and Ai Group. 1999. Weirdness indexing for logical document extrapolation and retrieval (wilder). In *The Eighth Text REtrieval Conference*.

Luisa Bentivogli, Pamela Forner, Bernardo Magnini, and Emanuele Pianta. 2004. Revising the wordnet domains hierarchy: semantics, coverage and balancing. In *Proceedings of the Workshop on Multilingual Linguistic Ressources*, MLR '04, pages 101–108.

Paul Buitelaar and Bogdan Sacaleanu. 2001. Ranking and selecting synsets by domain relevance. In *proceedings NAACL wordnet workshop*.

Kenneth Ward Church and Patrick Hanks. 1990. Word association norms, mutual information, and lexicography. *Comput. Linguist.*, 16(1):22–29.

Philipp Cimiano and Johanna Vlker. 2005. Text2onto - a framework for ontology learning and data-driven change discovery. In *Proceedings of the 10th International Conference on Applications of Natural Language to Information Systems (NLDB)*, volume 3513 of *Lecture Notes in Computer Science*, pages 227–238.

Fumiyo Fukumoto and Yoshimi Suzuki. 2011. Identification of domain-specific senses in a machine-readable dictionary. In *ACL (Short Papers)*, pages 552–557.

William A. Gale, Kenneth W. Church, and David Yarowsky. 1992. One sense per discourse. In *Proceedings of the workshop on Speech and Natural Language*, HLT '91, pages 233–237.

Aldo Gangemi, Nicola Guarino, Claudio Masolo, and Alessandro Oltramari. 2003. Sweetening wordnet with dolce. *AI Mag.*, 24(3):13–24.

Aitor Gonzalez-Agirre, Mauro Castillo, and German Rigau. 2012. A proposal for improving wordnet domains. In *Proceedings of Language Resources and Evaluation Conference*, pages 3457–3462.

Mitesh M. Khapra, Anup Kulkarni, Saurabh Sohoney, and Pushpak Bhattacharyya. 2010. All words domain adapted wsd: finding a middle ground between supervision and unsupervision. In *Proceedings of the 48th Annual Meeting of the Association for Computational Linguistics*, ACL '10, pages 1532–1541.

Jon Kleinberg and Éva Tardos. 2002. Approximation algorithms for classification problems with pairwise relationships: metric labeling and markov random fields. *J. ACM*, 49(5):616–639.

Vladimir Kolmogorov and Ramin Zabih. 2002. What energy functions can be minimized via graph cuts? In *Proceedings of the 7th European Conference on Computer Vision-Part III*, ECCV '02, pages 65–81.

Lung-Hao Lee, Yu-Ting Yu, and Chu-Ren Huang. 2009. Chinese wordnet domains: Bootstrapping chinese wordnet with semantic domain labels. In Olivia Kwong, editor, *PACLIC*, pages 288–296.

Bernardo Magnini and Gabriela Cavagli. 2000. Integrating subject field codes into wordnet. pages 1413–1418.

Bernardo Magnini, Giovanni Pezzulo, and Alfio Gliozzo. 2002a. The role of domain information in word sense disambiguation. *Natural Language Engineering*, 8:359–373.

Bernardo Magnini, Carlo Strapparava, Giovanni Pezzulo, and Alfio Gliozzo. 2002b. Comparing ontology-based and corpus-based domain annotations in wordnet. In *First International Global WordNet Conference, Mysore, India*.

Mark W. Schmidt and Karteek Alahari. 2011. Generalized fast approximate energy minimization via graph cuts: Alpha-expansion beta-shrink moves. *CoRR*, abs/1108.5710.

Richard Szeliski, Ramin Zabih, Daniel Scharstein, Olga Veksler, Vladimir Kolmogorov, Aseem Agarwala, Marshall Tappen, and Carsten Rother. 2008. A comparative study of energy minimization methods for markov random fields with smoothness-based priors. *IEEE Trans. Pattern Anal. Mach. Intell.*, 30(6):1068–1080.

Ma Xiaojuan and Christiane Fellbaum. 2012. Rethinking wordnet's domains. In *Proceedings of 6th International Global WordNet Conference*, Matsue, Japan, jan.

Wang Yanna and Zhou Zili. 2009. Domain ontology generation based on wordnet and internet. In *Proceedings of the International Conference on Management and Service Science, 2009. MASS '09*, pages 1 –5.

Chaoyong Zhu, Shumin Shi, and Haijun Zhang. 2011. Gloss-based word domain assignment. In *7th International Conference on Natural Language Processing and Knowledge Engineering (NLP-KE)*, pages 150–155.

# Parse Ranking with Semantic Dependencies and WordNet

**Xiaocheng Yin**[♠] **Jungjae Kim**[♠] **Zinaida Pozen**[◇♣] **Francis Bond**[♠]
[♠] **Nanyang Technological University**, Singapore
[◇] **University of Washington**, Seattle
yinx0005@e.ntu.edu.sg, jungjae.kim@ntu.edu.sg,
zpozen@gmail.com, bond@ieee.org

**Abstract**

In this paper, we investigate which features are useful for ranking semantic representations of text. We show that two methods of generalization improved results: extended grand-parenting and supertypes. The models are tested on a subset of SemCor that has been annotated with both Dependency Minimal Recursion Semantic representations and WordNet senses. Using both types of features gives a significant improvement in whole sentence parse selection accuracy over the baseline model.

## 1 Introduction

In this paper we investigate various features to improve the accuracy of semantic parse ranking. There has been considerable successful work on syntactic parse ranking and reranking (Toutanova et al., 2005; Collins and Koo, 2006; McClosky et al., 2006), but very little that uses pure semantic representations. With recent work on building semantic representations (from deep grammars such as LFG (Butt et al., 1999) and HPSG (Sag et al., 1999), directly through lambda calculus, or as in intermediate step in machine translation) the question of ranking them has become more important.

The closest related work is Fujita et al. (2010) who ranked parses using semantic features from Minimal Recursion Semantics (MRS) and syntactic trees, using a Maximum Entropy Ranker. They experimented with Japanese data, using the Hinoki Treebank (Bond et al., 2008), using primarily elementary dependencies: single arcs between predicates and their arguments. These can miss some important connections between predicates.

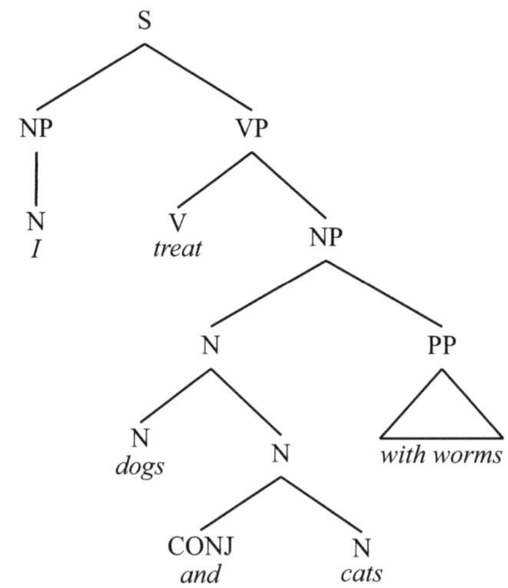


Figure 1: Syntactic view of sentence *"I treat dogs and cats with worms"*.

An example parse tree for *I treat dogs and cats with worms* is shown in Figure 1.[1], for the interpretation "I treat both dogs and cats that have worms" (not "I treat, using worms, dogs and cats" or any of the other possibilities)

The semantic representation we use is Dependency Minimal Recursion Semantics (DRMS: Copestake, 2009). The Minimal Recursion Semantics (MRS: Copestake et al., 2005) is a computationally tractable flat semantics that underspecifies quantifier scope. The Dependency MRS is an MRS representation format that keeps all the information from the MRS but is simpler to manipulate. DMRSs differ from syntactic dependency graphs in that the relations are defined between slightly abstract predicates, not between

[♣] Currently at PointInside, Inc.

[1] Simplified by omission of non-branching nodes.

surface forms. Some semantically empty surface tokens (such as infinitive *to*) are not included, while some predicates are inserted that are not in the original text (such as the null article).

A simplified MRS representation of our example sentence and its DMRS equivalent are shown in Figure 2.

In the DMRS, the basic links between the nodes are present. However, potentially interesting relations such as that between the verb *treat* and its conjoined arguments *dogs* and *cats* are not linked directly. Similarly, the relation between *dogs and cats* and *worms* is conveyed by the preposition *with*, which links them through its external argument (ARG1: *and*) and internal argument (ARG2: *worms*). There is no direct link. We investigate new features that make these links more direct (Section 3.2).

We also explore the significance of the effectiveness of links between words that are connected arbitrarily far away in the semantic graph (Section 3.2.3).

Finally, we experimented with generalizing over semantic classes. We used WordNet semantic files as supertypes to reduce data sparseness (Section 3.2.4). This will generalize the lexical semantics of the predicates, resulting in a reduction of feature size and ambiguity.

## 2 Previous Work

This paper follows up on the work of Fujita et al. (2010) in ranking MRS semantic representations, which was carried out for Japanese. We are conducting a similar investigation for English, and add new features and approaches. Fujita et al. (2010) worked with the Japanese Hinoki Corpus (Bond et al., 2008) data and used hypernym chains from the Goi-Taikei Japanese ontology (Ikehara et al., 1997) for variable-level semantic backoff. This is in contrast to the uniform WordNet semantic file backoff performed here. In addition, this work only focuses on MRS ranking, whereas Fujita et al. (2010) combined MRS features with syntactic features to improve syntactic parse ranking accuracy.

Our use of WordNet Semantic Files (SF) to reduce lexical feature sparseness is inspired by several recent papers. Agirre et al. (2008, 2011) have experimented with replacing open-class words with their SFs. Agirre et al. (2008) have shown an improvement in full parse and PP attachment scores with statistical constituency parsers using SFs. Agirre et al. (2011) have followed up on those results and re-trained a dependency parser on the data where words were replaced with their SFs. This resulted in a very modest labeled attachment score improvement, but with a significantly reduced feature set. In a recent HPSG work, MacKinlay et al. (2012) attempted to integrate lexical semantic features, including SF backoff, into a discriminative parse ranking model. However, this was not shown to help, presumably because the lexical semantic features were built from syntactic constituents rather than MRS predicates.

The ancestor features found to be helpful here are inspired by the use of grand-parenting in syntactic parse ranking (Toutanova et al., 2005) and chains in dependency parsing ranking (Le Roux et al., 2012).

## 3 Resources and Methodology

In this section we introduce the corpus we work on, and the features we extract from it.

### 3.1 Corpus: SemCor

To evaluate our ranking methods, we are using the Redwoods Treebank (Oepen et al., 2004) of manually disambiguated HPSG parses, storing full signs for each analysis and supporting export into a variety of formats, including the Dependency MRS (DMRS) format used in this work.

The HPSG parses in Redwoods are based on the English Resource Grammar (ERG; Flickinger, 2000) – a hand-crafted broad-coverage HPSG grammar of English.

For our experiments, we used a subset of the Redwoods Treebank, consisting of 2,590 sentences drawn from SemCor (Landes et al., 1998). In the SemCor corpus each of the sentences is tagged with WordNet senses created at Princeton University by the WordNet Project research team. The average length of the Redwoods SemCor sentences is 15.4 words, and the average number of parses is 247.

From the treebank we can export the DMRS. The choice of which words become predicates is slightly different in the SemCor/WordNet and the ERG. The ERG lexicon groups together all senses that have the same syntactic properties, making them underspecified for many sense differences. Thus elementary predicate $\mathsf{cat}_{n:1}$ could be any of the WordNet senses $\boldsymbol{cat}_{n:1}$ "feline mammal usu-

*I treat dogs and cats with worms.*

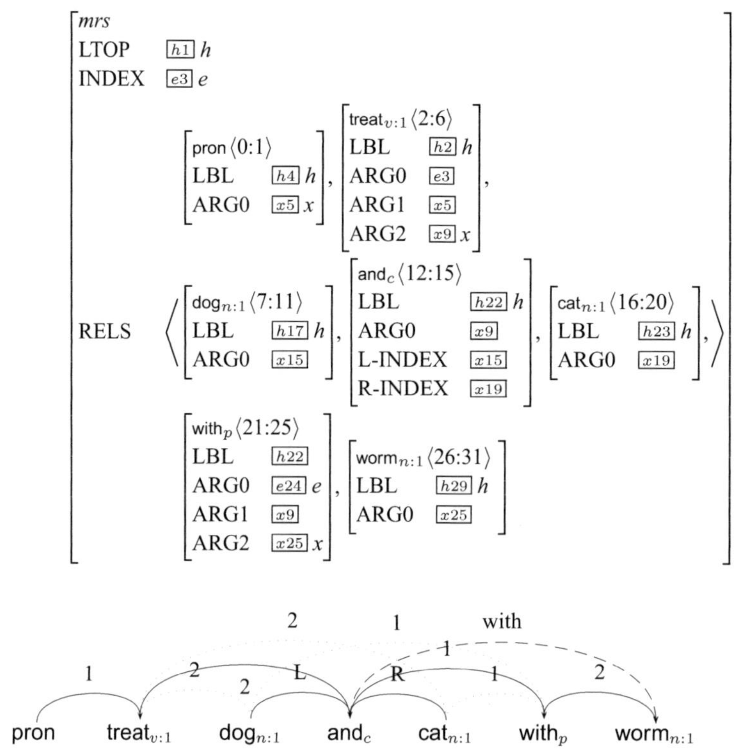


Simplified by omission of quantifiers
Dashed lines show Preposition (P) features
Dotted lines show Conjunction (LR) features
Arc labels show the roles: 1 is ARG1, 2 is ARG2, ....

Figure 2: MRS and DMRS for *I treat cats and dogs with worms.*

| | |
|---|---|
| $\mathtt{Tops}_n$ | $\mathtt{act}_n$ |
| $\mathtt{animal}_n$ | $\mathtt{artifact}_n$ |
| $\mathtt{attribute}_n$ | $\mathtt{body}_n$ |
| $\mathtt{cognition}_n$ | $\mathtt{communication}_n$ |
| $\mathtt{event}_n$ | $\mathtt{feeling}_n$ |
| $\mathtt{food}_n$ | $\mathtt{group}_n$ |
| $\mathtt{location}_n$ | $\mathtt{motive}_n$ |
| $\mathtt{object}_n$ | $\mathtt{person}_n$ |
| $\mathtt{phenomenon}_n$ | $\mathtt{plant}_n$ |
| $\mathtt{possession}_n$ | $\mathtt{process}_n$ |
| $\mathtt{quantity}_n$ | $\mathtt{relation}_n$ |
| $\mathtt{shape}_n$ | $\mathtt{state}_n$ |
| $\mathtt{substance}_n$ | $\mathtt{time}_n$ |

Table 1: WordNet Noun Semantic Files.

ally having thick soft fur and no ability to roar", ***cat***$_{n:2}$ "an informal term for a youth or man" and six more.[2] In some cases, DMRS decomposes a single predicate into multiple predicates (e.g. *here* into in$_p$ this$_q$ place$_n$). The ERG and WordNet also often make different decisions about what constitutes a multiword expression. For these reasons the mapping between the two annotations is not always straightforward. In this paper we use the mapping between the DRMS and WordNet annotations produced by Pozen (2013).

Using the mapping, we exploited the sense tagging of the SemCor in several ways. We experimented both with replacing elementary predicates with their synsets, their hypernyms at various levels and with their semantic files (Landes et al., 1998), which generalize the meanings of words that belong to the same broad semantic categories.[3] These dozens of generalized semantic tags help to address the issue of feature sparseness, compared to thousands of synsets. We show the semantic files for nouns and verbs in Tables 1 and 2. In this paper, we only report on the parse selection accuracy using semantic files to reduce ambiguity, as it gave the best results.

### 3.2 Semantic Dependency Features

In this section we introduce the baseline features for parse ranking.

Table 3 shows example features extracted from the DMRS depicted in Figure 2.Features 1–16 are

| | |
|---|---|
| $\mathtt{body}_v$ | $\mathtt{change}_v$ |
| $\mathtt{cognition}_v$ | $\mathtt{communication}_v$ |
| $\mathtt{competition}_v$ | $\mathtt{consumption}_v$ |
| $\mathtt{contact}_v$ | $\mathtt{creation}_v$ |
| $\mathtt{emotion}_v$ | $\mathtt{motion}_v$ |
| $\mathtt{perception}_v$ | $\mathtt{possession}_v$ |
| $\mathtt{social}_v$ | $\mathtt{stative}_v$ |
| $\mathtt{weather}_v$ | |

Table 2: WordNet Verb Semantic Files.

the semantic dependency features (Baseline). 17–18 are the conjunctive features (LR). 19–22 are the preposition role features (PR).

| # | Sample Features |
|---|---|
| 0 | ⟨0 treat$_{v:1}$ ARG1 pron ARG2 and$_c$⟩ |
| 1 | ⟨0 and$_c$ L-IND dog$_{n:1}$ R-IND cat$_{n:1}$⟩ |
| 2 | ⟨0 with$_p$ ARG1 and$_c$ ARG2 worm$_{n:1}$⟩ |
| 3 | ⟨1 treat$_{v:1}$ ARG1 pron⟩ |
| 4 | ⟨1 treat$_{v:1}$ ARG2 and$_c$⟩ |
| 5 | ⟨1 and$_c$ L-IND dog$_{n:1}$⟩ |
| 6 | ⟨1 and$_c$ R-IND cat$_{n:1}$⟩ |
| 7 | ⟨1 with$_p$ ARG1 and$_c$⟩ |
| 8 | ⟨1 with$_p$ ARG2 worm$_{n:1}$⟩ |
| 9 | ⟨2 treat$_{v:1}$ pron and$_c$⟩ |
| 10 | ⟨2 with$_p$ and$_c$ worm$_{n:1}$⟩ |
| 11 | ⟨3 treat$_{v:1}$ pron⟩ |
| 12 | ⟨3 treat$_{v:1}$ and$_c$⟩ |
| 13 | ⟨3 and$_c$ dog$_{n:1}$⟩ |
| 14 | ⟨3 and$_c$ cat$_{n:1}$⟩ |
| 15 | ⟨3 with$_p$ and$_c$⟩ |
| 16 | ⟨3 with$_p$ worm$_{n:1}$⟩ |
| 17 | ⟨1 treat$_{v:1}$ ARG2 dog$_{n:1}$⟩ |
| 18 | ⟨1 treat$_{v:1}$ ARG2 cat$_{n:1}$⟩ |
| 19 | ⟨ 0 and$_c$ L-IND dog$_{n:1}$ R-IND cat$_{n:1}$ **with**$_p$ worm$_{n:1}$ ⟩ |
| 20 | ⟨1 and$_c$**with**$_p$ worm$_{n:1}$⟩ |
| 21 | ⟨2 and$_c$ worm$_{n:1}$⟩ |
| 22 | ⟨3 and$_c$ worm$_{n:1}$⟩ |

Table 3: Features for the DMRS in Fig 2.

Baseline features are those that directly reflect the dependencies of the DMRS. In Table 3, feature type ⟨0⟩ (0–2) shows predicates with all their arguments. Feature type ⟨1⟩ (3–8) shows each argument individually. Feature type ⟨2⟩ shows all arguments without the argument types. Feature type ⟨3⟩ is the least specified, showing individual arguments without the labels. These types are the same as the MRS features of Toutanova et al. (2005) and

[2] Elementary predicates are shown in sans-serif font, ***WordNet senses*** in bold italic, **`WordNet semantic files`** are shown in bold typewriter.

[3] Semantic Files are also sometimes referred to as Semantic Fields, Lexical Fields or Supersenses.

the SEM-DEP features of Fujita et al. (2010).

### 3.2.1 Conjunctive Features

We further create two more features, called Left/Right Handle Features (LR), to link directly the two arguments of conjunctive relations with their parent, independently from the other argument. In Table 1, for example, the feature ⟨$\text{treat}_{v:1}$ ARG2 $\text{and}_c$⟩, although valid, does not convey the meaning of the sentence. Instead, we add the two LR features ⟨$\text{treat}_{v:1}$ ARG2 $\text{dog}_{n:1}$⟩ (feature 17) and ⟨$\text{treat}_{v:1}$ ARG2 $\text{cat}_{n:1}$⟩ (feature 18), which better model the conjunction relation.

### 3.2.2 Preposition Role Features

As shown in Figure 2, the node $\text{with}_p$ has two links: to $\text{and}_c$ (ARG1) and to $\text{worm}_{n:1}$ (ARG2). The two relations together indicate a noun-preposition-noun relationship. Instead of breaking the relationship into the two separate features, we introduce it, as a whole, as a new type of feature, where the two arguments of the preposition (e.g. $\text{and}_c$, $\text{worm}_{n:1}$) will have a direct relation via the preposition (e.g. $\text{with}_p$). We name these Preposition Role features (PR), as they are similar in spirit to semantic roles. Some sample PR features are given in Table 3, features 19–22.

The new features explicitly convey, for example, noun-preposition-noun relations. Parses containing features like *something at somewhere* can be further distinguished from parses containing *at somewhere* and *something at* separately. When the features become more representative, active parses are more likely to be selected, though with the cost of a larger feature set size.

As 4 types of features can be developed based on one relationship, a Preposition Role link would have 4 separate features. While the Conjunctive features mentioned in previous section give 2 to 4 additional features, Baseline-PR features normally give 4 more. Thus, the feature size of Baseline-PR model is larger than that of the Baseline-LR model.

### 3.2.3 Ancestor Features

While the semantic dependency features correspond to direct dependencies, we introduce a new type of features that represent indirect dependencies between ancestors and their descendants in the DMRS. For each predicate, we collect all its descendants linked through more than one dependency and create features to represent the indirect dependencies between the predicate and the descendants. We name these features Ancestor Features (AF).

| # | Sample Features |
|---|---|
| 0 | ⟨0 $\text{treat}_{v:1}$ ARG1 pron ARG2 $\text{and}_c$⟩ |
| 1 | ⟨0 $\text{and}_c$ L-IND $\text{dog}_{n:1}$ R-IND $\text{cat}_{n:1}$⟩ |
| 2 | ⟨0 $\text{treat}_{v:1}$ ARG2 $\text{dog}_{n:1}$ ARG2 $\text{cat}_{n:1}$⟩ |
| 3 | ⟨1 $\text{treat}_{v:1}$ ARG1 pron⟩ |
| 4 | ⟨1 $\text{treat}_{v:1}$ ARG2 $\text{and}_c$⟩ |
| 5 | ⟨1 $\text{treat}_{v:1}$ ARG2 $\text{dog}_{n:1}$⟩ |
| 6 | ⟨1 $\text{treat}_{v:1}$ ARG2 $\text{cat}_{n:1}$⟩ |
| 7 | ⟨1 $\text{and}_c$ L-IND $\text{dog}_{n:1}$⟩ |
| 8 | ⟨1 $\text{and}_c$ R-IND $\text{cat}_{n:1}$⟩ |
| 9 | ⟨2 $\text{treat}_{v:1}$ pron $\text{and}_c$⟩ |
| 10 | ⟨2 $\text{treat}_{v:1}$ $\text{dog}_{n:1}$ $\text{cat}_{n:1}$⟩ |
| 11 | ⟨3 $\text{treat}_{v:1}$ pron⟩ |
| 12 | ⟨3 $\text{treat}_{v:1}$ $\text{and}_c$⟩ |
| 13 | ⟨3 $\text{treat}_{v:1}$ $\text{dog}_{n:1}$⟩ |
| 14 | ⟨3 $\text{treat}_{v:1}$ $\text{cat}_{n:1}$⟩ |

Table 4: Ancestor Features (AF).

Table 4 has some sample AF features such as that linking from $\text{treat}_{v:1}$ to $\text{dog}_{n:1}$ and $\text{cat}_{n:1}$ (i.e. feature 2). This is a one-level ancestor, involving two predicates, while multi-level ancestors deal with more than two predicates linked in a sequence. Note that these are different from the LR features (features 15, 16 in Table 1), in that AF features include both arguments of a conjunction, for example, connecting the predicate $\text{treat}_{v:1}$ to its grandchildren $\text{dog}_{n:1}$ and $\text{cat}_{n:1}$ via the argument role of $\text{and}_c$ in the predicate (feature 2 in Table 4).

When a sentence has $n$ dependencies, our method generates $O(\frac{n(n-1)}{2}) = O(n^2)$ AF features. In the corpus we use, the dependency structure of a sentence typically has 4 levels. In practice the number of AF features is roughly triple the number of Baseline features. In the evaluation experiments, we investigated all the eight combinations of the three types of LR, PR, and AF features, where each combination is combined with the baseline features.

### 3.2.4 Semantic File Features

In the features up until now, words have been represented as elementary predicate semantic dependencies (SD). Because SemCor also has WordNet senses, we experiment with replacing open class words with their supertypes, in this case using the WordNet semantic files (SF). If a word is not matched to a WordNet synset we continue to use

| # | Sample Features |
|---|---|
| 0 | $\langle$0 **body**$_v$ ARG1 pron ARG2 and$_c\rangle$ |
| 1 | $\langle$0 and$_c$ L-IND **animal**$_n$ R-IND **animal**$_n\rangle$ |
| 2 | $\langle$0 with$_p$ ARG1 **and**$_c$ ARG2 **animal**$_n\rangle$ |
| 3 | $\langle$1 **body**$_v$ ARG1 pron$\rangle$ |
| 4 | $\langle$1 **body**$_v$ ARG2 and$_c\rangle$ |
| 5 | $\langle$1 and$_c$ L-IND **animal**$_n\rangle$ |
| 6 | $\langle$1 and$_c$ R-IND **animal**$_n\rangle$ |
| 7 | $\langle$1 with$_c$ ARG1 **animal**$_n\rangle$ |
| 8 | $\langle$1 with$_c$ ARG2 **animal**$_n\rangle$ |
| 9 | $\langle$2 **body**$_v$ pron and$_c\rangle$ |
| 10 | $\langle$2 with$_p$and$_c$ animal$_n\rangle$ |
| 11 | $\langle$3 **body**$_v$ pron$\rangle$ |
| 12 | $\langle$3 **body**$_v$ and$_c\rangle$ |
| 13 | $\langle$3 and$_c$ **animal**$_n\rangle$ |
| 14 | $\langle$3 and$_c$ **animal**$_n\rangle$ |
| 15 | $\langle$3 with$_c$ and$_c\rangle$ |
| 16 | $\langle$3 with$_c$ **animal**$_n\rangle$ |

Table 5: Baseline features with Semantic Files (SF).

the elementary predicate. This SF representation is also applied to the eight combinations of feature types. A sample of the features in the SF representations are given in Table 5.

Sometimes two features, such as 13 and 14 in Table 3, are replaced with the same feature, like 9 in Table 5, because dog$_{n:1}$ and cat$_{n:1}$ are both replaced with **animal**$_n$. There are about half as many Semantic File features as there are SD features.

## 4 Results

We set up the evaluation task as reranking of the top 500 Redwoods analyses, previously selected by the syntactic MaxEnt ranker. The subset of SemCor introduced in Section 3.1 is trained and tested with the features introduced in Section 3.2. We grouped the feature sets into two according to the two word representation of basic Semantic Dependencies (SD) and generalized Semantic Files (SF). Sometime two or more different parses of a sentence have the same set of features. That is, the features failed to distinguish between two parses: often because of spurious syntactic ambiguity that had no effect on the semantics. In this case we merged duplicate feature sets to reduce the ambiguity in machine learning. If an inactive parse has the same set of features as that of the active one, the resulting merged parse was treated as active.

| Features | Accuracy (%) | Features (×1,000) |
|---|---|---|
| SD-Baseline | 25.4 | 454 |
| SD+LR | 25.3 | 469 |
| SD+PR | 25.8 | 563 |
| SD+LR+PR | 25.6 | 582 |
| SD+AF | 24.8 | 1,430 |
| SD+AF+LR | **27.1** | 1,497 |
| SD+AF+PR | 25.8 | 1,761 |
| SD+AF+LR+PR | 26.3 | 1,842 |

Table 6: Parse selection results with SD.

| Features | Accuracy (%) | Features (×1,000) |
|---|---|---|
| SF-Baseline | 25.0 | 223 |
| SF+LR | 25.1 | 235 |
| SF+PR | 26.3 | 306 |
| SF+LR+PR | 26.3 | 321 |
| SF+AF | **28.2** | 1,051 |
| SF+AF+LR | 28.0 | 1,101 |
| SF+AF+PR | 28.1 | 1,310 |
| SF+AF+LR+PR | 27.7 | 1,375 |

Table 7: Parse selection results with SF.

We used TADM (Toolkit for Advanced Discriminative Modeling; Malouf, 2002) for the training and testing of our machine learning model, following Fujita et al. (2010). We carried out 10-fold cross-validation for evaluation. We measured the parse selection accuracy at the sentence level. A parse was considered correct only when all the dependencies of the parse are correct.

The results of parse selection based on SD and SF representations are shown in Tables 6 and 7. The addition of the ancestor features (AF) gives the most increase in the parse selection accuracy. This result indicates that indirect dependencies as well as direct dependencies in a successful parse frequently appear in other active parses. Second, the SF representation shows better results than the SD representation in most cases. The semantic abstraction of the semantic files reduces the problem of feature sparseness and is enough to effectively rerank parses, whose syntactic properties are already to some extent validated during parsing.

Third, the addition of the PR features also usually increases the parse selection accuracy. We plan to (semi-)automatically find more such multi-dependency structures whose combination shows better performance than the individual dependencies. Fourth, the LR features do not improve the accuracy significantly in most cases, though the SD+AF+LR combination shows the best results among the feature sets of the SD representation. This is understandable since the number of the LR features in our corpus is much smaller than those of the other features of SD, PR and AF. We need to test it with a bigger corpus.

## 5 Discussion

These results show the validity of our assumption that long distance features and supertypes are both useful for selecting the correct interpretation of a sentence. Currently the SD+AF+LR model is the best for using the elementary predicates. However the best overall results come from the SF+AF model when we generalize to the semantic files. In future work we will investigate on larger-sized and more richly annotated corpora so that we can discover more about the relation between feature size and parse selection accuracy. In addition, we expect that increasing the corpus size will lead directly to higher accuracy. Other avenues we would like to explore is backing off not to the semantic files, but rather to WordNet hypernyms at various levels.

These results show that generalizing to semantic supertypes allows us to build semantic ranking models that are not only smaller, but more accurate. In general, learning time was roughly proportional to the number of features, so a smaller model can be learned faster. We hypothesize that it is the combination of dependencies and supertypes that makes the difference: approaches that used semantic features on phrase structure trees (such as Bikel (2000) and MacKinlay et al. (2012)) have in general failed to get much improvement.

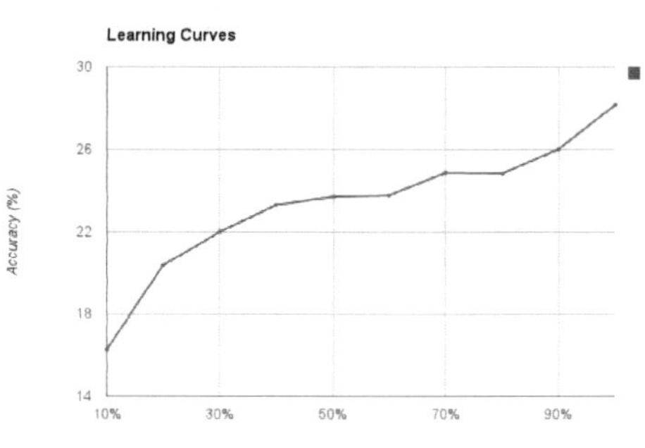


Figure 3: Learning curve for SF+AF.

The overall accuracy is still quite low, due principally to the lack of training data. We show the learning curves for the SF+AF configuration in Figure 3 (the other configurations are similar). The curve is still clearly rising: the accuracy of parse selection on our corpus is far from saturated. This observation gives us confidence that with a larger corpus the accuracy of parse selection will improve considerably. The learning curve in Fujita et al. (2010) showed similar results for the same amount of data, and increased rapidly with more (they had a larger corpus for Japanese).

As there are so far still very few corpora with both structural and lexical semantic annotation, we are currently investigating the use of automatic word sense disambiguation to create the features, in a similar way to Agirre et al. (2008). Finally, we would like to investigate even more features, such as the dependency chains of Le Roux et al. (2012).

One exciting possibility is projecting ranking features across languages: wordnet semantic files are the supertypes for all wordnets linked to the Princeton Wordnet, of which there are many (Bond and Foster, 2013). The predicates that are not in the wordnets are generally either named entities or from smallish closed sets of function words such as conjunctions, prepositions and pronouns. We are currently investigating mapping these between Japanese and English using transfer rules from an existing machine translation system (Bond et al., 2011). In principal, a small set of mappings for closed class words could allow us to quickly boot-strap a semantic ranking model for any language with a wordnet.

## 6 Conclusion

In summary, we showed some features that help parse selection. In the SD group, LR features together with AF features achieved a 1.75% improvement in accuracy over the basic Baseline model (25.36% → 27.12%). However, LR feature alone and AF feature alone both decrease the accuracy (25.36% → 25.28% and 25.36% → 24.84%). PR features and combination of PR and AF features both achieved small improvements (0.416% Baseline → Baseline+PR, 0.410% Baseline → Baseline-PR+AF). LR combined with PR features did not improve the accuracy.

When features get generalized to supertypes, as shown in the SF group, models with more features achieved higher accuracies with the best being the model with ancestor features (AF) added. This (SF+AF) achieved an improvement of 3.21% absolute over the baseline model (24.97% → 28.18%). Adding more features to AF only decreases the accuracy. Generalizing to semantic supertypes allows us to build dependency ranking models that are not only smaller, but more accurate.

### Acknowledgments

The authors are grateful to Mathieu Morey and other members of the Deep Linguistic Processing with HPSG Initiative along with other members of their research groups for many extremely helpful discussions.

## References

Eneko Agirre, Timothy Baldwin, and David Martinez. 2008. Improving parsing and PP attachment performance with sense information. In *Proceedings of the 46th Annual Meeting of the Association for Computational Linguistics (ACL HLT 2008)*, pages 317–325. Columbus, USA.

Eneko Agirre, Kepa Bengoetxea, Koldo Gojenola, and Joakim Nivre. 2011. Improving dependency parsing with semantic classes. *Proceedings of the 49th Annual Meeting of the Association for Computational Linguistics*, pages 699–703.

Daniel M. Bikel. 2000. A statistical model for parsing and word-sense disambiguation. In *Proceedings of the Joint SIGDAT Conference on Empirical Methods in Natural Language Processing and Very Large Corpora*, pages 155–163. Hong Kong.

Francis Bond and Ryan Foster. 2013. Linking and extending an open multilingual wordnet. In *51st Annual Meeting of the Association for Computational Linguistics: ACL-2013*, pages 1352–1362. Sofia. URL `http://aclweb.org/anthology/P13-1133`.

Francis Bond, Sanae Fujita, and Takaaki Tanaka. 2008. The Hinoki syntactic and semantic treebank of Japanese. *Language Resources and Evaluation*, 42(2):243–251. URL `http://dx.doi.org/10.1007/s10579-008-9062-z`, (Re-issue of DOI 10.1007/s10579-007-9036-6 as Springer lost the Japanese text).

Francis Bond, Stephan Oepen, Eric Nichols, Dan Flickinger, Erik Velldal, and Petter Haugereid. 2011. Deep open source machine translation. *Machine Translation*, 25(2):87–105. URL `http://dx.doi.org/10.1007/s10590-011-9099-4`, (Special Issue on Open source Machine Translation).

Miriam Butt, Tracy Holloway King, María-Eugenia Niño, and Frédérique Segond. 1999. *A Grammar Writer's Cookbook*. CSLI publications.

Michael Collins and Terry Koo. 2006. Discriminative reranking for natural language parsing. *Computational Linguistics*, 31(1).

Ann Copestake. 2009. Slacker semantics: Why superficiality, dependency and avoidance of commitment can be the right way to go. In *Proceedings of the 12th Conference of the European Chapter of the ACL (EACL 2009)*, pages 1–9. Athens.

Ann Copestake, Dan Flickinger, Ivan A. Sag, and Carl Pollard. 2005. Minimal Recursion Semantics. An introduction. *Research on Language and Computation*, 3(4):281–332.

Dan Flickinger. 2000. On building a more efficient grammar by exploiting types. *Natural Language Engineering*, 6 (1):15–28.

Sanae Fujita, Francis Bond, Takaaki Tanaka, and Stephan Oepen. 2010. Exploiting semantic information for HPSG parse selection. *Research on Language and Computation*, 8(1):1–22. URL `http://dx.doi.org/10.1007/s11168-010-9069-7`.

Satoru Ikehara, Masahiro Miyazaki, Satoshi Shirai, Akio Yokoo, Hiromi Nakaiwa, Kentaro Ogura, Yoshifumi Ooyama, and Yoshihiko Hayashi. 1997. *Goi-Taikei — A Japanese Lexicon*. Iwanami Shoten, Tokyo. 5 volumes/CDROM.

Shari Landes, Claudia Leacock, and Christiane Fellbaum. 1998. Building semantic concordances. In Christine Fellbaum, editor, *WordNet: An Electronic Lexical Database*, chapter 8, pages 199–216. MIT Press.

Joseph Le Roux, Benoit Favre, Alexis Nasr, and Seyed Abolghasem Mirroshandel. 2012. Generative constituent parsing and discriminative dependency reranking: Experiments on english and french. In *Proceedings of the ACL 2012 Joint Workshop on Statistical Parsing and Semantic Processing of Morphologically Rich Languages*, pages 89–99. Association for Computational Linguistics, Jeju, Republic of Korea. URL `http://www.aclweb.org/anthology/W12-3412`.

Andrew MacKinlay, Rebecca Dridan, Diana McCarthy, and Timothy Baldwin. 2012. The effects of semantic annotations on precision parse ranking. In *SEM 2012: The First Joint Conference on Lexical and Computational Semantics-*, volume 2, pages 228–236. Association for Computational Linguistics.

Robert Malouf. 2002. A comparison of algorithms for maximum entropy parameter estimation. In *CONLL-2002*, pages 49–55. Taipei, Taiwan.

David McClosky, Eugene Charniak, and Mark Johnson. 2006. Reranking and self-training for parser adaptation. In *44th Annual Meeting of the Association for Computational Linguistics and 21st International Conference on Computational Linguistics: COLING/ACL-2006*, pages 337–344.

Stephan Oepen, Dan Flickinger, Kristina Toutanova, and Christoper D. Manning. 2004. LinGO Redwoods: A rich and dynamic treebank for HPSG. *Research on Language and Computation*, 2(4):575–596.

Zinaida Pozen. 2013. *Using Lexical and Compositional Semantics to Improve HPSG Parse Selection*. Master's thesis, University of Washington. URL `https://digital.lib.washington.edu/researchworks/handle/1773/%23469`.

Ivan A. Sag, Tom Wasow, and Emily Bender. 1999. *Syntactic Theory: A Formal Introduction*. CSLI Publications, Stanford, second edition.

Kristina Toutanova, Christopher D. Manning, Dan Flickinger, and Stephan Oepen. 2005. Stochastic HPSG parse disambiguation using the Redwoods corpus. *Research on Language and Computation*, 3(1):83–105.

# Do not do processing, when you can look up: Towards a Discrimination Net for WSD

**Diptesh Kanojia**
IIT Bombay
dipteshkanojia@gmail.com

**Pushpak Bhattacharyya**
IIT Bombay
pb@cse.iitb.ac.in

**Raj Dabre**
IIT Bombay
prajdabre@gmail.com

**Siddhartha Gunti**
IIT Bombay
siddhartha.gunti191@gmail.com

**Manish Shrivastava**
IIT Bombay
mani.shrivastava@gmail.com

## Abstract

The task of Word Sense Disambiguation (WSD) incorporates in its definition the role of 'context'. We present our work on the development of a tool which allows for automatic acquisition and ranking of 'context clues' for WSD. These clue words are extracted from the contexts of words appearing in a large monolingual corpus. These mined collection of contextual clues form a *discrimination net* in the sense that for targeted WSD, navigation of the net leads to the correct sense of a word given its context. Utilizing this resource we intend to develop efficient and light weight WSD based on look up and navigation of memory-resident knowledge base, thereby avoiding heavy computation which often prevents incorporation of any serious WSD in MT and search. The need for large quantities of sense marked data too can be reduced.

## 1 Introduction

Word Sense Disambiguation (WSD) is formally defined as the task of computationally identifying senses of a word in a context. Chatterjee et al. (2011) showed that contextual evidence is the predominant parameter for human (and hence machine) sense disambiguation process.

Joshi et al. (2013) had conducted experiments on eye tracking for sense disambiguation in which they studied the cognitive aspects of human sense disambiguation. They demonstrated that annotators do not focus on sentential structure but look for specific words that help identify the domain of the word and narrow down the number of senses.

Kanojia et al. (2012) had developed a basic WordNet navigation and clue selection tool, "Sense Discrimination Tool", which we have studied and improved upon. We realized that this tool can be improved to include many useful functionalities, the most important being automated clue word acquisition using word context (see section 2) and clue ranking based on the relative importance of a clue word. Thus, to utilize context efficiently we have developed a tool which can help mark clues for each word sense along with providing weights indicating their importance. It can also automatically generate clue word suggestions from large monolingual corpus; leading to the development of a new resource for context based WSD. This tool will later evolve into a memory resident knowledge base whose look up and navigation can perform high quality, light weight WSD. This would avoid the need for sense marked data which it is expensive to create. Such a static WSD system will essentially amount to look up and navigation to discriminate amongst word senses, thereby avoiding expensive computation.

## 2 Clue Marker Tool[1]

"Sense Discrimination Tool" developed by Kanojia et al. (2012) provided simple functionality of allowing lexicographers to traverse WordNet senses and annotate them with clues which were added manually during this process.

The Clue Marker Tool which we present here has embedded within it a number of functionali-

[1] http://www.cfilt.iitb.ac.in/~diptesh/admin/login.php

ties which transcend beyond mere marking words with clues. It is language independent and we plan to expand it to many other languages later. For now we describe our work on Hindi. Refer to snapshots attached for each subsection. The tool allows for the following actions:

### 2.1 Centralized User Management

In order to track what work was done by which lexicographer we created a registration/login mechanism (Snapshot 1). This ensures that no one can tamper with the data and also determines how much work was done by a particular person. After the first registration the request is sent to the admin who can regulate the tool usage by the person.

### 2.2 Phonetic Typing and Devanagari Keyboard

We integrated the Google Transliterate API into our tool which simplifies the task of data entry. For people who find the phonetic typing difficult we have also incorporated a visual Devanagari keyboard.

### 2.3 WordNet Synsets Navigation

Wordnets have emerged as crucial resources for Natural Language Processing (NLP). They are lexical structures composed of synsets and semantic relations (Fellbaum, 1998). Our tool allows one to navigate through the complete Hindi WordNet (Narayan et al., 2002). One can proceed in a sequential manner by viewing previous or next synsets. If one wishes to view any arbitrary synset they can just type its 'id' in a search box and get redirected to it. One can also search for a word and the tool will display all the synsets that contain that word and the user can select any one.

### 2.4 Add Clues

Synset words, Gloss and Example are possible clue sources. We have provided a mechanism so that if a user selects any text on the page, it can be added to the clues box with a "add"/"add to clues" button (Snapshot 2). After the lexicographer is sure, she can "submit" the clues to make sure they are finally added to the database. Adding clues only from synset words, gloss or example can be quite restrictive and thus we incorporated a corpus search mechanism known as the concordancer search.

### 2.5 Concordancer Search

The concordancer is a tool in which, given a corpus and any word to be searched, it returns a set of sentences which contain the word (Snapshot 3). We provided mechanisms to control the number of sentences to be displayed for lexicographer's convenience. Any word from the sentences returned by the concordancer search results can also be added to the clue word list by the "add to clues" button. The corpus we used, initially, consisted of around 0.22 million sentences from tourism, health and BBC news corpus[2]. We then considered incorporating 0.45 million lines of Wikipedia corpus and 0.97 million lines of crawled news data. Thus we collated a total of approximately 1.4 million lines of monolingual corpus for Hindi.

### 2.6 Generate Clues automatically

Even with the above concordancer, the lexicographers still have to go through a large number of sentences to decide on the clue words. The primary feature of this tool is being able to generate clues automatically from concordancer sentences (Snapshot 4). To alleviate this problem we developed a mechanism to automatically generate candidate clue words. The lexicographer can click on the "search for possible clues" button to get a set of words which the tool proposes to be prominent clues. The procedure to generate the clue words is given below:

1. Select N sentences (N=10 for the results reported here) from the concordancer search results by using the first word of the synset as a search term.
2. Run the Hindi part of speech CRF tagger[3] on these sentences.
3. Select the nouns and verbs from the tagged words.
4. Remove stop words, noise and duplicates.

We select nouns and verbs because the lexicographers determined that they are the best candidates for clues. These are, however, not ordered by relative importance, which was the objective of developing the tool. We thus made investigations on the association between the clue words and the synset words leading to some interesting

[2] www.cfilt.iitb.ac.in/wsd/annotated_corpus/

[3] http://www.cfilt.iitb.ac.in/tools/POS_tagger.zip

| S. No. | Word | Clues |
|---|---|---|
| 1. | अपराध (*aparādha*) (crime) | **अपराधी** (*aparādhi* - criminal), **दण्ड**(*daṇḍa* - penalty), **सजा**(*sajā* - punishment), **हत्या**(*hatyā* - killing), **साधुजी**(*sādhuji* - sage), **चौंका**(*cauṅkā* - surprised), **बंगले**(*bangle* - bungalow), **लौटा**(*lautā* - return),**घटनाक्रम**(*ghatnākrama* – development), सोकर(*sokar* - slept) |
| 2. | पुष्पित (*puṣpita*) (flowering) | **आनंद**(*ānanda* - joy), **वनस्पति**(*vanaspati* - flora), **स्पर्श**(*sparśa* - touch), स्थिरता(*sthiratā* - stability), सखी(*sakhī* - girlfriend), **सम्पर्क**(*samparka* - contact), शांति(*śānti* – silence, peace), **पवन**(*pavana* - wind), **समन्वित** (*samanvita* - incorporated) |
| 3. | अनाथ (*anātha*) (orphan) | **अनाथों** (*anātho* - orphans), **अनाथालय**(*anāthālaya* - orphanage), **मां-बाप**(*maa-baap* - parents), बताती(*batāti* - inform), मारती(*mārti* – to hit), चलाना(*calānā* – to operate), मैनेजर(*mainējara* - manager), **असहाय**(*asahāya* - helpless), **खोकर**(*khokar* - lose) |
| 4. | अपमान (*apamāna*) (insult, affront) | **जनक**(*janak* - originator), **सहन**(*sahan* – to endure), **मरना**(*marnā* – to die), **समझ**(*samajh* - understanding), **कहे**(*kahe* - said), भूखों(*bhukho* - hungry), परीक्षित(*parikshita* - tested), सूचनाओं(*sucanao* - information), **मुँह**(*muñh* - mouth) |

Table 1: Clues after PMI ranking

results and insights which are given in the next section.

For each word in the list returned, we calculated a score and sorted the list based on this score. The result is a reordered list of clues presented to the lexicographers who reject the wrong ones. Since the best clues are at the top the lexicographers found their task much simpler than before.

## 3 Clue Words Ranking

We considered a set of 80 synsets and studied them to form an idea of the basis of ranking the clue words. We used Hindi Synsets for our study. For each synset:

1. Generate the set of possible/candidate clue words by corpus searching, POS tagging and filtering as described in section 2.6.
2. For each clue word generate scores
3. Sort list of scored clues in descending order and consider top 10 clues.

Scoring techniques which include the co-occurrence factor between two words seemed intuitive since they would rate the clues statistically. We studied some prominent scoring mechanisms such as contingency table measure and PMI given by Terra et al. (2003) amongst which PMI fared better.

### 3.1 Pointwise Mutual Information

PMI, a concept from information theory, is indicative of the degree of association between two words, in this case: the current synset member and the potential clue word. The formulae used are:

$$\mathrm{PMI(target, clue\ word)} = \log_2 \frac{\mathrm{p(target, clue\ word)}}{\mathrm{p(target)*p(clue\ word)}} \quad \ldots (3.1)$$

$$\mathrm{p(x,y)} = \frac{\#(\text{number of sentences containing x and y})}{\#(\text{number of sentences})} \quad \ldots (3.2)$$

$$\mathrm{p(x)} = \frac{\#(\text{number of sentences containing x })}{\#(\text{number of sentences})} \quad \ldots (3.3)$$

For words that are independent, then PMI is 0.

### 3.2 Results with PMI

We present in Table 1 above, four synsets for which there were strong clues after PMI based ranking. The clues in bold are relevant ones. Over the complete set of 80 words studied, an average of 5 relevant clue words occurred in the top 10 after PMI ranking. This situation freed the lexicographers from looking for clue words manually, by reading sentences from the concordancer search.

## 4 Synset reinforced clue ranking

In PMI based ranking, we would only consider the first word of a synset to retrieve clues which led the tool to produce the same set of clues for all synsets which had this word as the first word. We solved this problem by reinforcing the clues using other members of the given synset. We also use a different metric for clue word selection and ranking.

This modified clue acquisition mechanism, instead of using just the first word of the synset, uses the first three words of the synset. Using more members of the same synset helps in high-

| S. No. | Word senses | Top overlapped clues |
|---|---|---|
| 1. | जन्मा (*janma*) (born) | काल(*kaal* - time), मृत्यु(*mrityu* - death), रूप(*roop* – form, shape), आज(*aaj* - today), दुनिया(*duniya* - world), युग(*yuga* - era) |
| | जन्मा (*janma*) (originate) | प्रयोगशाला(*prayogshalaa* - laboratory), कारण(*kaaran* - reason), अनुसंधान(*anusandhaan* - research), अध्ययन(*adhyyan* - study), भाषा(*bhashaa* - language), तर्क(*tarka* - argument) |
| 2. | आदिवासी (*aadivaasi*) (tribe) | अभाव(*abhaav* - scarcity), कारण(*kaaran* - reason), प्रदेश(*Pradesh* - territory), शिक्षा(*shiksha* - education), जनजाति(*janjaati* – tribe, folk), भाषांतरण(*bhashaantaran* - translation), विवाद(*vivaada* - debate), अवस्थापन(*avasthaapan* – habitation, abode) |
| | आदिवासी (*aadivaasi*) (domicile) | जनसंख्या(*janasankhya* - population), राज्य(*rajya* - state), सीमाओं(*seemaon* - borders), संस्कृति(*sanskriti* - culture), आकलनों(*aakalanon* - estimations) |
| 3. | यूरोपीय,यूरोपी (*yuropiya, yuropi*) (related to Europe) | संघ(*sangha* - union), रूप(*roop* - form), देशों(*deshon* - countries), शक्ति(*shakti* - power), विश्व(*vishwa* - world) |
| | यूरोपी,यूरोपीय (*yuropi , yuropiya*) (European citizen) | भाषा(*bhasha* - language), लोगों(*logon* - people), परिवार(*parivaar* - family) |
| 4. | जल्दी (*jaldi*) (rapidity) | काम(*kaam* - work), कारण(*kaaran* - reason), लोग(*log* - people), अभिनय(*abhinaya* - acting), विषय(*vishaya* - topic), नुकसान(*nuksaan* - loss) |
| | जल्दी, सवेरे (*jaldi, savere*) (early morning) | स्नान(*snaana* - bath), सुबह(*subaha* - morning), दिन(*din* - day), दूध(*doodh* - milk), देर(*der* - delay), व्रत(*vrata* – fast, fasting) |

Table 2: Overlapped clues

lighting those clues which are more important for a given synset.

As before, we retrieve the sets of candidate clue words for each of the 3 synset words and then perform further processing. Instead of just top 10 clues we now consider as many as possible to ensure coverage. We find clue word overlaps between the three different sets of clues obtained. Those candidate clues which are present in more than one set are obviously good indicators of sense and are given a higher ranking. This added metric counters polysemy, even when first synset word is same for different senses, since having clues which are generated from members of the given synset would help greatly in disambiguating using the overlapping clues. Such clue overlaps would be able to help us distinguish between fine grained word senses and eliminate the unrelated sense, thus improving our accuracy. Table 2 presents such cases where clue overlaps are able to distinguish specifically between the different senses for the same word.

## 5 Error Analysis

For every wrong clue generated we studied the sentences from the concordancer which lead to its coming up. We believe that these wrong clues appear due to the following reasons:

### 5.1.1 Chance co-occurrence

Consider for अनाथ (*anātha*) (orphan) the clue word मैनेजर (manager). Here अनाथ mostly occurred with अनाथालय (orphanage) (a strong clue) which has an association with मैनेजर; but मैनेजर can occur with any organization like banks, companies and so on. Similarly, Proper nouns can also occur by chance without giving any information about the senses.

### 5.1.2 Lack of Context

Retrieval of relevant clue words is greatly affected by the sentences that are chosen to get the context. Currently, we are using 10 sentences from the concordancer output to get a list of potential clues. Using more sentences can help in some cases by providing more relevant clues. We have refrained from increasing this number to avoid runtime computation time. We expect to reduce pre-processing time to enable us to include more sentences.

### 5.1.3 Absence of word in corpus

The tool cannot provide any clues if the word is not present in the monolingual corpus. This can happen for two reasons: if the word is rare or if the word is not matched by the concordancer due to corpus tokenization errors. We realized that 1.4 million domain specific sentences can be restrictive. We are currently in the process of collecting more, clean and good quality, corpus from the web.

# 6 Discrimination Net

The tool is expected to produce a structured net (Figure 1) with the synset words (green) connected to the clues (yellow), as neighbors, with weighted edges given by the scoring mechanism, which for now is PMI. Using wordnet sematic relations, relevant clues can be brought closer to the sense that they indicate. This structured net will be further augmented by inclusion of semantic relations from WordNet to result in a *Discrimination Net*. To disambiguate a word using this net, we will calculate a score for all the senses of the word and select the sense with highest score based on its clues.

## 6.1 Scoring mechanism and sample

The score for a particular possible sense will be progressively calculated by traversing from clue words of the given synset in the net, while moving towards the sense word. We are in the process of developing a more efficient scoring mechanism than PMI which will help us in assigning relevant weightage to edges in the discrimination net and improve the potential clue score.

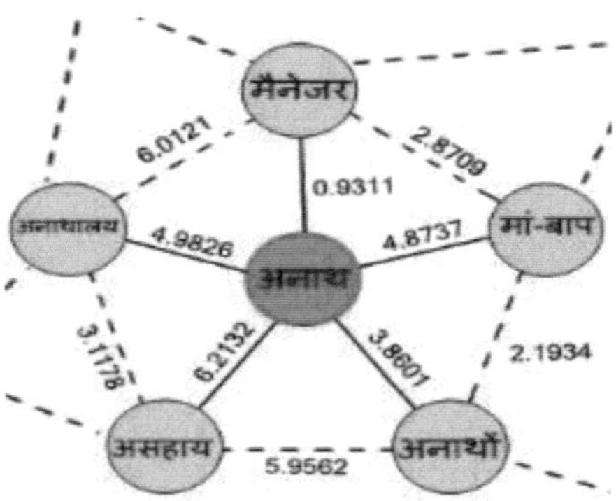


Figure 1: Discrimination Net Sample

# 7 Conclusions and Future work

We have described the Clue Marker Tool for word senses which allows lexicographers to select relevant clues from a set of ranked candidate clues to disambiguate the sense of the word under consideration. This tool, in addition to being a wordnet browser, is also a corpus browser by way of concordancer based searching. In order to generate high quality clues, we applied PMI based clue ranking and observed its efficacy. The tool is language independent, since by adding synsets of another language to the database and the POS tagger, the clue gathering process can be adapted for the new language. In future we plan to study better measures for clue ranking based on established statistical methods, along with augmenting the corpus to get improvements in generated clues. Finally, we plan to devise efficient and light weight WSD methods that will use the discrimination net, hopefully, bringing about a newer understanding of WSD.

# References


Pushpak Bhattacharyya, Debasri Chakrabarty, Dipak Narayan and Prabhakar Pande. 2002. An Experience in Building the Indo WordNet- a WordNet for Hindi, *International Conference on Global WordNet (GWC 02), Mysore, India.*

Pushpak Bhattacharyya, Arindam Chatterjee, Salil Joshi, Diptesh Kanojia and Akhlesh Meena. 2011. A Study of Human Sense annotation process: Man v/s Machine. *Global WordNet Conference, Matsue, Japan.*

Pushpak Bhattacharyya, Arindam Chatterjee, Salil Joshi and Diptesh Kanojia. 2012. Discrimination Net for Hindi. *COLING, Mumbai, India.*

Pushpak Bhattacharyya, Salil Joshi and Diptesh Kanojia. 2013. More than meets the eye: Study of Human Cognition in Sense Annotation. *NAACL HLT 2013, Atlanta, USA.*

Charles Clarke and Egidio Terra. 2003. Frequency Estimates for Statistical Word Similarity Measures. *NAACL HLT 2003, Edmonton, Canada.*

Christiane Fellbaum. 1998. WordNet: An Electronic Lexical Database. *Cambridge, MA: MIT Press.*

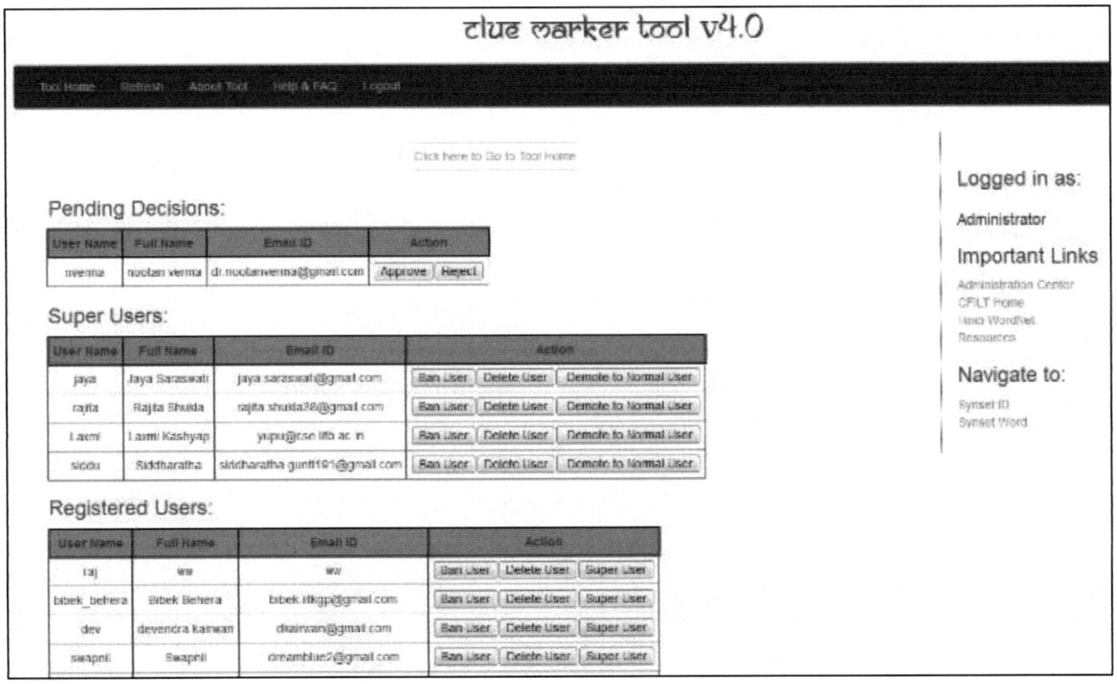


**Snapshot 1: Clue Marker tool user management**

**Snapshot 2: Clue Marker tool home / Data entry**

**Snapshot 3: Clue marker tool concordancer pane**

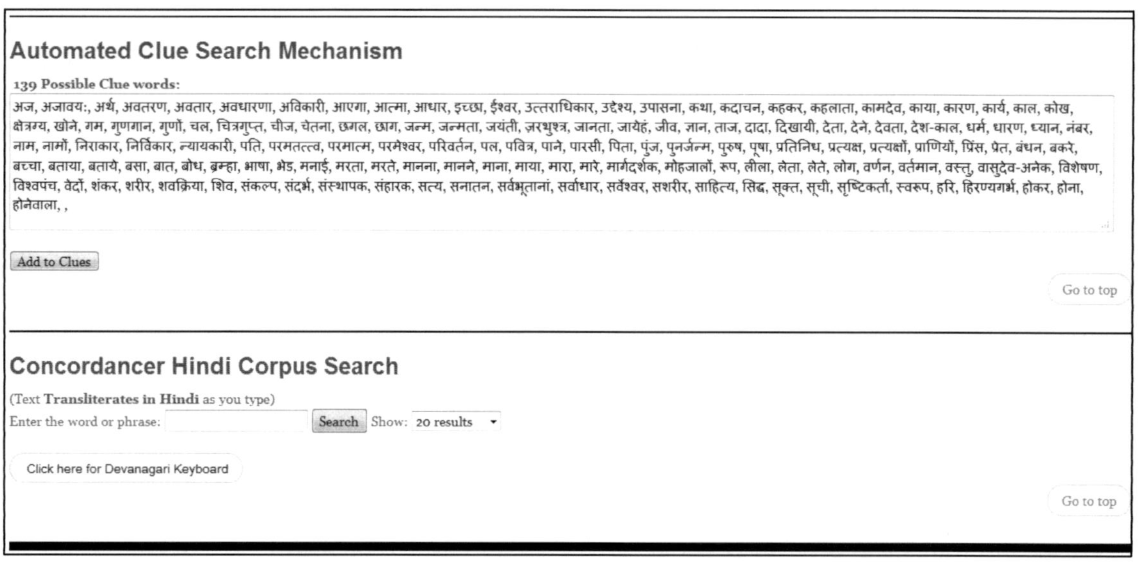


**Snapshot 4: Clue marker tool automated clue search**

# Elephant Beer and Shinto Gates: Managing Similar Concepts in a Multilingual Database

**Martin Benjamin**
EPFL Swiss Federal Institute of Technology
Lausanne, Switzerland
martin.benjamin@epfl.ch

## Abstract

This paper addresses problems in equivalence among concepts, within and between languages. The Kamusi Project has begun building a massively multilingual dictionary that relates as many languages as possible for which data can be gathered. In the process, we have encountered numerous complexities that we attempt to address through the design of our data structure. This paper presents the issues we have encountered, and discusses the solutions that we have developed.

## 1 Introduction

True synonyms are rare within a language, if synonyms are taken to be words that can stand in each other's place in all contexts. Even if you cannot propose a whisper's difference between the ideas of "snuggling" and "cuddling", you can "snuggle against" someone, but you cannot "cuddle against" them. In Swahili, "ndovu" and "tembo" are completely interchangeable when talking about elephants, but bring you different brands of beer when you ask for them in a bar. Each word must thus be treated differently in a dictionary, so that its particular nuances can be elaborated.

Between languages, it is quite common that terms exist for exactly the same concept. When speaking of colors, English "red" evokes essentially the same bloody hue as "rouge" in French or "nyekundu" in Swahili. An "elephant" is an elephant, whether it is "éléphant" or "ndovu". "Beer" and "bière" and "bia" are all beer. However, we do not expect other senses of a word to map identically in translation; we anticipate that a "red" grape in English might be "noir" in French.

These issues are not new to lexicographers, and this paper will not claim to advance our understanding of synonymy; a trio of recent articles in the International Journal of Lexicography (2013) by Adamska-Sałaciak, Gouws, and Murphy provide the context from which this paper is launched. What is new is the system that Kamusi is developing to produce a global dictionary that can catalogue synonyms within and across languages, and account for their subtle differences.

## 2 Monolingual Pillars and Multilingual Beams

The basic architecture of Kamusi was developed to handle cases like the examples above, which we now think of as the easy ones. The initial structure is two dimensional, with vertical pillars and horizontal beams.

The vertical axis is the monolingual entry for a term. Within a language, each term is entitled to as many entries as that particular sequence of letters has senses; "light" (not dark) is a different entry from "light" (not heavy) or "light" (not serious) or "light" (low calorie). Those entries can then be segregated into groups, so that a "light" (flame for a cigarette) is grouped with the verb "light" (ignite a fire) while "light" (a lamp) is grouped with "light" (a traffic signal). Within groups, entries can be ranked, so that "light" (a lamp) is listed above "light" (a traffic signal). The groups themselves can be ranked on a scientific or whimsical basis – a corpus count would place the groups for light (energy) and light (lamps) high on the list, but the decision about where to rank light comedy versus light soda can only be arbitrary. This vertical structure provides all the space needed to engage in the lexicographical challenge of giving a definition to each of a term's different senses. In order to support the horizontal beams, no entry is deemed complete in Kamusi unless it includes a definition written in its own language.

The horizontal axis is the same concept as expressed in different languages. "Light" (not dark) can be expressed with some term in German, another term in Japanese, and another one in Songhay. Once a concept from one language has been determined to be equivalent to a particular entry for a different language that is already in the system, we take the relationship to be transitive across all the other equivalents in all the other languages in the system. Because "red" for colors and "red" for grapes are two different entries on the vertical pillar in English, they connect to different horizontal beams, and we can weld on terms in different languages that match those varying concepts:

Red (color of blood) ↔ rouge ↔ nyekundu
↓
Red (color of wine) ↔ rouge ↔ nyekundu
↓
Red (color of grapes) ↔ noir ↔ zambarau

In this schema, "rouge" in French has its own monolingual pillar (color of blood, color of wine, type of cosmetic), as does "noir". It is clear what terms gloss each other between languages – one would not look up "red" and mistakenly use the color of blood to talk about grapes in either French or Swahili. Horizontal beams work perfectly when concepts are essentially the same across languages.

## 3 Mapping Inexact Concepts

Unfortunately for our architecture, however, languages do not map on a simple one-to-one basis. We have had to address five major problems with the internal wiring of our edifice.

1) Partial equivalence
2) No equivalent term
3) Different forms
4) Different parts of speech
5) Synonyms within a language

1. Partial equivalence. In English, we have ten fingers and ten toes, and the Dutch have ten "vingers" and ten "tenen". Romanians, however, have twenty "degete", and Swahili speakers have twenty "vidole". Nowhere is this a problem for glove makers, but it wreaks havoc for a multilingual dictionary. English and Dutch are full equivalents, as are Romanian and Swahili, but those two sets only partially match each other. Thus, the flow of transitivity is broken, and the nature of the partial relationships is ambiguous.

When establishing a relationship between terms in Kamusi, a contributor specifies whether they are "parallel", "similar", or "explanatory" (see the next section). Terms that are designated as "similar" disrupt the welding of the horizontal beam. We know that items that are added as parallel to "finger" will be transitive to the first set, and items that are parallel to "vidole" are parallel to the second set, and we can also infer the same similarity between new terms on either side of the divide. However, we cannot infer any inherent relationship between similarities that have not been documented; a language that had terms for each individual finger but no overriding category term, for example, would be similar to finger and vinger in a different way than it is similar to kidole and deget, and differently than the similarity between finger/vinger ↔ deget/kidole. The programming to chart similarities between transitive groups is not complete as of this writing.

Forthcoming programming will include two new features for similarities. First, each relationship pair will have a descriptive field in which differences can be explained in writing, in multiple languages. Second, users will be able to vote on the level of similarity (close, distant, barely comparable), and the votes can be aggregated into a graphic such as a Venn diagram to alert dictionary users about potential dangers in equivalence.

Partial equivalence is also addressed within Kamusi's vertical pillars. As discussed, each sense should have a definition of a term written in its own language. Each of these definitions can be further translated into any other language. Thus, an English definition of "finger" would refer to the ten digits of the hand, and the Romanian and Swahili translations of that definition, stored within the English concept of "finger", would also discuss the ten digits of the hand. Conversely, the Romanian definition of "deget" would refer to both hands and feet, and the English translation of that definition within the Romanian entry would contain that clarifying information for English readers.

2. No equivalent term. Numerous concepts that exist in one language do not exist in another. For example, Japanese has a term "torii" (鳥居) for the ceremonial gate to a Shinto shrine seen in the images above. "Torii" is not an English word, but we need a way to describe it in a Japanese-English dictionary. Our solution is to create an entry on the English side that is labeled "explanatory" of the Japanese term: "Shinto gate". This term does not become part of the larger English lexicon, but will be visible when a user looks up "torii" in Japanese or conducts a direct English-Japanese search.

Explanatory phrases come with their own complications. "Shinto gate" is an endpoint on the horizontal beam; one can add a French explanatory phrase for "torii", but that will not link to the English explanation. However, Okinawan does have the concept, and uses the term トリイ (torii). In this case, the relationship between Japanese and Okinawan is transitive, so we assume that English "Shinto gate" is explanatory of the Okinawan and any other languages that enter the parallel set.

Parallel relationships cannot be automatically inferred from explanations in the current Kamusi system. For example, "-simulia" in Swahili and "a povesti" in Romanian are both explained in English with the phrase "tell a story", but that relationship is not easily discoverable. Future programming will address this gap.

3. Different forms. Two languages might have the same concept, represented by the same part of speech, but approached from different directions. For example, placing a passive suffix on the Swahili verb "-abiri" (travel as a passenger) produces the verb "-abiriwa", which can translate to English as "be crossed" in the sense that a river is crossed by a ferry. Such misalignments occur ad infinitum between Bantu languages and English, and similar form differences occur throughout the data.

Kamusi has a tidy system for handling different forms of a word (although we do not have a tidy term, since neither "morphemes" nor "inflections" cover the concept; our current candidate is the coinage "morphlections"). When a language has a manageable number N of morphlections, such as the four possible forms of a Portuguese adjective, we create N minus one additional input boxes for that part of speech, which we label during the setup process (e.g., feminine singular, masculine plural, and feminine plural). A more automated system for large conjugation sets such as Romance verbs is on the agenda, and a fully automated system for machine-predictable agglutination parsing has already been developed for Swahili and should be transferable (not without tears) to languages from German to Xhosa.

This morphlection system makes it possible to list forms that do not normally appear in dictionaries, such as the passive verb form in English. "-Abiriwa" can then be linked to "be crossed" within the correct sense entry of "cross" (not betray, nor intersect, etc.). Everything that one needs to know in order to make sense of "be crossed" is contained within the English entry (it is the passive form of a verb meaning "to pass from one side to the other"), without having to create a full separate English entry to accommodate the Swahili formation. It also becomes possible to link morphlections from one language to morphlections in another, such as mapping the English past participle "crossed" to the French past participle "traversé". A search for a morphlection will pull up the full result for the canonical form, but show any relevant interlanguage links for the morphlection as well.

4. Different parts of speech. Although you may think your watch is on your left wrist, with "left" as an adjective, in Kirundi it is on your wrist leftly, with "bubamfu" as an adverb. Similarly, the verb "achtgeben" in German is expressed in English as an auxiliary verb plus an adjective, "be careful", and in French as an auxiliary verb plus a noun, "faire attention". A green cigar may be just a cigar with an adjective, but it greens as a verb ("guun") in the Aukan language of Suriname.

A monolingual dictionary should contain only the terms that exist in that language; "careful" is an English term, whereas "be careful" is a non-problematic construction of two terms that has no home in any English dictionary consulted for this paper, nor in the Princeton WordNet. Bilingual dictionaries, however, need ways to show how terms in one language are expressed in the other. As shown in the example below from WordReference.com, showing equivalence between languages in such cases is a struggle; "achtgeben" is glossed as "be careful", but "be careful" is shown on the English side as a usage example that does not track back to "achtgeben".

Wörterbuch Englisch-Deutsch © WordReference.com 2012:
**care·ful** ['keəfʊl] *adj (adv regelm)*

1. vorsichtig, achtsam:
**be careful!** nimm dich in Acht!;
**be careful to** *inf* darauf achten zu *inf*, nicht vergessen zu *inf*;
**be careful not to** *inf* sich hüten zu *inf*; aufpassen, dass nicht;
**be careful of your clothes!** gib acht auf deine Kleidung!

2. bedacht, achtsam (**of, for, about** auf *+akk*), umsichtig
3. sorgfältig, genau, gründlich: **a careful study**
4. *Br* sparsam

**Figure 1: "careful" in English-German translation, http://www.wordreference.com/ende/careful**

Wörterbuch Englisch-Deutsch © WordReference.com 2012:
**achtgeben** *v/i (irr, trennb, hat -ge-)* be careful;
**achtgebenauf** *(+akk)* watch, keep an eye on *umg*;
**gib acht!** look out!, (be) careful!

'**achtgeben**' also found in these entries:

Deutsch:
Acht - wachen
Englisch:
attend - heed - look to - mark - mind - watch

**Figure 2: "achtgeben" in German-English translation, http://www.wordreference.com/deen/achtgeben**

The Kamusi solution is to provide fields for "bridges". Though not implemented as of this writing, the monolingual entry for a term will also include the option for a contributor to "add a bridge" for a part of speech. The English adjective "careful" can be augmented with the verb bridge "be careful", and the French noun "attention" can have the verb bridge "faire attention". The English and French items can then be linked to German and become connected transitively along the horizontal beam, or they can be linked directly without the German intermediary. In either case, we do not crowd the monolingual side of a dictionary with unnecessary entries for differently-structured concepts from other languages, but we include the necessary information and make it discoverable.

5. Synonyms within a language. The Kamusi structure makes it easy to attach a synonym to a single sense of a word, such as matching "traverse" only to the sense of "cross" as passing from one side to the other. However, we face three additional challenges: a) whether the terms are exact equivalents, b) whether one term is preferred to another, and c) how they act in transitive translation sets.

a. When presenting glosses between languages, one has some latitude to stretch the notion of exact equivalence between terms; English "stool" can be linked as equivalent to Swahili "kigoda" even though a typical stool is much higher above the ground than a typical kigoda. Within a language, though, the subtle differences between terms arguably take on more significance. "Think" and "ponder" are synonyms in the WordNet sense of "reflect deeply on a subject", but there is a nuanced difference of degree.

As with bilingual glosses, forthcoming programming will provide the opportunity to categorize a synonym relationship as parallel or similar. Users will have the opportunity to rate the closeness of similar terms, and a comment field will provide the opportunity to stipulate the ways that synonyms differ. In the above example, "think" and "ponder" would likely be shown as parallel for the specific sense, but a comment that adheres to the relationship might explain that pondering is a somewhat more intense activity.

b. Within a group of terms that are listed as synonyms, a system is needed to rank those that are more prevalent. This is especially important when showing the set within a translation result, because language learners will have little independent basis to judge which term to use. A student of English would be hard pressed to select a best choice from among the options in the WordNet synset: "chew over, think over, meditate, ponder, excogitate, contemplate, muse, reflect, mull, mull over, ruminate, speculate". A chief complaint that Swahili teachers have about the Kamusi Project is that students tend to use the first entry of a search result, even if the display is alphabetical because the result has not yet been ranked, so essays are often submitted with some rather strange choices of vocabulary. Without a ranking system, English students worldwide will chew over problems more often than they ponder them, and they will excogitate more than they contemplate.

We have developed a simple tool (currently not online due to a change in our programming platform) that allows contributors to slide entries in a set up or down in relation to each other. A set can ultimately be locked down by a moderator, but we see the ranking tool as lightweight work that is a good use of crowd-source energy. Synonyms cannot easily be ranked based on corpus frequency results, because the work of determining the specific senses of homonyms is prohibitive. Future programming will simplify crowdsourcing even more, posing questions to users such as, "'Ponder' and 'think' are both defined as 'to reflect deeply on a subject.' Which do you use more often?" Without digressing into our plans for building Kamusi data through tightly-controlled input from the crowd, we can still propose that aggregated voting results will provide a somewhat scientific method to rank terms within a set of synonyms.

c. Monolingual synonyms within multilingual translation sets. "Ndovu" and "tembo" are both translations of "elephant" and "éléphant", but they are not translations of each other. In future, were we to link "ndovu" to "elephant" as a parallel translation, and then link "tembo" and "elephant", Kamusi will be savvy enough to recognize that "ndovu" and "tembo" are the same language, and therefore synonyms rather than translations. Conversely, if we have a set of synonyms in one language, and we link one of those terms to a term in another language, then we can create a transitive translation relationship for each of those synonyms. The coding for this feature will follow significant refinements to the behavior of translation sets that have just been completed as of this writing, with ramifications described in the conclusion.

## 4. Concluding thoughts: Integration with the Global WordNet

The questions of synonymy raised above are, of course, not new to WordNet. What is new is the potential that the Kamusi system offers for fine-tuning relationships identified as synonymous within a language, and for charting those identified semantic links across language WordNets.

As an example, the Princeton WordNet contains the synset: car/ auto/ automobile/ machine/ motorcar. UWN/MENTA maps the sense of that synset to the following French equivalents: automobile/ auto/ bagnole/ voiture/ wagon, and similar clusters or single terms in many other languages.

Tying five terms identified as synonyms in English with five terms identified as synonyms in French creates 25 pairs, each of which needs to be differentiated from homonyms on both sides. When the programming resources are available, Kamusi proposes to address this challenge through a process that engages the crowd to validate synsets within a language, and their glosses across languages. In the above example, crowd consensus might push "machine" out of the English synset, or bring "wheels" into the group. A similar process would be in effect on the French side. When a link is established between any item within a set of synonyms in one language, and another item within a set of synonyms in another language, then the computer establishes the existence of a relationship among all the entities.

What is significant about these links from one synonym to the next, and from one translation to the next, however, is that they are not absolute. With programming completed just in time for this paper to go to press, Kamusi charts degrees of separation between links that have been validated by humans and those that have been inferred by transitivity algorithms. Those degrees of separation will track through intra-language synonyms. Thus, if "wheels" is human-linked to "car", "car" is linked by hand to "voiture", and "voiture" is manually linked to "bagnole", then "wheels" and "bagnole" will be shown to be separated by three degrees. This will enable readers to make an educated judgment about the tightness of the association between any two terms. In addition, knowledgeable users will be able to help confirm, reject, or add nuance to computer-predicted linkages.

The programming to implement a smooth integration of WordNet data within the Kamusi framework has not yet advanced out of the conceptual stage, for two reasons. First, a variety of other tasks must be completed in order for working with WordNet data to be practical, particularly reestablishment of the grouping tool in a multilingual context, certain behaviors of morphlections, and the big upcoming task of developing an effective system of working with the crowd. Second, finances. Once those elements are in order, and we have had further conversations with members of the WordNet community to refine our approach, we look forward to seeing what can happen when we connect the extensive multilingual WordNet data sets with the lexicographical potential that the Kamusi framework makes possible.

## 5. References


Arleta Adamska-Sałaciak. 2013. Equivalence, Synonymy, and Sameness of Meaning in a Bilingual Dictionary, *Int J Lexicography* 26 (3): 329-345

Rufus H. Gouws. 2013. Contextual and Co-Textual Guidance Regarding Synonyms in General Bilingual Dictionaries, *Int J Lexicography* 26 (3): 346-361

M. Lynne Murphy. 2013. What We Talk About When We Talk About Synonyms: (and What it Can Tell Us About Thesauruses), *Int J Lexicography* 26 (3): 279-304

# Creation of Lexical Relations for IndoWordNet

**Ashish Narang**
CSED, Thapar University
Patiala India.
ash-
ish.narang6789@gmail.com

**Rajendra Kumar Sharma** SMCA,
Thapar University Pa-
tiala India.
rkshar-
ma@thapar.edu

**Parteek Kumar**
CSED, Thapar University Pa-
tiala India.
par-
teek.bhatia@thapar.edu

## Abstract

WordNet is an electronic lexical database available on-line as a powerful resource to the researchers in the area of computational linguistics, text processing and other related areas. WordNet for Hindi language has already been developed by IIT, Bombay. The Indian languages WordNets are being created using expansion approach from Hindi WordNet under IndoWordNet project. In expansion approach, semantic relations are borrowed from the reference language, while the lexical relations need to be created for each language, as these relations are language dependent. This paper describes the process of creation of lexical relations like antonym, compounding, conjunction and gradation for IndoWordNet. A lexical creation tool has been presented in this paper with provision to create lexical relations in target language on the basis of relations created in Hindi WordNet and with another provision to create lexical relations in target language without referring to Hindi WordNet. It has been observed that lexical relations for target language can be created easily on the basis of relations created in Hindi WordNet for Hindi in-family languages, while for the languages that do not fall in the same family provision of creation of lexical relation without referring to Hindi WordNet can be used.

## 1 Introduction

WordNet is a large lexical database of a language. In WordNet, words are grouped together according to their similarity of meanings. WordNet maintains concepts in a language, relations between concepts and their ontological details. Each concept in a language represents a synset. Synsets are basic building blocks of WordNet. Synset is composed of gloss, example sentences and set of synonym words that are used for the concept. Besides synset data, a WordNet maintains lexical and semantic relations. Lexical relations like antonomy and gradation are between the words in a language whereas semantic relations like hypernymy, hyponymy, meronymy, holonymy, entailment, troponymy and casuation are between concepts in a language. WordNet structure makes it a useful tool for computational linguistics and natural language processing. The major applications of WordNet are text categorization (Gabrilovich and Markovitch, 2004), text summarization (Bellare *et al.,* 2004), word sense disambiguation (Banerjee and Pedersen, 2002) and machine translation *etc.*

Recognizing the immense importance of lexical resources arises the necessity for creation of IndoWordNet project. IndoWordNet is a linked structure of WordNets of major Indian languages from Indo-Aryan, Dravidian and Sino-Tibetan families. The WordNets for these languages are being created using the expansion approach from the Hindi WordNet which was made available free for research in 2006. Using expansion approach, there is advantage of being able to borrow the semantic relations of a given source WordNet (Bhattacharyya, 2010). Lexical relations cannot be borrowed from source WordNet using expansion approach as they are language dependent. In order to create lexical relations for IndoWordNet languages, a lexical creation tool has been proposed in this paper with a provision to create lexical relations from source WordNet and as well as to create lexical relations for those words which are not covered in source WordNet.

## 2 Related Work

English WordNet is the first WordNet created in this field. The development of English WordNet started in 1985 (Miller, 1985) at the Cognitive Science Laboratory of Princeton University. The success of English WordNet has inspired several projects that aim at constructing the WordNet for other languages or to develop multilingual WordNet. EuroWordNet is a system of semantic network for European languages. The EuroWordNet project dealt with Dutch, Italian, Spanish, German, French, Czech, and Estonian languages (Vossen, 1998). BalkaNet WordNet project has developed WordNets for Bulgarian, Greek, Romanian, Serbian and Turkish languages (Tufis *et al.*, 2004).

In India, Hindi WordNet was developed in 2006 by IIT, Bombay. Later on Hindi WordNet was extended to Marathi WordNet. Currently IndoWordNet project, a linked structure of major Indian languages is in progress in India. Moreover, Indradhunsh Project a part of IndoWordNet project, aim at developing WordNets for seven major Indian languages, Bengali, Gujarati, Kashmiri, Konkani, Oriya, Punjabi and Urdu has been initiated in 2010. These Indian languages WordNets are being created using expansion approach from Hindi WordNet under the guidance of IIT, Bombay.

## 3 WordNet relations

WordNet contains the standard information found in dictionaries and thesauri. An additional feature of WordNet is its information about the relationships between words and synsets. The words and synsets in the WordNet are linked through two types of relations, *i.e.*, lexical and semantic relations. Lexical relation exists between the word forms while semantic relation exists between the concepts.

### 3.1 Semantic relations

Semantic relation is a relation between meanings, and since meanings can be represented by synsets, semantic relations can be considered as pointers between synsets (Tufis *et al.*, 2004). For example, hypernym/hyponym is a semantic relation. Consider two synsets given in (1) and (2).

{ਪੌਦਾ *paudā 'plant'*, ਬੂਟਾ *būṭā 'plant'*} ...(1)

{ਚਾਹ *cāh 'tea'*} ...(2)

Here, {ਪੌਦਾ *paudā 'plant'*, ਬੂਟਾ *būṭā 'plant'*} is hypernym of {ਚਾਹ *cāh 'tea'*} and {ਚਾਹ *cāh 'tea'*} is hyponym of {ਪੌਦਾ *paudā 'plant'*, ਬੂਟਾ *būṭā 'plant'*}. There are total thirteen semantic relations, namely, hypernymy, hyponymy, meronymy, holonymy, entailment, causation, troponymy, ability link, capability link, functional link, attributes, modifies noun and modifies verb exist in a WordNet.

Using expansion approach there is advantage of being able to borrow the semantic relations of a given WordNet. For example, consider two synsets in the source WordNet given in (3) and (4).

{चाय *chaie 'tea'*} ...(3)

{पौधा *paudha 'plant'*, पौदा *pauda 'plant'*} ...(4)

In Hindi WordNet (source), synset given by (4) is hypernymy of synset given by (3) and synset given by (3) is hyponym of synset given by (4). These two synsets also share hyperonymy/hyponymy relation in Punjabi (target) language. Since, the synset-id are kept same for all the languages, therefore, semantic relations from the source WordNet (Hindi) can be extended to all target languages with expansion approach.

### 3.2 Lexical Relations

Lexical relations are the relations between members of two different synsets. For example, consider two synsets given in (5) and (6).

{ਮੋਟਾ *mōṭā 'fat'*, ਭਾਰੀ *bhārī 'fat'*, ਸਥੂਲ *sathūl 'fat'*, ਥੂਲ *thūl 'fat'*,ਵਜਨੀ *vajnī 'fat'*} ...(5)

{ਪਤਲਾ *patlā 'thin'*, ਦੁਬਲਾ *dublā 'thin'*, ਕਮਜ਼ੋਰ *kamzōr 'thin'*, ਮਾੜਾ *māṛā 'thin'*} ...(6)

Here, synsets (5) and (6) are opposites but they do not share antonym relation. Antonym relation exists between two words not between two synsets. Here, words ਮੋਟਾ *mōṭā 'fat'* and ਪਤਲਾ *patlā 'thin'* are in antonym relation.

## 4 Lexical creation tool

In order to create the lexical relations for all the participating languages of IndoWordNet project, a lexical creation tool has been designed with provision to create lexical relations in target language on the basis of relations created in Hindi WordNet and with another provision to create lexical relations in target language without referring to Hindi WordNet. Lexical creation tool can create the following lexical relations.

- Antonym
- Compounding
- Conjunction
- Gradation

In the subsequent subsection the lexical creation tool has been presented by considering Punjabi as target language. However, the system is able to handle all languages participating in IndoWordNet project.

### 4.1 Antonymy creation tool With reference to Hindi WordNet

Antonymy is a lexical relation that exists between a pair of words that represent opposite meaning. The antonyms for Hindi WordNet have already been created. Antonyms for the Punjabi WordNet can be created from the antonyms of Hindi WordNet, but database design of Punjabi WordNet is different from Hindi WordNet. There is a need to design an interface which can bridge the gap between two different database designs and create the antonyms for the Punjabi WordNet from Hindi WordNet. Algortihm 4.1 has been used for creation of antonyms from Hindi WordNet. The algorithm is developed using IndoWordNet database design (IndoWordNet Database design, 2011) and Hindi WordNet database design followed by IIT, Bombay.

**Algorithm 4.1: Creation of Antonyms with reference to Hindi WordNet**

1. Extract ***synset_id*** of source Hindi ***synset_word*** from ***HWN_DB*** table.
2. Extract ***word_ids*** from ***wn_synset_word*** table, for the ***synset_id*** found in step 1.
3. For each ***word_id*** found in step 2, extract the corresponding words in target language from ***wn_word*** table.
4. Extract ***synset_id*** of antonym Hindi ***synset_word*** from ***tbl_noun_anto_direction*** table.
5. Extract ***word_ids*** from ***wn_synset_word*** table, for the ***synset_id*** found in step 4.
6. For each ***word_id*** found in step 5, extract corresponding words in target language from ***wn_word*** table.

**Description of Algorithm 4.1**

For example, for the word पूर्व *purav 'east'* in Hindi, system searches for source word in ***tbl_noun_anto_direction*** table and extract corresponding ***synset_id***, *i.e.*, 6898 as shown in Figure 1. For the given ***synset_id*** 6898, system refers to ***wn_synset_word*** table to extract the ***word_ids*** as shown in step 1 of Figure 1. For each of the ***word_id*** found, system retrieves the corresponding words in target language, *i.e.*, Punjabi from ***wn_word*** table as shown step 2 of Figure 1. The similar approach has been followed to find the antonym words for antonym ***synset_id.*** A user interface has been designed in Java to provide the relevant information to the end user as shown in Figure 2.

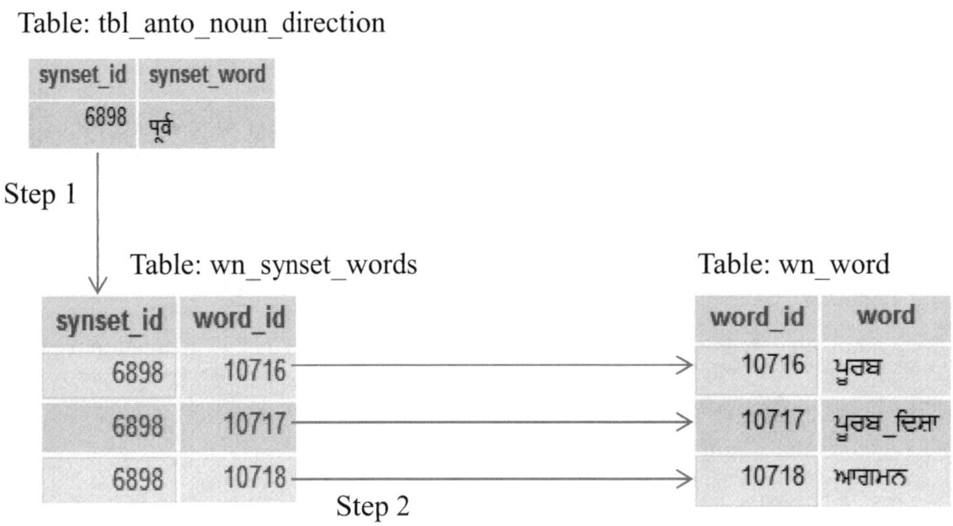


Figure 1: Extracting words corresponding to synset_id 6898

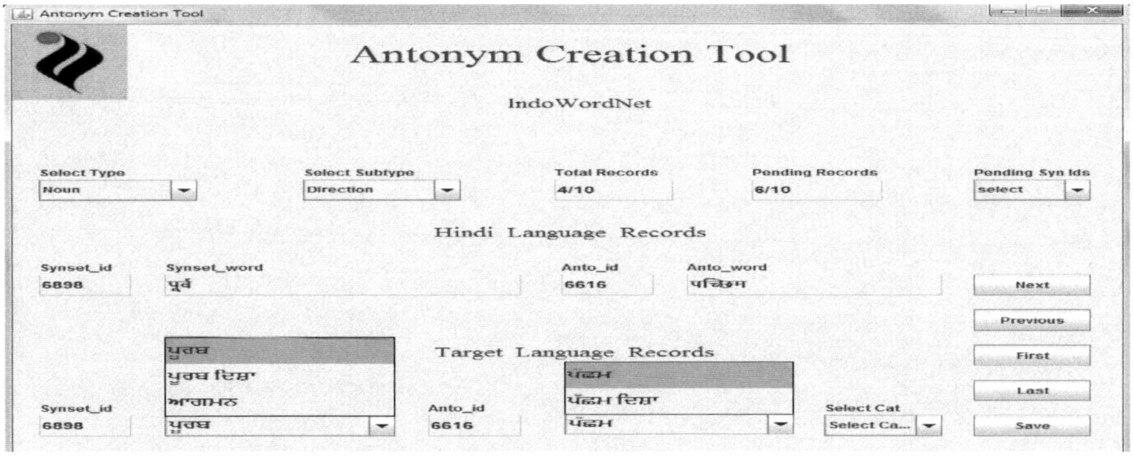


Figure 2: Interface for antonym creation tool with reference to Hindi WordNet

## 4.2 Antonymy creation tool without reference to Hindi WordNet

The antonym relation may also exist between the words which are not covered in Hindi WordNet, but may exist in the target language. This is a very common case for those Indian languages that do not belong to same language family as Hindi. There is need to design a tool which can create the antonyms for such words. The algorithm 4.2 has been designed for the creation of antonym for these words. The algorithm is developed using IndoWordNet database design (IndoWordNet Database design, 2011).

**Algorithm 4.2: Creation of Antonyms without reference to Hindi WordNet**

1. Extract ***word_id*** of the input word in target language from ***wn_word*** table.
2. Extract ***synset_ids*** from ***wn_synset_word*** table, for ***word_id*** found in step 1.
3. For each ***synset_id*** found in step 2, extract the corresponding concepts from ***wn_synset*** table.
4. Extract ***word_id*** of the input antonym word in target language from the ***wn_word*** table.
5. Extract ***synset_ids*** from ***wn_synset_word*** table, for ***word_id*** found in step 4.
6. For each ***synset_id*** found in step 5, extract the corresponding concepts from ***wn_synset*** table.

**Description of algorithm 4.2**

Let us consider an example for creation of antonym for input Punjabi word, ਚੰਗਾ *caṅgā 'good character'*, the system refers to ***wn_word*** table to extracts corresponding ***word_id*** as shown in Step 1 of Figure 3.

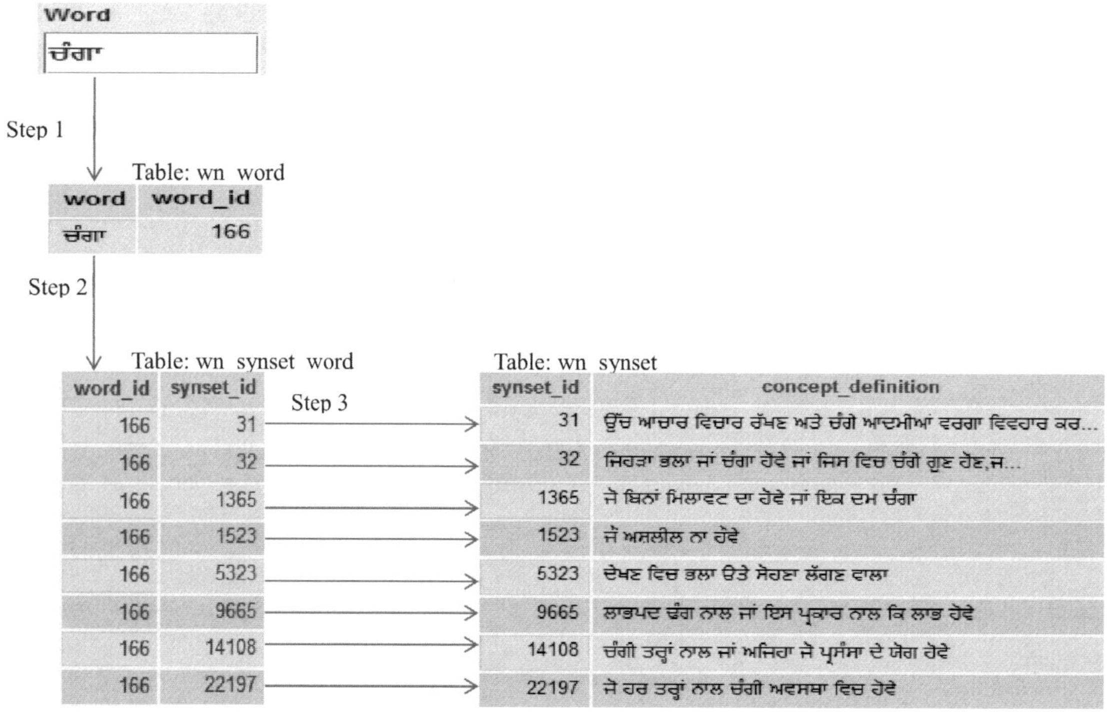


Figure 3: Extraction of concepts for the word ਚੰਗਾ *caṅgā 'good character'*

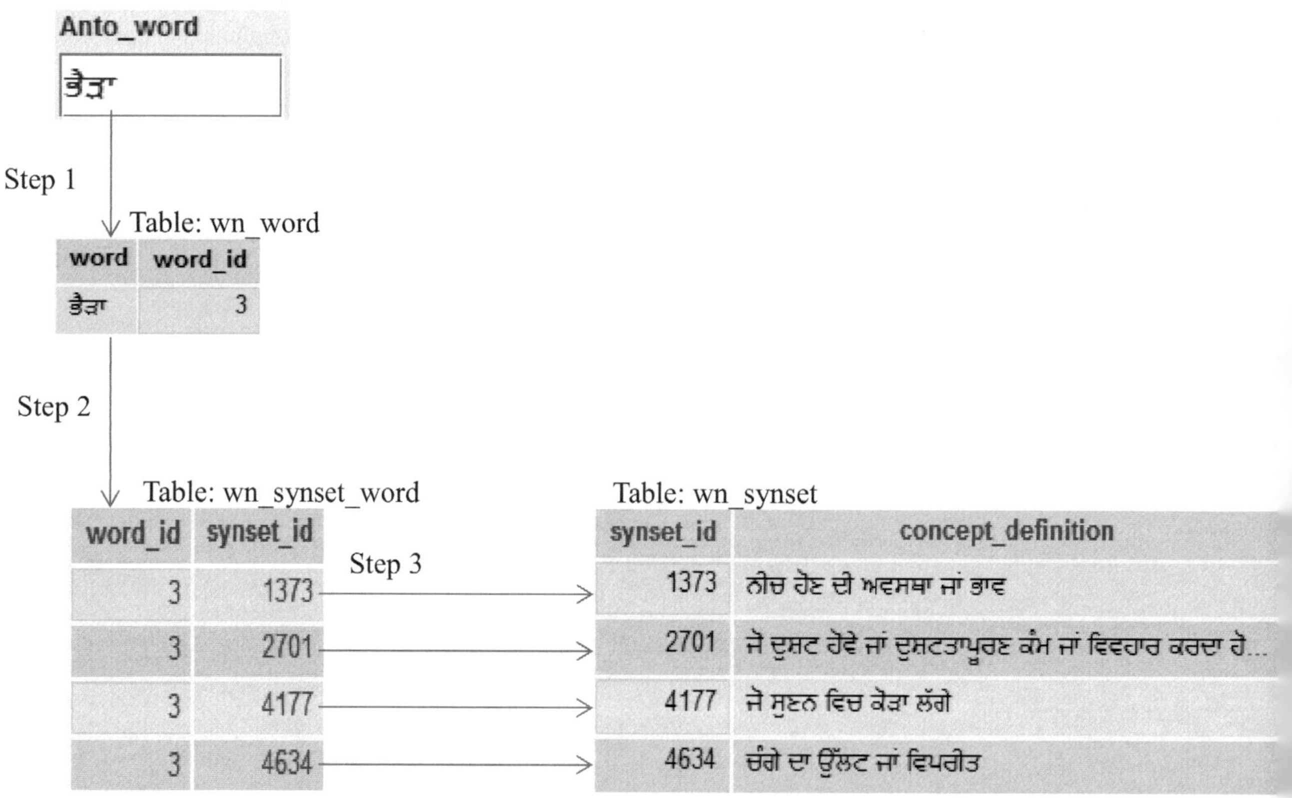


Figure 4: Extraction of concepts for the word ਭੈੜਾ *bhaiṛā 'charactterless'*

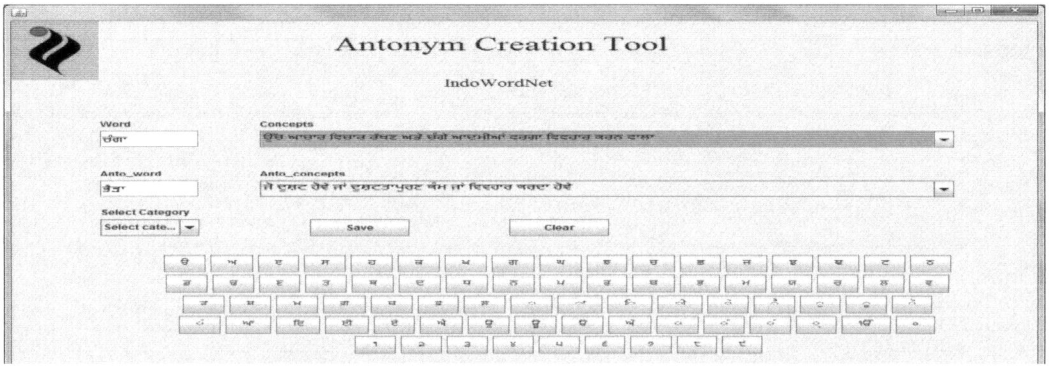


Figure 5: Interface for creation of antonyms without Hindi WordNet

For a given ***word_id***, system extracts ***synset_ids*** from ***wn_synset_word*** table. Concepts for extracted ***synset_id*** have been retrieved from ***wn_sysnset*** table as shown in step 3 given in Figure 3. The similar approach has been followed for corresponding input antonym word. The process of extraction of antonym word information is depicted in Figure 4.

A user interface has been designed in Java to provide relevant information to end user as shown in Figure 5.

### 4.3 Compounding creation tool

Compounding relation relates a compound word with its part word. A compound word is formed when two words are joined to form a new word. An interface has been designed to create such relations from compounding relations that already exist in Hindi WordNet. The tool reduces manual typing effort for the creation of compounding relation.

The snapshot of Compounding creation tool taking Hindi WordNet as basis is given in Figure 6.

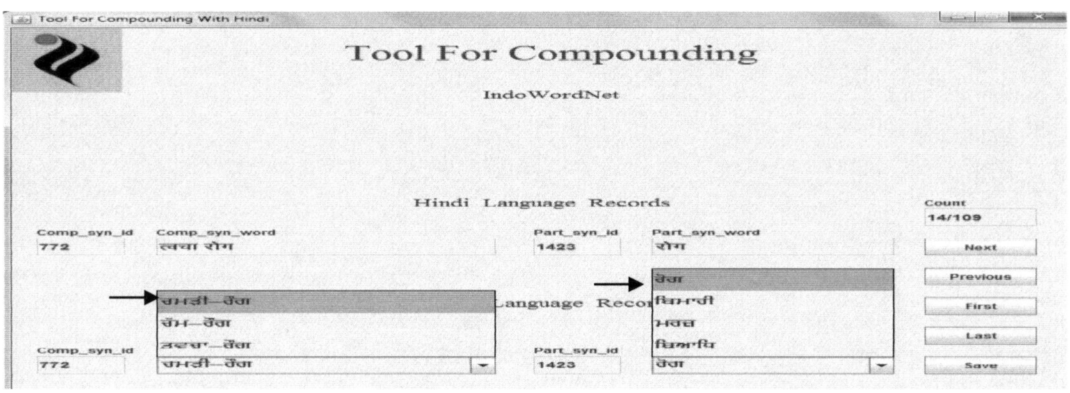


Figure 6: Compounding creation tool taking Hindi WordNet as basis

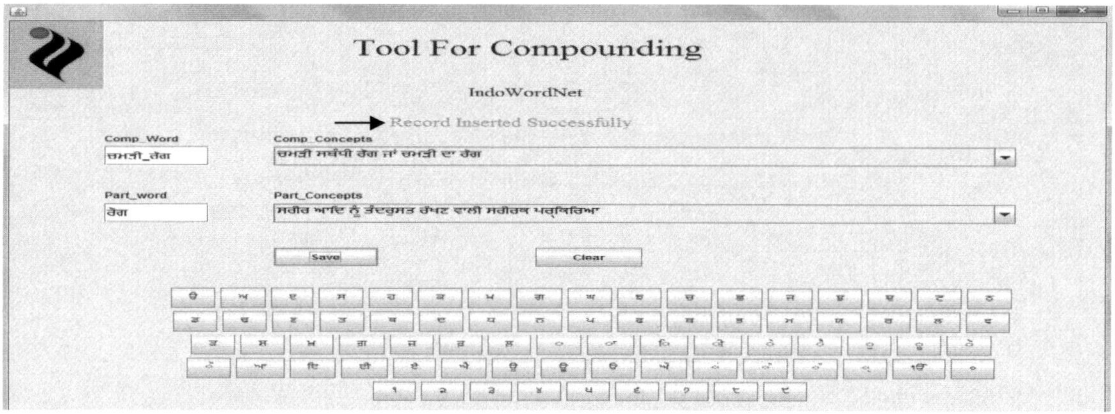


Figure 7: Compounding creation tool without taking Hindi WordNet as basis

A compounding relation may exist in target language between those words that are not covered by Hindi WordNet. For this a tool has been developed. The snapshot of compounding creation tool, without taking Hindi WordNet as basis is given in Figure 7.

### 4.4 Conjunction creation tool

Conjunction relation relates a conjunction word with its part word. The snapshot of conjunction creation tool taking Hindi WordNet as basis is given in Figure 8.

The snapshot of conjunction creation tool without taking Hindi WordNet as basis is given in Figure 9.

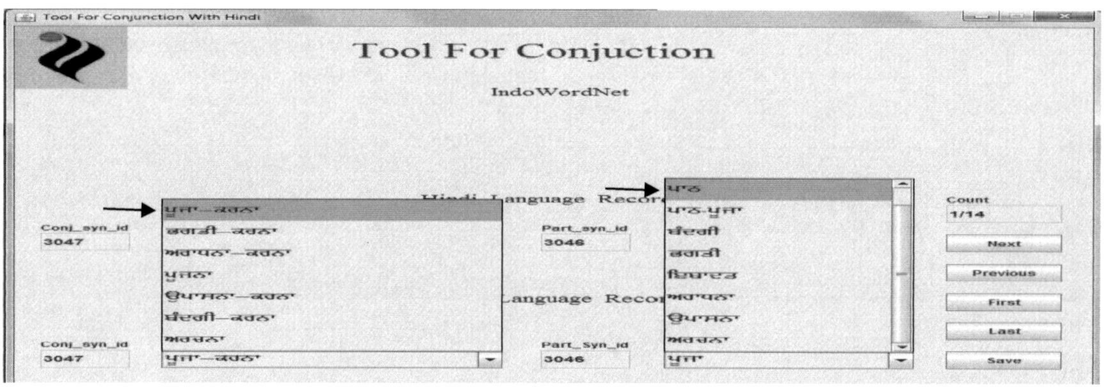


Figure 8: Conjunction creation tool taking Hindi WordNet as basis

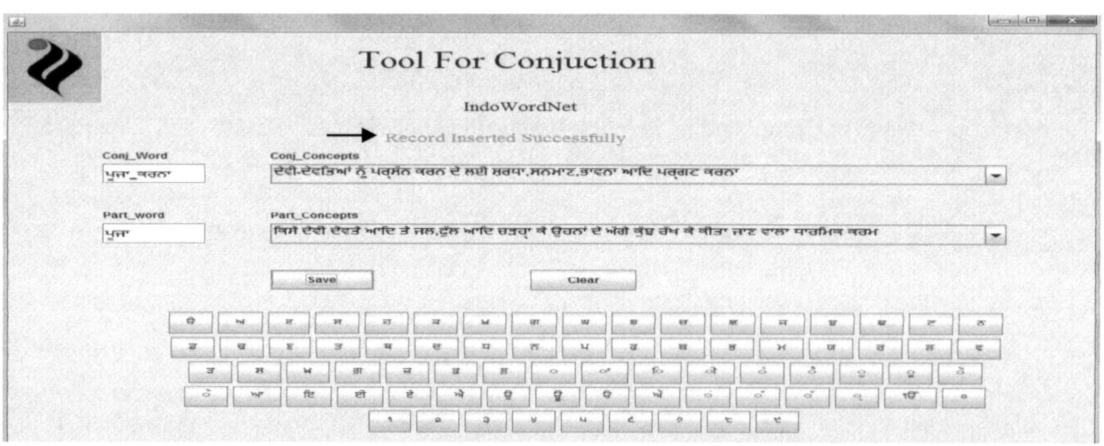


Figure 9: Conjunction creation tool without taking Hindi WordNet as basis

### 4.5 Gradation creation tool

Gradation is a lexical relation that exists between three word forms. It represents the intermediate concept between two opposite concepts. The snapshot of gradation creation tool taking Hindi WordNet as basis is given in Figure 10.

The snapshot of conjunction creation tool with out taking Hindi WordNet as basis is given in Figure 11.

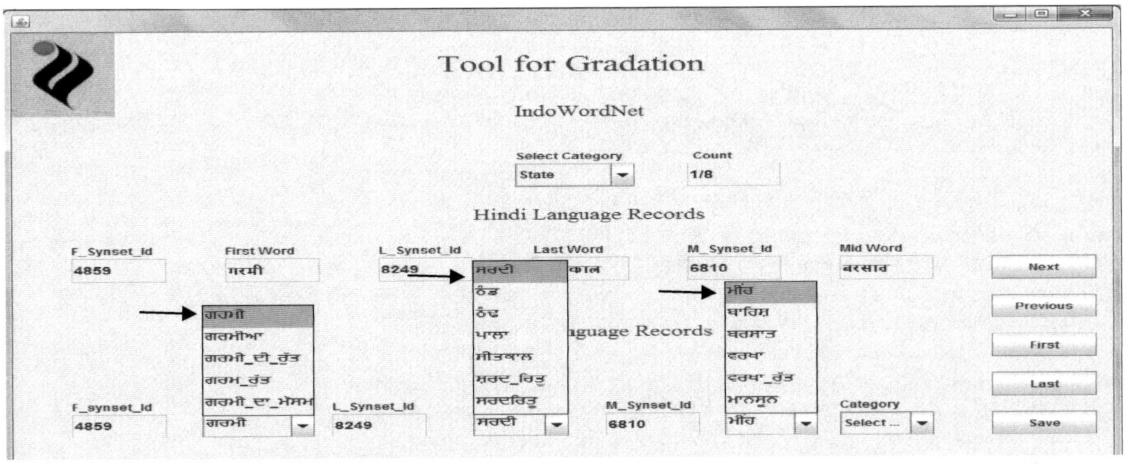


Figure 10: Gradation creation tool taking Hindi Wordnet as basis

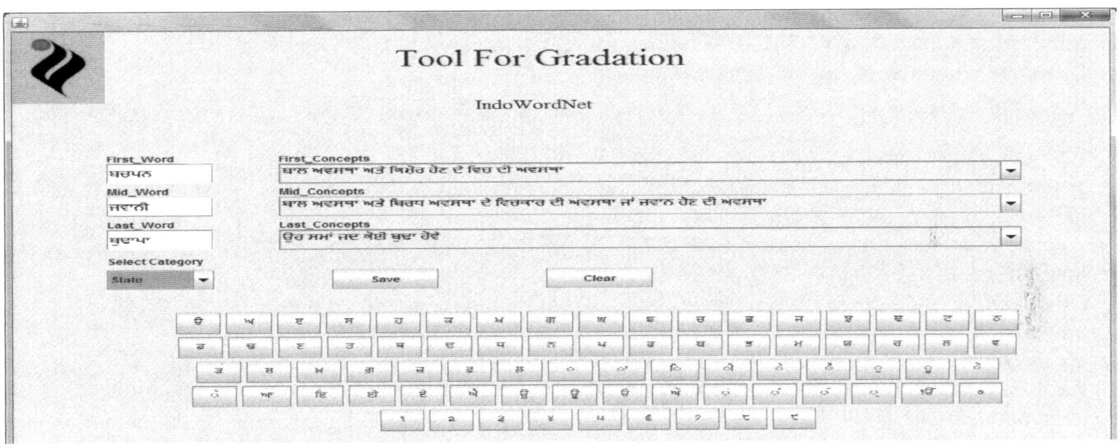


Figure 11: Gradation creation tool without taking Hindi WordNet as basis

## 5. Conclusion

Using expansion approach semantic relations are borrowed from the source language as they are same for all the languages. Lexical relations are language specific, so they cannot be borrowed from the source language. It has been observed that manual typing work can be reduced for Hindi in-family languages to a larger extent by creating lexical relations for target language on the basis of relations created in Hindi WordNet, while for languages that do not fall in the same family provision of creation of lexical relation without referring to Hindi WordNet will be helpful extensively.


## Acknowledgements

This work has been carried out under research project titled "Development of Indradhanush: An Integrated WordNet for Bengali, Guajarati, Kashmiri, Konkani, Oriya, Punjabi and Urdu" under the leadership of IIT Bombay and Goa University. This project is sponsored by MoCIT, Govt. of India. We also acknowledge the contribution of Punjabi University, Patiala team for the development of Punjabi WordNet.


## References


Dan Tufis, Dan Cristea and Sofia Stamou. 2004. Balkanet: Aims, methods, results and perspectives. A general overview. *Romanian J. Sci. Tech. Inform.* vol.7 (1-2), pp: 9-43.

Evgeniy Gabrilovich and Shaul Markovitch. 2004. Text Categorization with Many Redundant Features: Using Aggressive Feature Selection to Make SVMs Competitive with C4.5. In *21st International Conference on Machine Learning,* Canada, pp: 321-328.

George A. Miller. 1985. WordNet: A Dictionary Browser. In *First International Conference on Information in Data,* University of Waterloo, Canada.

George A. Miller, Richard Beckwith, Christiane Fellbaum, Derek Gross and Katherine Miller. 1990. Introduction to WordNet: An On-line Lexical Database. *International Journal of Lexicography*, pp: 235-244.

IndoWordNet Database Design. 2011. Tech. Rep. by Goa University, Goa.

Kedar Bellare, Anish D. Sarma, Atish D. Sarma, Navneet Loiwal, Vaibhav Mehta, Ganesh Rama-Krishnan and Pushpak Bhattacharyya. 2004. Generic Text Summarization Using WordNet. In *Language Resources Engineering Conference,* Barcelona.

Piek Vossen (ed.). 1998. EuroWordNet: A Multilingual Database with Lexical Semantic Networks. *Kluwer Academic Publishers*, Dordrecht.

Pushpak Bhattacharyya. 2010. IndoWordNet. In *Lexical Resources Engineering Conference Malta.*

Rupinderdeep Kaur, Rajendra K. Sharma, Suman Preet, and Parteek Bhatia. 2010. Punjabi WordNet Relations and Categorization of Synsets, In *3rd IndoWordNet Workshop, IIT Kharagpur*.

Satanjeev Banerjee and Ted Pedersen. 2002. An Adapted Lesk Algorithm for Word Sense Disambiguation Using WordNet. In *Third International Conference on Intelligent Text Processing and Computational Linguistics*, Mexico City, pp: 1-10.

# Swesaurus;
# *or*,
# The Frankenstein Approach to Wordnet Construction

**Lars Borin**
Språkbanken
Department of Swedish
University of Gothenburg
Gothenburg, Sweden
lars.borin@svenska.gu.se

**Markus Forsberg**
Språkbanken
Department of Swedish
University of Gothenburg
Gothenburg, Sweden
markus.forsberg@svenska.gu.se

## Abstract

Swesaurus is a freely available (under a CC-BY license) Swedish wordnet under construction, built primarily by scavenging and recycling information from a number of existing lexical resources. Among its more unusual characteristics are graded lexical-semantic relations and inclusion of all parts of speech, not only open-class items.

*The materials at present within my command hardly appeared adequate to so arduous an undertaking, but I doubted not that I should ultimately succeed. I prepared myself for a multitude of reverses; my operations might be incessantly baffled, and at last my work be imperfect, yet when I considered the improvement which every day takes place in science and mechanics, I was encouraged to hope my present attempts would at least lay the foundations of future success. Nor could I consider the magnitude and complexity of my plan as any argument of its impracticability. [...] After having formed this determination and having spent some months in successfully collecting and arranging my materials, I began.*
(Shelley, 1818, Ch. 4)

## 1 Introduction: Swesaurus – towards a quiltwork wordnet

Swesaurus is a Swedish open-source "protowordnet" under active development. The main novel methodological aspect of this development is its "quiltwork" – or "Frankenstein" – character. Swesaurus is being constructed mainly by scavenging and recycling lexical-semantic information from a number of existing lexical resources. Other noteworthy features of Swesaurus which distinguish it from most other wordnets is the fact that it does not practice "part-of-speech discrimination"; it constitutes a lexical-semantic resource encompassing all parts of speech (POS),[1] and its *graded* lexical-semantic relations.

In the literature we find basically two main approaches to (manual) wordnet construction (Vossen, 1998), viz. (1) the merging approach – based on language-specific lexicographical knowledge and where the synsets and their interrelations consequently respect the structure of the language in question, and where any linking to the English Princeton WordNet (PWN) is made subsequently to the wordnet construction – or (2) the extension approach – where the structure is imported wholesale using bilingual resources (dictionaries or translation corpora) from another language, typically English (PWN), and where the linking to the source wordnet consequently is part of the design. Good examples of wordnets built using the merging approach are the Danish wordnet DanNet (Pedersen et al., 2009) and the Polish wordnet plWordNet (Piasecki et al., 2009), while the extension approach can be well illustrated with the Finnish wordnet FinnWordNet (Lindén and Niemi, 2013), where a translation agency was employed for translating PWN into Finnish, or the two Norwegian wordnets (for the two written standards of Norwegian, Bokmål and Nynorsk), which were translated using partly automatic corpus-based methods, although not from PWN, but from DanNet.[2]

True to its quiltwork character, Swesaurus incorporates elements of both approaches. For most of the Swesaurus components, the merging approach has been the only choice, utilizing as they did information from pre-existing monolingual

[1] Recall that Princeton WordNet covers only the open parts of speech, the "content words", specifically nouns, verbs, adjectives, and adverbs. However, because of what seems to be a specific Anglo-Saxon lexicographical practice (Apresjan, 2002), numerals are also included in WordNet, classified as nouns (cardinals) or adjectives (ordinals).

[2] This makes eminent sense, given that one of the two Norwegian written standards is historically based on Danish.

Swedish resources, but in the case of the Core WordNet component, the extension approach has been used (see section 3.3).

The motivation for building Swesaurus is manifold. The utility of having a PWN-like resource for a language is often stated in the literature. Further, the work is driven in part by opportunity: The general resource harmonization and standardization activities described below in section 2 open the possibility of mining and compiling similar kinds of information from originally quite heterogeneous lexical resources, both as to their content, and above all with respect to their format.

## 2 The prerequisites: A unified lexical infastructure

The construction of Swesaurus would not be possible without the groundwork laid in the Swedish FrameNet++ project (Borin et al., 2010), the goals of which are threefold: (1) creation of an integrated lexical macro-resource; (2) construction of a Swedish framenet; and (3) creation of open resources.

Crucially, the first goal has been implemented on the content level through a decision on resource interlinking on the word sense level. As a consequence of this, a structured system of persistent identifiers has been designed for word senses, which are used as links among resources. This does not mean that the only possible kind of link is based on (word sense) identity. Especially with diachronic and cross-language links, other relations are needed, at least hyponymy/hyperonymy, expressed using `skos:narrower` and `skos:broader` (Miles and Bechhofer, 2009).

The macro-resource, of which Swesaurus is a part, is large and diverse, consisting of 23 lexical resources, ranging from the Swedish FrameNet to Old Swedish dictionaries, containing a total of 686,237 lexical entries at the time of writing. To be able to work productively with this macro-resource, we need good tools for interacting with the data, for abstracting, ordering, searching and visualizing the data itself, for inferring and presenting relations among data items, and for editing the data. To meet these demands, a generalized lexical infrastructure is under development (Borin et al., 2012a; Borin et al., 2013b), geared towards dealing with large networks of interconnected lexicons (Borin, 2010; Borin et al., 2010) that have been encoded in the LMF format (Lexical Markup Framework; see ISO 2008; Francopoulo 2013).

One essential component of the lexical infrastructure is a generic search interface that provides a plug-and-play search tool for resources already in LMF, where the LMF format is employed both internally within the infrastructure and, trivially, as an export format.

The lexical infrastructure also maintains a strong bidirectional connection to a general and flexible corpus infrastructure (Borin et al., 2012b). For example, the lexical information in the macro-resource is used in annotating the corpora, and the language examples for the lexical resources are retrieved from the corpus infrastructure.

A pervasive theme for both infrastructures is *openness*, which for the lexical infrastructure is demonstrated through its utilization of open standards and open-content licenses, as well as the daily publication of not only the resources but everything else that is available in-house, such as formal test protocols, change history and the tools themselves. The tools are available through a set of web services, which are open for others to use, and which provide a convenient way of accessing the lexical information programmatically.

## 3 The lexical resources

Below, we discuss the existing lexical resources underlying the component parts of Swesaurus and how they are processed for inclusion in Swesaurus.

### 3.1 SALDO

The lexical macro-resource described in section 2 is topologically a hub-and-spokes structure. There is one primary lexical resource, a pivot, to which all other resources are linked. This is SALDO (Borin et al., 2013a), a large (130K entries and 1.9M wordforms), freely available (under a Creative Commons Attribution license) morphological and lexical-semantic lexicon for modern Swedish. It has been selected as the pivot partly because of its size and quality, but also because its form and sense units are identified by carefully designed unique persistent identifiers (PIDs) to which the lexical information in other resources are linked.

The standard scenario for a new resource to be integrated into the macro-resource is to (partially) link its entries to the sense PIDs of SALDO. This cannot be done automatically on the level of word senses in the general case. However, like many other linguistic phenomena, the distribution of senses over lemmas in lexical resources is roughly Zipfian (Moon, 2000; Borin, 2010). Thus, the vast majority of the lemmas are monosemous, reducing the sense mapping problem to the much simpler problem of pairing up forms between lexical resources. This is ultimately what makes an endeavor such as Swesaurus feasible.

Doing this automatic pairing of forms typically has the effect that the ambiguity of a resource becomes explicit: the bulk of the resources associate lexical information to part-of-speech-tagged base forms, information not always valid for all senses of that base form. This is natural since most of the resources have initially been created for human consumption, and a human can usually deal with this kind of underspecification without problem. Some of these ambiguities can be resolved automatically – especially if information from several resources is combined – but in the end, manual work is required for complete disambiguation.

SALDO is a kind of lexical-semantic network, superficially similar to PWN, but quite different from it in the principles by which it is structured. SALDO is about the same age as PWN, and it was developed completely independently of the latter, inspired more by a Russian tradition of lexical description, rather than an Anglo-Saxon one; cf., for example, Igor' Mel'čuk's *Meaning – Text Model* (Mel'čuk, 1974).

The basic linguistic idea underlying the structure of SALDO is that, semantically speaking, the whole vocabulary of a language can be described as having a center – or core – and (consequently) a periphery. The notion of *core vocabulary* is familiar from several linguistic subdisciplines (Borin, 2012). In SALDO this idea is consistently applied down to the level of individual word senses. Thus, every entry in SALDO – representing a word sense – has one or more semantic descriptors, which are themselves also entries in the dictionary. All entries in SALDO (with one sole exception; see below) are actually occurring words or conventionalized or lexicalized multi-word units of the language.

One of the descriptors, called *primary*, is obligatory. The primary descriptor is the entry which better than any other entry fulfills two requirements: (1) it is a semantic neighbor of the entry to be described; and (2) it is more central than it. However, there is no requirement that the primary descriptor is of the same part of speech as the entry itself. Thus, the primary descriptor of *kniv* 'knife (n)' is *skära* 'cut (v)', and that of *lager* 'layer (n)' is *på* 'on (p)'.

Through the primary descriptors SALDO is a single tree, rooted by assigning an artifical top sense (called PRIM) as primary descriptor to the 42 topmost word senses.

That two words are semantic neighbors means that there is a direct semantic relationship between them (such as synonymy, hyponymy, meronymy, argument-predicate relationship, etc.). As could be seen from the examples given above, SALDO includes not only open-class words, but also pronouns, prepositions, conjunctions etc. In such cases closeness must sometimes be determined with respect to function or syntagmatic connections, rather than ("word-semantic") content.

Centrality is determined by means of several criteria: frequency, stylistic value, word formation, and traditional lexical-semantic relations all combine to determine which of two semantically neighboring words is to be considered more central.

Relevant to the Swesaurus endeavor, the primary descriptor will in practice quite often be either a hyperonym or synonym of the keyword. Thus, SALDO was mined for Swesaurus candidates by extracting all same-POS entry–primary descriptor pairs. In the process, some important special cases were recognized which require very little manual post-processing, such as noun compound entries where the form of the primary descriptor corresponds to the last member of the compound, e.g., *livförsäkring : försäkring* 'life insurance : insurance', and where the entry in the overwhelming majority of cases is a hyponym of the primary descriptor. In this way, a large number of synonyms, near-synonyms, hyperonyms, antonyms, and related senses could be extracted from SALDO, representing all parts of speech.

### 3.2 Synlex

Synlex (the People's Synonym Lexicon; Kann and Rosell 2006) is a lexical resource that has been created by asking members of the public – users of an online Swedish-English dictionary – to judge the degree of synonymy of a random, automatically generated synonym pair candidate, on a scale from 0 (not synonyms) to 5 (fully synonymous). A synonym pair list containing all pairs that average 3.0 or more on a large number of judgements is available for download under an open-source license. The latest version of the list at the time of writing is dated 2013-05-23, and contains 19,269 graded synonym pairs (38,538 if symmetry of synonymy is not taken into account).

The members of these pairs are words (i.e., text word forms) – not even part of speech is indicated – mainly dictionary base forms (lemmas), but sometimes inflected forms, and in some cases multi-word expressions. One problem then becomes, in the case of a word having as synonyms several other words – because of homonymy and polysemy – to determine how many senses we are dealing with. Also, for those familiar with PWN, we should add that synonymy relations in Synlex are sometimes between words with different POS, just as in EuroWordNet. Although in EuroWordNet this kind of synonymy is still formally distinct from within-POS synonymy, bearing the label XPOS_NEAR_SYNONYM (Alonge et al., 1998).

Since Synlex gives us access to graded synonymy, we may introduce the notion of fuzzy synsets into Swesaurus (Borin and Forsberg, 2010), i.e., synsets where a word's membership is a matter of degree (see section 4 for a discussion about synsets in Swesaurus).

#### 3.2.1 Wiktionary

Wiktionary is an undertaking similar to Wikipedia, but for collaborative writing of dictionaries rather than encyclopedias. The Swedish Wiktionary,[3] is a downloadable free resources that, among other things, contains some lexical-semantic relations. The work of extracting such relations from Wiktionary is hampered by the fact that the data set is only partially encoded with a formal structure. It is the responsibility of the writer to encode the different information categories in a lexical entry in the correct wiki format that was intended by the creator of Wiktionary, but no automatic check of the encoding is actually done. Since the result of a faulty encoding may actually look correct for the human eye, there are in practice a number of errors in Wiktionary that complicate the automatic information extraction.

We have experimented with extracting synonymy relations between words, with a resulting set of 10,529 synonymy pairs, of which 3,857 of the word pairs have members with only one sense in SALDO. Hence, no manual disambiguation is needed, so they may be incorporated immediately into Swesaurus. Some of the pairs are wrong, since some lexical entries contain information from other languages and relation within them. This results in a few cases where, e.g., a Swedish word is linked to a Polish one. In practice, this is not a major problem, since the linking to SALDO filters out those words that are not in SALDO.

The synonymy relations in Wiktionary are in general of higher quality than those in Synlex, which is to be expected since the author of a lexical entry in Wiktionary makes a conscious choice when assigning synonyms to a word, but Synlex, on the other hand, builds upon automatically generated word pairs, with the consequence that words that is not normally judged synonymous are sometimes assigned a degree greater than zero. For example, consider the pair *förlovning : förpliktelse* 'engagement to be married : obligation', the members of which are normally not considered to be synonymous, but when presented together and you are asked to quantify their synonymy degree, you may be tempted to give them at least a small degree of synonymy.

### 3.3 Core WordNet

As part of the EC-funded META-NORD project (2011–2013), a linking of the Princeton Core WordNet (CWN) to Swedish was completed and included in Swesaurus. The linkage was bootstrapped by using the Lexin basic Swedish-English dictionary (∼25,000 entries). Swedish lemmas in Lexin were automatically linked, in an overgenerating manner, to SALDO sense identifiers, giving us a set of senses for every lemma. The glosses of CWN were subsequently, via Lexin, linked to these sense sets. CWN has 5,000 entries, of which around 89% were covered by Lexin. Furthermore, 23% had a unique link to one SALDO sense, and the remaining an average ambiguity of 4.4 (a rather high ambiguity, but not unexpected for a core vocabulary).

### 3.4 The Gothenburg Semantic Database

The Gothenburg Semantic Database (SDB; Järborg 2001) is a lexical database for modern

[3] See `http://sv.wiktionary.org`

Swedish covering 61,000 entries with an extensive description inflection, morphology and meaning. Originally building on a lexicographical database that has been used in producing two modern Swedish reference dictionaries, SDB has been enriched with a deeper semantic description where many of the verb senses have been provided with semantic valency information using a set of about 40 general semantic roles and linked to example sentences in a corpus.

SDB holds two kinds of relevant lexical-semantic information: (1) explicit lexical semantic relations cross-referencing among different lexical entries (lemmas); and (2) implicit in its hierarchical organization of lexical entries into main senses and subsenses, typically corresponding to a superordinate–hyponym relation.

The linking of SDB senses to SALDO sense identifiers is ongoing. An initial automatic linking is now being manually checked and corrected. For those senses that are already processed in this way, the explicit lexical semantic relations have been included in Swesaurus, and some of the derived relations calculated (see section 4), while the entry-internal hierarchical relations present in SDB have not yet been extracted. In the process, it has become clear that the explicit relations are not consistent, and will need a good deal of manual correction, which is ongoing.

#### 3.4.1 Bring's thesaurus

The author of what is probably the first Swedish thesaurus, Sven Casper Bring (1842–1931) worked as a lawyer, district judge and translator. Besides practicing law, he published several translations from French, Italian and English to Swedish. His final work was an adaptation to Swedish of Roget's well-known *Thesaurus* (Bring, 1930). He writes in his preface to the book that he was inspired by similar adaptations that had taken place of Roget's Thesaurus to German.

Bring's thesaurus was digitized in the early 1990s and has since been made available under an open-content license. Work is ongoing to create a modernized version of Bring by using SALDO and other modern lexical resources in order to semi-automatically add modern vocabulary to it.

Like in Roget, the vocabulary included in Bring is divided into slightly over 1,000 "conceptual classes". Each class consists of a list of words, where, when there are enough relevant words, nouns are listed first, followed by verbs, and finally a mixed group containing adjectives, adverbs, interjections and phrases. Semicolons, together with paragraph structure, group words together, which are thought to be more closely semantically related. Semicolon groups often contain synonym clusters, with distance between words in a cluster roughly correlating to degree of synonymy, and we plan to explore how the semicolon groups can be used as a source for yet another Swesaurus component.

## 4 Some matters of method

Following a long tradition in lexicography and lexical semantics, we posit as primary semantic entities in all our lexical resources *word senses*, i.e., roughly the content side of the Saussurean linguistic sign, paired with a form side on the word level (a word, a conventionalized or lexicalized multiword expression, or, rarely, a sub-word-unit). Importantly in this connection, *synsets* are not primary entities in our resources.

As a corollary to the above, all lexical-semantic relations are between word senses only. Synonymy is simply one of these relations among many others. A PWN-style wordnet, on the other hand, does not have the synonymy relation at all. Synsets are defined through (one construal of) synonymy, but the relation itself is not present as such in the wordnet.

The decision not to allow synsets into Swesaurus as first-class citizens rests partly on tradition. Importantly, however, in doing this, we also avoid building in a strong assumption about the nature of synonymy into the foundations of our resource. Even though synonym dictionaries are among the oldest products of lexicography – even the Sumerians and Akkadians compiled them (Civil, 1990) – in practice synonymy has turned out to be a most slippery notion: While synonyms are self-evidently a central feature of language according to Lieber (1841, vii), they are "morally impossible" to Döderlein (1863, xii). Thus, in constructing Swesaurus we have opted for treating synsets as derived, from a possibly varying or changing definition of synonymy.

Ockham's razor also enters into the picture: Since word senses seem to be needed in any case, and to be in some sense more basic than synsets – more than half (54%) of the synsets in PWN have only one member, arguably a word sense – we see no pressing need to adopt the synset as basic notion.

This makes the basic information unit in Swesaurus the (word-sense) *relational triple*, whose three components are: (1) a source word sense; (2) a *graded* lexical-semantic relation; and (3) a target word sense. In addition, each triple has provenance information, i.e., from which resource it originates and whether it is primary or derived. The relations used so far in Swesaurus are the ones listed in Table 1.

At present, all derived relations except related-sense are generally taken to hold only within a part of speech – i.e., source and target words must have the same part of speech – although this may change in the future.[4] The related-sense relation is a catchall label covering a mixed bag of semantic and formal relations among word senses, both more loose "evocation" (Boyd-Graber et al., 2006) or "associative" (Borin et al., 2013a) semantic relations, and formal derivational relations, e.g., verbs and the corresponding deverbal nouns, nouns and their denominal adjectives, etc.

The resources generally have fragmentary information, for various reasons. From the logical properties of the relations follow certain inference rules which allow us to partly ameliorate this situation.

For example, the transitivity of most of the relations allows us to add many derived relational triples to Swesaurus. If we have the information that A is-a-synonym-of B and B is-a-synonym-of C, we can infer that A is-a-synonym-of C even in the absence of this explicit information. More subtle inferences are also possible, for example: If we have the explicit information that A is-a-hyponym-of B and C is-a-hyponym-of D and further that A is-a-cohyponym-of C, we can then infer that B is-a-synonym-of D.

[4]Some of the original synonym pairs in Synlex already cross part-of-speech boundaries, and even SDB has a small number of such examples, e.g. some color adjectives are listed as hyponyms of the noun *grundfärg* 'primary color'. Further, we note that especially in linguistic descriptions of languages with rich derivational morphological systems it is often taken for granted that, e.g., a verb and the corresponding deverbal action noun express the same concept – are synonymous – so that the difference between *to eat* (v.) and *the eating* (n.) is on a par with the tense difference between *eats* and *ate*. Both express the concept of eating, but in forms determined by the syntactic frame in which they are made to function (see, e.g., Fellbaum 2005). The differences are in both cases purely formal, not conceptual.

There are also some less obviously useful entailment relations, which however should be recognized both for completeness' sake and for implementing correct behavior in search and browsing tools, such as: Synonymy entails cohyponymy; and all other relations entail related-sense.

The consequence of this is that Swesaurus contains two kinds of relational triples: (1) primary triples, explicitly present in the sources; and (2) derived triples, automatically computed using the inference rules for triples.

"Wordnetified" versions of Swesaurus in addition contain synsets constructed through the transitive closure of the synonymy relation.

Graded relations complicate this picture, and it is not completely clear how to best use the degree information in computing derived relations. Consequently, we must be careful when deriving new synonym pairs in Synlex, especially if we iterate over already derived ones. A few pairs like the already mentioned *förlovning : förpliktelse* 'engagement to be married : obligation' may give rise to a large number of questionable synonymy pairs. A more conservative approach than general transitivity is to use the existing synonymy cliques in the derivation process, and only derive new synonyms if we create a new clique by deriving that synonym. This has been the strategy chosen for deriving new synonym pairs from Synlex.

According to the website of the *Global WordNet Association*,[5] "resources that follow the wordnet design" must include

- links to WordNet (Princeton or others that are linked to PWN)
- WN structure (minimally: synset, hyponymy)

Swesaurus marginally fulfills the first criterion – only the CWN component is linked to PWN – although we acknowledge the usefulness of such a linking, and are planning to extend it to the other components of Swesaurus. It also fails the second criterion, since there are no synsets at all in Swesaurus. However, as we have argued and shown above, A PWN-style wordnet – in fact, many different PWN-style wordnets – can be completely mechanically derived from Swesaurus, with synset sizes dependent on the synonymy degree threshold chosen for synset assembly. The synsets can then inherit selected lexical semantic relations from their member word senses.

[5]See http://globalwordnet.org/?page_id=38

| Relation | Logical properties |
|---|---|
| synonymy | symmetric, transitive |
| antonymy | symmetric |
| related-sense | symmetric, transitive(?) |
| hyponymy/subordinate sense | transitive, inverse of hyperonymy |
| hyperonymy/superordinate | transitive, inverse of hyponymy |
| cohyponymy | symmetric, transitive |
| partonymy | transitive(?), inverse of holonymy |
| holonymy | transitive(?), inverse of partonymy |

Table 1: Lexical-semantic relations used in Swesaurus

## 5 Conclusions and future work

All the activities listed in section 3 are ongoing to various degrees. In summary, approximate current numbers of primary and derived relational triples in the different Swesaurus components are as follows:

| Component | Primary | Derived |
|---|---|---|
| Synlex | 19,000 | 9,500 |
| Wiktionary | 4,000 | – |
| CWN | 4,500 | – |
| SDB | 10,000 | 13,500 |
| SALDO | 32,500 | – |

All numbers are for *normalized relational triples*, which means that symmetric relations are counted only once for a given word-sense pair, and that for relations with an inverse, only one of the two is present in the data. Thus, A is-an-antonym-of B will exclude the presence of B is-an-antonym-of A, and A is-a-hyperonym-of B will be transformed into B is-a-hyponym-of A.

We are already starting to see how genuine synergy could arise from the work described above. The flow of information is not one-way; instead, the derived lexical-semantic information made possible through the construction of Swesaurus may in its turn be used to enrich the original lexical resources. Synonyms may be a good source of new lexical units in a framenet, for instance, and the modernization of Bring's Thesaurus will probably be easier to accomplish using the lexical-semantic information from Swesaurus. We have already mentioned that semicolon groups in Bring are often made up of synonym clusters, but like its predecessor and model Roget, Bring, too, organizes many of its conceptual classes according to antonymies, making the antonymy information in Swesaurus a potential source of enrichment of Bring.

So far our work on Swesaurus has focused on the crosslinking and consequent synergistic enrichment of heterogeneous lexical resources. Another important line of research found in the literature on wordnet construction, but that we have not touched upon in this paper, concerns corpus-driven, machine-learning based methods for wordnet building. We have conducted some initial experiments based on a large Swedish corpus collection, and this is a direction which we plan to pursue further in the future. In this connection, a particularly intriguing question is to what extent near synonymy of the kind found in Synlex can be discovered automatically in corpora.

## Acknowledgments

The research presented here has been made possible through financial support from the Swedish Research Council (*Swedish FrameNet++* project, contract no 2010-6013), from the University of Gothenburg through its support of the Centre for Language Technology and through its support of Språkbanken (the Swedish Language Bank), and from the European Commission through its support of the META-NORD project under the ICT PSP Programme, grant agreement no 270899.

## References

Antonietta Alonge, Nicoletta Calzolari, Piek Vossen, Laura Bloksma, Irene Castellon, Maria Antonia Marti, and Wim Peters. 1998. The linguistic design of the EuroWordNet database. In Piek Vossen, editor, *EuroWordNet: A Multilingual Database with Lexical Semantic Networks for European Languages*. Kluwer, Dordrecht. Pages 19–43.

Yuri D. Apresjan. 2002. Principles of systematic lexicography. In Marie-Hélène Corréard, editor, *Lex-*

*icography and Natural Language Processing. A Festschrift in Honour of B. T. S. Atkins*. Euralex, Grenoble. Pages 91–104.

Lars Borin and Markus Forsberg. 2010. From the people's synonym dictionary to fuzzy synsets - first steps. In *Proceedings of the LREC 2010 workshop Semantic relations. Theory and Applications*, pages 18–25.

Lars Borin, Dana Danélls, Markus Forsberg, Dimitrios Kokkinakis, and Maria Toporowska Gronostaj. 2010. The past meets the present in Swedish FrameNet++. In *14th EURALEX International Congress*. Leeuwarden. EURALEX. Pages 269–281.

Lars Borin, Markus Forsberg, Leif-Jöran Olsson, and Jonatan Uppström. 2012a. The open lexical infrastructure of Språkbanken. In *Proceedings of LREC 2012*. Istanbul. ELRA. Pages 3598–3602.

Lars Borin, Markus Forsberg, and Johan Roxendal. 2012b. Korp – the corpus infrastructure of Språkbanken. In *Proceedings of LREC 2012*. Istanbul. ELRA. Pages 474–478.

Lars Borin, Markus Forsberg, and Lennart Lönngren. 2013a. SALDO: a touch of yin to WordNet's yang. *Language Resources and Evaluation*, May. Online first publication; DOI 10.1007/s10579-013-9233-4.

Lars Borin, Markus Forsberg, Leif-Jöran Olsson, Olof Olsson, and Jonatan Uppström. 2013b. The lexical editing system of karp. In *Kosem, I., Kallas, J., Gantar, P., Krek, S., Langemets, M., Tuulik, M. (eds.) 2013. Electronic lexicography in the 21st century: thinking outside the paper. Proceedings of the eLex 2013 conference, 17-19 October 2013, Tallinn, Estonia.*, volume 2013, pages 503–516.

Lars Borin. 2010. Med Zipf mot framtiden – en integrerad lexikonresurs för svensk språkteknologi. *LexicoNordica*, 17:35–54.

Lars Borin. 2012. Core vocabulary: A useful but mystical concept in some kinds of linguistics. In Diana Santos, Krister Lindén, and Wanjiku Ng'ang'a, editors, *Shall we play the Festschrift game? Essays on the occasion of Lauri Carlson's 60th birthday*. Springer, Berlin. Pages 53–65.

Jordan Boyd-Graber, Christiane Fellbaum, Daniel Osherson, and Robert Schapire. 2006. Adding dense, weighted connections to WordNet. In *GWC 2006 Proceedings*. Brno. Masaryk University. Pages 29–35.

Sven Casper Bring. 1930. *Svenskt ordförråd ordnat i begreppsklasser*. Hugo Gebers förlag, Stockholm.

Miguel Civil. 1990. Sumerian and Akkadian lexicography. In Oskar Reichmann Hausmann, Franz Josef and, Herbert Ernst Wiegand, and Ladislav Zgusta, editors, *Wörterbücher: Ein internationales Handbuch zur Lexikographie. Zweiter Teilband / Dictionaries: An international encyclopedia of lexicography. Second volume / Dictionnaires: Encyclopédie internationale de lexicographie. Tome second*. Walter de Gruyter, Berlin. Pages 1682–1686.

Ludwig Döderlein. 1863. The author's preface. In *Döderlein's hand-book of Latin synonymes. Translated by Rev. H.A. Arnold, B.A., with an introduction by S.H. Taylor, LL.D.* Warren F. Draper, Andover. Pages ix–xvi.

Christiane Fellbaum. 2005. Co-occurrence and antonymy. *International Journal of Lexicography*, 8(4):281–303.

Gil Francopoulo, editor. 2013. *LMF: Lexical Markup Framework*. ISTE/Wiley, London/Hoboken, NJ.

ISO. 2008. Language resource management – Lexical Markup Framework (LMF). International Standard ISO 24613:2008.

Jerker Järborg. 2001. Roller i Semantisk databas. Research Reports from the Department of Swedish No. GU-ISS-01-3. University of Gothenburg, Department of Swedish.

Viggo Kann and Magnus Rosell. 2006. Free construction of a free Swedish dictionary of synonyms. In *Proceedings of the 15th NODALIDA conference, Joensuu 2005*. Department of Linguistics, University of Joensuu. Pages 105–110.

Francis Lieber. 1841. Preface of the translator. In *Dictionary of Latin synonymes, for the use of schools and private students, with a complete index. By Lewis [Ludwig] Ramshorn. From the German by Francis Lieber*, Charles C. Little and James Brown. Pages iii–viii.

Krister Lindén and Jyrki Niemi. 2013. Is it possible to create a very large wordnet in 100 days? An evaluation. *Language Resources and Evaluation*, July. Online first publication; DOI 10.1007/s10579-013-9245-0.

Igor' A. Mel'čuk. 1974. *Opyt teorii lingvističeskih modelej «Smysl ↔ Tekst»*. Nauka, Moscow.

Alistair Miles and Sean Bechhofer. 2009. SKOS Simple Knowledge Organization System Reference. W3C Recommendation. `http://www.w3.org/TR/skos-reference/`.

Rosamund Moon. 2000. Lexicography and disambiguation: The size of the problem. *Computers and the Humanities*, 34(1–2):99–102.

Bolette Sandford Pedersen, Sanni Nimb, Jørg Asmussen, Nicolai Hartvig Sørensen, Lars Trap-Jensen, and Henrik Lorentzen. 2009. DanNet: The challenge of compiling a wordnet for Danish by reusing a monolingual dictionary. *Language Resources and Evaluation*, 43(3):269–299.

Maciej Piasecki, Stanisław Szpakowicz, and Bartosz Broda. 2009. *A Wordnet from the Ground Up*. Oficyna Wydawnicza Politechniki Wrocławskiej, Wrocław.

Mary Wollstonecraft Shelley. 1818. *Frankenstein; or, The Modern Prometheus*. Lackington, Hughes, Harding, Mavor & Jones, London.

Piek Vossen. 1998. Introduction to EuroWordNet. In Piek Vossen, editor, *EuroWordNet: A Multilingual Database with Lexical Semantic Networks for European Languages*. Kluwer, Dordrecht. Pages 1–17.

# Facilitating Multi-Lingual Sense Annotation: Human Mediated Lemmatizer

**Pushpak Bhattacharyya** IIT Bombay pushpakbh@gmail.com

**Ankit Bahuguna** IIT Bombay / TU Munich ankitbahuguna@outlook.com

**Lavita Talukdar** IIT Bombay lavita.talukdar@gmail.com

**Bornali Phukan** IIT Bombay bornali31phukan@gmail.com

## Abstract

Sense marked corpora is essential for supervised word sense disambiguation (WSD). The marked sense ids come from wordnets. However, words in corpora appear in morphed forms, while wordnets store lemma. This situation calls for accurate lemmatizers. *The lemma is the gateway to the wordnet.* However, the problem is that for many languages, lemmatizers do not exist, and this problem is not easy to solve, since rule based lemmatizers take time and require highly skilled linguists.Satistical stemmers on the other hand do not return legitimate lemma.

We present here a novel scheme for creating accurate lemmatizers quickly. These lemmatizers are *human mediated.* The key idea is that a trie is created out of the vocabulary of the language. The lemmatizing process consists in navigating the trie, trying to find a match between the input word and an entry in the trie. At the point of first mismatch, the yield of the subtree rooted at the partially matched node is output as the list of possible lemma. If the correct lemma does not appear in the list- as noted by a human lexicographer- backtracking is initiated. This can output more possibilities. A ranking function filters and orders the output list of lemma.

We have evaluated the performance of this human mediated lemmatizer for eighteen Indian Languages and five European languages. We have compared accuracy values against well known lemmatizers/stemmers like Morpha, Morfessor and Snowball stemmers, and observed superior performance in all cases. Our work shows a way of speedily creating human assisted accurate lemmatizers, thereby removing a difficult roadblock in many NLP tasks, e.g., sense annotation.

## 1 Introduction

Supervised WSD- the ruling paradigm for high accuracy sense determination- requires sense marked corpus in large quantity. Sense annotation is a difficult job, requiring linguistic expertise, knowledge of the topic and domain, and most importantly a fine sense of word meanings.

Most often the sense annotation task is accomplished by using a *Sense Marker Tool*, like the one described in Chatterjee *et. al.* (2010). This particular tool, equipped with an easy to use GUI facilitates the task of manually marking each word with the correct sense of the word, as available in the wordnet of the language. The tool has the wordnet sense repository resident in its memory. It displays the senses of word for the human annotator to choose from. The mentioned tool is extensively used by a number of language groups in India to produce high quality sense marked corpus. Figure 1 shows the Sense Marker Tool, where a user is marking the sense of the word "banks" in English.

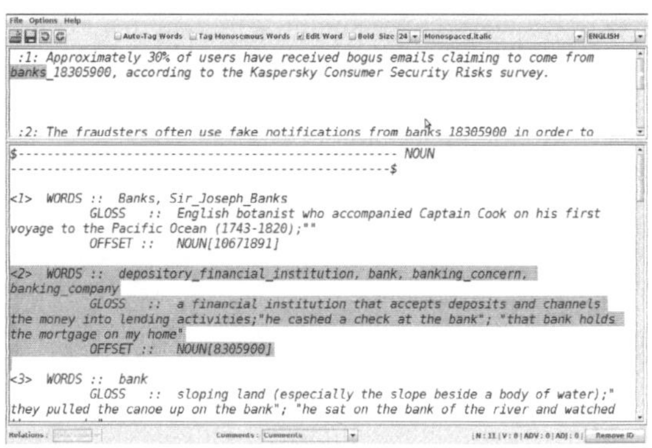


Figure 1: Sense Marking Tool - manually marking correct sense for English word "banks"

Now it is obvious that if the wordnet is to be accessed for the senses to be displayed, the lemma of the words must be available. The lemma is the gateway to the wordnet. Lemmatization is an important activity in many NLP applications. We stress at this point that our focus of attention is lemmatization and not stemming. As a process, stemming aims to reduce a set of words into a canonical form which may or may not be a *dictionary word* of the language. Lemmatization, on the other hand, always produces a legal root word of the language. To give an example, a stemmer can give rise to "ladi" from "ladies". But a lemmatizer will have to produce "lady". And if the senses of 'ladies' has to be found, the lemma 'lady' is required.

There are three basic approaches to lemmatization, *viz.*, affix removal (rule based systems), statistical (supervised/unsupervised) and hybrid (rule based + statistical). Developing a rule based system is an uphill task, requiring a number of language experts and enormous amount of time. Purely statistical systems fail exploit linguistic features, and produce non-dictionary lexemes. A hybrid system utilizes both the above mentioned approaches.

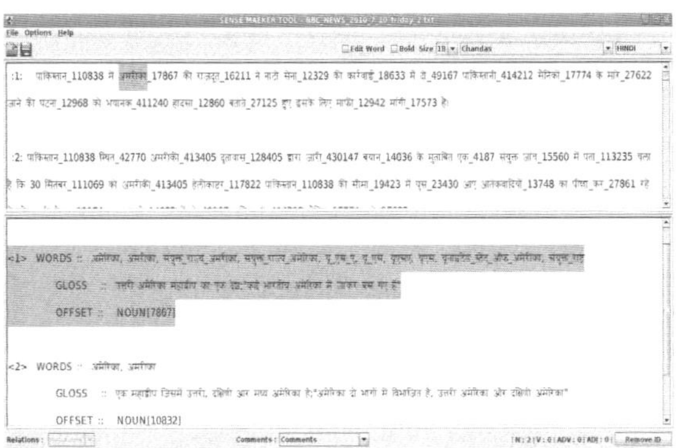

Figure 2: Sense Marking Tool - Input Language: Hindi

In this paper, we discuss an alternative approach to lemmatization which is quick, takes user help and is exact. The key idea is that a trie is created out of the vocabulary of the language. The lemmatizing process consists in navigating the trie, trying to find a match between the input word and an entry in the trie. *At the point of first mismatch- i.e., maximum prefix matching, the yield of the subtree rooted at the partially matched node is output as the list of possible lemma.* If the correct lemma does not appear in the list- as noted by a human lexicographer- a backtracking is initiated. This can output more possibilities, since the yield of a node at a higher level of the trie is output. A ranking function filters and orders the output list of lemma.

Our ultimate goal is to integrate the human mediated lemmatizer with the *Sense Marking Tool* (Figure 2).Currently, the tool supports the following 9 languages: English, Hindi, Marathi, Tamil, Telugu, Kannada, Malayalam, Bengali and Punjabi.

For Example, In Assamese:

Inflected Word Form: ঘৰলৈ (ghoroloi ~ to home)

Root Word: ঘৰ (ghor ~ home)

We give an example to give a feel for how our lemmatiser works. When a linguist tries to mark the correct sense of the inflected Assamese word as shown in Figure 3 ('gharalai' meaning 'in the house'), in the current scenario no output is displayed, but with our lemmatizer integrated, it will show the possible lemma of that word.

(ঘৰ ঘৰৰ ঘৰঘৰ ঘৰ-ঘৰ ঘৰচকা ঘৰহীন ঘৰুৱা)

Here, the correct lemma is shown at the top of the list, and the lemma can pull out the senses from the wordnet for the linguist to tag with.

The remainder of this paper is organized as follows. We describe related work and background in section 2. Section 3 explains the core of our human mediated lemmatiser. Implementation details are in Section 4. Experiments and results are discussed in Section 5. Comparison with existing stemmers/lemmatizers are in Section 6. Section 7 concludes the paper and points to future directions.

## 2 Related Work and Background

Lovins described the first stemmer (Lovins, 1968), which was developed specifically for IR/NLP applications. His approach consisted of the use of a manually developed list of 294 suffixes, each linked to 29 conditions, plus 35 transformation rules. For an input word, the suffix with an appropriate condition is checked and removed. Porter developed the Porter stemming algorithm (Porter, 1980) which became the most widely used stemming algorithm for English language. Later, he developed stemmers that covered Romance (French, Italian, Portuguese and Spanish), Germanic (Dutch and German) and Scandinavian languages (Danish, Norwegian and Swedish), as

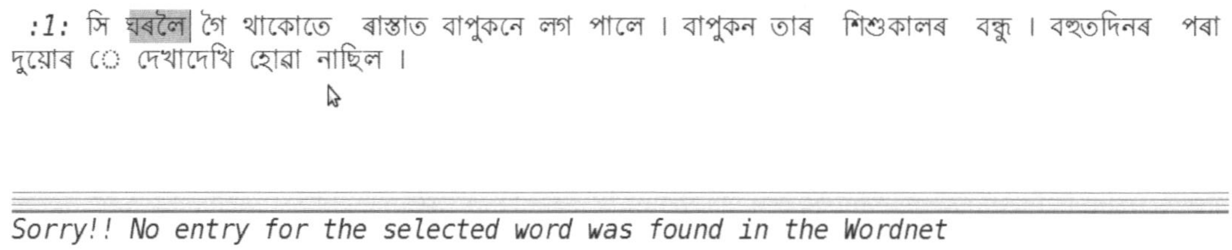


Figure 3: Tool shows no output for inflected Assamese word "ghoroloi" (highlighted) meaning *to home*.

well as Finnish and Russian (Porter, 2006). These stemmers were described in a very high level language known as Snowball[1].

A number of statistical approaches have been developed for stemming. Notable works include: Goldsmith's unsupervised algorithm for learning morphology of a language based on the Minimum Description Length (MDL) framework (Goldsmith, 2001; 2006). Creutz uses probabilistic maximum a posteriori (MAP) formulation for unsupervised morpheme segmentation (Creutz, 2005; 2007).

A few approaches are based on the application of Hidden Markov models (Melucci et al., 2003). In this technique, each word is considered to be composed of two parts "prefix" and "suffix". Here, HMM states are divided into two disjoint sets: *Prefix state* which generates the first part of the word and *Suffix state* which generates the last part of the word, if the word has a suffix. After a complete and trained HMM is available for a language, stemming can be performed directly.

Plisson proposed the most accepted rule based approach for lemmatization (Plisson et al., 2008). It is based on the word endings, where suffixes are removed or added to get the normalized word form. In another work, a method to automatically develop lemmatization rules to generate the lemma from the full form of a word was discussed (Jongejan et al., 2009). The lemmatizer was trained on Danish, Dutch, English, German, Greek, Icelandic, Norwegian, Polish, Slovene and Swedish full form-lemma pairs respectively.

Kimmo (Karttunen et al., 1983) is a two level morphological analyser containing a large set of morphophonemic rules. The work started in 1980 and the first implementation n LIST was available 3 years later.

Tarek El-Shishtawy proposed the first non-statistical Arabic lemmatizer algorithm (El-Shishtawy et al., 2012). He makes use of different Arabic language knowledge resources to generate accurate lemma form and its relevant features that support IR purposes and a maximum accuracy of 94.8% is reported.

OMA is a Turkish Morphological Analyzer which gives all possible analyses for a given word with the help of finite state technology. Two-level morphology is used to build the lexicon for a language (Ozturkmenoglu et al., 2012).

Grzegorz Chrupala (Chrupala et al., 2006) presented a simple data-driven context-sensitive approach to lemmatizating word forms. Shortest Edit Script (SES) between reversed input and output strings is computed to achieve this task. An SES describes the transformations that have to be applied to the input string (word form) in order to convert it to the output string (lemma).

As for lemmatizers for Indian languages, the earliest work by Ramanathan and Rao (2003) used manually sorted suffix list and performed longest match stripping for building a Hindi stemmer. Majumdar et. al (2007) developed YASS: Yet Another Suffix Stripper. Here conflation was viewed as a clustering problem with a-priory unknown number of clusters. They suggested several distance measures rewarding long matching prefixes and penalizing early mismatches. In a recent work related to Affix Stacking languages like Marathi, (Dabre et al., 2012) Finite State Machine (FSM) is used to develop a Marathi morphological Analyzer. In another approach, A Hindi Lemmatizer is proposed, where suffixes are stripped according to various rules and necessary addition of character(s) is done to get a proper root form (Paul et al., 2013). GRALE is a graph based lemmatizer for Bengali comprising two steps (Loponen et al., 2013). In the first, step it extracts the set of frequent suffixes and in the second step, a human manually identifies the case suffixes. Words are often considered as node and edge from node **u** to **v** exist if only **v** can be generated from **u** by addi-

[1]See `http://snowball.tartarus.org/`

tion of a suffix.

Unlike the above mentioned rule based and statistical approaches, our human mediated lemmatizer uses the properties of a "trie" data structure which allows retrieving *possible* lemma of a given inflected word, with human help at critical steps.

## 3 Our Approach to lemmatization

The scope of our work is suffix based morphology. We do not consider infix and prefix morphology. We first setup the data structure 'Trie' (Cormen et al., 2001) using the words in the wordnet of the language. Next, we match, byte by byte, the input word form and wordnet words. The output is all wordnet words which have the maximum prefix match with the input word. This is the "direct" variant of our lemmatizer.

The second or "backtrack" variant prints the results 'n' levels previous to the maximum matched prefix obtained in the 'direct' variant. The value of 'n' is usr controlled. A ranking function then decides the final output displayed to the user.

In Figure 5, a sample trie diagram is shown consisting of Hindi words given at Figure 4. The words are stored starting from a node subsequent to the root node, in a character by character unicode byte order.

| List of words |
|---|
| 1. कमरबन्द (kamarband ~ drawstring) |
| 2. कमरा (kamara ~ room) |
| 3. कमरी (kamari ~ small blanket) |
| 4. कमल (kamal ~ Lotus) |
| 5. लड (lad ~ fibril) |
| 6. लडकपन (ladakpan ~ childhood) |
| 7. लड़का (ladka ~ boy) |
| 8. लड़की (ladki ~ girl) |
| 9. लड़ना (ladna ~ fight) |

Figure 4: List of sample words.

At each level, we insert the characters of the word in an alphabetical order pertaining to unicode standard for different languages from left to right.

We illustrate the search in the trie with the example of the inflected word "लड़कियाँ" (ladkiyan, *i.e.,* girls). Our lemmatizer gives the following output:

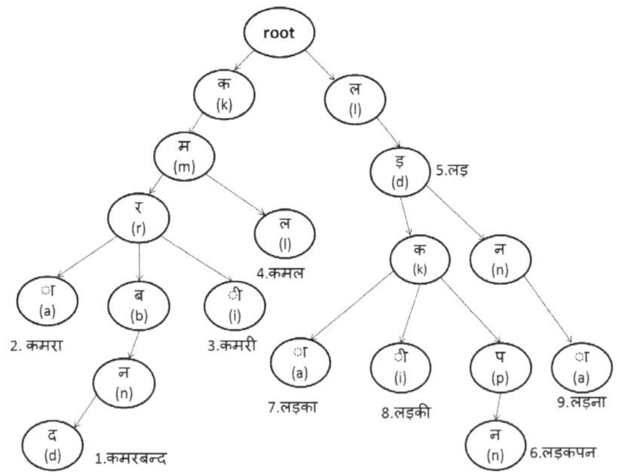


Figure 5: A simple trie storing Hindi words (kamarband, kamara, kamari, kamal, lad, ladakpan, ladka, ladki and ladna)

(ल लड़ लड़का लड़की लड़कपन लड़कोरी लड़कौरी)

From this result set, a trained lexicographer can easily pick the root word as "लड़की" (ladki, *i.e.,* girl). It is the user controlled backtracking which is novel and very useful in our lemmatizer. We elaborate on backtracking below.

### 3.1 Backtracking

We explain backtracking using the sample words in Figure 6 and the trie as shown in Figure 7.

| List of words |
|---|
| 1.असणे (asane ~ hold) |
| 2.असली (asali ~ real) |
| 3. आज (aaj ~ today) |

Figure 6: List of sample words : Backtracking.

We take the example of असलेले (*aslele*) which is an inflected form of the Marathi word असणे (*asane*). Here, when we call the first iterative procedure without backtracking, the word असली (*asali*) is given as output. Although, being a valid wordnet word, it is not the correct root form of the word असलेले. Hence, we perform a backtrack from असल (*asal*) to अस (*asa*) thereby getting असणे (*asane*) as one of the outputs.

An example involving two levels of backtracking is that of a Marathi word कापसाला (*kApsAlA*), which is an inflected form of the root word कापुस, (*kApusa*) *i.e.,* cotton). Here are the results from our lemmatizer:

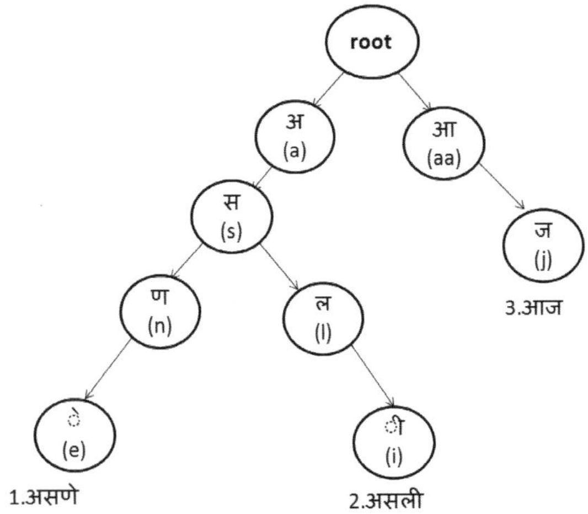


Figure 7: Search in Trie - Backtracking in case of Marathi word "असल्लेल्ले" (*aslele*)

Basic:
(क का काप कापसाचा)

1 - level backtrack:
(क का काप कापसी कापसाचा)

2 - level backtrack:
(क का काप कापड कापणे
कापरा कापरे कापसी कापूर कापूस
कापडेपट कापणावळ कापराचा
कापलेला कापसाचा कापाकापी)

Thus, we can find the root word कापुस at 10th position in the result list of two level backtrack.

### 3.2 Ranking Lemmatizer Results

Our lemmatizer by default prints out all the possible root forms given a queried word. We have employed a heuristic to filter the results and hence minimize the size of the result set:

1. Only those output matches are accepted whose length is smaller than or equal to the length of the queried word. This is based on an assumption that the root word length shall not be greater than the length of its equivalent inflected word form (we agree that this is not universally true; hence the word 'heuristic' for the pruning strategy).

2. The filtered results are sorted on the basis of the length (in an ascending order) which in most cases displays the root word earlier in a given set of words.

For example, in case of the Marathi word "असल्लेल्ले" (*aslele*) the ranking function receives a number of words as input, after a first level backtrack is performed (as shown in Figure 8). The function then applies the ranking heuristic based on length and then sorts them in their ascending order. Thus, the final lemmatizer output is generated with the root word असणे (*asane*) in first position.

Input to Rank Function:
असंख्य||असंगती||असंतुलित||असंतुलित_बल||असंतुष्ट||असंतुष्टता||असंतोषी||
असंदिग्ध||असंबद्ध||असंबद्धता||असंभव||असंभवनीय||असंभाव्य||असंभाव्यता||
असंमती||असंयत||असंयम||असंयमित||असंयमी||असंशायात्मक||असणे||असते
पण||असत्य||असत्यता||असनसियान||असन्माननीय||असफल_होणे||असभ्य||
असभ्यपणा||असभ्यपणे

LEMMATIZER OUTPUT:

(असणे असंभव असंयत असंयम असत्य असभ्य असंख्य असंगती असंमती
असंयमी असतेपण असंतोषी असंबद्ध असंयमित असत्यता)

Figure 8: Ranking of results - For Marathi word "असल्लेल्ले" (*aslele*)

## 4 Implementation

We have developed an on-line interface (Figure 9) and a downloadable Java based executable jar which can be used to test our implementation. The interface allows input from 18 different Indian languages (Hindi, Assamese, Bengali, Bodo, Gujarati, Kannada, Kashmiri, Konkani, Malayalam, Manipuri, Marathi, Nepali, Sanskrit, Tamil, Telugu, Punjabi, Urdu and Odiya) and 5 European languages (Italian, Danish, Hungarian, French and English) and they are linked to their respective lexical databases. For easy typing, a virtual keyboard is also provided. The first iteration of stemming is performed by clicking "Find" and backtracking is performed by clicking "Backtrack". The backtrack utility allows us to backtrack upto 8 levels and the level of backtrack is displayed in a field. This was implemented, since there are several inflected words in our test data which required a backtrack of more than one level to get the root word. The interface also has a facility to *upload* a text document related to a specific language. We can then download the results in an output file containing possible stems of all the words present in the input document. The human annotator can thus choose the correct lemma from the list of possible stems associated with each word.

## 5 Experiments and Results

We performed several experiments to evaluate the performance of the lemmatizer. The basis of our

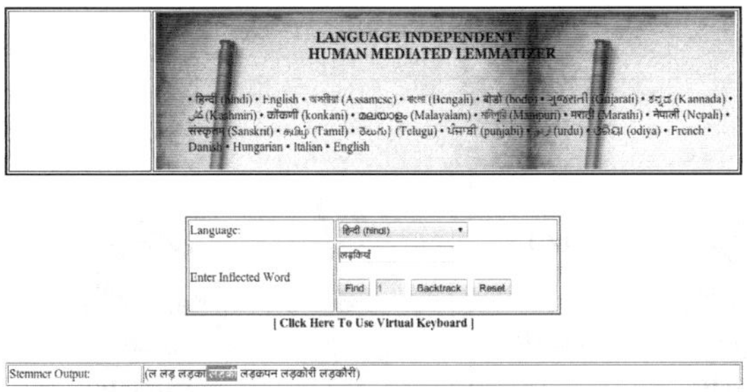


Figure 9: Online Interface - Language Independent Human Mediated Lemmatizer

evaluation was that for every inflected input word, a set of output root forms will be generated by the lemmatizer. **Even if one of the result in the top 10 from this set matches the root in the gold standard, then we consider our result to be correct.** Following this approach the accuracy of inflected nouns undergoing stemming is very high. Although, due to readjustment in verbs, for the first iteration without backtracking, our lemmatizer gives a fairly low accuracy. This can be further improved through backtracking, when we traversed the trie, one level up at a time. The first iteration of stemming gives result among the best five outputs and the backtracking approach gives among the best ten outputs. Interestingly, for inflected words in Italian our lemmatizer performs better when we include the results of one level backtrack as compared to a non-backtrack variant. The results for various languages are shown in Table 1 based on the lemmatizer's default variant, *i.e.*, without using backtrack feature.

### 5.1 Preparation of Gold Data

We prepared the gold data to perform evaluation for Hindi and Marathi languages, by using the domain specific sense marked corpus[2] which contains inflected words along with their root word forms. This corpus was created by trained lexicographers. Similarly, we had a sense marked corpus for Bengali, Assamese, Punjabi and Konkani.

For Dravidian languages like Malayalam and Kannada and for European languages like French and Italian, we had to perfrom manual evaluation as the sense marked data was unavailable. We did this, with a list of inflected words provided by native speakers and found remarkable precision in result.

[2]See `http://www.cfilt.iitb.ac.in/wsd/annotated_corpus/`

| Language | Corpus Type | Total Words | Precision Value |
|---|---|---|---|
| *Hindi* | Health | 8626 | 89.268 |
| *Hindi* | Tourism | 16076 | 87.953 |
| *Bengali* | Health | 11627 | 93.249 |
| *Bengali* | Tourism | 11305 | 93.199 |
| *Assamese* | General | 3740 | 96.791 |
| *Punjabi* | Tourism | 6130 | 98.347 |
| *Marathi* | Health | 11510 | 87.655 |
| *Marathi* | Tourism | 13176 | 85.620 |
| *Konkani* | Tourism | 12388 | 75.721 |
| *Malayalam** | General | 135 | 100.00 |
| *Kannada** | General | 39 | 84.615 |
| *Italian** | General | 42 | 88.095 # |
| *French** | General | 50 | 94.00 |

Table 1: Precision calculation for output produced by our lemmatizer based on the first variant, *i.e.*, without using backtrack feature. * denotes manual evaluation and # denotes one level backtracking.

### 5.2 Analysis

Errors are due to the following:

1. Agglutination in Marathi and Dravidian languages.

   Marathi and Dravidian languages like Kannada and Malayalam show the process of agglutination[3]. It is a process where a complex word is formed by combining morphemes each of which have a distinct grammatical or semantic meaning. Such words do not produce correct results in the first go, and we need to back track the trie upto a certain level to get the correct root form.

2. Suppletion.

   The term suppletion[4] implies that a gap in the paradigm was filled by a form "supplied" by a different paradigm. For example, the root word "go", has an irregular past tense form "went". For these irregular words the output of the lemmatizer is incorrect, as the root words are stored in their regular forms in the trie.

We have reported the precision scores (Table 1) for all the languages (except Italian) on the "direct" variant of our lemmatizer, *i.e.*, without using

[3]See `http://en.wikipedia.org/wiki/Agglutination`

[4]See `https://en.wikipedia.org/wiki/Suppletion`

| Corpus Name | Human Mediated Lemmatizer | Morpha | Snowball | Morfessor |
|---|---|---|---|---|
| English_General | 89.20 | 90.17 | 53.125 | 79.16 |
| Hindi_General | 90.83 | NA | NA | 26.14 |
| Marathi_General | 96.51 | NA | NA | 37.26 |

Table 2: Comparative Evaluation (precision values) of Human Mediated Lemmatizer [Without using Backtracking] against other classic stemming systems like Morpha, Snowball and Morfessor

backtrack feature. It is clear from our examples in Marathi viz. "असलेले" (*aslele*) and the scores reported in Italian that *precision improves when backtracking is used.*

## 6 Comparative evaluation with existing lemmatizers/stemmer

We compared performance of our system against three most commonly used lemmatizers/stemmers, *viz.* Morpha (Guido et al., 2001), Snowball [5] and Morfessor (Creutz, 2005; 2007). The results are shown in Table 2. Our lemmatizer works better than Morfessor for Hindi (up by 64%) and Marathi (up by 59%). For English, our lemmatizer outperforms Snowball by almost 36% and Morfessor by almost 10%. Although, as an exception, Morpha lemmatizer works better by about 1% in this case.

Snowball and Morpha lemmatizers are not available for Indian Languages and thus the results are marked with 'NA'. Morfessor being statistical in nature does not capture all the linguistic and morphological phenomenons associated with Indian languages and Snowball and Morpha are strictly rule based in nature and do not use any linguistic resource to validate the output. We have, of course, compared our lemmatizer with in-house rule based Hindi and Marathi morph analyzers. The Marathi Morphological Analyzer (Dabre et al., 2012) has an accuracy of 72.18%, with a usability of 94.33%, where as the in-house Hindi Morphological Analyzer[6] accuracy is close to 100% with average usability around 96.5% (Table 3). Here, usability is the percentage of total number of words analyzed out of total words in corpus.

However, these morph analysers have taken years to build with many false starts and false hits and misses. Compared to this, our human mediated lemmatizer was constructed in a few weeks' time. Once it was realized that we need lemmatizers for accessing senses of words, the system was built in no time. It is the preparation of gold data, generation of accuracy values and comparison with existing systems that took time.

[5] See http://snowball.tartarus.org/index.php

[6] See http://www.cfilt.iitb.ac.in/~ankitb/ma/

| | Nouns | Verbs |
|---|---|---|
| Total words in test Corpus | 14475 | 13160 |
| Correctly analyzed words | 13453 | 13044 |
| Unidentified words | 1022 | 116 |

Table 3: Hindi Morphological Analyzer - Results

## 7 Conclusion and future work

We gave an approach for developing light weight and quick-to-create human mediated lemmatizer. We applied the lemmatizer to 18 different Indian languages and 5 European languages. Our approach uses the longest prefix match functionality of a trie data structure. Without using any manually created rule list or statistical measure, we were able to find lemma of the input word within a ranked list of 5-15 outputs. The human annotator can thus choose from a small set of results and proceed with sense marking, thereby greatly helping the overall task of Machine Translation and Word Sense Disambiguation. We also confirm the fact that the combination of man and machine can identify the root to near 100 percent accuracy.

In future, we want to further prune of output list, making the ranking much more intelligent. Integration of the human mediated lemmatizer to all languages' sense marking task needs to be completed. Also we want to expand our work to include languages from different linguistic families.

## References

Arindam Chatterjee, Salil Rajeev Joshi, Mitesh M. Khapra and Pushpak Bhattacharyya 2010. *Introduction to Tools for IndoWordnet and Word Sense Disambiguation*, The 3rd IndoWordnet Workshop, Eighth International Conference on Natural Language Processing (ICON 2010), IIT Kharagpur, India.

Grzegorz Chrupala 2006. *Simple data-driven context-sensitive lemmatization* , Chrupaa, Grzegorz (2006) Simple data-driven context-sensitive lemmatization. In: SEPLN 2006, 13-15 September 2006, Zaragoza, Spain.

Thomas H. Cormen, Clifford Stein, Ronald L. Rivest and Charles E. Leiserson 2001. *Introduction to Algorithms*, 2nd Edition, ISBN:0070131511, McGraw-Hill Higher Education.

Mathis Creutz and Krista Lagus. 2005. *Unsupervised morpheme segmentation and morphology induction from text corpora using Morfessor 1.0.*, Technical Report A81, Publications in Computer and Information Science, Helsinki University of Technology.

Mathis Creutz and Krista Lagus. 2007. *Unsupervised models for morpheme segmentation and morphology learning*, Association for Computing Machinery Transactions on Speech and Language Processing, 4(1):1-34

Raj Dabre, Archana Amberkar and Pushpak Bhattacharyya 2012. *Morphology Analyser for Affix Stacking Languages: a case study in Marathi*, COLING 2012, Mumbai, India, 10-14 Dec, 2012.

Tarek El-Shishtawy and Fatma El-Ghannam 2012. *An Accurate Arabic Root-Based Lemmatizer for Information Retrieval Purposes*, IJCSI International Journal of Computer Science Issues, Vol. 9, Issue 1, No 3, January 2012 ISSN (Online): 1694-0814.

John A. Goldsmith 2001. *Unsupervised Learning of the morphology of a Natural Language*, Computational Linguistics, 27(2): 153-198

John A. Goldsmith 2006. *An algorithm for the unsupervised Learning of morphology*, Natural Language Engineering, 12(4): 353-371

Bart Jongejan and Hercules Dalianis 2009. *Automatic training of lemmatization rules that handle morphological changes in pre-, in- and suffixes alike*, Proceedings of the 47th Annual Meeting of the ACL and the 4th IJCNLP of the AFNLP, pages 145 - 153, Suntec, Singapore, 2-7 August 2009

Lauri Karttunen 1983. *KIMMO: A General Morphological Processor* , Texas Linguistic Forum, 22 (1983), 163-186.

Aki Loponen, Jiaul H. Paik and Kalervo Jarvelin 2013. *UTA Stemming and Lemmatization Experiments in the FIRE Bengali Ad Hoc Task* , Multilingual Information Access in South Asian Languages Lecture Notes in Computer Science Volume 7536, 2013, pp 258-268

J.B. Lovins 1968. *Development of a stemming algorithm*, Mechanical Translations and Computational Linguistics Vol.11 Nos 1 and 2, pp. 22-31.

Prasenjit Majumder, Mandar Mitra, Swapan K. Parui, Gobinda Kole, Pabitra Mitra, and Kalyankumar Datta. 2007. *YASS: Yet another suffix stripper*, Association for Computing Machinery Transactions on Information Systems, 25(4):18-38.

Prasenjit Majumder, Mandar Mitra and Kalyankumar Datta 2007. *Statistical vs Rule-Based Stemming for Monolingual French Retrieval*, Evaluation of Multilingual and Multi-modal Information Retrieval, Lecture Notes in Computer Science vol. 4370, ISBN 978-3-540-74998-1, Springer, Berlin, Heidelberg.

James Mayfield and Paul McNamee 2003. *Single N-gram Stemming*, SIGIR '03, Toronto, Canada.

Massimo Melucci and Nicola Orio 2003. *A novel method of Stemmer Generation Based on Hidden Markov Models*, CIKM '03, New Orleans, Louisiana, USA.

Guido Minnen,John Carroll and Darren Pearce. 2001. *Applied morphological processing of English*, Natural Language Engineering, 7(3). 207-223.

Okan Ozturkmenoglu and Adil Alpkocak 2012. *Comparison of different lemmatization approaches for information retrieval on Turkish text collection* , Innovations in Intelligent Systems and Applications (INISTA), 2012 International Symposium on.

Plisson Joël, Lavrac Nada, Mladenic Dunja 2008. *A rule based approach to word lemmatization*, Proceedings of 7th International Multi-conference Information Society, IS 2004, Institute Jozef Stefen, Ljubljana, pp.83-86, 2008

Snigdha Paul, Nisheeth Joshi and Iti Mathur 2013. *Development of a Hindi Lemmatizer*, CoRR, DBLP:journals/corr/abs/1305.6211 2013

M.F. Porter 1980. *An algorithm for suffix stripping*, Program; 14, 130-137

M.F. Porter 2006. *Stemming algorithms for various European languages*, Available at [URL] `http://snowball.tartarus.org/texts/stemmersoverview.html` As seen on May 16, 2013

Ananthakrishnan Ramanathan, and Durgesh D Rao 2003. *A Lightweight Stemmer for Hindi.* , Workshop on Computational Linguistics for South-Asian Languages, EACL

# VerbNet Workbench

**Indrek Jentson**
University of Tartu
Tartu, Estonia
indrek.jentson@ut.ee

## Abstract

In this paper a tool to manage a dataset for a VerbNet-like verb lexicon is presented. It was designed to allow users to create a verb lexicon for another language than English and at the same time use the same data structure as the English VerbNet. We take a look at the most relevant requirements of the software and will give an overview of the functionality achieved so far.

## 1 Introduction

In 2000 the verb lexicon for English was created by scientist from the University of Pennsylvania and named as VerbNet (Kipper et al., 2000). The following work has extended the content of the verb lexicon with many new verbs and verb classes (Kipper et al., 2006). Today in the English VerbNet version 3.2 there are 273 total main classes and 214 total subclasses with 6340 total verbs covered (Unified Verb Index, 2013).

Several works have shown that the VerbNet is very useful for NLP but till now a resource of this size and coverage exists only for English. There is no questions that similar verb lexicons for others languages are needed.

In recent work the question was asked - is it feasible to convert the English Verbnet into a similar verb lexicon for some other language and the following analysis for Estonian showed that in principle the class hierarchy, thematic roles with restrictions and semantic descriptions are reusable for such work (Jentson, 2013).

In order to start building a new verb lexicon for Estonian side-by-side with the English VerbNet the appropriate tool - VerbNet Workbench - was designed and implemented.

## 2 Requirements for the VerbNet Workbench

In order to understand exactly what kind of software is required to manage VerbNet data the most essential functional requirements (FR) were specified.

**FR1.** The system shall allow each user to choose a target language for the following work session.

FR1.1. The system shall allow an authenticated user to add a new language to the list of available languages.

**FR2.** The system must be completely compatible with the data structure of the English VerbNet.

FR2.1. The system shall allow to import the VerbNet data files for the selected language in XML format correspondent to XML schema `vn_schema-3.xsd` (VerbNet, 2013).

FR2.2. The system shall allow to export the VerbNet data files for the selected language in XML format with the XML scheme file consistent to the exported data.

**FR3.** The system shall allow an authenticated user to enter the following information in the context of the selected language:

1) the general data for a verb class together with a reference to the corresponding verb class in the English VerbNet;
2) the members of the verb class together with the references to the other language resources (for example the WordNet, the FrameNet etc);
3) the thematic roles with the selection restrictions for the arguments of the verb class;
4) the syntactic frames of the verb class, each containing an example, a syntactic template with the syntactic restrictions and a semantic description;

5) the subclasses of the verb class, they are with the same structure as the main class.

FR3.1. The system shall allow an authenticated user to insert new selection restrictions with the descriptions for the thematic roles.

FR3.2. The system shall allow an authenticated user to insert new syntactic restrictions with the descriptions.

FR3.3. The system shall allow an authenticated user to insert new predicates with the descriptions for the semantic descriptions.

**FR4.** The system shall allow an authenticated user to reserve a verb class for his/her work and publish the changed data only after the work is marked completed.

FR4.1. The system shall show to an authenticated user the list of verb classes reserved by that user.

FR4.2. The system shall prevent a user from reserving some verb class that is already reserved.

**FR5.** The system shall maintain all versions of the records for every verb class.

**FR6.** The system shall allow each user to search the verbs from the lexicon and list all the references to those verb classes where the verb is in the list of members.

In the process of designing and implementing the VerbNet Workbench software all those requirements were taken into account. From the non-functional requirements we highlight only one - the targeted system must be web-based in order to ensure its availability to all interested parties and to allow many linguists to work together on the VerbNet data.

## 3 Results: overview of functionality

In order to build the VerbNet Workbench we used the programming language Python 2.7 (2013) and the web application framework Django (Django Project, 2013). For data storage the database management system PostgreSQL 9.2 (2013) is used, but it is possible to use any relational database system supported by Django.

The UML class diagram of the necessary data model is presented on Figure 1. The main data object on the diagram is class *VNClass* the purpose of which is to hold data for the verb classes in the context of the chosen language. The list of verbs (class *Member*), thematic roles (class *ThematicRole*) and syntactic frames (class *Frame*) belongs to each verb class. For each syntactic frame, there is a data structure to describe the template (class *Syntax* etc) and the meaning (class *Semantics* etc) of the sentence.

In Table 1 there is a short overview of the functionality which is available to the users. Access to that functionality is divided between three user roles. The role 'User' belongs to any unauthenticated user who wants to use the prepared data. An authenticated user gets the role 'Contributor' and can additionally do everything that 'User' can do and the user with the role 'Administrator' has rights to do everything.

| Actor | Use Case |
|---|---|
| User | Choose a language |
| User | Browse a class hierarchy |
| User | View attributes of the verb class |
| User | Search for a verb class by given verb |
| User | Export the VerbNet dataset for chosen language (XML-files) |
| Contributor | Authenticate the user |
| Contributor | Define a new language |
| Contributor | Create a new verb class or subclass |
| Contributor | Enter information for attributes of the verb class |
| Contributor | Add the members to the verb class |
| Contributor | Change data of the verb class |
| Administrator | Import the VerbNet dataset for chosen language (XML-files) |
| Administrator | Manage the users |

Table 1. The overview of realized Use Cases

The usual scenario for entering new information to the database includes activities like choosing some verb class from the English VerbNet, entering an appropriate name for this verb class in the chosen working language, finding the class members (this can be started by translating the verbs in the same verb class of the

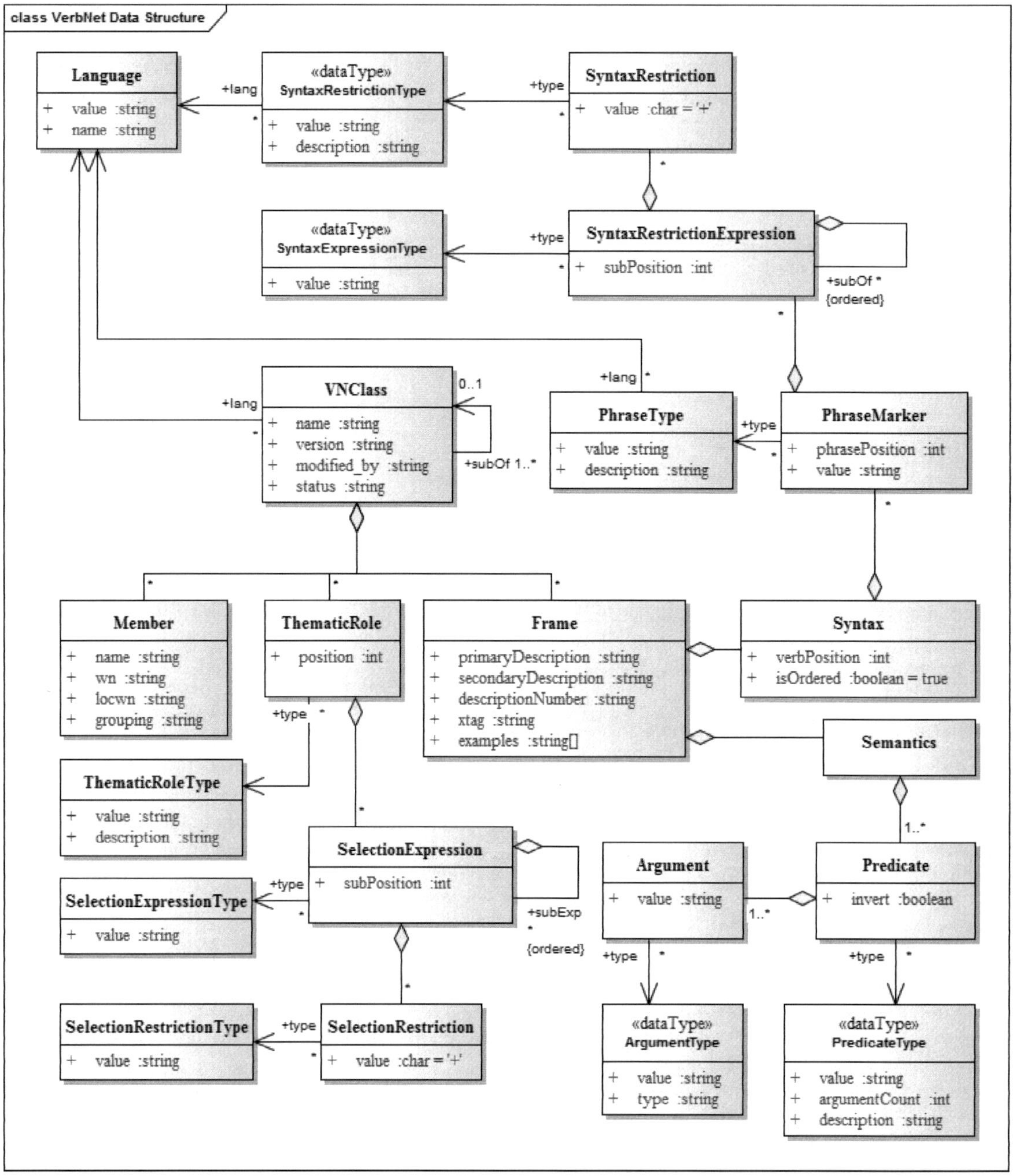


Figure 1. The data model for the VerbNet Workbench

English VerbNet) and defining the syntactic frames. Defining all suitable syntactic templates with the syntactic restrictions for the selected verb class is indeed the most challenging work in this process because there lay the main differences when we are looking from the point of view of another language.

This basic functionality allows linguists to start collecting information about the verbs for many different languages so that the data structure of the gathered information is compatible with the English VerbNet and the verb classes from one language are comparable to the verb classes from some other language.

## 4 Discussion: present and future challenges

The first user experience has shown that the tool allows data to be managed in such a way that all necessary information can be entered by the contributors and the users can browse, search and download data already collected. However, it is also observed that some advanced features would be helpful for data entry, enabling the necessary data type values to be selected and the amount of manual input reduced.

Referencing from the submitted data to other resources for the same language is currently implemented only on the description level. Functionality, which allows opening and viewing referenced resources such as Wordnet or Framenet, is depending on availability and access methods of each specific resource and the general approach is therefore complicated to implement.

## 5 Conclusion

It can be concluded that the main use cases with basic functionality are indeed realized, but more work is necessary in order to increase usability and user comfort. It is also planned to enable a localization of the application in order to provide the users with the possibility to use a preferred language for the user interface. A separate issue is drafting the user manual to give substantive guidelines for categorizing verbs and to explain the basic principles and the rules about compiling a verb class dataset.

We hope that the availability of the VerbNet Workbench will propitiate work on verb semantics and give the possibility to create a useful language resource for natural language processing in many languages.

## Reference


Indrek Jentson. 2013. *The Feasibility of Estonian VerbNet.* Estonian Papers in Applied Linguistics 9 (2013): 75-83.

Karin Kipper, Hoa Trang Dang and Martha Palmer. 2000. *Class-based construction of a verb lexicon.* Proceedings of the National Conference on Artificial Intelligence. Menlo Park, CA; Cambridge, MA; London; AAAI Press; MIT Press; 1999, 2000, 691–696.

Karin Kipper, Anna Korhonen, Neville Ryant and Martha Palmer. 2006. *Extending VerbNet with novel verb classes.* Proceedings of 5th international conference on Language Resources and Evaluation (2006), No. 2.2.

Django Project, `https://www.djangoproject.com/` (15.11.2013).

PostgreSQL, `http://www.postgresql.org/` (15.11.2013).

Python Programming Language, `http://www.python.org/` (15.11.2013).

Unified Verb Index, `http://verbs.colorado.edu/verb-index/` (15.11.2013).

VerbNet v3.2, `http://verbs.colorado.edu/verb-index/vn/verbnet-3.2.tar.gz` (15.11.2013)

# A Survey of WordNet Annotated Corpora

**Tommaso Petrolito**[⊕⊙] and **Francis Bond**[⊕]
[⊕]Linguistics and Multilingual Studies,
**Nanyang Technological University**, Singapore
[⊙] Informatica Umanistica,
**University of Pisa**, Italy
bond@ieee.org, tommasouni@gmail.com

## Abstract

This paper surveys the current state of wordnet sense annotated corpora. We look at corpora in any language, and describe them in terms of accessibility and usefulness. We finally discuss possibilities in increasing the interoperability of the corpora, especially across languages.

## 1 Introduction

There are over 60 different wordnet projects projects for more than 60 languages.[1] The first wordnet was the Princeton WordNet of English (Fellbaum, 1998) describing over 150,000 concepts. Many others have followed, even if with different coverage rates in each continent (Africa and central Asia are less covered than the other geographical regions), all around the world. So today there are many wordnets all sharing a similar structure, some of them freely available, others restricted to license owners.

Bond and Paik (2012) surveyed the available wordnets and evaluated them on two axes: how **accessible** (legally OK to use) and how **usable** (of sufficient quality, size and with a documented interface) (Ishida, 2006). In this paper we do the same for sense-annotated corpora. We restrict ourselves to those that use a wordnet as the sense inventory.

Sense annotated corpora can be classified according to several criteria. Some obvious ones are the language used; the lexicon used to determine the senses; the size; the license. In addition, another useful distinction is that between those that annotate **all words** and those that only annotate **some words**, typically either a sample of a few frequent words, or of a single part-of-speech. We will also distinguish those corpora that align to SemCor (Langone et al., 2004) the first wordnet annotated corpus. We will first describe it in some detail, as it is the most typical corpus, and then note where other corpora differ from it.

We have found more than 20 WordNet Annotated Corpora in more than 10 different languages. We describe them in the following Section 2, discuss some of the issues they raise in Section 3 and then plans for future work in 4.

[1]`http://globalwordnet.org/?page_id=38`

## 2 WordNet Annotated Corpora

We have tried to list all known corpora annotated with wordnet senses, in any language.[2] In most cases, information on size comes from the latest publication describing the corpus, or its web-page. Sometimes the data is from the corpus providers themselves, in which case we will note this. We have also put the information online as the Global Wordnet Association's *Wordnet Annotated Corpora* page (`http://globalwordnet.org/?page_id=241`). This will be kept up-to-date.

We divide the corpora into three groups: SemCor and its translations; non-English Corpora; and English Corpora. We summarize the corpora in Table 1, and then describe each one in more detail.

### 2.1 SemCor and Translations

#### 2.1.1 Princeton SemCor

The English SemCor corpus is a sense-tagged corpus of English created at Princeton University by the WordNet Project research team (Landes et al., 1998). It was created very early in the WordNet project (Miller et al., 1994), and was one of the first sense-tagged corpora produced for any language. The corpus consists of a subset of the Brown Corpus (700,000 words, with more than 200,000 sense-annotated) (Francis and Kucera, 1979), and it has been part-of-speech-tagged and sense-tagged. It is distributed under the Princeton Wordnet License.

For each sentence, open class words (or multi-word expressions) and named entities are tagged. Not all expressions are tagged. We give a (constructed) example in Figure 1. Note that the tagged synsets do not have to be continuous (as in *get up*) and that there are some untagged elements (typically multi word expressions, such as ***on one's feet***). Closed class words such as articles and prepositions are only tagged if they are part of a multi-word expression. The annotation is known to be imperfect: Bentivogli and Pianta (2005) estimate around 2.5% of the tags to be incorrect.

The Brown corpus has also been annotated with syntactic information by various other projects, including the Penn Treebank (Marcus et al., 1993); Susanne (Sampson, 1995) (also sense-annotated with the WordNet 1.6 senses in the SemiSusanne project by Powell (2005)) and Redwoods (Oepen et al., 2004; Flickinger,

[2]Although we may have missed some lexical sample corpora.

| Name | # words | # taggable | # tagged | lng | Wordnet | License | Semcor | Target |
|---|---|---|---|---|---|---|---|---|
| SemCor3.0-all | 360k | n/a | 193k | eng | WN 3.0 | wordnet | + | all |
| SemCor3.0-verbs | 317k | n/a | 41k | eng | WN 3.0 | wordnet | + | v |
| Jsemcor | 380k | 150k | 58k | jpn | Jpn WN | wordnet | + | all |
| MultiSemCor[a] | 269k | 121k | 93k | ita | MultiWN | CC BY 3.0 | + | all |
| | 258k | n/a | 120k | eng | WN 1.6 | CC BY 3.0 | | |
| SemCor EnRo | 176k | 89k | 48k | rum | BalkaNet | MSC ... | + | all |
| | 178k | n/a | n/a | eng | WN 2.0 | BY-NC-ND | | |
| BulSemCor[b] | 101k | n/a | 99k | bul | BulNet | web only | – | all+ |
| Eusemcor | 300k | n/a | n/a | baq | Basque WN | web only | – | all |
| spsemcor | 850k | n/a | 23k | spa | ESPWN1.6 | web only | – | n, v |
| AnCora | 500k | n/a | n/a | spa | EuroWN 1.6 | research only | – | n |
| | 500k | n/a | n/a | cat | EuroWN 1.6 | research only | | |
| DutchSemcor[c] | 500,000k | n/a | 283k | dut | Cornetto | n/a | – | all |
| TüBa-D/Z Treebank[d] | 1,365k | n/a | 18k | ger | GermaNet | none | – | some, v, n |
| WebCaGe | n/a | n/a | 11k | eng | GermaNet | CC BY-SA 3.0 | – | all |
| ISST | 306k | n/a | 81k | ita | ItalWN | research only | – | all |
| NTU-MC | 116k | 63k | 51k | eng | PWN | CC BY | – | all |
| | 106k | 67k | 36k | cmn | COW | CC BY | | |
| | 56k | 37k | 28k | ind | WN Bahasa | CC BY | | |
| | 49k | 20k | 15k | jpn | Jpn WN | CC BY | | |
| AQMAR Arabic SST[e] | 65k | n/a | 32k | ara | WN | CC BY-SA 3.0 | – | n, v |
| Jos100k[f] | 100k | n/a | 5k | slv | sloWNet | CC BY-NC 3.0 | – | some n |
| Hungarian WSD corpus | 16k | n/a | 5k | hun | HuWN | none | – | n, v, adj |
| KPWr | 438k | n/a | 9k | pol | plwordnet | CC BY 3.0 | – | some |
| Gloss Corpus | 1,621k | 656k | 449k | eng | WN 3.0 | wordnet | – | some |
| Groningen Meaning Bank | 1,020k | n/a | n/a | eng | WN | none | – | all |
| MASC | 504k | n/a | 100k | eng | WN 3.0 | none | – | v |
| DSO Corpus | n/a | n/a | 193k | eng | WN 1.5 | LDC | – | n, v |
| OntoNotes | 1,500k | n/a | n/a | eng | Coarse WN | LDC | – | n, v |
| SemLink | 78k | n/a | n/a | eng | Coarse WN | none | – | all |
| Senseval 3 | 5k | n/a | 2k | eng | WN 1.7.1 | none | – | all |
| SemEval-2013 Task 12[g] | 5k | n/a | n/a | eng | BabelNet | none | – | n |
| SemEval-2013 Task 13 | 141k | n/a | 5k | eng | BabelNet | none | – | n, v, adj |

Table 1: Corpora Tagged with Wordnet Senses

**a** According to Bentivogli and Pianta (2005) 23.4% of Italian words still need to be tagged, so we can estimate (given that 93k is the 76.6%) the content words at 121k.

**b** The annotations include both open-class and closed-class words.

**c** 282,503 tokens manually tagged by two annotators, anyway more than 400,000 have been manually tagged by at least one annotator and millions have been automatically tagged (information from the corpus providers themselves: Piek Vossen).

**d** The targets of the annotation are not all the nouns and verbs but only a selected set of 109 words (30 nouns and 79 verbs). The total number of annotations is 17,910 (information from the corpus providers themselves: Verena Henrich and Marie Hinrichs). The corpus is not currently available but it will be.

**e** According to Schneider et al. (2012) about half the tokens in the data are covered by a nominal supersense, so we can estimate (given that the tokens are 65k) the tagged tokens at 32k.

**f** Only the 100 most frequent nouns are annotated.

**g** The corpus is multilingual, in fact the same articles are available in other four languages:french, spanish, german and italian, respectively containing 3k tokens each, Frech, Spanish and German and 4k Italian)

$Kim_a$ $got_b$ $slowly_c$ $up_b$, the $children_d$ $were_e$ $already_f$ $on_g$ $their_g$ $feet_g$.

| ID | Lemma | Sense |
|---|---|---|
| a | Kim | **org** |
| b | get_up | $get\_up_4$ |
| c | slowly | $slowly_1$ |
| d | child | $child_1$ |
| e | be | $be_3$ |
| f | already | $already_1$ |
| g | on_one's_feet | **notag** |

Figure 1: SemCor Example

2011). The combination of syntactic and semantic information has been used in various parsing experiments (Bikel, 2000; Agirre et al., 2008). The corpus is divided into two parts: **semcor-all** in which 186 texts have all open-class words (such as nouns, verbs, adjectives and adverbs) semantically annotated. The SemCor component of all word types consists of 359,732 (Lupu et al., 2005) tokens of which 192,639 are semantically annotated. The second part, **semcor-verbs**, only has verbs senses annotated: 41,497 verbal occurrences from 316,814 tokens (Lupu et al., 2005).

### 2.1.2 MultiSemCor

MultiSemCor is an English/Italian parallel corpus created by translating the English SemCor corpus into Italian (Bentivogli and Pianta, 2005). In particular it consisted of the translation of 72% of the SemCor-all corpus. This sub-corpus was automatically word aligned and the semantic annotations were automatically projected from the English words to their Italian translation equivalents. The resulting corpus has texts aligned both at the sentence and word level, and annotated with part of speech, lemma and word sense (PWN 1.6). MultiSemCor version 1.1 contains 14,144 sentences and 261,283 tokens, 119,802 of which are annotated with senses. Words that did not project from English were not tagged: an estimated 23.4% of the concepts that should be tagged are not. The MultiSemCor project includes a MultiSemCor Web Interface (Ranieri et al., 2004). It provides for two distinct browsing modalities. In the *text-oriented* modality (*MSC Browser*), for each bi-text (109/116 aligned texts working actually[3]) the user has access to the alignment at the sentence and word level, and to the dictionary. "MultiSemCor+" (as defined by Lupu et al. (2005)) is a more recent extension that also contains the the Romanian SemCor (Section 2.1.3, Lupu et al., 2005). This new project represents a first test bed for multilingual semantic disambiguation experiments. We can browse the same aligned texts in Romanian and English on the MultiSemCor Browser. Currently the English-Romanian modality has only a subset of the Italian: 12/116 aligned texts.

### 2.1.3 SemCor En-Ro corpus and RoSemCor

Even if the monolingual Romanian corpus is not so clearly available while the multilingual one is distributed open and free under MS Commons-BY-NC-ND [4]. En-Ro SemCor contains a total of 178,499 words for English and 175,603 words for Romanian (Lupu et al., 2005; Ion, 2007). The English SemCor texts have been translated into Romanian and the sentence and paragraph annotations have been observed. The sense transfer from English to Romanian follows closely the WSDTool procedure (a wordsense disambiguation algorithm described by Ion (2007)). From a total of 88,874 occurrences of content words in Romanian, 54.54% received sense annotation by the transfer procedure.

### 2.1.4 Jsemcor

Japanese Sem-Cor (JSemCor: Bond et al., 2012) is a sense-tagged corpus for the Japanese Wordnet (Isahara et al., 2008), based on translation of the subset of English SemCor used in MultiSemCor (Section refsec:multisemcor) with senses projected across from English. In this case, of the 150,555 content words only 58,265 are sense tagged. Jsemcor is a SemCor corpus: the texts are aligned to the correspondent English SemCor texts both at the sentence and word level. The transfer process left 39% of the senses untagged because of the fundamental differences between Japanese and English. A major cause of lexical gaps is part-of-speech mismatches. The license is similar to the Princeton WordNet License, so the data is freely available.

## 2.2 Independent Corpora for other languages

Most projects sense-tag existing annotated corpora for their languages. This means that they can take advantage of the work that has gone into pre-processing them, and also be used with other annotations.

### 2.2.1 BulSemCor

The Bulgarian Semantically Annotated Corpus (Koeva et al., 2010) is part of the Bulgarian Brown Corpus (balanced but not aligned to the English Brown Corpus, so BullSemCor is a NonSemCor corpus). It consists of 811 excerpts each containing 100+ words: the total size of the source corpus is 101,062 tokens.[5] Each lexical item (simple or compound word) which occurs in the particular context in BulSemCor is assigned manually the unique semantic or grammatical meaning from the Bulgarian wordnet. The result is a lemmatised POS and sense-annotated corpus of units of running text. Unlike most wordnet corpora, the annotation includes both open-class and closed-class words. Sense distinctions in the closed word classes have been drawn primarily from corpus evidence. The sense-annotated corpus consists of 99,480 lexical units annotated with the most appropriate synset from the Bulgarian wordnet (BulNet). The corpus excerpts are offered under MS NoRedistribution NonCommercial license [6] for free, it is also possible to query the corpus online. The restrictions on use and redistribution mean that corpus is not considered open source.

### 2.2.2 Eusemcor and spsemcor

The University of the Basque Country and the Department of Software, Technical University of Catalonia have produced two browsing-online-only corpora: Eusemcor (Basque Semcor) and spsemcor (Spanish Semcor) (Agirre et al., 2006). Eusemcor was compiled with samples from a balanced corpus and a newspaper corpus. It comprises 300,000 words in total. Agirre et al. (2006) point out that as Basque is an agglutinative language, it has a higher lemma/word rate than English, so in parallel corpora it would allow to think that 300,000 words in Basque are comparable to 500.000 words in English. The process of tagging the new corpus was

[3] `multisemcor.fbk.eu/frameset1.php`

[4] `http://meta-net.eu/meta-share/meta-share-licenses/META-SHARE=%20COMMONS_BYNCND%20v1.0.pdf`

[5] `dcl.bas.bg/en/corpora_en.html#SemC`

[6] `http://www.meta-net.eu/meta-share/meta-share-licenses/META-SHARE%20NonCommercial%20NoRedistribution%20NoDerivatives%20For-a-fee-v%201.0.pdf`

used in this case mainly to extend the Basque WordNet adding the eventual missing needed senses. Spsemcor is a part of SenSem, a databank of Spanish which maps a corpus and a verbal database. The SenSem corpus consists of 25,000 sentences, 100 for each of the 250 most frequent verbs of Spanish (Davies, 2002). Sentences are tagged at both syntactic and semantic levels: verb sense, phrase and construction types, aspect, argument functions and semantic roles. In the Spsemcor part of SenSem the noun heads were tagged with the Spanish WordNet 1.6: 23,307 forms for 3,693 noun lemmas of the SenSem corpus have been semantically annotated (Climent et al., 2012). This corresponds to the 82.6% of the total amount of verbal arguments in the corpus. Both Eusemcor and Spsemcor are only available for online browsing.

#### 2.2.3 AnCora

AnCora (Martí et al., 2007) are two multilingual corpora of 500,000 words each: a Catalan corpus (AnCora-CAT) and a Spanish (AnCora-ESP) one, built in an incrementally way from the previous 3LB corpora.[7] In this way, 400,000 words were added to each corpus coming from different press sources (mainly newspapers). The AnCora corpora were annotated at different levels of linguistic description: the whole Catalan corpus is annotated with morphological, syntactic, and semantic information; as for Spanish, the morphological and syntactic levels are already completed, while the semantic annotation covers 40% of the corpus (200,000 words). The lexical semantic annotation consists in assigning each noun in the corpora its sense. This process was carried out manually and the senses repository is WordNet. Each noun was assigned either a WordNet sense or a label indicating a special circumstance.

#### 2.2.4 DutchSemCor

DutchSemCor is a sense-tagged corpus with senses and domain tags from the Cornetto lexical database (Vossen et al., 2011). In DutchSemCor about 282,503 tokens for 2,870 nouns, verbs and adjectives (11,982 senses) have been manually tagged by two annotators, resulting in 25 examples on average per sense (anyway more than 400,000 have been manually tagged by at least one annotator and millions have been automatically tagged). The examples mainly come from existing corpora collected in the projects CGN (9 millions words: Van Eerten, 2007), D-Coi, and SoNaR (500 millions words: Oostdijk, 2008), but also additional examples from the Dutch websites have been added. DutchSemCor is not available, but excerpts and statistics are freely downloadable.

[7] Read Civit and Martí (2004) for 3LB-ESP and Civit et al. (2004) for 3LB-CAT

#### 2.2.5 TüBa-D/Z Treebank

Henrich and Hinrichs (2013) have manually annotated the TüBa-D/Z Treebank[8] with GermaNet senses with the goal of providing a gold standard for word sense disambiguation. The underlying resource is a German newspaper corpus manually annotated at various levels of grammar. The sense inventory used for tagging word senses is taken from GermaNet. With the sense annotation for a selected set of 109 words (30 nouns and 79 verbs) occurring 17,910 times in the TüBa-D/Z, the treebank currently represents the largest manually sense-annotated corpus available for GermaNet. The corpus is not currently available but it will be made freely available in a future release at the TüBa-D/Z Sense Annotations webpage.[9]

#### 2.2.6 WebCaGe

WebCaGe is a web-harvested corpus annotated with GermaNet senses, the largest sense-annotated corpus available for German (Henrich et al., 2012). WebCaGe includes example sentences from the German Wiktionary (46,457 German words) and additional material collected by following the links to Wikipedia, the Gutenberg archive, and other web-based materials. Wiktionary (7,644 tagged word tokens) and Wikipedia (1,732) contribute by far the largest subsets of the total number of tagged word tokens (10,750) compared with the external webpages (589) and the Gutenberg texts (785). These tokens belong to 2,607 distinct polysemous words contained in GermaNet, among which there are 211 adjectives, 1,499 nouns, and 897 verbs. On average, these words have 2.9 senses in GermaNet (2.4 for adjectives, 2.6 for nouns, and 3.6 for verbs). WebCaGe is distributed under the Creative Commons Attribution-ShareAlike 3.0 Unported License (CC BY-SA 3.0) [10]

#### 2.2.7 ISST

ISST is the Italian Syntactic-Semantic Treebank (Montemagni et al., 2003) a multi-layered annotated corpus of Italian. ISST has a five-level structure covering orthographic, morpho-syntactic, syntactic and semantic levels of linguistic description. The fifth level deals with lexico-semantic annotation, which is carried out in terms of sense tagging of lexical heads (nouns, verbs and adjectives) augmented with other types of semantic information: ItalWordNet (Italian part of the EuroWordNet Project) is the reference lexical resource used for the sense tagging task. The ISST corpus consists of 305,547 word tokens (composing a balanced corpus for a total of 215,606 tokens and a specialized

[8] www.sfs.unituebingen.de/en/ascl/resources/corpora/tueba-dz.html

[9] http://www.sfs.uni-tuebingen.de/en/ascl/resources/corpora/sense-annotated-tueba-dz.html

[10] http://creativecommons.org/licenses/by-sa/3.0/

corpus, amounting to 89,941 tokens, with texts belonging to the financial domain) of which 81,236 content words are sense annotated. ISST was made available for research purposes in 2010 (Dei Rossi et al., 2011).

#### 2.2.8 NTU-MC

The NTU-Multilingual Corpus is a corpus designed to be multilingual from the start. It contains parallel text in eight languages: English (eng), Mandarin Chinese (cmn), Japanese (cpn), Indonesian (ind), Korean (kor), Arabic (arb), Vietnamese (vie) and Thai (tha) (Tan and Bond, 2012). Text is in three genres: short stories, essays and tourism. All the text is translated from English. The text is being sense annotated (Open Multilingual Wordnet[11] senses) in Chinese, English, Japanese and Indonesian (tourist data only; Bond et al., 2013). Tagging is still underway, snapshots are available from `compling.hss.ntu.edu.sg/ntumc`. The sizes of the different subcorpora are given in Table 1. There is more data for Chinese and English, with less for Indonesian and Japanese.

#### 2.2.9 AQMAR Arabic SST

This is a 65,000-token corpus[12] of 28 Arabic Wikipedia articles (selected from the topical domains of history, sports, science, and technology) hand-annotated for nominal supersenses (40 coarse lexical semantic classes, 25 for nouns, 15 for verbs, originating in WordNet). It extends the Named Entity Corpus[13] and was developed by Nathan Schneider, Behrang Mohit, Kemal Oflazer, and Noah Smith (Schneider et al., 2012) as part of the AQMAR project.[14] This dataset is released under the Creative Commons Attribution-ShareAlike 3.0 Unported license (CC BY-SA 3.0).

#### 2.2.10 Jos100k

The Jos100k corpus of Slovene contains 100,000 words of sampled paragraphs from the FidaPLUS corpus.[15] It is meant to serve as a reference annotated corpus of Slovene: its manually-validated annotations cover three level of linguistic description (morphosyntactic, syntactic and semantic). All the occurences of 100 most frequent nouns are annotated with their concept (synset id) from the Slovene WordNet sloWNet. The corpus is now at the version 2.0 and is freely available (CC BY-NC 3.0 [16]) for browsing and downloading at the project webpage: `nl.ijs.si/jos/jos100k-en.html`. An online browser for concordances is available here `nl.ijs.si/jos/cqp/` and a lot of documenting information is available as TEI corpus.[17]

[11] `compling.hss.ntu.edu.sg/omw`

[12] `www.ark.cs.cmu.edu/ArabicSST/`

[13] `www.ark.cs.cmu.edu/ArabicNER/`

[14] `www.ark.cs.cmu.edu/AQMAR/`

[15] `www.fidaplus.net/`

[16] `http://creativecommons.org/licenses/by-nc/3.0/deed.en`

[17] `http://www.tei-c.org/release/doc/tei-p5-doc/en/html/ref-teiCorpus.html`

#### 2.2.11 Hungarian word sense disambiguated corpus

The Hungarian WSD corpus (Vincze et al., 2008), contains 39 suitable word form samples selected (the most frequent words with more than one well-defined senses) for the purpose of word sense disambiguation. There are 300-500 samples for each word (so more or less 16,000 thousands samples). The Hungarian National Corpus and its Heti Világgazdaság (HVG) subcorpus provided the basis for corpus text selection and senses are from the Hungarian WordNet (HuWN) [18]. This corpus is a fine-grained lexical sample corpus.The corpus follows the SemEval XML format (not validable XML).

#### 2.2.12 KPWr Polish Corpus of Wroclaw University

The Polish Corpus of Wroclaw University (Broda et al., 2012) represents written and spoken Polish. All the documents are freely available under the Creative Commons Attribution 3.0 Unported Licence[19]. The texts are organized in 14 categories (blogs, science, stenographic recordings, dialogue, contemporary prose, past prose, law, long press articles, short press articles, popular science and textbooks, wikipedia, religion, official texts and technical texts). The annotations are on the level of chunks and selected predicate-argument relations, named entities, relations between named entities, anaphora relations and word senses (plwordnet[20] senses). The corpus contains totally 438,327 words with 9157 tagged (for selected lexems) and has been been developed by The WrocUT Language Technology Group G4.19, Artificial Intelligence Department at the Institute of Informatics, Wroclaw University of Technology.

### 2.3 Other English Corpora

As is common for language resources, there are more for English than for any other language.

#### 2.3.1 WordNet Gloss Corpus

In the Princeton WordNet Gloss Corpus Word,the definitions (or glosses) of WordNet's synsets are manually linked to the context-appropriate sense in WordNet. The corpus contains 1,621,129[21] tokens with 449,355 sense tagged (330,499 manually + 118,856 automatically) on 656,066 taggable words and globs (the tagged ones + 206,711 untagged). The wordnet definitions have been translated into many languages, including Albanian (Ruci, 2008), Japanese (Bond et al., 2010), Korean (Yoon et al., 2009) and Spanish (Fernández-Montraveta et al., 2008). Further, the glosses are useful for unsupervised sense disambiguation techniques such

[18] `http://www.inf.u-szeged.hu/rgai/HuWN`

[19] `http://creativecommons.org/licences/by/3.0/legalcode`

[20] `plwordnet.pwr.wroc.pl/wordnet`

[21] `wordnet.princeton.edu/glosstag.shtml`

as LESK (Lesk, 1986): and it has been shown for another resource that having the glosses disambiguated improves the accuracy of extended LESK (Baldwin et al., 2008).

### 2.3.2 Groningen Meaning Bank

The Groningen Meaning Bank (GMB), is a free corpus of English (1,020,367 tokens) developed at the University of Groningen, comprises thousands of texts in raw and tokenised format, tags for part of speech, named entities and lexical categories (word senses from WordNet, among other things), and discourse representation structures compatible with first-order logic (Basile et al., 2012). The senses are mostly automatically annotated, though part of them are manually corrected through the GMB wiki-like interface: `gmb.let.rug.nl/explorer`. The current (development) version of the GMB is accessible via the GMB Explorer: everbody is explicitly invited to contribute to the GMB by providing corrections to existing linguistic annotations with the simplicity made possible by such a wiki-like environment. Anyone can register via the GMB Explorer and check, improve, or discuss linguistic annotations. Stable releases are made available periodically and are freely available from the downloads webpage. Data from the Wordrobe[22] platform is also used to correct word senses in the GMB, applying the very innovative crowdsourcing technique "Game with a Purpose" (GWAP): rewarding contributors with entertainment rather than money. The design and the first results of Wordrobe are presented in Venhuizen et al. (2013).

### 2.3.3 MASC

MASC (Manually Annotated Sub-Corpus) is a part of the American National Corpus (Ide, 2012) with multiple layers of annotations in a common format that can be used either individually or together, and (unlike, for example, OntoNotes) to which others can add annotations. MASC currently contains nineteen genres of spoken and written language data in roughly equal amounts, covers a wide range of written genres, including emerging social media genres (tweets, blogs). The entire MASC is annotated for logical structure, token and sentence boundaries, part of speech and lemma, shallow parse (noun and verb chunks), named entities (person, location, organization, date), and Penn Treebank syntax. Portions of MASC are also annotated for additional phenomena, including 40,000 of full-text FrameNet frame element annotations and PropBank, TimeML, and opinion annotations over a roughly 50,000 subset of the data. MASC also includes sense-tags for 1,000 occurrences of each of 100 words chosen by the WordNet and FrameNet teams (100,000 annotated occurrences), described in (Ide, 2012). The sense-tagged data are distributed as a separate sentence corpus with links to the original documents in which they appear. Where MASC does not contain 1000 occurrences of a given word, additional sentences were drawn from the OANC. All annotations have either been manually produced or automatically produced and hand-validated. MASC is distributed without license or other restrictions.

[22] `gmb.let.rug.nl/wordrobe.php`

### 2.3.4 DSO Corpus of Sense-Tagged English

This sense tagged corpus was provided by Ng and Lee (1996) of the Defence Science Organisation (DSO) of Singapore and has been hand tagged by 12 undergraduates from the Linguistics Program of the National University of Singapore. It contains sense-tagged word occurrences for 121 nouns and 70 verbs which are among the most frequently occurring and ambiguous words in English. These sentences are taken from the Brown corpus and the Wall Street Journal corpus. About 192,800 word occurrences have been hand tagged with WordNet 1.5 senses. It is distributed on the Linguistic Data Consortium Catalogue[23] (LDC) under different licences for LDC Members (free for 1997 members) and Non-Members.

### 2.3.5 OntoNotes

OntoNotes Release 5.0[24] is the final release of the OntoNotes project,[25] a collaborative effort between BBN Technologies, the University of Colorado, the University of Pennsylvania and the University of Southern Californias Information Sciences Institute. The goal of the project was to annotate a large corpus comprising various genres of text (news, conversational telephone speech, weblogs, usenet newsgroups, broadcast, talk shows) in three languages (English, Chinese, and Arabic) with structural information (syntax and predicate argument structure) and shallow semantics (word sense linked to an ontology and coreference). OntoNotes Release 5.0 contains the content of earlier releases and adds source data from and/or additional annotations for, newswire (News), broadcast news (BN), broadcast conversation (BC), telephone conversation (Tele) and web data (Web) in English and Chinese and newswire data in Arabic. Also contained is English pivot text (Old Testament and New Testament text). This cumulative publication consists of 2.9 million words. Its semantic representation includes word sense disambiguation for nouns and verbs. The sense annotation is done on coarse grained clusters of wordnet senses (OntoNotes Sense Groups) for 1.5 million words of English.

### 2.3.6 SemLink

SemLink is a project whose aim is to link together different lexical resources via set of mappings. These mappings could make it possible to combine the different information provided by these different lexical

[23] `catalog.ldc.upenn.edu/LDC97T12`

[24] `catalog.ldc.upenn.edu/LDC2013T19`

[25] `www.bbn.com/ontonotes/`

resources for tasks such as inferencing. Currently SemLink contains mappings between PropBank,[26] VerbNet,[27] FrameNet[28] and WordNet[29](which is again represented by the OntoNotes Sense Groups). The content of all four of these resources can be browsed on-line using the Unified Verb Index.[30] The SemLink corpus is the WSJ portion of the Penn TreeBank, currently at Version 1.2.2c with approximately 78,000 tokens. The corpus is freely downloadable and browsable on the SemLink project webpage.[31]

### 2.4 Senseval and SemEval tasks and lexical samples

SemEval (Semantic Evaluation) is an ongoing series of evaluations of computational semantic analysis systems. The first three evaluations, Senseval-1 through Senseval-3, were focused on word sense disambiguation, then Senseval evolved from the Senseval word sense evaluation series to the new SemEval series. In fact during the fourth workshop, SemEval-2007 (SemEval-1), the nature of the tasks evolved to include semantic analysis tasks outside of word sense disambiguation. Each of these evaluations provided some lexical samples or little corpora. Here we list the most recent and relevant.

#### 2.4.1 Senseval 1-3

The first SENSEVAL took place in 1998, for English, French and Italian, culminating in a workshop. Senseval 1[32] provided a corpus containing 12,000+ instances of 35 words, and a practice run corpus distributed prior to Senseval 1, containing 20,000+ instances of 38 words. In 2001 Senseval 2 provided a corpus containing 12,000+ instances of 73 words. For the "English all-words task" at the Senseval-3, Snyder and Palmer (2005) prepared a sense-tagged corpus: 5,000 words from two Wall Street Journal articles (editorial domain the first, news story the second one) and one excerpt from the Brown Corpus (fiction). All verbs, nouns and adjectives have been double annotated with WordNet 1.7.1 senses, and then adjudicated and corrected by a third person. The total tagged words are 2,212 (given that some of these are multiwords the total number of tags is 2,081). All the data (ill-formed XML) produced for Senseval are freely available at the Senseval web page, but are also available at the Pedersen's webpage [33] in a partially corrected but still ill-formed XML version.

#### 2.4.2 Line, Hard, Serve and Interest Corpora

Pedersen has also collected and converted to the Senseval 2 format the corpora for ***line***, ***hard*** and ***serve***, each with 4,000+ noun instances, tagged with 6, 3 and 4 wordnet senses repectively Leacock et al. (1993), along with the ***interest*** corpus (2,369 instances from the ACL/DCI Treebank tagged with 6 LDOCE senses described by Bruce and Wiebe (1994)). All these resources are freely available at the Ted Pedersen's webpage[34].

#### 2.4.3 SemEval07–13

Many other resources are available at the SemEval2007[35], SemEval2010[36], SemEval2012[37] and SemEval2013[38] websites. In particular we have to mention Semeval-2013 Task 12 (all nouns tagged with WordNet 3.0 senses) and SemEval-2013 Task 13. The Task 12 test set consisted of 13 articles (Navigli et al., 2013) obtained from the datasets available from the 2010, 2011 and 2012 editions of the workshop on Statistical Machine Translation (WSMT). The articles cover different domains, ranging from sports to financial news. The same article was available in 4 different languages (English, French, German and Spanish). In order to cover Italian, an Italian native speaker manually translated each article from English into Italian, with the support of an English mother tongue advisor. In Table 1 we show for each language the number of words of running text, together with the number of multiword expressions and named entities annotated, from the 13 articles. The Task 13 (Jurgens and Klapaftis, 2013) has a lexical sample corpus for 20 nouns, 20 verbs, and 10 adjectives, tagged with WordNet 3.1 senses. In the dataset there are 4664 instances (on 141k tokens) and will soon be available on its task website[39]. Task 13's dataset (Jurgens and Klapaftis, 2013) covers multiple genres of text (spoken, newswire, fiction, etc.) and has annotations when multiple senses apply, with around 11% annotated with at least two senses that are weighted by applicability.

## 3 Discussion

Currently, there is no widely adopted format for wordnet annotated corpora (even if the ISO TC37/SC4 group[40] is working on the principles of semantic annotation[41]): every institution uses its own format, and very little sharing of tools to manipulate the data. This is despite much work on corpus standards. With the

[26] `verbs.colorado.edu/~mpalmer/projects/ace.html`
[27] `verbs.colorado.edu/~mpalmer/projects/verbnet.html`
[28] `framenet.icsi.berkeley.edu/fndrupal/`
[29] `wordnet.princeton.edu/`
[30] `verbs.colorado.edu/verb-index/`
[31] `verbs.colorado.edu/semlink/`
[32] `www.senseval.org/`
[33] `www.d.umn.edu/~tpederse/data.html`
[34] `www.d.umn.edu/~tpederse/data.html`
[35] `www.senseval.org/`
[36] `semeval2.fbk.eu/semeval2.php?location=data`
[37] `www.cs.york.ac.uk/semeval-2012/`
[38] `www.cs.york.ac.uk/semeval-2013/`
[39] `www.aclweb.org/anthology/S/S13/S13-2049.pdf`
[40] `www.tc37sc4.org/index.php`
[41] `www.iso.org/iso/home/store/catalogue_tc/catalogue_detail.htm?csnumber=60581`

exception of the MultiWordNet, the corpora are not linked with the wordnets in an online interface. For those languages with sense tagged corpora, there are generally between 10–100 thousand tagged entries: far fewer than the number of senses in the wordnets. This means that most wordnet entries have no example in the corpus. Kilgariff and Rosenzweig (2000) argued that tagging all words was not useful from the lexicographers point of view: it is better to have 50-100 examples for each word, than 1 or 2 for many. However, for research into lexical semantics and the distribution of words, as well as the use of semantic classes as backoff in other processing, it is necessary to tag all words. This is the most common form of annotation. Most projects point out that the much of the time spent in annotation is in fact in adding new word senses — this is still a very hard problem.

English has the most sense tagged data, followed by Dutch, then Italian, Japanese and Romanian (assuming that much of the Bulgarian is closed class words). The last three are all tagging through projection — this is an efficient way to bootstrap sense annotation.

There are two projects that have created multilingual corpora. The first is the MultiSemCor project, which grew out of the MultiWordNet. Construction of multiple wordnets and corpora went hand in hand. They inspired a similar approach for Japanese. Their MultiSemCor Browser (Ranieri et al., 2004) is probably the best and most useful tool for researchers interested in studying multilingual information. Even so, there is still much to do. There are only two non-English corpora currently available and the browser works only with English-Italian/Romanian: there are no links between Italian and Romanian.

Building a new translated semcor is difficult for at least three reasons. The first problem is that the wordnet annotated corpora don't update their sense tagging system (based on a precise wordnet version) when the English WordNet and SemCor do. If your wordnet is linked to a different version, in order to combine them into a single multilingual structure, we have to map to a common version.

The second problem is the variety of formats used. So sometimes even if a corpus is legally available, there could be still a technical hurdle before it becomes easily accessible. Conversion to a common format is the obvious solution. Finally, translating SemCor is in itself expensive, even though it may be worth it due to the richness of the existing annotation that can be projected across.

The second multi-lingual project is the NTU Multilingual Corpus. Instead of translating an existing sense tagged corpus, they chose to choose texts already freely available in multiple languages, and use the translations to guide the annotation. This was more expensive to annotate at first, but has the potential to cheaply expand to more languages: projecting from the existing annotations.

One possible explanation for the lack of coordination in tools and formats is that many of the large corpora are not open-source (Dutch, DSO, Romanian, Spanish, Basque, WebCaGe, ISST). It is therefore not legally possible for people to reformat and redistribute the corpora. In contrast, the open English corpora have been mapped to the latest version of Wordnet and the same format and made available.[42] As more corpora are released under open licenses, we expect this state to improve.

## 4 Future Work

We would like to further the usefulness of the multilingual corpora in several ways. The first is to align the English, Italian, Romanian and Japanese translations of SemCor. We will then use English as a pivot to link Italian, Romanian and Japanese. When all four languages are aligned, we can use the translations to disambiguate and check the senses, as well as trying to make the projection more robust. The second is to do this with the NTU-multilingual corpus: make it compatible with MultiSemCor, align through English and refine. This will make it easier to add other languages: the Sherlock Holmes short stories and the Cathedral and the Bazaar have many translations. The third is to do this with the Wordnet Gloss Corpus: linking definitions in other languages to make a multilingual gloss corpus. It would also be interesting to use definitions from other sources (such as Wiktionary) to make an aligned sense-tagged paraphrase corpus. Finally (or in parallel) we would like to make these corpora all searchable, and linked to the Wordnet Grid (Pease et al., 2008; Bond and Foster, 2013).

## 5 Conclusions

All these observations about the compatibility troubles in the construction process of multilingual wordnet annotated corpora point at a clear fact: the more we standardize our data formats, and the more we open and share freely our resources and tools the easier and the faster will be the development of new resources all over the world.


### Acknowledgments

This research was supported in part by the Erasmus Mundus Action 2 program MULTI of the European Union, grant agreement number 2009-5259-5. We would like to thank Anja Weisscher and Piek Vossen for their help in adding the information to the Global Wordnet Association page. We would also like to thank Shan Wang, Verena Henrich, Marie Hinrichs, Valerio Basile, Behrang M., Christiane D. Fellbaum, Ng Hwee Tou, David Jurgens, Mathieu Lafourcade, Orin Hargraves, Tomaz Erjavec, Vincze Veronika and Marcin Oleksy for their help and information.


[42] You can find SemCor, Senseval 2 and 3 here, `www.cse.unt.edu/~rada/downloads.html#semcor`

## References


Eneko Agirre, Izaskun Aldezabal, Jone Etxeberria, Eli Izagirre, Karmele Mendizabal, Eli Pociello, and Mikel Quintian. 2006. Improving the Basque wordnet by corpus annotation. In *In Proceedings of Third International WordNet Conference*, pages 287–290. Jeju Island, Korea.

Eneko Agirre, Timothy Baldwin, and David Martinez. 2008. Improving parsing and pp attachment performance with sense information. In *Proceedings of the 46th Annual Meeting of the Association for Computational Linguistics (ACL HLT 2008)*, pages 317–325. Columbus, USA.

Timothy Baldwin, Su Nam Kim, Francis Bond, Sanae Fujita, David Martinez, and Takaaki Tanaka. 2008. MRD-based word sense disambiguation: Further extending Lesk. In *International Joint Conference on Natural Language Processing 2008*, pages 775–780. Hyderabad, India.

Valerio Basile, Johan Bos, Kilian Evang, and Noortje Venhuizen. 2012. Developing a large semantically annotated corpus. In *LREC*, volume 12, pages 3196–3200.

Luisa Bentivogli and Emanuele Pianta. 2005. Exploiting parallel texts in the creation of multilingual semantically annotated resources: the multisemcor corpus. *Natural Language Engineering*, 11(3):247–261.

Daniel M. Bikel. 2000. A statistical model for parsing and word-sense disambiguation. In *Student Research Workshop at ACL 2000*, pages 1–7. Hong Kong.

Francis Bond, Timothy Baldwin, Richard Fothergill, and Kiyotaka Uchimoto. 2012. Japanese semcor: A sense-tagged corpus of japanese. In *Proceedings of the 6th International Conference of the Global WordNet Association (GWC)*.

Francis Bond and Ryan Foster. 2013. Linking and extending an open multilingual wordnet. In *51th Annual Meeting of the Association for Computational Linguistics and the Human Language Technologies*, pages 1352–1362. Sofia. URL `http://aclweb.org/anthology/P13-1133`.

Francis Bond, Hitoshi Isahara, Kiyotaka Uchimoto, Takayuki Kuribayashi, and Kyoko Kanzaki. 2010. Japanese WordNet 1.0. In *16th Annual Meeting of the Association for Natural Language Processing*, pages A5–3. Tokyo.

Francis Bond and Kyonghee Paik. 2012. A survey of wordnets and their licenses. In *Proceedings of the 6th Global WordNet Conference (GWC 2012)*. Matsue. 64–71.

Francis Bond, Shan Wang, Eshley Huini Gao, Hazel Shuwen Mok, and Jeanette Yiwen Tan. 2013. Developing parallel sense-tagged corpora with wordnets. In *Proceedings of the 7th Linguistic Annotation Workshop and Interoperability with Discourse*, page 149–158. Association for Computational Linguistics, Sofia, Bulgaria.

Bartosz Broda, Michał Marcińczuk, Marek Maziarz, Adam Radziszewski, and Adam Wardyński. 2012. KPWr: Towards a Free Corpus of Polish. In Nicoletta Calzolari, Khalid Choukri, Thierry Declerck, Mehmet Uğur Doğan, Bente Maegaard, Joseph Mariani, Jan Odijk, and Stelios Piperidis, editors, *Proceedings of LREC'12*. ELRA, Istanbul, Turkey.

F. Rebecca Bruce and M. Janyce Wiebe. 1994. Word-sense disambiguation using decomposable models. In *Proceedings of the 32nd Annual Meeting of the Association for Computational Linguistics*, pages 139–146.

Monsterrat Civit, Núria Bufı, and Pilar Valverde. 2004. Building cat3lb: a treebank for catalan. In *Proceedings of the SALTMIL Workshop at LREC 2004*, pages 48–51.

Montserrat Civit and Ma Antònia Martí. 2004. Building cast3lb: A spanish treebank. *Research on Language and Computation*, 2(4):549–574.

Salvador Climent, Marta Coll-Florit, Marina Lloberes, and German Rigau. 2012. Semantic hand tagging of the SenSem corpus using Spanish wordnet senses. In *GWC 2012 6th International Global Wordnet Conference*, page 72.

Mark Davies. 2002. Un corpus anotado de 100.000. 000 palabras del español histórico y moderno. *Procesamiento del lenguaje natural*, 29:21–27.

Stefano Dei Rossi, Giulia Di Pietro, and Maria Simi. 2011. Evalita 2011: Description and results of the supersense tagging task. *Evalita 2011*.

Christine Fellbaum, editor. 1998. *WordNet: An Electronic Lexical Database*. MIT Press.

Ana Fernández-Montraveta, Gloria Vázquez, and Christiane Fellbaum. 2008. The spanish version of wordnet 3.0. *Text Resources and Lexical Knowledge. Mouton de Gruyter*, pages 175–182.

Dan Flickinger. 2011. Accuracy vs. robustness in grammar engineering. In E. M. Bender and J. E. Arnold, editors, *Language from a Cognitive Perspective: Grammar, Usage, and Processing*, pages 31–50. CSLI Publications.

W. Nelson Francis and Henry Kucera. 1979. *BROWN CORPUS MANUAL*. Brown University, Rhode Island, third edition. (`http://khnt.aksis.uib.no/icame/manuals/brown/`).

Verena Henrich and Erhard Hinrichs. 2013. Extending the tüba-d/z treebank with germanet sense annotation. In Iryna Gurevych, Chris Biemann, and Torsten Zesch, editors, *Language Processing and Knowledge in the Web*, volume 8105 of *Lecture Notes in Computer Science*, pages 89–96. Springer Berlin Heidelberg. URL `http://dx.doi.org/10.1007/978-3-642-40722-2_9`.

Verena Henrich, Erhard Hinrichs, and Tatiana Vodolazova. 2012. Webcage: a web-harvested corpus annotated with germanet senses. In *Proceedings of the 13th Conference of the European Chapter of the Association for Computational Linguistics*, pages 387–396. Association for Computational Linguistics, EACL, Avignon, France.

Nancy Ide. 2012. Multimasc: An open linguistic infrastructure for language research. In *Proceedings of the Fifth Workshop on Building and Using Comparable Corpora*. Istanbul.

Radu Ion. 2007. *Metode de dezambiguizare semantica automata. Aplicat ii pentru limbile englezas i romana*. Ph.D. thesis, ACADEMIA ROMANA, Institutul de Cercet ari pentru Inteligenta Artificiala, Bucarest.

Hitoshi Isahara, Francis Bond, Kiyotaka Uchimoto, Masao Utiyama, and Kyoko Kanzaki. 2008. Development of the Japanese WordNet. In *Sixth International conference on Language Resources and Evaluation (LREC 2008)*. Marrakech.

Toru Ishida. 2006. Language grid: An infrastructure for intercultural collaboration. In *IEEE/IPSJ Symposium on Applications and the Internet (SAINT-06)*, pages 96–100. URL `http://langrid.nict.go.jp/file/langrid20060211.pdf`, (keynote address).

David Jurgens and Ioannis Klapaftis. 2013. Semeval-2013 task 13: Word sense induction for graded and non-graded senses. In *Proceedings of the 7th International Workshop on Semantic Evaluation*.

Adam Kilgariff and Joseph Rosenzweig. 2000. Framework and results for English SENSEVAL. *Computers and the Humanities*, 34(1-2):15–48. Special Issue on SENSEVAL.

Svetla Koeva, Svetlozara Leseva, Ekaterina Tarpomanova, Borislav Rizov, Tsvetana Dimitrova, and Hristina Kukova. 2010. Bulgarian sense annotated corpus - results and achievements. In M. Tadić, M. Dimitrova-Vulchanova, and S. Koeva, editors, *Proceedings of the 7th International Conference of Formal Approaches to South Slavic and Balkan Languages*, pages 41–48. FASSBL-7, Dubrovnik, Croatia.

Shari Landes, Claudia Leacock, and Christiane Fellbaum. 1998. Building semantic concordances. In Fellbaum (1998), chapter 8, pages 199–216.

Helen Langone, Benjamin R. Haskell, and George A. Miller. 2004. Annotating wordnet. In *Workshop On Frontiers In Corpus Annotation*, pages 63–69. ACL, Boston.

C. Leacock, G. Towell, and E. Voorhees. 1993. Corpus-based statistical sense resolution. In *Proceedings of the ARPA Workshop on Human Language Technology*, pages 260–265.

Michael Lesk. 1986. Automatic sense disambiguation: How to tell a pine cone from an ice cream cone. In *Proceedings of the 1986 SIGDOC Conference*, pages 24–26. ACM, New York.

Monica Lupu, Diana Trandabat, and Maria Husarciuc. 2005. A Romanian semcor aligned to the English and Italian multisemcor. In *Proceedings 1st ROMANCE FrameNet Workshop at EUROLAN 2005 Summer School*, pages 20–27. EUROLAN, Cluj-Napoca, Romania.

Mitchell P Marcus, Mary Ann Marcinkiewicz, and Beatrice Santorini. 1993. Building a large annotated corpus of English: The Penn treebank. *Computational linguistics*, 19(2):313–330.

Maria Antònia Martí, Mariona Taulé, Manu Bertran, and Lluís Màrquez. 2007. Ancora: Multilingual and multilevel annotated corpora. *MS, Universitat de Barcelona*.

George A. Miller, Martin Chodorow, Shari Landes, Claudia Leacock, and Robert G. Thomas. 1994. Using a semantic concordance for sense identification. In *Proceedings of the ARPA Human Language Technology Workshop*, pages 240–243. ARPA.

Simonetta Montemagni, Francesco Barsotti, Marco Battista, Nicoletta Calzolari, Ornella Corazzari, Alessandro Lenci, Antonio Zampolli, Francesca Fanciulli, Maria Massetani, Remo Raffaelli, Roberto Basili, MariaTeresa Pazienza, Dario Saracino, Fabio Zanzotto, Nadia Mana, Fabio Pianesi, and Rodolfo Delmonte. 2003. Building the Italian syntactic-semantic treebank. In Anne Abeillé, editor, *Treebanks*, volume 20 of *Text, Speech and Language Technology*, pages 189–210. Springer Netherlands.

Roberto Navigli, David Jurgens, and Daniele Vannella. 2013. Semeval-2013 task 12: Multilingual word sense disambiguation. In *Proceedings of the 7th International Workshop on Semantic Evaluation (SemEval 2013), in conjunction with the Second Joint Conference on Lexical and Computational Semantics (* SEM 2013), Atlanta, Georgia*, pages 14–15.

Hwee Tou Ng and Hian Beng Lee. 1996. Integrating multiple knowledge sources to disambiguate word sense: An exemplar-based approach. In *Proceedings of the 34th annual meeting on Association for Computational Linguistics*, pages 40–47.

Stephan Oepen, Dan Flickinger, Kristina Toutanova, and Christoper D. Manning. 2004. LinGO redwoods: A rich and dynamic treebank for HPSG. *Research on Language and Computation*, 2(4):575–596.

NHJ Oostdijk. 2008. Sonar: Stevin nederlandstalig referentiecorpus.

Adam Pease, Christine Fellbaum, and Piek Vossen. 2008. Building the global wordnet grid. In *Proceedings of the CIL-18 Workshop on Linguistic Studies of Ontology*. Seoul. URL `http://www.adampease.org/professional/Grid2008.pdf`.

Christopher Mark Powell. 2005. *From E-Language to I-Language: Foundations of a Pre-Processor for the Construction Integration Model*. Ph.D. thesis, Oxford Brookes University.

Marcello Ranieri, Emanuele Pianta, and Luisa Bentivogli. 2004. Browsing multilingual information with the multisemcor web interface. In *Proceedings of the LREC 2004 Satellite Workshop on The Amazing Utility of Parallel and Comparable Corpora*, pages 38–41. LREC.

Ervin Ruci. 2008. On the current state of Albanet and related applications. Technical report, University of Vlora. (`http://fjalnet.com/technicalreportalbanet.pdf`).

Geoffrey Sampson. 1995. In *English for the Computer: The SUSANNE Corpus and Analytic Scheme*, pages +499 pp. Oxford: Clarendon Press, University of Sussex.

Nathan Schneider, Behrang Mohit, Kemal Oflazer, and Noah A Smith. 2012. Coarse lexical semantic annotation with supersenses: an arabic case study. In *Proceedings of the 50th Annual Meeting of the Association for Computational Linguistics: Short Papers-Volume 2*, pages 253–258. Association for Computational Linguistics.

Benjamin Snyder and Martha Palmer. 2005. The english all-words task. In *Third International Workshop on the Evaluation of Systems for the Semantic Analysis of Text (SENSEVAL-3)*, pages 41–43.

Liling Tan and Francis Bond. 2012. Building and annotating the linguistically diverse NTU-MC (NTU-multilingual corpus). *International Journal of Asian Language Processing*, 22(4):161–174.

Laura Van Eerten. 2007. Over het corpus gesproken nederlands. *Nederlandse Taalkunde*, 12(3):194–215.

Noortje J Venhuizen, Valerio Basile, Kilian Evang, and Johan Bos. 2013. Gamification for word sense labeling. In *Proc. 10th International Conference on Computational Semantics (IWCS-2013)*, pages 397–403.

Veronika Vincze, György Szarvas, Attila Almási, Dóra Szauter, Róbert Ormándi, Richárd Farkas, Csaba Hatvani, and János Csirik. 2008. Hungarian word-sense disambiguated corpus. In *LREC*.

Piek Vossen, Attila Görög, Fons Laan, Maarten van Gompel, Rubén Izquierdo, and Antal van den Bosch. 2011. Dutchsemcor: building a semantically annotated corpus for Dutch. *Proceedings of eLex*, pages 286–296.

Aesun Yoon, Soonhee Hwang, Eunroung Lee, and Hyuk-Chul Kwon. 2009. Construction of Korean wordnet KorLex 1.5. *Journal of KIISE: Software and Applications*, 36(1):92–108.

# A Quantitative Analysis of Synset of Assamese Wordnet: Its Position and Timeline


**Shikhar Kr. Sarma**
Gauhati University
Guwahati,Assam,India.
sks001@gmail.com

**Dibyajyoti Sarmah**
Gauhati University
Guwahati,Assam,India.
dibyasarmah@gmail.com

**Ratul Deka**
Gauhati University
Guwahati,Assam,India.
rdeka8258@gmail.com

**Anup Kr. Barman**
Gauhati University
Guwahati,Assam,India.
anupbarman.gu@gmail.com

**Jumi Sarmah**
Gauhati University
Guwahati,Assam,India.
jumis884@gmail.com

**Himadri Bharali**
Gauhati University
Guwahati,Assam,India.
himadri0001@gmail.com

**Mayashree Mahanta**
Gauhati University
Guwahati,Assam,India.
mayashreemahanta@gmail.com

**Umesh Deka**
Gauhati University
Guwahati,Assam,India.
deka_umesh@rediffmail.com



## Abstract

The synsets in Assamese Wordnet play a significant role in the enrichment of Assamese language. These synsets are built depending on the intuition the native speakers of the language. There is no fixed rule in the arranging the positions of each synset. The present paper mainly aims to make a quantitative comparison of every synset position of Wordnet seeing the occurrences of these synsets in corpus of Assamese (approximately 1.5 million words). The experimental result of this comparison is represented with the help of diagrams. Again, it is an attempt to highlight the timeline of each synsets of Wordnet based on the corpus. It is dealt with the change of the synonymous word forms in course of times.


## 1 Introduction

Language is a central feature of human identity. Language is the identity of that particular community. No community can survive without a language. The language of the communities live in India is very ancient and rich. Similarly, Assamese language is also one of the ancient and rich languages of the north-eastern languages. Assamese has been regarded as a rich language with its own script and written literary texts since the ancient times. Assamese language belongs to the Satam group of the Indo-European language family. The main root of this language lies to the Indo-Aryan languages.

Dr. Banikanta Kakati has classified the development of Assamese language into three stages (Kakati, 2008):

### A. Early Assamese (14th to 16th century A.D.)

This period again may be divided into a) Pre-Vaishnavite and b) Vaishnavite sub-periods. The earliest known Assamese writer is Hema Saraswati, who wrote a small poem 'Prahlad Charit'. Sankardeva, the great Vaishnavite reformer in Assam, born in 1449 A.D. composed religious songs and drama. In his popularly known as Braja-Bali idioms (Goswami, 1983).

### B. Middle Assamese (17th to 19th century A.D.)

The main characteristic of this period is the historical writings initiated under the inspiration of the Ahom court. These historical writings in prose are known as Buranjis. In the Ahom court, historical Chronicles were at first composed in their original Tibeto-Chinese languages, but when the Ahom rulers adopted Assamese as the court language, historical chronicles began to be written in Assamese. The language is essentially modern except for slight alterations in grammar and spelling.

### C. Modern Assamese

The modern Assamese period begins with the publication of the Bible in Assamese by American Baptist Missionaries in the first quarter of the 19th century. The currently prevalent standard Asamiya has its roots in the Sibasagar dialect of Eastern Assam. The American Baptist Missionaries were the first to use this dialect in translating the Bible in 1813 A.D. In 1836 A.D., they started a monthly periodical called Arunodoy and in 1848 A.D., Nathan Brown published the first book on Assamese grammar. The Missionaries published the first Assamese-English Dictionary compiled by Miles Bronson in 1867 A.D. The Sibasagar Asamiya dialect came to be formally recognized as the Standard Asamiya dialect when it was made the official language of the state by the schools, courts, and Govt. officers in 1872. This Standard language is accepted by all other Asamiya dialect as the standard norm and was used for all formal occasions – in writing, in the classroom, in meetings, in the courts and offices and for inter-dialect communication also.

## 2 Assamese Corpus

The term 'corpus' is used to refer to a collection of linguistic data (covering spoken and written) in a language for some specific purposes and these data are to stored, managed and analyzed in digital format. There is a huge amount of corpus in Assamese language consisting of approximately 15 or 20 lakh words based on the various Assamese literary or non-literary texts (such as magazines, newspaper, dramas, novels, stories, articles etc.). Words are collected from various texts ranging from 19th to 21st centuries (Sarma et al., 2012).

## 3 Assamese Wordnet

Wordnet is a repository of words of a language. Wordnet is basically a synonymous lexical database. Vocabulary plays a main role in building Wordnet. Assamese language possesses a huge amount of vocabulary; it becomes easy to build Wordnet in the language. The task of Assamese Wordnet building is almost ready to provide us with all the lexical words. Yet there are still many words in the language those need to be entered (Sarma et al., 2010).

Assamese Wordnet is built on the basis of Hindi Wordnet (Sarma et al., 2012). Here, words are shown according to the sense of the given context or sentence and accordingly, we can derive different meanings from them. For example, the Assamese word '*paani, and 'farkaal*" has different meaning according to its sense in the context.

Paani (noun) –

Paanir para bemar hoi
Kaamtu paani hoi gol

Farkaal (Adjective) – Bataratu bar farkaal (not rainy)

- Raam farkaal monar maanuh
- Khuala manar manuh (Free minded)
- Path farkaal hoise (not muddy, dry)

## 4 Quantitative Analysis

The main aim of quantitative analysis is a complete description. Quantitative analysis allows for fine distinctions to be drawn because it is not necessary to the data into a finite number of classifications.

The resulting corpus contains over 1.5 billion words and 14958 Assamese Wordnet synset data. Initially, we have tried to find out the position of corpus and synset data. The synset category is classified as noun, verb, adjective and adverb for Assamese Wordnet. Here, we compare the frequency of Wordnet synset to the frequencies of Corpus data.

Some results of words position analysis in Assamese Wordnet with Corpus are mentioned below:

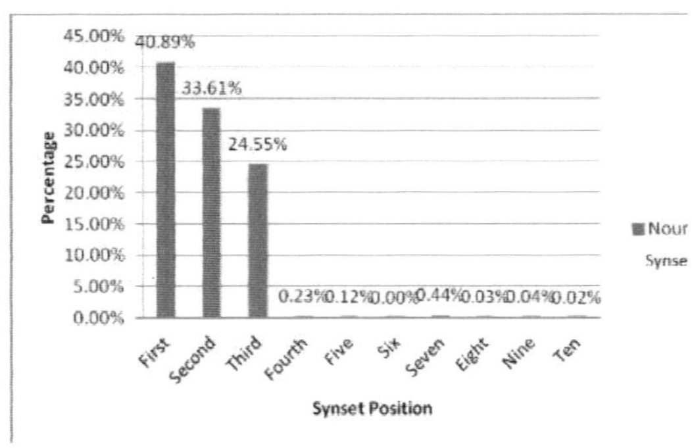


Figure 1: Position analysis of Noun Synset

In Figure 1, we have shown Synset Positions of Noun in Assamese Corpus. For the First position we have found 40.89%, for the second and third 33.61% and 24.55% respectively and so on. Similarly in Figure 2, Figure 3, Figure 4 we have shown Synset Positions and analysis of verb, adverb and adjective in Assamese Corpus.

Finally in Figure 5, it is clear that the finding of first position is always higher than the remaining synset position.

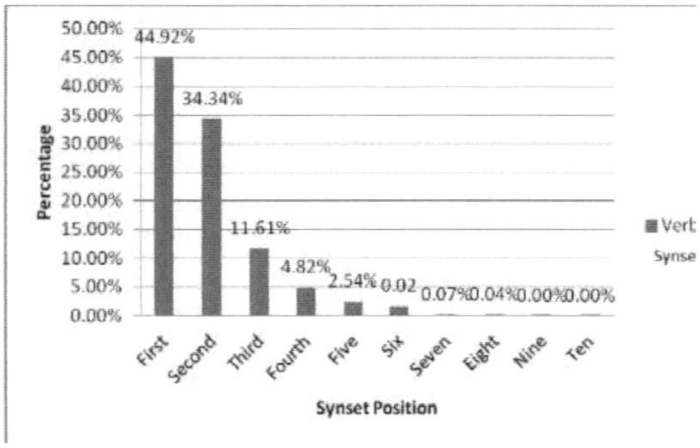


Figure 2: Position analysis of Verb Synset

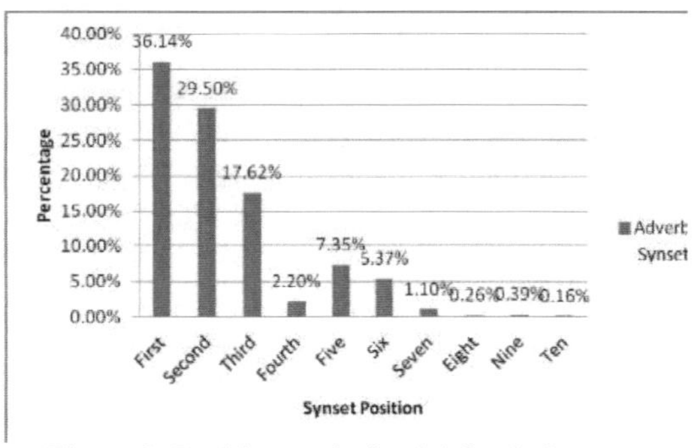


Figure 3: Position analysis of Adverb Synset

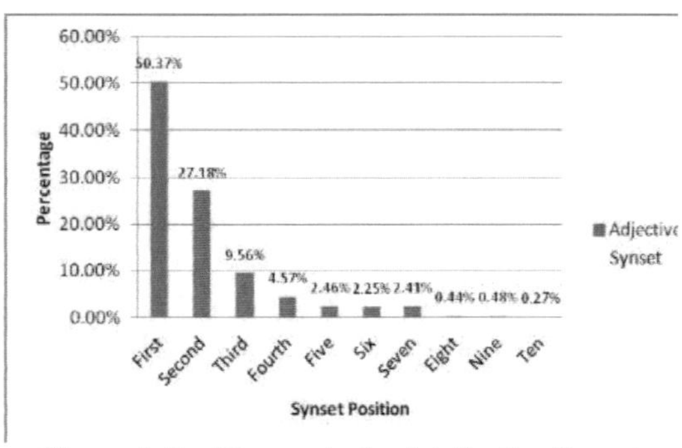


Figure 4: Position analysis of Adjective Synset

Final Result of Analysis

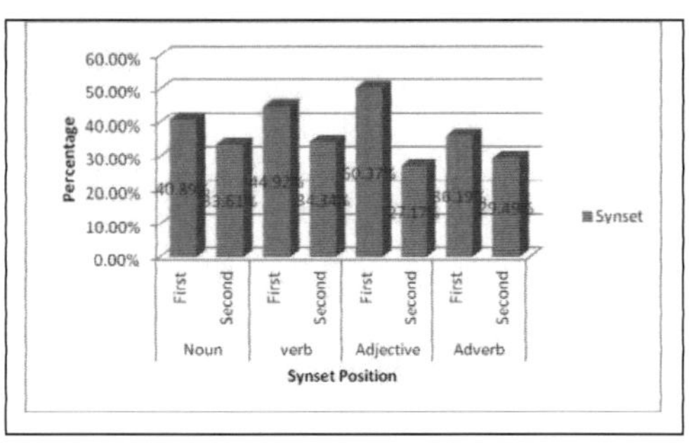


Figure 5: Final result of analysis

## 5 Timeline of Words

Wordnet has been built taking various words of hundred years. There are 38 synset positions in Wordnet. Especially, words are found to be most frequently used in the synset positions like 1st, 2nd and 3rd which cover a period from 1900 to 1995. It is worth mentioning here that we have not found any synonymous words after the synset position 17. Most of the words starting from synset position no. 1 to 5 we have seen words have became change from the old Assamese to modern forms. Thus, it has enriched the words in Assamese language.

While studying the synset in Assamese language, it is seen that most of the words used by the Christian missionaries have not been used at present times. It does not mean that these words have disappeared completely, but these are used less frequently with change in the forms of those words.

Examples of words change in Assamese language are mentioned below:

| Synset Position | Forms of 20th Century | Present Forms |
|---|---|---|
| 3 | সইত Soit (true)(1918) | সত্য Satya(true) |
| 7 | আৰাৱ‘aaraaw’(high sound) (1963) | চিঞৰ ‘chiyar’(high sound) |
| 7 | ক্লেশ ‘klesh’ (sorrow)(1900) | বেদনা‘bedanaa’ (sorrow) |
| 3 | ব্যাঘ্র ‘byaghra’ (tiger) | বাঘ ‘baagh’ (tiger) |
| 11 | কৰাইচ ‘karaaich’ (miser) (1938) | কৃপণ ‘kripan’(miser) |

Table 1: Word Change of Assamese Language

In Table 1 we have shown the Synset Position in 1st Column and in the 2nd and 3rd column we have shown the words forms of 20th century and present day respectively.

## Conclusion

The present paper makes an examination on the timeline of synset positions of Assamese Wordnet. In order to perform this task, mainly we refer to Assamese corpus covering time period from 1900 to 2008. In this corpus, there are more than 1.5 million texts. We consider all the synsets of Assamese Wordnet entered till date as it is in a developing stage. First we determine the timeline of all the corpus entries and secondly we map up these entries with their corresponding synset entries. While mapping we also consider the respective positions of each synset entries. After analysis the data, we basically found that from first to fifth position of synset entries are occurred frequently in the time period of our given corpus. But the results varied from different word categories those are clearly depicted in the above sections.

## References


Golock C. Goswami. 1983. *Structure of Assamese*, Gauhati University , Assam Guwahati,Assam

Banikanta Kakati. 2008. *Assamese: Its Formation and Development*, Lawayers Book Stall, Guwahati , Assam

Shikhar Kr. Sarma, Moromi Gogoi, Rakesh Medhi, Utpal Saikia. 2010. *Foundation and Structure of Developing an AssameseWordnet*, Department of Computer Science Gauhati University, Proceedings of the 5th Global Wordnet Conference,Narosa Publishing House.

Shikhar Kr. Sarma, Utpal Saikia, Mayashree Mahanta, Himadri Bharali. 2012, Assamese Vocabulary and Assamese Wordnet Building: An Analysis. Global Wordnet Conference, Matsue, Japan

Shikhar Kr. Sarma, Himadri Bharali, Ambeswar Gogoi, Anup Barman. *A Structured Approach for Building Assamese Corpus*: Insights, Applications and Challenges, coling 2012, India

# An Analytical Study of Synonymy in Assamese Language Using WorldNet: Classification and Structure

**Shikhar Kr. Sarma**
Gauhati University
Guwahati,Assam,India.
sks001@gmail.com

**Himadri Bharali**
Gauhati University
Guwahati,Assam,India.
himadri0001@gmail.com

**Mayashree Mahanta**
Gauhati University
Guwahati,Assam,India.
mayashreemahanta@gmail.com

**Utpal Saikia**
Gauhati University
Guwahati,Assam,India.
utpal.sk@gmail.com

**Dibyajyoti Sarmah**
Gauhati University
Guwahati,Assam,India.
dibyasarmah@gmail.com

**Abstract**

The present paper aims to categorize different types of synonymous words and also to highlight their synonymic pattern as well as grammatical categories found in Wordnet of Assamese language. Synonymy is an important component of vocabulary of the language. It establishes lexical relation between words. In fact, the term 'synonymy' is applied to the two or more words which share the same semantic features. WorldNet is a lexical database consisting of synsets. A synset is constructed by assembling a set of synonyms that together define a unique sense and synset is the basic foundation of Wordnet. Assamese language is rich in synonyms. In Assamese WorldNet, more than 20,000 synsets are entered under the categories of Noun, Verb, Adverb and Adjective. These synsets can of different types according to their semantic similarity, connotation, denotation, stylistic variations etc.

## 1 Introduction

Synonym is an important feature of the vocabulary of any language. But it is very difficult to give a clear, precise and correct definition of synonymy. There are various approaches with numerous definitions of synonym and types of synonyms. Linguistically, two or more words in the same language with very closely related meaning are called synonyms. It is to be mentioned here that synonyms does not mean the 'sameness of meaning' as there is no two terms with completely identical meaning. It is generally accepted that complete synonym is rare in natural language. The discussion of synonyms comes under the study of lexical relation. Lexical relation analyses the meaning of the words in the language which have related meanings. The idea of synonym is not only applied to lexical items, but also idioms, larger expressions, of course. A lexicographer builds a synonym dictionary depending on the words which share the same semantic features in a given language.

The present paper deals with lexical synonyms of the same word class, not with the phrasal synonyms. We will categorize the synonymous words considering the semantic features of the words they share based on Assamese Wordnet. Besides, it is also an attempt to point out the synonymic pattern and the grammatical categories of synsets in Wordnet.

## 2 A rapid sketch of Assamese Language

Assamese is the easternmost New Indo-Aryan language spoken in the Brahmaputra valley comprising at present six districts with Lakhimpur in the extreme east and Goalpara in the west. Tibeto-Burman and the Khasi are the important ones. According to the 1991 census report, the number of speakers of the language is almost 100000 billions. However, it is spoken as a second language by a considerable number of speakers of Tibeto-Burman languages like Bodo, Mising and Karbi. Traditionally, it has served as the lingua-franca or pidgin in the neighbouring states of Nagaland and Arunachal Pradesh.

The word 'Assamese' is an English one based on the anglicized form 'Assam' from the native word 'Asam'. The word Assam was connected with the Shan invaders of the Brahmaputra valley during the 13th century. In modern Assamese, Shan invaders of the 13th century are termed as 'Ahoms'.

Presence of Assamese language dated back to the literatures of Charyapadas, written by Budhist scholars. The Assamese language present in charyapadas reflects its evolutionary stages in initial state. Literatures with distinct Assamese language are found from the Kavyas of the pre Sankari era. This was in 13th century AD. From that time onwards pure Assamese language with its structured forms evolved (Goswami, 1983). Assamese script is derived from Brahmi script. It played a vital role in the evolution of the Indian script. The rock inscription and copper plate from 5th to 9th century showed the evolution of Assamese script. There are eight vowel phonemes in Assamese. There are twenty-one consonant and two semi-vowel phonemes in the Standard Colloquial Assamese (Kakati, 2008).

## 2 A Brief Discussion of Assamese Vocabulary

The scope of Assamese vocabulary is very vast. It consists of words of Sanskrit origin, Non-Aryan words, dialect oriented words. Besides Assamese socio-cultural influences are also perceived in the vocabulary of the language. It is to be noted here that Assamese still lacks a common vocabulary dictionary in the language. Moreover, no dictionary was found in the early and the middle ages. The selected modern dictionaries are – '*A Dictionary in Assamese and English by Miles Bronson*' (1867); 'Hemkosh' (1900), by Hemchandra Barua and later it is compiled by Debananda Barua (the 14th edition) which included 1, 54,428 words; '*Chandrakanta Abhidhan*' (2004, 3rd edition) '*Adhunik Asomiya Sabdakosh*' (2007, 9th edition), '*Asamiya Jatiya Abhidhan*' (2010) and many other vocabulary dictionaries are available in Assamese language. No common standard vocabulary dictionary has been made till today. Many critics have prepared vocabulary lists in their own way. Earlier philologists like Kaliram Medhi and Banikanta kakati had classified vocabulary list in their own style.

Kaliram Medhi in 'Asomiya Byakaran aru Bhasatattva' has provided a classification Assamese vocabulary such as 'tatsama', 'tatbhava' and 'desaja'. But his 'Desaja' words are shown as loan words in which maximum words are Perso-Arabic words (Pathak, 2004). Therefore, his vocabulary classification cannot be taken as valid. On the other hand, though Banikanta Kakati's classification of Assamese vocabulary covers almost all the aspects, yet his classification also cannot be regarded as valid one.

It is interesting to note here that there are a large amount of loan words in Assamese language. In day-to-day life these loan words have been used extremely to express feelings, ideas etc. Moreover, it is seen that Perso-Arabic words have been used in Assamese language. These words occupy a significant status in Assamese language.

Assamese vocabulary can be divided into the following heads (Sarma et al., 2012):

1. Aryan or words of Sanskrit origin
   a. Tatsama
   b. Semi-tatsama
   c. Tadbhava
2. Non-Aryan words
   a. Austro-Asiatic
   b. Tibeto-Burmese
   c. Tai-Ahom
   d. Dravidian
3. Loan words
   a. Words coming from N.I.A. languages
   b. Foreign Words
   i.Persian
   ii.Arabic
   iii.Portugese
   iv.English
   c. Loan translations
      i.Translated words
      ii.Terminology
4. Unclassified words
   a. Hybrid
   b. Onomatopoetic
   c. Compound

## 3 Wordnet and Synonym Sets Building in Assamese Language

Wordnet is a repository of words of a language. It is basically a synonymous lexical database. The words are classed together according to their similarity of meanings. Vocabulary plays a main role in building Wordnet. The task of Assamese Wordnet building is almost ready to provide us with all the lexical words. Though Assamese wordnet tries to cover all the Assamese word forms, yet there are still many words in the language those need to be entered (Sarma et al., 2010)

### 3.1 Classification of Synonymy in Assamese

Assamese language is rich in synonyms. We can classify synonyms under the following three heads:

1. Absolute synonymy:

Words can be called absolutely synonymous if they share the complete semantic features in all contexts of occurrences. However, it is generally recognized that absolute synonyms are almost non-existent. Though it is very rare, it certainly exists in Assamese languages. It is limited mostly to dialectical variations and technical or institutional terms. For example:

বিদ্যালয় 'bidyaaloi' (school): পঢ়াশালী, পাঠশালা 'parhaashaalii, haathshaalaa'

খবৰ 'khabar' (news): বাতৰি, সংবাদ, সংবাদ পত্ৰ, বাতৰি কাকত 'baatari, sangbaad, sangbaad hatra, baatari kaakati'

2. Stylistic synonymy:

Stylistic synonyms are words conveying the same concept but differing in stylistic connotations. Stylistic synonymy is very common in Assamese language. For example-

মৃৎযু 'mrityu' (death):

মৰণ, প্ৰয়াণ, প্ৰাণৎযাগ, মহাপ্ৰয়াণ, বৈকুণ্ঠ প্ৰয়াণ, তিৰোধান, তিৰোভাৱ, কাল, লোকান্তৰ,কালগ্ৰাম, দেহাৱসান 'maran, prayaan, praantyaag, mahaaprayaan,boikuntha prayaan, tirodhaan, tirobhaabh, kaal, lokaantar, kaalagraam, dehaawasaan'

সুন্দৰ 'sundar' (beautiful): ধুনীয়া,দেখনিয়াৰ,ৰূপহ, মোহনীয়,নয়নাভিৰাম,চকুত লগা, চকু জুৰোৱা, নয়ন জুৰোৱা, বিতোপন,চকুত চমক লগোৱা 'dhuniaa, dekhaniyaar, rupah, mohaniiya, nayanaabhiraam, sakut lagaa, saku juruwaa, nayan juruwaa, sakut samak lagowaa'

3. Ideographic synonymy:

Ideographic synonyms convey the same concept but differ in denotations. It is also called denotation based synonymy. For example-

টুকুৰা 'tukuraa' (a piece): চকল, ডোখৰ 'chakal, dokhar'

খং 'khong' (anger): ক্ৰোধ, ৰাগ, কোপ, ক্ৰোধাগ্নি 'krodh, raag, kop, krodhaagni'

Apart from these, we can have the following more synonym types in Assamese language depending on its resemblance of meaning, distribution, style, form etc.

### 3.2 Near Synonymy

Near synonyms are those words whose meaning is relatively close or more or less similar, but not fully intersubstitutable. They vary in terms of their shades of denotation, connotation, implicature, emphasis or register. Near synonyms are extensively found in Assamese. For example:

ভাল 'bhaal' (good): সজ্জন,সৎ 'sajjan, sat'

All these words denote the quality of goodness. But they differ from one another in respect to their denotational meaning. The word ভাল 'bhaal' is a generic term, whereas সজ্জন 'sajjan' is more particular applicable only to human being. Besides, সৎ 'sat' conforms to both animate and inanimate things. The usages of these synsets are shown below-

ভাল 'bhaal' - ভাল ব্যক্তি/ কাম/ কিতাপ 'bhaal byakti/kaam/kitaap' (good person/work/book)

সজ্জন 'sajjan'- সজ্জন ব্যক্তি/ *কাম/ *কিতাপ

সৎ 'sat'- সৎ ব্যক্তি/ কাম/ *কিতাপ

Near-synonyms can vary as follows-

| Type of variation | Examples |
|---|---|
| Collocational | কৰ্ম, চাকৰি '*karma, chaakari*' (work) |
| Stylistic, formality | সন্মানীয়, মাননীয়, মান্যবৰ '*sanmaniiya, maananiiya, maanyabar*' (honourable) |
| Stylistic, forced | ধ্বংস, পতন '*dhansha, patan*' (destruction) |
| Expressed attitude | ক্ষীণ, লাহী, শুকান '*khin, laahii, sukaan*'(*thin*) |
| Emotive | মা, আই, মাতৃ '*maa, aai, matri*' (mother) |
| Continuousness | নিগৰা, বোৱা '*nigaraa, bowaa*' (to drip, to flow) |
| Fuzzy boundary | বননি, বন, হাবি, জংঘল, অৰণ্য '*banani, ban, haabi, janghal, aranya*' (wood) |

Table 1: Type of variation

The first column in the table 1 represents the various classifications of Near-synonyms and in the next column, the examples of respective Near-synonym types are given accordingly. The above mentioned Near-synonym variations are seemed to be almost near in their meanings, but most of them differ in their distributions. The distribution of the first type of variation of Near-synonym in the Table 1 is shown below:

Collocational: কৰ্ম স্থান '*karma sthaan)* (work place)

চাকৰি *স্থান '*chaakari sthaan*' (Work place)

## 3.3 Connotation Based Synonymy

More modern approach to classify synonyms may be based on definition of synonymous words differing in connotation. The scope of connotation based synonyms is very vast one. Connotation based synonyms in Assamese language are categorized in the following types:

a. Connotation of degree or intensity: আচৰিত, অবাক, স্তম্ভিত '*aacharit, abaak, stambhita*' (surprise)
b. Connotation of duration: জুমি চোৱা, ভূমুকিয়াই চোৱা *'jupi chowaa, jumi chowaa, bhuumukiyaai chowaa'* (to peep)
c. Emotive Connotation: অকলশৰীয়া, শূন্যতা *'akalshariiyaa, shunyataa'* (loneliness)
d. Evaluative Connotative: It conveys speaker's attitude as good or bad. For example: প্ৰখ্যাত, জনাজাত, বিখ্যাত *'pryakhyaat, janaajaat, bikhyaat'* (famous)
e. Causative Connotation: পকা, পৰিপক্ক হোৱা *'pakaa, paripakka howaa'* (to ripe)
f. Connotation of manner: সোনকালে, ততালিকে, খৰকৈ, শীঘ্ৰে *'sonkaale, tataalike, kharkoi, shiighre'* (fast)

## 3.4 Cognitive Synonymy

Cognitive synonymy is also known as descriptive, propositional or referential synonymy. Cognitive synonym is sometimes described as incomplete synonymy (Lyons, 1981), or non-absolute or partial synonymy (Lyons, 1996). Cognitive synonymy highlights the fact that though not all speakers of a language will necessarily use, yet they may understand it well. Cognitive synonymy is also termed as denotative synonymy (Stanojević, 2009) It analyzes sense and denotation. Examples of Cognitive synonyms-

গোপন 'gopan' (secret): অপ্ৰকাশ্য, গুপ্ত, গুপুত 'aprakaashya, gupta, guput'

দেউতা 'deutaa' (father): পিতা, পাপা, পিতাই, আতা, বাবা, পিতৃ 'pitaa, paapaa, pitai, aataa, baabaa, pitri'

## 3.5 Euphemism Synonymy

Euphemism is the substitution of words of mild or vague connotations for expressions rough, unpleasant. These kinds of synonyms are important linguistic tools that are inherent in our language. Most of the people like to use in day to day conversation. The use of such words is both social and emotional. Euphemism deals with the touchy or taboo subjects (like sex, personal appearance or religion) without hurting or upsetting others (Radulović, 2012). As a matter of fact, euphemism can be of two types: (a) Positive euphemisms increase acceptability such as, domesticity, institutional, economical etc., and (b) negative euphemisms decrease negative values that are associated with negative phenomena such as, war, drunkenness, crime, poverty (Rawson, 1981). For example:

Positive euphemism: স্তন '*stan*' (breast): পিয়াহ, পয়োধৰ, পয়োভাৰ, কুচকুম্ভ, ওহাৰ, বাত '

Negative euphemism: বেশ্যা '*beshyaa*' (prostitute): গণিকা, ৰেণ্ডী, দেহোপজীৱী, পতিতা, নটিনী '*ganikaa, rendii, dehohajiibii, patitaa, natinii*'

## 4 Synonymic Pattern and Grammatical Catagories in Assamese Wordnet

There is no fixed pattern of synonymous words in a synset in Assamese wordnet. Sometimes only one word is provided for one concept in the Wordnet. In certain concepts, it covers up to 38 synonymous words. Here, we can take the following example:

Concept: AG: ঘেহুঁ আদিৰ বিশেষ প্ৰকাৰৰ খহটা চূৰ্ণ

EG: milled product of durum wheat (or other hard wheat) used in pasta

Synset: চুজি *'suji'*

Concept: AG: ধৰ্ম গ্ৰন্থৰ দ্বাৰা স্বীকৃত এক সৰ্ব্বোচ্চ সত্তা, যি সৃষ্টিৰ গৰাকী

EG: the supernatural being conceived as the perfect and omnipotent and omniscient originator and ruler of the universe; the object of worship in monotheistic religions

Synset: ভগৱান, ঈশ্বৰ, প্ৰভু, বিধাতা, পৰমপিতা, দয়াময়, সৃষ্টিকৰ্তা, পৰমব্ৰহ্ম, জগদীশ, অন্তৰ্যামী, ভুৱনেশ্বৰ, কৰুণাময়, নেদেখাজনা, ওপৰৰজনা, জগজীৱ, মংগলময়, সৰ্বমংগলময়, সনাতন, বিভু, ধাতা, বিধাতাপুৰুষ, জগদীশ্বৰ, জগৎপিতা, জগৎপতি, জগতকৰ্তা, জগতস্ৰষ্টা, জগজীউ, পৰমেশ্বৰ, পৰাৎপৰ, ইচ্ছাময়, পৰমাত্মা, ত্ৰিজগতপতি, ত্ৰিলোকপতি, পৰমানন্দ, নিয়ন্তা, চিন্তামণি, ভবেশ, নিৰাকাৰ '*bhagawaan, iishwar, prabhu, bidhaataa, parampitaa, dayaamoy, sristikartaa, parambrahma, jagadiish, antarjaamii, bhuwaneswar, karunaamoy, nedekhaajanaa, oprarjanaa, jagajiiwa, mangalmoy, sarbamangalmoy, sanaatan, bibhu, dhaataa, bidhaataapurush, jagadiishwar, jagatpitaa, jagatpati, jagatkartaa, jagatsrastaa, jagajiiu, parameshwar, paraatpar, issaamoy, paramaatmaa, trijagatpati, trilokpati, haramaananda, niyantaa, chintaamoni, bhabesh, niraakaar*'

Apart from these, Assamese Wordnet considers only Noun, Verb, Adverb and Adjective class. But there are evidences of synonymous words in closed classes also like preposition, conjunction and Interjection etc. It may be the reason that we can find large amount synonymous words from the open classes and also can be compared with the other languages easily.

Examples of Synsets according to grammatical categories are given below:

Noun: কাগজ, কাকত, তুলাপাত, পেপাৰ 'kaagaj, kaakat, tulaapaat, pepaar' (paper)

Verb: নচা, নৃত্য কৰা 'nachaa, nritya karaa' (to dance)

Adverb: ওচৰতে,কাষতে,সমীপতে,গুৰিতে,অদূৰতে '*osarate, kaashate, samiipate, gurite, aduurate*' (near)

Adjective: অধম, প্ৰবলতাহীন, কম, অপ্ৰবল, বেয়া, নিকৃষ্ট 'adham, prabalataahiin, kam, aprabal, beyaa, nikrista' (bad)

## 5 Conclusion

Synonymy plays a vital role in the field of lexical study. It paves the way for wordnet building in any natural language. Synonyms in Assamese wordnet cover a large amount of lexical words coprising the grammatical categories, such as noun, verb, adverb, adjectives. Accordingly, we classify synonyms into certain types in Assamese language.

It is to be mentioned here that while building synonym sets in Assamese wordnet, dialectical forms are not considered. Besides, though borrowed words are included in synset building in Assamese, but the numbers are very limited. Yet, there are many foreign words which we use them as native words in day to day communication. This kind of discussion will be dealt later sometime. Yet, wordnet with all its synsets have succeeded in representing Assamese language in a very systematic and novel way.

## References


Hemchandra Barua. 1900. *Hemkosh*, ed. and published by Debananda Barua.

Miles Bronson. 1867. *Dictionary in Assamese and English*

Sumanta Chaliha.2007. *Adhunik Asomiya Sabdakosh*, Bani Mandir, Ghy

Golock C. Goswami. 1983. *Structure of Assamese*, Gauhati University, Assam Guwahati,Assam

Banikanta Kakati. 2008. *Assamese: Its Formation and Development*, Lawyers Book Stall, Guwahati , Assam

John Lyons. 1977. *Semantics*. Vol.1. Cambridge: Cambridge University Press.

John Lyons. 1981. *Language and Linguistics: An Introduction*, CUP, Cambridge.

John Lyons. 1996. *Linguistic Semantics*, CUP, Cambridge.

Maheswar Neog and Upendranath Goswami ed., 2004, C*handrakanta Abhidhan,* Publication Deptt. Gauhati University

Ramesh Pathak. 2004. *Studies in Assamese Vocabulary*, Anita Pathak, Guwahati, Assam

Milica Radulović: *Expressing Values in Positive and Negative Euphemism*. Facta Universitatis, Series: Linguistics and Literature Vol. 10, No 1, 2012, pp. 19 – 28

Hugh Rawson.1981. *A Dictionary of Euphemisms and Other Doubletalk*. New York: Crown Publishers, Inc.

Debabrat Sarma. 2010. *Asamiya Jatiya Abhidhan*, Asom Jatiya Prakash

Shikhar Kr Sarma,Utpal Saikia, Mayashree Mahanta, Himadri Bharali. 2012, *Assamese Vocabulary and Assamese Wordnet Building: An Analysis*. Global Wordnet Conference, Matsue, Japan

Shikhar Kr. Sarma, Moromi Gogoi, Rakesh Medhi and Utpal Saikia. 2010. *Foundation and Structure of Developing an AssameseWordnet*, Department of Computer Science Gauhati University, Proceedings of the 5th Global Wordnet Conference,Narosa Publishing House.

Maja Stanojević. *Cognitive Synonomy: A General Overview*, Linguistics and Literature Vol. 7, No 2, 2009, pp. 193 – 200, Facta Universitatis

# Assamese WordNet based Quality Enhancement of Bilingual Machine Translation System

**Anup Kumar Barman**
Dept. of IT
Gauhati University
Guwahati, India
anupbarman.gu@gmail.com

**Jumi Sarmah**
Dept. of IT
Gauhati University
Guwahati, India
jumis884@gmail.com

**Prof. Shikhar Kumar Sarma**
Dept. of IT
Gauhati University
Guwahati, India
sks001@gmail.com

## Abstract

Machine Translation is a task to translate the text from a source language to a target language in an automatic manner. Here, we describe a system that translate the English language to Assamese language text which is based on Phrase based statistical translation technique. To overcome the translation problem related with highly open word class like Proper Noun or the Out Of Vocabulary words we develop a transliteration system which is also embedded with our translation system. We enhance the translation output by replacing words with their most appropriate synonymous word for that particular context with the help of Assamese WordNet Synset. This Machine Translation system outcomes with a reasonable translation output when analyzed by linguist for Assamese language which is a less computationally aware language among the Indian languages.

## 1 Introduction

Machine Translation (MT) is a system that can automatically generate translation output from source language to target language. In country like India, the MT system are very much essential due to their language diversity. The highly increasing rate of digital information indicates the top level requirement of MT system so that every people irrespective to their language can acquire and utilize those information. There are basically three approaches to develop a MT system which are Rule based approach, Statistical approach and some Hybrid approaches. In Rule based approach, various naturally occurring phenomenon on source language text are investigated and then extract them as some rules and analyze them to fit to embed for generating target language text. By using some parser from the source text they produce some intermediate representation and then the target language text is generated from the intermediate representation. In Statistical approach, to train up various parameters large number of parallel corpus are required. A Statistical approach derives with a better result when the size of the corpus is increased. Here, the best translation are performed based on some decision. Some Example based approaches are also used to translate the source language text to target language text. Due to the less amount of digitized documents as the parallel corpus some tries to correct their statistical translation output by using some Linguistic Rules. Such type of approaches are considered to be the hybrid approaches.

Assamese is a language spoken by the North-East people of India. It is one of the less computationally aware Indian language belonging to the Indo-Aryan Family. It is spoken by approximately 14 million people of the North-East region of India. Unfortunately, this language has less amount of computational linguistic resources. The linguistics researches are still in traditional mode. But, recently some researchers have made a deliberate attempt to study Assamese language from technological perspective. They have started to work in the development and enrichment of the language of Assamese in the field of Natural Language Processing (NLP). The Machine Translation task for Assamese language is very difficult as the amount of parallel corpus is very less.

WordNet, a lexical database was developed by Prof George A Miller for English language in 1985. Based on English WordNet structure, Indo-WordNet was being developed. Assamese WordNet was developed as a part of the Indo-WordNet project. Assamese WordNet, a lexical database was first developed in Gauhati University, 2009 by (Sarma et al., 2010). Assamese

WordNet comprises of contents that are linked to both English and Hindi WordNet. A combination of dictionary and thesaurus, Assamese WordNet comprises of four major components. They are ID which act as a primary key for identifying any synset in WordNet, CAT indicates the Parts Of Speech category, SYNSET lists the synonymous words in a most used frequency order and GLOSS describes the concept of any synset. GLOSS consist of Text-Definition and Example-Sentence. Text Definition contains concepts denoted by synset and Example shows the use of any synset entry. There are various semantic relation that occur between synsets in WordNet. They are Hypernymy-Hyponymy(IS-A/Kind of), Entailment-Troponymy (Manner-of for verbs), Meronymy-Holonymy (HAS-A/ PART-WHOLE). Synset, the basic building block of WordNet can explore the semantically related terms. For instance these words খাৰু (kharu: Bangles), কংকণ (kankan: Bangles), কঙ্কণ (kangkan: Bangles) describes the same concept হাতত পিন্ধা এবিধ গহনা (haatat pindhaa ebidh gahanaa:*A hand wearing ornament*).This structure of WordNet helps in automatic text analysis and various artificial intelligence applications as a combination of dictionary and thesaurus. Assamese WordNet has been used for a number of different purposes in text analysis such as Automatic document classification (Sarmah et al., 2012), Automatic text summarization (Kalita et al., 2012) etc. Here, we tried to use the Assamese WordNet basically the synsets for fine tuning the translated output by replacing words with their most appropriate synonymous word for that particular sentence.

This paper presents a MT system for English-Assamese which is based on Statistical Phrase based translation approach. Here we first developed a MOSES based translation system which we consider as the baseline translation system. For linguistically open class Proper Noun or some other Out of vocabulary words we implemented a MOSES based transliteration system which transliterate the English word to Assamese word in Character level. Then we embed this transliteration system with our Base line Translation system. The output of the new system was enhanced by mapping the words with Assamese WordNet synset so that we can put the most appropriate synonymous word for that particular sentence. This will give us a more relevant translation output when reviewed by some linguistic persons.

This paper further continues with a description of Previous Notable Work done while implementing a MT system for other Indian Languages in Section2, Section3 portrays our methodology to implement a English-Assamese MT system . This section starts with a description of tools used in implementing our system, an explanation of our English-Assamese parallel corpus, a system architecture where it gives us a overview of our baseline translation system, an elaboration of our transliteration system and the process of enhancing the translation output through mapping with the Assamese WordNet synsets. Section4 analyzes the result of our system. Finally conclusions are drawn in section5.

## 2 Related Study

Though spoken by major population of North-East India, Assamese language is still behind in computational perspective, basically processing the MT system. No work on MT system was researched or developed for Indian language like Assamese till date. To develop any MT system for a specific language requires collaboration among computer researchers, linguistics and expert manual translators. Although in languages like English or some other foreign language, the MT task is very well processed, the Machine Translation in Indian languages is still an open problem. MT in Indian languages was developed using various approaches.

(Devi et al., 2010; Goyal and Lehal, 2009) used Direct Machine Translation Systems for languages Hindi and Punjabi respectively. Another one MT system was developed based on the Paninian Grammar (Goyal and Lehal, 2010) using this approach. The other approach found while developing an MT system for Indian Languages is the Rule based approach. In rule based approach Transfer based machine translation is used in (Saha, 2005; Bandyopadhyay S, 2000) where there are three modules - analyzed, transfer and generation module. One another Transfer based MT system was developed at Resource Centre for Indian Language Technology solution (Dwivedi and Sukhadeve, 2010) to translate English to Canada Text. Pseudo Interlingua approach of Rule Based was used to develop Anglabharti MT system for translating English to Indian languages. To reduce the human labour than the Rule based approach a Corpus-based MT approach was used. In statistical approach, the open source software like GIZA++ can be used to align the parallel corpus and then the aligned corpus is processed to generate the Phrase based Translation model. Tool like SRILM may be used to generate the statistical language model. The Phrase based MOSES decoder can be used to translate the sentences after finding the translation model and language model. Statistical MT system for English-Hindi (Ahsan et al., 2010) and English-Malayalam was developed by using English-Hindi and English-Malayalam parallel corpus. Some Example based MT system was developed where the hypothesis is that a translation will be considered as most appropriate if it was occurred previously. Anubharti is an example based MT system which was developed by IIT kanpur (Sinha, 2004) where some grammatical analysis was also performed to reduce the size of the parallel corpus.

## 3 Our Approach

This section describes verious software tools used for developing our proposed Machine Translation system, portrays our system architecture and description of each modules of our system.

### 3.1 Used Tools

In order to develop an English -Assamese Machine Translation System we used various open source software tools. The phrase based machine translation system MOSES (Koehn et al., 2007) is used to perform the translation task. Through this statistical machine translation tool we train up a translation module by using English-Assamese Parallel corpus. MOSES implies an efficient search algorithm called beam-search which can quickly find the highest probability translation from huge numbers of choices. Another statistical machine translation toolkit GIZA++ (Och and Ney, 2003) was used to align our parallel corpus. For alignment task, GIZA++ is used to train IBM models 1-5 and HMM word alignment model. To generate the word classes which is necessary for training the aligned models this machine translation toolkit uses mkcls tool. A bilingual dictionary can be produced from that parallel corpus using GIZA++. We use SRILM toolkit to develop a statistical language model which has been under development in the SRI Speech Technology and Research Laboratory since 1995. In SRILM (Stolke, 2002) a set of C++ class libraries are available to implement a language model. To accomplish some standard task like training a language model or testing on data there are also a set of executable programs and some auxiliary scripts which are built on top of these class libraries. We run all these toolkits on LINUX platform.

### 3.2 System Architecture

In our English-Assamese MT system, we integrated the baseline statistical MT model with a statistical transliteration model. The transliteration model helps us to improve the translation output by providing the transliteration basically for Proper Noun or some other Out of vocabulary(OOV) words. Mapping the translated output with WordNet synset gives us more suitable synonymous word for that specific sentence. Below given a architecture diagram for our MT system.

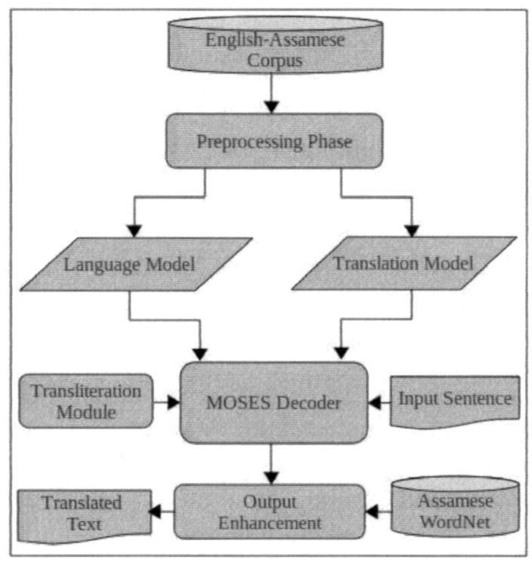


Figure 1: System Diagram

### 3.3 Data

Since digitized documents for Assamese language are very less in amount so to collect the parallel corpus for MT task was very difficult. For our approach, we prepare a parallel corpus of English-Assamese at Gauhati University NLP lab. This parallel-corpus contains data basically of tourism domain. In our parallel-corpus there were 100 files for each English and Assamese language. This parallel-corpus contains a collection of 14,371 English sentences with their respective translations in Assamese language. The corpus contains 326804 and 267224 words for English and Assamese language respectively. To fit this parallel-corpus in our translation model we follow

the below pre-processing steps-
**File Format Conversion**:- We converted the file format of each file from UTF-16 to UTF-8 and we convert the line encoding from Windows to Unix/Linux.
**Sentence Extraction**:- Sentences were extracted from XML mark-up text.
**Corpus Cleaning**:- We clean-up the whole parallel-corpus by removing all unwanted characters, junk values and blank spaces etc.
**Sentence Alignment**:- We align each English sentence with respective Assamese sentences.

### 3.4 Baseline Translation System

To set-up our baseline translation system for English-Assamese we use the English-Assamese parallel corpus. By using the GIZA++ toolkit, we convert this sentence aligned parallel corpus to word aligned corpus and then processed them to fit in our phrase based translation model. We use the SRILM tool to develop our statistical language model from our corpus. For phrase based translation, we use MOSES decoder after getting the translation model and language model. To make this MOSES system learn we use this English-Assamese parallel corpus. Sample output of our Baseline Translation system is given below:

| SNo. | English Text | Assamese Text |
|---|---|---|
| 1. | Tiger is India's national animal | ব্যাঘ্র ভাৰতৰ ৰাষ্ট্ৰীয় জন্তু |
| 2. | Tiger is a violent animal | ব্যাঘ্র হিংসুক জন্তু |
| 3. | Mumbai is an ancient city | Mumbai আদিম চহৰ |
| 4. | Assam is a beautiful state | Assam ধুনীয়া ৰাজ্য |
| 5. | Times of India | সময় ভাৰত |

Table 1: Output of Baseline Translation

### 3.5 Transliteration System

Since Assamese is a less computationally aware language, the parallel corpus is very less in size. Moreover, for some linguistically open word class like Proper Noun are very less available in the parallel corpus. The statistical MT system, acquires knowledge from the trained English-Assamese parallel corpus. From the above Table 1 which shows the results of our baseline translation system, we found that some words which are translated as source input word is. Those non-translated words are not found in the trained parallel corpus of English-Assamese. To overcome the translation problem basically related with Proper Noun word we develop a Statistical transliteration system. But, for other Out of vocabulary words we cannot implement the transliteration system since transliteration cannot represent the concept of those word in target language. To implement our transliteration system, we collect nearly 0.1 million unique Proper Noun in English and we transliterate them to Assamese. For transliteration, we consider each Proper Noun as a sequence of characters separated by a space. Then we create the language model by using SRILM tool. For alignment purpose , we use the same GIZA++ tool. Then we train up the MOSES decoder by using the Name Entity parallel corpus for English Assamese. We take the best output from n numbers of output from our statistical transliteration system. Output are also generated with a space in between each character. Finally, we combine this characters to get our transliterated output. Following Table 2 shows the sample result of our statistical transliteration system.

| SNo. | Input Term | Transliterated Term |
|---|---|---|
| 1. | Mumbai | মুম্বাই |
| 2. | Assam | অসম |
| 3. | Times of India | টাইমচ্ অফ ইণ্ডিয়া |
| 4. | Rajasthan | ৰাজস্থান |
| 5. | Brahmaputra | ব্ৰহ্মপুত্ৰ |

Table 2: Output of Transliteration System

### 3.6 Combined System

A combined system was formed by combining the statistical transliteration with the baseline translation system. The statistical transliteration system is only for Proper Noun. We use one Named Entity dictionary comprising 1 lakh English Named Entities to recognize the Named Entities. The transliterated form was XML marked up. These XML files later were provided as an external knowledge to MOSES decoder for decoding. Combined system gives us the output provided by the baseline system with the Transliterated System. Following Table 3 shows the result of our combined system.

| SNo. | English Text | Assamese Text |
|---|---|---|
| 1. | Tiger is India's national animal | ব্যাঘ্র ভাৰতৰ ৰাষ্ট্ৰীয় জন্তু |
| 2. | Tiger is a violent animal | ব্যাঘ্র হিংসুক জন্তু |
| 3. | Mumbai is an ancient city | মুম্বাই আদিম চহৰ |
| 4. | Assam is a beautiful state | অসম ধুনীয়া ৰাজ্য |
| 5. | Times of India | টাইমচ্ অফ ইণ্ডিয়া |

Table 3: Output of Combined System

| SNo. | English Text | Assamese Text |
|---|---|---|
| 1. | Tiger is India's national animal | বাঘ ভাৰতৰ ৰাষ্ট্ৰীয় জন্তু |
| 2. | Tiger is a violent animal | ব্যাঘ্র হিংস্র জন্তু |
| 3. | Mumbai is an ancient city | মুম্বাই প্ৰাচীন চহৰ |
| 4. | Assam is a beautiful state | অসম ধুনীয়া ৰাজ্য |
| 5. | Times of India | টাইমচ্ অফ ইণ্ডিয়া |

Table 4: A sample of Final Output

### 3.7 Enhancement Using WordNet

The representation of a single concept using various words (synonymous words) in one language made influence in MT task. All synonymous words are not equally appropriate for all sentences in terms of their context. In a statistical MT system, for a source language term the most weighted target language term is always selected for every sentence containing that term without considering the appropriateness of that sentence. But, in natural language one individual concept is represented by using various synonymous term in various sentences. To overcome this statistical MT problem, we take help of the lexical resource Assamese WordNet where the set of synonymous terms to represent each concept are available. We enhance the output of our Combined System by selecting the appropriate synonymous term for that sentence through mapping each term to their respective WordNet synset. Selection of the appropriate synonymous terms in context of various sentences was done by checking manually through some Linguist fellows. Then we replace each term by the using the selected synonymous term so that our statistical MT output becomes more relevant in terms of Assamese language. Following Table 4 shows the final translation output after enhancement of the output produced by the combined system using Assamese WordNet.

## 4 Result Analysis

To evaluate our system performance, we take 500 English sentences for testing our statistical MT system. In the above tables, we show a sample output of each modules. Table 1 shows the baseline system's output where some of the Proper Nouns like India was translated to ভাৰত(Bharat:*India*) and some others remain the same like Mumbai and Assam. In Table 2 we show a sample output of our Transliterated system. The statistical transliterated system outcomes with a state-of-art accuracy. Then we mixed the Statistical Baseline System and Transliteration system to produce a combined system and a sample output of the system is shown in Table 3. Here the translation problem related with Proper Noun was solved with the proper transliteration form of them. As shown in Table 3 the term Assam, Mumbai, Times Of India was transliterated to অসম(*assam*),মুম্বাই(*Mumbai*), টাইমচ্ অফ ইণ্ডিয়া(*Times of India*) respectively which were not correct in Table1. Our combined system translation output was more or less correct but there are several words which are not appropriate for that specific sentence. To handle that type of inappropriateness problem we enhance our combined system output by mapping each term to their respective synset i.e, if a synset s have n entries for a word w in a sentence st then we have n number of possibilities to replace that particular word. Now we discover all possible such sentences which was later judged by the linguist to determine the most appropriate one. As in Table 3, we have seen that for the English sentence -Mumbai is an ancient city, the output is মুম্বাই আদিম চহৰ (*mumbai aadim sahar*)but the term আদিম(*aadim* )is not relevant to that particular sentence. In Assamese WordNet, there is a synset পুৰণি, পুৰণা, প্ৰাচীন, পুৰাতন, পুৰাকালীন, প্ৰাক্-কালীন, আদিম. Id 1661 where including this word আদিম there are seven synonymous words. Among these, the term পুৰণি(*puroni*) is the most appropriate as per linguist judgement. In our 1st and 2nd example sentences the words like ব্যাঘ্র and হিংসুক are replaced with the most appropriate synset terms বাঘ and হিংস্র respectively. In this way, we found the enhance result of our combined system's translation output which is depicted in Table 4.

## 5 Conclusions

We sum up our translation task by developing a English-Assamese translation system which is a combination of a statical phrase based translation and a statistical transliteration system and later the output was fine tuned by using Assamese WordNet. This introducing English-Assamese Statistical MT system gains a satisfactory output. The more strength of the parallel-corpus better the result of the Statistical MT system. Assamese is a less computationally aware language so the strength of English-Assamese parallel-corpus is weak. A statistical transliteration module is also embedded with our translation system so that we can overcome the translation problem related with Proper Nouns and some out-of vocabulary words. The transliteration module with a good accuracy helped in improving our translation system's performance. Also the lexical resource Assamese WordNet gives us a significant improvement in our translation output by providing the most accurate synonymous word for a specific context. A state-of-art translation results are generated by our Statistical MT system. As this is a first approach towards developing a English-Assamese Machine Translation system this will contribute significantly towards Assamese Natural Language Processing.

## References


Arafat Ahsan, Prasanth Kolachina, Sudheer Kolachina, Dipti Misra Sharma and Rajeev Sangal. 2010. *Coupling Statistical Machine Translation with Rule-based Transfer and Generation.* In Proceedings of AMTA- The Ninth Conference of the Association for Machine Translation in the Americas. Denver, Colorado,.2010.

Sivaji Bandyopadhyay. 2000. *ANUBAAD - The Translator from English to Indian Languages.* In Proceedings of VIIth State Science and Technology Congress, Calcutta, India, 2000.

Sobha Lalitha Devi, Pravin Pralayankar, S. Maneka, T. Bakiyavathi, R.V.S. Ram and V. Kavitha. 2010. *Verb Transfer in a Tamil to Hindi Machine Translation System.* In Proccedings of International Conference of Asian Language Processing, 2010, Harbin, China, pp. 261-264.

Sanjay Kumar Dwivedi and Pramod Premdas Sukhadeve. 2010. *Machine translation systems in Indian perspective.* Journal of computer science, pp.1082-1087,2010.

Vishal Goyal and Gurpreet Singh Lehal. 2009. *Evaluation of Hindi to Punjabi Machine Translation System.* International Journal of Computer Science Issues, vol4 no1, 2009, pp. 36-39.

Vishal Goyal and Gurpreet Singh Lehal. 2010. *Web Based Hindi to Punjabi Machine Translation System.* Journal of Emerging Technologies in Web Intelligence, Vol.2, 2010, pp.148-151.

Chandan Kalita, Navanath Saharia and Utpal Sharma. 2012. *An Extractive Approach of Text Summarization of Assamese using WordNet.* In Proccedings of 6th International Global WordNet Conference (GWC 12) Japan, January 9-13 2012, pp. 149-154.

Philipp Koehn, Hieu Hoang, Alexandra Birch, Chris Callison-Burch, Marcello Federico, Nicola Bertoldi, Brooke Cowan, Wade Shen,Christine Moran, Richard Zens, Chris Dyer, Ondej Bojar, Alexandra Constantin and Evan Herbst. 2007. *Moses: Open Source Toolkit for Statistical Machine Translation.* In Annual Meeting of the Association for Computational Linguistics(ACL),2007.

Franz Josef Och and Hermann Ney. 2003. *A systematic comparison of various statistical alignment models.* Computational Linguistics, 29(1):19-51,2003.

Goutam Kumar Saha. 2005. *The EB-Anubad translator: A hybrid scheme.* Journal of Zhejiang University SCIENCE 2005, ISSN 1009-3095, pp.1047-1050.

Shikhar Kr. Sarma, Moromi Gogoi, Utpal Saikia and Rakesh Medhi 2010. *Foundation and structure of Developing Assamese WordNet.* In Proceedings of 5th International Conference of the Global WordNet Association.

Jumi Sarmah, Navanath Saharia and Shikhar Kr. Sarma. 2012. *A Novel Approach for classification of Document using Assamese WordNet.* In Procceedings of 6th International Global WordNet Conference (GWC 12) Japan, January 9-13 2012, pp. 324-329.

R. Mahesh K. Sinha. 2004. *An Engineering Perspective of Machine Translation: AnglaBharti-II and AnuBharti-II Architectures.* In Proceedings of International Symposium on Machine Translation, NLP and Translation Support System (iSTRANS- 2004), November 17-19, 2004.

Andreas Stolke. 2002. *SRILM-an extensible language modeling toolkit.* In Proceedings of the ICSLP,2002.

# Morphosemantic relations between verbs in Croatian WordNet

**Krešimir Šojat**
Faculty of Humanities and Social Sciences, University of Zagreb, Croatia
ksojat@ffzg.hr

**Matea Srebačić**
University of Zagreb, Croatia
msrebaci@unizg.hr

## Abstract

This paper deals with morphosemantic relations between Croatian verbs and discusses their inclusion in Croatian WordNet. Morphosemantic relations refer to semantic relations between morphologically related verbs, i.e., between verbs from the same derivational family. A derivational family consists of verbs with the same lexical morpheme grouped around a base form. Generally, a verb with the simplest morphological structure serves as a base form for derivational processes. In Croatian, verbs are derived from base forms through prefixation and suffixation. Both derivational processes trigger aspectual and semantic changes. The focus is on semantic relations that regularly appear in various derivational families and consequently in various semantic fields. It is argued that these morphosemantic relations are crucial for the further development of Croatian WordNet.

## 1 Introduction

Croatian WordNet is a lexical database built through the so-called expand model (Vossen, 1998), i.e., by translating and adapting synsets from Princeton WordNet (further *PWN*) into Croatian. The building of Croatian WordNet (*CroWN*) can roughly be divided into two major phases. The first phase consisted of the translation and adaptation of the so-called basic concept sets from the multilingual projects EuroWordNet (*EWN*) and BalkaNet (*BN*) (cf. (Raffaelli et al., 2008). At present, CroWN contains 10,000 synsets. 8500 of these are from the basic concept sets of EWN and BN. Each synset was manually translated and provided with meaning definitions and usage examples. Synsets contain lexical units of the same part of speech. Since CroWN is a relatively small resource, the second phase of the project is primarily oriented toward its enlargement. Approximately 1500 noun synsets were added using the same procedure. This freely available version of CroWN contains 7391 noun synsets, 2318 verb synsets, and 310 adjective synsets.[1] As the numbers indicate, nouns make up almost 75% of the whole lexicon.[2] Such a strong predominance of this part of speech was a motivation to make CroWN a more balanced and representative resource for Croatian. The second phase of the project is primarily focused on enlarging the number of verbal synsets. However, this task required a re-examination of the building strategy applied so far.

## 2 Motivation

We decided to re-examine our building strategy for two reasons. The first pertains to differences between English and Croatian verbs that are more significant than was assumed. The second reason is an attempt to speed up the building of CroWN by using other available language resources for Croatian. As far as the first reason is concerned, the lexical hierarchies and word senses from PWN in numerous cases differ significantly from the lexical meaning, number of senses, and sense relations in their Croatian counterparts. For example, the verb *dati* appears in 28 synsets in CroWN (i.e. it is marked for 28 senses), but such a particularization of meaning is a consequence of the adopted expand model, and does not reflect its true semantic structure. Alt-

---

[1] CroWN can be downloaded from the following site: `http://meta-share.ffzg.hr/repository/browse/croatian-wordnet/`

[2] Similar situation is frequent in other wordnets. Maziarz et al. (2012) provide detailed statistics of POS distribution across major wordnets.

hough *dati* is a highly polysemous verb in Croatian, we found only 12 different senses of this verb listed in various monolingual dictionaries.[3] Apart from issues concerning conceptual systems and semantic representation, rich derivational processes between Croatian verbs bring about relations that cannot be captured by presently used semantic relations.[4] Verbs in Croatian are derived from other verbs by prefixation and suffixation. Both processes can trigger a change in aspect and the addition of a new semantic component to the base form. In accordance with Binnick (1991), we treat aspect as a grammatical feature, but predictable shifts in meaning, frequently referred to as *Aktionsarten*, as lexical features, pertaining to classes of verbs. This distinction is reflected in the structure of verbal synsets in CroWN. True aspectual pairs, i.e., imperfectives and perfectives denoting completion of an action, are members of the same synset. The lexical meaning of these perfectives differs from imperfectives only in this temporal distinction. Apart from aspectual change, semantic components brought by affixes can produce combinations that, in terms of meaning, can vary from compositional to completely idiosyncratic. E.g., the verb *crtati* 'to draw$_{ipf}$' has a true aspectual pair *nacrtati* 'to draw$_{pf}$', but there are six other prefixed perfectives as well: 1. *pre+crtati* 'to copy (by drawing)$_{pf}$', 2. *pod+crtati* 'to underline$_{pf}$', 3. *o+crtati* 'to outline$_{pf}$', 4. *is+crtati* 'to draw completely$_{pf}$', 5. *u+crtati* 'to draw into$_{pf}$', and 6. *za+crtati* 'to make a plan$_{pf}$'. The same prefixes can be used with other base forms, e.g. *pre+pisati* 'to copy (by writing)$_{pf}$', *pre+slikati* 'to copy (by painting)$_{pf}$. The base form *crtati* 'to draw$_{ipf}$' can also be suffixed, e.g. 1. *crt-k-ati* 'to draw$_{ipf}$, diminutive', 2. *crt-kar-ati* 'to draw$_{ipf}$, pejorative'.[5] Suffixes with diminutive and pejorative meanings can also combine with other base forms. We pose two basic questions: Which semantic regularities can be spotted in combinations of particular affixes and various base forms? and How can thereby established morphosemantic relations be used in our further work? In order to address these issues, as well as to speed up the building of CroWN, we have decided to use data from CroDeriV, a large morphological database of Croatian verbs. In the following section we shall briefly describe this resource (for a full description, see Šojat et al., 2012).

## 3 CroDeriV

CroDeriV is a computational lexicon containing data on the morphological structure of approximately 14 300 Croatian verbs collected from freely available dictionaries and corpora. The compiled verbal lemmas were analyzed for morphemes with a rule-based approach and the results were checked manually. Each lexical entry in CroDeriV consists of verbs decomposed into morphemes and linguistic metadata. The structure for all analyzed verbs consists of 11 morpheme slots and covers all combinations of recorded lexical and grammatical morphemes. There are four types of slots for morphemes: (1) derivational prefixes (four slots), (2) the lexical part (three slots – in the majority of cases only one is filled, the three slots are provided for verbal compounds of two roots and an interfix), (3) derivational and conjugational suffixes (three slots), and (4) infinitive ending (one slot). The metadata in lexical entries indicate verbal aspect and types of reflexivity.[6] The database enables queries across the full derivational span of a particular base form and provides extensive data about the distribution and frequency of affixes in the derivation of Croatian verbs.[7] In the following section, the underlying analysis of affixal meanings is described.

## 4 Affixal Meanings

The majority of verbal prefixes in Croatian developed from prepositions, and the original locative component pervades in their meaning. However, they are highly polysemous units and in various combinations they can differently modify the meaning of base forms. For example, the

[3] More examples can be found in Šojat et al. (2012: 111 – 112).

[4] We use the same semantic relations between verbal synsets as in EWN and BN. These relations are synonymy, hyponymy/hypernymy, antonymy, cause, and subevent.

[5] Suffixes *-k-* and *-kar-* occupy the first position on the right side of the verbal root *crt-*. The full morphological analysis of the verbs *crtati, crtkati* and *crtkarati* is thus: *crt-ø-ø-a-ti, crt-k-ø-a-ti* and *crt-kar-ø-a-ti* (cf. Section 3).

[6] CroDeriV resembles databases like CatVar for English (`http://clipdemos.umiacs.umd.edu/catvar`) and Unimorph for Russian (`http://courses.washington.edu/unimorph/index.html`).

[7] For data on the productivity and frequency of affixes in Croatian, see Šojat et al. (2013).

verbal prefix *na-* 'on' can have at least eight different meanings (divided further into several subgroups) in combinations with various base forms:

1) pure aspectual meaning: *pisati* 'to write$_{ipf}$' – *napisati* 'to write$_{pf}$'

2) locative meanings:

a. top-down: *baciti* 'to throw$_{pf}$' – *nabaciti* 'to throw onto$_{pf}$'

b. proximity: *letjeti* 'to fly$_{ipf}$' – *naletjeti* 'to bump into$_{pf}$'

c. putting something on something: *slagati* 'to pile$_{ipf}$' – *naslagati* 'to pile one on another$_{pf}$'

3) inchoativity: *trunuti* 'to rot$_{ipf}$' – *natrunuti* 'to begin to rot$_{pf}$'

4) distributivity: *bacati* 'to throw$_{ipf}$' – *nabacati* 'to throw one by one$_{pf}$'

5) sufficiency: *jesti* 'to eat$_{ipf}$' – *najesti se* 'to stuff oneself$_{pf}$'

6) excessiveness: *piti* 'to drink$_{ipf}$' – *napiti se* 'to get drunk$_{pf}$'

7) addition: *gomilati* 'to accumulate$_{ipf}$' – *nagomilati* 'to accumulate a lot of X$_{pf}$'

8) intensitiy:

a. low intensity: *gristi* 'to bite$_{ipf}$' – *nagristi* 'to bite a bit$_{pf}$'

b. high intensity: *pisati* 'to write$_{ipf}$' – *napisati se* 'to tire oneself with writing$_{pf}$'

All 19 verbal prefixes recorded in CroDeriV were analyzed in the same manner.[8] This analysis enabled the recognition of the same or similar semantic components shared by different prefixes as well as the division of prefixal meanings into four major semantic groups. The four major groups of prefixal meanings are location, time, quantity, and manner. Each group has several subgroups. An analysis of suffixal meanings yielded an additional semantic group of diminutive and pejorative verbs.[9] Before further discussion, we shall briefly present the morphosemantic relations between verbs in other Slavic wordnets and compare them with the relations used in CroWN.

## 5 Related Work

Rich derivational morphology in Slavic languages and problems faced in the building of Czech, Bulgarian, and Serbian wordnets are discussed in Pala and Hlaváčková (2007), Koeva (2008), and Koeva et al. (2008). The discussion refers mainly to derivational relations across different parts of speech. Pala and Hlaváčková (2007) list 14 derivational processes in Czech introduced into Czech WordNet as relations between derived and base forms. This results in a "two-level network", where the higher level includes semantic relations between synsets, and the lower level includes derivational relations between single synset members. Although the verb-verb pairs are linked through prefixation, this relation is not used in further analysis. Koeva (2008) points out the relation between verbal aspectual pairs as the most productive derivational relation in Bulgarian and argues that perfective and imperfective verbs in Bulgarian WordNet should be split into separate synsets. While the hypernymy would be based on imperfective verbs only, synsets would be linked with the morphosemantic relation aspect. Relations between prefixed derivatives and base forms, apart from aspectual, are not discussed. The work presented in Koeva et al. (2008) concerning Serbian WordNet refers mainly to derivational relations across different parts of speech. Aspectual pairs in Serbian WordNet are members of the same synset. The most elaborate account of relations between verbs in Slavic is given in Maziarz et al. (2011) and Maziarz et al. (2012). In Polish WordNet 2.0 aspectual pairs are kept apart and lexical hierarchies consist of either perfective or imperfective verbs. Relations between verbs are divided into purely semantic relations (e.g., synonymy, hyponymy, meronymy holonymy, antonymy, processuality, causality, inchoativity, presupposition, and preceding) and derivationally-motivated relations (e.g., pure aspectuality, secondary aspectuality, iterativity, and derivationality). Some of the relations hold between lexical units (word-sense pairs, e.g., antonymy or pure aspectuality), while others hold between synsets (e.g., hyponymy and processuality). In CroWN, pure aspectual pairs are members of the same synset. Pure aspectual pairs are determined primarily by the test of secondary imperfectivization (cf. Jelaska, 2005; Maziarz et al., 2011), but also by additional criteria pertaining to semantics of affixes. The relation of pure aspectuality exists between a base form and a derivative with an affix which does not contain any other semantic components except perfectiveness, e.g. *pisati* 'to write$_{ipf}$' – *napisati* 'to write$_{pf}$' are members of the same synset. The same holds for iterative verbs

[8] These prefixes are: *do-, iz-, na-, nad-, o-/ob-, obez-, od-, po-, pod-, pre-, pred-, pri-, pro-, raz-, s-, su-, u-, uz-,* and *za-*.

[9] An analysis of prefixal meanings is given in Šojat et al. (2012); suffixal meanings are discussed in Šojat et al. (2013).

and perfective base forms. Although iterative verbs have the additional semantic component of repetitiveness, they differ from their perfectives only in this temporal component. E.g., *pisati* 'to write$_{ipf}$' – *prepisati* 'to copy by writing$_{pf}$' are not members of the same synset. However, *prepisati* 'to copy by writing$_{pf}$' – *prepisivati* 'to copy by writing$_{ipf\text{-}iter}$' are members of the same synset. Each synset member is tagged with one of the following aspect labels: IPF, PF, BI, or ITER, representing imperfective, perfective, bi-aspectual and iterative forms. This distinction is also reflected in different aspectual forms used in definitions, although they are structurally and semantically the same. Finally, all morphosemantic relations in CroWN discussed below hold between single members of synsets, i.e. lexical units, and not between whole synsets.

## 6 Morphosemantic Relations in CroWN

Morphosemantic relations are based on overlapping components of affixal meanings in combinations with various base forms. The analysis described in Section 4 enabled the classification of affixal meanings into four broad semantic groups for prefixes and one for suffixes. Four major groups for prefixes – location, time, quantity, and manner – are further divided into subgroups (28 in total). Morphosemantic relations and a variety of sub-relations based upon this classification are listed below:

1. PREFIXES:
   a) **location group**: bottom-up, top-down, proximity, through, apart, to/towards, over, into, around, under, re-location, behind, across, from
   b) **time group**: inchoativity, finitiveness, distributivity, preceding
   c) **quantity group**: sufficiency (+/-), excessiveness, intensity (+/-), exceeding, deprivation, addition
   d) **manner group**: inter-connection, change of property.

SUFFIXES:
   a) **diminutive group**: diminutive, pejorative

As far as the semantic impact of prefixes is concerned, relations in the *location* group predominantly hold between verbs of movement, but also between numerous other base verbs and derivatives with spatial relations pervading their lexical meaning (e.g., *udahnuti* 'to inhale' or *uvući* 'to drag into'). Derivatives in *time* group refer to different phases of actions denoted by base verbs (e.g., beginning or termination). The subtype *distributivity* is on the border between the *time* and *quantity* groups since the derivatives denote repetitive actions performed by one or more agents on one or more objects. Since distributive actions are performed iteratively, this relation is listed in the *time* group. Relations from the *quantity* group hold when derivatives denote various degrees of an action (e.g. *naraditi se* 'to tire oneself out (with work)', *najesti se* 'to eat one's fill'). The smallest group – *manner* – contains only two relations denoting changes of properties (e.g., *uprljati se* 'to become dirty') and actions performed in a specific manner (e.g. *sufinancirati* 'to co-finance'). The semantic impact of suffixes is limited to diminutive and pejorative meaning expressed by derivatives (e.g., *jeduckati* 'to nibble'). The aim of this classification is to establish the set of morphosemantic relations and use them within derivational families of verbs in CroWN. To determine which verbs are derivationally related and therefore are candidates for further analysis, we compared the list of verbs from CroWN and CroDeriV. All verbs from the 2318 verbal synsets in CroWN are recorded in CroDeriV.

The full list of verbs from CroWN was filtered into those sharing the same root. The list of verbs recognized as derivatives comprises 2530 base forms and prefixed derivatives. This list was further filtered for verbs marked as aspectual pairs in CroWN. In the next step, prefixed forms were segmented into prefixes and base forms. Thus we obtained 572 base forms and 1476 derivatives as candidates for the assignment of morphosemantic relations. In the final step, the relations were manually assigned to derivationally related verbs from CroWN. When no morphosemantic relation was appropriate due to the idiosyncratic nature of the combinations, we tagged this relation as DERIV (144 verbs).

The result of the whole procedure is a list of 572 base forms and 1186 prefixed verbs marked for morphosemantic relations. There are also 19 lexical units marked as diminutives in CroWN. In CroDeriV, derivational suffixes for diminutives always occupy the first slot to the right of the root (cf. Section 3). Table 1 contains the overall frequency of relations in four major groups as well as the frequency of the three most prominent subrelations for prefixed derivatives (*manner* contains only two subrelations). The last row indicates the frequency of suffixed derivatives.

| Group | Freq | Subgroup | Freq |
|---|---|---|---|
| Loc | 598 | loc_apart | 141 |
| | | loc_around | 87 |
| | | loc_from | 70 |
| Time | 276 | time_fin | 132 |
| | | time_inch | 109 |
| | | time_distr | 28 |
| Quan | 190 | quan_int | 126 |
| | | quan_exc | 25 |
| | | quan_suff | 20 |
| Mann | 122 | mann_prop | 88 |
| | | mann_conn | 34 |
| Dim | 19 | pejorative | 8 |

Table 1: Frequency of MS relations in CroWN

## 7 Discussion and Future Work

None of the discussed morphosemantic relations between members of different synsets can be completely subsumed by any of semantic relations between synsets in terms of semantic content. Base verbs and their derivatives are frequently not members of same lexical hierarchies, such as synsets containing derivationally related verbs like *ići* 'to go', *ući* 'to go into', *izaći* 'to go out' and *otići* 'to go away'. Although the verbs *ući* and *izaći* are marked as antonyms, the relatedness of the whole group is not indicated. The relation cause partially overlaps with our morphosemantic relation change of property, but cause cannot encompass reflexive non-agentive counterpart pairs of transitive verbs in Slavic (e.g. *topiti se – otopiti se* 'to melt$_{ipf-pf}$'' – *to become soft or liquid* vs. *topiti – otopiti* 'to melt$_{ipf-pf}$' – *to cause to become soft or liquid.* The relation of subevent refers to two simultaneous actions or to an action which is a part of the action denoted by another synset, but it does not reflect particular parts of events, such as its beginning or terminating point, as morphosemantic relations of inchoativity or finitiveness do. In order to capture the semantic relatedness between verbs usually scattered across different hierarchies, we have introduced a set of 28 morphosemantic relations. This "two-level network," as defined by Pala and Hlaváčková (2007), along with extensive data from CroDeriV, provides an excellent basis for further work. Although CroDeriV does not contain data about lexical meaning and semantic relations between verbs, information about the morphological structure of verbs proved valuable for the detection of derivationally related verbs and the assignment of morphosemanic relations. Information about complete derivational families is also valuable for the further expansion of CroWN, which is one of our primary goals. It can be used both to complete already present derivational families and to introduce new ones. Finally, the importance of morphosemantic relations in the description of the verbal system in Croatian can be demonstrated with the Croatian verb *gristi* 'to bite$_{ipf}$'. This verb appears in CroWN only in this form, whereas CroDeriV contains ten other derivatives from this base form. Only the derivative marked with the relation DERIVED in Figure 1 below can be straightforwardly connected to other synsets in CroWN via semantic relations. All other derivatives, i.e., 90% of this derivational family, should be connected to this base form primarily by morphosemantic relations as described here. Although the full set of morphosemantic relations as discussed here provides a more densed and fine-grained structure of the Croatian lexicon, we are aware that in numerous cases it is hard to maintain the consistency and clear-cut distinctions among 28 presented relations. However, we are convinced that even a set of morphosemantic relations limited to four major groups of prefixed derivatives (location, time, quantity and manner) and one group of suffixed derivatives (diminutive/pejorative) can substantially enrich wordnets for Slavic languages.

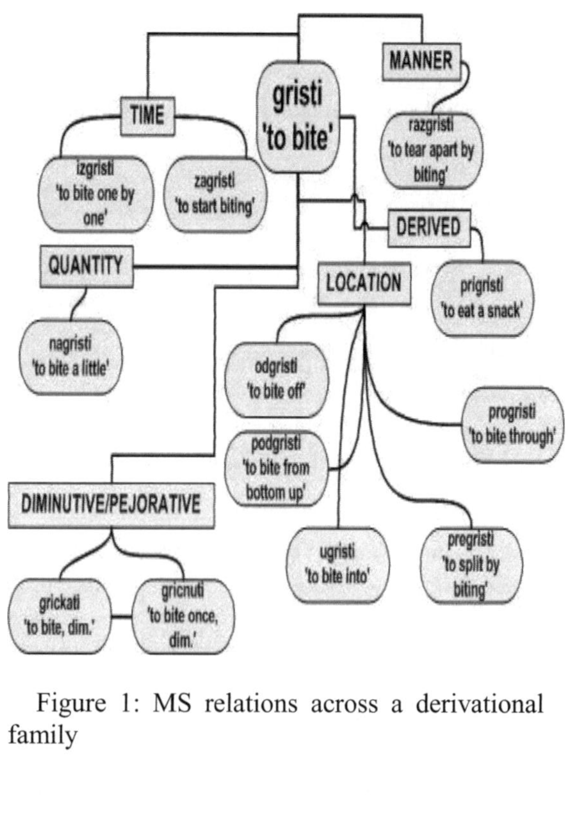


Figure 1: MS relations across a derivational family

## Acknowledgements

The research was supported by MZOS RH project 130-1300646-1002 and partially by XLike project (FP7, Grant 288342).

## References

Robert I. Binnick. 1991. *Time and the Verb: A Guide to Tense & Aspect*. Oxford University Press, Oxford, UK.

Zrinka Jelaska. 2005. *Hrvatski kao drugi i strani jezik*. Hrvatska sveučilišna naklada: Zagreb.

Svetla Koeva. 2008. Derivational and Morphosemantic Relations in Bulgarian WordNet. *Proceedings of the Intelligent Information Systems 2008*, 359–368.

Svetla Koeva, Cvetana Krstev and Duško Vitas. 2008. Morpho-semantic Relations in WordNet – a Case Study for two Slavic Languages. *Proceedings of the 4th Global WordNet Conference*, 239–254.

Marek Maziarz, Maciej Piasecki, Stanislaw Szpakowicz, Joanna Rabiega-Wisniewska, Bozena Hojka 2011. Semantic Relations between Verbs in Polish WordNet 2.0. *Cognitive studies*, 11:183–200.

Marek Maziarz, Maciej Piasecki and Stanisław Szpakowicz. 2012. An Implementation of a System of Verb Relations in plWordNet 2.0. *Proceedings of the 6th Global WordNet Conference*, 181–188.

Karel Pala and Dana Hlaváčková. 2007. Derivational Relations in Czech WordNet. *Proceedings of the Workshop on Balto-Slavonic Languages*, 75–81.

Ida Raffaelli, Marko Tadić, Božo Bekavac, Željko Agić 2008. Building Croatian WordNet. *Proceedings of the 4th Global WordNet Conference,* 349-360.

Krešimir Šojat, Matea Srebačić and Marko Tadić. 2012. Derivational and Semantic Relations of Croatian Verbs. *Journal of Language Modelling*, 0 (1): 111-142.

Krešimir Šojat, Matea Srebačić and Vanja Štefanec. 2013. CroDeriV i morfološka raščlamba hrvatskoga glagola. *Suvremena lingvistika*, 39 (75): 75 – 96.

Piek Vossen. (Ed.) 1998. *EuroWordNet. A Multilingual Database with Lexical Semantic Networks,* Kluwer Academic Publishers, Dodrecht, Boston, London.

# News about the Romanian Wordnet

**Verginica Barbu Mititelu**
RACAI
13, Calea 13 Septembrie
Bucharest 050711, Romania
vergi@racai.ro

**Ştefan Daniel Dumitrescu**
RACAI
13, Calea 13 Septembrie
Bucharest 050711, Romania
sdumitrescu@racai.ro

**Dan Tufiş**
RACAI
13, Calea 13 Septembrie
Bucharest 050711, Romania
tufis@racai.ro

## Abstract

There are more than 60 wordnets worldwide; the Romanian wordnet is among those that are maintained and further developed. Begun within the BalkaNet project and further enriched in various (application oriented) projects, it was used in word sense disambiguation, machine translation and question answering with promising results. We present here the latest qualitative and quantitative improvements of our lexical resource, special attention being paid to derivational relations, the latest statistics, as well as the development of an Application Programming Interface, meant to facilitate work with the wordnet, both for its further development purposes and for its use in applications. In the context of creating a common European research infrastructure network, our wordnet is licensed through META-SHARE, being freely available for scientific purposes.

## 1 Introduction

The development of the Romanian wordnet (RoWN henceforth) started within BalkaNet project[1]. Afterwards, it has been developed and maintained within several projects by the Natural Language Processing (NLP) group of the Romanian Academy Research Institute for Artificial Intelligence (RACAI): ROTEL[2], STAR[3], SIR-RESDEC[4], ACCURAT[5], METANET4U[6], the Romanian Academy research plan.

Within BalkaNet a core of 18000 synsets was created. They were aligned to the Princeton WordNet (PWN) versions available throughout time, respectively version 2.0 at the end of the project. Among those synsets there were more than 400 that lexicalize concepts specific to the Balkan area. These were implemented in all six languages of the project (Bulgarian, Czech, Greek, Romanian, Serbian, Turkish) and were linked to hypernym synsets, already existing in PWN, so they were not left dangling in the network.

RoWN contains words belonging both to the general vocabulary and to various domains of activity. Throughout time, we aimed at a complete coverage of the basic common sets from EuroWordNet[7], of the 1984 corpus[8], of the newspaper articles corpus NAACL2003[9], of the Acquis Communautaire corpus and the Eurovoc thesaurus[10], of VerbNet 3.1[11], and as much as possible from the ROWikipedia lexical stock.

Two basic development principles have always been followed: the Hierarchy Preservation

[1] http://www.dblab.upatras.gr/balkanet
[2] http://www.ai.ici.ro/rotel_eng/index.htm
[3] http://www.racai.ro/star
[4] http://www2.racai.ro/sir-resdec
[5] http://www.accurat-project.eu/, http://valhalla.racai.ro/accurat/index.php?page=despre
[6] http://www.racai.ro/metanet4u-racai
[7] http://www.illc.uva.nl/EuroWordNet
[8] http://nl.ijs.si/ME/Vault/CD/docs/1984.html
[9] http://ws.racai.ro:9191/repository/browse/the-naacl-2003-english-romanian-corpus/da86dc2efb6811e2a8ad00237df3e35886f019db7a16437f801cba30dd6ab209
[10] http://optima.jrc.it/Acquis/JRC-Acquis.3.0/doc/README_Acquis-Communautaire-corpus_JRC.html
[11] http://verbs.colorado.edu/~mpalmer/projects/verbnet.html

Principle (HPP) (according to which the hierarchical structure of the concepts in a wordnet is the same irrespective of the natural language for which the wordnet is developed) and the Conceptual Density Principle (which ensures that once a concept is selected to be implemented, all its ancestors up to the unique beginners are also selected, thus preventing the existence of dangling nodes) (Tufiş et al., 2004). The former principle was the assumption behind our development methodology, namely the expand method. The latter ensured the lack of dangling nodes in the nouns and verbs hierarchies. As a consequence of the way we chose to create our language resource, the lexical density has never been our preoccupation, thus there are many words that do not occur in as many synsets as how many meanings they have. Nevertheless, we do not exclude such an objective from our further developments.

At present, RoWN is aligned to PWN version 3.0. Details about the way we performed the alignment from PWN 2.0 to PWN 3.0 and about the way we solved the encountered problems (the n:1 or 1:n matches between synsets in the two versions) are presented in Tufiş et al. (2013).

RoWN is licensed through META-SHARE[12] (). It is free for academic research, but restricted for commercial use.

In this paper we present the latest qualitative and quantitative improvements of our lexical resource, the latest statistics (Section 3), special attention being paid to derivational relations (Section 4), as well as the development of an Application Programming Interface, meant to facilitate work with the wordnet, both for its further development purposes and for its use in applications (Section 5). Our intentions for further development are included in the Conclusions section. Before proceeding, we enumerate the applications in which our team used RoWN and which, throughout time, influenced our decisions about the concepts to be further implemented in the network.

## 2 Uses of RoWN

Ion and Tufiş (2009) and Ion and Ştefănescu (2011) describe word sense disambiguation (WSD) methods that make use of wordnets: the former is set in a multilingual environment and the WSD is done with the help of aligned wordnets. The latter is set in a monolingual environment and the WSD is done with the help of the lexical chains established between the co-occurring words in the text, chains whose length is calculated in the wordnet. The assumption is that the shorter the lexical chain, the more similar the words. The length of the lexical chain depends on the number of relations marked in the network. The results in the multilingual environment are reported as better than those in the monolingual one.

For a Question Answering (QA) system, RoWN was used for expanding the query introduced by the user (Ion et al., 2008) with words semantically related (i.e., synonyms, hypo- and hyperonyms) to the ones it contained. Moreover, RoWN was also used in the last phase, that of ranking the found results by calculating the semantic distance, again as a lexical chain, between the words introduced by the user and those occurring in the text. It was noticed that the relations with the greatest contribution at calculating the score are hyponymy and derivational relations.

Aligned wordnets are valuable sources of cross-language equivalents, especially multiword terms, in machine translation.

## 3 Latest Quantitative Developments

Lately our efforts of implementing new synsets aimed at a complete coverage of VerbNet 3.1, with the prospect of creating a syntactic parser for Romanian.

The up-to-date statistics about RoWN are presented in Table 1 and 2 below. In the former, PoS stands for part of speech, S for synset, L for literal, UL for unique literals and NL for nonlexicalized synsets. Obeying the HPP stated above implies the transfer of the hierarchies from PWN into RoWN. The lack of perfect equivalences among languages is widely known; nevertheless, we chose to disregard it. Moreover, there are lexical gaps in all languages. We call them nonlexicalized concepts and represent them as empty synsets. For example, for the PWN verbal synset {zip_up:1} (gloss: close with a zipper) there is no literal in the corresponding Romanian synset. However, such synsets do not lack relations: the corresponding ones from PWN are transferred into RoWN.

[12] http://ws.racai.ro:9191/repository/browse/18

| PoS | S | L | UL | NL |
|---|---|---|---|---|
| Nouns | 41063 | 56532 | 52009 | 1839 |
| Verbs | 10397 | 16484 | 14210 | 759 |
| Adjective | 4822 | 8203 | 7407 | 79 |
| Adverbs | 3066 | 4019 | 3248 | 110 |
| TOTAL | 59348 | 85238 | 75656 | 2787 |

Table 1: Statistics about synsets and literals in RoWN.

| Relation | Number |
|---|---|
| hypo/hyperonymy | 48316 |
| instance_hypo/hyperonymy | 3889 |
| antonym | 4131 |
| similar_to | 4838 |
| verb_group | 1530 |
| member_holonym | 2047 |
| part_holonym | 5573 |
| substance_holonym | 410 |
| also_see | 1333 |
| attribute | 958 |
| cause | 196 |
| entailment | 371 |

Table 2. Semantic relations in RoWN.

It is worth noticing that antonymy, which is a lexical relation in PWN, is represented as a semantic one in RoWN. The conceptual opposition between the synsets is more useful in various applications than the mere antonymy between two literals.

With the exception of *attribute* relation, all the others enumerated in Table 2 link synsets with literals of the same part of speech. A path between two words of a different part of speech, about which any speaker would say they are related, although not impossible to find, would be too long, thus providing wrong information about the similarity between those words.

## 4 Derivational Relations

Using RoWN in applications, as presented above, showed unnatural lexical chains, such as one of the possible chains between *inventator* "inventor" and *inventa* "to invent":

**inventator**(1.1) *instance_hyponym* James_Watt(x)
James_Watt(x) *instance_hypernym* inginer(1.1)
inginer(1.1) *hyponym* inginer_software(1)
inginer_software(1) *domain_member_TOPIC* ştiinţa_calculatoarelor(x)
ştiinţa_calculatoarelor(x) *domain_TOPIC* programa(3)
programa(3) *hyponym* crea_mental(1)
crea_mental(1) *hypernym* **inventa**(1)

The strangeness of this example results from the intricate path from *inventator* to *inventa*, uncommon for whatever speaker of Romanian: *inventator – James Watt – inginer* "engineer" – *inginer software* "software engineer" – *programa* "to program" – *crea mental* "to create by mental act" – *inventa*.

Faced with a number of such cases, we decided to implement derivational relations into our wordnet.

This type of relations exists in other wordnets as well: the Turkish WordNet (Bilgin et al., 2004), PWN (Fellbaum et al., 2007), the Czech WordNet (Pala and Hlaváčková, 2007), the Polish WordNet (Piasecki et al., 2012), the Estonian one (Kahusk, et al., 2010). Given the language-specific character of such relations, each team undertook their own strategy for finding the relations in their wordnet. However, there are teams that transferred the derivational relations in PWN and then validated them: this is the case for the Bulgarian WordNet (Koeva, 2008), the Serbian (Koeva et al., 2008) and the Finnish one (Lindén and Niemi, 2013).

Whereas most of the undertakings above aimed at expanding the network with new synsets derivationally linked with the literals already in the wordnet, we were interested in adding such relations between literals that are in the synsets. No extension was intended, at least for the moment.

We discuss below some theoretical aspects of derivational relations and the significance of their representation in a wordnet and then present the methodology we adopted for identifying and annotating them in RoWN.

### 4.1 Pre-requisites

Derivation is one means of creating new words in a language from existing morphemes, i.e. the smallest units of a language that have their own meaning. It ensures both formal and semantic relatedness between the root and the derived word: the formal relatedness is ensured by the fact that the root and the derived word contain (almost) the same string of letters that represent the root, while the semantic relatedness is ensured by the compositionality of meaning of the derived word: its meaning is a sum of the meaning of the root and the meaning of the affix(es). Thus, the Romanian words *alerga* "run" and *alergător* "runner" are derivationally related: the latter is obtained from the former by adding the suffix *-ător* (after removing *-a*, the infinitive suffix) and it means "the one who runs". However, derivational relations cannot be established for all meanings of these words: when considered with their proper meaning, they are related, but when *alerga* is considered with its figurative meaning "to try hard to get something", it does not establish a derivational relation with *alergător*, as it has not developed any related figurative meaning.

In the derivation process only one affix of a type is added. So, a prefix and a suffix can be added to a root in the same derivation step, but never two suffixes or/and two prefixes. If a word contains more than two affixes of the same type, then they were attached in different steps in the derivation.

### 4.2 Identifying derivational relations between literals in RoWN

Having available a list of (492) Romanian affixes and the list of (31872) simple literals in RoWN, we searched for pairs of literals ($literal_1$ and $literal_2$) such that $literal_1$ +/- affix(es) = $literal_2$. The "+" version covers progressive derivation, while the "-" version covers backformation. We allowed for at most 2 affixes, but of different types, as discussed above. The results are presented in Table 3:

| Derivation type | Number of derived words | Percent |
|---|---|---|
| **Prefixation** | 2862 | 17.43 |
| **Suffixation** | 13556 | 82.57 |
| **TOTAL** | 16418 | |

Table 3. Derivational relations between simple literals in RoWN.

The percents are reasonable: it is a well-known fact that prefixation is weakly productive in Romanian, unlike suffixation.

We subjected the found pairs to an automatic and then a manual validation. For the former, we enriched the list of affixes with information about the part of speech of the words to which they can attach and of the words they help create. The list is available at www.racai.ro/~vergi under Research. For example, the suffix *-a* can be attached to nouns or to adjectives to create verbs:

*-a* n>v a>v

Examples include: *buton* ("button") + *-a* > *butona* ("to channel-surf"), *scurt* ("short") + *-a* > *scurta* ("to shorten").

Afterwards we proceeded to a manual validation of the whole number of pairs. The results are presented in Table 4: for each type of derivation (DT) (prefixation P or suffixation S), from the found pairs (column 2) we present the number of those passing the automatic validation (AV) in column 3 and then of those that passed the manual validation (MV) in column 4; the last column presents the percent of manually validated pairs for each derivation type.

| DT | Found | AV | MV | % |
|---|---|---|---|---|
| P | 2862 | 2621 | 1990 | 69.53 |
| S | 13556 | 8345 | 8452 | 62.35 |
| TOTAL | 16418 | 10966 | 10442 | |

Table 4. Validated pairs.

Examples of pairs that passed the automatic validation but not the manual one include: *prinde* "to catch" – *surprinde* "to surprise", *abate* "to deviate" – *abator* "slaughter house".

### 4.3 Sense level annotation

Having already established that derivational relations need to be marked at the word sense level, not for all senses of the words in a pair, the next necessary step is to calculate the Cartesian product of the sets of synsets in which the members of the validated pairs occur. Thus, for the 10442 pairs of literals resulted after manual validation, we calculated the Cartesian product for each pair, obtaining a total of 101729 pairs of synsets. They display formal relatedness and, in order to mark a derivational relation for them, it is also necessary to subject them to a semantic evaluation. A linguist goes through them and whenever semantic similarity is noticed, the pair is labeled with one of the 57 semantic labels we established: 16 for prefixed words (together, subsumption, opposition, mero, eliminate, iterative, through, repeat, imply, similitude, instead, aug, before, anti, out, back) and 41 for suffixed ones (subsumption, member_holo, member_mero, substance_holo, substance_mero, ingredient_holo, holonym, part, agent, result, location, of_origin, job, state, period, undergoer, instrument, sound, cause, container, vehicle, body_part, material, destination, gender, wife, dim, aug, object_made_by, subject_to, by_means_of, clothes, event, abstract, colour, tax, make_become, make_acquire, manner, similitude, related).

The most frequently attached semantic labels are: for prefixed words: opposition (*neesențial* "unessential" – *essential* "essential") (792), subsumption (*subclasă* "subclass" – *clasă* "class") (363), repeat (*reaprinde* "reignite" – *aprinde* "ignite") (305); for suffixed words: related (*călduros* "warm" – *căldură* "warmth") (1294), event (*împărtăşanie* "communion" – *împărtăşi* "commune") (699), abstract (*cerință* "requirement" – *cere* "require") (490), manner (*primejdios* "dangerous" - *primejdie* "danger") (436), agent (*linguşitor* "adulator" – *linguşi* "adulate") (394). At the end of the article, in the Annex, containing Table7 and Table 8, we present the semantic labels and their frequencies for prefixed and, respectively, suffixed words, accompanied by examples.

### 4.4 Statistics about derivational relations

Going through 55849 such pairs of synsets, we obtained the results in Table 5.

| | Prefixed | Suffixed | TOTAL |
|---|---|---|---|
| **Pairs subject to validation** | 30132 | 25717 | 55849 |
| **Validated pairs** | 3145 | 13916 | 17061 |
| **Percent** | 10.43 | 89.64 | **30.55** |

Table 5. Semantically annotated pairs.

The aim of marking these derivational relations was to increase the number of links between synsets, especially between synsets of different parts of speech. For the validated pairs we included in Table 6 statistics about the derivational relations involving words of the same and of different part of speech. It is obvious that, on the whole, adding derivational relations to a wordnet increases the number of cross-part of speech (PoS) relations.

| | Same PoS % | Cross PoS % |
|---|---|---|
| Prefixed | 97 | 3 |
| Suffixed | 15 | 85 |
| TOTAL | 38 | **62** |

Table 6. Distribution of derivational relation on PoS.

## 5 RoWordNetLib

We have built an Application Programming Interface (API) for RoWN, called RoWordNetLib, meant as a tool to aid quick implementations of RoWN into both research-oriented and industry applications. When designing it, we envisaged a tool that should be easy to use, easy to extend and that would offer a sufficiently large array of functionalities. The chosen programming language is Java.
The main functionalities that RoWordNetLib provides are:

- Input/Output for working with XML-based RoWN files;
- Methods for working with the semantic network itself (RoWordNet objects containing RoWN);
- Set operations for working with multiple RoWordNet objects (reunion, intersection, complement, difference, merge, etc.);
- Basic Word Sense Disambiguation (WSD) algorithms;
- Similarity Metrics (both distance-based and semantic).

The API's uses can be classified as (1) internal – it helps to facilitate the continuous work of enriching RoWN and (2) external – to quicken the development of Romanian-enabled smart applications. By providing set operations like difference, intersection or reunion on RoWordNet objects, more people can work in parallel on RoWN and then easily join their versions into a single wordnet, thus easing its development. Externally, wordnets are successfully used to perform word sense disambiguation, information retrieval, information extraction, machine translation, automatic text classification and summarization.

RoWordNetLib is structured into several packages, each with its assigned functionality. The main packages are: 'data', 'io', 'op' and 'wsd'.

The 'data' package contains the data structures RoWordNetLib uses internally. Its structure is simple, following the way the data is naturally structured in a wordnet: a RoWordNet object contains an array of Synset objects which are indexed by the synset ID for retrieval speed. Each Synset object contains a number of primitive types as well as an array of Literal objects and an array of Relation objects. A Literal object contains a word and an associated sense. A Relation object contains a relation (string) that points to a target synset (defined as an ID), as well as optionally having a source and target literal for cases where the relation is not between synsets but between two synsets' particular literals.

The 'io' package provides input and output functions. The most important I/O function is reading and writing RoWordNet objects in their native XML format.

The 'op' package provides different operational tools: (1) set operation methods for joining, intersecting, complementing, etc., multiple RoWordNet objects; (2) through the BFWalk class, the ability to perform a breadth-first walk through the RoWN semantic network; (3) a number of distance-based and semantic similarity measures (Resnik, 1995) for measuring the closeness of concepts (lexicalized by literals in synsets).

The 'wsd' package implements two Word Sense Disambiguation algorithms: Lesk (1986) and an adapted version of Lesk. They are used to obtain information content values for synsets in RoWN given an arbitrary Romanian text as the input corpus, which is further used to enable the semantic similarity measures.

## 6 Conclusions and Further Work

RoWN is a valuable resource for the Romanian language and the NLP group of RACAI uses it in most of their applications. We presented here our latest qualitative and quantitative achievements.

Further enrichment of RoWN is a constant preoccupation of our team. It follows all the time the other interests of the group. For instance, the last set of implemented synsets was made up of verbs exclusively, given our present interest to cover VerbNet 3.1, with the prospect of creating a parser for Romanian.

Increasing the density of relations between synsets in order to make RoWN more effective in applications was obtained by adding derivational relations. Although they are relations between literals, the semantic labels we attached to them can be viewed as a link between the synsets to which the respective literals belong. After finishing the semantic annotation of the derivative pairs, we could try to expand the network with automatically derived words. For Romanian an experiment of automatically deriving words is reported by Petic (2011), who used very productive and reliable affixes. With the list of affixes and their combination possibilities (available at www.racai.ro/~vergi under Research) that we have created, we can dare test new cases of automatic derivation for Romanian.

## Reference


Orhan Bilgin, Özlem Çetinoglu, and Kemal Oflazer. 2004. Morphosemantic relations in and across wordnets: A study based on Turkish. P. Sojka, K. Pala, P. Smrz, C. Fellbaum, P. Vossen (Eds.), *Proceedings of GWC.*

Christiane Fellbaum, Anne Osherson, and Peter E. Clark. 2007. Putting Semantics into WordNet's "Morphosemantic" Links. *Proceedings of the 3rd Language and Technology Conference.*

Radu Ion and Dan Ştefănescu. 2011. Unsupervised Word Sense Disambiguation with Lexical Chains and Graph-Based Context Formalization. Zygmunt Vetulani (ed.): *LTC 2009*, Lecture Notes in Artificial Intelligence, 6562/2011: 435—443.

Radu Ion and Dan Tufiş. 2009. Multilingual versus Monolingual Word Sense Disambiguation. *International Journal of Speech Technology*; 12 (2-3):113-124.

Radu Ion, Dan Ştefănescu, Alexandru Ceauşu, and Dan Tufiş. 2008. RACAI's QA System at the Romanian-Romanian Multiple Language Question Answering (QA@CLEF2008) Main Task. Carol Peters et al. (eds.) *Working Notes for the CLEF 2008 Workshop*: 10.

Neeme Kahusk, Kadri Kerner, and Kadri Vider. 2010. Enriching Estonian WordNet with Derivations and Semantic Relations. *Proceeding of the 2010 conference on Human Language Technologies – The Baltic Perspective*:195-200.

Svetla Koeva. 2008. Derivational and Morphosemantic Relations in Bulgarian Wordnet. *Intelligent Information Systems*; XVI:359-369.

Svetla Koeva, Cvetana Krstev, and Duško Vitas. 2008. Morpho-semantic Relations in Wordnet – A Case Study for two Slavic Languages. *Proceedings of the Fourth Global WordNet Conference:*239-254.

Michael Lesk. 1986. Automatic sense disambiguation using machine readable dictionaries: How to tell a pine cone from an ice cream cone. *5th SIGDOC*:24-26.

Krister Lindén and Jyrki Niemi. 2013. Is it possible to create a very large wordnet in 100 days? An evaluation. *Language Resources and Evaluation*, http://link.springer.com/article/10.1007%2Fs10579-013-9245-0.

Karel Pala and Dana Hlaváčková, D. 2007. Derivational relations in Czech Wordnet. *Proceedings of the Workshop on Balto-Slavonic Natural Language Processing*: 75-81.

Mircea Petic. 2011. Generative mechanisms of Romanian derivational morphology. *Memoirs of the Scientific Section of the Romanian Academy*. Series IV, Tome XXXIV:21-30.

Maciej Piasecki, Radoslaw Ramocki, and Marek Maziarz. 2012. Recognition of Polish Derivational Relations Based on Supervised Learning Scheme. *Proceedings of LREC 2012*: 916-922.

Philip Resnik. 1995. Using information content to evaluate semantic similarity in a taxonomy. *14th International Joint Conference on Artificial Intelligence*.

Dan Tufiş, Dan Cristea, and Sofia Stamou. 2004. BalkaNet: Aims, Methods, Results and Perspectives. A General Overview. *Romanian Journal on Information Science and Technology*; 7:9-34.

Dan Tufiş, Verginica Barbu Mititelu, Dan Ştefănescu, Radu Ion. 2013. The Romanian Wordnet in a Nutshell. *Language Resources and Evaluation*, http://link.springer.com/article/10.1007%2Fs10579-013-9230-7.

**Annex**

| **Label** | **Occurrences** | **Example** |
|---|---|---|
| BACK | 2 | reflux “low tide” – flux “high tide” |
| TOGETHER | 29 | întreţese “interweave” – ţese “weave” |
| AUG | 5 | supraabundenţă “overabundance” – abundenţă “abundance” |
| OUT | 1 | epidermal “epidermis” – derma “dermis” |
| SIMILITUDE | 61 | reţine “withhold” – ţine “hold” |
| IMPLY | 26 | desconsidera “disconsider” – considera “consider” |
| THROUGH | 5 | răzbate “get through” – bate “beat” |
| MERO | 17 | suprafaţă “surface” – faţă “face” |
| BEFORE | 14 | preambalare “prepacking” – ambalare “packing” |
| OPPOSITION | 792 | neesenţial “unessential” – esenţial “essential” |
| REPEAT | 305 | reaprinde “reignite” – aprinde “ignite” |
| SUBSUMPTION | 363 | subclasă “subclass” – clasă “class” |
| ANTI | 10 | anticolinesterază “anticholinesterase” – colinesterază “cholinesterase” |
| INSTEAD | 6 | vicepreşedinte “vicepresident” – preşedinte “president” |
| ITERATIVE | 2 | răsfoi “thumb through” – foaie “leaf” |
| ELIMINATE | 9 | deşela “override” – şale “loin” |

Tabel 7. Semantic labels for prefixed words and their frequency in RoWN.

| **Label** | **Occurrences** | **Example** |
|---|---|---|
| RELATED | 1294 | călduros “warm” – căldură “warmth” |
| SOUND | 163 | bufneală “plunk” – bufni “to plunk” |
| STATE | 284 | îndoială “doubt” – îndoi “to doubt” |
| DESTINATION | 5 | patentant “patentee” – patenta “to patent” |
| AUG | 1 | grăsan “big fat person” – gras “fat” |
| SIMILITUDE | 115 | încărcătură “loading” – încărcare “loading” |
| PERIOD | 43 | bătrâneţe “old age” – bătrân “old” |
| JOB | 179 | semănător “sower” – semăna “sow” |
| PART | 12 | optime “eighth” – opt “eight” |
| MEMBER_MERO | 17 | orăşean “town dweller” – oraş |

| | | |
|---|---|---|
| | | "town" |
| BY_MEANS_OF | 104 | opreliște "obstructor" – opri "obstruct" |
| CAUSE | 19 | umezeală "dampness" – umezi "to damp" |
| MEMBER_HOLO | 37 | soldățime "soldiery" – soldat "soldier" |
| RESULT | 227 | tencuială "plastering" – tencui "plaster" |
| SUBJECT_TO | 19 | chinui "to anguish" – chin "anguish" |
| ABSTRACT | 490 | cerință "requirement" – cere "require" |
| SUBSUMPTION | 42 | căpetenie "headman" – cap "head" |
| OF_ORIGIN | 29 | sătean "villager" – sat "village" |
| EVENT | 699 | împărtășanie "communion" – împărtăși "to commune" |
| INSTRUMENT | 84 | ondulator "crimper" – ondula "to crimp" |
| INGREDIENT_HOLO | 1 | sticlărie "glass work" – sticlă "glass" |
| TIME | 1 | cătănie "period of military service" – cătană "serviceman" |
| MANNER | 436 | primejdios "dangerous" – primejdie "danger" |
| MAKE_ACQUIRE | 110 | îndigui "to dam" – dig "dam" |
| CONTAINER | 17 | afișier "board" – afiș "poster" |
| HOLONYM | 26 | pieptar "vest" – piept "breast of a garment" |
| DIM | 50 | căsuță "little house" – casă |

| | | |
|---|---|---|
| | | "house" |
| OBJECT_MADE_BY | 50 | chinezărie "Chinese work" – chinez "Chinese" |
| CLOTHES | 1 | pieptar "vest" – piept "breast" |
| SUBSTANCE_HOLO | 2 | cerat "waxy" – ceară "wax" |
| AGENT | 394 | lingușitor "adulator" – linguși "adulate" |
| LOCATION | 87 | cărămidărie "brickyard" – cărămidă "brick" |
| MATERIAL | 4 | îndulcitor "sweetener" – îndulci "sweeten" |
| UNDERGOER | 47 | setos "thirsty" – sete "thirst" |
| COLOUR | 19 | cenușiu "ashen" – cenușă "ash" |
| GENDER | 13 | călugăriță "nun" – călugăr "monk" |
| SUBSTANCE_MERO | 1 | ricină "ricin" – ricin "castor oil plant" |
| MAKE_BECOME | 89 | caricaturize "to caricature" – caricatură "caricature" |

Tabel 8. Semantic labels for suffixed words and their frequency in RoWN.

# On shape classifiers, their metaphorical extension(s) and wordnet potentials

**Francesca Quattri**
The Hong Kong Polytechnic University
Hong Kong
francesca.quattri@connect.polyu.hk

**Abstract**

This paper aims at highlighting the complex lexico-semantic information entailed in Chinese shape classifiers. The study is based on a selection of the same as derived from extensive literature. The goal is to introduce shape information in wordnets in a comprehensive way starting by shape classifiers. The suggestion is to map them not just as information coercers, but also as lexical items (nouns, verbs, adjectives). The paper also explores the metaphorical implications that can be derived from classifiers in this double function.

## 1 Introduction

Classifiers belong to some of the most complex issues in the grammars of the languages that own them (e. g. Japanese, Chinese, Korean, Thai). The approach to classifiers as not just grammatical, but also lexical items, has already been paved. (Mok, Huini and Bond, 2012; Paik and Bond, 2002) and (Bond and Paik, 2000) have for instance conducted research on classifiers and Wordnet® (WN), mainly focusing on the generation / prediction of classifiers from WN or from a common ontology.

In this paper, some Chinese shape classifiers are taken into account. Upon the claim made in literature that they enhance shape-related properties entailed in the nouns they collocate with (as described in Section 2), three major claims are made. (I) Classifiers (as for this study, shape ones) can trigger shape-related information from the noun they accompany, but (II) they can also pass the shape-related information they already contain to the nouns that follow (which makes this information transfer bi-, and not just mono-directional).

In order to understand point II, it needs to be pointed out that, although classifiers are defined as morphemes specifying the semantic class of the nouns that follows, they can be nouns, verbs and adjectives at the same time (a fact that remains rather unmentioned in the referred literature). Once this fact is acknowledged, the afore assumed bi-directionality of lexico-semantic information from classifier to noun sounds feasible.

In the proposed examples, cases are also shown in which the *liason* between classifier and noun may be shallow (meaning that it is unclear how the shape-related classifier can possibly match with a certain noun). For these cases, it is suggested that (III) the bond between shape classifier and noun that follows is justifiable through metaphorical extension.

The author believes that the introduction of classifiers as elements of meaning derivation and meaning extension can be of interest for the wordnet community.

All the points in the research stress the need to consider classifiers and shape-related information in wordnets in greater detail. The research also tries to justify the use of classifiers in commonsense language.

The choice of selecting shape over other kinds of classifiers, as well as the hypothesis of a metaphorical justification in their use in language are inscribed in the bigger frame of current research (Quattri, 2013a; Quattri, 2013b).

## 2 Shape classifiers as lexico-semantic information carriers

According to (Huang and Ahrens, 2003), classifiers coerce information from the noun they accompany. This kind of retrieved information helps to better specify the noun into kind, event or individual. The authors, together with (Imai, Saalbach and Stern, 2010), categorize classifiers according to the properties that they extract from the noun they collocate with, including ShapeAttributes, such as length, or roundness, or flatness.[1]

Although not explicitly stated, it seems that other authors apply the similar value to classifiers, i. e. of being elements that coerce or extract information from the event or object that comes after them. For instance, according to ((Sera, Johnson and Yichun, 2013):5–7), the Chinese classifier 條 tiáo reflects the length and flexibility entailed in the objects it carries (e. g. a rope, or a snake). 支 zhī stresses length and rigidity, while 個 ge is a more universal classifier, thus partly a shape-related one. For (Sera, Johnson and Yichun, 2013), the use of 條，支 and 個 in Chinese, counts, among other shape classifiers in their research, for 56.5% of general use.

Once the monodirectionality between classifier *y* and noun *x* is implied, some authors either categorically deny, or hardly prove,[2] the existence of a hierarchical relations among the different morphemes.

In this paper, a new approach to classifiers is proposed, with the following assumptions: (I) Classifiers can trigger information from the noun they accompany but (II) they are not just morphemes, but also proper words (nouns, verbs and / or adjectives) with proper meaning/s. This acknowledged, it is assumed that the meaning that a classifier coerces from a noun may be contained in the classifier itself and transferred to the word it accompanies. (III) When the matching between classifier and noun appears shallow, there might exist a metaphorical motivation that enables to justify the use of that specific morpheme for that specific noun.

Let's propose some examples as evidence.

Take for instance the classifier 張 zhāng. When used as a verb, the word means 'to spread up', 'to stretch', 'to expand', while when used as a noun it means 'string'. Not surprisingly, when acting as morpheme, 張 accompanies nouns which define long, flat objects, such as bows, tables, or pieces of paper (II). Yet, 張 also matches to words like 'mouth' (一張嘴 yī zhāngzuǐ) or ballot (一張選票 yī zhāng xuǎnpiào). One feasible justification is that both the body part and the vote are visually synthesized, the first as something flat (sort of string), the second as the real instrument that enables a vote to be casted. Since both objects stand in the mental eye for something else, we call them metaphorical extension of the real meaning, triggered by the classifier 張 (III).

管 (兒) guǎn(r) stands in Chinese for 'tube' or 'pipe'. The word also acts as classifier for tube-shaped objects, such as flutes and toothpaste tubes. Literature does not provide a precise specification of the association of 管 to these nouns, so it may be possible to assume that the ShapeAttribute length is triggered either by the noun (I), or by the classifier (II).

Another case of vagueness in the determination of what coerces what is provided by the case of 片 piàn. In 一片吐司 yī piàn tǔsī , a piece of bread, the ShapeAttribute flatness is entailed in, and can therefore derived from either 片 piàn as word (also meaning 'slice'), or from 土司 tǔsī, 'sliced bread'. In this uncertainty, one might use this example as evidence for (I). On the contrary, in the case of in 一片地 yī piàn dì, a (flat) piece of land, one can state with almost no doubt that the ShapeAttribute flatness derives from 片 and not from 地 (II), since the latter simply means 'land', 'place', 'earth', 'ground'.

團 tuán corresponds to the English verb 'to roll', 'to roll into a ball', 'to gather'. As a noun, it translates into 'regiment', 'group', 'society', 'body' (which metaphorically can all stand for conglomeration of substance, or "mass" of people). As adjective, 團 stands for 'circular', 'round', 'collective'. As a classifier, 團 collocates with round objects, such as doughs (一團麵團 yī tuán miàntuán).[3] Cases like this, where the metaphorical extension is assumed to be found in the classifier as a noun, have been marked separately in fig. 1, and could be considered a further extension of point (III) (IIIa).

In some cases, metaphorical extensions can be more than assumed. Their justification may lie in the lexical derivation that the word / classifier has inherited from another meaning which conceptually stands in a higher position (as in the case of a node-synset relation).

[1]The upper ontology SUMO (`www.ontologyportal.com`) maps these shape features differently. Length is for istance mapped as LengthMeasure, roundness as ShapeAttribute, flatness as VisualAttribute or SpatialRelation. The author has decided to represent all these shape-related features as subsumed to the self-defined upper concept ShapeAttribute (as in fig. 1).

[2]For reference: Adams and Conklin (1973), Allan (1977), Croft (1994), Denny (1986), Downing (1996), also cited under ((Imai, Saalbach and Stern, 2010):485ff.)

[3]Notice the presence of 團 as suffix of the Chinese word for 'dough', 麵團.

One example for these cases is the Chinese correspondent for English 'tree', 木 mù. The radical can be a semantic or a phonetic component. From 木 derive at least four shape classifiers (which carry 木 in their character): 本 běn, 根 gēn and 株 zhū. When used as proper nouns, all three mean 'root'. The *part_of* relation between classifier and radical is quite straightforward; the metaphorical extension (III) might lie in the fact that from the physical 'root' derives a virtual root, or 'basis', 'foundation' (both words count among the meanings of the three classifiers as nouns). The metaphorization process does not stop at the level of radical-classifier, but seems to continue in some of the expressions generated by the word (e. g. 我們必須找到問題的根源 wǒmen bìxū zhǎodào wèntí de gēnyuán, literally "we must find the root of the problem", with 根源 gēnyuán meaning 'root' - for 'cause' and 'origin').

Another important aspect regarding classifiers that has been noticed from thorough investigations of several shape ones, is the fact that classifiers (when acting either as coercer or borrower of shape information) select specific information within the wide range of possible ShapeAttribute(s). For instance, although 本 běn, 根 gēn and 株 zhū are all used as classifiers for plants and trees, each of them highlight a particular shape, position, or size of the plants and trees they collocate with.

The same observation on selective information can be drawn from the use, in commonsense language, of the word / classifier 顆 kē (e. g. 一颗西瓜 yī kē xīguā, one melon), when for instance compared to 粒 lì (e. g. 一粒子彈 yī lì zǐdàn one bullet). Although both classifiers are used to enhance the shape attribute of roundness, they collocate with different sized objects. 顆 classifies "solid round objects" (such as small spheres, pearls, corn grains, teeth, hearts and satellites), 粒 on the contrary classifies "small round things" (such as peas, bullets, peanuts, pills, grains).[4]

Eventually, what needs to be reminded with regards to classifiers (that should be further stressed in the case shape classifiers are introduced in wordnets) is their "conceptual polysemy". An example can be 條 tiáo. 條 classifies long, flexible, bendable objects, both animate and inanimate. When combined to nouns, this cluster of shape attributes is not evoked by 條 all at once. For instance, when combined with 'shorts' (一條短褲 yī tiáo duǎnkù), only the length of the shorts is highlighted, not their flexibility or viscosity. The selected information retrieved by 條 appears even clearer when compared to 個 ge, most probably the most generic Chinese classifier, usable to classify people and objects in general.

This process of selective information retrieval shows that classifiers act upon the noun they carry with a sort of "selective inference" (Hobbs, 1983a; Hobbs, 1983b). Hobbs associates this to the thinking process and in particular to metaphors, claiming that the meaning of metaphors is only fully understandable if retrieved within their context of use.

A disclaimer needs to be made on the selected examples. The Chinese language is an upper concept itself, and stands for a conundrum of different languages and dialects which constitute the World Chineses. It derives that what sounds as a natural linguistic combination for some might sound exotic for others. The classifiers presented in this study have been extracted from a long list of academic articles and books on the matter, hereby only partially cited (selected reference). The shape classifies that have been selected represent the ones that are mostly cited in examples and that have been consensually defined as shape ones by the majority of the consulted authors. There still remains some disagreement among mother tongue speakers. For instance, according to some of them, the Chinese classifier 枝 zhī, presented by some authors as shape classifier for non-living objects and therefore also reported in fig. 1, is used in commonsense language in rare or specific cases. Other colleagues have claimed that the use of 顆 kē as classifier for 'melon' sounds unnatural, since the shape classifier seems to match with round yet small objects (e. g. 一顆蘋果 yī kē píngguǒ one apple).

Eventually, given the short nature of this paper, implications about the distinction between classifiers, measure words and quantifiers[5], or shape-*based* and shape-*related* classifiers[6] could not be

[4]Information partially retrieved from CEDICT, Chinese-English dictionary, http://cdict.net/

[5]For measure words, classifiers, quantifiers, also see: (Her and Hsieh, 2010)(Shi, 1996)(Zhang and Schmitt, 1998)(Aikhenvald, 2000), Li (1924), Wang (1937), Lü (1953) (in (Song, 2009), ((Chao, 1968):584–620) and Tao (1990:312, in (Huang and Ahrens, 2003)).

[6]Among the authors consulted for the definition of shape-

further deepened.

## 3 Future work

Current wordnets do not encode shape information, and lack a comprehensive mapping of classifiers.

This svelte research aims to show how much lexico-semantic knowledge can be retrieved from these small units of language and their possible metaphorical implications. Its inclusion in wordnets (also married with an ontological analysis, as fig. 1 tries to show) can be beneficiary for both language users and language learners.

The project can be framed within a bigger effort to collect comprehensive information on classifiers (not just shape ones), provided general consensus on their use and meanings. For instance, Hantology (Chou and Huang, 2010)[7] could be further tailored by inserting classifiers. Because the database currently mainly focuses on radicals and characters, classifiers (e. g. 團), are mapped as characters. Since characters are then linked to all the words they respectively generate, it results that one character is often mapped to several upper concepts. The author is aware that the metaphorical extensions of meaning hereby presented are subject to personal interpretation, but this should be nevertheless valued as a primary attempt to try to justify the collocational structure that exists between Chinese classifiers and nouns. Also, given the apparent discrepancy between the use of classifiers in commonsense language and in written language, as mentioned above, it might also be interesting to draw a comparison between real-word and formal use of classifiers in Chinese (starting by 普通話 pǔtōnghuà or Mandarin).

Another already initiated extension of the study can include the cross-linguistic comparison of classifiers, in the search for common patterns, starting by ground literature such as (Matsumoto, 1993; Matsumoto, 1986; Paik and Bond, 2002).


## Acknowledgments

The author greatly thanks Dr. Jiajuan Xiong for the revision of the Chinese entries. Any remaining errors are of the author.


*based* and shape-*related* classifiers are: (Shi, 1996), Tai and Chao (1995, in (Shi, 1996)), (Yichun, Wu and Chung, 2011) and (Sera, Johnson and Yichun, 2013).

[7]See http://hantology.sinica.edu.tw/

**Further notes on fig. 1**

For 條，間，座: ((Song, 2009):27), citing Li (1924/1925). For 條 and 枝、支 also (Sera, Johnson and Yichun, 2013). For 條 also(Imai, Saalbach and Stern, 2010)

For 筐 and 抽屜: ((Song, 2009):17), citing (Chao, 1968). Also ((Song, 2009): 103): "As a classifier, it is used in front of the nouns denoting objects or things in the shape of a long and hollow cylinder, such as writing brush, a gun, a flute, or a tube of toothpaste".

For 張: ((Song, 2009): 18), citing (Chao, 1968). Chao defines classifiers like 張"temporary" measures, because the classifier can be used as both word (with the classifier 個) and classifier. For 張 also (Liang, 2008), ((Srinivasan, 2010): 179) and (Imai, Saalbach and Stern, 2010). Notice that although 張，抽屜，筐 are defined by Chao as "measure word", they all pass the 的 test[a] , and are therefore hereby considered classifiers.

For 條: ((Song, 2009): 100): "[⋯] long objects, such as long benches, long sofas, sausages, boats; long shapes in landscapes and mountain ranges; rivers, watercourses, and pipelines; roads, paths and ways; items and articles in written documents; certain body parts of humans, such as arms, legs, tails, tongues, intestines and people's lives; and certain animals, such as snakes, fish, dogs and cows." For 條 also ((Srinivasan, 2010): 179) and ((Gao and Malt, 2009): 1125).

For 枝: ((Song, 2009): 91): "As a classifier, it is used for classifying sticks and long shaped objects such as writing brushes, pens, pencils, candles, rifles; military troops; songs and music; measurement of light and electronic power [⋯]".

For 股: ((Song, 2009):88).

For 顆 kē, 糰 tuán, 粒 lì, 塊 kuài, 片 piàn and 張 zhāng (exception cases) : (Liang, 2008).

For 根 gēn : ((Srinivasan, 2010): 179).

[a]More on 的 as distinguisher between classifier and measure word: (Her and Hsieh, 2010)

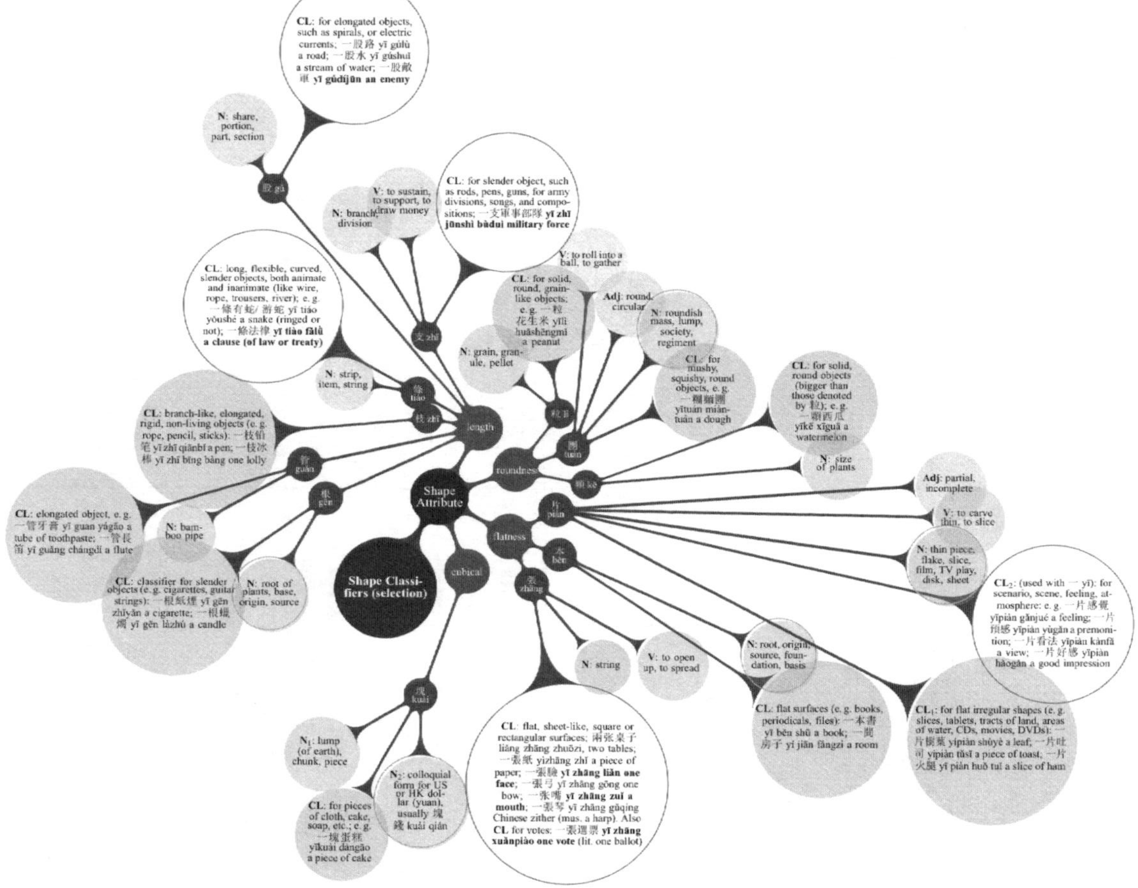


**Figure 1:** Extract of a possible representation of shape classifiers[a]

## Selected References


Alexandra Y. Aikhenvald. 2000. *Classifiers: A Typology of Noun Categorization Devices.* Oxford University Press, Oxford, NY.

Francis Bond and Kyonghee Paik. 2000. Reusing an ontology to generate numeral classifiers. *Proceedings of the 18th International Conference on Computational Linguistics (COLING 2000)*, 90-96.

Yuen-Ren Chao. 1968. *A Grammar of Spoken Chinese*. University of California, California.

Ya-Min Chou and Chu-Ren Huang. 2010. Hantology: Conceptual system discovery based on orthographic convention. In: Chu-Ren Huang, Nicoletta Calzolari, Aldo Gangemi, Alessandro Lenci, Alessandro Oltramari and Laurent Prévot, *Ontology and the Lexicon: A Natural Language Processing Perspective*. Cambridge University Press, Cambridge, London.

Ming Y. Gao and Barbara C. Malt. 2009. Mental representation and cognitive consequences of Chinese individual classifiers. *Language and Cognitive Processes*, 24(7/8): 1124–1179.

One-Soon Her and Chen-Tien Hsieh. 2010. On the semantic distinction between classifiers and measure words in Chinese. *Language and Linguistics*, 11(2):527–551.

Jerry Hobbs. 1983a. Metaphor interpretation and selective inferencing, cognitive processes in understanding metaphors (part I). *Empirical Studies of the Arts*, 1(1):17–33.

Jerry Hobbs. 1983b. Metaphor interpretation and selective inferencing, cognitive processes in understanding metaphor (part II). *Empirical Studies of the Arts*, 1(2):125–141.

Chu-Ren Huang and Kathleen Ahrens. 2003. Individuals, kinds and events: Classifier coercion of noun. *Language Sciences*, 25(4): 353–373.

Chu-Ren Huang, Ke-Jiann Chen and Ching-Hsiung Lai (*eds.*). 1997. *Mandarin Daily Dictionary of Chinese Classifiers*. Mandarin Daily Press, Taipei, Taiwan.

Chu-Ren Huang, Ru-Yng Chang and Hsiang-Bin Lee. 2010. In: Chu-Ren Huang, Nicoletta Calzolari, Aldo Gangemi, Alessandro Lenci, Alessandro Oltramari and Laurent Prévot, *Ontology and the Lexicon: A Natural Language Processing Perspective*. Cambridge University Press, Cambridge, London.

Mutsumi Imai, Henrik Saalbach and Elsbeth Stern. 2010. Are Chinese and German children taxonomic, thematic, or shape biased? Influence on classifiers and cultural contexts. *Frontiers in Cultural Psychology*, 1(194) (unspecified page no.).[8]

Neal Szu-Yen Liang. 2008. The acquisition of Chinese shape classifiers by L2 adult learners. *Proceedings of the 20th North American Conference on Chinese Linguistics NACCL-20*, volume 1:309–326. Columbus, Ohio, The Ohio State University, April 2008.

Yō Matsumoto. 1993. Japanese numeral classifiers: A study of semantic categories and lexical organization. *Linguistics*, 31(1993): 667–713.

Yō Matsumoto. 1986. The Japanese classifier -hon. A prototype-semantic analysis. *Sophia Linguistica*, 20(21):73–81.

Hazel Shu Wen Mok, Heshley Gao Huini and Francis Bond. 2012. Using WordNet to predict numeral classifiers in Chinese and Japanese. *Proceedings of the 6th Global WordNet Conference*, January 9-13, 2012, Matsue, JP.

Kyonghee Paik and Francis Bond. 2012. Spatial representation and shape classifiers in Japanese and Korean. In: David Beaver, Stefan Kaufmann, Brady Clark and Louis Casillas (eds.), *The Construction of Meaning*. CSLI Publications, Stanford, 163–180.

Kyonghee Paik and Francis Bond. 2001. Multilingual general of numeral classifiers using a common ontology. *Proceedings of the 19th International Conference on Computer*


[8] Further reference under: `http://www.frontiersin.org/cultural_psychology/10.3389/fpsyg.2010.00194/abstract`

*Processing of Oriental Languages (ICCPOL 01)*, 141–147.

Francesca Quattri 2013a. Square, zero, kitchen, start: Insights on cross-linguistic conceptual encoding. *Proceedings of the 2nd International Workshop on Computational Creativity, Concept Invention and General Intelligence (C3GI 13)*, volume 2.

Francesca Quattri 2013b. The misanderstanding about shapes: What we think shapes are and what they are not. *The 21st Annual Conference of the International Association of Chinese Linguistics (IACL 13).*

Maria D. Sera, Kaitlin R. Johnson and Jenny Yichun. 2013. Classifiers augment and maintain shape-based categorization in Mandarin speakers. *Language and Cognition*, 5(1):1–23.

Yu-Zhi Shi. 1996. Proportion of extensional dimensions: The primary cognitive basis for shape-based classifiers in Chinese. *Journal of the Chinese Language Teachers Association* 31(2):37–59.

Jiang Song. 2009. *The Semantic Structure of Chinese Classifiers and Its Implications for Linguistic Relativity*. Doctoral dissertation, University of Hawai'i.

Mahesh Srinivasan. 2010. Do classifiers predict differences in cognitive processing? A study of nominal classification in Mandarin Chinese. *Language and Cognition*, 2(2): 177–190.

Shi Zhang and Bernd Schmitt. 1998. Language-dependent classification: The mental representation of classifiers in cognition, memory and evaluation. *Journal of Experimantal Psychology* 4(3):375–385.

Jenny Yichun, Kuo Jiun-Shiung Wu and Shu-Chuang Chung. 2011. Computer-assisted learning of Chinese shape classifiers. 《華語文教學研究》 8(2):99–122.

# Leveraging Morpho-semantics for the Discovery of Relations in Chinese Wordnet


**Shu-Kai Hsieh**
Graduate Institute of Linguistics
National Taiwan University
Taipei, Taiwan
shukaihsieh@ntu.edu.tw

**Yu-Yun Chang**
Graduate Institute of Linguistics
National Taiwan University
Taipei, Taiwan
yuyun.unita@gmail.com



## Abstract

Semantic relations of different types have played an important role in wordnet, and have been widely recognized in various fields. In recent years, with the growing interests of constructing semantic network in support of intelligent systems, automatic semantic relation discovery has become an urgent task. This paper aims to extract semantic relations relying on the *in situ* morpho-semantic structure in Chinese which can dispense of an outside source such as corpus or web data. Manual evaluation of thousands of word pairs shows that most relations can be successful predicted. We believe that it can serve as a valuable starting point in complementing with other approaches, which will hold promise for the robust lexical relations acquisition.


## 1 Introduction

Semantic relations are at the core of WordNet-alike architecture, and constitute the essential and integral part of linguistic and conceptual knowledge formalization. However, the manual labeling task of semantic relations is very laborious.

To minimize the labor, in recent years, automatic ways of extracting semantic relations from textual data have been proposed. Among these methods, extensive works have been done based on the so-called *pattern-based* approaches, which was pioneered by (Hearst, 1992). The patterns predefined or plucked out of a corpus are often referred to as *lexico-syntactic patterns*, which serve as an information marker for a certain relation between two concepts. Later representative works using such approaches include (Cimiano et al., 2005), and (Pantel and Pennacchiotti, 2006), etc. Pattern-based extraction has shown quite reasonable success characterized by a (relatively) high precision rate, but suffers from a very low recall resulting from the fact that the patterns are rare in corpora. Remedies against the problem involve exploiting scaled data from the web (Cimiano et al., 2005), but runs the risk of influenced by the web genre (Alain, 2010).

To enrich the relations coverage in Chinese Wordnet (CWN), in this paper, we propose an *in situ* approach by exploiting the morph-semantic information. This method, simple and straightforward as it seems, does not incur the difficulties associated with *lexical gaps* in cross-language mapping that any translation-based model would encounter; and it is also economic and complementary with previous approaches in that we can dispense of an outside corpus resource.

In what follows, Section 2 gives a brief summary of lexical semantic relations acquisition from two perspectives. Section 3 explains the proposed methods for the automatic discovery of semantic relations, which are the main focus of this study. Section 4 shows the experiment results and discussion. Finally, we conclude this paper in Section 5.

## 2 Relations in Chinese Wordnet

Modelling on English WordNet, CWN has been launched by Academia Sinica in 2006 and continuously broadened its scope (Huang et al., 2010).[1]. The initial version of CWN contains a manually created fine-grained senses repository but sparse relations. However, semantic relation labeling is a time-consuming and labor-demanding task. Two main methods were employed to automatic relation acquisition.

### 2.1 Bilingual Bootstrapping Approach

Though lexical semantic relations (LSRs) could be presumed to be *more* universal than word senses in human languages, a direct

[1]Freely available at http://lope.linguistics.ntu.edu.tw/cwn

copying or simple porting of LSRs from one wordnet to another could possibly lead to invalid relations in the target wordnet. A broader view on the underlying inference logic of cross-language LSRs with 26 rules was first proposed by (Huang et al., 2002) and formally introduced in (Hsieh, 2009). A series of large-scaled bilingual bootstrapping experiments showed substantial improvements (with 55% precision) over baseline model (47%). However, it was also reported that among the correctly predicted LSRs, a large portion (c.a. 60%) belongs to *non-lexical relations* such as `similar to`, `pertainym`, `also see`, etc.

To look deeper into the issues, second experiment focusing only on the `hypernymy-troponymy` among the verbs was conducted. The bootstrapping model returned totally 12214 verb pairs mapped from WordNet 3.0, which were manually evaluated. The analysis shows that around 50% verb pairs can be recognized as fit in CWN, however, two main error types are identified: [1] Lexicalization of verbs: similar to the problems of lexical gap appeared in the cross-language sense mapping, a single word in English often has meanings that require several words in Chinese to explain. By analyzing the results, it is found that many verbs could not be described by a single lexeme in Chinese. [2] Mismatch of synset: other than the above, there are cases when the hypernymy-troponymy relations of the verb pairs are approved, but the synset that CWN chooses is not the same with that of PWN. This could be due to the different semantic ranges between CWN and PWN hypernymy-troponymy pairs, or due to the subtlety of sense division when the sense levels are similar.

The bilingual bootstrapping experiments showed that lexical relations turn out to be not subject to automatic importing and would still require tremendous human efforts of validations.

### 2.2 Pattern-based Approach

There has been a variety of studies on the automatic acquisition of lexical semantic relations, Hearst (Hearst, 1992) first proposed a *lexico-syntactic pattern* based method for automatic acquisition of hyponymy from unrestricted texts, and since then automatically finding semantic relations by using various pattern-based algorithm has become the most common approach.

We (Lo et al., 2008) have tried to define some patterns (e.g., *a manner of*) to extract troponymy among verbs in Chinese. To avoid the interference of unnecessary contextual information which may include modal verbs, hedging, negation that often occur in different corpus genres, we applied the proposed patterns on the gloss of CWN. The results were evaluated with the substitution tests. Substitution test is commonly used in linguistic literature (Tsai et al., 2002); EuroWordnet provided linguistic tests for each semantic relation to examine the validity. In (Tsai et al., 2002), sentence formulae were created following the frame in EuroWordnet to examine the validity of certain semantic relations in Chinese. Linguistic semantic tests help researcher check if two word meanings have a certain kind of semantic relation or not, and further ensure the quality and consistence of the database. Therefore, following the previous framework, a set of sentence formulae based on properties of troponymy was created to verify the correctness of hypernymy-troponymy verb pairs. However, due to data sparseness, the system can achieve only high precision but low recall.

## 3 Morpho-semantic Linkage

Instead of assuming any *external context* in which words to be linked appear, we propose to exploit the *language-internal evidence* manifested at the morpho-syntactic levels in Chinese, which is assumably guided by underlying semantic composition of morphemes.

### 3.1 Morpho-semantics in WordNets

The idea of exploiting morpho-semantic information for the enrichment of WordNet has been discussed and implemented in the WordNet community for a while. (Miller and Fellbaum, 2003) first described the importance of adding "morphosemantic links" to WordNet, with later works (Fellbaum et al., 2009) on the classification of regular polysemous patterns of morphosemantic V-N pairs related via *-er* affixation (e.g., *build-builder*).

The notion of *morpho-semantic links* (MSLs) has been applied to other (morphologically-rich) languages such as Czech (Pala and Hlaváčková, 2007) (in terms of `D-relations`), Turkish (Bilgin et al., 2004) and Bantu languages (Bosch et al., 2008). It is worth of mentioning that the proposed *morpho-semantic relations* or *derivational relations* are relations that hold among literals (lemmas) rather than synsets, which leaves some room of discussion about the extra level these relations should be anchored because neither *paradigmatic* nor *syntagmatic* relations would fit.

It is note here that for morphologically-poor languages like Chinese, the MSLs are quite different in that they do not exist between *stems* and *suffixes*, but between *word-to-be/word-used-to-be* morphemes instead. This has the practical advantages for the enrichment of existing paradigmatic relations, as we will introduce in the following.

### 3.2 Probing Morpho-Semantic Relations in Chinese

The vast majority of Chinese characters represent the *morphemes*. It has been always a controversy over the notion of *wordhood* in the lexical history of Chinese. In a way any Chinese character can be seen as *word-to-be* or *word-used-to-be* morphemes. Given the fact that the relative predominance of the mono-syllabic *word* in ancient Chinese has shifted to bi-syllabic words in modern Chinese, the huge semantic weight carried by the morphemes has made the idea of *character-centered* lexicon deeply ingrained in Chinese mind. Orthographically, the lack of word delimiter (such as space) in texts worsens the achievement of consensus regarding the distinction between words, compounds and phrases, and thus makes the segmentation a long-standing heated topic in Chinese NLP.

We follow the cognitive-functional stance in the respect that lexicon and syntax form a continuum rather than two strictly separated modules. We argue that the *Morpho-Semantic Relations* (MSRs), i.e., the ways morphemes combine to form composite meanings, can function as the organic linkage in revealing the composition mechanism among the continuum of different lexical units in varied contexts. In terms of WordNet's paradigmatic relations, this means that morpho-semantic information in Chinese can be used to identify these relations based on the *position* and *semantic role* of morphemes in modification.

In the case of Verb-Verb (compound) words, where the word is composed of two verbal morphemes, linguistics have sorted out different types resulting from the interplay of morphemes within (Li and Thompson, 1981). For instance, for the type of so-called 'parallel' VV compounds, $V_1$ (verb in the first position) and $V_2$ (verb in the second position) share the similar meaning (`near synonyms`), such as *bang-zhu* 'help-assist' (help), *fang-qi* 'loosen-abandon' (give up). With a fine-grained sense analysis, we can label the `troponymy` between $V_1$ and $V_1V_2$, where $V_1$ is widely recognized as the component that carries heavier semantic load in VV compound (a.k.a. *left-headedness*).

In the case of Noun-Noun (compound) words, e.g., *noodle-shop* 'mian-dian' (noodle shop), where the word is composed of two nominal morphemes, the $N_1$*modifier* - $N_2$*head* structure is prevalently observed (a.k.a. *right-headedness*). The linkage between $N_1N_2$ and $N2$ can be labeled as `hypernymy-hyponymy`.

## 4 From MSL to Lexical Semantic Relations

### 4.1 Hypothesis

As argued in previous section, *Morpho-Semantic Linkage* abound in abundant relational knowledge. In this study, we aim to enrich the CWN with relations leveraged by operationalizing MSL.

The automatic labeling of the lexical semantic relations on word-pairs is quite straightforward. For $N_1N_2$ compounds, $\prec N_1N_2, N_2\succ$ pairs are labeled with `hypernymy-hyponymy`, and $\prec N_1N_2, N_1\succ$ pairs are labeled with `meronymy-holonymy`.

The cases of VV compounds are trickier, the flow of judgement is shown in algorithm 1. When $V_1$ has `synonymy` or `near-synonymy` with $V_2$, then $V_1V_2$ are troponyms of both $V_1$ and $V_2$. If $V_2$ is on the list of 完住掉開壞成, which is a subclass of the VV compounds that are often called *resultative compounds*, for there is a *causal relation* between the event represented by the first compound of such a compound and the event/state represented by the second component.

```
Data: VV compounds
Result: Labeled relations between V1V2
        and V1/V2
initialization (POS tagging);
if V1 is V2 then
  | return troponymy;
else
  | if V2 is 完住掉開壞成 then
  |   | return causality;
  | if V2 is 上下來去進回出落入向往過起
  | then
  |   | return directional;
  | end
  | else
  |   | return pertainymy;
  | end
end
```

**Algorithm 1:** Pseudo code for relations labeling between $V_1V_2$ and $V_1/V2$

### 4.2 Experiments

In this section, we discuss the experiment we designed, the evaluation and error analysis.

The first step is to create a list of term pairs, which a total of 561,703 words covered in CWN [2], Sinica BOW [3], and Ministry of Education Online Chinese Dictionary [4]. In this experiment, we focus only on bi-syllabic words represented by two characters, which constitute the largest proportion of Chinese vocabulary repository.

In order to filter out a coarse-grained bi-syllabic word list, only both characters of a bi-syllabic word that could be found in the big word list, are preserved. Additionally, four principles are applied to construct a more fine-grained word list: [1] the part-of-speech tags of both characters within a bi-syllabic word should be NN or VV; [2] bi-syllabic words containing metaphors are excluded; [3] bi-syllabic morphemic word (e.g., 齷齪 (sordid)) or archaic words (e.g.,搗家) are not included; and [4] proper nouns, (e.g., 成龍(Jackie Chan)) are not considered. Therefore, a list with 1482 bi-syllabic words are produced. Using the hypotheses proposed in section 4.1, the relations are automatically labelled on the related word pairs.

A manual evaluation of the resulting semantic relations lists was conducted. We have created a wiki-based collaborative platform[5] on which registered users can contribute to CWN by adding new entries, editing existing ones and rating one another's contribution to ensure the quality of collective intelligence (Lee et al, 2013). Figure 1 shows the snapshot of the system.

With three linguistic graduate students judging the correctness, the inter-annotator agreement measured by `Fleiss kappa` (Fleiss, 1971) was used, which is defined as:

$$k = \frac{\overline{P} - \overline{P_e}}{1 - \overline{P_e}}$$

where the numerator expresses the degree of agreement actually achieved, and the denominator the degree of agreement that is possible above chance. As a result, it's interesting to see that there is a very poor agreement between three raters ($k = -0.7069972$) on the predicted relations of $\prec W_1 - W_1W_2 \succ$, which also gets low precision rate; while agreement achieves a moderate degree (with $k = 0.5835113$) on the predicted relations of $\prec W_2 - W_1W_2 \succ$, which also gets high performance in precision.[6] Figure 2 shows the enrichment of relations through the experiment.

### 4.3 Discussion

The experiment we carried out gives rise to some issues for discussion. Table 1 shows the performance for each predicted relation. When we scrutinize the portion with low precision rate, we found that the problematic cases are mostly from the predicted `meronymy-holonymy` relations between NN compounds, i.e., $\prec N_1N_2 - N_1 \succ$. It is in fact not surprising in that the definition of *part-whole* is not easily stated, and the judgement criteria in the previous literature are not unproblematic too. For instance, given the restrictive rules

[2]See `http://lope.linguistics.ntu.edu.tw/cwn/`

[3]See `http://bow.sinica.edu.tw/`

[4]See `http://dict.revised.moe.edu.tw/`

[5]See `http://lope.linguistics.ntu.edu.tw/cwikin/`

[6]The results will be accessible at `http://140.112.147.131/`

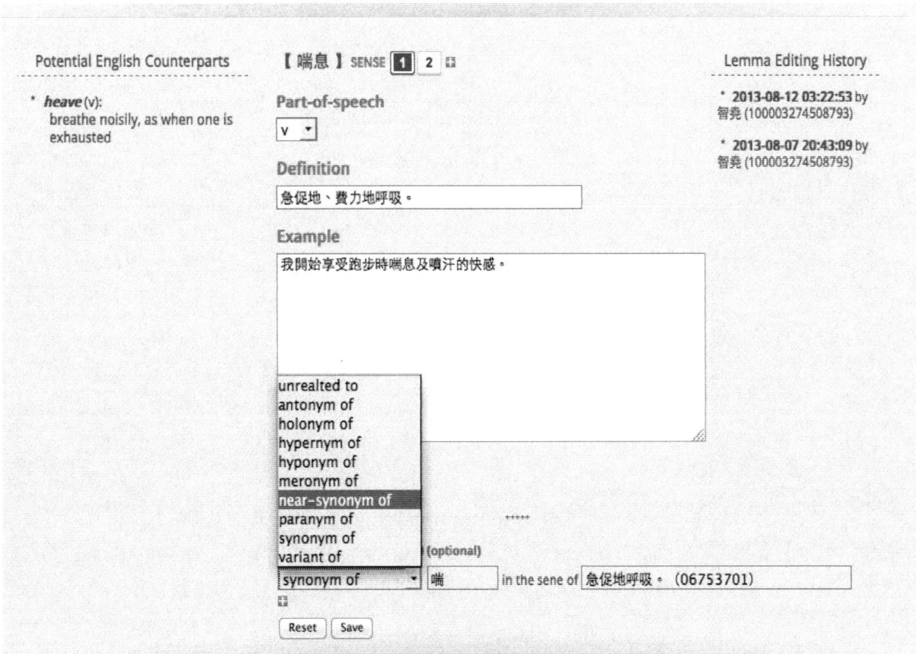


Figure 1: User graphical interface of CWIKIN

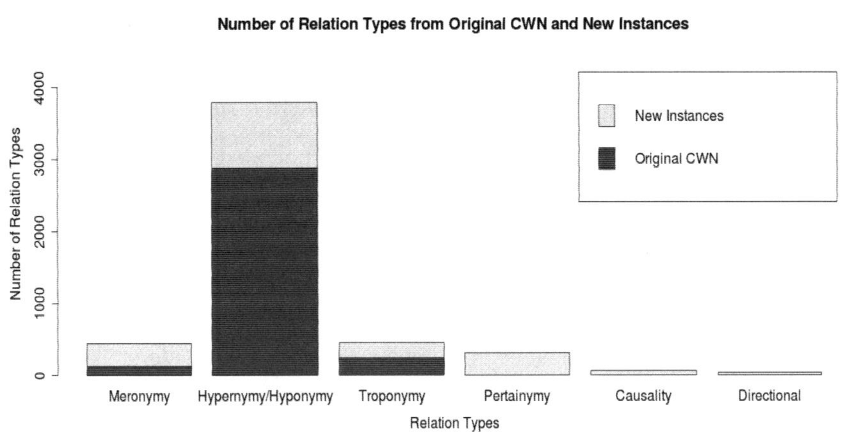


Figure 2: Relations added

that Cruse (1986) sets on the meronymy relation with the co-existence of both the '$N_1N_2$ is part of $N_1$' and '$N_1$ has $N_1N_2$' paraphrases, the raters did not all agree that the relation hold between 黨部 (party headquarter) and 黨 (political party).

Another main error sources come from the predicted `troponymy-hypernymy` relations between $\prec V_1V_2 - V_1 \succ$. Recall that we hypothesize that if $V_1$ and $V_2$ are synonymous, then $V_1V_2$ is automatically labeled as troponym of $V_1$. The errors arose here can be mainly ascribed to the lack of consistent Chinese thesaurus. In this experiment, the CWN synset (fine-grained synonym determination) and CILIN semantic class (coarse-grained synonym determination) are integrated for prediction, both has different criteria regarding the sameness or nearness of senses between two verbs. In addition, no proper rules for the evaluation of troponymy among raters constitute the difficulties as well.

Furthermore, there are two points can be made. [1], the experiment of relation discovery is conducted at the level of word-lemma, not concept(word-sense), in terms of wordnet, the generic label 'semantic relations' are regarded as the relation occurring between *linguistic units* rather than between concepts (i.e., *synsets.*) Currently, the predicted relations are presumably connected with the first sense of the word lemma in CWN. A fine-grained annotation will be left for future work. [2], in the evaluation task, when the raters did not agree with the predicted relation type, they also provide proper relation types for the pair, which are not *named relations* explicitly defined in WordNet. For example, the *qualia modification* between certain $N_1N_2$ and $N_2$, such as 肉醬(meat sauce) - 醬(sauce). This is different from patterned-based approaches where a *bottom-up* methodology is taken because named and explicitly defined semantic relations of interest are presumed before lexico-syntactic patterns are extracted and utilized to search for instances of the relations

## 5 Conclusion

Lexical semantic relations offers rich linguistic and conceptual knowledge information and are the most to fill in for wordnets. Semantic relations extraction has been one of the most important tasks in many fields. The challenges pertaining to this task are multifaceted. The most active *pattern-based* approaches provide a reasonable solution, but poses difficulties as well.

In this paper, we have presented a *linguistic alternative* to the task in Chinese by resorting to resources of language in itself. Rather than focusing on the *patterns design - relation extraction* model, a notion of *Morpo-semantic links* is proposed to support the extraction and labeling of a wide variety of semantic relations in Chinese. The experiment shows that it is possible to discover semantic relations without being influenced by corpus size and genres. This simple strategy can also serve as the linguistic baseline for related works.

Future works include: [1] extending to VN and NV compounds (Song and Qiu, 1981), and more fined-grained classification of semantic relations among these word-pairs, and [2] mapping with Japanese Wordnet where an amount of Chinese characters are employed for advanced cross-linguistic validation. We also hope that the work presented here will shed new light on the understanding of morpho-semantic representation of natural languages.

## References


Alain Auger and Caroline Barrière (eds). 2010. *Probing Semantic Relations.* John Benjamins Publishing, Amsterdam/Philadelphia.

Orhan Bilgin, Özlem Çetinoglu and Kemal Oflazer. 2004. Morphosemantic Relations In and Across Wordnets: A Study Based on Turkish. In: *Proceedings of the Second Global WordNet Conference*, 60–66.

Sonja Bosch, Christiane Fellbaum and Karel Pala. 2008. Enhancing WordNets with Morphological Relations: A Case Study from Czech, English and Zulu. In: *Proceedings of the Fourth Global WordNet Conference*, 74–90.

Philipp Cimiano, Aleksander Pivk Lars, Schmidt-Thieme and Steffen Staab. 2005. Learning Taxonomic Relations from Heterogeneous Sources of

| Word Pairs | Type of Relations | Precision | Observations |
|---|---|---|---|
| W1-W1W2 | Meronymy | 33% | 956 |
| | Pertainymy | 25% | 352 |
| | Troponymy | 29% | 174 |
| W2-W1W2 | Causality | 90% | 73 |
| | Directional | 90% | 43 |
| | Hypernymy/Hyponymy | 95% | 956 |
| | Pertainymy | 93% | 241 |
| | Troponymy | 92% | 169 |

Table 1: Inter-annotator agreement across all relations


Evidence. In: Buitelaar (eds),*Ontology Learning from Text: Methods, Evaluation and Applications*, 55–73.

Christiane Fellbaum, Anne Osherson, and Peter. E. Clark. 2009. Putting Semantics into WordNet's "Morphosemantic" Links. In: Zygmunt Vetulani and Hans Uszkoreit (eds). *Human Language Technology. Challenges of the Information Society*, 350-358.

Joseph. L. Fleiss. 1971. Measuring Nominal Scale Agreement among Many Raters. *Psychological Bulletin*, 76(5): 378–382.

Marti A. Hearst. 1992. Automatic Acquisition of Hyponyms from Large Text Corpora. In: *Proceedings of the Fourth International Conference on Computational Linguistics (COLING)*, 539–545.

Shu-Kai Hsieh. 2009. Formal Description of Lexical Semantic Relations. *Concentric: Studies in Linguistics*, 35(1):87–109.

Chu-Ren Huang, I-Ju Tseng, and Dylan Tsai. 2002. Translating Lexical Semantic Relations. In: *SEMANET '02 Proceedings of the 2002 workshop on Building and using Semantic Networks*, 1–7.

Chu-Ren Huang,Shu-Kai Hsieh,Jia-Fei Hong,Yun-Zhu Chen,I-Li Su,Yong-Xiang Chen and Sheng-Wei Huang. 2010. Chinese Wordnet: Design, Implementation, and Application of an Infrastructure for Cross-Lingual Knowledge Processing. *Journal of Chinese Information Processing*, 24(2):14–23.

Chih-Yao Lee, Yu-Yun Chang, Shu-Kai Hsieh, Jia-Fei Hong and Chu-Ren Huang. 2013. *CWIKIN: A wiki that Helps Quicken the Development of Chinese Wordnet.* The 8th International Conference of the Asian Association for Lexicography. Bali, Indonesia.

Charles N. Li and Sandra A. Thompson. 1981. *Mandarin Chinese: A Functional Reference Grammar.* Berkeley: University of California Press.

Chiao-Shan Lo, Yi-Rung Chen, Chih-Yu Lin, and Shu-Kai Hsieh. 2008. Automatic Labeling of Troponymy for Chinese Verbs. In: *Proceedings of the 20th Conference on Computational Linguistics and Speech Processing (ROCLING).*

George Miller and Christiane Fellbaum. 2003. Morphosemantic Links in WordNet. *Traitement Automatique de Langue*, 44(2):69–80.

Karel Pala and Dana Hlaváčková. 2007. Derivational Relations in Czech WordNet. In: *ACL '07 Proceedings of the Workshop on Balto-Slavonic Natural Language Processing: Information Extraction and Enabling Technologies.* Stroudsburg, PA, USA.

Patrick Pantel and Marco Pennacchiotti. 2006. Espresso: Leveraging Generic Patterns for Automatically Harvesting Semantic Relations. In: *Proceedings of Conference on Computational Linguistics / Association for Computational Linguistics (COLING/ACL-06).*

Gerardo Sierra, Rodrigo Alarcón, César Aguilar and Carme Bach. 2010. Definitional Verbal Patterns for Semantic Relation Extraction. In: Alain Auger and Caroline Barrière (eds). *Probing Semantic Relations.* John Benjamins Publishing, Amsterdam/Philadelphia.

Zuoyan Song and Qiu Likun. 2013. Qualia Relations in Chinese Nominal Compounds Containing Verbal Elements. *International Journal of Knowledge and Language Processing*, 28(1):114–133.

Dylan B. Tsai, Chu-Ren Huang, Shu-Chuan Tseng, Elanna J.I.Lin, Keh-jiann Chen and Yuan-hsun Chuang. 2002. Chinese Lexical Semantic Relations: Definition and Classification Criteria. *Journal of Chinese Information Processing*, 2002(4):21–31.

# Aligning an Italian WordNet with a Lexicographic Dictionary: Coping with limited data


| Tommaso Caselli | Carlo Strapparava | Laure Vieu | Guido Vetere |
|---|---|---|---|
| TrentoRISE | FBK-HLT | LOA-CNR & IRIT-CNRS | IBM CAS |
| Via Sommarive, 18 | Via Sommarive, 18 | 118 route de Narbonne | P.zza Manci, 17 |
| Povo (TN) IT-38123 | Povo (TN) IT-38123 | Toulouse F-31062 | Povo (TN) IT-38123 |
| t.caselli@trentorise.eu | strappa@fbk.eu | vieu@irit.fr | gvetere@it.ibm.com |



## Abstract

This work describes the evaluations of two approaches, Lexical Matching and Sense Similarity, for word sense alignment between MultiWordNet and a lexicographic dictionary, Senso Comune De Mauro, when having few sense descriptions (MultiWordNet) and no structure over senses (Senso Comune De Mauro). The results obtained from the merging of the two approaches are satisfying, with F1 values of 0.47 for verbs and 0.64 for nouns.


## 1 Introduction

This work is situated in the field of word sense alignment, a research area which has seen an increasing interest in recent years and which is a key requirement for achieving semantic interoperability between different lexical-semantic resources (Matuschek and Gurevych, 2013). Our goal is to automatically import high-quality glosses in Italian in MultiWordNet (Pianta et al., 2002) (MWN) by aligning its synsets to the entries of a lexicographic dictionary, namely the Senso Comune De Mauro (SCDM), thus providing Italian with a more complete and robust version of MWN. For SCDM, the linking of the entries with MWN plays a double role. On the one hand, it will introduce lexical-semantic relations, thus facilitating its use for NLP tasks in Italian, and, on the other hand, it will make SCDM a structurally and semantically interoperable resource for Italian, to which other lexical-semantic resources (both in Italian, such as PAROLE-SIMPLE-CLIPS (Ruimy et al., 2003), and in English, such as VerbNet (Kipper Schuler, 2005), among others), sense annotated corpora (e.g. the MultiSemCor corpus (Bentivogli and Pianta, 2005)), and Web-based encyclopedia (e.g. Wikipedia) can be connected.

At this stage of development we focused on the alignment of verbs and nouns. The remaining of this paper is organized as follows. Section 2 will state the task and describe the characteristics of the two lexica. In Section 3 some related works and the perculiarities of our work are discussed. The approaches we have adopted are described in Section 4. The evaluation is carried out in Section 5, including an error analysis. Finally, in Section 6 conclusions and future works are reported.

## 2 Problem Description and Resources

Following (Matuschek and Gurevych, 2013), word sense alignment (WSA) can be formally defined as a list of pairs of senses from two lexical-semantic resources. A pair of aligned senses denotes the same meaning. For instance, taken the two senses of the word "*day*" "`amount of hours of work done in one day` and "`the recurring hours established by contract or usage for work`" (taken from translated SCDM and MWN, respectively), they must be aligned as they are clearly equivalent.

### 2.1 MultiWordNet

MWN is a computational multilingual lexicon perfectly aligned to Princeton WN 1.6. As in WN, concepts are organized in synonym sets (*synsets*) which are hierarchically connected by means of hypernym relations (*is_a*). Additional semantic relations such as meronymy, troponymy, nearest synonym and others are encoded as well. The Italian section of MWN is composed of 38,653 synsets, with 4,985 synsets for verbs and 28,517 synsets for nouns. Each synset is accompanied by a gloss describing its meaning and, when present, one or more examples of use. Only 3,177 glosses (8,21%) are in Italian and, in particular, 402 for verbs and 2,481 for nouns.

### 2.2 Senso Comune De Mauro

The SCDM lexicon is part of a larger research initiative, *Senso Comune*[1] (Oltramari et al. (2013)).

[1] `http://www.sensocomune.it`

Senso Comune aims at building an open knowledge base for the Italian language, designed as a crowd-sourced initiative that stands on the solid ground of an ontological formalization and well-established lexical resources. The lexicon entries have been obtained from the De Mauro GRADIT dictionary and consists in the 2,071 most frequent Italian words, for a total of 11,939 fundamental senses. As for verbs we have 3,827 senses, corresponding to 643 lemmas, with an average polysemy of 5.9 senses per lemma. As for nouns we have 4,586 senses, corresponding to 1,111 lemmas with an average polysemy of 4.12 senses per lemma. In SCDM, word senses are encoded following lexicographic principles and are associated with lexicographic examples of usage.

Senso Comune comprises three modules: i.) a top level module for basic ontological concepts; ii.) a lexical module for linguistic and lexicographic structures; and iii.) a frame module for modeling the predicative structure of verbs and nouns. The top level ontology is inspired by DOLCE (Descriptive Ontology for Linguistic and Cognitive Engineering) (Masolo et al., 2002). All nominal entries have been manually classified according to the ontological concepts and an ontological classification of verb entries will start in the near future. With respect to MWN, word senses are not hierarchically structured and no semantic relation is encoded. Senses of polysemous entries have a flat representation, one following the other.

## 3 Related Works

Previous works in word sense alignment can be divided into two main groups: a.) approaches and frameworks which aim at linking lexica based on different models to WN synsets (Rigau and Eneko (1995); Navigli (2006); Roventini et al. (2007)) or language resources, such as Wikipedia (Ruiz-Casado et al. (2005); Mihalcea (2007); Niemann and Gurevych (2011)), and b.) approaches towards the merging of different language resources (Gurevych et al. (2012); Navigli and Ponzetto (2012)). Our work clearly fits into the first group. While different methods are employed (similarity-based approaches *vs.* graph-based approaches), common elements of these works are: i.) the extensive use of lexical knowledge based on the sense descriptions such as the WN glosses or an article first paragraph as in the case of Wikipedia; and ii.) the extension of the basic sense descriptions with additional information such as hypernyms for WN entries, domains labels or categories for dictionaries or Wikipedia entries so as to expand the set of available information, thus improving the quality of the alignments.

As for our task, the most similar work is (Navigli, 2006) where entries from a lexicographic dictionary, namely the Oxford English Dictionary (OED), are mapped to WN. The author adopts and compares two methods: a.) a pure lexical matching function based on the notion of lexical overlap (Lesk, 1986) of the lemmas in the sense descriptions; and b.) a semantic matching based on a knowledge-based WSD system, Structural Semantic Interconnections (SSI), built upon WN and enriched with collocation information representing semantic relatedness between sense pairs. In this latter approach, first each sense description in WN and in the OED is disambiguated by means of SSI with respect to the WN sense inventory, thus obtaining a semantic description as a bag of concepts. Then, two senses are matched if a relation edge is identified between the concepts in the description of each sense in the two lexica. Both approaches are evaluated with respect to a manually created gold standard. The author reports an overall F1 measure of 73.84% for lexical matching, and of 83.11% for semantic matching.

With respect to the SCDM, the OED has some advantages, namely i.) the distinction between core senses and subsenses for polysemous entries; ii.) the presence of hypernyms explicitly signalled; and iii.) domain labels associated with word senses. Such kind of information is not present in the SCDM where senses are presented as a flat list and no enrichment of the sense descriptions with additional information is available, except for the ontological tagging of nouns. Moreover, the low number of MWN glosses in Italian prevents a straightforward application of state-of-the-art methods for sense alignment. MWN sense descriptions must be built up from other sources. Thus, the main issue we are facing is related to data sparseness, that is how to tackle sense alignment when we have few descriptions in Italian (MWN side) and few meta-data and no structure over senses (SCDM side).

## 4 Methodology

The automatic alignment of senses has been conducted by applying two approaches for constructing the sense representations of the resources and evaluation.

### 4.1 Lexical Match

In the first approach, Lexical Match, for each word $w$ and for each sense $s$ in the given resources $R \in$ {MWN, SCDM} we constructed a sense descriptions $d_R(s)$ as a bag of words in Italian. Provided the different characteristics of the two resources, two different types of bag of words have been built. As for the SCDM, the bag of words is represented by the lexical items in the textual definition of $s_w$, automatically lemmatized and part-of-speech analyzed with the TextPro tool suite (Pianta et al., 2008) with standard stopword removal. On the other hand, for each synset, $S$, and for each part of speech in analysis, the sense description of each MWN synset was built by optionally exploiting:

- the set of synset words in a synset excluding $w$;
- the set of direct hypernyms of $s$ in the taxonomy hierarchy in MWN;
- the set of synset words in MWN standing in the relation of *nearest synonyms* with $s$;
- the set of synset words in MWN composing the manually disambiguated glosses of $s$ from the "Princeton Annotated Gloss Corpus"[2]. To extract the corresponding Italian synset(s), we have ported MWN to WN 30;
- the set of synset words in MWN composing the gloss of $s$ in Italian (when available);
- for verbs, the set of synset words in MWN standing in the relations of *entailment/is_entailed*, *causes/is_caused* with $s$;
- for nouns, the set of synset words in MWN standing in the relations of *part_of/has_part*, *has_member/is_member* with $s$.

The alignment of senses is based on the notion of lexical overlap. We used `Text::Similarity` v.0.09 module[3], and in particular the method `Text::Similarity::Overlaps`, to obtain the overlap value between two bags of words of $s_w$. Text similarity is based on counting the number of overlapping tokens between the two strings, normalized by the length of the strings.

One of the well known limitation of the Lexical Match approach is the so called "lexical gap" problem (Meyer and Gurevych, 2011), i.e. a reduced number of overlapping words. To overcome this limit, we have exploited a newly developed multilingual resource, BabelNet (Navigli and Ponzetto, 2012), which has been obtained by merging together WN synsets and Wikipedia pages with an accuracy of 83%. It contains 4,683,031 nominal glosses (2,985,243 of which are in English). In BabelNet English WN 3.0 synsets have been aligned to their corresponding Wikipedia pages and then extended to other languages, including Italian, by exploiting Wikipedia language links and WN mappings. As for our task, we have retained only those BabelNet entries which have a corresponding synset word in MWN. In this way, we have extended the bag of words representation of nominal entries for MWN synsets by adding the Italian Wikipedia glosses from BabelNet.

### 4.2 Sense Similarity

In the second approach, Sense Similarity, the basis for sense alignment is the Personalized Page Rank (PPR) algorithm (Eneko and Soroa, 2009) relying on a lexical-semantic knowledge base model as a graph $G$ = (V, E) as available in the UKB tool suite[4]. As knowledge base we have used WN 3.0 extended with the "Princeton Annotated Gloss Corpus". Each vertex $v$ of the graph is a synset, and the edges represent semantic relations between synsets (e.g. hyperonymy, hyponymy, etc.). The PPR algorithm ranks the vertices in a graph according to their importance within the set and assigns stronger initial probabilities to certain kinds of vertices in the graph. The result of the PPR algorithm is a vector whose elements denotes the probability for the corresponding vertex that a jumper ends on that vertex if randomly following the edges of the graph.

To obtain the PPR vector for a sense $s$ of the

[2] See http://wordnet.princeton.edu/glosstag.shtml

[3] http://www.d.umn.edu/~tpederse/text-similarity.html

[4] See http://ixa2.si.ehu.es/ukb/

SCDM, we have translated the Italian textual definitions in English by means of a state-of-the-art Machine Translation system[5], automatically lemmatized and part-of-speech analyzed with the TextPro tool suite, remove standard stopwords and applied the UKB tool suite. The PPR vector is a thus semantic representation overall the entire WN synsets of the textual definition of $s$ in SCDM.

As for the MWN synsets, we have exploited its conversion to WN 3.0. Instead of building the PPR vector by means of the lexical items, we have passed to the UKB tool suite the WN synset id, thus assuming that the MWN synset is already disambiguated.
Given two PPR vectors, namely $ppr_{mwn}$ and $ppr_{scdm}$ for the MWN synset $w_{syn}$ and for the SCDM sense $w_{scdm}$, we calculated their cosine similarity. On the basis of the similarity score, the sense pair is considered as aligned or not.

## 5 Experiments and Evaluation

### 5.1 Gold Standards

To evaluate the reliability of the two approaches with respect to our data, we developed two different gold standards, one for verbs and one for nouns.

The verb gold standard is composed by 44 lemmas selected according to corpus frequency (highly frequent lemmas in the La Repubblica Corpus (Baroni et al., 2004)) and patterns in terms of semantic and syntactic features[6]. It is composed by 350 aligned sense pairs obtained by manually mapping the MWN synsets to their corresponding senses in the SCDM lexicon. These verbs corresponds to 279 synsets and 424 senses in the SCDM. Overall, 211 of the 279 MWN synsets have a corresponding sense in the SCDM (i.e. SCDM covers 84.22% of the MWN senses in the data set), while 235 out of 424 SCDM senses have a correspondence in MWN (i.e MWN covers 49.76% of the SCDM senses). Average degree of polysemy for MWN entries is 6.34, while for the SCDM is 9.63.

The noun gold standard is composed by 46 lemmas selected according to frequency and polysemy with respect to the fundamental senses in the SCDM (each lemma must have at least two fundamental senses in the SCDM). On the basis of the manual alignment, we have obtained 166 aligned sense pairs. The noun lemmas correspond to 229 synsets and 216 senses in the SCDM. Overall, 134 of the 229 MWN synsets have a corresponding sense in the SCDM (i.e. SCDM covers 53.71% of the MWN senses in the data set), while 123 out of 216 SCDM senses have a correspondence in MWN (i.e MWN covers 62.03% of the SCDM senses). Average degree of polysemy for MWN entries is 4.97, while for the SCDM is 4.69. The difference in terms of coverage with respect to the verbs is clearly due to two aspects, namely i.) the restrictions of the SCDM entries to the fundamental senses; ii.) the higher coverage in terms of nouns synsets of MWN with respect to the verbal ones.

Though small, the size of the gold standards is representative of the two lexica. In particular, the 279 verbs synsets yield 3,319 possible sense pairs, i.e. 11.8 SCDM senses per synset on average. As for nouns, the 229 nominal synsets yield 1,414 sense pairs, i.e. 6.13 SCDM senses on average.

### 5.2 Results

The evaluation has been performed by computing Precision (the ratio of the correct alignment with respect to all proposed alignments), Recall (the ratio of extracted correct alignment with respect to the alignments in the gold standard), F-measure (the harmonic mean of Precision and Recall calculated as $2PR/P + R$) and Accuracy (the precentage of the correctly identifed alignments and non alignments). As baseline, we have implemented a random match algorithm, *rand*, which for the same word $w$ in SCDM and in MWN assigns a random SCDM sense to each synset with $w$ as synset word, returning a one-to-one alignment. The selection of the correct alignments has been obtained by applying two types of thresholds with respect to all proposed alignments (the "no_threshold" row in the tables): i.) a simple cut-off at specified values (0.1; 0.2); ii.) the selection of the maximum score (either lesk measure or cosine; row "max_score" in the tables) between each synset $S$ and the proposed aligned senses of the SCDM. As for the maximum score threshold, we have retained as good alignments also instances of a tie, thus allowing the possibility of having one MWN synset aligned to more than one SCDM sense.

[5] We use Google Translate API.

[6] A subset of these verbs have been taken from (Jezek and Quochi, 2010)

| Lexical Match | P | R | F1 | Acc. |
|---|---|---|---|---|
| Verb SYN - no_threshold | 0.41 | 0.29 | **0.34** | 0.864 |
| Verb SYN - $\geq$ 0.1 | 0.42 | 0.26 | 0.32 | 0.874 |
| Verb SYN - $\geq$ 0.2 | 0.54 | 0.11 | 0.18 | 0.901 |
| Verb SYN - max_score | 0.59 | 0.19 | **0.29** | **0.909** |
| Verb SREL - no_threshold | 0.38 | 0.32 | **0.35** | 0.786 |
| Verb SREL - $\geq$ 0.1 | 0.40 | 0.27 | 0.32 | 0.781 |
| Verb SREL - $\geq$ 0.2 | 0.53 | 0.11 | 0.18 | 0.863 |
| Verb SREL - max_score | 0.60 | 0.20 | **0.30** | **0.908** |
| Verb - `rand` | 0.15 | 0.06 | 0.08 | |

| Lexical Match | P | R | F1 | Acc |
|---|---|---|---|---|
| Noun SYN - no_threshold | 0.52 | 0.59 | **0.55** | 0.885 |
| Noun SYN - $\geq$ 0.1 | 0.58 | 0.41 | 0.48 | 0.901 |
| Noun SYN - $\geq$ 0.2 | 0.71 | 0.16 | 0.26 | 0.904 |
| Noun SYN - max_score | 0.69 | 0.42 | **0.52** | **0.920** |
| Noun SREL - no_threshold | 0.49 | 0.60 | **0.54** | 0.877 |
| Noun SREL - $\geq$ 0.1 | 0.60 | 0.40 | 0.48 | 0.905 |
| Noun SREL - $\geq$ 0.2 | 0.71 | 0.13 | 0.22 | 0.902 |
| Noun SREL - max_score | 0.69 | 0.42 | **0.52** | **0.921** |
| Noun - `rand` | 0.17 | 0.12 | 0.14 | |

Table 1: Results for automatic alignment based on Lexical Match for SYN and SREL sense representations.

### 5.2.1 Lexical Match Results

We have analyzed different combinations of the sense representation of a synset. We developed two basic representations: SYN, which is composed by the set of synset words excluding the target word *w* to be aligned, all of its direct hypernyms, the set of synset words in MWN standing in the relation of *nearest synonyms* and the synset words obtained from the "Princeton Annotated Gloss Corpus"; and SREL, which contains all the items of SYN plus the the synset words included in the selected set of semantic relations. The results are reported in Table 1.
As the figures show, all synset configurations outperform the baseline `rand` for both parts of speech in analysis. However, it is interesting to observe that the alignment of noun senses performs much better than that for verbs in both sense representations and with all filtering methods. On the basis of the alignment method (i.e. lexical overlap) such a difference in performance provides interesting data on the two resources in analysis. A manual exploration of the data in the configurations both for verbs and nouns has highlighted that, on the one hand, we suffer from data sparseness on the SCDM side as no extension of the sense description of the glosses is possible, and, on the other hand, that senses are described in ways that are semantically equivalent but with different lexical items.

As for verbs the Recall with no filtering (no_threshold) has extremely low levels, ranging from 0.32 for SREL to 0.29 for SYN. The SREL sense representation outperforms SYN when no filtering is applied only in terms of Recall (+0.03), thus signaling that the additional semantic relations play a very limited role in the description of verb senses without providing real additional information to match data in the SCDM glosses. Furthermore, the difference in performance of the SREL configuration is not statistically significant with respect to the SYN configuration ($p > 0.05$).

The situation looks different for nouns where, although low, the no threshold Recall values range between 0.60 (SREL) to 0.59 (for SYN). As for the two basic configurations, SYN and SREL, the results show that SYN is more accurate and that the impact of additional semantic relations, though it slightly improves the Recall, is not statistically signiticant ($p > 0.05$).

Both for verbs and nouns we decided to select the SYN basic configuration as the best sense representation because it has a simpler bag-of-words and better Precision. To improve the results, we have extended this basic representation with the lexical items in the corresponding glosses of BabelNet (+BABEL) (only for nouns) and the lexical items of the MWN Italian glosses (+IT) (for verbs and nouns)[7]. The results are illustrated in Table 2.

In both cases, the extension of the basic sense representations with additional data is positive, namely for Recall. Notice that for verbs the presence of Italian MWN glosses improves the alignment results (for the no-threshold filter, F1=0.37 vs. F=0.35 for SREL and F1=0.34 for SYN) as they introduce information which better represents the sense definition than the synset words in the bag of words representations and overcomes missing information in the WN 3.0 annotated glosses. For instance, consider the following example for the verb "*rendere*" [to make]. In example 1a) the two senses are aligned with a very low lexical overlap score as there is only one word in com-

[7] The Italian MWN glosses for the items in the Golds are present for 24% senses of verbs and 30% senses of nouns, respectively

| Lexical Match | P | R | F1 |
|---|---|---|---|
| Verb SYN+IT - no_threshold | 0.36 | 0.38 | **0.37** |
| Verb SYN+IT - $\geq$ 0.1 | 0.38 | 0.31 | 0.34 |
| Verb SYN+IT - $\geq$ 0.2 | 0.51 | 0.13 | 0.20 |
| Verb SYN+IT - max_score | **0.63** | 0.23 | **0.34** |
| Noun SYN+BABEL - no_threshold | 0.47 | 0.66 | **0.56** |
| Noun SYN+BABEL - $\geq$ 0.1 | 0.58 | 0.40 | 0.47 |
| Noun SYN+BABEL - $\geq$ 0.2 | 0.69 | 0.12 | 0.21 |
| Noun SYN+BABEL - max_score | **0.69** | 0.44 | **0.55** |
| Noun SYN+BABEL+IT - no_threshold | 0.47 | 0.66 | **0.55** |
| Noun SYN+BABEL+IT - $\geq$ 0.1 | 0.53 | 0.43 | 0.48 |
| Noun SYN+BABEL+IT - $\geq$ 0.2 | 0.71 | 0.18 | 0.28 |
| Noun SYN+BABEL+IT - max_score | **0.66** | 0.45 | **0.54** |

Table 2: Results for Lexical Match alignment with extensions with BabelNet data and MWN Italian glosses.

mon (“*fare*”), while in 1b) the presence of the Italian glosses in the synset sense increases the lexical match score as it matches both words in the gloss in the SCDM. The lexical items of the sense descriptions are reported in Italian, matching words are in bold.

1a. `**fare** essere mettere` [synset_id v—00080274 ]
`**fare** diventare` [SCDM_id 243356]

1b. **fare** essere mettere **diventare** [synset_id v—00080274 ]
**fare** **diventare** [SCDM_id 243356 ]

The positive effect of the original Italian data for verbs points out a further issue for our task, namely that the derivation of sense representations of MWN synsets by means of synset words (including the sense annotated glosses of WN 3.0) is not as powerful as having at disposal original glosses.

Similarly, for nouns we register an improvement in Recall at a low or null cost for Precision for all filtering methods, with the exclusion of the no threshold filtering. Precision for SYN+BABEL+IT with maximum score filtering is lowered with respect to the extension with the BabelNet data only (P=0.66 for SYN+BABEL+IT *vs.* P=0.69 for SYN+BABEL)[8]. To better clarify these results, consider the following example for the noun “*palla*” [ball]. In the example 2a) the two senses are not aligned as there are no matching words, while in 2b) the extension by means of the BabelNet data provides a sufficient number of matching items for aligning the two senses. As for the previous example, the lexical items of the sense descriptions are reported in Italian, matching words are in bold.

2a. pallone oggetto cosa balocco partita battere bocciare circolare rotondo tondo [synset_id n—02240791 ]
sfera dimensione variabile materiale diverso cuoio gomma avorio pieno gonfiare aria usare numeroso gioco sport [SCDM_id 241637]

2b. pallone oggetto cosa balocco partita battere bocciare circolare rotondo tondo palla essere oggetto sferico **usare** vario **sport** **gioco** esempio calcio pallacanestro pallavolo biliardo bowling [synset_id n—02240791 ]
sfera dimensione variabile materiale diverso cuoio gomma avorio pieno gonfiare aria **usare** numeroso **gioco** **sport** [SCDM_id 241637]

Concerning the filtering of the proposed alignments, the maximum score filter provides the best results for Precision at a low cost in terms of Recall, with F1 scores for verbs ranging from 0.34 (SYN+IT) to 0.29 (SYN), and from 0.55 (SYN+BABEL) to 0.52 (SYN and SREL) for nouns. It is interesting to point out a further difference in performance between verbs and nouns. In particular, for verbs we can observe that the filtering based on maximum score has lower F1 values with respect to the no threshold baseline in all sense descriptions. As for nouns, on the contrary, both the two basic sense descriptions, SYN and SREL, and the SYN+BABEL configuration have comparable F1 values between the no threshold and the maximum score data. Nevertheless, the filtering based on the maximum score improves the quality of the proposed alignment by removing lots of false positives both for verbs and nouns (for verbs P=0.59 for SYN, P=0.60

[8] Excluding the BabelNet data and running the alignment only with the Italian glosses, SYN+IT, with maximum score filtering, gives F1=0.52 which is the same as SYN and SREL, and lower that SYN+BABEL.

for SREL, and P=0.63 for SYN+IT; for nouns, P=0.69 for SYN, SREL, and SYN+BABEL, P=0.66 for SYN+BABEL+IT) without impacting on the number of good instances retrieved (for verbs R=0.19 for SYN, R=0.20 for SREL, and R=0.23 for SYN+IT; for nouns R=0.42 for SYN and SREL, R=0.44 for SYN+BABEL; R=0.45 for SYN+BABEL+IT).

### 5.2.2 Similarity Measure Results

The results for the Similarity Measure obtained from the Personalized Page Rank algorithm on the basis of the vectors described in Section 4.2 are illustrated in Table 3.

| **Similarity Measure** | **P** | **R** | **F1** |
|---|---|---|---|
| Verb - no_threshold | 0.10 | 0.9 | 0.19 |
| Verb - $\geq$ 0.1 | 0.47 | 0.25 | **0.32** |
| Verb - $\geq$ 0.2 | **0.66** | 0.16 | 0.26 |
| Verb - max_score | 0.42 | 0.20 | 0.27 |
| Verb - `rand` | 0.15 | 0.06 | 0.08 |
| Noun - no_threshold | 0.12 | 0.94 | 0.21 |
| Noun - $\geq$ 0.1 | 0.52 | 0.32 | **0.40** |
| Noun - $\geq$ 0.2 | **0.77** | 0.21 | 0.33 |
| Noun - max_score | 0.42 | 0.38 | 0.40 |
| Noun - `rand` | 0.17 | 0.12 | 0.14 |

Table 3: Results for automatic alignment based on Similarity Score.

Similarly to the Lexical Match, the Personalized Page Rank approach outperforms the baseline `rand`. Overall, the differences in performance with the Lexical Match results are not immediate. In general, as the Recall values for no threshold filtering show, almost all aligned sense pairs of the gold are retrieved, outperforming the Lexical Match. Clearly, this difference is strictly related to the different nature of the sense descriptions, i.e. a *semantic* representation based on a lexical knowledge graph, which is able to catch semantically related items out of the scope for the Lexical Match approach.

By observing the figures for verbs, we notice that the simple cut-off thresholds provide better results with respect to the maximum score. The best F1 score (F1=0.32) is obtained when setting the cosine similarity to 0.1, though Precision is less than 0.50 (namely, 0.47). When compared with threshold value of 0.1 of the Lexical Match, the Personalized Page Rank method yields the best Precision (P=0.47 *vs.* P=0.42 for Verb SYN, P=0.38 for Verb SYN+IT, and P=0.40 for Verb SREL). Similar observations can be done when the threshold is set to 0.2. In this latter case, Personalized Page Rank yields the best Precision score for verbs with respect to all other filtering methods and the Lexical Match results obtained with maximum score (P=0.66 *vs.* P=0.59 for Verb SYN, P=0.63 for Verb SYN+IT, and P=0.60 for Verb SREL).

The analysis for nouns is more complex. Apparently, the Personalized Page Rank approach has lower F1 scores with respect to all Lexical Match sense configurations and filtering methods, including the no threshold score of the basic sense descriptions (respectively, F1=0.55 for SYN, F1=0.54 for SREL, F1=0.21 for Personalized Page Rank). However, when maximizing Precision for the Personalized Page Rank (threshold 0.2), the algorithm provides better performances (F1=0.33) with respect to Lexical Match on the same filtering method, minimizing the drop of Recall (R=0.21; +0.09 with respect to SYN+BABEL with same threshold; + 0.08 with respect to SREL; +0.05 with respect to SYN, respectively).

The better performance of the simple cut-off thresholds with respect to the maximum score is due to the fact that aligning senses by means of semantic similarity provides a larger set of alignments and facilitates the identification of multiple alignments, i.e. one-to-many.

### 5.2.3 Merging Lexical Match and Sense Similarity

As the two approaches are different in nature both with respect to the creation of the sense descriptions (simple bag of words *vs.* semantic representation) and to the methods with which the alignment pairs are extracted and computed, we have developed a further set of experiments by merging together the results obtained from the best sense descriptions and best filtering methods for Lexical Match and Semantic Similarity. As parameters for the identification of the best results we have taken into account the Precision and F1 values. Excluding the presence of Italian data from the sense descriptions of the Lexical Match approach due to their sparseness, we selected the SYN sense description filtered with maximum score for verbs (P=0.59, F1=0.29) and the SYN+BABEL sense description filtered with maximum score for nouns (P=0.69; F1=0.55). As for the Personalized Page Rank approach, we have selected both for verbs and nouns the cut-off threshold at 0.2. The results are reported in Table 4.

| Merged | P | R | F1 |
|---|---|---|---|
| Verb - SYN+ppr02 | 0.61 | 0.38 | **0.47** |
| Noun - SYN+BABEL+ppr02 | 0.67 | 0.61 | **0.64** |

Table 4: Results for automatic alignment merging the best results from Lexical Match and Sense Similarity.

The combination of the best results yields the best performance for both parts of speech compared to the stand-alone approaches. In particular, for verbs we obtain an F1=0.47, with an improvement of 0.18 points with respect to SYN and of 21 points with respect to Personalized Page Rank with threshold 0.2. Similar improvements can be observed for nouns, where SYN+BABEL+ppr02 has an F1=0.64, with an improvement of 9 points with respect to SYN+BABEL and of 31 points with respect to Personalized Page Rank with threshold 0.2. In both cases the performance gains originate from the higher precision of the Personalized Page Rank approach which minimizes the data sparseness of the SCDM lexicon.

## 6 Conclusion and Future Work

This paper focuses on the automatic alignment of senses from two different resources when few data are available. In particular, the lack of Italian glosses in MWN and the absence of any kind of structured information in the SCDM dictionary posed a serious issue for the application of state-of-the-art techniques for sense alignment.

We experimented with two different approaches: Lexical Match and Sense Similarity obtained from Personalized Page Rank. In all cases, when filtering the data we are facing low scores for Recall which point out issues namely related to data sparseness in our lexica. By comparing the results of the two approaches, we can observe that: i.) the Personalized Page Rank yields the best Precision with respect to Lexical Match; ii.) Lexical Match, with a simple sense description configuration (i.e. the SYN configurations for verbs and nouns), is still a powerful approach for this kind of tasks; the exploitation of additional semantically related items (e.g. SREL for verbs) or additional sense descriptors (e.g. SYN+BABEL for nouns), though good in principle, has a limited contribution to solve the "lexical gap" problem in our case and points out differences in the way word senses are encoded in the two lexica; and iii.) Personalized Page Rank vectors and Lexical Match appears to qualify as complementary methods for achieving reliable sense alignments, namely when dealing with few data. Our approach provides satisfying results both for verb and noun sense alignment, with an overall F1=0.47 for verbs and an F1=0.64 for nouns. The better results for nouns are strictly related to the definitions of the senses which mainly relies on synonym words and hypernyms. On the other hand, verbs tend to have more abstract definitions and the contribution of additional semantic relations (i.e. the SREL configuration) is poor.

Future work will concentrate on two aspects by exploiting the sense alignment results. The aligned sense pairs will be used for sense clustering as a strategy to reduce the sense descriptions in MWN and in SCDM. Existing clustering of WN senses (e.g. Navigli (2006)) will be used as a starting point and for subsequent evaluation. Furthermore, we aim at importing the ontological classes of SCDM in MWN. This aspect will be useful for the identification of possible taxonomical errors in the MWN hierarchy and boostrap better sense alignments.

## References

Marco Baroni, Silvia Bernardini, Federica Comastri, Lorenzo Piccioni, Alessandra Volpi, Guy Aston, and Marco Mazzoleni. 2004. Introducing the "`la Repubblica`" corpus: A large, annotated, `TEI(XML)`-compliant corpus of newspaper italian. In *Proceedings of the Fourth International conference on Language Resources and Evaluation (LREC-04)*.

Luisa Bentivogli and Emanuele Pianta. 2005. Exploiting parallel texts in the creation of multilingual semantically annotated resources: the MultiSemCor Corpus. *Natural Language Engineering*, 11:247–261, 8.

Agirre Eneko and Aitor Soroa. 2009. Personalizing PageRank for Word Sense Disambiguation. In *Proceedings of the 12th conference of the European chapter of the Association for Computational Linguistics (EACL-2009)*, Athens, Greece.

Iryna Gurevych, Judith Eckle-Kohler, Silvana Hartmann, Michael Matuschek, Christian M. Meyer, and Christian Wirth. 2012. Uby - a large-scale unified lexical-semantic resource based on LMF. In *Proceedings of the 13th Conference of the European Chapter of the Association for Computational Linguistics (EACL 2012)*.

Elisabetta Jezek and Valeria Quochi. 2010. Capturing coercions in texts: a first annotation exercise. In *Proceedings of the Seventh conference on International Language Resources and Evaluation (LREC'10)*, pages 1464–1471, Valletta, Malta. European Language Resources Association (ELRA).

Karin Kipper Schuler. 2005. *Verbnet: a broad-coverage, comprehensive verb lexicon*. Ph.D. thesis, Philadelphia, PA, USA. AAI3179808.

Michael Lesk. 1986. Automatic sense disambiguation using machine readable dictionaries: how to tell a pine code from an ice cream cone. In *Proc. of 5th Conf. on Systems Documentation*. ACM Press.

Claudio Masolo, Aldo Gangemi, Nicola Guarino, Alessandro Oltramari, and Luc Schneider. 2002. Wonderweb deliverable D17: the wonderweb library of foundational ontologies. Technical report.

Michael Matuschek and Iryna Gurevych. 2013. Dijkstra-wsa: A graph-based approach to word sense alignment. *Transactions of the Association for Computational Linguistics (TACL)*, 2:to appear.

Michael Meyer and Iryna Gurevych. 2011. What psycholinguists know about chemistry: Aligning Wiktionary and WordNet for increased domain coverage. In *Proceedings of the 5th International Joint Conference on Natural Language Processing (IJCNLP)*.

Rada Mihalcea. 2007. Using Wikipedia for automatic word sense disambiguation. In *Human Language Technologies 2007: The Conference of the North American Chapter of the Association for Computational Linguistics; Proceedings of the Main Conference*, Rochester, New York.

Roberto Navigli and Simone Paolo Ponzetto. 2012. BabelNet: The automatic construction, evaluation and application of a wide-coverage multilingual semantic network. *Artificial Intelligence*, 193:217–250.

Roberto Navigli. 2006. Meaningful clustering of senses helps boost word sense disambiguation performance. In *Proceedings of the* $44^{th}$ *Annual Meeting of the Association for Computational Linguistics joint with the* $21^{st}$ *International Conference on Computational Linguistics (COLING-ACL)*, Sydney, Australia.

Elisabeth Niemann and Iryna Gurevych. 2011. The peoples web meets linguistic knowledge: Automatic sense alignment of Wikipedia and WordNet. In *Proceedings of the 9th International Conference on Computational Semantics*, pages 205–214, Singapore, January.

Alessandro Oltramari, Guido Vetere, Isabella Chiari, Elisabetta Jezek, Fabio Massimo Zanzotto, Malvina Nissim, and Aldo Gangemi. 2013. Senso Comune: A collaborative knowledge resource for italian. In I. Gurevych and J. Kim, editors, *The Peoples Web Meets NLP, Theory and Applications of Natural Language Processing*, pages 45–67. Springer-Verlag, Berlin Heidelberg.

Emanuele Pianta, Luisa Bentivogli, and Cristian Girardi. 2002. MultiWordNet: developing an aligned multilingual database. In *First International Conference on Global WordNet*, Mysore, India.

Emanuele Pianta, Cristian Girardi, and Roberto Zanoli. 2008. TextPro Tool Suite. In *Proceedings of the Sixth International Conference on Language Resources and Evaluation (LREC-08)*, volume CD-ROM, Marrakech, Morocco. European Language Resources Association (ELRA).

German Rigau and Agirre Eneko. 1995. Disambiguating bilingual nominal entries against WordNet. In *Proceedings of workshop The Computational Lexicon, 7th European Summer School in Logic, Language and Information*, Barcelona, Spain.

Adriana Roventini, Nilda Ruimy, Rita Marinelli, Marisa Ulivieri, and Michele Mammini. 2007. Mapping concrete entities from PAROLE-SIMPLE-CLIPS to ItalWordNet: Methodology and results. In *Proceedings of the 45th Annual Meeting of the Association for Computational Linguistics Companion Volume Proceedings of the Demo and Poster Sessions*, Prague, Czech Republic, June.

Nilda Ruimy, Monica Monachini, Elisabetta Gola, Nicoletta Calzolari, Maria Cristina Del Fiorentino, Marisa Ulivieri, and Sergio Rossi. 2003. A computational semantic lexicon of italian: *SIMPLE. Linguistica Computazionale XVIII-XIX, Pisa*, pages 821–64.

Maria Ruiz-Casado, Enrique Alfonseca, and Pablo Castells. 2005. Automatic assignment of Wikipedia encyclopedic entries to WordNet synsets. In *Proceedings of the Third international conference on Advances in Web Intelligence*, AWIC'05, Berlin, Heidelberg. Springer-Verlag.

# Terminology in WordNet and in plWordNet

**Marta Dobrowolska**
Institute of Informatics
Wrocław University of Technology
Wrocław, Poland
martadobr@gmail.com

**Stan Szpakowicz**
Institute of Computer Science
Polish Academy of Sciences
Warsaw, Poland
&
School of Electrical Engineering
and Computer Science
University of Ottawa
Ottawa, Ontario, Canada
szpak@eecs.uottawa.ca

## Abstract

We examine the strategies of organizing terminological information in WordNet, and describe an analogous strategy of adding terminological senses of lexical units to plWordNet, a large Polish wordnet. Wordnet builders must cope with differences in lexical and terminological definitions of a term, and with the boundaries between terminological and lexical information. A somewhat adjusted strategy is required for Polish, though both WordNet and plWordNet rely mainly on semantic relations in organizing the terminological and general-language units. The proposed guidelines for plWordNet, built on several distinct combinations of denotation and connotation, have a solid theoretical underpinning but will require a large-scale verification of their effectiveness in practice.

## 1 Introduction

The study of lexicography invokes three types of definition: lexicographic, encyclopedic and terminological.

> The object of a lexicographic definition is [...] the verbal representation, the word itself; the object of the terminological definition is the concept, the abstract representation of the entity existing in the real world (Hudon, 1998, pp. 80-81).

The third definition type describes the real-world object itself, recalling everything that is known about it (Hudon, 1998, p. 81). The three types broadly correspond to linguistic dictionaries, encyclopaedias and specialised dictionaries respectively. It would be very unlikely, however, to find a purely linguistic dictionary with entries devoid of encyclopaedic or terminological elements. Section 2 describes how different kinds of information can be included in a dictionary entry, how they are combined or separated. We first compare lexicographic and encyclopaedic aspects of definitions, and then consider how the lexicographic and terminological aspects are related. Section 3 presents data from Princeton WordNet[1] (Fellbaum, 1998) and demonstrates the strategies used by its authors to solve the problem of the kinds-of- information diversity. Section 4 proposes guidelines for adding terminology to plWordNet, a large Polish wordnet. The problem of the diversity of kinds of information can be framed as three questions:

1. What relations should link units differing in the kind of knowledge to which they refer?
2. Are the relations sufficient to pinpoint the differences between stylistic registers?
3. How do glosses help diversify PWN units by the kind of knowledge they represent?

## 2 Lexicography versus terminology

Svensén (2009, p. 289) holds that most lexicographers consider boundaries between linguistic and encyclopaedic information to be fluid, and often

[1] abbreviated as PWN throughout this paper

find it hard to define what to regard as linguistic or encyclopaedic. An encyclopaedic definition may be included in typologies of lexical definitions:

> maximally rich definition, reflecting world knowledge rather than merely knowledge of the language, contains all kinds of highly specific information and a lot of practical which is not universally invalid (Geeraerts, 2003, p. 90).

It is, however, impossible to distinguish between lexical and encyclopaedic information:

> in the final account, the lexical information is determined by the encyclopaedic fact of particular real-world features. Thus the lexical information is derivable from and not independent of the encyclopaedic information [...] (Bauer, 2005, p. 127).

Some words, mainly nouns but also verbs and adjectives, should have a considerably stronger direct connection with the world than function words such as pronouns, conjunctions and prepositions (Svensén, 2009, p. 292). Dictionaries, depending on the amount and organization of the encyclopaedic element, occupy different positions on the scale of encyclopaedicity. Differences occur at the level of entries as well:

- an encyclopaedic entry is mainly headed by a common noun or a proper name, a linguistic entry – by any type of word;
- a linguistic entry is attached to the item serving as a lemma, whereas an encyclopaedic entry dealing with a certain subject could have another lemma without having to change the content of the entry (Svensén, 2009, p. 290);
- a linguistic entry may contain information about lexical and grammatical collocations of lexical units, their pragmatic functions, syntactic behaviour and so on (Fuertes-Olivera and Arribas-Baño, 2008, p. 2).

Definitions of technical and other specialized terms, like encyclopaedic definitions, do not relate to linguistic units with their universally understandable and accepted meanings, but to specific concepts established in their areas of knowledge. Traditional terminology also declares the independence of linguistics and follows its own rigorous principles:

- the onomasiological perspective (how to express a given concept);
- univocity (one term should only refer to one, clear-cut concept);
- synchrony (focus on the present meaning of terms);
- compliance of the definitions with ISO standards (Temmerman, 2000).

This may suggest a vast distance between terminography and lexicography (which treats those principles as options), but many lexicographers note that these two sciences should meet on several planes. One of the mentioned fields is Language for Specific Purposes (LSP), a term currently used to refer to specialized communication. The methodological confluence between terminography and lexicography is driven by a move away from the concept as the centre of attention.

> This change of emphasis has deep methodological repercussion, which imply the abandoning of the traditional method of onomasiological work in favor of semasiological approach which has a great deal in common with lexicography (Fuertes-Olivera and Arribas-Baño, 2008, p. 8).

Confluences between terminology and lexicology were the focus of the experiment which was designed to check whether the application of the terminological definitions will streamline the process of human-based subject indexing. Terms and descriptors (basic thesaurus units, selected to represent a specific concept in a thesaurus and in indexed documents) share these essential properties (Hudon, 1998, pp. 72-73):

- they represent single concepts in a domain,
- they are signs founded in natural language,
- they reflect language patterns established in a field of specialty.

Whereas definitions are the key component of a term bank, the heart of a thesaurus has traditionally been its relational structure. Hudon concludes, however, that definitions and relationships are assigned complementary roles in a terminological thesaurus. Definitions precisely characterize the meaning of the descriptor, while relationships pinpoint the place of the unit in the lexical hierarchy (Hudon, 1998, p. 78).

We will tackle the questions posed in Section 1, given that PWN is (among other things) a kind of thesaurus which contains both definitions and relations, and that lexical, encyclopaedic and terminological information is interrelated.

## 3 Terminology in PWN

In its role as a thesaurus, PWN brings together, often in the same synsets, elements of general language usage and LSP units absent from general-purpose dictionaries. Experts and laymen sometimes react differently to the same word,[2] and some words are not even in a typical layman's idiolect.[3] Svensén (2009, p. 243) notes: "To the expert, the extension of a technical terms is often small [...] whereas the intension is large".

Terminological definitions tend to refer to other terms. In a wordnet, therefore, the presence of a terminological synset requires the presence of its hypernyms, hyponyms, meronyms and so on. It makes little practical sense to put specialist language in a separate network. The difference between the professional and lay point of view is seldom clear, and even if it were, it might be too subtle to be captured by semantic relations alone.

We see two methods of putting terminology in a wordnet when the same denotation corresponds to a terminological and a general connotation:

- create two lexical units and differentiate them by the hypernyms of their two synsets;
- create one lexical unit and define it by two or more hypernyms of the synset to which it belongs (or by one hypernym if both meanings have the same *genus proximum*).

Lay and specialist meanings may also differ both in connotation and denotation. For example, the PWN 3.0 synsets ***star 1*** and ***star 3*** refer to different concepts but have the same hyponym ***celestial body, heavenly body***. The difference is signalled by glosses, by other relations (the scientific term ***star 1*** has two holonyms and several instances), and by domain (***star 1*** is linked to astronomy).

[2]Such a word has the same denotation (literal meaning), but different connotations (intepretations).

[3]Try *penicillamine*, *enterotoxin* and *modiolus* without peeking in a dictionary!

Another strategy is needed when two or more different lemmas have the same denotation, but different connotations and probably different stylistic registers. Should units belonging to general language and LSP be placed in one synset, or should they be linked by the another semantic relation, such as hyponymy (the general meaning as a hypernym of the specialist sense) or some form of relatedness?

We examined a sample of 200 nouns drawn independently and at random from a homogeneous population of PWN nouns. There are 94 common nouns belonging to general language (including those both in general and specialist registers, *e.g.*, western hemisphere), 20 proper names and 86 terms. Interestingly, most of those 200 nouns have glosses without a usage example. Only 23 synsets have usage examples and just one of them is a terminological synset. One can observe a tendency: the less encyclopaedic the noun, the more likely its usage is to be noted. Grammatical and lexical collocations are typically the kind of linguistic information not necessary in an encyclopaedic definition (Fuertes-Olivera and Arribas-Baño, 2008, p. 2).

Coming back to the role of glosses (question 3 in Section 1): they may contain information which is distinctly lexical (*e.g.*, usage examples) or encyclopaedic (*e.g.*, dates of birth and death), and so signal the character of the concept. They do not, however, pinpoint all the necessary features of terms, because they are not terminological definitions as discussed by Hudon (1998, p. 81).

A significant part of the sample, 32 lexical units, belongs to the biological taxonomy. Synsets referring to taxonomic definitions often contain several lexical units: purely scientific terms, such as Latin names of the taxa, as well as names in the vernacular. In this case, the strategy is to join in one synset all units, no matter to what register of language they belong. That is the case of the synset ***oxeye daisy 2, ox-eyed daisy 1, marguerite 1, moon daisy 1, white daisy 1, Leucanthemum vulgare 1, Chrysanthemum leucanthemum 1***.

Merging different kinds of knowledge and thus registers of language is also noticeable outside synsets, in relations between them. For example, another taxon name from our sample, ***genus Colaptes 1***, is a holonym of ***flicker 2***. It is not a species but a general name of certain woodpeckers, and its hyponyms are the names of the species of such woodpeckers. This is one of many examples of the impossibility of organising lexical and terminological synsets in independent networks. On the other hand, to distinguish terminology from general language, terms are often linked by several *domain* relations to synsets which refer to certain domains. Such relations signal that some synsets (*e.g.,* atom) are members of the domains named by other synsets (*e.g.,* physics, chemistry). This relation has three types: topic, region and usage.

As it happens, our sample does not contain units which have counterparts with the same lemma and denotation, but different connotation, which would be signalled by double hypernymy. This may suggest that the strategy adopted by PWN authors is to not single out senses on the grounds of subtle differences of lay and specialist knowledge, but to concentrate on the same denotation.

## 4 A design for plWordNet

The basic element of plWordNet is not a synset, but a lexical unit (Maziarz et al., 2013), which can be assigned its own register/stylistic label and a gloss containing a usage example. It is, then, appropriate to consider distinct meanings of the same unit in different language registers. Taking into account the connection between a lemma, denotation and connotation, we propose a strategy of putting terminology into plWordNet, which considers three cases. The guidelines have already been put to a practical test: they inform the work of a team charged with adding terminology to plWordNet.

**Case 1**

There are two different words: a (technical) term and a word from general language, with the same denotation but different connotations, *e.g., kot domowy* 'domestic cat' and *kot* 'cat'. When two words denote the same object, their register determines whether they land in one synset or in two synsets. In plWordNet, certain pairs of registers are considered close, others – distant (Maziarz et al., 2014). The specialist and general registers are close, so we put *kot domowy* and *kot* in the same synset. Substantially different registers, *e.g.,* specialist and obsolete, are distant, so we put *pies* 'domestic dog' and *sobaka* 'dog (a borrowing from Russian, obsolete and stylistically marked in contemporary Polish)' in different synsets and link those synsets by relatedness.

**Case 2**

There is one word with two connotations but one denotation, *e.g., krew* 'blood'.[4] The boundary between specialist and general knowledge is not sharp: elements of specialist knowledge can enter the general vocabulary. So, we create one unit but describe it in two ways: it should have both terminological and lexical hyponyms.

**Case 3**

There is one word with two connotations, as well as two denotation, *e.g., para 1* 'a substance in the gas phase at a temperature lower than its critical point' (vapour) and *para 2* 'the hot mist that appears when water is boiled' (steam). We insert two lexical units and describe them differently. Different meanings of one word can be closely related. Consider, *e.g.,* the word *jeżyna*: ***jeżyna 1*** '*Rubus* L.' is a hypernym of ***jeżyna 3*** 'blackberry bush'. As this example shows, general words can be defined, via hyponymy and hypernymy, by specialist terms.

The meaning of lexical units and synsets in plWordNet – as in any wordnet – is defined principally by semantic relations. Whatever defining phrases appear in glosses have an auxiliary character. On the other hand, the role of stylistic register is noteworthy: they allow the reconstruction of specialist definition paths and distinguish them from general-language paths. We note that labels play the same role as *domain* relations in PWN.

The distinction between general and specialist registers may sometimes lead to an excessive specialisation of the meanings. This effect can be significantly reduced if encyclopaedic and lexical information is placed in the same synset.

## 5 Conclusions

This study has proposed a precise strategy of adding terminological senses of lexical units to plWordNet. We began by investigating the strategies adopted by the authors of PWN. While discussing the choices, we considered three aspects of a lexical unit: its lemma, denotation and connotation. There are, naturally, differences between PWN and plWordNet, due to the typological differences between the languages and the to the model adopted for plWordNet (Maziarz et al., 2013). Some choices made in the two wordnets

[4]The terminological definition is "a connective tissue composed of blood cells suspended in blood plasma", and the general-language definition is "a red fluid in animals circulating in veins and arteries".

are quite dissimilar: plWordNet avoids, for example, putting in one synset units with the same denotation, but with distant stylistic registers. It appears that register values will play a more significant role in plWordNet than in PWN, and more emphasis will be placed on differences in connotation. We observed, however, two similarities between the English and Polish wordnet. They both reflect the fluidity of the boundaries between specialist and general knowledge, and in both of them semantic relations remain the principal tool for defining senses.

The accuracy and effectiveness of the strategy we have proposed in this paper must be verified in practice by a large team of plWordNet builders. The observations thus gathered may also lead to a refinement of the strategy. The ultimate test of plWordNet with terminology in place will be its successful applications, but that is quite beyond the scope of this paper.

## Acknowledgment

Financed by the Polish National Centre for Research and Development project SyNaT.

## References

Laurie Bauer. 2005. The Illusory Distinction between Lexical and Encyclopedic Information. In Arne Zettersten Henrik Gottlieb, Jens Erik Mogensen, editor, *Proc. Eleventh International Symposium on Lexicography, May 2002, University of Copenhagen*, pages 111–116.

Christiane Fellbaum, editor. 1998. *WordNet – An Electronic Lexical Database*. The MIT Press.

Pedro A. Fuertes-Olivera and Ascensión Arribas-Baño. 2008. *Pedagogical Specialised Lexicography: The representation of meaning in English and Spanish business dictionaries*, volume 11 of *Terminology and Lexicography Research and Practice*. John Benjamins.

Dirk Geeraerts. 2003. Meaning and definition. In Piet van Sterkenburg, editor, *A practical guide to lexicography*, pages 83–93. John Benjamins.

Michèle Hudon. 1998. *An assessment of the usefulness of standardized definitions in a thesaurus through interindexer terminological consistency measurements*. PhD thesis, University of Toronto.

Marek Maziarz, Maciej Piasecki, and Stanisław Szpakowicz. 2013. The chicken-and-egg problem in wordnet design: synonymy, synsets and constitutive relations. *Language Resources and Evaluation*, 47(3):769–796.

Marek Maziarz, Maciej Piasecki, Ewa Rudnicka, and Stan Szpakowicz. 2014. Registers in the System of Semantic Relations in plWordNet. In *Proc. Global WordNet Conference*, Tartu, Estonia.

Bo Svensén. 2009. *A handbook of lexicography: the theory and practice of dictionary-making*. Cambridge University Press.

Rita Temmerman. 2000. *Towards New Ways of Terminology Description: The sociocognitive approach*, volume 3 of *Terminology and Lexicography Research and Practice*. John Benjamins.

# plWordNet as the Cornerstone of a Toolkit of Lexico-semantic Resources

**Marek Maziarz**
**Maciej Piasecki**
**Ewa Rudnicka**
Institute of Informatics
Wrocław University of Technology
Wrocław, Poland
mawroc@gmail.com
maciej.piasecki@pwr.wroc.pl
ewa.rudnicka78@gmail.com

**Stan Szpakowicz**
Institute of Computer Science
Polish Academy of Sciences
Warsaw, Poland
&
School of Electrical Engineering
and Computer Science
University of Ottawa
Ottawa, Ontario, Canada
szpak@eecs.uottawa.ca

## Abstract

A wordnet is many things to many people: a graph of inter-related lexicalised concepts, a taxonomy, a thesaurus, and so on. A wordnet makes good sense as the mainstay of any deep automated semantic analysis of text. We have begun the construction of a multi-component, multi-use toolkit of natural language processing tools with plWordNet, a very large Polish wordnet, at its centre. The components will include plWordNet and its mapping onto an ontology (the upper level and elements of the middle level), a lexicon of proper names and a semantic valency lexicon. Some of those elements will be aligned with plWordNet, and there will be a mapping onto Princeton WordNet. Several challenging applications will show the utility of the toolkit in practice.

## 1 How wordnets evolve

Wordnets start small but quickly grow to account for much of the lexical material of the given language. The size of version 3.1 of Princeton WordNet (PWN) (Fellbaum, 1998) is a *de facto* standard, even if this mature wordnet also keeps growing, albeit slowly.[1] One of the resources which approach this size standard is plWordNet (Piasecki et al., 2009), now in version 2.1. Languages change continually, so lexicographers never rest, but one can still ask when the development of a wordnet ought to slow down, and whether there is an appropriate steady state of a wordnet. That clearly is a loaded question, and much depends on the language. For example, suppose that a wordnet for a richly inflected language with complex and varied derivation was originally a translation of PWN. Such a wordnet should, sooner or later, acquire semantic relations which account accurately for its unique lexical system..

A wordnet, even as developed as PWN, GermaNet (Hamp and Feldweg, 1997) or plWordNet (Maziarz et al., 2013a), serves many natural language processing (NLP) applications, yet it seems neither feasible nor necessary to remake wordnets into universal NLP resources. Instead, we propose to mark clear boundaries around a wordnet (what it should and what it should not include), and treat it as a pivotal element of an organic toolkit of inter-connected tools and resources for the semantic analysis of texts, along with the auxiliary morphological and syntactic analysis tools. Our case study is such a toolkit, now under development, centred on plWordNet 3.0 (also in development), and intended first and foremost for research in the humanities.

In the remainder of the paper, we present the main design assumptions and principles of that project. We explain how comprehensive we want plWordNet 3.0 to become, what size and what coverage we envisage. We attempt to describe how the toolkit will be built around plWordNet, and we outline plans for its large-scale illustrative applications in several domains. We discuss how the components of the toolkit will be expanded or constructed: plWordNet 3.0, its mapping to an ontology, and a semantic lexicon of proper names. We also briefly present resources for morphological and structural description, as-

[1] PWN began as a test of a theory of human semantic representation and memory (Collins and Quillian, 1969). It now features a comprehensive vocabulary, a set of universally useful semantic relations, glosses, links to ontologies, and more.

sociated with the plWordNet system, among them a lexicon of lexico-syntactic structures of multi-word expressions and a valency lexicon linked to plWordNet but developed independently.

This work is meant to take several years of initial effort and years of maintenance. We cannot answer many design questions *yet*, but many will be answered as the project unfolds. That is to say. we want to interlace theory and practice.

## 2 The cornerstone

### 2.1 The model of plWordNet

There is a rather unfortunate tendency to treat wordnets as a substitute for ontologies (which are perhaps less well known and less easily available to the NLP community), but significant differences are clear when one compares an ontology with a wordnet understood as a lexico-semantic resource (Prévot et al., 2010). A systems of concepts in a wordnet must be expressed entirely in a natural language – unlike ontologies. A strict knowledge representation is required in an ontology, but a wordnet works through words. The inherent ambiguity of the lexical material makes very formal definitions infeasible. In particular, synonymy is a matter of degree, while concepts in an ontology should be defined with certainty. A rigorous construction of an ontology is not easy insofar as language intuitions "get in the way". For example, PWN contains a network of conceptual relations between synsets which represent *lexicalised concepts*, but – unsurprisingly – no formal definition of the notion of *concept* has been put forward yet. PWN's structure was shaped by the lexico-semantic dependencies among words, not by formal properties of an ontology structure.[2]

Corpus analysis can help recognise lexico-semantic relations for inclusion in a wordnet. Practical substitution tests can be formulated for individual relations without committing to any particular theory of lexical semantic or human cognition, in the spirit of *minimal commitment* (Maziarz et al., 2013b). A wordnet so conceived provides a description of the lexical system which is well defined and grounded in language data. It can also be built up at a considerably low cost and with a high degree of consistency.

Corpus-based wordnet development, which has led to plWordNet 2.1, assumes a very large monolingual corpus as the main source of lexical knowledge. Software tools facilitate corpus browsing and semi-automatic knowledge extraction (Piasecki et al., 2009). Dictionaries and encyclopedias are consulted in order, if necessary. This rigorous procedure limits the variability of editing decisions by circumscribing the role of linguistic intuition, though intuition still has its place as a final recourse.

A wordnet based very closely on language data is easier to develop when its primitive is a *linguistically* motivated construct: the lemma-sense pair which we call the *lexical unit* (LU). The plWordNet model, described in detail in (Maziarz et al., 2013b), considers lexico-semantic relations between LUs. LUs are grouped into synsets if they share lexico-semantic relations from a pre-defined repertory, called *constitutive relations*. They must be fairly *frequent* (to describe many LUs), *shared* among LUs (to define groups), *grounded* in the linguistic tradition (to facilitate their consistent understanding) and, if possible, already *used* in other wordnets (to improve compatibility). One of the effects is that synonymy is not a primary relation. It is derived from other lexico-semantic relations, notably hyponymy and hypernymy, which are much simpler to recognise consistently. A relation between two synsets is directly derived from lexico-semantic relations, and it is effectively an abbreviation for a set of links defined for all pairs of LUs from both synsets.

Not every lexico-semantic relation qualifies as a constitutive relation. For example, antonymy is not shared widely enough, and there are no "co-antonyms" for the same LU. Antonymy obviously belongs in a wordnet, but not as a defining factor. Another example: plWordNet does not directly include derivational relations which describe transformations of the basic morphological word forms. It only records lexico-semantic relations signalled by those formal transformations. For example, the same morpheme can be used to create forms of different meanings, so in each case we describe a different specific lexico-semantic relation rather than the formal dependencies among word forms (Piasecki et al., 2012b).

When we wrote precise definitions and substitution tests, we realised that several factors systematically constrain linking large sub-classes of LUs by lexico-semantic relations. Three of those fac-

[2] Put another way, there can be a disconnect between the "straitjacket" of an ontology and the inevitable vagueness and context-dependence of actual texts.

tors, stylistic registers, verb aspect and semantic verb classes, apply frequently enough to allow explicit treatment in the relation definitions (Maziarz et al., 2013b). They refer to the properties of LUs, so we call them *constitutive features*. Relations strictly limited to verbs of the same aspect and semantic class include hyponymy and several specific entailment relations such as inchoativity. Registers explain many situations when pragmatic limitations prevent LUs with the same denotation from being used in the same contexts. Such LUs do share some relations, so constraining relation definitions by register compatibility helps shape the wordnet structure consistently.

Glosses may play a secondary role in a representation of lexical meaning based on the relational paradigm, but writing them helps wordnet editors work with polysemous lemmas. They are also helpful for human users and very useful in applications. Automatically extracted usage examples, equally secondary, are very popular with users in linguistics. We will, therefore, place plWordNet 3.0 glosses and examples in for as many LUs as possible, though the final numbers are hard to put now on this laborious process.

The system of lexico-semantic relations in plWordNet 3.0 will not differ much from plWordNet 2.1. The verb hypernymy structure putting verbs into semantic classes may have to be adjusted. The adverb network must be built from scratch. It will also be important to increase network density for the existing relation types.[3]

The whole plWordNet 3.0, together with all associated resources and mappings, will be naturally available on an *open* WordNet-style licence.

## 2.2 Size matters

Table 1 shows that plWordNet 2.1 comes close in size to PWN 3.1: nearly the same number of synsets, and about 2/3 of the lemmas and LUs. We want the vocabulary to correspond to the contents of a large morpho-syntactic dictionary (Saloni et al., 2012) commonly used when processing Polish texts, but the coverage is still far from that number.[4] The target size of plWordNet 3.0 is not easy to set *a priori*, but we know that it is better to count lemmas than synsets (assuming that all senses of

[3]There are 3.99 relations per noun synset, 3.06 relations per verb synset, 1.56 per adjective synset inplWordNet 2.1. In PWN: 3.54 for nouns, 2.21 for verbs and 2.43 for adjectives.

[4](Saloni et al., 2012) has around 200,000 lexemes (our lemmas), but that includes many proper names.

| POS | synsets | lemmas | LUs | avs |
|---|---|---|---|---|
| N-PWN | 82,115 | 117,798 | 146,347 | 1.78 |
| N-plWN | 80,950 | 78,184 | 110,913 | 1.37 |
| V-PWN | 13,767 | 11,529 | 25,047 | 1.81 |
| V-plWN | 21,770 | 17,518 | 32,037 | 1.47 |
| A-PWN | 18,156 | 21,785 | 30,004 | 1.65 |
| A-plWN | 15,113 | 11,651 | 18,748 | 1.25 |

Table 1: The count of Noun/Verb/Adjective synsets, lemmas and LUs by part of speech (POS), and average synset size (avs), in PWN 3.1 (PWN) and plWordNet 2.1 (plWN).

a lemma are accounted for).[5] Note that infrequent words need a representation in wordnets more than frequent words, well described by knowledge automatically extracted from a large corpus. Measures of semantic relatedness tend to be useless for lemmas appearing less than 50 times in a corpus of more than 1 billion tokens (Piasecki et al., 2009). That said, it is unrealistic to aim for a wordnet with full coverage of a frequency list based on a very large corpus.

It is hard to say just how many words there are in a language, never mind newest coinage. Corpora, even huge, are not complete enough (Kornai, 2002; Gale and Sampson, 1995, p. 218). One might assess a lower bound of the vocabulary size from existing dictionary sizes, or calculate it analytically with corpus and statistical methods.

English is often assumed to have the most words. The Oxford English Dictionary (Simpson, 2013) contains 300k main entries (± lemmas) and 600k word forms, but no freshest neologisms. There are even larger dictionaries: *Woordenboek der Nederlandsche Taal* with 430k entries (Nijhoff, 2001) and a 330k dictionary of Grimm brothers (Grimm, 1999); both are contemporary *and* historical. A comparable Polish dictionary from the early 1900s has 280k entries (Karłowicz et al., 1900–1927; Piotrowski, 2003, p. 604). Modern dictionaries of general Polish have fewer entries: 130k (Zgółkowa, 1994–2005), 125k (180k LUs) (Doroszewski, 1963–1969), 100k (150k LUs) (Dubisz, 2004), 45k (100k LUs) (Bańko, 2000). They do not contain many specialised words and senses from science, technology, culture and so on, appropriate for a wordnet.

[5]The number of lemmas covered tells how many out-of-vocabulary words to expect during processing.

| corpus | corpus size | # entries |
|---|---|---|
| Cobuild (1986) | 18M | 19.8k |
| Cobuild Bank of English (1993) | 121M | 45.2k |
| Bank of English (2001) | 450M | 93.0k |
| plWordNet | 1,800M | ≈174.0k |

Table 2: Dictionary size in entries as a function of corpus size according to Krishnamurthy. For comparison – the estimates for plWordNet.

| | # entries |
|---|---|
| Polish dictionaries | 100-250k |
| plWordNet corpus, 10+ lemmas [K] | 174k |
| doubled plWordNet corpus, 0+ lemmas [GT] | +200k |

Table 3: Potential lemma count for plWordNet. Estimates due to Krishnamurthy [K] and Good & Toulmin [GT].

Krishnamurthy (2002) ties the corpus size to the number of lemmas which occur 10+ times. We added an extrapolation for plWordNet (Table 2): 174k lemmas, a little more than we propose to have in plWordNet 3.0.[6]

If we could double our current corpus, the approximation in (Good and Toulmin, 1956; Efron and Thisted, 1975, eq. 2.7) would be useful:

$$\hat{\Delta} = \sum_{x=1}^{\infty}(-1)^{x+1}n_x,$$

$\hat{\Delta}$ is the size of a new vocabulary found in the new part of the corpus, $n_x$ is number of word types used $x$ times in the source corpus (before doubling). This gives 1,322,850 new word types for the doubled plWordNet corpus. Standard deviation is given by formula (2.10) in (Efron and Thisted, 1975) :

$$S = \sqrt{var\hat{\Delta}} = \sqrt{\sum_{x=1}^{\infty} n_x} \approx \pm 42\text{k word types.}$$

This approximation, however, takes into account proper names, foreign words, typos and so on (Kornai, 2002, p. 83), undesirable in our wordnet. Even if we conservatively assume 15% "real" words,[7] we can count on some 200k additional lemmas. Multi-word lexical units would not be included in that estimate. See Table 3 for details.

In the end, we set the target size of plWordNet 3.0 arbitrarily at 200,000 lemmas: a lot, but it accords with the largest Polish dictionaries and with corpus statistics – and with the policy of accounting for rare lemmas. The completion is expected at the end of 2015. The number of synsets (218,000) and LUs (250,000) has been estimated by extrapolating the lemma-LU-synset ratios in plWordNet 2.1.

The size of plWordNet has already far exceeded the vocabulary of the average Polish user – by design. A wordnet should outstrip traditional dictionaries if it is to be part of language tools which work on the Internet scale (with practically limitless vocabulary) and without the benefit of human language intuition. plWordNet 3.0 will be part of the CLARIN language technology infrastructure[8] aimed at delivering research tools for processing text and speech resources in the very broad domain of the humanities and social sciences.

Not all applications benefit from a large wordnet. Word-sense disambiguation may suffer if there are too many too fine sense distinctions, but the granularity of the senses and the size in lemmas are not strictly correlated. The former is more a matter of a construction decision, with relatively infrequent cases of a lemma of the general register assigned new specific senses.[9]

Wordnet construction based on knowledge extracted from a large corpus (Piasecki et al., 2009; Piasecki et al., 2012a) reaches its limits when the most frequent vocabulary has been accounted for.[10] A Polish corpus of significantly more than the present 1.8 billion words is much harder to make than it would be for English if one wants to preserve quality.[11] Pattern-based relation extraction, better with low frequencies, tend to be less complete and less productive than statistical distribution-based methods. We will have to supplement corpus data with knowledge from such structured text resources as Wikipedia.

[6]This estimation was given by a regression curve:

$$N_{10+} = 6.67t^{0.477} \approx 6.67\sqrt{t},$$

where $t$ is the corpus size and $N_{10+}$ is the number of words with 10 or more corpus occurrences; the coefficient of determination equals 0.996. The equality is of a power-law kind, as Guiraud's law (Guiraud, 1954).

[7]Indeed, we found 15 common words in a 100-word sample taken from the plWordNet corpus frequency list.

[8]See `http://nlp.pwr.wroc.pl/clarin` and `http://clarin.eu`

[9]A small example: *dryl* 'drill' means an exercise or an ape, the latter very rare.

[10]Any measure of semantic relatedness works fine for 1,000 occurrences per one billion words, deteriorates for 100 occurrences and practically fails for 10.

[11]Language errors and irregularities quickly decrease the quality of morpho-syntactic preprocessing.

### 2.3 The quality

The current phase of our long-term project begins with plWordNet 2.1: version 2.0 with improvements due to the application of automated diagnostic tools, and a continually growing mapping to PWN 3.1. The development of plWordNet has been consistently carried out in WordnetLoom, a wordnet editor with advanced graphical editing capabilities and a palette of corpus search, dictionary search, structure checking and bookkeeping tools (Piasecki et al., 2013). WordnetLoom imposes many constraints on the wordnet relation structures, but we have discovered that more is required. New rules include the following:

- simple structural errors, such as the presence of lexical units (LUs) without synsets or links without the obligatory inverse counterpart for symmetric relations;
- general semantic errors such as hypernymy and meronymy cycles, more than one relation linking a pair of synsets, or direct and indirect relations linking mutually a pair of synsets;
- specific semantic rules developed for selected domains and hypernymy branches.

## 3 The toolkit of lexico-semantic resources

### 3.1 Multi-word expressions

Multi-word Expressions (MWEs), a substantial part of the lexicon, are under-represented in dictionaries and on frequency list. With effective MWE detection, a very large corpus is the most reliable source of MWEs, but (inconveniently) morphological analysis handles their elements separately. We will expand the dictionary of lexico-morpho-syntactic MWE structures from (Kurc et al., 2012) to more than 60000 MWEs in a separate resource linked to plWordNet 3.0.

### 3.2 Proper names

We treat proper names (PNs) as separate from the lexicon: very few PNs are present in general dictionaries. That is why they do not belong in lexico-semantic resources. In particular, hyponymy does not really apply. An entity denoted by a PN is an *instance* of a *type*. PNs are primarily characterised by their referents, not by their semantic properties revealed in use examples. One must know the referent of the given PN in order to to interpret it unambiguously. The instance/type relations are not lexico-semantic relations, so PNs can in principle be linked directly to an ontology, not to a wordnet. There are, however, two arguments in favour of linking PNs *via* a wordnet:

1. lexico-syntactic contexts which signal *instance of* links can be collected for many PNs and common nouns;
2. for various good reasons, PNs are already well represented in several wordnets.

As to argument 2: selected PNs are described in plWordNet because they are the derivational bases from which certain classes of frequent nouns and adjectives are derived, cf (Maziarz et al., 2011). Such PNs are part of the wordnet and are linked by plWordNet instance/type relations.

Argument 1 is even more important for us. We plan to describe semantically a very large number of PNs, and do it semi-automatically based on the information extracted from a large corpus (Kurc et al., 2013). Such information can support linking to a wordnet, but not directly to an ontology. Definite noun phrases are also used as anaphoric expressions to refer to and substitute PNs. Heads of such NPs are types for the substituted PNs or hypernyms of the proper types. That is yet another argument for linking PNs to an ontology via the wordnet as an intermediary.

A PN semantic lexicon will then be a separate resource linked to plWordNet 3.0 and through it to an ontology – more below. We will build up to 2.5 million Polish PNs an existing resource of 1.4 million.[12] The number of semantic categories will go from the present 52 up to more than 100. The categories will be mapped to plWordNet 3.0 synsets, providing a default link for each PN belonging to the given category. A more fine-grained mapping may be considered for selected categories such as persons. The PN lexicon is meant to be dynamic: it will be automatically expanded given any new corpus for a specific domain.

### 3.3 Wordnets and mapping

Unlike many other national wordnets constructed by the transfer and merge method, plWordNet has been built independently of PWN. That was a conscious choice motivated by the desire to offer a faithful description of a lexico-semantic system of Polish language, uninfluenced by the structure and

[12] See `http://nlp.pwr.wroc.pl/pl/narzedzia-i-zasoby/nelexicon`

content of PWN. Only when the core of plWordNet was constructed did we start its mapping to PWN (Rudnicka et al., 2012; Kędzia et al., 2013), noting a number of contrasts resulting from differences between lexical systems of English and Polish (*e.g.,* lexical gaps, lexicalised grammatical categories, different structuring of information) as well as in the content and structural design of the two networks.

The development of plWordNet 2.0 was independent of PWN (other than its evident influence as a general model). The mapping to PWN was manual, bottom-up, for selected domains – person, artefact, location, time, food and communication (Rudnicka et al., 2012). It was extended in plWordNet 2.1 to round out the coverage of those domains and to include PWN's core synsets (those representing the most frequent word senses) (Boyd-Graber et al., 2006). All this will facilitate linking to Open Multilingual Wordnet (Bond and Foster, 2013) and perhaps other similar resources.

The procedure considers several candidate inter-lingual relations (I-relations) in strict order. Initially, we placed inter-register I-synonymy – differently stylistically-marked words with close meaning – low on the decision list. It is, however, a well-defined choice when a marked Polish LU occurs in plWordNet but its counterpart is not in PWN, or even cannot be lexicalised in English. Now inter-register I-synonymy is next after I-synonymy. The same applies to inter-lingual partial synonymy, when there is a partial overlap of meaning and structure between the source and target synsets. The overlap is immediately visible, so partial synonymy can be assigned right after dismissing full synonymy. When neither I-synonymy applies, I-hyponymy is considered (it has turned out to be the most frequent I-relation), then I-hypernymy, I-meronymy and I-holonymy.

Manual mapping onto PWN is also an opportunity to verify plWordNet's content and structure, and repair errors. Linguists who did not create some part of plWordNet take a second look at it. The mapping procedure (Rudnicka et al., 2012) relies on the comparison of the relation structures for the corresponding synsets, so potential flaws in the hypernymy structure on either side can be discovered, especially because WordnetLoom visualises such structures (many levels down and up). The overall workload doubles in practice. Manual mapping takes nearly as long as wordnet construction, but if it includes verification then result is a lexical resource which allows a deep comparison of the two lexical resources on a very large scale.

The whole plWordNet 3.0 will be mapped onto PWN 3.1 (Rudnicka et al., 2012; Kędzia et al., 2013), and differences in lexical coverage will likely be a problem. A virtual supplement to Princeton WordNet 3.1 may be necessary to make the mapping work for Polish material not present yet on the English side (and give a boost to future multilingual applications). Gaps and discrepancies will be recorded and presented to the Princeton WordNet team. The mapping has thus far focussed on nouns. Extending it to verbs and adjectives may require a revised procedure.

### 3.4 The ontology

In plWordNet project we have deliberately kept the wordnet separate from any ontology, although we are aware that such a relationship must be established sooner or later. plWordNet has been built as a faithful description of the Polish lexical system providing an interface between the lexicon and abstract concept structures of an ontology.

Ontologies make concepts unambiguous, but natural language does not allow such "luxuries". Usage constrains meaning, and stylistic register is a case in point. Some lexical-semantic relations can link only words of identical or at least compatible registers.[13] Such considerations should be reflected in the wordnet structure. Constraints on registers in plWordNet 2.1 are part of the definitions of selected lexico-semantic relations: hyponymy and hypernymy can only connect words of compatible registers, inter-register synonymy accounts for near-synonymy with a tolerable register difference, and so on.

A wordnet's expressive power rests primarily on the lexico-semantic relations it encodes. One might say that, in the relational paradigm, all supplementary data, *e.g.,* glosses, are secondary, but such a strict position would yield wordnets inadequate for applications. Given that ontologies contain a different kind of information, it makes sense to create a mapping from a wordnet to an ontology and thus associate concepts with their lexical embodiment. Clearly, there is much linguistic knowledge not expressible by lexico-semantic relations, but it could appear in resources of other

[13] By way of illustration, two Polish words mean 'girl', but only *dziewczyna* is stylistically neutral, while *laska* is strongly marked as colloquial.

types linked to wordnets, such as syntactic and semantic valency frames (Hajnicz, 2012).

In theory, any ontology would work with plWordNet, but SUMO (Pease, 2011) ought to be favoured. There is a mapping from PWN (Peace and Fellbaum, 2010), and other wordnets linked to it are linked to SUMO at least indirectly. The manually constructed plWordNet-to-PWN mapping will help automate SUMO linking. I-synonymy links can be unambiguously mapped over. In other cases, ambiguity causes trouble, *e.g.,* between I-hypernymy and instances of SUMO hyponymy. Synsets in plWordNet and abstract SUMO concepts may have to be linked manually. The ontology mapping will enable the construction of an advanced shallow-semantic parser for Polish which builds a partial semantic representation from concepts acquired in SUMO via plWordNet. The ontology mapping will also facilitate linking plWordNet 3.0 to the Global WordNet Grid,[14] and will support the building of multilingual resources and applications.

## 4 The expectations

The construction of plWordNet 3.0 has started in July 2013. Complete plWordNet hypernymy branches are mapped to PWN in parallel by people other than those who built those branches. We expect plWordNet 3.0 to become a comprehensive wordnet (>200,000 lemmas) and one of the largest ever Polish dictionaries of any kind. The whole toolkit of semantic resources, completed by the end of 2015, will include plWordNet 3.0, a dynamic lexicon of 2.5 million PNs linked to plWordNet, a mapping plWordNet-PWN and a mapping of plWordNet to the top-level SUMO ontology plus selected medium-level ontologies. The lexico-syntactic structure of plWordNet MWEs (at least 60,000 lemmas) will be described in an associated resource. The toolkit will also be integrated with a syntactico-semantic valence lexicon.

The whole complex system of resources and tools (*e.g.,* for MWE and PN extraction), developed for the needs of the CLARIN project, is intended to be a strong, universal basis for applications and for further resources and tools, *e.g.,* a wordnet-based lexical similarity measure.

The modularly constructed toolkit will have a layered architecture of large software systems. Different layers of lexical knowledge will be separate but linked, *e.g.,* a relational description of lexical meaning in a wordnet and its formal interpretation in an ontology, or lexical meaning and facts represented by PNs. Each layer is based on limited set of notions and principles, can be used separately and upgraded.

[14] See `http://globalwordnet.org/?page_id=67`


## Acknowledgments

Co-financed by the Polish Ministry of Education and Science, Project CLARIN-PL, and the Polish National Centre for Research and Development project SyNaT.


## References


Mirosław Bańko, editor. 2000. *Inny słownik języka polskiego PWN [Another dictionary of Polish]*, volume 1-2. Polish Scientific Publishers PWN, Warszawa.

Francis Bond and Ryan Foster. 2013. Linking and Extending an Open Multilingual Wordnet. In *Proc. 51st Annual Meeting of the ACL (Volume 1: Long Papers)*, Sofia, Bulgaria. Pages 1352–1362.

Jordan Boyd-Graber, Christiane Fellbaum, Daniel Osherson, and Robert Schapire. 2006. Adding dense, weighted connections to WordNet. In *Proc. Third International WordNet Conf.*

Alan M. Collins and M. Ross Quillian. 1969. Retrieval Time from Semantic Memory. *Journal of Verbal Learning and Verbal Behavior*, 8(2):240–247.

Witold Doroszewski, editor. 1963–1969. *Słownik języka polskiego [A dictionary of the Polish language]*. Państwowe Wydawnictwo Naukowe.

Stanisław Dubisz, editor. 2004. *Uniwersalny słownik języka polskiego [A universal dictionary of Polish], electronic version 1.0*. Polish Scientific Publishers PWN.

Bradley Efron and Ronald Thisted. 1975. Estimating the Number of Unseen Species (How Many Words Did Shakespeare Know)? Technical report, Division of Biostatistics, Stanford University, California.

Christiane Fellbaum, editor. 1998. *WordNet – An Electronic Lexical Database*. The MIT Press.

William A. Gale and Geoffrey Sampson. 1995. Good-Turing Frequency Estimation without Tears. *Journal of Quantitative Linguistics*, 2(3):217–237.

I. J. Good and G. H. Toulmin. 1956. The Number of New Species, and the Increase in Population Coverage, when a Sample is Increased. *Biometrika*, 43:45–63.

Jacob Grimm. 1999. *Deutsches Wörterbuch [The German Dictionary]*. Deutsche Taschenbuch Verlag.

Pierre Guiraud. 1954. *Les caractères statistiques du vocabulaire*. Presses Universitaires de France, Paris.

Elżbieta Hajnicz. 2012. Similarity-based Method of Detecting Diathesis Alternations in Semantic Valence Dictionary of Polish Verbs. In *Security and Intelligent Information Systems, SIIS 2011, Warsaw, Poland, Revised Selected Papers*, volume 7053 of *Lecture Notes in Computer Science*. Springer-Verlag. Pages 345–358.

Birgit Hamp and Helmut Feldweg. 1997. GermaNet – a Lexical-Semantic Net for German. In *Proc. ACL Workshop on Automatic Information Extraction and Building of Lexical Semantic Resources for NLP Applications*, pages 9–15.

Chu-Ren Huang, Nicoletta Calzolari, Aldo Gangemi, Alessandro Oltramari, and Laurent Prévot, editors. 2010. *Ontology and the Lexicon. A Natural Languge Processing Perspective*. Studies in Natural Languge Processing. Cambridge University Press.

Jan Karłowicz, Adam Antoni Kryński, and Władysław Niedźwiedzki, editors. 1900–1927. *Słownik języka polskiego [A dictionary of the Polish language]*. Warszawa.

András Kornai. 2002. How many words are there? *Glottometrics*, 4:61–86.

Ramesh Krishnamurthy. 2002. Corpus size for lexicography. Corpora list archive, ⟨http://torvald.aksis.uib.no/corpora/2002-3/0254.html⟩.

Roman Kurc, Maciej Piasecki, and Bartosz Broda. 2012. Constraint Based Description of Polish Multiword Expressions. In *Proc. Eight International Conf. on Language Resources and Evaluation (LREC'12)*, Istanbul, Turkey. Pages 2408–2413.

Roman Kurc, Maciej Piasecki, and Stan Szpakowicz. 2013. Automatic Construction of a Dynamic Thesaurus for Proper Names. In A. Przepiórkowski et al., editor, *Computational Linguistics – Applications*, volume 467 of *Studies in Computational Intelligence*. Springer.

Paweł Kędzia, Maciej Piasecki, Ewa Rudnicka, and Konrad Przybycień. 2013. Automatic Prompt System in the Process of Mapping plWordNet on Princeton WordNet. *Cognitive Studies*. to appear.

Marek Maziarz, Maciej Piasecki, Joanna Rabiega-Wiśniewska, and Stanisław Szpakowicz. 2011. Semantic Relations among Nouns in Polish WordNet Grounded in Lexicographic and Semantic Tradition. *Cognitive Studies*, 11:161–181. ⟨http://www.eecs.uottawa.ca/~szpak/pub/\\Maziarz_et_al_CS2011a.pdf⟩.

Marek Maziarz, Maciej Piasecki, Ewa Rudnicka, and Stan Szpakowicz. 2013a. Beyond the transfer-and-merge wordnet construction: plWordNet and a comparison with WordNet. In G. Angelova, K. Bontcheva, and R. Mitkov, editors, *Proc. Int.l Conf. on Recent Advances in Natural Language Processing*, Hissar, Bulgaria.

Marek Maziarz, Maciej Piasecki, and Stanisław Szpakowicz. 2013b. The chicken-and-egg problem in wordnet design: synonymy, synsets and constitutive relations. *Language Resources and Evaluation*, 47(3):769–796.

M. Nijhoff. 2001. *Woordenboek der Nederlandsche Taal [Dictionary of the Dutch Language]*. Instituut voor Nederlandse Lexicologie. First published in 1863.

Adam Peace and Christiane Fellbaum. 2010. Formal ontology as interlingua: the SUMO and WordNet linking project and Global WordNet. In Huang et al. (Huang et al., 2010).

Adam Pease. 2011. *Ontology - A Practical Guide*. Articulate Software Press, Angwin, CA.

Maciej Piasecki, Stanisław Szpakowicz, and Bartosz Broda. 2009. *A Wordnet from the Ground Up*. Wrocław University of Technology Press. ⟨http://www.eecs.uottawa.ca/~szpak/pub/\\A_Wordnet_from_the_Ground_Up.zip⟩.

Maciej Piasecki, Roman Kurc, Radosław Ramocki, and Bartosz Broda. 2012a. Lexical Activation Area Attachment Algorithm for Wordnet Expansion. In Allan Ramsay and Gennady Agre, editors, *Proc. 15th International Conf. on Artificial Intelligence: Methodology, Systems, Applications*, volume 7557 of *Lecture Notes in Computer Science*, Varna, Bulgaria. Springer. Pages 23–31.

Maciej Piasecki, Radosław Ramocki, and Marek Maziarz. 2012b. Automated Generation of Derivative Relations in the Wordnet Expansion Perspective. In *Proc. 6th Global Wordnet Conf.*, Matsue, Japan.

Maciej Piasecki, Michał Marcińczuk, Radosław Ramocki, and Marek Maziarz. 2013. WordNet-Loom: a WordNet development system integrating form-based and graph-based perspectives. *International Journal of Data Mining, Modelling and Management*, 5(3):210–232.

Tadeusz Piotrowski, 2003. *Współczesny język polski [Contemporary Polish], edited by Jerzy Bartmiński*, chapter Słowniki języka polskiego [Dictionaries of Polish]. Marie Curie-Sklodowska University Press, Lublin.

Laurent Prévot, Chu-Ren Huang, Nicoletta Calzolari, Aldo Gangemi, Alessandro Lenci, and Alessandro Oltramari, 2010. *Ontology and the lexicon: a multidisciplinary perspective*, chapter 1. In Huang et al. (Huang et al., 2010), pages 3–24.

Ewa Rudnicka, Marek Maziarz, Maciej Piasecki, and Stan Szpakowicz. 2012. A Strategy of Mapping Polish WordNet onto Princeton WordNet. In *Proc. COLING 2012, posters*, pages 1039–1048.

Zygmunt Saloni, Marcin Woliński, Robert Wołosz, Włodzimierz Gruszczyński, and Danuta Skowrońska. 2012. *Słownik gramatyczny języka polskiego [A grammatical dictionary of Polish*. Warsaw University.

John Simpson. 2013. *Oxford English Dictionary*. Oxford University Press. ⟨http://www.oed.com/⟩.

Halina Zgółkowa, editor. 1994–2005. *Praktyczny słownik współczesnej polszczyzny [A practical dictionary of contemporary Polish]*. Wydawnictwo Kurpisz.

# Some Structural Tests for Wordnets, with Results

**Ahti Lohk**
Tallinn University of Technology
Akademeia tee 15a
Tallinn, Estonia
ahti.lohk@ttu.ee

**Heili Orav**
University of Tartu
Liivi 2
Tartu, Estonia
heili.orav@ut.ee

**Leo Võhandu**
Tallinn University of Technology
Akademeia tee 15a
Tallinn, Estonia
leo.vohandu@ttu.ee

## Abstract

This paper proposes some test-patterns (viewed as sub-structures) to evaluate the hierarchical structure of wordnets. By observing hierarchical structure, both top-down and bottom-up experiments are carried out on four wordnets: Princeton WordNet (version 3.1), Cornetto (version 2.0), the Polish Wordnet (version 2.0) and the Estonian Wordnet (version 67). The top-down approach is used to find small hierarchies, which are defined as having up to three levels of subordinates starting from unique beginners (rootsynsets). The bottom-up perspective is looking at the links that appear due to polysemy, and yet these are not. These redundant links form "asymmetric ring topology", and should be eliminated. Finally, an additional particular feature of large closed subsets will be introduced. Addressed views provide an opportunity to evaluate and/or improve the structure of wordnet hierarchies. This paper also provides an overview of the current status of these four wordnets from the according to our proposed test patterns.

## 1 Introduction

No linguist doubts the importance of wordnets. There are currently about 60 different wordnets worldwide. There are different views on the amount of information that is put into the system of synsets. But Miller and Fellbaum's primary goal, to create a large hypernym/hyponym relational style synset system is the same everywhere. Groups of specialists are involved in every implementation of wordnet for a given language. Every specialist has her/his subjective view about the relational connections between synsets.

It is important that every team has a strong belief in the high quality of the system they have created.

The theory and practice of building and checking computer chips with many millions of elements has proven that one has to build an independent test system to check designer created connections. As wordnets are similarly complex systems, we aim to build such a test system for wordnets.

The task of tests is to create lists of different types of inconsistencies which any Wordnet has at the given moment. Structural inconsistencies do not always translate to a wordnet error. The last word in checking wordnet lists always belongs to a lexicographer. What is truly crucial is that such lists are comprehensive. Tests must check all structurally weak areas of a given wordnet at any given moment.

After a lexicographer has made needed corrections, there follows a repetition of the same test. Such an iterative process has only one goal – to come to a clear understanding of all the weak places a given test can find.

Every created test has a different power. Some tests point with 100% probability to an error made by a lexicographer, although the error rate is usually below 100%. Such tests also have an important lexicographic value, as a long list of inconsistencies usually points to a complicated linguistic problem lacking a unique solution.

In this article we study only hypernym/hyponym relations.

## 2 Background of the wordnets

### 2.1 Princeton WordNet (PrWN)

Wordnets (Fellbaum, 1998) have emerged as one of the basic standard lexical resources in the language technology field. Princeton WordNet (PrWN) and most other wordnets are structured into synsets. A synset is usually described as capturing a lexicalised concept. Synsets are linked by conceptual relations with names borrowed from linguistic work on lexical semantics, such as hypernymy, holonymy, meronymy and so on.

More than 60 languages followed suit for building wordnets for their vernacular and very different compilation strategies have been applied. Some teams have decided to translate PrWN and adjust the result of that translation. Some wordnet developers have chosen an opposite route, such as expanding from the most frequent words or from top concepts as it has seen in ontological approaches.

The following is a brief introductory description of three databases from the Fenno-Ugric language family, and the Germanic and Slavic branches of the Indo-European language family.

### 2.2 Cornetto

The goal of Cornetto[1] was to build a lexical semantic database for Dutch, following the structure and content of Wordnet and FrameNet. Cornetto comprises information from two electronic dictionaries: the *Referentie Bestand Nederlands*, which contains FrameNet-like structures, and the *Dutch wordnet* (DWN) which utilises typical wordnet structures. DWN has a similar structure as the English WordNet although the top-level hierarchy was developed from an ontological framework and more horizontal relations are defined. The database has 70,371 synsets and 119,108 lexical units.

### 2.3 Polish Wordnet (plWN)

Work on PolNet began in 2005 (Derwojedowa, 2008), and its thesaurus is currently composed of nearly 116,000 synonym sets. The plWN development was organised in an incremental way, starting with general and frequently used vocabulary. The most frequent words from a reference corpus of the Polish language were selected.

### 2.4 Estonian Wordnet (EstWN)

The Estonian Wordnet began as part of the EuroWordNet project (Vossen, 1998), and was built by translating base concepts from English to allow monolingual extension. Words (literals) to be included were selected on frequency basis from corpora. Extensions have been compiled manually from Estonian monolingual dictionaries and other monolingual resources. After the start several methods have been used, for example domain-specific, i.e there have been dealt with semantic fields like architecture, transportation etc, there are some endeavors to add derivatives automatically and the results have been used of sense disambiguation process. Version 67 of EstWN consists of 60,434 synsets, including 82,515 words.

[1] http://www2.let.vu.nl/oz/cltl/cornetto/index.html

## 3 Related works

The most similar research to our paper has been done by Tom Richens, who has studied the anomalies in the WordNet verb hierarchies (Richens, 2008). Under the notion of topological anomalies, he notes three types of sub-structures in the hierararchical structure of WordNet that should be checked: "cycles", "rings" (these in turn are classified into "asymmetric ring topology" and "symmetric ring topology") and "dual inheritance". He emphasizes that if "dual ineritance" (which also includes "asymmetric ring topology" and "symmetric ring topology") appears, it merits investigation.

In his paper, Richens refers to the work of Pavel Smrž (Smrž, 2004) and Yang Liu (Liu, 2004). Smrž proposes twenty-seven tests for quality control in wordnet development. In most cases these tests are dealing with editing errors like "empty ID, POS, SYNONYM, SENSE (XML validation)" or "duplicate literals in one synset", but some of them are errors of hierarchical structure, like "cycles", "dangling uplinks", "structural difference from PWN and other wordnets", "multi-parent relations".

Lin proves and refers to two kind of hypernymy faults in WordNet (about version 2.0): rings and isolators, and asserts that "In the future, some amendments should be made to solve these issues during the evolution of WordNet" (Liu, 2004).

Research about quality and evaluation of WordNet are made also by Aron N. Kaplan et al. (Kaplan, 2001), Philippe Martin (Martin, 2003), Raghuvar Nadig (Nadig, 2008) and Tomáš Čapek (Čapek, 2012).

## 4 Top-down view, small hierarchies

A top-down view of the structure will begin walking through the unique beginner separating all hierarchical structures (see Fig. 2), which end after the root of the concept on three next levels. This view can be useful for detecting small hierarchies that have somehow remained unconnected to a higher hierarchy. A large number of small hierarchies points to a lack of feedback (see Table 1).

PrWN was originally constructed with 25 unique beginners (rootsynset). These rootsynsets were later connected to a single unique beginner labeled "entity" (Miller, 2007). From Table 1, it can be seen that in the PrWN there are only 11

| Princeton WordNet | |
|---|---|
| rootsynset | **352** (n-12, v-340, a-0) |
| 1 add. level | 155 (n-11, v-144, a-0) |
| 2 add. levels | 81 (n-0, v-81, a-0) |
| 3 add. levels | 48 (n-0, v-48, a-0) |
| **Cornetto** | |
| rootsynset | **497** (a-454, n-2, v-2, r-12, c-27) |
| 1 add. level | 285 (a-263, r-11, c-1) |
| 2 add. levels | 148 (a-137, r-1, c-10) |
| 3 add. levels | 40 (a-37, n-1, c-2) |
| **Polish WordNet** | |
| rootsynset | **861** (n-531, v-35, j-295) |
| 1 add. level | 586 (n-335, v-25, j-226) |
| 2 add. levels | 159 (n-100, v-9, j-50) |
| 3 add. levels | 49 (n-34, v-0, j-15) |
| **Estonian WordNet** | |
| rootsynset | **169** (n-129, v-4, a-36) |
| 1 add. level | 128 (n-94, v-0, a-34) |
| 2 add. levels | 18 (n-16, v-0, a-2) |
| 3 add. levels | 6 (n-6, v-0, a-0) |

Table 1: Number of rootsynsets and number of hierarchies that have only up to three additional levels of subordinates. (Numbers in brackets are about parts of speech as it is shown in every WordNet database.)

noun root synsets with one additional level of hierarchy, which is probably either due to human error, or unfinished work.

According to Table 1, Cornetto has only two noun and two verb hierarchies. That shows that every added synset is located directly into a large hierarchy. (Rootsynsets for the nouns are iets:2 and niets:1, translated as "something" and "nothing".)

The much smaller number of Estonian Wordnet's rootsynsets (169) is due to the fact that the team has gradually started to take into account the specific nature of the information obtained by structural tests. For example, in version 65, the number of rootsynsets was 303. Most of the decrease in rootsynsets is due to the fall of noun rootsysets has been reduced from 248 to 129.

It may be wise to take advantage of the low number of verb root concepts of EstWN to improve other wordnets' verb hierarchies. This is certainly the case when the number of root concepts is too big.

The number of small hierarchies can be reduced considerably trying to locate them in the bigger hierarchy. This approach is a particular issue in the noun and verb trees.

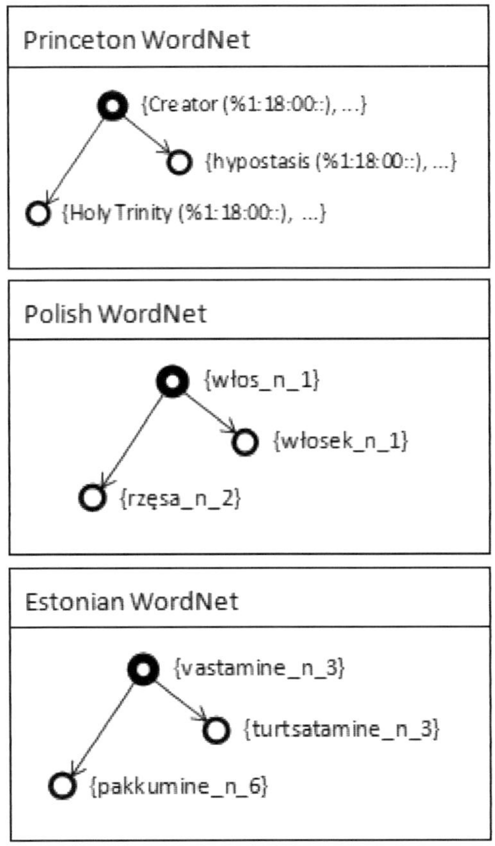


Figure 1: Small hierarchies. Rootsynsets with one additional level.

## 5 Bottom-up view, asymmetric ring topology

In this view, we are moving from lower level synsets to higher ones starting from synsets with many parents and separating substructures where such synsets are related to other synset directly and indirectly (see Fig. 2). The resulting subset is also referred to as a asymmetric ring topology (Richens, 2008) (see Table 2). This sub-structure may occur if lexicographers have created a new, more precise link to another synset, forgot to remove the previous relation. In this case one synset is connected to hypernym-synsets twice - directly and indirectly through other hypernym-synset (see Fig. 2)

## 6 The Largest Closed Subset (LGS)

LGS in hierarchical structures has been regarded as a coherent bipartite graph (Lohk, 2013).

| | Synsets with many parents | Asymmetric ring topology |
|---|---|---|
| PrWN | 1,425 | 30 |
| Cornetto | 2,438 | 306 |
| plWN | 10,942 | 476 |
| EstWN | 1,167 | 69 |

Table 2: Synsets with many parents and asymmetric ring topology numerically

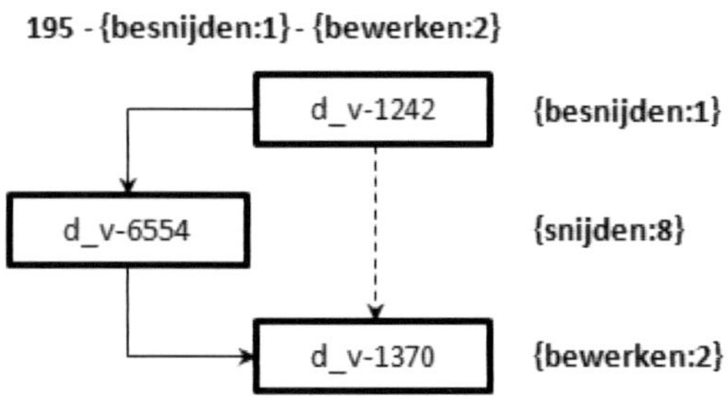


Figure 2: Asymmetric ring topology seen in Cornetto

In many cases LGS seems to be like particular feature of the hierarchical structure that links different hierarchical structures started from unique beginners. It is remarkable that in many cases the upper base of the bipartite graph consists of root-synsets (see Table 3). Authors think that this conflict arises because the concepts of the root level are put to the same level with non-roots.

In Figure 3 an artificially constructed hierachical structure with one unique beginner (root node) has been shown. Closed subsets are highlighted by rectangles. Our interest is to find only the biggest ones, this is possible when a closed subsynset has at least two parents (represented with thick lines).

According to Figure 3 and Table 3 lower nodes in a closed subset are related to the first number in the second column of the table and upper nodes in a closed subset are related to the second number also in the second column of the table.

In the case of PrWN, every upper base synset in the bipartite graph belongs to the synset "entity;" in the case of Cornetto, to "iets:2" (in eng: "something"); and in the case of EstWN into "olev" (in eng: essive). Cornetto has one more large closed subset, related to verbs. As can be see in Table 1, the overall number of verb hi-

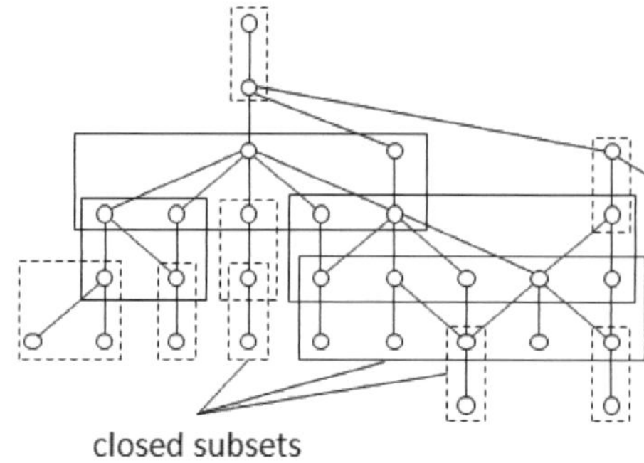


Figure 3: Artifically constructed tree of the WordNet with closed subsets

| | The biggest closed subset | Root synsets in closed subset | Synsets of closed subsets that are connected to root synsets |
|---|---|---|---|
| PrWN | 1,064 x 126 | 0 | 1 |
| Cornetto[1] | 11,032 x 589 | 0 | 1 |
| Cornetto[2] | 4,423 x 545 | 1 | 2 |
| plWN | 30,794 x 4,683 | 142 | 76 |
| EstWN | 1,526 x 66 | 8 | 1 |

Table 3: The largest closed subsets

erarchy is two and second big closed subset of Cornetto (in Table 3) connects these two (root synsets {afspelen:1, gebeuren:1, ..} and {zijn:7, uitmaken:2, vormen:5}).

While PrWN is obviously the most studied (see WordNet bibliography[2]) and Cornetto has a commercial version[3], it can be assumed that their hierarchical structure has received more attention (see Table 3, the number of rootsynsets in closed subset is in the case of PrWN and Cornetto 0).

Earlier tests with the Slovenian Wordnet (version 3.0) showed that a very large closed set may not be typical for all wordnets. It turned out that the largest closed subset size in this case was only 248 x 3.

LGS and closed subsets with many hypeonyms may be generally useful if the hypernyms in the upper base of closed sets are separated and their levels of concept are evaluated. Additionally, LGS seems to indicate the correctness (or uncorrectness) of the hierarchical structure, although this

[2] http://lit.csci.unt.edu/~wordnet/

[3] http://tst-centrale.org/nl/producten/lexica/cornetto/7-56

claim has not been definitively verified.

## 7 Discussion and Conclusion

The most difficult issue for wordnet compilers with regard to noun hierarchical relationships is to find the top hypernyms. The same also occurs in regard to finding the top concepts for the most frequent verbs, both transitive and intransitive. As for adjectives, the situation is even more unclear, as wordnets for various languages deal with adjectives differently. In some wordnets, adjectives are hierarchical (as seen in Table 1: Cornetto, EstWN), but in PWN, adjectives have different types of" semantic connections.

One analyses only the short hierarchies in all wordnet variants, (root level plus up to 3 lower levels) one comes to the realisation that new add-ons for wordnets have created a situation in which missing feedback has lost the information required to correctly connect synsets.

All wordnets studied here show that the expansion process requires strong and effective feedback.

As is made clear by Table 1, in the top-down perspective, three of the four wordnets studied here require either verb or noun hierarchy correction. However, as Cornetto has only two hierarchies for nouns and verbs, it has somehow excluded small hierarchies. This shows that Cornettos team is using different tools or/and ways for add-ons.

## References


Magdalena Derwojedowa, Maciej Piasecki, Stanislaw Szpakowicz, Magdalena Zawislawska and Bartosz Broda. 2008. *Words, Concepts and Relations in the Construction of Polish WordNet* In Proceedings of the Fourth Global WordNet Conference - GWC 2008. pp: 162–177.

Tomáš Čapek. 2012. *SENEQA – System for Quality Testing of Wordnet Data.* Proceedings of 6th International Global Wordnet Conference. Matsue, Japan, 9-13 January 2012. pp: 400-404.

Christiane D. Fellbaum. 1998. *WordNet An Electronic Lexical Database* Cambridge, Massachusetts, London, England: The MIT Press

Aaron N. Kaplan and Lenhart K. Schubert. 2001. *Measuring and improving the quality of world knowledge extracted from WordNet.* University of Rochester, Rochester, NY.

Yang Liu, Jiangsheng Yu, Zhengshan Wen and Shiwen Yu. 2004. *Two Kinds of Hypernymy Faults in WordNet: the Cases of Ring and Isolator.* Proceedings of the Second Global WordNet Conference. Brno, Czech Republic, 20-23 January 2004. pp: 347-351.

Ahti Lohk, Ottokar Tilk and Leo Võhandu . 2013. *How to Create Order in Large Closed Subsets of WordNet-type Dictionaries* Estonian Papers in Applied Linguistics 9 pp: 149–160.

Philippe Martin. 2003. *Correction and extension of WordNet 1.7* Conceptual Structures for Knowledge Creation and Communication: Springer. pp: 160–173.

George A. Miller. and Christiane D. Fellbaum. 2007. *WordNet then and now* Lang Resources & Evaluation, Volume 41, Issue 2. pp: 209–214.

Nadig Raghuvar, Ramanand J and Bhattacharyya Pushpak. 2008. *Automatic Evaluation of Wordnet Synonyms and Hypernyms* Proceedings of ICON-2008: 6th International Conference of Natural Language Processing.

Tom Richens. 2008. *Anomalies in the wordnet verb hierarchy* Proceedings of the 22nd Inter-national Conference on Computational Linguistics: COLING-ACL 2008. pp: 729–736.

Piek Vossen. 1998. *EuroWordNet: A Multilingual Database with Lexical Semantic Networks* Dordrecht: Kluwer Academic Publishers.

Pavel Smrž. 2004. *Quality Control for Wordnet Development.* Proceedings of the Second Global WordNet Conference. Brno, Czech Republic, 20-23 January 2004. pp: 206-212.

# Fusion of Multiple Semantic Networks and Human Association

**Hitoshi Isahara**
Toyohashi University of Technology
Toyohashi, Aichi, Japan
isahara@tut.jp

**Kyoko Kanzaki**
Toyohashi University of Technology
Toyohashi, Aichi, Japan
kanzaki@imc.tut.ac.jp

**Eiko Yamamoto**
Gifu Shotoku Gakuen University
Gifu, Japan
eiko@gifu.shotoku.ac.jp

**Takayuki Kuribayashi**
Toyohashi University of Technology
Toyohashi, Aichi, Japan.
kuribayashi@lang.cs.tut.ac.jp

**Michinaga Otsuka**
Toyohashi University of Technology
Toyohashi, Aichi, Japan
michinaga@lang.cs.tut.ac.jp

## Abstract

We are trying to construct a conceptual system that accurately represents human thoughts by fusing of semantic networks. As semantic networks to fuse, we use the Japanese Wordnet which is a thesaurus made manually based on linguistic intuition and the knowledge acquired automatically from the actual text stored in the huge corpus. Such knowledge are represented as mutual relations of the concepts of words. In order to acquire such relations, we focus on the case relations in sentences and calculate inclusive relations of co-occurrence by using Complementary Similarity Measure. As an application and verification of the conceptual system created, we try to simulate human associations by using the conceptual system. As an experimental result, we found the obvious difference in generated association links between using the semantic network of Japanese Wordnet and using the fused semantic networks with Japanese Wordnet and the acquired mutual relations.

## 1 Introduction

In systems that support human creativity and search, a dictionary data similar to human perception is required. Human do not think in only classification knowledge. It is insufficient for the systems which support human cognitive processes to utilize only those existing language resources such as thesauri that summarize word senses and conceptual relationships of words. Because humans express their thoughts with words, it is valid to acquire knowledge from their actual utterances and contexts reflecting their thoughts.

In this study, we are trying to construct a conceptual system that accurately represents human thoughts by fusing of semantic networks. As semantic networks to fuse, we use the following two kinds of knowledge structure. As the first one, we used the Japanese Wordnet (Isahara et al, 2008) which is a thesaurus made manually based on linguistic intuition. As the second one, we use the knowledge acquired automatically from the actual text stored in the huge corpus. Such knowledge are represented as mutual relations of the concepts of words. In order to acquire such relations, we focus on the case relations in sentences such as "case and statement," "verb and object" and "subject and verb," and calculate inclusive relations of co-occurrence by using Complementary Similarity Measure (CSM) (Hagita and Sawaki, 1995; Yamamoto et al., 2005).

As an application and verification of the conceptual system created, we try to simulate human associations by using the conceptual system. Concretely, we first conduct an experiment on the association with a stimulus word, and create the association network based on the experimental result by using our conceptual system. Then, we visualize the structure of the created association networks and analyze them as networks. As an experimental result, we found the obvious difference in generated association links between using the semantic network of Japanese Wordnet and using the fused semantic networks with Japanese Wordnet and the acquired mutual relations.

## 2 Experimental Data

To realize our aim described above, we create new knowledge structure by combining the Wordnet which is manual made thesaurus with taxonomical information and the mutual relations between words which is extracted from actual text in a huge web corpus. In this section, we explain data for our experiment.

### 2.1 Japanese Wordnet

As for Wordnet, we use Japanese Wordnet version 1.1, whose specifications are shown in Table 1.

| | |
|---|---|
| Number of words | 93,834 |
| Number of senses | 158,058 |
| Number of synlinks | 283,600 |
| Number of synset | 57,238 |
| Number of gloss | 135,692 |
| Number of example sentence | 48,276 |

Table 1. Specifications of Japanese Wordnet

### 2.2 CSM data

In this study, we utilize the knowledge based on human utterances to construct a semantic network as a representation of human thought. We use Complementary Similarity Measure (CSM) to acquire such knowledge from the actual text.

CSM is an asymmetry and noise-resistant measure. Values obtained by CSM indicate relations between words, such as Hypernym-Hyponym. We named data obtained in these process "CSM data." Comparing the Japanese Wordnet and the CSM data, we found a lot of words and word relations that retrieved from web corpus but that have not been stored in the Wordnet. Therefore, we constructed new conceptual system based on the Japanese Wordnet that enriched by conceptual relationships with word pairs in CSM data.

### 2.3 Experimental data based on case relation

In our experiment, we use web corpus with 500 million Japanese sentences (Kawahara and Kurohashi, 2006). We analyze syntactically 500 million sentences and extract pairs of words having co-occurrence relations in an actual sentence by focusing on case relation, namely modified/modifier relationship. Then, we calculate CSM value for each pairs, after we reduce some noises in the extracted pairs by setting a threshold value.

To estimate inclusive relations between words, we applied the method based on the CSM, which estimates inclusive relations between two vectors (Yamamoto et al., 2011). By using an appearance pattern as a feature vector for each word in treating linguistic resource such as a corpus or document collection, we have reported being able to determine a relation between two words according to the inclusive relation estimated by the CSM value.

The Japanese language has case-marking particles that indicate the semantic relation between two words in a dependency relation. Then, using the syntactic analysis result of the web corpus, we collected words in case (dependency) relations.

We considered the meaning of some case relations as follows.

Subject and Verb (SV)

The set of verbs that occur with certain kinds of nouns as their subject represents the behavior of the noun. To extract this relation, we use case-marking particle <ga>.

For example, if "dog" occurs with "eat" and "bear," and "animal" occurs with "fly", "eat", and "bear", then we considers that "dog is an animal" since the behavior of "dog" is a subset of (or included in) the behavior of "animal."

Verb and Object (VO)

The set of verbs that occur with certain kinds of nouns as their object represents "how to treat." To extract this relation, we use case-marking particle <wo>.

For example, as "criminal" often appears as an object of the verb "catch," we can imagine that a criminal is a person who tend to be caught.

Noun and Sentence (NS)

For each noun N in a sentence S, we can regard that N co-occurs with S. In other words, nouns appearing in same sentence have a relationship each other. They tend to be together in one specific scene in a real world. In our experiment, we extracted such relations by gathering nouns in a sentence with case-marking particles <ga>, <no>, <wo>, and <de>.

| | NS | SV | VO | SO-S | SO-O |
|---|---|---|---|---|---|
| Number of extracted words | 4,676,041 | 1,449,150 | 1,503,255 | 395,734 | 346,531 |
| Threshold | 10 | 2 | 3 | 2 | 2 |
| Number after elimination | 246,717 | 176,511 | 114,336 | 31,531 | 32,703 |
| Number of links with positive CSM value | 19,279,434 | 1,908,489,076 | 718,477,958 | 27,801,885 | 46,351,392 |

SO-S means nouns in subject position classified by similarities of nouns in object position in a sentence. SO-O is vice versa.

Table 2. Statistics of extracted words and relations

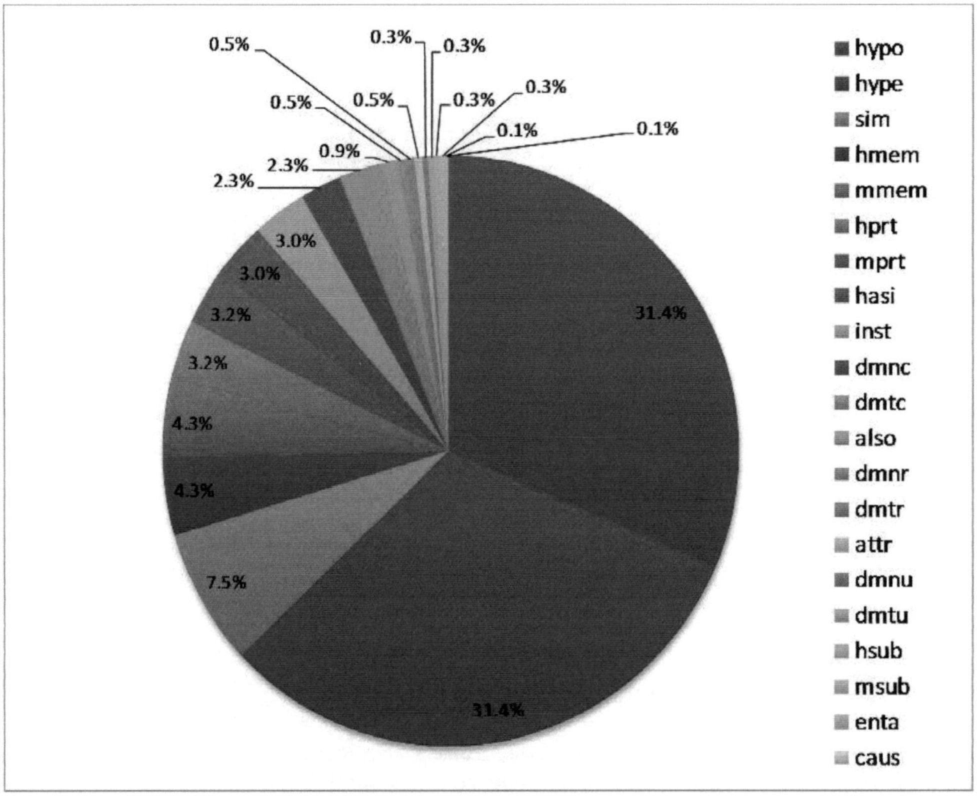


Figure 1. Breakdown of links in Japanese Wordnet

Subject and Object (SO)

This co-occurrence relation is the combination of a subject and an object for same verb.

For example, in the sentence "a human eats a bread", "human" and "bread" are extracted as a combination.

As described above, we calculate the similarity between two words based on the word co-occurrence by using CSM. To do this, we represent by a binary vector experimental data which extracted from corpora based on the case relation; the vector corresponds to the appearance pattern of a noun. We apply the CSM for the calculation (Yamamoto et al. 2005). Parameters for calculating the CSM-value correspond to the number of dimensions in each situation.

Table 2 shows the number of extracted words, the number of extracted words after the elimination by a threshold, its threshold (number of occurrence) and combination of words which has positive CSM value, for each case relation.

In this paper, we use NS data, because it could extract enough number of data with variety of CSM values.

## 3 Comparison between Japanese Wordnet and CSM data

In this section, we compare Japanese Wordnet with relation between concepts and CSM data which consists of links between two words with its CSM value.

As shown in Table 1, there are 286,300 synlink entries in Japanese Wordnet. Among them, 178,178 entries (63%) are taxonomical links such as hyponym and hypernym. Figure 1 shows the statistics of links in Japanese Wordnet.

As shown in Table 2, we extracted 19,279,434 links which have positive CSM value from our experiments. We chose top 5% of these links by setting a CSM value as a threshold (926,653 links). We use this extracted and eliminated CSM data, i.e. word links with CSM value, for comparison with Japanese Wordnet. The result of comparison are shown in Table 3.

In Table 3, "Number of data" means that the number of links (or relations) extracted automatically by our system. "Percentage for all CSM data" is the percentage of the data among all extracted and eliminated CSM data.

"No wordid" means that one or two words related to this link of CSM data are not stored in Japanese Wordnet. As shown in Table 3, about 63% of data contain words which are not stored in Japanese Wordnet. It shows that CSM data which was extracted automatically from huge corpus are useful to improve the coverage of vocabulary which appears in the real text.

"No synlink" means there is no relation between two synsets in Japanese Wordnet, which correspond to two words in each CSM data. 37% of CSM data are categorized into this class. This category means we can add new relations (links) into Japanese Wordnet based on the cooccurrency between words in the huge corpus.

"Same synset" means that two words in CSM data are treated as synonyms in the Japanese Wordnet. "Hypernym," "hyponym" and others, which are not shown in Table 2, means that two words are already stored in Japanese wordnet properly. We found 1,415 such relations by this experiments, i.e. Hypernym (578), Hyponym (475) and others (362).

| Relation | Number of data | Percentage for all CSM data |
|---|---|---|
| No wordid | 582555 | 62.8666 |
| No synlink | 341868 | 36.8928 |
| Same synset | 815 | 0.08795 |
| Hypernym | 578 | 0.06238 |
| Hyponym | 475 | 0.05126 |

Table 3. Comparison between Japanese Wordnet and CSM data

## 4 Creation of New Knowledge System by Fusing Two Network Structure

In this section, we construct a conceptual system by fusing of semantic networks, i.e. Japanese Wordnet and set of word links extracted by CSM based method.

As CSM can extract many relations between words from the input data, i.e. huge corpus, we decided to set a threshold of CSM value to eliminate the number of links to fuse. We add links after elimination to Japanese Wordnet. There are 178,178 links stored in Japanese Wordnet as hyponym or hypernym. Among them, relations between nouns are 151,700. As we could get 151,604 relations with the threshold of 8200, we set the threshold 8200, and add these 151,604 relations to Japanese Wordnet, which means that we enlarge twice in size of conceptual system.

## 5 Human Association

### 5.1 Experiments by Human Subject

In order to verify our new concept system, we conducted experiments about human association with human subjects.

If a concept structure resembles to human knowledge structure, connecting two concepts in the concept structure means simulating human associations from one concept to the other. Wordnet resembles taxonomical knowledge that human made, and CSM data (NS data) shows the knowledge of scenes which humans picture in mind. Combining these two different kinds of knowledge, we are trying to create human knowledge structure which resembles more than other existing knowledge systems.

Figure 2. Experiments by high school pupils

We presented test sheet with 11 stimulus nouns to 51 participants (31 university students and 20 senior high school pupils), and asked them to write down what s/he associated by each stimulus words (Figure 2).

If we can find shorter connections of links between a stimulus word and an associated word via our system than Japanese Wordnet, our system is closer to knowledge structure of humans than Wordnet, at least from the viewpoint of associations by humans.

We made network of conceptual links between a stimulus word and associated words for visibility purpose.

For stimulus words, we use 11 nouns (music, curry, apple, soccer, scissors, communication, love, arm, pasta, school, vegetable), which were mostly selected by the following conditions;

Word stored in the Japanese Wordnet.
Concrete object.
Possibility of associations.
General word, not too specific.

With 11 stimulus words and 20 high school participants, we got a total of 1,456 words including 690 different words, such as "music: jazz, disco and rock" and "curry: rice, carrot."

### 5.2 Consideration to Simulate Associations

Figure 3 shows the association network using Pajek (Pajek—Program for large network analysis) for stimulus word "腕 ude 'arm' " by new concept system. Here association network means set of links between stimulus word and associated words. In Figure 3, only a stimulus word and associated words which are directly connected to a stimulus word or associated words are visualized in order to consider the relations between associated words.

There are "腕 ude 'arm' " and "アーム aamu 'arm' " in the Left-hand side of the figure. As both "腕 ude 'arm' " and "アーム aamu 'arm' " are in the same synset of Japanese Wordnet, this association, i.e. from "腕 ude 'arm' " to "アーム aamu 'arm' ", is a kind of paraphrase. The associated words shown in the middle of the figure are words directly associated from a stimulus words, such as "筋肉 kinniku 'muscle' ". There is "料理人 ryorinin 'cook' " which is different direction of association to other associated words. This association is caused by the polysemous feature of Japanese word "腕 ude 'arm' ", i.e. physical arm and ability about a technique. The word in the right-hand side of Figure 3, such as "タンパク質 tanpakushitsu 'protein' " can be thought as associations not directly from arm but via an associated word in the middle, e.g.,

"腕 ude 'arm' "
--- "筋肉 kinniku 'muscle' "
--- "タンパク質 tanpakushitsu 'protein' "

"腕 ude 'arm' "
--- "体 karada 'body' "
--- "服 fuku 'clothes' "

In order to make detailed discussion, we have to explore more about human association and network structure we created, however, current simple network seems to reflect procedure of human associations to a certain degree.

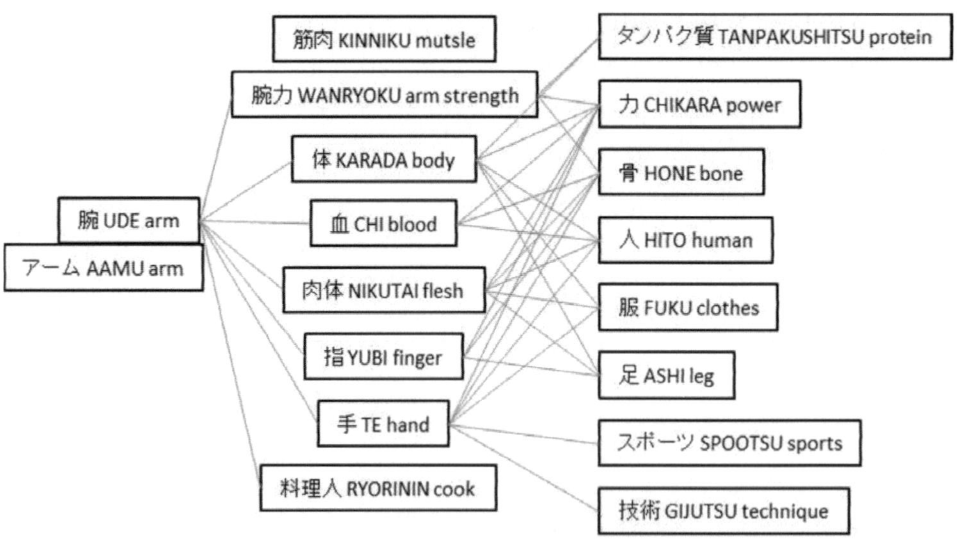

Figure 3. Partial association network for "腕 ude 'arm' "

## 6 Conclusion

In this study, we proposed and constructed a new conceptual system that by fusing of two different kinds of semantic networks. As semantic networks to fuse, we used the Japanese Wordnet which is a thesaurus made manually based on linguistic intuition and the new type of semantic structure which comes from the knowledge based on human utterances that are mutual relations of the concepts acquired automatically from the actual text.

In order to verify our new concept system, we conducted experiments by human subjects. We discussed the possibility of humanlike associations with our system.

We will consider tuning values assigned to each link of network precisely based on real associations conducted by humans by using simulation technology and huge computer power.

## References


Norihiro Hagita and Minako Sawaki, 1995. Robust recognition of degraded machine-printed characters using complementary similarity measure and error-correction learning. *Proceedings of SPIE – The International Society for Optical Engineering,* 2442:236-244.

Hitoshi Isahara, Francis Bond, Kiyotaka Uchimoto, Masao Utiyama and Kyoko Kanzaki, 2008. Development of Japanese WordNet, LREC2008, Marrakech.

Daisuke Kawahara and Sadao Kurohashi, 2006. A Fully-lexicalized Probabilistic Model for Japanese Syntactic and Case Structure Analysis, *In Proceedings of HLT-NAACL2006*, 176-183.

Pajek—Program for large network analysis. Version 2.05. Available from: `http://vlado.fmf.uni-lj.si/pub/networks/pajek/`

Eiko Yamamoto, Kyoko Kanzaki and Hitoshi Isahara, 2005. Extraction of hierarchies based on inclusion of co-occurring words with frequency information. *Proceedings of IJCAI 2005*, 1166-1172.

Eiko Yamamoto and Hitoshi Isahara, 2011. Creative Information Retrieval Using Thematically Related Words. *Information Extraction from the Internet*, Chapter 13, iConcept Press

# Semi-Automatic Extension of Sanskrit Wordnet using Bilingual Dictionary

**Sudha Bhingardive**
Center for Indian Language Technology,
Indian Institute of Technology Bombay
sudha@cse.iitb.ac.in

**Tanuja Ajotikar**
Department of Humanities and Social Sciences,
Indian Institute of Technology Bombay
gtanu30@gmail.com

**Irawati Kulkarni**
Center for Indian Language Technology,
Indian Institute of Technology Bombay
irawatikulkarni@gmail.com

**Malhar Kulkarni**
Department of Humanities and Social Sciences,
Indian Institute Technology Bombay
malhar@iitb.ac.in

**Pushpak Bhattacharyya**
Center for Indian Language Technology,
Indian Institute Technology Bombay
pb@cse.iitb.ac.in

## Abstract

In this paper, we report our methods and results of using, for the first time, semi-automatic approach to enhance an Indian language Wordnet. We apply our methods to enhancing an already existing Sanskrit Wordnet created from Hindi Wordnet (which is created from Princeton Wordnet) using expansion approach. We base our experiment on an existing bilingual Sanskrit English Dictionary and show how lemma in this dictionary can be mapped to Princeton Wordnet through which corresponding Sanskrit synsets can be populated by Sanskrit lexemes. This our method will also show how absence of resources of a pair of languages need not be an obstacle, if another resource of one of them is available. Sanskrit being historically related to languages of Indo-European family, we believe that this semi-automatic approach will help enhance Wordnets of other Indian languages of the same family.

## 1 Introduction

Wordnet is a lexical semantic network, widely used in various applications of natural language processing. Princeton wordnet (PWN) is the mother of all Wordnets (Fellbaum, 1988). It was created at the Cognitive Science Laboratory of Princeton University. EuroWordNet (Vossen, 1998; Vossen, 2000), CoreNet (Choi, 2004), IndoWordNet (Bhattacharyya, 2010), HowNet (Zhendong, 2000), MultiWordNet (Bentivogli, 2000; Bentivogli and Pianta 2000), BabelNet (Navigli, 2012) and so many other Nets are also some of the most commonly used semantic networks.

PWN is manually created using the knowledge from various dictionaries. Several Wordnets are created semi-automatically using the expansion approach from PWN. Many of them use bilingual dictionaries or Wikipedia. This type of creation saves enormous manual efforts and time. However, it demands high quality machine-readable resources in the respective languages.

Sanskrit wordnet (SWN) (Kulkarni *et.al*, 2010) is manually created using the expansion approach from Hindi wordnet (HWN), which in turn was created from the Princeton Wordnet. The current status of Sanskrit wordnet is stated in Table 1.

**Total synsets**: 22912 **Total unique words**: 44950

| POS | Noun | Verb | Adverb | Adjective |
|---|---|---|---|---|
| synset counts | 17413 | 1246 | 263 | 3990 |

Table 1: Sanskrit wordnet current status

## 2 Motivation

In this work, we aim to report our experiences to populate SWN by a semi-automated approach. Currently, manual approach is used which is time consuming and tedious. Following are the reasons that make manual approach time consuming.

### 2.1 Large number of synonyms for a Sanskrit word

In the available lexical literature of Sanskrit (given below in Section 3), normal range for number of words in any synset varies between 1–20 *e.g., līlā* [a game (6 synset members)], *vṛddhaḥ* [an old man (20 synset members)], *bhakṣaṇam* [an act of eating (20 synset members)]. Synsets with only one word are common in the cases of coined words, instrument names and kinship relations. However, some synsets exceed this limit and have huge number of words as its members. We note below some of the prominent phenomena.

- Synsets expressing concepts in the domain of mythology, culture, religion and philosophy contain large number of words *e.g., viṣṇuḥ* [Hindu deity (127 synset members)], *somaḥ* [a God (120 sysnet members)], *yuddha* [a war (97 synset members)], *sūryaḥ* [the Sun (85 synset members)], *samudraḥ* [an ocean (synset members)].
- Synsets of noun/adjective category containing words with features of derivational morphology tend to have large number of words *e.g., dyutimat* [bright (246 synset members)], *Shikhin* [one who possesses antenna (40 synset members)].
- The process of compound formation in Sanskrit allows creation of multiple synonyms and therefore synsets containing such compounds tend to have large number of words *e.g., devaalaya* [house of gods = temple (50 synset members)], *alpamati* [one who possesses little intellect (40 synset members)].

For creating above mentioned synsets, lexicographers gathered information from various resources, *e.g.,* while creating a concept of *yuddha* (a war), 97 words were collected from various lexical resources given below: Spoken Sanskrit Dictionary[1] (7 words), Apate's Sanskrit-English Dictionar[2] (7 words), Monier William's English–Sanskrit Dictionary[3] (57 words) and Shabdakalpadrum (80 words).

After collecting the words, duplicate words were eliminated. Words representing proper meanings are entered in the synset. This process is monetarily expensive and time consuming. Automatic approach can help populate such synsets using bilingual dictionaries. In the process there will be over-generation which will have to be controlled by manual approach.

### 2.2 Appropriate selection of words for creating synsets

While creating the synsets, appropriate selection of words is required to express the precise meaning. In Hindu texts, which are mainly in Sanskrit there are various names for a single deity *e.g., Viṣṇu* (Hindu deity) has 132 names, *Kṛṣṇa* has 132 names and *Rāma* has 67 names. For creating synsets of these deities one must be very careful as *Kṛṣṇa* and *Rāma* are incarnations of *Viṣṇu* and can easily get interchanged and thereby affecting the intended meaning.

The road-map of the paper is as follows. Section 3 presents the related work. Section 4 explains the methodology used for extension of SWN. Section 5 illustrates results. Outcomes are presented in Section 6. Section 7 includes conclusion and future work.

## 3 Related Work

Most of the Wordnets are created by expansion approach using PWN. Several Wordnets have tried to increase their coverage using various automatic or semi-automatic approaches. Some of them are listed below. CoreNet (Choi, 2004) is an automatically constructed Wordnet, which uses a Japanese–Korean electronic dictionary. Korean words are programmatically generated during translation from Japanese. BabelNet (Navigli, 2012) is a very large, wide-coverage, multilingual semantic network. This resource is created by mapping a multilingual encyclopedic knowledge repository (Wikipedia) and a computational lexicon of English (PWN). The integration is performed via an automatic mapping and by filling in lexical gaps in resource-poor languages with the

[1] http://spokensanskrit.de/
[2] http://www.aa.tufs.ac.jp/~tjun/sktdic/
[3] http://www.sanskrit-lexicon.uni-koeln.de/monier/mwauthorities/mwauth_SktDevaUnicode.html#record_Lalit_

aid of Machine Translation. This provides concepts and named entities, lexicalized in many languages and connected with large amounts of semantic relations. Chinese Wordnet (Renjie Xu, 2008) is developed in an automatic manner by translating English words to Chinese using Chinese–English dictionary. Czech wordnet (Karel Pala, 2008) is automatically extended from PWN using machine-readable bilingual dictionary. Polish WordNet (M. Derwojedowa, 2008) is designed semi-automatically by extracting lexical relations from the large Polish corpora. Lexicographers are used for mapping these relations with PWN.

### 3.1 Why was Monier William's Sanskrit–English dictionary used for extending SWN?

We have used the publicly available Monier William's Sanskrit–English dictionary for SWN semi-automatic extension. The list of all the texts used by Monier Williams is publicly available. This dictionary includes over 1, 80, 000 words and definitions. All entries are organized according to the root of a word, the *dhatu*, which offers better understanding of the meaning of the word. It includes special references to cognate Indo-European languages as well as literary citations. It provides precise meanings for the words in the Vedic literature, which is useful for studying the scriptures. This is one of the most comprehensive and useful Sanskrit–English dictionaries. The other reason for using this dictionary for the present purpose, fortunately, is availability. Out of all the lexical resources mentioned above, only this is available in program readable format which makes this resource singularly important from the point of view of present research. One of the outputs of the use of this resource is extraction of proper nouns. We have automatically extracted them and added to SWN without linking them to PWN. This method is explained in Section 4.2.

## 4 Methodologies used for extending SWN

SWN is created by expansion approach from HWN, which was in turn created by PWN.

Figure 1: SWN manual creation

Our selected resource is in Sanskrit and English. Therefore, in order to utilize it for the present purpose we have to link PWN directly to SWN.

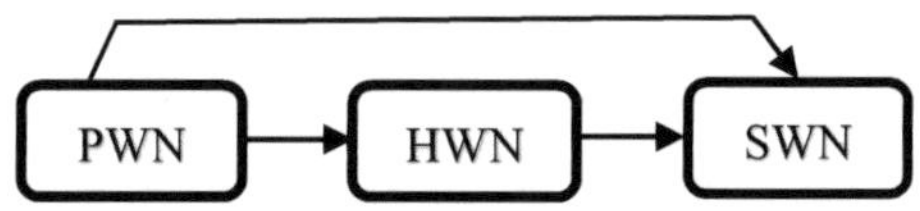


Figure 2: SWN semi-automatic creation

We link Sanskrit–English dictionary to PWN by using a heuristic. This will be automatic approach. These linkages are validated by lexicographers. This will be manual approach. Thus we will populate SWN by semi-automatic approach using this resource.

### 4.1 Heuristics used for linking William's dictionary to PWN

William's dictionary contains Sanskrit words along with its English description. The description is concise for most of the Sanskrit words, *e.g.*, *kamala* (lotus) has the description 'a lotus'. In comparison, PWN glosses are descriptive as shown in Figure 3.

| | | |
|---|---|---|
| **MW Dictionary** | **Word:** *kamala* | **English Definition** a lotus |
| **Princeton Wordnet** | **Synset:** lotus, Indian lotus, sacred lotus, Nelumbonucifera | **Gloss/Definition** native to eastern Asia; widely cultivated for its large pink or white flowers) |

Figure 3: Dictionary and PWN entry for *kamala* (a lotus)

Finding the maximum overlap between the description words in dictionary and PWN gloss words is not efficient as we get several possible mappings. It is monetarily expensive and time consuming to generate and validate these mappings. Therefore, this type of heuristic is not suitable for linking dictionary to PWN.

William's dictionary is a very rich resource in Sanskrit language, which is useful for extending the SWN. Hence, we linked dictionary to PWN using a heuristic, which finds the maximum overlap between description words in dictionary and words in PWN synsets. Using this heuristic, the dictionary entries are linked to PWN. We got 14653 single and 55059 multiple possible mappings. Lexicographers are in the process of validating these mappings. The architecture diagram of the process is shown in Figure 4. Following are the steps for the procedure to link dictionary to PWN.

- For a Sanskrit word $S_w$, from dictionary, its equivalent English description is taken and its maximum overlap with words in the PWN synsets is found.
- $S_w$ is directly mapped to the synset if the word in the description is found to be monosemous in PWN.
- The mapping is evaluated manually if the word in the description is found to be polysemous in PWN.

After successful mapping, all Sanskrit words are added in SWN.

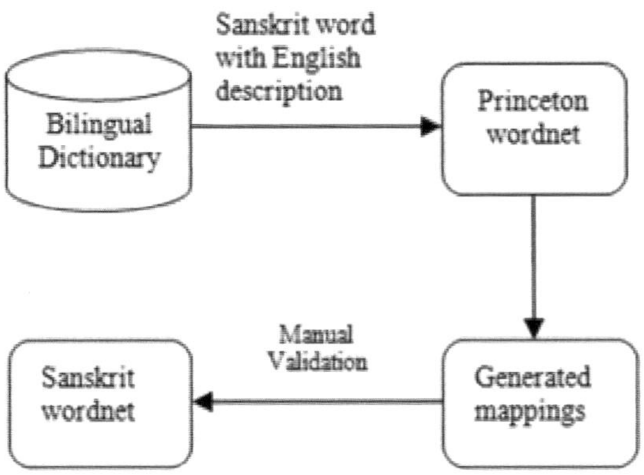


Figure 4: Architecture diagram

This task can be explained with the help of an example, for the word '*kartr*' (spinner), we found three possible mappings in PWN. For validating these multiple possible mappings, we designed an interface as shown in Figure 5. It provides various functionalities on mappings *viz.,* display, search, validate and delete. A lexicographer will select an appropriate mapping with the synset in PWN of correct sense.

After manual validation, all dictionary entries with valid mappings are inserted into the Sanskrit wordnet. Adding of all the dictionary entries maually requires excessive efforts. Thus, a semi-automatic approach will save these excessive manual efforts.

### 4.2 Other automatic application of Wiliam's dictionary to populate SWN

If the English description of the Sanskrit word began with the phrase 'Name of a', all such words can be considered as proper nouns. For example, the word '*Brahamhapuri'* has the description, 'Name of a location'. Currently all proper nouns are part of the Wordnet. However, it is yet to be decided whether these are maintained in a separate gazetteer (gazetteers are those which contain entities themselves that are proper nouns), which will in turn link to SWN. If it is decided that they are to be treated as a part of Wordnet then it would add 14,339 synsets to SWN.

Some of the extracted nouns are class names. For example, the word '*Ustika'* has the description 'Name of a kind of plant' and the word '*Bhaumadevalipi*' has the description 'Name of a kind writing'. Both these words are class names. All class names are not stored in a gazetteer. They are very much stored in the SWN. So far, fifty-five class names are extracted from the dictionary and stored in SWN.

## 5 Results

As discussed in Section 4.1 we are linking dictionary with PWN. There are 14, 653 Sanskrit words for which single mappings were found in PWN and 55, 059 words for which multiple mappings were found in PWN. The work of these mappings is still under validation process. We have extracted 14,339 proper nouns from dictionary, which are not covered by SWN.

These proper nouns must get inserted into SWN as these are most frequent occurrences in Sanskrit literature. Current synset coverage status of SWN is illustrated in Table 1. After adding dictionary entries, SWN coverage will increase considerably. With this semi-automatic approach, SWN will be a richer lexical resource in Sanskrit language.

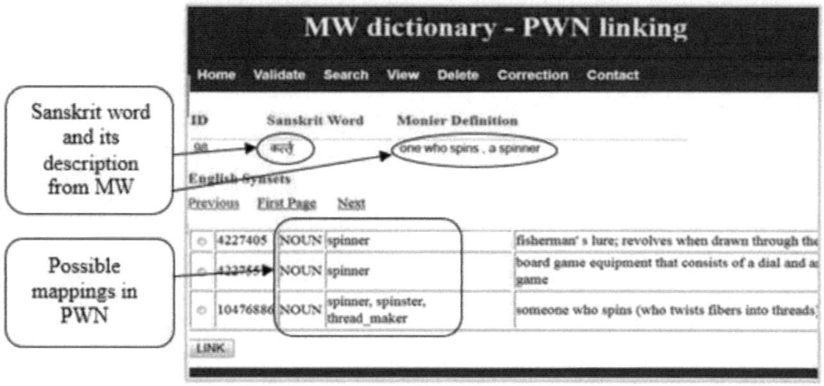


Figure 5: Interface for validating multiple possible mappings

## 6 Outcomes: Improving SWN-HWN-PWN linkages

6.1 SWN synsets can be corrected with the help of William's dictionary. For example, in SWN, one synset containing the word '*dīptiḥ*' is linked to the sense of 'luster' in PWN. However, in William's dictionary sense of '*dīptiḥ*' is {Brightness, Slight, splendor, beauty} which is different than this already linked to PWN sense (luster). As this dictionary is considered as an authentic lexical resource for Sanskrit we can remove the word '*dīptiḥ*' from the corresponding SWN synset.

6.2 Coverage of HWN will also improve with the help of dictionary. For example, dictionary provides the same English meaning 'moonless' for all the Sanskrit words namely '*acandra*', '*naṣṭacandra*', '*niḥsomaka*', and '*visoma*'. In the existing HWN, the concept of 'moonless' is not available. It is also not covered in SWN as it is created using expansion approach from HWN. The above mentioned words form a synset and can be added to SWN and then be further borrowed in HWN. In this way, we are also increasing the HWN coverage using dictionary and SWN as shown below.

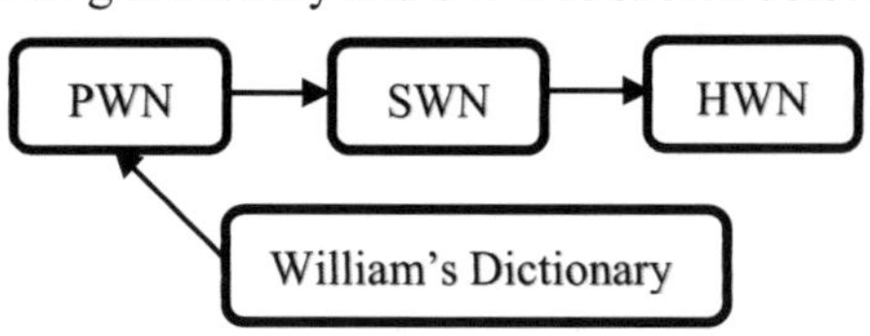


Figure 6: HWN enriched with SWN and William's dictionary

6.3 Some existing SWN synsets are not linked with PWN as SWN–PWN linking is via HWN. We are also improving these linkages using the dictionary. For example, an HWN synset corresponding to one of the synsets of *vilāsin* in SWN, is not linked with PWN. English description of *vilāsin* is given as '*coquettish*' in the William's dictionary. Both Sanskrit and English interpretation are under the same POS category of adjective. Thus, now we can link this SWN synset to PWN synset. In this way we are improving SWN–HWN–PWN linkages.

## 7 Conclusion and Future work

We have attempted to implement a semi-automatic approach for Sanskrit wordnet extension using Monier William's Sanskrit–English dictionary. Dictionary entries are automatically extracted and linked to PWN which need manual validation. For this purpose we have created a tool (Figure 5) which is language independent and therefore can be adopted by other similar language pairs. Post manual validation, all these entries will be inserted to SWN. Also, we have automatically extracted proper nouns from dictionary, which play an important role in Sanskrit literature. With the help of this approach we are correcting existing synset members of SWN and existing SWN–HWN–PWN linkages. HWN coverage can also be increased with the help of this approach. Following this approach, we will generate all semantic and lexical relations automatically from the same bilingual dictionary. This work can be extended using other resources like Böhtlingk and Roth's Sanskrit–German dictionary along with Monier William's dictionary for learning some useful patterns to make SWN a rich resource in Sanskrit language.

## Acknowledgements

We thank to Dr. Peter Scharf, President, Sanskrit Library, United States of America, for providing the database. We acknowledge the work which provides an XML encoding of the Monier Williams Sanskrit-English Dictionary which was done in collaboration between the Institute of Indology and Tamil Studies (IITS) of the University of Cologne and Brown University's Sanskrit Department.

## References

Luisa Bentivogli, Emanuele Pianta and Fabio Pianesi, 2000. Coping with lexical gaps when building aligned multilingual wordnets, In Proceedings of LREC2000, Athens, Greece.

Luisa Bentivogli, Emanuele Pianta, 2000. Looking for lexical gaps, Proceedings of Euralex, Stuttgart, Germany.

Pushpak Bhattacharyya, 2010. IndoWordNet, Lexical Resources Engineering Conference (LREC), Malta.

Key-Sun Choi and Hee-Sook Bae, 2004. Procedures and Problems in Korean-Chinese-Japanese Wordnet with Shared Semantic Hierarchy, GWC2004.

Magdalena Derwojedowa, Maciej Piasecki, Stanisaw Szpakowicz, Magdalena Zawisawska and Bartosz Broda, 2008. Words, concepts and relations in the construction of Polish WordNet, In Proceedings of the Global WordNet Conference, Seged, Hungary.

Dong Zhen Dong, 1988. Knowledge Description: What, How and Who? , In Proceedings of the International Symposium on Electronic Dictionaries, Tokyo, Japan.

Christiane Fellbaum, 1998. WordNet: An Electronic Database, MIT Press, Cambridge, MA.

Marti Hearst, 1992. Automatic Acquisition of Hyponyms from Large Text Corpora, Proc. of International Conference on Computational Linguistics, COLING1992.

Malhar Kulkarni, Chaitali Dangarikar, Irawati Kulkarni, Abhishek Nanda and Pushpak Bhattacharyya, 2010. Introducing Sanskrit Wordnet, 5th International Conference on Global Wordnet (GWC2010), Mumbai.

Malhar Kulkarni, 2008. Lexicographic traditions in India and Sanskrit, Journal of Language Technology, (1) pp. 160-165.

Roberto Navigli and Simone Ponzetto, 2012. BabelNet: The Automatic Construction, Evaluation and Application of a Wide-Coverage Multilingual Semantic Network, Artificial Intelligence, Elsevier.

Karel Pala, Dana Hlaváčková, and Vašek, 2008. Semi-automatic Linking of New Czech Synsets Using Princeton WordNet, Intelligent Information Systems.

Madhukar Mangesh Patkar, 1981. History of Sanskrit Lexicography, Munshiram Manoharlal Publishers, Delhi.

Ellen Riloff and Rosie Jones, 1999. Learning Dictionaries for Information Extraction using Multilevel Bootstrapping, Proc. of National Conference on Artificial Intelligence.

Piek Vossen, 2002. Euro WordNet General Document, University of Amsterdam.

Piek Vossen, 1998. EuroWordNet: A Multilingual Database with Lexical Semantic Networks, Kluwer, Dordrecht, Netherlands.

Renjie Xu, Zhiqiang Gao, Yingji Pan, Yuzhong Qu, Zhisheng Huang, 2008. An Integrated Approach for Automatic Construction of Bilingual Chinese-English WordNet, ASWC 2008, LNCS 5367, 302–314.

# Registers in the System of Semantic Relations in plWordNet

**Marek Maziarz**
**Maciej Piasecki**
**Ewa Rudnicka**
Institute of Informatics
Wrocław University of Technology
Wrocław, Poland
mawroc@gmail.com
maciej.piasecki@pwr.wroc.pl
ewa.rudnicka78@gmail.com

**Stan Szpakowicz**
Institute of Computer Science
Polish Academy of Sciences
Warsaw, Poland
&
School of Electrical Engineering
and Computer Science
University of Ottawa
Ottawa, Ontario, Canada
szpak@eecs.uottawa.ca

## Abstract

Lexicalised concepts are represented in wordnets by word-sense pairs. The strength of markedness is one of the factors which influence word use. Stylistically unmarked words are largely context-neutral. Technical terms, obsolete words, "officialese", slangs, obscenities and so on are all marked, often strongly, and that limits their use considerably. We discuss the position of register and markedness in wordnets with respect to semantic relations, and we list typical values of register. We illustrate the discussion with the system of registers in plWordNet, the largest Polish wordnet. We present a decision tree for the assignment of marking labels, and examine the consistency of the editing decisions based on that tree.

## 1 Introduction

A dense network of lexico-semantic relations is the feature that best differentiates a wordnet from other types of dictionaries and thesauri. Wordnets are organised into synsets and lexical units (LUs), whose meaning is crucially determined just by such relations. The inventories of relations, usually based on the findings in lexical semantics, seem largely comparable across wordnets, but specific definitions and strategies of applications vary. Wordnets also vary in the amount of typical dictionary information encoded. An apt example of such variation is the treatment of stylistic registers, as well as broad semantic domains, to which a given synset or LU belongs.

Lexico-semantic relations are the principal determinant of lexical meaning in plWordNet. Marking often constrains those relations; some of them cannot hold between LUs of incompatible registers. Semantics can constrain derivationally based relations, *e.g.,* femininity is limited to the nouns denoting animals and humans. Among verbs there are also relations limited to the particular aspect or verb class, like hyponymy or inchoativity (Maziarz et al., 2013, section 4).

Registers, semantic domains and verb classes are attributes. It is far from obvious how to put attributive information into an inherently relational structure of a wordnet. Princeton WordNet (PWN) represents semantic domains by synsets in two roles: elements of the lexical system and meta-information which characterises those elements. To associate a synset with a domain, a domain relation links it with another synset which represents that domain. Attributes of LUs can also be represented by sub-dividing those LUs into classes. This mechanism has been present in PWN from the beginning. There are, *e.g.,* separate bases for parts of speech or semantic domains, represented by the so-called lexicographers' files.

Registers have a major role to play in shaping the structure of plWordNet. We will continue the practice of making registers figure in the definitions of lexico-semantic relations, but we will analyse them, and introduce register values into plWordNet, very systematically. To begin with, we need an appropriate set of marking labels. It should streamline the description of lexico-semantic relations, facilitate future plWordNet applications, and ensure the consistency of the linguists' decisions.

Section 2 of the paper recaps the model of the semantic relation system in plWordNet. Section 3 serves as an overview of related work insofar as it contributes to our intended use of the marking labels for the enrichment of the wordnet-based description of lexical meaning. Section 4 presents the details of the markedness labelling in plWordNet. Section 5 reports on a small, carefully arranged experiment meant to determine how consistent marking can be expected given a precise procedure in the form of a decision tree. Section 6 offers a few conclusions based on our experience, and briefly discusses our expectations for the ongoing development of plWordNet.

## 2 Constitutive relations and registers

A wordnet is founded on synonymy. Its basic unit, the synset, is a group of *lexical units* (LUs).[1] Although synonymy is undoubtedly key, wordnets vary as to how it is defined and applied. The creators of PWN (Miller et al., 1993; Fellbaum, 1998) adopt a very strict definition of synonymy usually attributed to Leibniz,[2] but realistically make it context-dependent. The effect is a take on synonymy which is linguistically satisfying but insufficiently accurate: the wordnet authors' intuition largely dictates what LUs go into a synset. Moreover, a synset is often understood as a set of synonymous LUs, while synonymous LUs are understood as elements of the same synset. Such circularity is hard to make operational.

The interdependence of the notions of synonymy and synset, and the subjectivity of authorial judgement, can be avoided. Maziarz et al. (2013) propose a different perspective. The LU, rather than the synset, becomes the basic structure in plWordNet. As Vossen (2002) notes, the central relations – synonymy, hyponymy, hypernymy, meronymy and holonymy – are lexical: they hold between words, not between concepts. A PWN synset denotes a *lexicalized concept*, and *conceptual* relations link synsets, but those relations have a lexico-semantic origin. Our model derives synset content and synonymy from a carefully constructed set of *constitutive relations* between LUs. The construction is discussed in (Maziarz et al., 2013); the focus of this paper is on the properties which help constitutive lexico-semantic relations determine synsets.

The constitutive relations in plWordNet are hyponymy, hypernymy, meronymy and holonymy, plus verb-specific relations of presupposition, preceding, cause, processuality, state, iterativity and inchoativity (Maziarz et al. (2011) discuss the details), and adjective-specific relations of value (of an attribute), gradation and modifier (Maziarz et al., 2012b). They are supplemented by *constitutive features*: verb aspect and semantic class, and register.

A wordnet describes lexical meaning primarily via semantic relations, so it is important for a constitutive relation to be fairly widespread in the network. A high degree of sharing among groups of LUs is necessary because a constitutive relation underlies grouping LUs into synsets. It also helps if a constitutive relation is well established in linguistics: linguists who are wordnet editors will encounter fewer misunderstanding. Finally, a constitutive relations which accords with the wordnet practice will make for better compatibility among wordnets (Maziarz et al., 2013).

Verbs of different aspect participate in different lexico-semantic relations, *e.g.*, a hypernym cannot be replaced by the other element of its aspectual pair. The value of aspect thus constrains selected verb relations (Maziarz et al., 2012a). Semantic verb classes also restrict links for some verb relations. The verb classification is based on a Vendlerian typology. A hierarchy of verb classes has been implemented in plWordNet as a hypernymy hierarchy of *artificial lexical units*, each naming a different class. Verbs in a given class are hyponyms of the corresponding artificial LU.

Stylistic registers have been introduced into plWordNet relation definitions; they appear in guidelines and in some substitution tests. With every editing decision a linguist must recognise the registers of the LUs and synsets to be linked. The marking labels represent pragmatic features of LU usage, so it seems natural to have register values encoded explicitly.

A synset in plWordNet is a set of lexical units which are connected to the rest of the network by the same set of instances of constitutive relations, and have compatible values of the constitutive features. Note how this definition does *not* refer to

[1] We understand the *lexical unit* informally as a lemma-sense pair.

[2] "Two words are said to be synonyms if one can be used in a statement in place of the other without changing the meaning of the statement."

synonymy. Once synset membership has been decided, its elements are understood to be in the relation of synonymy.

It now becomes crucial to recognise accurately the connectivity afforded by the constitutive relations. Linguists who build the wordnet are assisted by conditions in the definitions of relations (such conditions often refer to registers and semantic classes) and by substitution tests. Vossen (2002) discusses tests for semantic correspondence, which did not take into account the differences in register or usage, often essential for the possibility of contextual interchangeability.

Lexical units which have nearly the same sense but significantly differ in register are put into separate synsets, but the proximity is not lost: those synsets become linked by inter-register synonymy. That relation is weaker than synonymy with respect to sharing. Synsets linked by inter-register synonymy share a hypernym, but *not* hyponym sets, and clearly have different register values.

Consider an example: *komputer* 'computer' has an obsolete inter-register synonym *mózg elektronowy* 'electronic brain'. Figure 1 shows hyponymy to *urządzenie elektroniczne* 'electronic device', which is shared.[3] There is, however, a hyponym *komputer cyfrowy* 'digital computer', a specialist term which should not be linked to the obsolete term for a computer.[4] The terms *komputer* and *mózg elektronowy* have the same denotation but different linguistic contexts of use.

The model and the development of plWordNet comply with a form of minimal commitment principle: make as few assumptions as possible about the construction process. First of all, the model avoids references to theories of cognition and specific theories of lexical semantics. By minimising the theoretical underpinning and grounding all editing decisions on the language data observable in a corpus, we try to focus on the lexical system regardless of the reasons why it is organised as it is. We thus hope to make the wordnet theory-neutral and ready for use in a wide range of applications.

Minimal commitment does not preclude a *mapping* to an ontology. Such a mapping supplements the linguistic dependencies recorded in the wordnet with a theoretical interpretation: the cognitive principles of the ontology. The wordnet describes lexico-semantic relation of varying, possibly complex, background and origin, while the ontology mapping shows a possible relation between the lexical system and the internal cognitive structure of concepts. A potential plus is the possibility of considering different ontologies as the mapping target, and so different interpretations of the lexical dependencies.

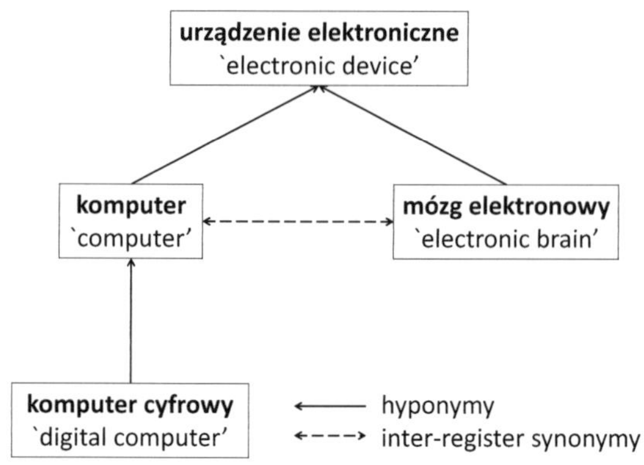


Figure 1: Inter-register synonymy between LUs from different registers.

## 3 Markedness in lexicography and in Princeton WordNet

Svensén (2009) notes that lexicographers refer as *marked* to the part of the vocabulary with additional pragmatic features which narrow the usage to a specific context or group of speakers. Such distinction includes, but is not limited to, different stylistic registers. Svensén adopts the classification of "diasystematic marking in a contemporary general purpose dictionary" (Hausmann, 1989), organised along 11 criteria: time, place, nationality, medium, socio-cultural, formality, text type, technicality, frequency, attitude and normativity. An unmarked centre and a marked periphery[5] are established for each criterion. The main peripheries include "archaism-neologism; regionalism, dialect word; foreign word; spoken-written sociolects; formal-informal; poetic, literary, journalese; technical language; rare; connoted; and incorrect". In a dictionary, the location of a lexical item in a periphery is signalled by a label, *e.g., arch* 'archaic', *AmE* 'American English' or

[3]In plWordNet, a hyponymy link from X to Y means "X is a hyponym of Y" rather than "X has a hyponym Y".

[4]The substitution test "If it is *a digital computer*, then it must be *an electronic brain*." sounds distinctly funny.

[5]or peripheries, because for some criteria there can be more than one periphery

*poet* 'poetic'.

Wordnets vary with respect to the ways and degree of coding markedness. PWN signals markedness with a special DOMAIN - MEMBER OF A DOMAIN relation with three sub-types: TOPIC, REGION and USAGE. It can be established between synsets in the same grammatical category or between cateories. The subtype names correspond to the criteria of marking (Hausmann, 1989). Surprisingly, noun synsets play the role of specific labels within particular subtypes. PWN 3.0 has 438 labels pertaining to DOMAIN TERM TOPIC, 166 labels to DOMAIN TERM REGION, and 29 labels to DOMAIN TERM USAGE.

A closer look at the specific label instances within the selected domains shows that some of them belong to different peripheries of Svensén (2009) / Hausmann (1989). The TOPIC domain includes such labels as, *e.g.,* 'archeology', 'Arthurian legend' or 'auto racing'. The USAGE domain includes, *e.g.,* 'archaism', 'African American Vernacular English' and 'colloquialism'. REGION seems to be built most consistently: in principle it concerns dialectal names. It could thus be treated as an equivalent of the 'regionalism-dialect word' periphery. Yet, some of those links signal only geographical membership, but not dialectal variation. Consider, for example, the relation DOMAIN TERM REGION between {Polynesia} and {Austronesia}. It is clearly not the case that *Polynesia* is a dialect word used mainly in, or coming from, Austronesia.

Polish lexicography distinguishes groups of marking (register) labels not unlike those we showed above: diachronic, stylistic, emotional, terminological (professional, scientific), diastratic, diatopic (geographical), diafrequential (Dubisz, 2006; Engelking et al., 1989). The consistency of marking is low. Lexicographers point out mistakes and dubious decisions in the dictionary-making process (Kurkiewicz, 2007).[6] Not only do dictionaries label the same lexical units differently (Engelking et al., 1989), but the label lists vary significantly (*exemplum* (Dubisz, 2006) and (Kurkiewicz, 2007)). There also are too many labels (ca. 20-30 main and more than 100 secondary categories), so it is virtually impossible to mark the semantico-pragmatic constraints with any degree of consensus.

Several sets of criteria have emerged during the lexicographic debates in Poland. We find the set proposed by Buttler and Markowski (1998) to be the most interesting. Three semantico-pragmatic features are posited: `official`, `specialist`, `emotional` (or `emotionally marked`, or `expressive`). Their +/- (present/absent values) define a space in which all language variants or styles can be placed. Thus, general language could be characterised by {`-official`, `-specialist`, `-emotional`}, and literary style by {`+official`, `-specialist`, `-emotional`}.

## 4 Registers in plWordNet

Although in plWordNet 2.0 registers did influence relations, they were not introduced explicitly. In order to gain high consistency, we have decided to mark labels explicitly, and to create detailed guidelines for the lexicographers.

The set of plWordNet marking labels is inspired by Buttler and Markowski (1998) and by Kurkiewicz (2007). As does the Great Dictionary of Polish (Kurkiewicz, 2007; Żmigrodzki, 2012), we aim to lower the overall number of labels by about an order of magnitude. In the end, we have distinguished nine marking labels, with general (unmarked) language as the tenth register:[7]

- **obsolete** – this label marks LUs which are outdated, typically used only by elderly or (rarely) middle-aged people;
- **regional** – LUs from a dialect, well known to (but not used by) almost all Poles;
- **terminological** {`+off`, `+spec`, `-emo`} – LUs used by specialists, scientists, engineers,

[6]Consider *metal* 'one listening to heavy metal music' and *wywiad* 'interview'. Dubisz (2006) labels the former `youth language`, the latter – `journalism`. Żmigrodzki (2012) assigns `music` to the former and no label to the latter.

This is not only the malady of Polish lexicography. In English and German dictionaries, words also carry assorted register labels. Svensén (2009, p. 316) notes: "Different dictionaries may use different labels, and the categories represented by the labels may have different ranges in different dictionaries. Moreover, there may be differences in labelling practice, so that, in one dictionary, fewer or more lexical items are regarded as formal or informal, correct or incorrect, etc., than in another one (Haussman 1989: 650)."

For example, *Oxford English Dictionary* (Simpson, 2013) equips the word *malady* with the label `literary`, while *Cambridge Dictionaries Online* (Heacock, 1995 2011) consider it `formal`. The word *freak* is `informal` in (Simpson, 2013), but has no label (!) in (Heacock, 1995 2011).

[7]We abbreviate the three features from (Buttler and Markowski, 1998) as `off` = official, `spec` = specialist, `emo` = emotional.

and generally professionals;

- **argot/slang** {-off, +spec, +emo} – LUs used by a particular social group or a small/local community;

- **literary** {+off, -spec, ±emo} – this label marks high style vocabulary, especially LUs used only in literature or in speeches;

- **official** {+off, -spec, -emo} – LUs used on official and formal occasions, mainly in communication between citizens and representatives of state institutions;[8]

- **vulgar** {-off, -spec, +emo} – crude vocabulary, LUs with very restricted acceptable usage;

- **popular** {-off, -spec, +emo} – LUs which might be used in a familiar context, but normally not acceptable in other situations;

- **colloquial** {-off, -spec, +emo} – vocabulary used informally, in a free style, but with low acceptability in official situations;

- **general** {±off, -spec, -emo} – LUs which could be used virtually in every situation.

To help plWordNet editors maintain consistency, we have designed a series of substitution tests in the form of a decision tree. The editor systematically inspects the semantic features ±spec, ±off and ±emo for a given LU, as well as more specific pragmatic features. The tree appears in Figure 2. Consider Example 1 (the prerequisite is italicised, the actual test is set in roman):

**Example 1** (regional)

> **Test**. *The LU* pyra 'potato' *may have equivalents in other regions of Poland or in general language*. The Poles know the LU pyra and recognise it as regional.[9]

The test is applied right after the diachronic criterion (Figure 2, obs). If the prerequisite and the test proper both hold, the LU pyra is marked as regional. The test fails if either part disagrees with the plWordNet editor's intuition.

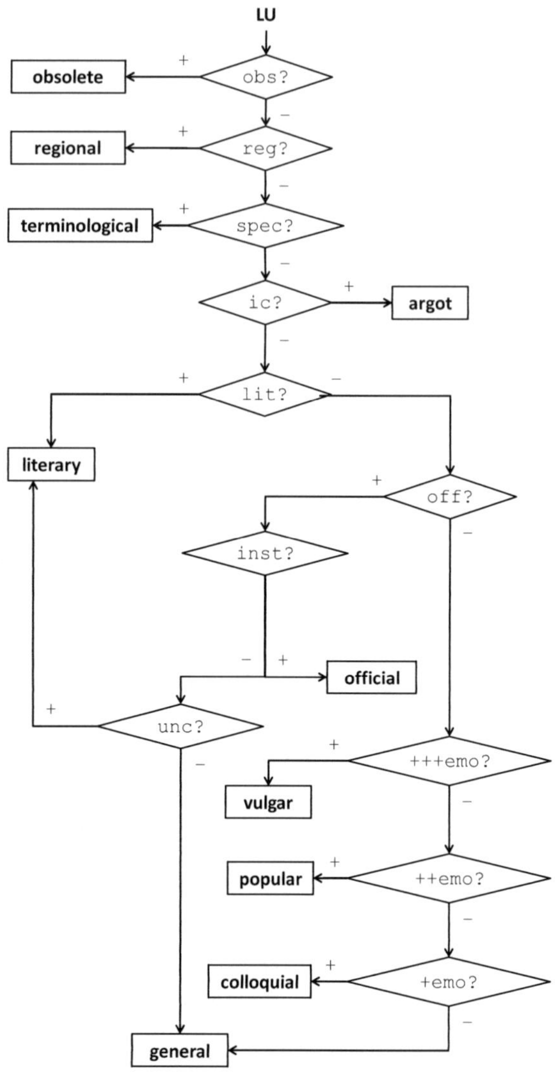


Figure 2: Substitution tests for markedness in plWordNet. Legend: +++emo = emotionally marked LU unacceptable in most situations (that includes vulgarity), ++emo = emotionally marked LU acceptable only in familiar situations, +emo = emotionally marked LU acceptable in some familiar situations and when talking to strangers, ic = LU from a slang or argot, inst = LU used only in communication with state institutions, lit = LU used only in literature, obs = used by the elderly, off = language suitable for official situations, reg = regional LU, spec = LU used only by specialists, unc = LU unsuitable for common communication.

[8] Such language develops around any bureaucracy.

[9] It is used in Greater Poland.

Example 2 shows a two-step test: consider a (possibly) vulgar noun first in an unofficial situation of talking to a stranger, and then in a very official situation.

**Example 2** (`vulgar`)

> **Test 1**. *Imagine that you meet a stranger in the street and talk a while. You have just used the LU* `skurwiel` 'son of a bitch'. Your interlocutor will most likely think that you are crude.
>
> **Test 2**. *Imagine yourself in the middle of a very official or public situation (you are in the presence of an elder, your superior, president of the Polish Republic, a professor, a bishop, or you are being interviewed on TV news). You have just used the LU* `skurwiel` 'son of a bitch'. Your interlocutor – or TV viewer – will most likely think that you are crude.

The substitution tests are applied in a cascade of filters. An LU which passes through all filters must land in the final bin – the general register.

## 5 The stability of the substitution tests

To ensure that the marking labels introduced in Section 4 can be applied with sufficient consistency, we examined the inter-rater agreement between two plWordNet editors who independently marked a sample of LUs. They were given a document with detailed guidelines and complete tests, and a spreadsheet with 385 noun LUs randomly drawn from plWordNet (a simple random sample, proper names and gerunds excluded).

Figure 3 presents the histograms of the counts of marking labels in the 385-LU sample. The most frequently assigned registers are terminology, general language, and literary and colloquial styles. These four account for more than 90% of the sample. Both editors found terminology to be the most frequent register, and neither found the *vulgar* label necessary. If we were to extrapolate, we could venture a broad guess on the approximate distribution of register values of LUs in plWordNet:

- $\frac{2}{5}$ in the terminology register,
- $\frac{1}{3}$ in the general register,
- $\frac{1}{6}$ in the literary style,

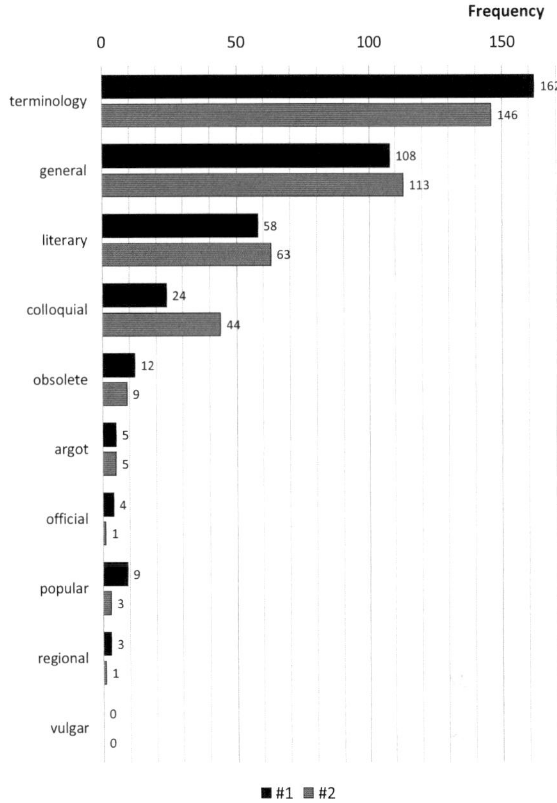


Figure 3: Counts of stylistic register values in a 385-LU sample from plWordNet, with two raters.

- $\frac{1}{12}$ in the colloquial style,
- $\frac{1}{12}$ in the remaining registers.

The annotators are in reasonable agreement, as measured by Cohen's kappa: $\kappa = 0.645$ with the confidence interval 0.586-0.722 (Table 1).[10] According to Landis and Koch (1977, p. 165), the confidence interval covers two values of agreement strength: moderate and substantial.

It is commonly assumed that only $\kappa \geq 0.8$ guarantees reliable results in computational linguistics, and $\kappa$ in 0.67-0.8 is tolerable. Reidsma and Carletta (2007) show that this rule of thumb does not always work. Sometimes lower $\kappa$ makes the results reliable, sometimes even $\kappa \geq 0.8$ does not suffice. The authors recommend checking whether differences between annotators are systematic or random,[11] so we have decided also to put our data

[10] The confidence interval was calculated by simple percentile bootstrap (DiCiccio and Efron, 1996; DiCiccio and Romano, 1988) suitable for Cohen's $\kappa$ (Artstein and Poesio, 2008).

[11] The former is a real problem for computational methods,

| label system | Cohen's $\kappa$ | confidence interval of $\kappa$ | $p$-value of $\chi^2$ test |
|---|---|---|---|
| 10 labels | 0.645 | 0.586-0.722 | 0.03962 |
| 5 labels | 0.722 | 0.657-0.785 | 0.02686 |

Table 1: Inter-rater agreement of two annotators assigning marking labels to nouns from plWordNet. Confidence intervals are calculated by the percentile bootstrap method, n = 10000 resamplings, $\alpha$ = 0.05. $P$-values are calculated for the $\chi^2$ tests of independence. The 10-label system was described in Section 4. The 5-label system equates compatible labels, as described in this section.

through a non-parametric $\chi^2$ test of independence. The $p$-value is 0.03962, so we do not reject the null hypothesis that the plWordNet editors' choices are distributed similarly at 1% significance level.

The Cohen's $\kappa$ value will increase if there are fewer marking labels. One fairly obvious way of doing that is to consider as *compatible* those marking label bins whose definitions are close; see the decision tree in Figure 2:

- `general` ≈ `literary` ≈ `colloquial`,
- `official` ≈ `terminology` ≈ `argot`,
- `vulgar` ≈ `popular`.

This boosts Cohen's kappa to 0.722 with a very good confidence interval of 0.657-0.785. Now the $\kappa$ is in the area of substantial agreement of Landis and Koch. The $\chi^2$ test for the new labelling system again leads us to the fortunate assumption that distributions of editor choices are similar at 1% significance level (so none of the editors has any bias). Fewer labels, narrow and high inter-rater agreement, but somewhat less information...

## 6 Conclusions

The model proposed for plWordNet bases the grouping of lexical units (LUs) into synsets on *constitutive relations*. In order to match the language data even more accurately, we enriched the definitions of some of the semantic relations. We added constraints which refer to verb aspect, verb semantic classes and registers. Those features play a central role in shaping the wordnet relation structure, so we named them *constitutive features*.[12]

the latter it not a threat.

[12]It is *attributive* information in an inherently *relational* system, but there is no contradiction. This information only helps constrain semantic relations, which remain the principal vehicle for the description of lexical meaning.

Registers appear to be particularly important, because they characterise all parts of speech covered by plWordNet, and they link the pragmatics of usage in a simple manner with the lexico-semantic description in the relational paradigm. That is why registers in plWordNet will now explicitly characterise LUs.

A review of the linguistic study of registers has suggested a set of ten registers, including the default unmarked register. We have also designed rules for register identification in the form of a decision tree, and made them a mandatory element of the guidelines for wordnet editors. We ran an annotation experiment in which two linguists independently assigned register values to a representative sample. We conclude that LUs can be given register labels with acceptable inter-annotator agreement.

Our wordnet model follows the minimal commitment principle. We only consider a small set of homogeneous and quite carefully specified basic notions. The whole system of semantic relations and synsets in a wordnet is directly derived from the linguistic lexico-semantic relations and from language data. The structure of the wordnet is closer to language facts, because it is derived from the lexico-semantic relations between LUs which can largely be observed directly in corpus data. That is why the adopted wordnet model facilitates semi-automated wordnet expansion using knowledge extracted from corpora. The systematic introduction of registers allows us to take into account elements of pragmatics without giving up the conceptual simplicity of the model.

## Acknowledgment

Co-financed by the Polish Ministry of Education and Science, Project CLARIN-PL, and the European Innovative Economy Programme project POIG.01.01.02-14-013/09.

## References

Ron Artstein and Massimo Poesio. 2008. Inter-Coder Agreement for Computational Linguistics. *Computational Linguistics*, 34(4):555–596.

Danuta Buttler and Andrzej Markowski. 1998. Słownictwo wspólnoodmianowe, książkowe i potoczne współczesnej polszczyzny [The general, bookish and colloquial vocabulary of contemporary Polish].

*Język a Kultura [Language and Culture]*, 1:179–203.

Thomas J. DiCiccio and Bradley Efron. 1996. Bootstrap Confidence Intervals. *Statistical Science*, 11(3):189–212.

Thomas J. DiCiccio and Joseph P. Romano. 1988. A Review of Bootstrap Confidence Intervals. *Journal of the Royal Statistical Society. Series B (Methodological)*, 50(3):338–354.

Stanisław Dubisz. 2006. Wstęp [introduction]. In Stanisław Dubisz, editor, *Uniwersalny słownik języka polskiego PWN. Wersja 3.0 (elektroniczna na CD) [A universal dictionary of Polish. Version 3.0 (electronic on CD)]*. Polish Scientific Publishers PWN.

Anna Engelking, Andrzej Markowski, and Elżbieta Weiss. 1989. Kwalifikatory w słownikach – próba systematyzacji [Qualifiers in dictionaries – an attempt to systematise]. *Poradnik Językowy [Language Guide]*, pages 300–309.

Christiane Fellbaum, editor. 1998. *WordNet – An Electronic Lexical Database*. The MIT Press.

Franz Josef Hausmann. 1989. Die Markierung im allgemeinen einsprachigen Wörterbuch: eine Übersicht. In Franz Josef Hausmann, Oskar Reichmann, Herbert Ernst Wiegand, and Ladislav Zgusta, editors, *Wörterbücher. Ein internationales Handbuch zur Lexikographie*, volume 5.1, pages 649–657. De Gruyter.

Paul Heacock, editor. 1995-2011. *Cambridge Dictionaries Online*. Cambridge University Press.

Juliusz Kurkiewicz. 2007. Kwalifikatory w wielkim słowniku języka polskiego [Qualifiers in the great dictionary of Polish]. In Piotr Żmigrodzki and Renata Przybylska, editors, *Nowe studia leksykograficzne [New lexicographic studies]*. Wydawnictwo Lexis.

J. Richard Landis and Gary G. Koch. 1977. The Measurement of Observer Agreement for Categorical Data. *Biometrics*, 33(1):159–174.

Marek Maziarz, Maciej Piasecki, Stanisław Szpakowicz, Joanna Rabiega-Wiśniewska, and Bożena Hojka. 2011. Semantic Relations between Verbs in Polish Wordnet 2.0. *Cognitive Studies*, 11.

Marek Maziarz, Maciej Piasecki, and Stan Szpakowicz. 2012a. An Implementation of a System of Verb Relations in plWordNet 2.0. In Christiane Fellbaum and Piek Vossen, editors, *Proc. 6th International Global Wordnet Conference*, pages 181–188, Matsue, Japan, January. The Global WordNet Association. ⟨www.globalwordnet.org/gwa/proceedings/gwc2012.pdf⟩.

Marek Maziarz, Stanisław Szpakowicz, and Maciej Piasecki. 2012b. Semantic Relations among Adjectives in Polish WordNet 2.0: A New Relation Set, Discussion and Evaluation. *Cognitive Studies*, 12.

Marek Maziarz, Maciej Piasecki, and Stanisław Szpakowicz. 2013. The chicken-and-egg problem in wordnet design: synonymy, synsets and constitutive relations. *Language Resources and Evaluation*, 47(3):769–796.

George A. Miller, Richard Beckwith, Christiane Fellbaum, Derek Gross, and Katherine J. Miller. 1993. Introduction to WordNet: an on-line lexical database. Unpublished, one of "Five Papers" ⟨ftp://ftp.cogsci.princeton.edu/pub/wordnet/5papers.ps⟩.

Dennis Reidsma and Jean Carletta. 2007. Reliability measurement without limits. *Computational Linguistics*, 1(1):1–8.

John Simpson. 2013. *Oxford English Dictionary*. Oxford University Press. ⟨www.oed.com/⟩.

Bo Svensén. 2009. *A handbook of lexicography: the theory and practice of dictionary-making*. Cambridge University Press.

Piek Vossen. 2002. EuroWordNet General Document Version 3. Technical report, University of Amsterdam.

Piotr Żmigrodzki, editor. 2012. *Wielki słownik języka polskiego: Zasady opracowania [A great dictionary of Polish: The principles of compilation]*. Institute of Polish Language, Polish Academy of Sciences.

# IndoWordnet Visualizer: A Graphical User Interface for Browsing and Exploring Wordnets of Indian Languages

**Devendra Singh Chaplot** **Sudha Bhingardive** **Pushpak Bhattacharyya**
Department of Computer Science and Engineering,
IIT Bombay, Powai,
Mumbai, 400076.
{chaplot,sudha,pb}@cse.iitb.ac.in

## Abstract

In this paper, we are presenting a graphical user interface to browse and explore the IndoWordnet lexical database for various Indian languages. IndoWordnet visualizer extracts the related concepts for a given word and displays a sub graph containing those concepts. The interface is enhanced with different features in order to provide flexibility to the user. IndoWordnet visualizer is made publically available. Though it was initially constructed for making the wordnet validation process easier, it is proving to be very useful in analyzing various Natural Language Processing tasks, *viz.*, Semantic relatedness, Word Sense Disambiguation, Information Retrieval, Textual Entailment, *etc.*

## 1 Introduction

IndoWordnet (Bhattacharyya, 2010) is a linked lexical knowledge base consisting of wordnets of various Indian languages, where each wordnet is composed of synsets and semantic relations. This resource is very useful for various NLP applications *viz.,* Machine Translation, Word Sense Disambiguation, Sentimental Analysis, Information Retrieval, *etc.* But to use this knowledge in an effective way, a set of tools are required to query, retrieve and visualize information from this knowledge base. Data visualization is the study of the visual representation of data, meaning "information that has been abstracted in some schematic form, including attributes or variables for the units of information" (Friendly, 2008). The main goal of visualization is to organize information clearly and effectively through graphical means. We have developed a user interface that provides a graphical representation of IndoWordnet. Till date, no such tool was developed for visualizing the wordnet database for Indian languages. The visualizer we developed takes a word from a specific language as an input and displays the related concepts of that word depending upon its semantic and lexical relations with other words in the wordnet.

This paper is organized as follows. Section 2 covers a related work. Section 3 gives an overview of IndoWordnet. Section 4 describes IndoWordnet visualizer. Section 5 gives implementation details. Conclusion and future work are covered in Section 6.

## 2 Related Work

There are many wordnet visualizers available for browsing and exploring wordnets to better understand the concepts and semantic relations between them. Some of them include BabelNet explorer (Navigli, 2013), AndreOrd (Johannsen and Pedersen, 2011), Visuwords[1], Nodebox[2], WordTies (Pedersen *et. al* 2013), WordVis (Vercruysse and Kuiper, 2011) *etc*. BabelNet explorer is designed for visualizing the lexical database BabelNet (Navigli and Ponzetto, 2012). It uses the tree layout for visualization which allows intuitive navigation. It covers English, Italian, Catalan, Spanish, German and French languages. AndreOrd is the wordnet browser developed for the Danish wordnet, DanNet. It uses the open source framework Ruby on Rails and the graphing toolkit Protovis[3]. Visuwords is the online graphical dictionary designed for accessing Princeton WorNet (Fellbaum, 1998). It uses a force-directed graph layout for visualizing the synset structure. Nodebox visualizer provides the static layout. It does not use any color or shape encoding in the graph. WordTies is the wordnet visualizer designed for Nordic and Baltic wordnets. It covers seven monolingual and four bilingual wordnets. It has been made available via

[1] http://www.visuwords.com/
[2] http://nodebox.net/code/index.php/WordNet
[3] http://vis.stanford.edu/protovis/

META-SHARE[4] through the META-NORD project.

## 3 Overview of IndoWordnet

IndoWordnet is the most useful multilingual lexical resource in Indian languages. Hindi wordnet is created manually using lexical knowledge from various dictionaries. Wordnets other than Hindi have been created by using expansion approach with Hindi as a pivot language. It includes 18 Indian languages [5] *viz.,* Assamese, Bengali, Bodo, Gujarati, Kannada, Kashmiri, Nepali, Kashmiri, Konkani, Malayalam, Manipuri, Marathi, Nepali, Odiya, Punjabi, Sanskrit, Tamil, Telugu, Urdu, *etc.* Expansion approach makes use of the fact that there are several 'universal concepts' which are independent of the language. If one language has synsets for universal concepts, then it makes sense to borrow this work for some other language. For such universal concepts, the semantic relations remain same across the languages. Hence one can directly borrow them for other languages. This principle is used in the creation of IndoWordnet. All the semantic relations for universal synsets are defined in Hindi and are borrowed by other languages. Expansion approach works very well for closely related languages like 'Hindi and Marathi'. The current statistics of the IndoWordnet is shown in Table 1.

| Languages | Synset count |
|---|---|
| Assamese | 14258 |
| Bodo | 15785 |
| Bengali | 36345 |
| Gujarati | 35581 |
| Hindi | 38283 |
| Kashmiri | 29466 |
| Konkani | 32370 |
| Kannada | 14674 |
| Malayalam | 12108 |
| Manipuri | 16315 |
| Marathi | 28055 |
| Nepali | 11713 |
| Punjabi | 32364 |
| Sanskrit | 22912 |
| Tamil | 20297 |
| Telugu | 20057 |
| Urdu | 31008 |

**Table 1: Current statistics of the IndoWordnet**

IndoWordnet stores various relations among words and synsets. These relations give an important knowledge about the language structure. These are categorized under two labels *viz.,* lexical relations and semantic relations.

### 3.1 Lexical Relations

Lexical relations are present between the words. IndoWordnet contains different types of lexical relations listed below,

- Gradation (state, size, light, gender, temperature, color, time, quality, action, manner) (for all parts-of-speech)
- Antonymy (action, amount, direction, gender, personality, place, quality, size, state, time, color, manner) (for all parts-of-speech)
- Compound (for nouns)
- Conjunction(for verbs)

### 3.2 Semantic Relations

Semantic relations are present between the synsets. Different types of semantic relations are given below,

- Hypernymy (for noun and verbs)
- Holonymy ( nouns)
- Meronymy (component object, member collection, feature, activity, place, area, face, state, portion, mass, resource, process, position, area)
- Troponymy (for verbs)
- Similar Attribute (between noun and adjective)
- Function verb (between noun and verb)
- Ability verb (between noun and verb)
- Capability verb (between noun and verb)
- Also see
- Adverb modifies verb (between adverb and verb)
- Causative (for verb)

[4] http://www.meta-share.org

[5] Wordnets for Indian languages are developed in IndoWordNet project. Wordnets are available in following Indian languages: Assamese, Bodo, Bengali, English, Gujarati, Hindi, Kashmiri, Konkani, Kannada, Malayalam, Manipuri, Marathi, Nepali, Punjabi, Sanskrit, Tamil, Telugu and Urdu. These languages cover 3 different language families, Indo Aryan, Sino-Tebetian and Dravidian. http://www.cfilt.iitb.ac.in/indowordnet

- Entailment (for verb)
- Near synset
- Adjective modifies noun (between adjective and noun)

IndoWordnet provides extra relations (Narayan *et. al.,* 2002) in comparison with Princeton wordnet, *e.g.*, gradation, causative form, nominal and verbal compounds, conjunction *etc.* All these relations are covered in IndoWordnet Visualizer. User can see these relations and understand them better visually. All these relations are used while finding the related concepts of a given word. The need to make entirely different explorer for IndoWordnet lies in its difference from other wordnets in terms of the structure and relations. The entirely different format makes it difficult to import other visualizers directly. Manually going through the wordnet relations takes very large time. Visualizer makes this process extremely efficient and intuitive. This motivated us to create a new visualizer for IndoWordnet. Developed GUI is enriched with various facilities as explained in Section 4.

## 4 IndoWordnet Visualizer

IndoWordnet visualizer is designed for visualizing the IndoWordnet database. It is made publically available on IndoWordnet website[6]. Related concepts of a given input word are extracted at different levels and a sub graph is displayed on a screen. The user interface layout and its features are described below.

### 4.1 User Interface Layout

The interface of the visualizer consists of following I/O features.

The input to the interface consists of:

- Text-box for the word to browse and explore
- Drop-box to select a language (Indian languages)
- Drop-box to select visualization options

The output of the interface consists of:

- A graphical view of all related words and concepts in a respective language for a given input word. (Screenshot 2)

6 http://www.cfilt.iitb.ac.in/indowordnet/

- Download option is provided for retrieving related words and concepts which can act as a good context clue for a given input word.

### 4.2 Features

Interface is enhanced with the following features, which provide flexibility to the user to visualize the wordnet database.

- Nodes are automatically arranged on the screen according to physics and depending on the total number of nodes. The repulsion between the nodes and the link distance is optimally calculated so as to display all nodes clearly. Here, nodes are nothing but the concepts from IndoWordnet. For a given input word, all related concepts are extracted from IndoWordnet and are displayed at appropriate positions on the screen.
- The size of the node varies according to the number of its immediate neighbor. A node consisting large number of neighbors is bigger in size than a node with less number of neighbors. This highlights more frequent words against less frequent ones.
- When a user moves a mouse pointer over a particular node, it highlights all its immediate neighbors along with that node. (Screenshot 6)
- When a user moves a mouse pointer over a particular edge, it highlights the type of relation exist between the nodes. Different color encodings are used for displaying the lexical and semantic relations. (Screenshot 3)
- User can click, drag, expand and fix nodes for better visibility. (Screenshot 4)
- Zoom in and zoom out facilities are also provided.
- When a user clicks on a node all its semantic information is displayed on the screen. It includes synset id, synset words, gloss, and example sentence.
- Download option is provided in order to get all the information displayed on a screen which is helpful for different NLP applications.

### 4.3 Visualization Schemes

In an interface, we provided two types of visual schemes.

1. By the number of levels
2. By the number of nodes

In the first scheme, for a given concept, related concepts are extracted according to different levels *e.g.,* immediate neighbors, neighbors of immediate neighbors and so on. Sometimes due to large number of neighboring concepts user may face difficulty in visualization. For example, for the Hindi concept 'मानवकृति' (man-made) given below, the number of extracted related concepts at different levels are shown in Table 2.

**Hindi concept:**

**Synset:**
मानव कृति, **मानवकृति**, मानव-कृति, मानव निर्मित वस्तु, मानव-कृत वस्तु, कृत्रिम वस्तु (Human work, man-made object, human - integrated object, artificial object)

**Gloss/example:**
मानव द्वारा बनाई या तैयार की हुई वस्तु "यह मुगलकालीन मानव कृति है"
(An object made or produced by man - A masterpiece of Mughal's era.)

As number of levels increases, number of nodes (related concepts) for the concept also increases drastically. It is very difficult to render such kind of concepts on a screen. That's why we provided a second visualization scheme in which user has been given a facility to choose number of nodes to be displayed on the screen (Screenshot 7).

| Level | Number of related concepts |
|---|---|
| 1 | 432 |
| 2 | 2019 |
| 3 | 5213 |
| 4 | 11597 |
| 5 | 16409 |
| 6 | 18983 |

**Table 2: Number of related concepts for the word 'मानव कृति' (manavakruti) (man-made) at different levels**

## 5 Implementation details

The front-end of the IndoWordnet Visualizer uses Data Driven Documents (D3) JavaScript library, which allows us to present the data of nodes and edges from the back-end, graphically. This library allows us to define geometry for nodes and edges so as to automatically arrange them efficiently, while also allowing the user to click, drag and fix any node for better visibility. The library uses Scalable Vector Graphics (SVG), which allows us to zoom into the graph without pixelating the nodes, links or labels. The superiority of D3 lies in its support for dynamic behavior allowing user-friendly interaction and animation.

## 6 Conclusion and Future Work

We have presented the IndoWordnet visualizer which can be used for browsing and exploring IndoWordnet lexical database. It is enhanced with various functionalities in order to provide flexibility to the user. It is very useful for wordnet validation process. It can be used in various Natural Language Processing applications *viz.,* Word Sense Disambiguation, Information Retrieval, Semantic Relatedness *etc.* IndoWordnet visualizer is under development and some more features are yet to be included like generating the minimum sub graph between two given concepts.

## References


Pushpak Bhattacharyya, 2010. "IndoWordnet", Lexical Resources Engineering Conference (LREC 2010), Malta.

Christiane Fellbaum, 1998. "WordNet: An Electronic Database", MIT Press, Cambridge, MA.

Michael Friendly, 2008. "Milestones in the history of thematic cartography, statistical graphics, and data visualization", National Sciences and Engineering Research, Council of Canada.

Anders Johannsen and Bolette Pedersen, 2011. "Andre ord" – a Wordnet Browser for the Danish Wordnet, DanNet, NODALIDA 2011 Conference Proceedings, pp. 295–298.

Dipak Narayan, Debasri Chakrabarty, Prabhakar Pande and Pushpak Bhattacharyya, 2002. " An Experience in Building the IndoWordNet - a WordNet for Hindi", International Conference on Global WordNet (GWC), Mysore, India.

Roberto Navigli, 2013. "A Quick Tour of BabelNet1.1", CICLing 2013, Part I, LNCS 7816, pp. 25–37.

Roberto Navigli and Simone Ponzetto, 2012. "BabelNetXplorer: A Platform for Multilingual Lexical Knowledge Base Access", France.

Bolette Pedersen, Lars Borin, Markus Forsberg, Neeme Kahusk, Krister Lindén, Jyrki Niemi, Niklas Nisbeth, Lars Nygaard, Heili Orav, Eirikur Rögnvaldsson, Mitchel Seaton, Kadri Vider, Kaarlo Voionmaa, 2013. "Nordic and Baltic wordnets aligned and compared through WordTies", Proceedings of the 19th Nordic Conference of Computational Linguistics (NODALIDA), 2013.

Steven Vercruysse and Martin Kuiper, 2011. "WordVis: JavaScript and Animation to Visualize the WordNet Relational Dictionary" in Proceedings of the Third International Conference on Intelligent Human Computer Interaction (IHCI 2011), Prague, Czech Republic, August, 2011

## Screenshots

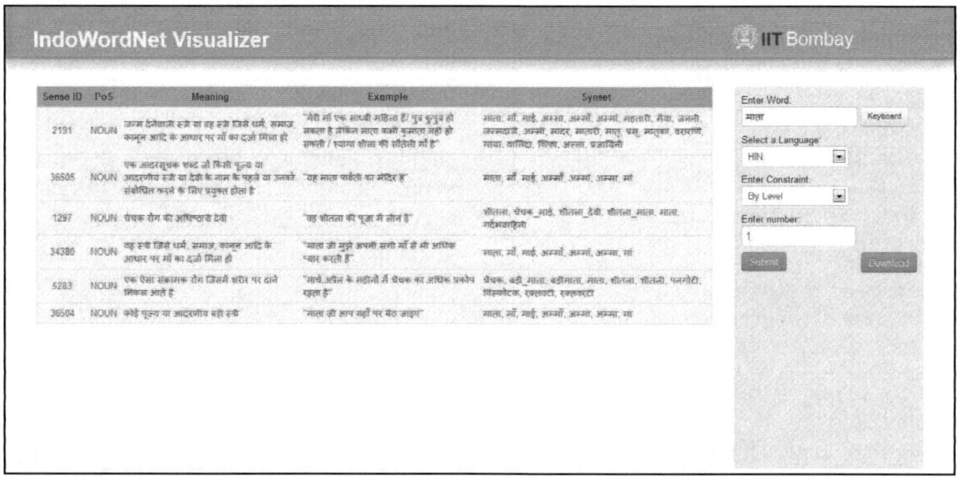


**Screenshot 1**: For a given Hindi word '*maata*' (mother), all its senses are displayed on a screen. User can see the graph of a particular sense by clicking on it.

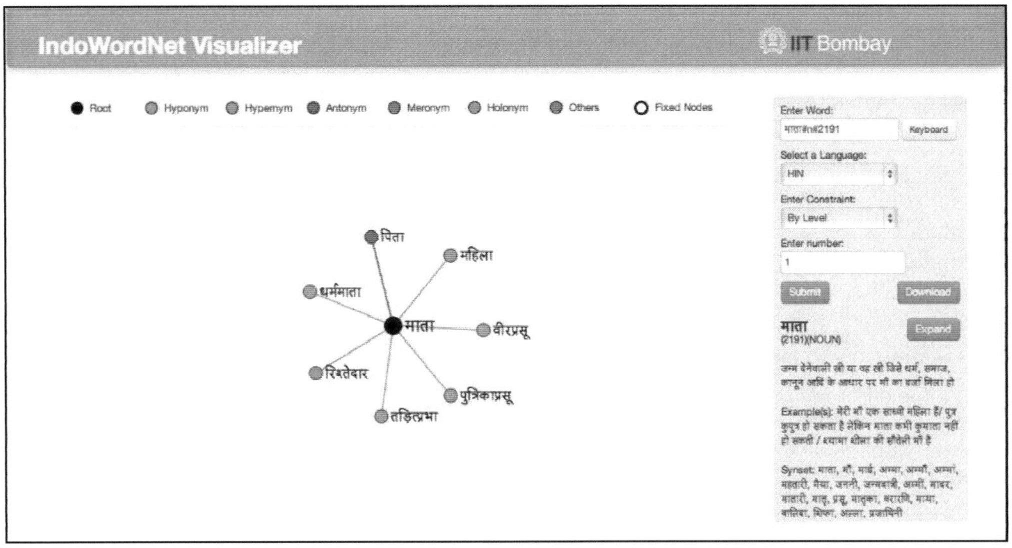


**Screenshot 2**: Graph for a Hindi word '*maata*' (mother) with level 1
All related concepts of '*maata*' are displayed in a graph along with its semantic information on right side

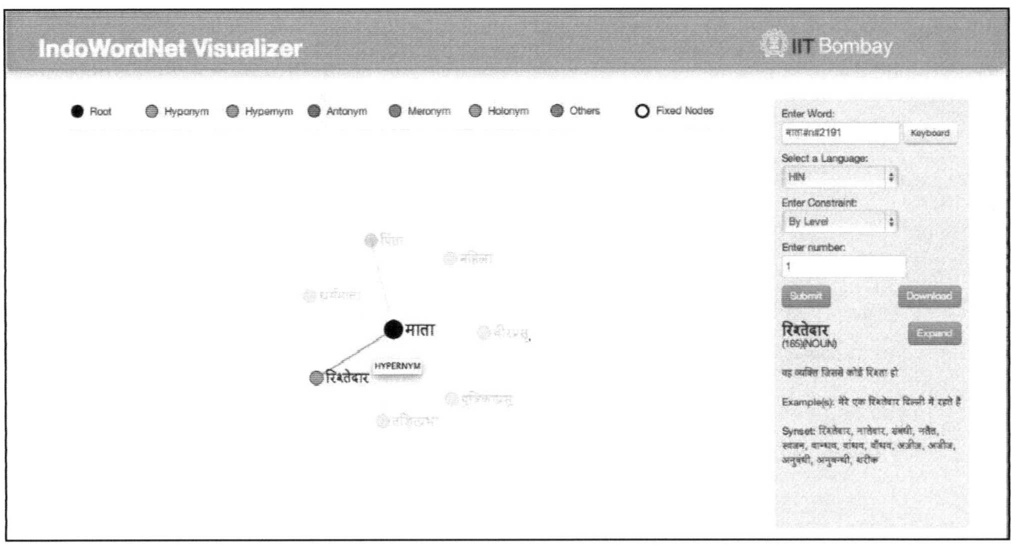


**Screenshot 3**: Graph for a Hindi word '*maata'* (mother) with level 1
When we move mouse pointer over the edge its relation is displayed.

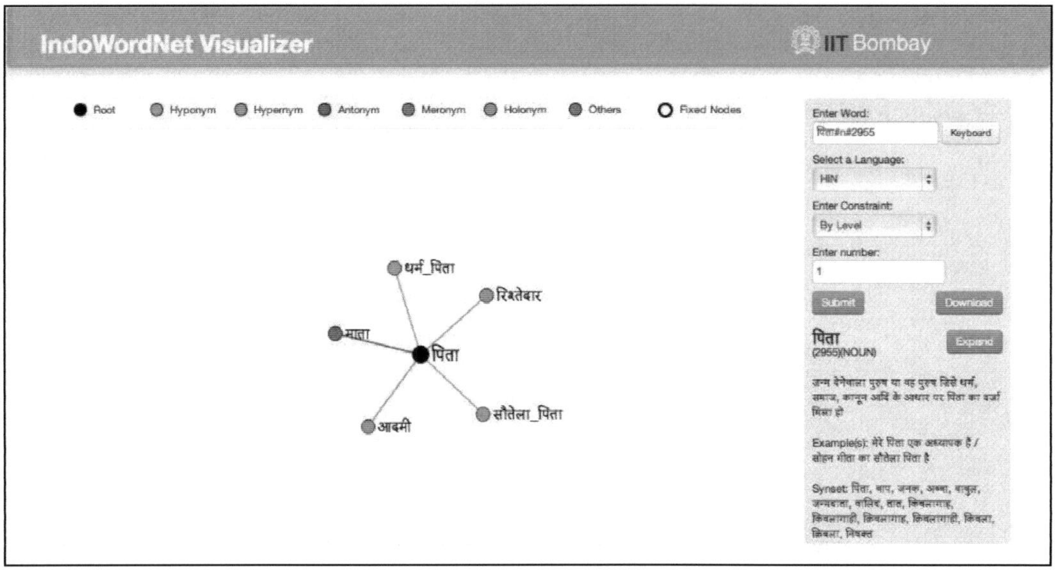


**Screenshot 4**: Graph for a Hindi word *'pita'* (father) with level 1

(In screenshot 2, if we expand node *'pita'* then this graph is generated)

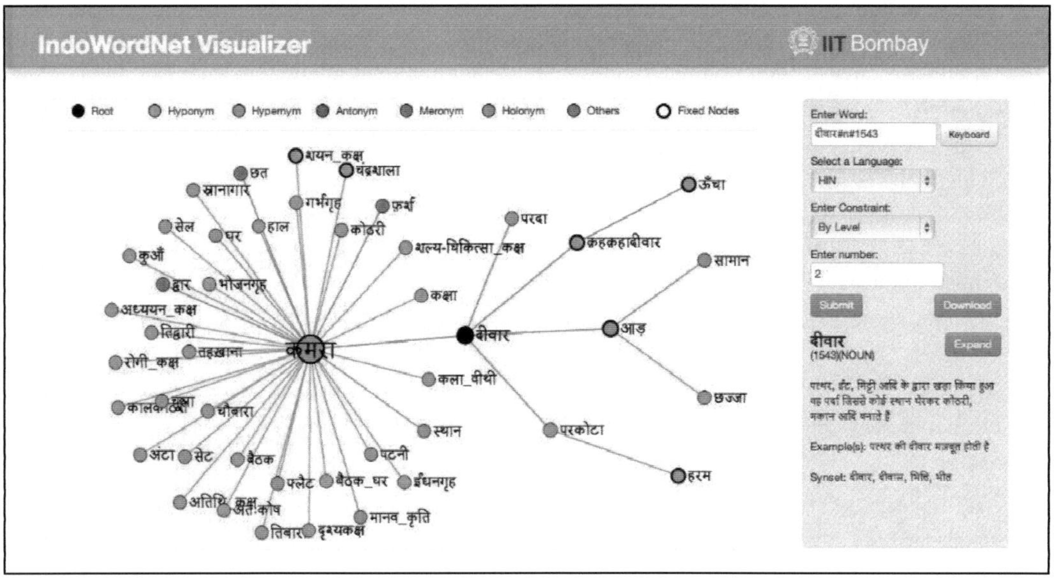


**Screenshot 5**: Graph for a Hindi word '*diwar*' (wall) with level 2

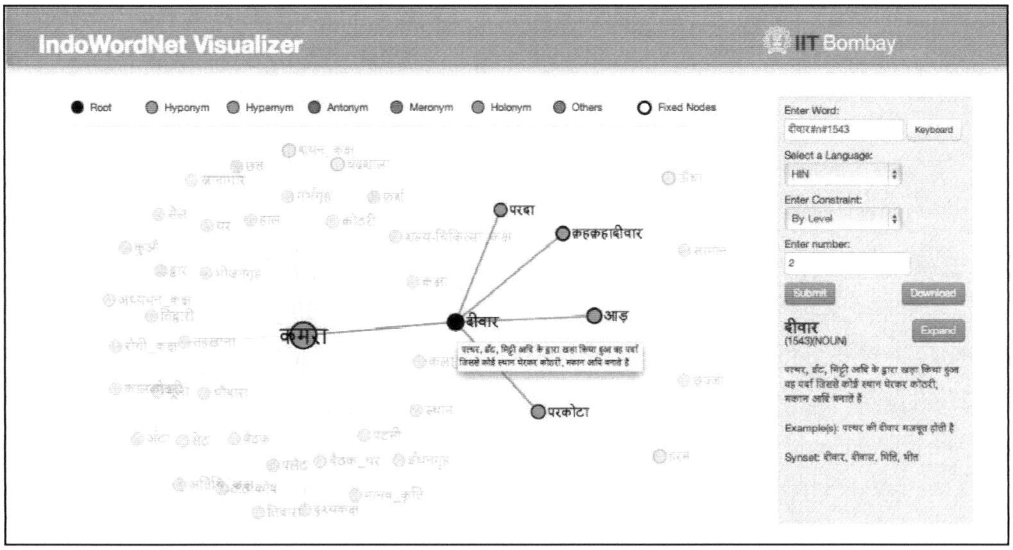


**Screenshot 6**: Graph for a Hindi word '*diwar'* (wall) with level 2. On mouse hover it highlights its synsets and only immediate neighbors (concepts)

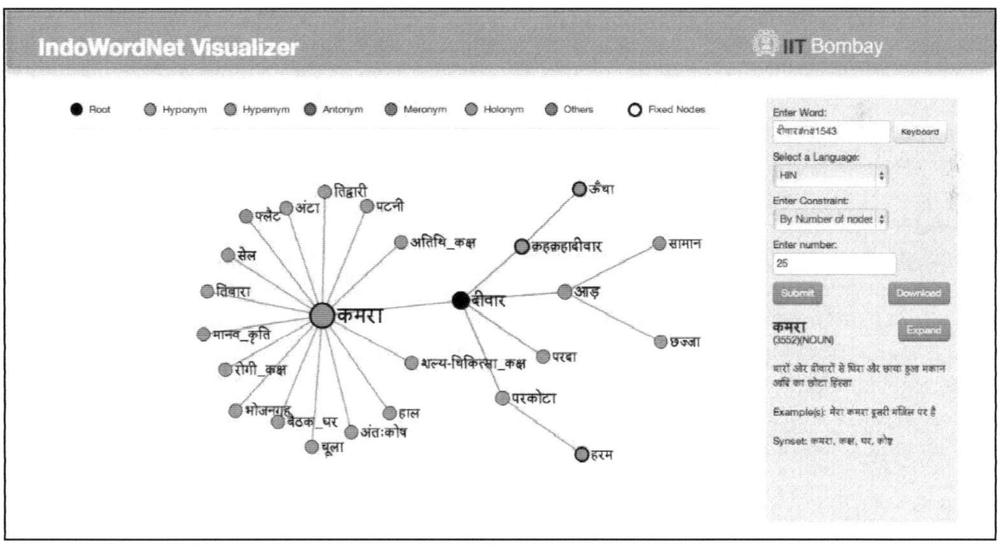


**Screenshot 7**: Graph for a Hindi word '*diwar*' (wall) with 25 number of nodes on a screen. This is another type of visual display scheme, where user can specify how many number of nodes he/she wants to display on a screen

# Towards Building Lexical Ontology via Cross-Language Matching

**Mamoun Abu Helou**
Birzeit University
Birzeit, Palestine
mabuhelou@birzeit.edu

**Matteo Palmonari**
Milano Biccoca University
Milano, Italy
palmonari@disco.unimib.it

**Mustafa Jarrar**
Birzeit University
Birzeit, Palestine
mjarrar@birzeit.edu

**Christiane Fellbaum**
Princeton University
Princeton, United State
fellbaum@princeton.edu

## Abstract

In this paper, we introduce a methodology for mapping linguistic ontologies lexicalized across different languages. We present a classification-based semantics for mappings of lexicalized concepts across different languages. We propose an experiment for validating the proposed cross-language mapping semantics, and discuss its role in creating a gold standard that can be used in assessing cross-language matching systems.

## 1 Introduction and Motivation

Sharing data on the Web meaningfully requires capturing the semantics behind the data. On the word level, meaning can be represented in digital lexical resources (lexicons) that are amenable to automatic processing and reasoning for a range of intra- and interlingual applications.

A *lexicon* is the inventory of word forms and meanings of a language. Each lexical entry specifies several linguistic properties of a word (such as its phonetics, morphology, and syntax) as well as its semantics. In a relational model of the lexicon, a words meaning is reflected in its relations to other words (Miller and Fellbaum 1991).

With the emergence of the Semantic Web, ontologies have gained great attention in research as well as in industry for enabling knowledge representation and sharing. An *ontology* in general, is a formal representation of critical knowledge that enables different systems sharing this knowledge to communicate meaningfully. Ontologies are perceived as language-independent representations of concepts and their interrelations, thereby allowing intelligent agents and applications to access and interpret the Web contents automatically.

Because some lexicons combine aspects of a lexicon with those of an ontology, they are often called linguistic ontologies (Hirst 2004, Jarrar 2010). A *linguistic ontology* can be seen both as a lexicon and as an ontology (Hirst 2004; Jarrar 2010), and is significantly different from domain ontologies. Because it is not constructed for a specific domain. Linguistic ontologies can be seen as semantic networks covering most common concepts in a natural language and provide knowledge structured on lexical items (words) of a language by relating them according to their meanings (concepts).

One such commonly used linguistic ontology is WordNet (Fellbaum 1998). WordNet was conceived as a lexicon, but the emergence of wordnets in other languages and the need to map them have raised the need to consider not just the lexical inventory of these languages (i.e., the word forms, word senses and their interrelations) but also their conceptual inventory, a set of categories of objects (concepts) that share the same properties and the relations among them.

In this paper we discuss the role of cross-language ontology matching methods in linking linguistic ontologies in different languages. In particular we investigate the semantics of cross-language mappings, and the problem of creating a gold standard to evaluate alternative ontology matching methods. We propose a classification-based semantic approach for mappings among concepts lexicalizations. We define a linguistic-based classification task that allows us to support the design of experiments to validate cross-language mappings and to enable us to build a gold standard that can be used to assess the performance of automatic cross-language matchers. Then, such mapping methods can be used to discover mappings at large-scale and solve the problem of creating large-scale linguistic ontologies in a (semi)-automatic way.

**The construction of linguistic ontologies** followed the success of WordNet and was motivated by the need for similarly structured lexicons for individual and multiple languages (multi-language lexicons). Both the "merge" (where a wordnet is first built manually from scratch) and the "expand" model (which proceeds largely by translation, Vossen 1998) are used to build wordnets in languages other than English. EuroWordNet (Vossen 2004) and MultiWordNet (Pianta et al. 2002) cover a number of European languages. In the EuroWordNet approach both models were used. Mappings among the different wordnets are represented in the Inter-Lingual Index, which is considered to be language independent. Whenever possible, entities from the individual wordnets are linked to the Inter-Lingual Index by means of equivalence and near-equivalence relations. MultiWordNet applied the expand model, and all wordnets are aligned as strictly as possible to the English WordNet under the assumption that most of the concepts are universally shared. However, Vossen (1996) argued that wordnets developed using the expand technique are overly influenced by English WordNet and thus retain its mistakes and structural drawbacks. However, the merge model strategy is more labor and cost-intensive. Wordnets for many languages have been constructed under the guidelines of Global WordNet Association[1], which aims to coordinate the production and linking of wordnets.

**Automatic construction of wordnets** is another method for building and linking wordnets, using machine translation techniques. The BabelNet project (Navigli and Ponzetto, 2012) used machine translation to provide equivalents in various languages for English WordNet synsets. While this approach might be suitable for certain NLP applications (de Melo and Weikum, 2012), it usually fails to account for the fact that different languages encode subtle socio-cultural aspects that do not always have straightforward translation equivalents. Cimiano et al. (2010) argued that translation tools (to some extent) might remove the language barrier but not necessarily the socio-cultural one; there is a need to find the appropriate word sense of the translated word that is not reflected in the literal translation equivalent. Moreover, Hirst (2004) argued that languages do not cover exactly the same part of the lexicon and, even where they seem to be common, several concepts are lexicalized differently.

**Ontology-based cross-language matching** is the process of establishing correspondences (find relations) among the ontological resources from two independent ontologies where each ontology is lexicalized in a different natural language (Spohr et al. 2011).

A common approach for cross-language ontology matching is based on transforming a cross-language matching problem into a mono-language one by translating the ontology elements of one ontology in the language adopted by the other ontology using automatic machine translation tools (e.g., Fu et al. 2012). Spohr et al. (2011) argued that the quality of machine translation systems is limited and depends greatly on the pair of languages considered. As a consequence, a pure *translation-based* approach is not sufficient to find a significant amount of mappings.

Although some techniques such as explicit semantic analysis (Gabrilovich and Markovitch 2007) proved to perform well in cross-language ontology matching (Narducci et al. 2013), it is important to understand how reliable automatic matching methods are in this domain. Before selecting and/or extending the more appropriate existing cross-language ontology matching techniques, we need to be able to compare alternative methods and to assess the quality of their output. Moreover we recognized that although a variety of cross-language ontology matching methods have been proposed, the semantic nature of cross-language mappings that cross-language ontology matching methods are expected to find has not been sufficiently investigated.

This motivated us to understand the *formal semantics of mappings among linguistic ontologies – lexicalization patterns across different languages*, and to investigate the specification of their intended meaning. In other words, providing a formal interpretation of the mapping semantics allows us to define a set of inference rules and to derive mappings (relations) from a set of existing mappings.

The research presented here aims to contribute to the Arabic Ontology project (Jarrar 2011). Our idea is to semi-automate this process by (1) matching Arabic concepts to English WordNet concepts, and (2) deriving the semantic relations among the Arabic concepts using relations among concepts in the English WordNet.

[1] http://globalwordnet.org/

The rest of the paper is structured as follows. In section 2, we introduce the Arabic Ontology project and describe the semi-automatic method by which it was created. Section 3 describes the cross-lingual ontology matching problem. In section 4, we illustrate the proposed approach. In section 5, we define an experimental setting for validating the proposed approach and its role in creating a gold standard for assessing cross-language mapping methods. In section 6, we conclude and outline possible future steps.

## 2 The Arabic Ontology

The Arabic Ontology (Jarrar 2010) aims to build a linguistic ontology for Arabic. The Arabic Ontology is a formal representation (using FOL) of the concepts that the Arabic terms convey. The Arabic Ontology can be seen and used as an *Arabic wordnet*; however, unlike WordNet, the Arabic Ontology is logically and philosophically well-founded, and follows strict ontological principles (Jarrar 2011).

The "*top levels*" of the Arabic Ontology are derived from philosophical notions (Jarrar et al. 2013), which are used to ensure the ontological correctness of the lower levels. The top levels of the Arabic Ontology constitute a classification of the most abstract concepts (i.e., meanings) of the Arabic terms. All concepts in the Arabic Ontology are classified under these top levels. These concepts are designed based on a deep investigation of the philosophy literature and well-recognized upper level ontologies like BFO (Smith. 1998), DOLCE (Gangemi et al. 2003a), SUMO (Niles and Pease 2001), and KYOTO (Casillas at al. 2009).

### 2.1 Semi-automatic Construction of the Arabic Ontology via Cross-Language Matching

In addition to that the Arabic Ontology that is being built manually at Sina Institute in Birzeit University [2], there are also hundreds of dictionaries that have been digitized and integrated into one lexical database. This database provides a good source for Arabic synsets (concepts), but lack semantic relations among the concepts. We argue that, by mapping such Arabic concepts into their conceptually equivalences in WordNet, one can (automatically) infer the relations among the Arabic concepts from the relations among the English concepts. The resultant relations can provide an initial set of relations that can be manually validated and corrected.

However, mapping synsets lexicalized in different languages is a challenging task. Cross-language ontology matching techniques (Spohr 2011; Fu 2012) can play a crucial role in bootstrapping the creation of large linguistic ontologies and, for analogous reasons, in enriching existent ontologies. We also remark that the above considerations do not apply to the Arabic ontology only, but our definitions and approach are general and can be reused for other languages.

## 3 Cross-Lingual Ontology Matching

Euzenat and Shvaiko (2007) defined *ontology matching* as a process that tries to establish *correspondences* among semantically related ontological entities, without explicitly specifying the natural languages used to label the ontological entities (e.g., concepts, relations, descriptions, and comments). We recall the definition of correspondence (mapping) presented in [Jung et al., 2009].

***Definition 1***: *Correspondence*, Given a source ontology $O_S$, a target ontology $O_T$ , and a set of alignment relations $\mathcal{R}$, a correspondence is a quadruple: *correspondence:=* $< c_S; c_T; r; n>$, $c_S \in O_S$, $c_T \in O_T$ . Where $r \in \mathcal{R}$, a set of alignment relations (e.g., $\equiv$, $\sqsubseteq$, or $\perp$), and $n \in [0, 1]$ is a confidence level (i.e., measure of confidence in the fact that the correspondence holds).

The largest part of the ontology matching strategies (see, Shvaiko and Euzenat 2013) involve syntactic and lexical comparisons, making ontologies for different languages very difficult to match. Ontology entities are expressed in natural language by associating them with terms (i.e., a lexicon) that belong to one (or more) natural languages. We denote the term *lexicalization* as the process of associating ontology entities with a set of terms that belongs to a set of natural languages, and the term *lingualization* as the process of retrieving the set of languages that the associated terms belong to.

According to Spohr et al. (2011), an ontology $O$ is lexicalized in a given language $l$, if the ontology terms are lingualized in language $l$, such that $l$ belong to the set of natural languages $L$ $(l \in L)$. Ontologies can be lexicalized in one language (monolingual ontology), two languages

[2] http://sites.birzeit.edu/comp/ArabicOntology/

(bilingual ontology) or more languages (multilingual ontology). Spohr and his colleagues also distinguished between the matching tasks based on the number of languages used to lexicalize the ontology terms.

Given two ontologies $O_S$ and $O_T$ , which are lexicalized in two sets of natural languages $L_S$ and $L_T$ respectively, we can define the cross-language ontology matching as the process of establishing relations or correspondences among ontological resources from two independent ontologies, where each ontology is lexicalized in (a) different natural language(s), but they do not share any language.

In the recent past, a *translation-based* approach has been used to transform the cross-language problem into a mono-language ontology matching one (e.g., Fu 2012). However, the cultural-linguistic barriers (Gracia et al. 2012) still need to be overcome in terms of the mapping process and techniques, as well as to formally define the semantic mappings that align concepts lexicalized across different natural languages. That is, the semantics of mapping among concepts lexicalized in different natural languages is still unsolved.

In general, a community of users (speakers) would consider two concepts that are lexicalized in two languages to be equivalent if both terms are used to indicate the same meaning in a given context. The context (or discourse) that a community of speakers shares in order to decide if these two terms (lexemes) refer to the same concept is "not only to explain what people say, but also how they say it. Lexical choice, syntax, and many other properties of the formal style of this speech are controlled by the parliamentary context" (Van Dijk, 2006).

Our main objective is to define the semantics of cross-language mapping among concepts lexicalization. This includes the formal representation and interpretation (i.e., formal semantic) of these mappings. We start from definitions and approaches proposed for mono-language ontology matching and we extend them to cross-language ontology matching.

# 4 Mapping Semantics in Cross-Language Ontology Matching

This section presents the classification-based interpretation for the cross-language mapping problem. We discuss the extension of the definition of the classification-based approach from formal interpretation (Atencia et al. 2012) to an interpretation that covers the concept lexicalization.

## 4.1 Classification-based Interpretation of Mappings

Ontology mapping can be seen as an expression that establishes relations among elements of two (or more) heterogeneous ontologies. A crisp mapping tells us that a certain concept is related to other concepts in different ontologies and specifies the type of relations, which are typically a set of formal relations $\{\equiv, \sqsubseteq, or \perp\}$. A *weighted mapping* ( see definition 2) in addition associates a number (weight) to those relations. We start from the definition of weighted mapping and its semantic presented in (Atencia et al. 2012) that we recall below.

***Definition 2***: *Weighted Mapping*, Given two ontologies $O_1$ and $O_2$, a weighted mapping from $O_1$ to $O_2$ is a quadruple: *weighed mapping:=* $\langle C, D, r, [\mathrm{a}, \mathrm{b}]\rangle$, where $C$ and $D$ are two concepts such that $C \in O_1$ and $D \in O_2$, $r \in \{\sqsubseteq, \equiv, \sqsupseteq, \perp\}$, *a* and *b* are real numbers in the unit interval [0, 1].

Intuitively, the semantics of the mapping $\langle C, D, r, [\mathrm{a}, \mathrm{b}]\rangle$ is that the relation *r* maps the concept $C$ to the concept $D$ with a confidence that falls into the closed interval $[\mathrm{a}, \mathrm{b}]$, where *a* and *b* represent respectively the lower and upper bounds of such an interval.

Following a standard model-theoretic *formal semantics* based concepts are intuitively interpreted as set of instances. An interpretation $\mathfrak{I}$ is a pair $\mathfrak{I} = \langle \Delta^{\mathfrak{I}}, \cdot^{\mathfrak{I}} \rangle$ where $\Delta^{\mathfrak{I}}$ is a non-empty set, called domain of interpretation $\mathfrak{I}$, and $\cdot^{\mathfrak{I}}$ is a function that interprets each concept (class) $C$ in the set of concepts $\mathcal{C}$ as a non empty subset of $\Delta^{\mathfrak{I}}$, and each instance identifier $(x \in X)$ as an element of $\Delta^{\mathfrak{I}}$. Intuitively, for a given ontology $O$, if $\mathcal{C}$ is a set of concepts, $\mathcal{R}$ is a set of relations, and $X$ is a set of shared individuals. Then $C^{\mathfrak{I}} \subseteq \Delta^{\mathfrak{I}}$ for $C \in \mathcal{C}$, $r^{\mathfrak{I}} \subseteq \Delta^{\mathfrak{I}} \times \Delta^{\mathfrak{I}}$ for $r \in \mathcal{R}$, and $x \in \Delta^{\mathfrak{I}}$ for $x \in X$.

**Weighted mappings semantics**, Atencia et al. (2012) provide a formal semantics of weighted mapping among independent ontologies, that assumes a classification-based interpretation of mappings. Let $C$ be a concept of $O_1$ and $x_k$ an individual of *X*; we define *X* as a *shared context* (domain) of the mapping. We say that $x_k$ is classified under $C$ according to $\mathfrak{I}_1$ if $x_k^{\mathfrak{I}_1} \in C^{\mathfrak{I}_1}$. Then, the set $C_X^{\mathfrak{I}_1} = \{x \in X \mid x^{\mathfrak{I}_1} \in C^{\mathfrak{I}_1}\}$

represents the subset of individuals of $X$ classified under $C$ according to $\mathfrak{I}_1$. Note that $C_X^{\mathfrak{I}_1}$ is a subset of $X$ ($C_X^{\mathfrak{I}_1} \subseteq X$), whereas $C^{\mathfrak{I}_1}$ is a subset of the domain of the interpretation $\mathfrak{I}_1$ ($C^{\mathfrak{I}_1} \subseteq \Delta^{\mathfrak{I}_1}$). In addition, $C_X^{\mathfrak{I}_1}$ is always a finite set, while $C^{\mathfrak{I}_1}$ may be infinite.

Figure 1, demonstrates the extensional meaning between two concepts $C$ and $D$ in the ontology $O_1$ and ontology $O_2$ respectively, with the classification-based mapping approach. $\mathfrak{I}_1$ and $\mathfrak{I}_2$ represent respectively an interpretation of $O_1$ and $O_2$. $\Delta^{\mathfrak{I}_1}$ and $\Delta^{\mathfrak{I}_2}$ represent the domain of interpretation of $\mathfrak{I}_1$ and $\mathfrak{I}_2$, respectively. The sets $C_X^{\mathfrak{I}_1}$ and $D_X^{\mathfrak{I}_2}$ represent the subsets of individuals $x_k$ in $X$ classified under $C$ according to $\mathfrak{I}_1$, and under $D$ according to $\mathfrak{I}_2$, respectively. The Individuals $z$ and $y$ represent individuals that do not belong to $X$.

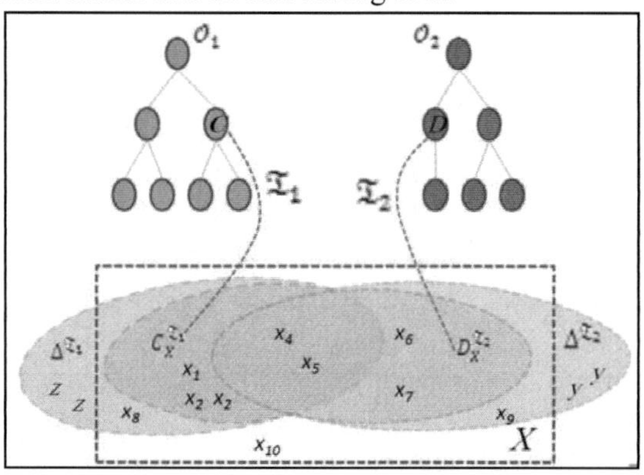

Figure 1: The extensional meaning of a concept and the common interpretation context.

The classification-based approach examines the relation among two concepts $C$ and $D$ that are in the ontology $O_1$ and $O_2$ respectively, by considering a common context (the shared domain $X$), defined as a set of common instances classified under the two ontology concepts. The different types of mappings $\langle C, D, r, [a,b]\rangle$ are obtained by looking at the different relation $r \in \{\sqsubseteq, \sqsupseteq, \equiv, \perp\}$. Atencia et al. use precision, recall, and F-measure, as used in the context of classification tasks, for the formalization of weighted subsumptions ($\sqsubseteq, \sqsupseteq$) and equivalence ($\equiv$)relations, respectively.

Following the classification perspective, a weighted subsumptions mapping $\langle C, D, \sqsubseteq, [a,b]\rangle$ interpreted as follows : the number of individuals of $X$ classified under C according to $\mathfrak{I}_1$ which are (re-)classified under D according to $\mathfrak{I}_2$. The weighted mapping can be seen as the recall of $C_X^{\mathfrak{I}_1}$ w.r.t $D_X^{\mathfrak{I}_2}$.

$$R\left(C_X^{\mathfrak{I}_1}, D_X^{\mathfrak{I}_2}\right) = \frac{\left|C_X^{\mathfrak{I}_1} \cap D_X^{\mathfrak{I}_2}\right|}{\left|C_X^{\mathfrak{I}_1}\right|} \in [a,b]$$

In the same way, the weighted mapping $\langle C, D, \sqsupseteq, [a,b]\rangle$ which falls in the confidence level interval $[a,b]$, is used to express the number of individuals of $X$ classified by $D$ according to $\mathfrak{I}_2$which are (re-) classified under $C$ according to $\mathfrak{I}_1$. Then the weighted mapping can be seen as the precision of $D_X^{\mathfrak{I}_2}$ *w.r.t* $C_X^{\mathfrak{I}_1}$.

$$P\left(C_X^{\mathfrak{I}_1}, D_X^{\mathfrak{I}_2}\right) = \frac{\left|C_X^{\mathfrak{I}_1} \cap D_X^{\mathfrak{I}_2}\right|}{\left|D_X^{\mathfrak{I}_2}\right|} \in [a,b]$$

Intuitively, the F-measure can be used to express the equivalence relation that aligns two concepts $C$ and $D$ where $\langle C, D, \equiv, [a,b]\rangle$ represent that F-measure falls into the confidence interval $[a,b]$. The F-measure is the harmonic mean of precision and recall. Typically the F-measure is used to evaluate the global quality of a classifier, the *F-measure* of $C_X^{\mathfrak{I}_1}$ and $D_X^{\mathfrak{I}_2}$ is defined as:

$$F\left(C_X^{\mathfrak{I}_1}, D_X^{\mathfrak{I}_2}\right) = 2.\frac{\left|C_X^{\mathfrak{I}_1} \cap D_X^{\mathfrak{I}_2}\right|}{\left|C_X^{\mathfrak{I}_1}\right| + \left|D_X^{\mathfrak{I}_2}\right|} \in [a,b]$$

An interesting point in the above weighted mapping definition is the use of an interval [a,b] to define an uncertain (yet bounded) weight associated with a mapping. Using such intervals - as a more general notation for mapping weights - we can define the equivalence relation as a conjunction of the two subsumption relations. This in particular gives the notion of logical consequences of weighted mappings that allows to define a set of inference rules to derive a mapping from a set of existing mappings. For instance, if we have weighted mappings $\langle C, D, \sqsubseteq, [h,j]\rangle$ and $\langle C, D, \sqsupseteq, [e,f]\rangle$, then we can derive the equivalence weighted mapping $\langle C, D, \equiv, [v,w]\rangle$ with $v = \min(h,e)$ and $w = \max(j,f)$.

Notice that, if we consider the usual definition of equivalence in DLs in terms of subsumption: $\langle C \equiv D\rangle$ *iff* $\langle C \sqsubseteq D\rangle$ and $\langle C \sqsupseteq D\rangle$, when dealing with single weight values for precision ($\sqsupseteq$) and recall ($\sqsubseteq$) instead of intervals, it is usually impossible to combine them into a single value by simple conjunction (Atencia et al. 2012). Nevertheless, generally ontology matchers are used to return a single confidence level value, for instance, $n$. Accordingly, to represent the value $n$ by means of the weighted mapping interval [a, b], the authors (Atencia et al. 2012) suggest to use a pointwise interval; we can assume that $a$=$b$, then $n$=[a, a]. Thus, we can simply present the weighted mapping relation as $\langle C, D, r, n\rangle$.

Assume that the set of individuals $\{x_1, \ldots, x_{10}\}$ (see Figure 1) are classified under $O_1$and $O_2$. If the individuals $\{x_1, \ldots, x_5\}$ are classified under concepts $C \in O_1$ and the elements $\{x_4, \ldots, x_7\}$ are classified under the concept $D \in O_2$, we can represent the subsumption relations $\langle C, D, \sqsubseteq, 0.4\rangle$ and $\langle C, D, \sqsupseteq, 0.5\rangle$ by computing the recall and precision, respectively. Then we can deduce the equivalence relation between $C$ and $D$ by computing the F-measure $\langle D, C, \equiv, 0.44\rangle$.

### 4.2 Classification-based Interpretation of Mappings in Cross-Language Ontologies

In what follow, we extend (Atencia et al. 2012) approach, which fits our problem and provides a good foundation for the cross-language mapping problem for several reasons. Many matching methods, in particular those for cross-language ontology matching, use metrics that evaluate the overlap between the entities (e.g., ontology individuals, documents, pieces of text) that are classified under two concepts. Also, the approach provides a very general definition of classification context (the set of instances considered for the interpretation of mappings), which can support the definition of a formal framework to interpret translations among ontology concepts that are lexicalized in different languages. Atencia et al. assume a formal interpretation of a concept denoted as class of instances in an interpretation domain.

Classification is interpreted as the task to establish whether an instance $i$ is member of a class $C$, i.e., if $i$ belongs to the extension of $C$. This extensional interpretation cannot be directly applied for ontologies that are not formally represented and interpreted in set theoretic semantics. For instance, when we annotate a document we can consider the concept as classifying an object, but the interpretation of classification here is different; in this case, saying that a concept classifies an object means that the concept represents the topic of the document. If we consider a sentence and we want to disambiguate the meaning of the words in it, we can consider the *disambiguation task* as a form of classification, namely, the classification of a word as occurrence of a word sense in the sentence.

We *hypothesize* that in order to share a meaning (concept) we have to share a domain of interpretation, and this domain represents the shared context of a community of languages speakers. Considering the extensional based approach, particularly the case of cross-lingual extensional meaning of a concept, we should keep in mind that according to a given shared context, it is *not* necessary that all objects classified under $C_S$ ($x \in C_{X,S}^{\mathfrak{I}_1}$) are also instances under $D_T$ ($x \in D_{X,T}^{\mathfrak{I}_2}$) according to an interpretation $\mathfrak{I}_1$ and $\mathfrak{I}_2$, respectively. It happens that an object $x \in C_{X,S}^{\mathfrak{I}_1}$ might *not* exist in the other language (or, ontology) ($x \notin D_{X,T}^{\mathfrak{I}_2}$), or even it might be classified under another concept such as ($x \in E_{X,T}^{\mathfrak{I}_2}$).

Recall that a synset is a set of words that all lexicalize and denote the same concept. Such words, called synonyms, are equivalent in that they carry the same meaning, even when not all synonyms are stylistically felicitous in all contexts. For example, the phrase "empty vessel" sounds good, while "vacant vassal" does not; "empty" is more frequently used than vacant in this context, in spite of the fact that both adjectives convey the same meaning. Note that "empty" and "vacant" are freely interchangeable when modifying nouns like "room" and "house."

Consider a corpus of sentences, where each sentence expresses a context and a word in the sentence represent the usage of a concept. If a majority of speakers (i.e., bilingual native speakers or lexicographers) can substitute two words, each belonging to a different language, in a sentence and both words indicate the same sense (meaning), then they can be used interchangeably to refer to the same concept (word sense).

We *hypothesize* that, if speakers can substitute two words in a given context, then these words are synonyms and give an equivalent meaning (concept) (Miller and Fellbaum 1991). This is valid also for intra- and interlingual substitution, as concepts are independent of specific languages. We assume the above hypothesis but, instead of considering the cross-language substitutability of words themselves, we consider the cross-language substitutability of meanings associated with these words, by referring to *co-disambiguation* (see definition 3) of words across ontologies in different languages.

**Definition 3**: *Co-disambiguation Task*, let *WSD*($w_i$) be a function called Word Sense Disambiguation, such that $w_i$ is an occurrence of the word $w$ in a sentence $S$. *WSD* associates $w_i$ with a sense in a lexicon (e.g., WordNet). Accordingly, we can define a *cross-language WSD* function *CL-WSD*$_{[L1>L2]}$($w_i$), such that *CL-WSD* associates a word $w_i$ in a language $L_1$

(where $L_1$ is the language used in *S*) with a sense in a lexicon lexicalized in another language $L_2$.

By extending the classification-based semantics defined in (Atencia et al. 2012) with the consideration of the *CL-WSD* classification task, we map a sense $C$ (lexicalized in $w_1$ using $L_1$) to a sense $D$ (lexicalized in $w_2$ using $L_2$) (i.e., represent conceptually-equivalence word senses) if *most* of the bilingual speakers accept that $CL\text{-}WSD_{[L1>L2]}(w_1) = C$, and $CL\text{-}WSD_{[L1>L2]}(w_1) = D$. At the same time accept that $CL\text{-}WSD_{[L2>L1]}(w_2) = C$, and $CL\text{-}WSD_{[L2>L1]}(w_2) = D$.

For example, in the sentence "the student sat around the table (طاولة) to eat their lunch", the words "table" and (طاولة, pronounced Tawlah) indicates the same meaning (a table at which meals are served). If most of the speakers would co-disambiguate "table" with the English word sense $Table_n^3$ (the third noun sense in WordNet for table - a piece of furniture with tableware for a meal laid out on it), and with the Arabic word sense{طاولة Tawlah, منضدة Mndada, مائدة Ma'ad, سفرة Soufra}, then $Table_3^n$ and {طاولة Tawlah, منضدة Mndada, مائدة Ma'ad , سفرة Soufra} denote the same concept.

In another words, if the substitution of the words does not change the meaning of the context, then they are conceptually equivalent. In view of this, *CL-WSD* can be seen as a classifier, where the number of agreements among the lexicographers (bilingual speakers) expresses the confidence (i.e., the weight) of the mapping.

The speakers perform the *CL-WSD* tasks, and the mapping between two word senses depends on a frequency-based function that measures the degree in which the two senses in two different languages co-disambiguate the same word sense in multiple contexts (sentences). Suppose we have a corpus of English sentences, we find a word $w_{en}$ that appears in these sentences. We disambiguate each occurrence of $w_{en,i}$ with an English word sense $C_i$ ; we disambiguate each occurrence of $w_{en,i}$ with a synset $D_i$ in Arabic. As a result of this operation we found two sets of distinct concepts $\bar{C}$ and $\bar{D}$ that have been used to disambiguate $w_{en}$ respectively in English and Arabic. For each $C_i \in \bar{C}$ we count the number of $C_i$ that has been co-disambiguated with every $D_i \in \bar{D}$. The co-disambiguation fraction of the two concepts $C$ and $D$ represent the degree at which we can consider $C$ *as a subclass of* $D$.

Although we use a classification task that differs from the one proposed in (Atencia et al. 2012), we can still use the inference rule they proposed to reason about mappings, to infer new mappings from existing mappings. Moreover, using the *CL-WSD* function as a classification task to evaluate the existence of relations among concepts, we can define a method to establish reference relationships between concepts by performing *CL-WSD* on sentence corpuses

## 5 Experiment Design for Cross-Language Mapping Validation

We present an experimental setting whereby the proposed cross-language mapping semantics can be evaluated and a gold standard to assess the quality and to compare alternative cross-language mapping methods can be generated.

In order to validate the equivalent relation we need to perform the following *CL-WSD* classification tasks: given a parallel corpus ( or two corpuses) which lexicalized in English and Arabic. We disambiguate each occurrence of $w_{en,i}$ in English sentences with a word sense $C_i$ and $D_i$ in English and Arabic respectively. In this way, we obtain two sets of distinct concepts $\bar{C}$ and $\bar{D}$ that have been used to disambiguate the English word $w_{en}$ respectively in senses form English and Arabic. For each $C_i \in \bar{C}$ we count how many times $C_i$ has been co-disambiguated with every $D_i \in \bar{D}$. The co-disambiguation count for the two concepts $C$ and $D$ represent the degree (confidence level) at which we can consider $C$ *as a subclass of* $D$.

In the same way, we disambiguate each occurrence of $w_{ar,i}$ in Arabic sentences with a word sense $C_i$ and $D_i$ in English and Arabic respectively. The distinct set of concepts $\bar{C}$ and $\bar{D}$ have been used to disambiguate the Arabic word $w_{ar}$ respectively in senses from English and Arabic. For each $D_i \in \bar{D}$ we count the number that $D_i$ has been co-disambiguated with every $C_i \in \bar{C}$. The proportion of the co-disambiguation for the two concepts $D$ and $C$ represent the confidence level at which we can consider $D$ *as a subclass of* $C$.

Then we use the F-measure to interpret the confidence level of the equivalent relation that aligns the two concepts $C$ and $D$.

However, it might be difficult and costly to make such experiment at large scale. One way is to use available sense annotated corpuses. Nevertheless, such an Arabic corpus is not available. Therefore, we propose to mine the subclass relations starting form a sense annotated English corpus, we *CL-WSD* the English words with the equivalent Arabic senses, and then we check if these relations can be converted to equivalence relations by exploiting the structure (relations) of the WordNet.

The proposed experiment corresponds to a classification task; asking bilingual speakers to perform a $CL\text{-}WSD_{[En>Ar]}$ classification task. We collect sentences from *"Princeton Annotated Gloss Corpus"*, a corpus of manually annotated WordNet synset definitions (glosses). The selected sentences are annotated with at least one sense that belongs to *"Core WordNet"*. The reason for selecting Core WordNet concepts is that they represent the most frequent and salient concepts and thus can shared among many or most languages. Accordingly, we hypothesize that mapping the core WordNet concepts to the equivalent Arabic concepts will form the core for the Arabic Ontology. Then we can extend it to include more cultural and language-specific concepts.

For each English word sense, a number of bilingual speakers (lexicographers) are asked to provide the equivalent Arabic word sense. For each word sense, the lexicographers substitute the English word with one of the Arabic synsets, which have been developed at Sina Institute and classified under the top levels. Using available bilingual dictionaries the lexicographers select the best translation. In Figure 2, in the sentence "the act of starting to construct a *house*", the English word "house" was *CL-WSD* with the English sense $house_1^n$ and the Arabic sense (منزل, Mnzel)[3]. For the same sentence we substitute the sense $house_1^n$ with its direct hypernym (subclass) sense $home_1^n$ from the WordNet. We *CL-WSD* the sense $home_1^n$ with the Arabic sense (بيت, Baet). Ideally, we should be able to deduce the subclass relation between (منزل) and (بيت).

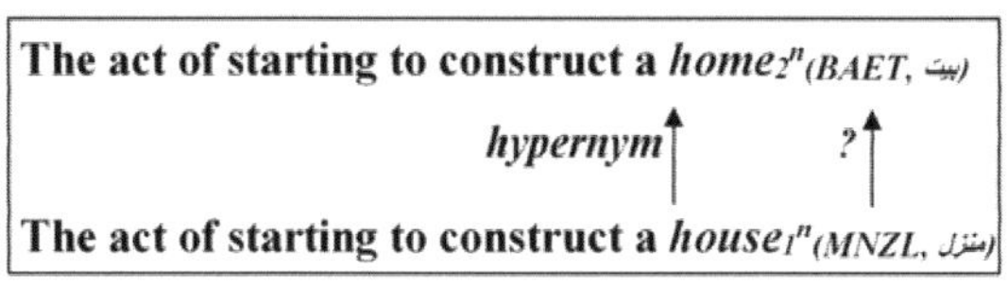


Figure 2: Example of *CL-WSD* task and a possible inference.

However, as mentioned before, not every concept is lexicalized in both (all) languages. The mappings thus obtained will form an initial semantic network. However, conflicts and overlaps might exist. The top levels concepts can control and eliminate part of this problem. For example, the associated concepts should be classified under the same top concept. This direction of work also taking into account the relations confidence level will be pursued in the future.

We plan to experiment with the proposed mapping approach on a large scale by considering all 5,000 Core WordNet concepts and to simulate the majority of speakers by incorporation larger number of bilingual speakers (lexicographers). We suggest adopting a crowdsourcing method (e.g., Amazon Mechanical Turkey (Sarasua et al. 2012) to collect feedback from larger number of lexicographers. A significance result of a full-scale version of the proposed experiment is to generate a gold standard for cross-language mappings. That can be used to assess the various automatic cross-language matching systems as well to validate the proposed semantic mapping. Thereby selecting or extending such mapping methods that can be used to discover mappings at large-scale and solve the problem of creating large-scale linguistic ontologies in a (semi)-automatic way. Moreover, we can validate the language-dependence hypothesis of the salient (core) concepts. In addition, we plan to investigate the explicit semantic analysis approach in the cross-language mapping settings (Sorg and Cimiano 2012) to enhance the word sense selection (conceptual translation) task.

## 6 Conclusion and Future Works

We introduced a classification-based mapping for cross-language matching purposes. We illustrated the proposed approach and outlined future steps. We plan to implement a large-scale experiment that covers the Core WordNet concepts and to adopt a crowdsourcing method to simulate the community agreements. In addition to bilingual dictionaries for word senses selection (conceptual translation), explicit semantic analysis techniques will be used. Moreover, we plan to investigate the extent to which the process of (semi)- automated creation is suitable for creating a linguistic ontology. We will formally define the mapping weight based on the proposed *CL-WSD* task. Finally, we aim to define and develop algorithms for semantic relations inference and to validate such methods using the cross-language mappings gold standard.

---

[3] Translation was obtained using Wikipedia inter-lingual links.

## Acknowledgments

This research is funded by EU FP7 SIERA project (no. 295006).

## References

Manuel Atencia, Alexander Borgida, Jérôme Euzenat, Chiara Ghidini and Luciano Serafini. 2012. A formal semantics for weighted ontology mappings. In ISWC-2012, pp17-33.

Philipp Cimiano, Elena Montiel-Ponsoda, Paul Buitelaar, Mauricio Espinoza and Asunción Gómez-Pérez. 2010. A note on ontology localization. Applied Ontology, 5(2).

Arantza Casillas, Arantza Diaz de Illarraza, Kike Fernandez, Koldo Gojenola, Egoitz Laparra, German Rigau, Aitor Soroa. 2009. The Kyoto Project. In Proc. SEPLN´09, Spain, September.

Gerard de Melo and Gerhard Weikum. 2012. Constructing and utilizing wordnets using statistical methods. Language Resources and Evaluation, 46(2):287-311.

Jérôme Euzenat and Pavel Shvaiko. 2007. Ontology matching. Springer.

Christiane Fellbaum., editor. 1998. WordNet: An Electronic Lexical Database (Language, Speech, and Communication). The MIT Press.

Bo Fu, Rob Brennan and Declan O'Sullivan. 2012. A configurable translation-based cross-lingual ontology mapping system to adjust mapping outcomes. Journal of Web Semantics, (V15)15-36.

Evgeniy Gabrilovich and Shaul Markovitch. 2007. Computing semantic relatedness using wikipediabased explicit semantic analysis. In Proceedings of the 20th IJCAI'07, pp1606–1611, San Francisco, CA, USA.

Jorge Garcia, Elena Montiel-Ponsoda, Philipp Cimiano, Asunción Gómez-Pérez, Paul Buitelaar, John McCrae. 2012. Challenges for the multilingual web of data. JWS. (V11):63-71.

Aldo Gangemi, Nicola Guarino, Claudio Masolo and Alessandro Oltramari. 2003a. Sweetening WordNet With DOLCE, AI Magazine, 24(2003), pp. 13–24.

Graeme Hirst. 2004. Ontology and the Lexicon, in Handbook on Ontologies and Information Systems. eds. S. Staab and R. Studer. Heidelberg: Springer.

Mustafa Jarrar., 2010. The Arabic Ontology. Lecture Notes, Knowledge Engineering Course (SCOM7348), Birzeit University, Palestine.

Mustafa Jarrar. 2011. Building a Formal Arabic Ontology (Invited Paper). In proceedings of the Experts Meeting on Arabic Ontologies and Semantic Networks. Alecso, Arab League. Tunis.

Mustafa Jarrar, Hiba Olwan, Rana Rishmawi. 2013. Classification of the most Abstract Concepts in Arabic - The Top Levels of the Arabic Ontology. Technical Report, Version 1. Sina Institute, Birzeit University, Palestine.

Jung Jason J. Jung, Anne Håkansson and Ronald Hartung, 2009. Indirect Alignment between Multilingual Ontologies: A Case Study of Korean and Swedish Ontologies. In Proc. of the 3rd Inter. KES, LNAI 5559, pp.233-241.

George A. Miller and Christiane Fellbaum. 1991. Semantic networks of English. Cognition, 41, 197-229.

Fedelucio Narducci, Matteo Palmonari and Giovanni Semeraro.2013. Cross-language Semantic Retrieval and Linking of E-gov Services. 12th ISWC, October, Australia

Ian Niles and Adam Pease. 2001. Towards a Standard Upper Ontology, in The 2nd International Conference on (FOIS-2001), Ogunquit, Maine.

Emanuele Pianta, Luisa Bentivogli, Christian Girardi. 2002. MultiWordNet: developing an aligned multilingual database. 1st GWC, India, January.

Barry Smith. 1998. The Basic Tools of Formal Ontology, in Nicola Guarino (ed.), Formal Ontology in Information Systems. Amsterdam, Oxford, Tokyo, Washington, DC: IOS Press (FAIA-98), 19-28

Philipp Sorg and Philipp Cimiano. 2012. Exploiting Wikipedia for cross-lingual and multilingual information retrieval. Data&Know. Eng.,74:26–45.

Dennis Spohr, Laura Hollink and Philipp Cimiano. 2011. A machine learning approach to multilingual and cross-lingual ontology matching. In Proc. of ISWC-11, Springer.

Pavel Shvaiko and Jérôme Euzenat. 2013. Ontology matching: State of the art and future challenges. IEEE Trans. Know. Data Eng., 25(1):158-176.

Cristina Sarasua, Elena Simperl and Natalya F. Noy. 2012. CROWDMAP: Crowdsourcing Ontology Alignment with Microtasks. In ISWC-2012,. Springer.

Teun A. Van Dijk. 2006. Discourse context and cognition . Discourse Studies, 8:159-177.

Piek Vossen. 1996. Right or wrong. combining lexical resources in the EuroWordNet project. In Pro. of Euralex-96, page 715728, Goetheborg.

Piek Vossen. 1998. Introduction to Eurowordnet. Computers and the Humanities, 32(2):7389.

Piek Vossen. 2004. EuroWordNet: a multilingual database of autonomous and language-specific wordnets connected via an Inter-Lingual-Index. International Journal of Lexicography, Vol.17.

# Morphosyntactic discrepancies in representing the adjective equivalent in African WordNet with reference to Northern Sotho

**Mampaka Lydia Mojapelo**

University of South Africa

Department of African Languages

mojapml@unisa.ac.za

## Abstract

This paper aims to highlight morphosyntactic discrepancies encountered in representing the adjective equivalent in African WordNet, with reference to Northern Sotho. Northern Sotho is an agglutinating language with rich and productive morphology. The language also features a disjunctive orthographic system. The orthography determines the attachment selection of morphemes. The immediate issue, in this paper, is the absence of a one-to-one correspondence between the adjective in English and that in Northern Sotho. The meaning equivalent of the English adjective covers more than one morphosyntactic category in Northern Sotho. In addition, the categories' structural diversity has a bearing on representation considerations. In some of these categories the stem suffices to represent the specific category unambiguously while in others there is a need to incorporate affixes with the stem. The challenge is to categorize semantic equivalents of the English adjective as such, while retaining their separate morphosyntactic tags in Northern Sotho, in harmony with the typology of the language. The present paper proposes morphologically feasible ways of representing this varied equivalent of the English adjective in Northern Sotho.

## 1 Introduction

African WordNet[1] seeks to build WordNets for all indigenous official languages of South Africa, which will be linked to one another. Northern Sotho[2] is one of the languages in African WordNet. So far in the project the work covers the verbs, nouns, and few adjectives. This presentation is based on the experiences with the adjective in the project so far. Like many languages African WordNet is expanded from the Princeton WordNet[3]. Being cognisant of dissimilar typologies of the source and target languages, as well as language-specific cultural and historical orientations, African WordNet is geared towards customisation to the African context.

The aim of this paper is to highlight morphosyntactic discrepancies encountered with the Northern Sotho equivalent of the adjective in African WordNet. It also proposes morphologically feasible ways in which the equivalent can be represented. Synsets are linked to one another through conceptual-semantic and lexical relations. WordNet therefore links together not only lexical items but, more significantly, the senses that the lexical items represent. It may be possible for a sense to be lexicalised in both the source and the target language without necessarily carrying the same morphosyntactic tag. This presentation will not go into the broad theoretical issues attending adjectives; rather the focus will be on the meaning equivalent of the English adjective in Northern Sotho, which is the target language, given typological differences between the two languages and differences in morphological structures of the equivalents in the target

[1] http://www.globalwordnet.org

[2] Northern Sotho (Sesotho sa Leboa) also known as Sepedi, one of the dialects, is a Niger-Congo Bantu language (Guthrie's zone S30)

[3] http://wordnet.princeton.edu

language. Each morphosyntactic category in Northen Sotho will be discussed separately and will conclude with a proposed representation in the database.

## 2 Semantic function of the adjective

English will be used as springboard here because it is the source language for the expand approach adopted for African WordNet. The semantic function of the English adjective, be it attributive or relational (Miller, 1978), is universal, namely to modify the noun. Morphologically, apart from the core adjectives which may also be morphologically affected through inflection, English adjectives include denominals and deverbals (Peters and Peters, 2000). Furthermore, there are also other different morphosyntactic constructions that are used in modifying the noun, such as the genitive and relative clause. For the purpose of this presentation and in context with African WordNet, the discussion will be confined to the English lexical entry with POS tag adjective, such as *purple*, *murdered*, *cute* and *little* and how they are rendered in the African WordNet.

The immediate issue, first of all, is the absence of a one-to-one correspondence between the adjective in English and that in Northern Sotho (Poulos and Louwrens, 1994). Northern Sotho has a limited number of adjectival stems, which is by no means a reflection of the language's capacity to produce qualifications for the noun. It is not always possible to use an adjective to convey a concept in Northern Sotho that is expressed by an English adjective. Traditional Northern Sotho grammars identify four morphosyntactic categories (the adjective, descriptive possessive [genitive], relative and enumerative) to perform this semantic function (Ziervogel et al., 1969; Poulos and Louwrens 1994). Moreover, each of these equivalents of the English adjective assumes a different prefix depending on the class of the noun it modifies. Some of the stems are unambiguous without affixes and some need affixes to make sense or to identify them with the relevant functional category. The issue is that a lexicalised equivalent of the sense expressed by an English adjective cannot be ignored on the grounds that it is not an adjective, nor can it be categorized as an adjective while it is not. It remains a challenge, specifically in this word category, that the source and target language differ on structural level. The next sections explore the ways in which each of the morphosyntactic categories can be represented, given their dynamic structures.

## 3 Northen Sotho equivalents of the English adjective adjective

The English adjective can be rendered by an adjective, possessive, relative or enumerative in Northern Sotho. The next sections discuss three of these morphosyntactic categories, illustrating and substantiating proposed representation strategies.

### 3.1 The adjective

Some English concepts expressed by adjectives are also expressed by adjectives in Northern Sotho. The structure of a Northern Sotho adjective is sketched as follows:

<table>
<tr><td>(Head noun)</td><td colspan="3">Adjective</td></tr>
<tr><td></td><td colspan="2">adjectival agreement</td><td>adjectival stem</td></tr>
<tr><td></td><td>Demonstrative</td><td>Adjectival prefix</td><td></td></tr>
</table>

Figure 1: The structure of a Northern Sotho adjective

The following example has a class 1 noun as head:

***Mo***nna [***yo mo***telele]

CL1-man CL1-Dem CL1-Pref-tall

/man that is tall/

'A tall man'

The head noun is given consideration in the structure because it influences the morphological structure of the adjective as a whole. For example, both parts of the adjectival agreement (in bold italics) agree with the head noun and will therefore change every time a noun from a different class is being modified. For this reason only the basic adjectival stem is captured as equivalent of the English adjective. The following examples illustrate the point made:

***Mo**nna [**yo mo**telele]*

'A *tall* man'

***Mo**nna [**yo mo**šweu]*

'A *light-complexioned* man'

***Ba**nna [**ba ba**ntši]*

'*Many* men'

The adjectival stem *-telele* (tall/long), for example, can be used to qualify nouns from various classes, as illustrated below:

Class 1: ***Mo**nna [**yo mo**telele]*

'A *tall* man'

Class 3: ***Mo**hlare [**wo mo**telele]*

'A *tall* tree'

Class 5: ***Le**phodisa [**le le**telele]*

'A *tall* policeman'

Class 6: ***Ma**phodisa [**a ma**telele]*

'*Tall* policemen'

Class 7: ***Se**timela [**se se**telele]*

'A *long* train'

Class 9: *Kota [**ye** telele]*

'A *tall/long* pole'

For the reasons mentioned and illustrated above the Northern Sotho adjective stem *-botse* (beautiful/cute/precious/dinky/pretty) appears in African WordNet as illustrated in Figure 2 to Figure 4:

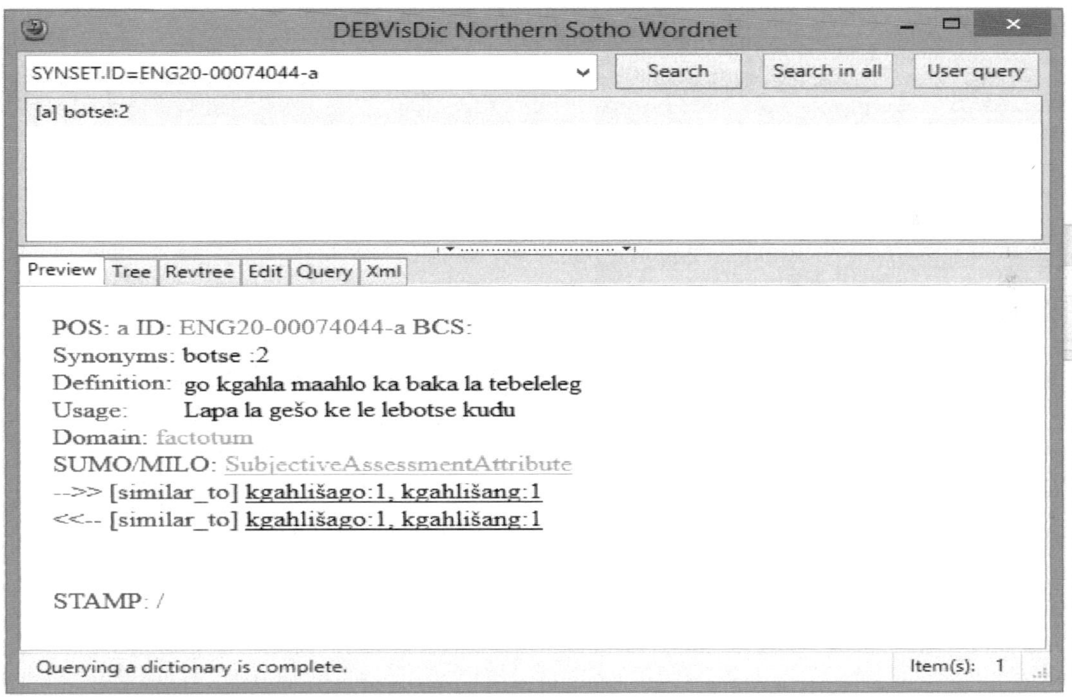


Figure 2: Adjective *beautiful:2*: aesthetically pleasing

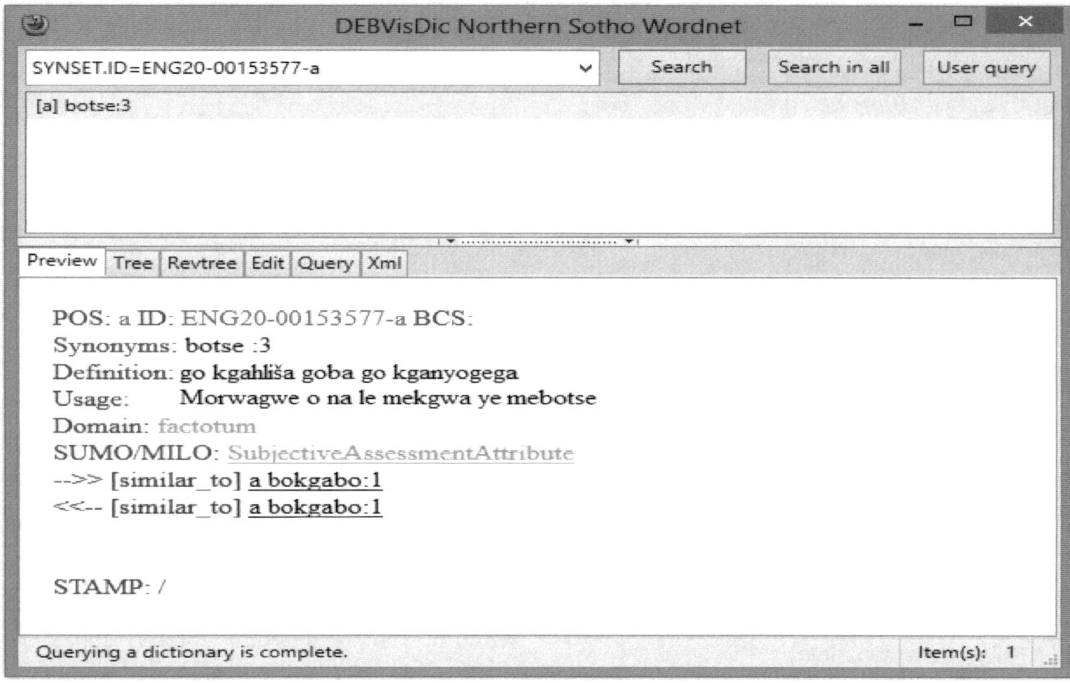


Figure 3: Adjective *cute:2,precious:3*: obviously contrived to charm

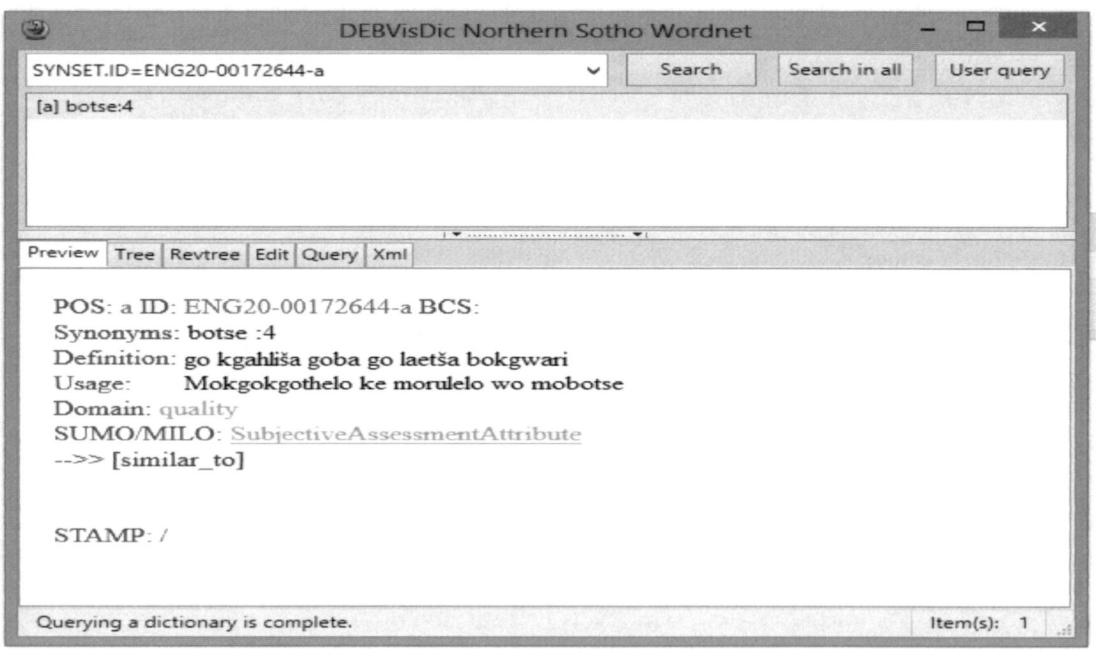


Figure 4: Adjective *dinky:2* (British informal) pretty and neat

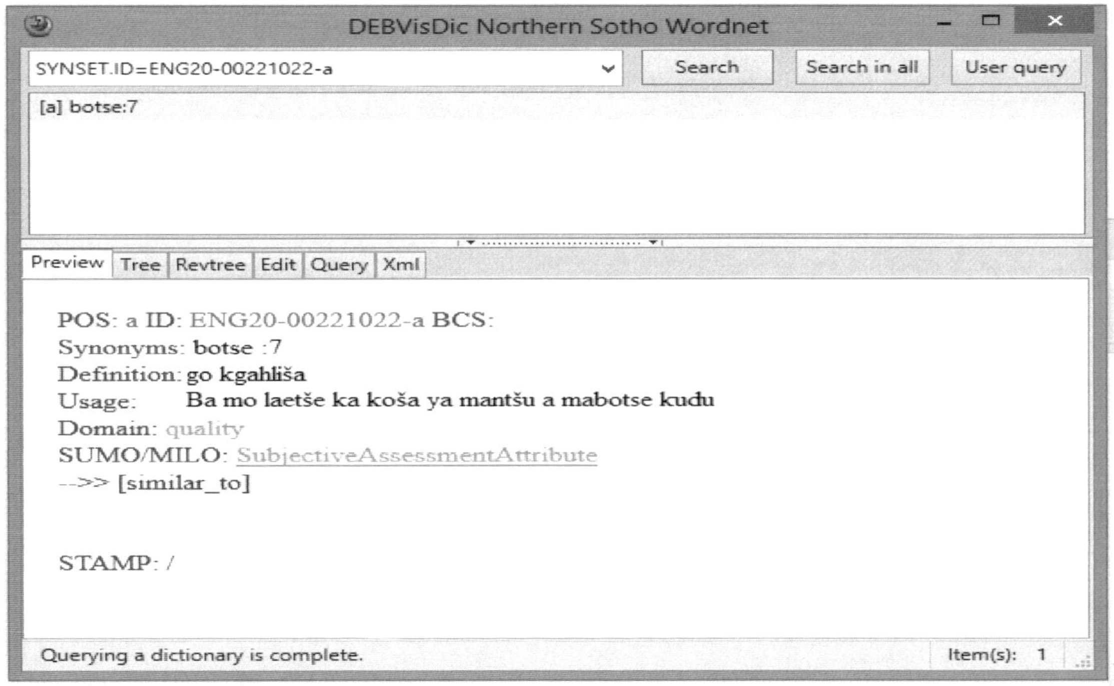


Figure 5: Adjective *pretty:1* pleasing by delicacy or grace; not imposing

Some English adjectives do not have adjective equivalents in Northern Sotho, but the senses are represented by different morphosyntactic categories.

## 3.2 Descriptive possessive/genitive

The genitive or possessive construction in general serves two semantic functions. It can be used for direct possession or ownership, and for describing the feature or quality of the noun (Poulos and Louwrens, 1994). It is the latter that is under discussion here. The descriptive possessive or genitive construction may serve as the cognitive-semantic equivalent of the English adjective. The general genitive/possessive structure is as follows:

| (Head noun) | Genitive | | |
|---|---|---|---|
| | genitive agreement | | Noun |
| | subject agreement | genitive **a** | |

Figure 6: The genitive/possessive construction

The following example of a possessive construction has a class 1 noun as head:

***Mo**nna* [***wa** senatla*]

CL1-man CL1-Dem CL7-strong individual

/man of strong individual/

'A strong man'

The first issue with the genitive is that the agreement comprises two components which behave differently. The subject agreement component is dependent on the head noun while genitive **a** is invariant. Secondly, the complement is a noun phrase, which is just another noun without the genitive agreement. To encode it unambiguously we need to include the invariant part of the genitive agreement with the complement, which is the descriptive part serving as equivalent to the English adjective. First, the invariant part of the genitive agreement is applicable to every head noun and, secondly, it makes the complement noun phrase duly interpreted as a descriptive. The first part of the genitive agreement will thus be unreliable as illustrated below (in italics):

Class 1: *Mo*nna [*w*a senatla]

'A strong man'

Class 5: *Le*ho [*l***a** go tia]

'A strong wooden spoon'

Class 9: Kala [*y***a** boleta]

'A soft branch'

Class 10: *Di*nku [*tš***a** bohlokwa]

'Important sheep'

The Northern Sotho descriptive possessive/ genitive as equivalent of the English adjective appears in African WordNet as follows:

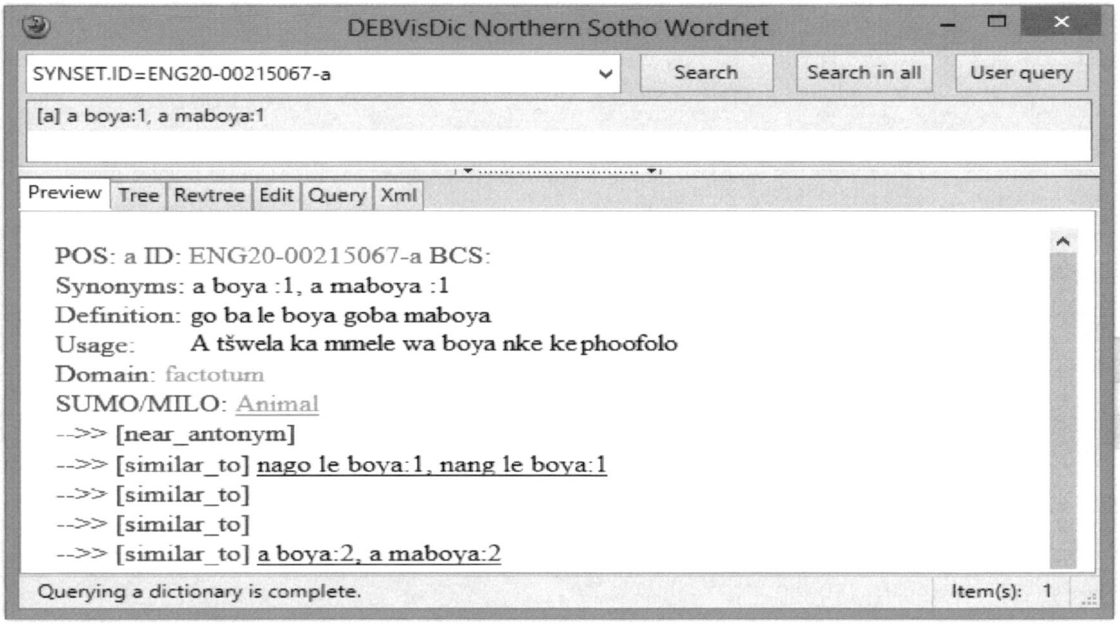


Figure 7: Adjective *hairy*:1 having or covered with hair

## 3.3 The relative

Traditional Northern Sotho grammars (and those of other Sotho languages) distinguish between the verbal and nominal relative (Poulos and Louwrens, 1994; Ziervogel, Lombard and Mokgokong, 1969). What is traditionally known as a nominal relative is called a 'new attributive adjective' by Creissels (2011) based on differentiation between word level and phrase level. The reason for this difference or overlap is that the Northern Sotho relative (both verbal and nominal) can also be a conceptual-semantic equivalent of the English adjective.

The verbal relative is further divided into the direct and indirect forms.

**Verbal relative**

A class 5 noun serves as head in the following examples:

Direct: ***Lephodisa*** [***le*** ***le*** *thuntšhago*]

CL5-policeman CL5-Dem CL5-SM shoot-SUFF-*go*

/Policeman that shoots/

Indirect: ***Lephodisa*** [***le*** *ba* ***le*** *thuntšhago*]

CL5-policeman CL5-Dem CL1-SM CL5-OC shoot-SUFF-*go*

/Policeman that they shoot/

'Policeman that is being shot'

For illustration we shall use only the direct relative clause, given that the same principles apply to the indirect relative. Figure 8 illustrates the structure of the direct verbal relative in Northern Sotho, as equivalent of the English adjective:

<table>
<tr><td rowspan="1">(Head noun)</td><td colspan="4">verbal relative</td></tr>
<tr><td></td><td colspan="2">Relative agreement</td><td>Verb stem</td><td>Suffix *go/ng*</td></tr>
<tr><td></td><td>Dem</td><td>subject agreement</td><td></td><td></td></tr>
</table>

Figure 8: The structure of the direct relative

Both parts of the relative agreement, namely the demonstrative (Dem) and the subject agreement depend on the head noun. Northern Sotho has two variant suffixes for the verbal relative, namely *-go* and *-ng*. The affixes *-go* and *-ng* on the verb stem indicate that its function is not to be a verb, but to qualify the noun. Both suffixes are equally recognised in Northern Sotho. Exclusion of variant parts of the verbal relative is not problematic because they are written disjunctively from the stem. Therefore only the verb stem, with the attached suffix, is recorded.

The Northern Sotho verbal relative as equivalent of the English adjective appears in African WordNet as follows:

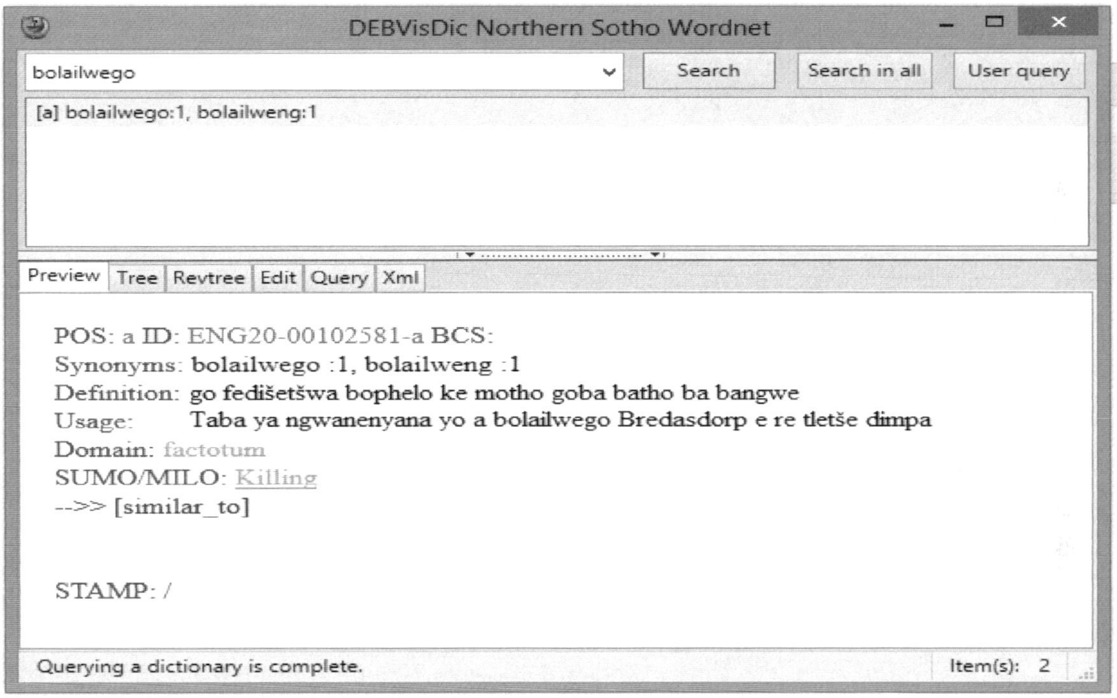


Figure 9: Adjective *murdered*:1 killed unlawfully

**Nominal relative**

The structure of the nominal relative is as follows:

<table>
<tr><td>(Head noun)</td><td colspan="2">Nominal relative</td></tr>
<tr><td></td><td>Nominal relative agreement (resembles Dem)</td><td>Noun</td></tr>
</table>

Figure 10: The structure of the nominal relative

A class 7 noun serves as head in the following example:

***Se**gotlane* [***se** bohlale*]

CL7-toddler CL7-Dem CL14-cleverness

/toddler that is clever/

'clever toddler'

Semantically the nominal relative can link to the noun through cross-POS relations (Marrafa and Mandes, 2006) – and similarly, the verbal relative to the verb.

## 4 Lexical semantic and morphosyntactic challenges to sort out along the way

Concepts such as worse (232954-a) and worst (2309979-a) are not easy to represent without including that which is 'worse or worst', or an adverb. Selection restrictions also have a bearing on this point as 'their meaning is determined … by the headnoun that they modify' (Fellbaum, 1998).

Other strategies used in the language to extend or refine a qualifying concept include the diminutive affix and reduplication. For example, yo motelele***nyana***/yo motelele***tšana*** (diminutive) and yo motelele*telele* (reduplication), which normally serve for gradability of various adjectival concepts as is the case with English degrees of comparison. While it is generally not necessary to include degrees of comparison in the database, some English concepts are perceived as being at various points on a continuum, where reduplication and adverbs are employed to differentiate them from others. Other challenges attending these forms include the frequent case that the diminutive involves phonological processes; whereas in reduplication there is no limit to the number of times the adjectival stem can be repeated, and for reduplication involving monosyllabic stems the adjectival prefix has to interfere repeatedly, for example:

Adjectival stem *-so* (black; dark):

***bo**rokgo* ***bjo*** ***bo**so* (A pair of black trousers): *borokgo bjo* ***boso**bo**so**bo**so*** (for intensity)

## 5 Concluding remarks

The lack of one-to-one correspondence between the adjective in English and in Northern Sotho results in the English adjective equivalent being represented by various morphosyntactic categories in Northern Sotho. Given their structural differences, these Northern Sotho equivalents require distinctive consideration in representing them in a manner that will be consistent with the language system. The proposal is that while it is understandable that only stems be considered, invariant parts that are separate from the stem but that will help to disambiguate it be retained (for example, ***a*** in the descriptive possessive construction). The suffix ***go*** or ***ng*** of the verbal relative also marks it as different from the verb. The challenge with the representation in African WordNet is that while they are all meaning equivalents of the same English word category, they straddle a number of morphosyntactic categories in Northern Sotho, which nevertheless share a semantic function.

While the nominal relative base is a noun, it selects nouns from classes 11 and 14 and is unlikely to be problematic. The enumerative has been left out of the discussion because their occurrence is not as wide as that of the categories discussed.

## References


Denis Creissels. 2011. The 'new adjectives' of Tswana. Paper presented at the WC2010 conference, Rome, 24-26 March 2010, revised April 2011. Viewed from http://reissels-new_adjectives.pdf

Christiane Fellbaum.1998. A semantic network of English: the mother of all wordnets. In Piek Vossen (ed.) *EuroWordNet:A Multilingual Databse with Lexical Semantic Networks*. Kluwer Academic Publishers, Dordrecht, pages 137-148.

Palmira Marrafa and Sara Mendes. 2006. Modeling adjectives in computational relational lexica. *Proceedings of the COLING/ALC Main Conference* Poster Session, Sydney, July 2006, pages 555-562.

Katherine J. Miller. 1998. Modifiers in WordNet. In Christiane Fellbaum (ed.) *WordNet: an electronic lexical database,* The MIT Press, Cambridge, MA, pages 47-68.

Ivonne Peters and Wim Peters. 2000. The Treatment of Adjectives in SIMPLE: Theoretical Observations, *Proceedings of LREC 2000.*

George Poulos and Louis J. Louwrens. 1994. *A linguistic analysis of Northern Sotho.* Via Afrika, Pretoria.

Dirk Ziervogel, Daniel P. Lombard and Pothinus C. Mokgokong. 1969. *A Handbook of the Northern Sotho Language*, Van Schaik, Pretoria.

# First steps towards a Predicate Matrix

**Maddalen López de Lacalle**
IXA group, UPV/EHU
Donostia, Spain
maddalen.lopezdelacalle@ehu.es

**Egoitz Laparra**
IXA group, UPV/EHU
Donostia, Spain
egoitz.laparra@ehu.es

**German Rigau**
IXA group, UPV/EHU
Donostia, Spain
german.rigau@ehu.es

## Abstract

This paper presents the first steps towards building the Predicate Matrix, a new lexical resource resulting from the integration of multiple sources of predicate information including FrameNet (Baker et al., 1997), VerbNet (Kipper, 2005), PropBank (Palmer et al., 2005) and WordNet (Fellbaum, 1998). By using the Predicate Matrix, we expect to provide a more robust interoperable lexicon by discovering and solving inherent inconsistencies among the resources. Moreover, we plan to extend the coverage of current predicate resources (by including from WordNet morphologically related nominal and verbal concepts), to enrich WordNet with predicate information, and possibly to extend predicate information to languages other than English (by exploiting the local wordnets aligned to the English WordNet).

## 1 Introduction

Predicate models such as FrameNet (Baker et al., 1997), VerbNet (Kipper, 2005) or PropBank (Palmer et al., 2005) are core resources in most advanced NLP tasks, such as Question Answering, Textual Entailment or Information Extraction. Most of the systems with Natural Language Understanding capabilities require a large and precise amount of semantic knowledge at the predicate-argument level. This type of knowledge allows to identify the underlying typical participants of a particular event independently of its realization in the text. Thus, using these models, different linguistic phenomena expressing the same event, such as active/passive transformations, verb alternations, nominalizations, implicit realizations can be harmonized into a common semantic representation. In fact, lately, several systems have been developed for shallow semantic parsing an explicit and implicit semantic role labeling using these resources (Erk and Pado, 2004), (Shi and Mihalcea, 2005), (Giuglea and Moschitti, 2006), (Laparra and Rigau, 2013).

However, building large and rich enough predicate models for broad–coverage semantic processing takes a great deal of expensive manual effort involving large research groups during long periods of development. In fact, the coverage of currently available predicate-argument resources is still far from complete. For example, (Burchardt et al., 2005) or (Shen and Lapata, 2007) indicate the limited coverage of FrameNet as one of the main problems of this resource. In fact, FrameNet1.5 covers around 10,000 lexical-units while for instance, WordNet3.0 contains more than 150,000 words. Furthermore, the same effort should be invested for each different language (Subirats and Petruck, 2003). Moreover, most previous research efforts on the integration of resources targeted at knowledge about nouns and named entities rather than predicate knowledge. Well known examples are YAGO (Suchanek et al., 2007), Freebase (Bollacker et al., 2008), DBPedia (Bizer et al., 2009), BabelNet (Navigli and Ponzetto, 2010) or UBY (Gurevych et al., 2012).

Following the line of previous works (Shi and Mihalcea, 2005), (Burchardt et al., 2005), (Johansson and Nugues, 2007), (Pennacchiotti et al., 2008), (Cao et al., 2008), (Tonelli and Pianta, 2009), (Laparra et al., 2010), we will also focus on the integration of predicate information. We start from the basis of SemLink (Palmer, 2009). SemLink aimed to connect together different predicate resources such as FrameNet (Baker et al., 1997), VerbNet (Kipper, 2005), PropBank (Palmer et al., 2005) and WordNet (Fellbaum, 1998). However, its coverage is still far from complete.

The Predicate Matrix, the resource resulting from the work presented in this paper, will allow to extend the coverage of current predicate resources (by including from WordNet closely related nominal and verbal concepts), to discover inherent inconsistencies among the resources, to enrich WordNet with predicate information, and possibly to extend predicate information to languages other than English (by exploiting the local wordnets aligned to the English WordNet). Moreover, the Predicate Matrix uses WordNet as a central resource. In that way, each row (or line) in the matrix presents partial predicate information related to a particular WordNet word sense.

First, as SemLink takes VerbNet as the central resource, we present a complete study of the coverage of the mappings between each resource included in SemLink to VerbNet. We describe the coverage and gaps of these mappings with respect to the lexical entries and the role structures of each resource. Second, we exploit WordNet to propose straightforward methods to discover incosistencies among the resources as well as to extend their coverage towards a more complete and robust predicate lexicon.

## 2 Sources of Predicate information

As a starting point for building the Predicate Matrix, we consider the sources of predicate knowledge connected to SemLink.

**SemLink**[1] (Palmer, 2009) is a project whose aim is to link together different predicate resources establishing a set of mappings. These mappings make it possible to combine the different information provided by the different lexical resources for tasks such as inferencing, consistency checking, interoperable semantic role labelling, etc. Currently, SemLink provides partial mappings to VerbNet (Kipper, 2005), PropBank (Palmer et al., 2005), FrameNet (Baker et al., 1997) and WordNet (Fellbaum, 1998).

**FrameNet** [2] (Baker et al., 1997) is a very rich semantic resource that contains descriptions and corpus annotations of English words following the paradigm of Frame Semantics (Fillmore, 1976). In frame semantics, a Frame corresponds to a scenario that involves the interaction of a set of typical participants, playing a particular role in the scenario. FrameNet groups words or lexical-units (LUs hereinafter) into coherent semantic classes or frames, and each frame is further characterized by a list of participants or frame-elements (FEs hereinafter). Different senses for a word are represented in FrameNet by assigning different frames.

**PropBank** [3] (Palmer et al., 2005) aims to provide a wide corpus annotated with information about semantic propositions, including relations between the predicates and their arguments. PropBank also contains a description of the frame structures, called framesets, of each sense of every verb that belong to its lexicon. Unlike other similar resources, as FrameNet, PropBank defines the arguments, or roles, of each verb individually. In consecuence, it becomes a hard task obtaning a generalization of the frame structures over the verbs.

**VerbNet** [4] (Kipper, 2005) is a hierarchical domain-independent broad-coverage verb lexicon for English. VerbNet is organized into verb classes extending (Levin, 1993) classes through refinement and addition of subclasses to achieve syntactic and semantic coherence among members of a class. Each verb class in VerbNet is completely described by thematic-roles, selectional restrictions on the arguments, and frames consisting of a syntactic description and semantic predicates.

**WordNet** [5] (Fellbaum, 1998) is by far the most widely-used knowledge base. In fact, WordNet is being used world-wide for anchoring different types of semantic knowledge including wordnets for languages other than English (Gonzalez-Agirre et al., 2012a). It contains manually coded information about English nouns, verbs, adjectives and adverbs and is organized around the notion of a *synset*. A synset is a set of words with the same part-of-speech that can be interchanged in a certain context. For example, <*learn*, *study*, *read*, *take*> form a synset because they can be used to refer to the same concept. A synset is often further described by a gloss, in this case: *"be a student of a certain subject"* and by explicit semantic relations to other synsets. Each synset represents a concept that are related with an large number of semantic relations, including hypernymy/hyponymy, meronymy/holonymy, antonymy, entailment, etc.

Obviously, we can also exploit the existing SemLink mappings to aid semi-automatic or fully automatic extensions of the current mapping coverage, in order to increase the overall overlapping.

[1] `http://verbs.colorado.edu/semlink/`
[2] `http://framenet.icsi.berkeley.edu/`
[3] `http://verbs.colorado.edu/~mpalmer/projects/ace.html`
[4] `http://verbs.colorado.edu/~mpalmer/projects/verbnet.html`
[5] `http://wordnet.princeton.edu/`

## 3 SemLink coverage

As SemLink uses VerbNet as the central resource, we present a complete study of the coverage of the mappings between each resource included in SemLink to VerbNet.

### 3.1 WordNet and VerbNet aligment

Although VerbNet is one of largest verb lexicons available it does not reach the coverage of the verbal part of WordNet. While WordNet contains **25,047** different verb senses there are just **6,293** predicates in VerbNet classes. This means that the mapping between both resources is, obviously, incomplete. Specifically there are **18,559** senses of WordNet, corresponding to **9,995** different lemmas, that have not been assigned to any VerbNet predicate. Many of these cases appear because of the distinct granularities of both resources. In fact **6,120** WordNet senses (corresponding to **2,099** lemmas) that are not mapped to VerbNet belong to lemmas that have at least another WordNet sense properly mapped to VerbNet. For instance, Table 1 shows the mapping between the verb *drown* in WordNet and VerbNet. Note that only two of the five WordNet senses are assigned to VerbNet.

| WordNet | VerbNet | |
|---|---|---|
| sense | member | class |
| drown%2:30:00:: | drown | 40.7 |
| drown%2:31:00:: | drown<br>drown | 42.2<br>40.7 |
| drown%2:30:02:: | - | - |
| drown%2:35:00:: | - | - |
| drown%2:42:00:: | - | - |

Table 1: WordNet to VerbNet aligment for *drown*$_v$

The rest of missing senses correspond to those cases where the lemma does not exist in the VerbNet lexicon (**7,320** lemmas and **11,201** senses). For example the verb *abort* does not appear in VerbNet since its three WordNet senses are not part of SemLink. The remaining cases (**1,443** WordNet senses and **576** lemmas) correspond to lemmas that exist in both resources but there is no sense mapping between them. For instance, there is no mapping between the WordNet sense *harm%2:29:00::* and the VerbNet verb that belongs to the class 31-1.

Moreover, SemLink does not provide mappings to WordNet senses for **1,077** VerbNet predicates. **304** of these VerbNet predicates share the same lemma with some other VerbNet sense that is already mapped to a WordNet sense. This is the case of *reveal* as shown in Table 2.

| VerbNet | | WordNet |
|---|---|---|
| member | class | sense |
| reveal | 29.2 | reveal%2:32:00 |
| reveal | 37.7 | reveal%2:32:00 |
| reveal | 37.10 | reveal%2:32:00 |
| reveal | 48.1.2 | - |
| reveal | 78 | - |

Table 2: VerbNet to WordNet aligment for *reveal*$_v$

From the rest of missing members, **574** correspond to those cases the lemma of the predicate also exists in WordNet (like the example of *harm* explained previously). Finally, there are only **199** verb senses in VerbNet whose lemmas do not exist in WordNet. For example: *africanize*$_v$, *backfill*$_v$ or *carbonify*$_v$.

### 3.2 PropBank and VerbNet aligment

The mapping between PropBank and VerbNet introduces additional complexity to the comparison of both resources. In this case, aligning the lexicon means that the arguments of the PropBank predicates must be aligned to the VerbNet thematic-roles.

First, regarding the lexicon mapping, once again, the differences in the coverages of the resources impede to obtain a complete alignment. From the **6,181** different PropBank predicates (comprising **4,552** lemmas), just **3,558** have their corresponding VerbNet predicate in SemLink. That is, **2,623** PropBank predicates have no correspondances to VerbNet. However, all the lemmas of PropBank are contained within the VerbNet lexicon. This means that for each one of the **2,623** missing predicates from PropBank there exists at least another predicate with the same lemma that is mapped to VerbNet. That is the case of the PropBank predicate *abandon.02*, shown in Table 3.

| PropBank | VerbNet | |
|---|---|---|
| predicate | member | class |
| accept.01 | accept<br>accept<br>accept | 13.5.2<br>29.2-1-1<br>77 |
| abandon.01 | abandon | 51.2 |
| abandon.02 | - | - |

Table 3: PropBank to VerbNet aligments for *accept*$_v$ and *abandon*$_v$

On the other hand, we found that the number of VerbNet predicates that are not aligned to PropBank is smaller than the number of PropBank predicates not aligned to VerbNet. That is, up to **4,736** of the **6,293** VerbNet predicates are aligned to PropBank while only **1,557** VerbNet predicates are not aligned to PropBank. Moreover, **298** of these VerbNet predicates do not exist in the PropBank lexicon, for instance $arrogate_v$, $deconstruct_v$, $mewl_v$ or $sprint_v$. Finally, there are **312** VerbNet predicates whose lemmas (**265** in total) are actually part of the PropBank lexicon but there is no aligment for them. For example, the predicate $offload_v$ of the VerbNet class *wipe_manner-10.4.1* is not connected to the PropBank predicate *offload.01*. Table 4 shows some aligments from VerbNet to PropBank.

| VerbNet | | PropBank |
|---|---|---|
| member | class | predicate |
| laugh | 40.2 | laugh.01 |
| flow | 47.2 | flow.01 |
| flow | 48.1.1 | - |

Table 4: VerbNet to PropBank aligments for $laugh_v$ and $flow_v$

Regarding the PropBank arguments and the VerbNet thematic-roles, **7,915** out of **15,871** arguments from PropBank[6] are mapped to a thematic-role from VerbNet[7]. That is, around a half of the total PropBank arguments, leaving out the remaining **7,956** arguments. From the opposite point of view, **9,682** out of **17,382** thematic-roles from VerbNet are included in the SemLink mapping. This means that **7,700** thematic-roles are not aligned to any PropBank argument. Table 5 contains some examples of existing and also missing mappings between PropBank arguments and VerbNet thematic-roles.

### 3.3 FrameNet and VerbNet aligment

The alingment between FrameNet and VerbNet proves to be very incomplete. For example, only **1,730** lexical-units from FrameNet[8] are aligned to, at least, one VerbNet predicate[9]. This number represents only 16% out of the total **10,195** lexical-units of FrameNet. Table 6 presents some aligments between VerbNet predicates and FrameNet lexical-units.

[6]Arguments of particular PropBank predicates. For instance, Arg0 of *paint.01*.

[7]Thematic-roles of particular VerbNet predicates. For instance, Agent of $paint_v$.

[8]Lexical-units of particular FrameNet frames. For instance, $sell_v$ from the frame *Commerce_sell*.

[9]Predicate of a particular VerbNet class. For instance, $sell_v$ from 13.1-1 VerbNet class.

| VerbNet | | PropBank | |
|---|---|---|---|
| predicate | them-role | predicate | argument |
| paint 9.9 | Agent | paint.01 | A0 |
| paint 9.9 | Destination | paint.01 | A1 |
| paint 9.9 | Theme | paint.01 | A2 |
| plant 9.7 | Agent | - | - |
| plant 9.7 | Destination | - | - |
| plant 9.7 | Theme | - | - |
| abandon 51.2 | Theme | abandon.01 | A0 |
| - | - | abandon.01 | A1 |
| - | - | abandon.01 | A2 |

Table 5: Some aligments between VerbNet thematic-roles and PropBank arguments

| VerbNet | | FrameNet | |
|---|---|---|---|
| class | member | frame | lexical-unit |
| 13.1-1 | sell | Commerce_sell | sell.v |
| 13.5.1 | buy | Commerce_buy | buy.v |
| 53.1-1 | delay | Hindering | delay.v |
| 53.1-1 | delay | Change_event_time | - |
| 13.5.3 | employ | Employing | - |
| 105 | employ | Using | - |

Table 6: Some aligments between VerbNet predicates and FrameNet lexical-units (LUs)

SemLink also includes the alignment between the roles of both resources. However, unlike PropBank the roles of FrameNet, that are called frame-elements, are defined at frame-level and not at predicate level. Therefore, the mapping of the VerbNet thematic-roles and the frame-elements of FrameNet is defined between VerbNet classes and FrameNet frames. Table 7 presents an example of the aligment of some roles from both resources for the VerbNet class 54.1. A VerbNet predicate member of this class has been aligned to the WordNet sense *total%2:42:00*.

| VerbNet | | FrameNet | |
|---|---|---|---|
| class | thematic-role | frame | frame-element |
| 54.1 | Agent | Adding_up | Cognizer |
| 54.1 | Theme | Adding_up | Numbers |
| 54.1 | Value | Adding_up | Result |

Table 7: Some aligments between VerbNet thematic-roles and FrameNet frame-elements (FEs)

Once again, the mapping between VerbNet and FrameNet presents significant gaps and miss-matches. For instance, just **825** of the **7,124** frame-elements of FrameNet[10] are linked to a VerbNet thematic-role. That is, **88%** of the frame-elements from FrameNet are not aligned to any VerbNet thematic-role. Moreover, only **262** frames out of **795** have at least one frame-element aligned to a VerbNet thematic-role. That is, just a few frames are used in the mapping. However, it also seems that, at a class level, most of the VerbNet thematic-roles appear to be aligned to at least one frame-element. VerbNet covers **787** different thematic-roles[11]. From these, **541** appear to be aligned to a FrameNet frame-element. In other words, it seems that just **246** thematic-roles are missing from the mapping provided by SemLink. Table 8 presents some class level aligments between VerbNet thematic-roles and FrameNet frame-elements (FEs).

| VerbNet | | FrameNet | |
|---|---|---|---|
| class | thematic-role | frame | frame-element |
| 10.10 | Agent | - | - |
| 10.10 | Attribute | - | - |
| 10.10 | Source | - | - |
| 10.10 | Theme | - | - |
| 48.3 | Theme | Catastrophe | Undesirable_Event |
| 48.3 | Location | Catastrophe | Place |
| 48.3 | Location | Catastrophe | Time |
| - | - | Catastrophe | Cause |
| - | - | Catastrophe | Circumstances |
| - | - | Catastrophe | Degree |
| - | - | Catastrophe | Manner |
| - | - | Catastrophe | Undergoer |
| - | - | Addiction | Addict |
| - | - | Addiction | Addictant |
| - | - | Addiction | Compeller |
| - | - | Addiction | Degree |
| - | - | Addiction | State |

Table 8: Some aligments between VerbNet thematic-roles and FrameNet frame-elements (FEs)

## 4 Using WordNet to cross-check predicate information

In this section, as a proof-of-concept, we will show a simple way to exploit WordNet for validating the predicate information appearing in SemLink. We apply a very simple method to check the consistency of VerbNet. Consider the following WordNet synset<*understand, read, interpret, translate*> with the gloss *"make sense of a language"* and the example sentences *"She understands French; Can you read Greek?"*. As synonyms, these verbs denote the same concept and are interchangeable in many contexts. However, in SemLink *read%2:31:04* appears aligned with the VerbNet class learn-14-1[12] while one of its synonyms *understand%2:31:03* appears aligned to the VerbNet class comprehend-87.2[13]. Moreover, the thematic-roles of both classes are different. Learn-14-1 has the following thematic-roles Agent (with semantic type [+animate]), Topic and Source while comprehend-87.2 has Experiencer (with semantic type [+animate or +organization]), Attribute and Stimulus. Are both sets of thematic-roles compatible? Complementary? Is one of them incorrect? Should we joint them? Maybe is the aligment incorrect? Is perhaps the synset definition?

Following with this example, the VerbNet predicate $understand_v$ has no connection to FrameNet, but its VerbNet class comprehend-87.2-1 has some other verbal predicates aligned to FrameNet. For instance, $apprehend_v$, $comprehend_v$ and $grasp_v$ are linked to the Grasp[14] FrameNet frame. Among the lexical-units corresponding to the Grasp frame it appears also the verbal predicate $understand_v$. This means that possibly, this verbal predicate should also be aligned to the FrameNet frame Grasp. The core frame-elements (roles) of this frame are Cognizer (with semantic type Sentient), Faculty and Phenomenon. Is this set of roles compatible with the previous ones?

## 5 Using WordNet to extend SemLink

As we have seen in Section 3, the mapping between the different sources of predicate information is far from being complete. However, the existing aligments also offer a very interesting source of information to be systematically exploited. In fact, we are devising a number of simple automatic methods to extend SemLink by exploiting simple properties from WordNet. As a proof-of-concept, we present in this section two very simple approaches to extend the coverage of the mapping between VerbNet predicates and

[10]Frame-elements of a particular FrameNet frame. For instance, the frame-element Cognizer for the *Adding_up* frame

[11]Role of a particular VerbNet class. For instance, Agent of VerbNet class 10.10

[12]http://verbs.colorado.edu/verb-index/vn/learn-14.php#learn-14-1

[13]http://verbs.colorado.edu/verb-index/vn/comprehend-87.2.php#comprehend-87.2-1

[14]https://framenet2.icsi.berkeley.edu/fnReports/data/frame/Grasp.xml

WordNet senses. Moreover, we also plan to use additional semantic resources that use WordNet as a backbone. For instance, exploiting those knowledge resources integrated into the Multilingual Central Repository[15] (MCR) (Atserias et al., 2004; Gonzalez-Agirre et al., 2012a) to extend automatically the aligment of the different sources of predicate information (VerbNet, PropBank, FrameNet and WordNet). Following the line of previous works, in order to assign more WordNet verb senses to VerbNet predicates, we also plan to apply more sophisticated word-sense disambiguation algorithms to semantically coherent groups of predicates (Laparra et al., 2010).

### 5.1 VerbNet Monosemous predicates

Monosemous verbs from WordNet can be directly assigned to VerbNet predicates still without a WordNet aligment. This very simple strategy solves **240** aligments. In this way, VerbNet predicates such as *divulge*$_v$, *exhume*$_v$, *mutate*$_v$ or *upload*$_v$ obtain a corresponding WordNet word sense[16]. Remember that only **576** lemmas from VerbNet were not aligned to WordNet.

### 5.2 WordNet synonyms

A very straightforward method to extend the mapping between WordNet and VerbNet consists on including synonyms of already aligned WordNet senses as new members of the corresponding VerbNet class. Obviously, this method expects that WordNet synomyms share the same predicate information. For instance, the predicate *desert*$_v$ member of the VerbNet class leave-51.2-1 appears to be assigned to desert%2:31:00 WordNet verbal sense. In WordNet, this word sense also has three synonyms, *abandon*$_v$, *forsake*$_v$ and *desolate*$_v$. Obviously, these three verbal senses can also be assigned to the same VerbNet class. This simple approach can create up to **5,075** new members of VerbNet classes (corresponding to **4,616** different WordNet word senses). For instance, Table 9 presents two productive examples. Moreover, applying this method **103** VerbNet predicates without mapping to WordNet in SemLink are aligned to a WordNet word sense.

[15] `http://adimen.si.ehu.es/MCR`

[16] Obviously, these aligments can be considered just as suggestions to be revised later on manually.

| VerbNet | WordNet | New |
|---|---|---|
| leave-51.2.1 | desert%2:31:00 | abandon%2:31:00:: <br> forsake%2:31:00:: <br> desolate%2:31:00:: |
| remove-10.1 | retract%2:32:00 | abjure%2:32:00:: <br> recant%2:32:00:: <br> forswear%2:32:00:: <br> resile%2:32:00:: |

Table 9: New WordNet senses aligned to VerbNet

## 6 A first version of the Predicate Matrix

We already produced a preliminary version of the Predicate Matrix[17]. The original SemLink in a Predicate Matrix form resulted in 36,174 rows (corresponding to 6,556 WordNet word senses). By applying the synonyms method described in the previous section the Predicate Matrix extended to 69,508 rows (10,984 WordNet word senses). Finally, by applying the monosemous method, the Predicate Matrix further extended to 70,391 rows (11,146 WordNet word senses).

Table 10 presents a full example of the information that is currently available in the Predicate Matrix including the new mappings obtained by the methods described in the previous section. Each row of this Table represents the mapping of a role over the different resources and includes all the aligned knowledge about its corresponding verb. The Table presents the cases obtained originally from SemLink, denoted as *SEMLINK*, and the cases inferred following the methods explained previously, identified as *SYNONYMS* or *MONOSEMIC* depending on the case. The Table also includes the following fields: the lemma and the class in VerbNet, the sense of the verb in WordNet, the thematic-role in VerbNet, the Frame of FrameNet, the corresponding lexical-entry and frame-element of FrameNet, the predicate in PropBank and its argument, the offset of the sense in WordNet and the knowledge associated with that sense in the MCR, such as the Adimen-SUMO (Álvez et al., 2012) and the new WordNet domain aligned to WordNet 3.0 (González-Agirre et al., 2012b) features as well as the Base Level Concept (Izquierdo et al., 2007) of the sense. Finaly, each line also includes the frequency and the number of relations of the WordNet word sense.

[17] `http://adimen.si.ehu.es/web/PredicateMatrix`

## 7 Conclusions and future work

We are now producing and studying initial versions of the Predicate Matrix by exploiting SemLink and applying very simple methods to extend and validate its content. By developping more advanced versions of the Predicate Matrix, we expect to provide a more robust and interoperable predicate lexicon. We plan to discover and solve inherent inconsistencies among the integrated resources. Moreover, we plan to extend the coverage of current predicate resources (by including from WordNet morphologically related nominal and verbal concepts, by exploiting also FrameNet information, etc.), to enrich WordNet with predicate information, and possibly to extend predicate information to languages other than English (by exploiting the local wordnets aligned to the English WordNet) and predicate information from other languages. For instance, the Ancora Spanish corpus and lexicon (Taulé et al., 2008).

## Acknowledgment

We are grateful to the anonymous reviewers for their insightful comments. This work has been partially funded by SKaTer (TIN2012-38584-C06-02), OpeNER (FP7-ICT-2011-SME-DCL-296451) and NewsReader (FP7-ICT-2011-8-316404), as well as the READERS project with the financial support of MINECO, ANR (convention ANR-12-CHRI-0004-03) and EPSRC (EP/K017845/1) in the framework of ERA-NET CHIST-ERA (UE FP7/2007-2013).

## References

Javier Álvez, Paqui Lucio, and German Rigau. 2012. Adimen-sumo: Reengineering an ontology for first-order reasoning. *International Journal on Semantic Web and Information Systems (IJSWIS)*, 8(4):80–116.

Jordi Atserias, Luís Villarejo, German Rigau, Eneko Agirre, John Carroll, Bernardo Magnini, and Piek Vossen. 2004. The meaning multilingual central repository. In *Proceedings of GWC*, Brno, Czech Republic.

Collin F. Baker, Charles J. Fillmore, and John B. Lowe. 1997. The berkeley framenet project. In *COLING/ACL'98*, Montreal, Canada.

Christian Bizer, Jens Lehmann, Georgi Kobilarov, Sören Auer, Christian Becker, Richard Cyganiak, and Sebastian Hellmann. 2009. Dbpedia-a crystallization point for the web of data. *Web Semantics: Science, Services and Agents on the World Wide Web*, 7(3):154–165.

Kurt Bollacker, Colin Evans, Praveen Paritosh, Tim Sturge, and Jamie Taylor. 2008. Freebase: a collaboratively created graph database for structuring human knowledge. In *Proceedings of the 2008 ACM SIGMOD international conference on Management of data*, pages 1247–1250. ACM.

Aljoscha Burchardt, Katrin Erk, and Anette Frank. 2005. A WordNet Detour to FrameNet. In *Proceedings of the GLDV 2005 GermaNet II Workshop*, pages 408–421, Bonn, Germany.

Diego De Cao, Danilo Croce, Marco Pennacchiotti, and Roberto Basili. 2008. Combining word sense and usage for modeling frame semantics. In *Proceedings of The Symposium on Semantics in Systems for Text Processing (STEP 2008)*, Venice, Italy.

Katrin Erk and Sebastian Pado. 2004. A powerful and versatile xml format for representing role-semantic annotation. In *Proceedings of LREC-2004*, Lisbon.

Christiane Fellbaum, editor. 1998. *WordNet. An Electronic Lexical Database*. The MIT Press.

Charles J. Fillmore. 1976. Frame semantics and the nature of language. In *Annals of the New York Academy of Sciences: Conference on the Origin and Development of Language and Speech*, volume 280, pages 20–32, New York.

Ana-Maria Giuglea and Alessandro Moschitti. 2006. Semantic role labeling via framenet, verbnet and propbank. In *Proceedings of COLING-ACL 2006*, pages 929–936, Morristown, NJ, USA. ACL.

Aitor Gonzalez-Agirre, Egoitz Laparra, and German Rigau. 2012a. Multilingual central repository version 3.0. In *LREC*, pages 2525–2529.

Aitor González-Agirre, German Rigau, and Mauro Castillo. 2012b. A graph-based method to improve wordnet domains. In *CICLING*, pages 17–28. Springer.

Iryna Gurevych, Judith Eckle-Kohler, Silvana Hartmann, Michael Matuschek, Christian M Meyer, and Christian Wirth. 2012. Uby: A large-scale unified lexical-semantic resource based on lmf. In *Proceedings of EACL*, pages 580–590.

Rubén Izquierdo, Armando Suárez, and German Rigau. 2007. Exploring the automatic selection of basic level concepts. In *Proceedings of RANLP*, volume 7. Citeseer.

Richard Johansson and Pierre Nugues. 2007. Using WordNet to extend FrameNet coverage. In *Proceedings of the Workshop on Building Frame-semantic Resources for Scandinavian and Baltic Languages, at NODALIDA*, Tartu, Estonia, May 24.

| VERSION | VN_LEMA | VN_CLASS | WN_SENSE | VN_THEMROLE | FN_FRAME | FN_LEXENT | FN_ROLE | PB_ROLESET | PB_ARG | MCR_iliOffset | MCR_SUMO | MCR_Domain | WN_BLC | WN_SENSEFREC | WN_SYNSET_REL_NUM |
|---|---|---|---|---|---|---|---|---|---|---|---|---|---|---|---|
| SEMLINK | stutter | 37.3 | stutter%2:32:00 | Agent | Communication_manner | 565 | Speaker | stutter.01 | 0 | ili-30-00981544-v | Communication | factotum | speak%2:32:00 | 2 | 006 |
| SEMLINK | stutter | 37.3 | stutter%2:32:00 | Recipient | Communication_manner | 565 | Addressee | stutter.01 | 2 | ili-30-00981544-v | Communication | factotum | speak%2:32:00 | 2 | 006 |
| SEMLINK | stutter | 37.3 | stutter%2:32:00 | Topic | Communication_manner | 565 | Message | stutter.01 | 1 | ili-30-00981544-v | Communication | factotum | speak%2:32:00 | 2 | 006 |
| SEMLINK | stutter | 37.3 | stutter%2:32:00 | Topic | Communication_manner | 565 | Topic | stutter.01 | 1 | ili-30-00981544-v | Communication | factotum | speak%2:32:00 | 2 | 006 |
| SEMLINK | stammer | 37.3 | stammer%2:32:00 | Agent | Communication_manner | 564 | Speaker | NULL | NULL | ili-30-00981544-v | Communication | factotum | speak%2:32:00 | 6 | 006 |
| SEMLINK | stammer | 37.3 | stammer%2:32:00 | Recipient | Communication_manner | 564 | Addressee | NULL | NULL | ili-30-00981544-v | Communication | factotum | speak%2:32:00 | 6 | 006 |
| SEMLINK | stammer | 37.3 | stammer%2:32:00 | Topic | Communication_manner | 564 | Message | NULL | NULL | ili-30-00981544-v | Communication | factotum | speak%2:32:00 | 6 | 006 |
| SEMLINK | stammer | 37.3 | stammer%2:32:00 | Topic | Communication_manner | 564 | Topic | NULL | NULL | ili-30-00981544-v | Communication | factotum | speak%2:32:00 | 6 | 006 |
| SYNONYMS | bumble | 37.3 | bumble%2:32:00 | Agent | Communication_manner | 565 | Speaker | stutter.01 | 0 | ili-30-00981544-v | Communication | factotum | speak%2:32:00 | 2 | 006 |
| SYNONYMS | bumble | 37.3 | bumble%2:32:00 | Recipient | Communication_manner | 565 | Addressee | stutter.01 | 2 | ili-30-00981544-v | Communication | factotum | speak%2:32:00 | 2 | 006 |
| SYNONYMS | bumble | 37.3 | bumble%2:32:00 | Topic | Communication_manner | 565 | Message | stutter.01 | 1 | ili-30-00981544-v | Communication | factotum | speak%2:32:00 | 2 | 006 |
| SYNONYMS | bumble | 37.3 | bumble%2:32:00 | Topic | Communication_manner | 565 | Topic | stutter.01 | 1 | ili-30-00981544-v | Communication | factotum | speak%2:32:00 | 2 | 006 |
| SYNONYMS | bumble | 37.3 | bumble%2:32:00 | Agent | Communication_manner | 564 | Speaker | NULL | NULL | ili-30-00981544-v | Communication | factotum | speak%2:32:00 | 6 | 006 |
| SYNONYMS | bumble | 37.3 | bumble%2:32:00 | Recipient | Communication_manner | 564 | Addressee | NULL | NULL | ili-30-00981544-v | Communication | factotum | speak%2:32:00 | 6 | 006 |
| SYNONYMS | bumble | 37.3 | bumble%2:32:00 | Topic | Communication_manner | 564 | Message | NULL | NULL | ili-30-00981544-v | Communication | factotum | speak%2:32:00 | 6 | 006 |
| SYNONYMS | bumble | 37.3 | bumble%2:32:00 | Topic | Communication_manner | 564 | Topic | NULL | NULL | ili-30-00981544-v | Communication | factotum | speak%2:32:00 | 6 | 006 |
| SYNONYMS | falter | 37.3 | falter%2:32:00 | Agent | Communication_manner | 565 | Speaker | stutter.01 | 0 | ili-30-00981544-v | Communication | factotum | speak%2:32:00 | 2 | 006 |
| SYNONYMS | falter | 37.3 | falter%2:32:00 | Recipient | Communication_manner | 565 | Addressee | stutter.01 | 2 | ili-30-00981544-v | Communication | factotum | speak%2:32:00 | 2 | 006 |
| SYNONYMS | falter | 37.3 | falter%2:32:00 | Topic | Communication_manner | 565 | Message | stutter.01 | 1 | ili-30-00981544-v | Communication | factotum | speak%2:32:00 | 2 | 006 |
| SYNONYMS | falter | 37.3 | falter%2:32:00 | Topic | Communication_manner | 565 | Topic | stutter.01 | 1 | ili-30-00981544-v | Communication | factotum | speak%2:32:00 | 2 | 006 |
| SYNONYMS | falter | 37.3 | falter%2:32:00 | Agent | Communication_manner | 564 | Speaker | NULL | NULL | ili-30-00981544-v | Communication | factotum | speak%2:32:00 | 6 | 006 |
| SYNONYMS | falter | 37.3 | falter%2:32:00 | Recipient | Communication_manner | 564 | Addressee | NULL | NULL | ili-30-00981544-v | Communication | factotum | speak%2:32:00 | 6 | 006 |
| SYNONYMS | falter | 37.3 | falter%2:32:00 | Topic | Communication_manner | 564 | Message | NULL | NULL | ili-30-00981544-v | Communication | factotum | speak%2:32:00 | 6 | 006 |
| SYNONYMS | falter | 37.3 | falter%2:32:00 | Topic | Communication_manner | 564 | Topic | NULL | NULL | ili-30-00981544-v | Communication | factotum | speak%2:32:00 | 6 | 006 |
| SEMLINK | squeak | 37.3 | squeak%2:39:00 | Agent | Communication_noise | 612 | Speaker | squeak.01 | 0 | ili-30-02171664-v | SoundAttribute | factotum | sound%2:39:00 | 3 | 007 |
| SEMLINK | squeak | 37.3 | squeak%2:39:00 | Recipient | Communication_noise | 612 | Addressee | squeak.01 | NULL | ili-30-02171664-v | SoundAttribute | factotum | sound%2:39:00 | 3 | 007 |
| SEMLINK | squeak | 37.3 | squeak%2:39:00 | Topic | Communication_noise | 612 | Message | squeak.01 | 1 | ili-30-02171664-v | SoundAttribute | factotum | sound%2:39:00 | 3 | 007 |
| SEMLINK | squeak | 37.3 | squeak%2:39:00 | Topic | Communication_noise | 612 | Topic | squeak.01 | 1 | ili-30-02171664-v | SoundAttribute | factotum | sound%2:39:00 | 3 | 007 |
| SEMLINK | screech | 37.3 | screech%2:39:00 | Agent | Communication_noise | 604 | Speaker | screech.03 | 0 | ili-30-02171664-v | SoundAttribute | factotum | sound%2:39:00 | 5 | 007 |
| SEMLINK | screech | 37.3 | screech%2:39:00 | Recipient | Communication_noise | 604 | Addressee | screech.03 | 2 | ili-30-02171664-v | SoundAttribute | factotum | sound%2:39:00 | 5 | 007 |
| SEMLINK | screech | 37.3 | screech%2:39:00 | Topic | Communication_noise | 604 | Message | screech.03 | 1 | ili-30-02171664-v | SoundAttribute | factotum | sound%2:39:00 | 5 | 007 |
| SEMLINK | screech | 37.3 | screech%2:39:00 | Topic | Communication_noise | 604 | Topic | screech.03 | 1 | ili-30-02171664-v | SoundAttribute | factotum | sound%2:39:00 | 5 | 007 |
| SYNONYMS | screak | 37.3 | screak%2:39:00 | Agent | Communication_noise | 612 | Speaker | squeak.01 | 0 | ili-30-02171664-v | SoundAttribute | factotum | sound%2:39:00 | 3 | 007 |
| SYNONYMS | screak | 37.3 | screak%2:39:00 | Recipient | Communication_noise | 612 | Addressee | squeak.01 | NULL | ili-30-02171664-v | SoundAttribute | factotum | sound%2:39:00 | 3 | 007 |
| SYNONYMS | screak | 37.3 | screak%2:39:00 | Topic | Communication_noise | 612 | Message | squeak.01 | 1 | ili-30-02171664-v | SoundAttribute | factotum | sound%2:39:00 | 3 | 007 |
| SYNONYMS | screak | 37.3 | screak%2:39:00 | Topic | Communication_noise | 612 | Topic | squeak.01 | 1 | ili-30-02171664-v | SoundAttribute | factotum | sound%2:39:00 | 3 | 007 |
| SYNONYMS | screak | 37.3 | screak%2:39:00 | Recipient | Communication_noise | 604 | Addressee | screech.03 | 2 | ili-30-02171664-v | SoundAttribute | factotum | sound%2:39:00 | 5 | 007 |
| SYNONYMS | screak | 37.3 | screak%2:39:00 | Topic | Communication_noise | 604 | Message | screech.03 | 1 | ili-30-02171664-v | SoundAttribute | factotum | sound%2:39:00 | 5 | 007 |
| SYNONYMS | screak | 37.3 | screak%2:39:00 | Topic | Communication_noise | 604 | Topic | screech.03 | 1 | ili-30-02171664-v | SoundAttribute | factotum | sound%2:39:00 | 5 | 007 |
| SYNONYMS | screak | 37.3 | screak%2:39:00 | Agent | Communication_noise | 604 | Speaker | screech.03 | 0 | ili-30-02171664-v | SoundAttribute | factotum | sound%2:39:00 | 5 | 007 |
| SYNONYMS | whine | 37.3 | whine%2:39:00 | Agent | Communication_noise | 612 | Speaker | squeak.01 | 0 | ili-30-02171664-v | SoundAttribute | factotum | sound%2:39:00 | 3 | 007 |
| SYNONYMS | whine | 37.3 | whine%2:39:00 | Recipient | Communication_noise | 612 | Addressee | squeak.01 | NULL | ili-30-02171664-v | SoundAttribute | factotum | sound%2:39:00 | 3 | 007 |
| SYNONYMS | whine | 37.3 | whine%2:39:00 | Topic | Communication_noise | 612 | Message | squeak.01 | 1 | ili-30-02171664-v | SoundAttribute | factotum | sound%2:39:00 | 3 | 007 |
| SYNONYMS | whine | 37.3 | whine%2:39:00 | Topic | Communication_noise | 612 | Topic | squeak.01 | 1 | ili-30-02171664-v | SoundAttribute | factotum | sound%2:39:00 | 3 | 007 |
| SYNONYMS | whine | 37.3 | whine%2:39:00 | Agent | Communication_noise | 604 | Speaker | screech.03 | 0 | ili-30-02171664-v | SoundAttribute | factotum | sound%2:39:00 | 5 | 007 |
| SYNONYMS | whine | 37.3 | whine%2:39:00 | Recipient | Communication_noise | 604 | Addressee | screech.03 | 2 | ili-30-02171664-v | SoundAttribute | factotum | sound%2:39:00 | 5 | 007 |
| SYNONYMS | whine | 37.3 | whine%2:39:00 | Topic | Communication_noise | 604 | Message | screech.03 | 1 | ili-30-02171664-v | SoundAttribute | factotum | sound%2:39:00 | 5 | 007 |
| SYNONYMS | whine | 37.3 | whine%2:39:00 | Topic | Communication_noise | 604 | Topic | screech.03 | 1 | ili-30-02171664-v | SoundAttribute | factotum | sound%2:39:00 | 5 | 007 |
| MONOSEMIC | natter | 37.3 | natter%2:32:00 | Agent | Communication_manner | 547 | Speaker | chatter.01 | 0 | ili-30-01038666-v | Communication | factotum | communicate%2:32:00 | 1 | 011 |
| MONOSEMIC | natter | 37.3 | natter%2:32:00 | Topic | Communication_manner | 547 | Message | chatter.01 | 1 | ili-30-01038666-v | Communication | factotum | communicate%2:32:00 | 1 | 011 |
| MONOSEMIC | natter | 37.3 | natter%2:32:00 | Topic | Communication_manner | 547 | Topic | chatter.01 | 1 | ili-30-01038666-v | Communication | factotum | communicate%2:32:00 | 1 | 011 |
| MONOSEMIC | natter | 37.3 | natter%2:32:00 | Recipient | Communication_manner | 547 | Addressee | chatter.01 | NULL | ili-30-01038666-v | Communication | factotum | communicate%2:32:00 | 1 | 011 |
| MONOSEMIC | prattle | 37.3 | prattle%2:32:00 | Agent | Communication_manner | 547 | Speaker | chatter.01 | 0 | ili-30-01036804-v | Communication | factotum | speak%2:32:00 | 1 | 015 |
| MONOSEMIC | prattle | 37.3 | prattle%2:32:00 | Topic | Communication_manner | 547 | Message | chatter.01 | 1 | ili-30-01036804-v | Communication | factotum | speak%2:32:00 | 1 | 015 |
| MONOSEMIC | prattle | 37.3 | prattle%2:32:00 | Topic | Communication_manner | 547 | Topic | chatter.01 | 1 | ili-30-01036804-v | Communication | factotum | speak%2:32:00 | 1 | 015 |
| MONOSEMIC | prattle | 37.3 | prattle%2:32:00 | Recipient | Communication_manner | 547 | Addressee | chatter.01 | NULL | ili-30-01036804-v | Communication | factotum | speak%2:32:00 | 1 | 015 |
| MONOSEMIC | rant | 37.3 | rant%2:32:00 | Agent | Communication_manner | 551 | Speaker | jabber.01 | 0 | ili-30-01051956-v | Communication | factotum | speak%2:32:00 | 2 | 011 |
| MONOSEMIC | rant | 37.3 | rant%2:32:00 | Topic | Communication_manner | 551 | Message | jabber.01 | 1 | ili-30-01051956-v | Communication | factotum | speak%2:32:00 | 2 | 011 |
| MONOSEMIC | rant | 37.3 | rant%2:32:00 | Topic | Communication_manner | 551 | Topic | jabber.01 | 1 | ili-30-01051956-v | Communication | factotum | speak%2:32:00 | 2 | 011 |
| MONOSEMIC | rant | 37.3 | rant%2:32:00 | Recipient | Communication_manner | 551 | Addressee | jabber.01 | 2 | ili-30-01051956-v | Communication | factotum | speak%2:32:00 | 2 | 011 |

Table 10: Partial view of the current content of the Predicate Matrix

Karen Kipper. 2005. *VerbNet: A broad-coverage, comprehensive verb lexicon*. Ph.D. thesis, University of Pennsylvania.

Egoitz Laparra and German Rigau. 2013. Impar: A deterministic algorithm for implicit semantic role labelling. In *Proceedings of the 51st Annual Meeting of the Association for Computational Linguistics (ACL 2013)*, pages 33–41.

Egoitz Laparra, German Rigau, and Montse Cuadros. 2010. Exploring the integration of wordnet and framenet. In *Proceedings of the 5th Global WordNet Conference (GWC 2010), Mumbai, India*.

Beth Levin. 1993. *English verb classes and alternations: A preliminary investigation*, volume 348. University of Chicago press Chicago.

Roberto Navigli and Simone Paolo Ponzetto. 2010. Babelnet: Building a very large multilingual semantic network. In *Proceedings of the 48th annual meeting of ACL*, pages 216–225.

Martha Palmer, Daniel Gildea, and Paul Kingsbury. 2005. The proposition bank: An annotated corpus of semantic roles. *Computational Linguistics*, 31(1):71–106, March.

Martha Palmer. 2009. Semlink: Linking propbank, verbnet and framenet. In *Proceedings of the Generative Lexicon Conference*, pages 9–15.

Marco Pennacchiotti, Diego De Cao, Roberto Basili, Danilo Croce, and Michael Roth. 2008. Automatic induction of FrameNet lexical units. In *Proceedings of EMNLP*.

Dan Shen and Mirella Lapata. 2007. Using semantic roles to improve question answering. In *Proceedings of the Joint Conference on (EMNLP-CoNLL)*, pages 12–21.

Lei Shi and Rada Mihalcea. 2005. Putting pieces together: Combining framenet, verbnet and wordnet for robust semantic parsing. In *Proceedings of CICLing*, Mexico.

Carlos Subirats and Miriam R.L. Petruck. 2003. Surprise: Spanish framenet! In *Proceedings of the International Congress of Linguists*, Praga.

Fabian M. Suchanek, Gjergji Kasneci, and Gerhard Weikum. 2007. Yago: A Core of Semantic Knowledge. In *WWW conference*, New York, NY, USA. ACM Press.

Mariona Taulé, Maria Antònia Martí, and Marta Recasens. 2008. Ancora: Multilevel annotated corpora for catalan and spanish. In *LREC*.

Sara Tonelli and Emanuele Pianta. 2009. A novel approach to mapping framenet lexical units to wordnet synsets. In *Proceedings of IWCS-8*, Tilburg, The Netherlands.

# Reducing False Positives in the Construction of Adjective Scales

**Alice Zhang**
Princeton University
Princeton, New Jersey, USA.
alicez@princeton.edu

## Abstract

Many adjectives that appear to be synonyms of one another differ in their intensity. Distinguishing the nuances between adjective synonyms is vital to linguistic understanding of a language, but WordNet currently does not encode the relative intensities of adjective synonyms that lie on the scale. Sheinman & Tokunaga (2009) proposed a solution of constructing Adjective Scales by data mining a web corpus. However, this process suffers from some limitations, most notably that of False Positives, which inaccurately suggest that adjective **X** is more or less intense than **Y**.

This paper classifies the types of false positives that Sheinman's method generates, then proposes a method to diminish the quantity of these false positives using linguistic searches in WordNet.

## 1 Introduction

Adjectives are currently represented in WordNet in a dumbbell structure, such that antonymous adjective pairs like "wet-dry" and "early-late" are connected with a single antonym link. Each word of the antonym pair is represented as one of two centroids on the dumbbells, and each of their synonyms are spread out radially around the centroid. This representation is problematic because 1) it suggests that all adjectives within a synset are equally similar to the centroid and 2) because many similar adjectives are misclassified as members of the same clusters, indicating that they describe the same types of objects, when in reality they are very different.

In their paper *Large, huge or gigantic?: Identifying and encoding intensity relations in WordNet*, Sheinman et al. (2013) proposed a method to uncover the differing intensity relationships amongst a set of adjective synonyms by mining a web corpus. In particular, Sheinman noticed particular patterns that occurred naturally in English speech that already codified the intensity relationships between the adjectives that were used within the pattern. For example, one of these semantic patterns is "X **but not** Y," where **Y** is implied to be more intense than **X**, e.g. "good but not great" implies that "great" is more intense than its synonym "good" based merely on the pattern "**X** but not **Y**" In fact, these patterns occur in both directions, such that while some patterns imply that **X** is more intense than **Y**, while others imply that **X** is less intense than **Y**. By discovering pairs of adjectives that occurred in the natural patterns, Sheinman was able to construct scales of adjective synonyms, where each adjective was listed according to its relative intensity.

While Sheinman's method seems, in large part, successful in constructing adjective scales, it also suffers from limitations of false positives, which appear when certain adjective pairs show up in the linguistic patterns, but do not actually indicate that adjective **Y** is more or less intense than **X**. For instance, the natural phrase "good but not good enough" would seem to suggest that "good" is more intense than "good" based merely on the battern "**X** but not **Y**," even though this is not true. These false positives are significant: a simple Google News search of the phrase "hot but not" will return false positives for over half of the results. This paper classifies the different types of false positives that can be generated and proposes an algorithm that utilizes WordNet to be able to detect these false positives.

## 2 Type A False Positives

### 2.1 Classification

**Type A** false positives are phrases where adjective **Y** is classified as being more intense than adjective

| Intense Patterns |
| --- |
| (is / are) X but not Y |
| (is / are) very X Y |
| extremely X Y |
| not X (hardy / barely / let alone) Y |
| X (but / yet / though) never Y |
| X (but / yet / though) hardly Y |
| X (even / perhaps) Y |
| X (perhaps / and) even Y |
| X (almost / no / if not / sometimes) Y |
| **Mild Patterns** |
| if not X at least Y |
| but Y but X enough |
| not Y (just / merely / only) X |
| not Y not even X |
| not Y but still very X |
| though not Y (at least X) |
| Y (very / unbelievably) X |

**Table 1** Examples of the linguistic patterns that Sheinman et al. noticed in natural language. X and Y represent adjectives such that X is more intense than Y.

**X**, even though both **X** and **Y** fall on the same adjective scale, but **Y** is not more intense than **X**. In particular, Type A False Positives can be further classified into three particular types: repetitions, antonyms, and reversals.

**Repetitions** occur when both adjectives **X** and **Y** are the same word. For example, one naturally occurring English phrase that follows the "X **but not** Y" pattern that Sheinman noted is the phrase "It was good, but not good enough." Another example would be the phrase "It was good, but not as good as it could have been." In both instances, the two adjectives that are being compared cannot have one be more intense than the other because they are the same.

**Antonyms** occur when **X** and **Y** are direct antonyms of one another - both **X** and **Y** fall on the same scale, but they cannot be synonyms of one another because they lie on opposite ends of the same scale. For example, consider the following sentence: "He is not tall, but not short either." Sheinman's method would falsely classify "short" as a more intense synonym to the word "tall," which is a misclassification.

Finally, **reversals** occur where **X** and **Y** are real adjective synonyms of one another, but **X** is a more intense adjective than **Y**. For example, the sentences "This artifact is ancient, perhaps even old enough to have existed before dinosaurs," "The water was scorching, but not hot enough to kill the bacteria," and "President Taft was extremely obese, fat to the point of getting stuck in his own bathtub" are all instances that would seem, based on Sheinman's method, to suggest that **Y** is more intense than **X**, when in reality, **X** is more intense than **Y**.

### 2.2 Correcting Type A False Positives

To identify Type A false positives, one only needs an algorithm that can detect instances of repetitions, antonyms, and reversals.

Checking for repetitions is a trivial task: one simply needs to determine if **X** and **Y** are the same word.

To detect antonyms, one can take advantage of the pointers that are built into WordNet to check if any of the direct or indirect antonyms of **X** is equal to **Y**, or alternatively, that any of the direct or indirect antonyms of **Y** is equal to **X**.

Finally, we can fix reversals by taking advantage of a web database. Let the phrase $p_1$ be the original phrase, and let $p_2$ be the original phrase with $X$ and $Y$ swapped. After conducting queries on a search engine for both $p_1$ and $p_2$, we can determine that the query for which more results appear is the correct intensity ordering of the two adjectives.

## 3 Type B False Positives

### 3.1 Classification

The second type of false positives is **Type B** false positives, which are phrases wherein **Y** is inaccurately classified as being a more intense synonym of **X** because **X** and **Y** are adjectives that do not fall on the same scale.

For example, consider the sentence "Stevie Wonder is very good, but not lyrical." Using Sheinman's method of pattern extraction, one would falsely infer that "lyrical" is a more intense synonym to "good," which cannot be true, as "lyrical" is not even a synonym for "good", much less a more intense form of it.

Furthermore, Type B false positives occur frequently in human speech, as it is very common to switch scales when using a particular pattern.

### 3.2 Correction with Level 1 Searches

The most straightforward way of fixing Type B false positives is to performa simple search, testing to see if **X** falls under the synset - a word's set of synonyms - of **Y**, or if **Y** falls under the synset of **x**. This term can be classified as a Level 1 search.

Level 1 searches are searches conducted in WordNet, wherein only the two synsets of words **X** and **Y** will be explored. They differ from Level 2 searches, which increase the depth of the search. In general, a Level N search searches through a set of words *w*, then a Level N+1 search will search through all synsets for each word contained in *w*. Thus a Level 2 search will search through all the synsets of words contained in synsets of words **X** and **Y**.

The Level 1 searches are successfully able to eliminate a large number of Type B false positives. For instance, TYPEB-LEVEL1 can correctly identify "good but not lyrical" and "tasty but not expensive" as false positives.

These types of false positives are interesting because they reveal innate patterns of cultural thinking. People sometimes associate a given quality or attribute with another, such as price and quality. A phrase such as "wealthy but not arrogant" might seem to suggest that human thinking associates the wealthy as having arrogant qualities, or a phrase such as "fat but not jolly" might seem to suggest that a culture views associates fat people with being jolly. Future work might be to further investigate Type B false positives to extract cultural associations from the linguistic patterns.

The problem is that Level 1 searches overgenerate the number of false positives. The following table lists a collection of instances where the Level 1 searches classify the phrases as a false positive, even though intuition as an English speaker tells us otherwise.

| X | Y | LEVEL1(X, Y) |
|---|---|---|
| good | wonderful | true |
| good | awesome | true |
| good | amazing | true |
| wonderful | awesome | true |
| elephantine | monstrous | true |
| gnomish | pocket-size | true |

**Table 2** Misclassified examples from a Level 1 search.

As evidenced, these examples suggest that Level-1 searches overgenerate the actual number of false positives. Further investigation allows us to see why: if we take all of the words included in the synset of $good$ and all the words included in the synset of $wonderful$, we can observe that neither word appears in the other's synset.

However, we can observe that triangulation appears in the synsets: $great$ appears as one of the words contained in the synset of $good$, and the words $great$ and $wonderful$ both have the word $extraordinary$ contained in both their synsets. Something that is $good$ must also be $great$, which is also $extraordinary$. Since something $wonderful$ is also $extraordinary$, it follows that $good$ and $wonderful$ are, indeed, true synonyms of one another.

### 3.3 Correction with Level 2 Searches

We have observed that two synonymous words that differ in intensity may not be included in each other's synsets, but may nonetheless share a common word between the two synsets. The word $wonderful$ does not appear in the synset of $good$ and $good$ does not appear in the synset of $wonderful$, but both $good$ and $wonderful$ share $great$ in their synsets. This leads us to believe that many of the falsely identified false positives could be eliminated by performing a Level 2 search instead of a Level 1 search.

A Level 2 search performs its searches one level deeper. A Level 2 search chooses one of the pair $(X, Y)$ as its base, and then calculates the synset of the other word. For each word in the synset, the Level 2 search performs a Level 1 search against the base word that it chose earlier. Then, it switches the base word and performs the same set of Level 1 searches on the opposite synset. For each Level 1 search, if the the algorithm has found a word common to both $X$ and $Y$'s synsets, the checker identifies the pair as a false positive. Otherwise, if every synset pair has been searched and no word has been found common to both synsets, the algorithm identifies the pair as a false positive. The pseudocode for a Level 2 search is given in Algorithm 1.

### 3.4 Results

Performing Level-2 searches on Type B false positives eliminates overgeneration of false positives, but also yields the problem of undergeneration because of word sense disambiguation. Each of the

**Algorithm 1** This function returns $true$ if phrase $X$ and $Y$ are identified as being a Type B false positive, and returns $false$ otherwise.

**procedure** TYPEB-LEVEL2($X, Y$)
  $synset_x \leftarrow$ GETADJECTIVESYNSET($X$)
  **for all** $i$ in $synset_x$ **do** ▷ Search for $Y$ in the synsets of $X$
    **if** TYPEA($i, Y$) is $false$ and TYPEB-LEVEL1($i, Y$) is $false$ **then**
      **return** false
  $synset_y \leftarrow$ GETADJECTIVESYNSET($Y$)
  **for all** $i$ in $synset_y$ **do** ▷ Search for $X$ in the synsets of $Y$
    **if** TYPEA($i, X$) is $false$ and TYPEB-LEVEL1($i, X$) is $false$ **then**
      **return** false
  **return** true

synsets contain so many different senses that a Level-2 search could easily identify two words as synonyms based off of a faulty "common word." Sample adjective queries are shown in the table below, along with the adjective pair that was found to be a successful Level-1 pair and the word that the two adjectives held in common.

| (X, Y) | Adj. Pair | Common Adj. |
|---|---|---|
| tall, thin | tall, thin | gangling |
| fat, smart | fat, intense | thick |
| short, rich | rich, dumpy | fat |
| happy, tasty | tasty, prosperous | rich |
| fat, red | red, rich | colorful |
| tall, awful | tall, tremendous | large |
| up, wide | up, broad | high |
| big, pretty | big, pretty | bad |
| strong, fat | strong, fat | fertile |
| good, big | good, large | ample |
| fat, atomic | fat, little | dumpy |
| sad, fat | sad, heavy | distressing |

**Table 3** Misclassified examples from a Level 2 search.

Our goal now is to reconcile the undergeneration of Level 1 searches with the overgeneration of the Level 2 searches. We do not consider searches deeper than a Level 2 search, because a Level 2 search already overgenerates.

## 4 Attributes

WordNet pointers contain information about a word's attribute, which stores the word's category, e.g. "size" for the adjectives "big" and "small." Adding checks that discard words of different attributes successfuly eliminates all the searches stored in Table 3.

The pseudocode for the altered algorithm, which includes attribute checks, is included as Algorithm 3. Running this altered algorithm corrects all of the results found in Table 3.

**Algorithm 2** Returns $true$ if $X$ and $Y$ are Type B false positives, and $false$ otherwise.

**procedure** TYPEB-LEVEL2-ATTR($X, Y$)
  $A_x \leftarrow$ GETATTRIBUTE($X$)
  $A_y \leftarrow$ GETATTRIBUTE($Y$)
  **if** $A_x$ is not $null$ and $A_y$ is not $null$ and $A_x$ is not equal to $A_y$ **then**
    **return** true
  $synset_x \leftarrow$ GETADJECTIVESYNSET($X$)
  **for all** $i$ in $synset_x$ **do**
    $A_i \leftarrow$ GETATTRIBUTE($i$)
    **if** $A_y$ is not $null$ and $A_i$ is not $null$ and $A_y$ is not $A_i$ **then**
      **continue**
    **if** TYPEA($i, Y$) is $false$ and TYPEB-LEVEL1($i, Y$) is $false$ **then**
      **return** false
  $synset_y \leftarrow$ GETADJECTIVESYNSET($Y$)
  **for all** $i$ in $synset_y$ **do**
    $A_i \leftarrow$ GETATTRIBUTE($i$)
    **if** $A_x$ is not $null$ and $A_i$ is not $null$ and $A_x$ is not $A_i$ **then**
      **continue**
    **if** TYPEA($i, X$) is $false$ and TYPEB-LEVEL1($i, X$) is $false$ **then**
      **return** false
  **return** true

### 4.1 Limitations

The most notable limitation is that the set of adjectives that have attributes is extremely small, and are thus susceptible to all of the pitfalls of the Level-2 searches described in Algorithm 3. In fact, most of the adjectives contained in WordNet do not have attribute pointers. Our algorithm could be substantially improved by encoding the attribute pointer more consistently in WordNet.

There are also a few exceptional cases, where

two adjectives are actually synonyms, but WordNet gives the two words different pointers. For example, the word "good" has an attribute of "quality" whereas the word "extraordinary" has an attribute of "ordinariness." Speakers of the English language can recognize that "good" and "extraordinary" are synonyms, but the algorithm would immediately reject them because they have different attributes.

### 4.2 Results

To test the algorithm, we ran four adjective pairs on it, selecting the phrases by the following criteria: 1) Returning a high enough number of hits on Google News so that the results can be considered significant, 2) Returning a low enough number of hits on Google News so that it is not overstrenuous to hand-classify each of the results, and 3) Adjectives that could be represented on a scale.

The searches were run by typing the pattern into a Google News search query in quotes (e.g. "hot but not"). Then, each search was classified by running it into the False Positive Checker described in Algorithm 1, and the accuracy of the classifications were checked by hand.

Overall, the False Positive Checker returns robust results for most adjectives. The vast majority of the errors occured because their attribute pointers returned $null$, leaving them susceptible to the Type 2 errors.

Altogether, for the two example searches listed above, the algorithm had 18 misclassifications out of 823 search results, for a total accuracy of 97.81%. All 823 instances described in Table 4 are instances of positives generated by Sheinman's method, but classifying these as true positives or false positives is left up to our algorithm. The high degree of accuracy from from the searches suggests that this algorithm is successfully able to classify Sheinman's phrases a true positives or false positives. If one could encode adjective attributes more consistently in WordNet, most of these errors would be able to be eliminated.

### 4.3 Limitations of WordNet

All of our searches rely on the ability of WordNet to classify adjectives correctly. However, many of our searches using the False Positive Checker indicate that there are gaps in WordNet's structure. More specifically, limitations on attribute pointers make it difficult to completely eliminate the appearance of false positives in Sheinman's method.

| phrase | misclassified/total | percentage |
|---|---|---|
| hot but not | 9/148 | 93.92% |
| big but not | 5/423 | 98.82% |
| old but not | 2/136 | 98.53% |
| happy but not | 2/116 | 98.28% |
| Total | 18/823 | 97.81% |

**Table 4** Accuracy of phrases searched on Google News.

Furthermore, synset membership is not always consistent with human intuition. For instance, both the words "subatomic" and "gnomish" might be included in the synset for "small," but "subatomic" is used to describe particles, whereas "gnomish" is used to describe people. These flaws suggest that WordNet needs to be more consistent in its attribute pointers for adjectives, as well as in how it links its adjectives together in synsets. In order to consistently be able to detect the false positive errors using Sheinman's method, it is vital for WordNet to be improve the quality of synsets, as well as to vastly expand the coverage of its attribute pointers.

Finally, the dumbbell structure of WordNet as it is renders it difficult to encode adjective scales within each synset. For future use, it would be important to rework the organization of WordNet such that adjective scales could be extracted more easily.

## 5 Conclusion

**Type A** false positives suggest that adjectives **X** and **Y** are on the same scale, but that **Y** is not more intense than **X**. There are three types of Type A false positives: repetitions, antonyms, and reversals, and all of these can be corrected relatively easily. **Type B** false positives occur when **X** and **Y** are not synonyms of one another and also do not fall on th same scale. Performing a Level 1 search on WordNet undergenerates false positives, but a Level 2 search overgenerates them. To solve this issue, we must use the attribute pointers, which can accurately classify the category of many of the adjectives contained in WordNet.

After conducting tests, the False Positive Checker accurately classified 97.81% of all phrases conducted through a test. These results could be further improved by improving the structure of WordNet by improving both the precision and the coverage of its attribute pointer.

All in all, the ability to distinguish the differing intensities of adjective synonyms is vital to being able to master the nuances of the English language. By improving the accuracy of Sheinman's method, we can continue to improve our ability to encode these unstated nuances into a lexical tool.

## 6 Acknowledgments

I would like to thank my advisor, Professor Christiane Fellbaum, for her support and guidance in helping me with this paper. She has provided valuable assistance to the undertaking of the work summarized here. I am also grateful to Princeton University's Student Activities Funding Engine (SAFE) for their generous sponsorship of my travel to the Global WordNet Conference.

## References

Fellbaum, Christiane. 1998. *WordNet: an electronic lexical database.* MIT Press WordNet is available from http://www.cogsci.princeton.edu/wn. 2010.

Vera Sheinman, Christiane Fellbaum, Isaac Julien, Peter Schulam, Takenobu Tokunaga. 2013. Large, huge or gigantic? Identifying and encoding intensity relations among adjectives in WordNet. *Language Resources and Evaluation*, 47:1-20.

Vera Sheinman, Takenobu Tokunaga. 2009. Adjscales: Differentiating between similar adjectives for language learners. *Proceedings of the International conference on computer supported education (CSEDU-09), 229-235.*

Mark Finlayson. 2013. Java Wordnet Interface (JWI) 2.2.4. MIT. http://projects.csail.mit.edu/jwi/.

# Embedding NomLex-BR nominalizations into OpenWordnet-PT

**Livy Maria Real Coelho**
Univ. Federal do Paraná
Curitiba, Brazil
livyreal@gmail.com

**Alexandre Rademaker**
IBM Research Brazil and EMAp/FGV
Rio de Janeiro, Brazil
alexrad@br.ibm.com

**Valeria de Paiva**
Nuance Communications
Sunnyvale, CA, USA
valeria.depaiva@gmail.com

**Gerard de Melo**
IIIS, Tsinghua University
Beijing, China
gdm@demelo.org

## Abstract

This paper presents NomLex-BR, a lexical resource describing Brazilian Portuguese nominalizations, and its integration with OpenWordnet-PT. We first describe the original English NOMLEX lexical resource and how we used it to bootstrap a Portuguese version. Subsequently, we describe how this lexicon can be embedded into OpenWordnet-PT, which facilitates its use and helps spot-checking both the bigger integrated resource and the original lexicon. Lastly, we outline some of the other, more substantial work that we plan to engage for the project of using linguistic insights for knowledge representation in Portuguese.

## 1 Introduction

To help investigate the semantics of deverbal nominalizations, and its implications for Natural Language Processing applications such as electronic ontologies, question answering, or information retrieval, it is useful to have a lexicon of such nominalizations. Our aim, in this paper, is to describe the production and distribution of an open-source, fully available RDF-packaged lexicon of deverbal nominalizations in Brazilian Portuguese, as well as a (still in progress) semantically annotated corpus of examples of these deverbal nouns. More generally we are interested in producing lexical resources for Portuguese that allow us to reason about the semantics of sentences in natural language.

We focus on nominalizations in this work, for several reasons. Deverbal nouns, or nominalizations, can pose serious challenges for knowledge-representation systems. A sentence like "Alexander destroyed the city in 332 BC" can easily be parsed and its semantic arguments, such as the agent of destruction (Alexander), the thing destroyed (the city), and the time (332 BC), are readily obtained for a proposed logical representation of the sentence. By contrast, a sentence like "Alexander's destruction of the city happened in 332 BC" is typically much harder to deal with. It describes the same event of destruction, with the same semantic arguments, but these are much harder to obtain automatically by syntactically parsing the sentence, for most parsers.

Nominalizations have been studied for more than four decades (Chomsky, 1970; Grimshaw, 1990; Alexiadou, 2001). While most of these works describe nominalizations' behavior through a syntactic or morphological point of view, recently, the study of nominalizations has focused also on semantic and ontological phenomena (Hamm and Kamp, 2009; Real and Retoré, 2013). With regard to lexical studies, deverbal nouns are particularly well-studied in English, with the NOMLEX project (Macleod et al., 1998) providing a well-established, open access baseline for corresponding results in other languages. Our work on NomLex-BR builds up from previous work on nominalizations in English (Gurevich et al., 2006). This previous work extended the coverage of NOMLEX's English norminalizations, via the use of Xerox PARC's state-of-the-art NLP system XLE (Maxwell and Kaplan, 1996) and some simple, but effective heuristics, and compared it to NOMLEX-PLUS (Meyers et al., 2004), the state-of-the-art in 2004. Our work here is an attempt at building the basic blocks underlying that work on nominalizations, for Portuguese. Our assumption was that the work done for English can be suitably adapted and re-used for Portuguese, if we keep the language comparisons in place. Additionally, we hoped to learn and adapt from the French experience with nominalizations, described in the Nomage project (Balvet et al., 2011).

The original version of NOMLEX is a small resource of only around a thousand nominalizations, which seemed ideal to be used as a basis for our project. The original NOMLEX was constructed starting out with nominalizations with the suffixes *-ion*, *-ment* and *-er*, taking samples of the most frequent words in a list of nouns from a combination of the Brown Corpus and the Wall Street Journal (about 1 million words of each). Words with these kinds of suffixes tend to be erudite words and these tend to work similarly in different (but related) languages. This was the original working hypothesis, which seems confirmed, to some degree, by our prototype.

To construct our lexicon, we first translated the easiest nominalizations into Portuguese, such as *construction/ construção* and *writer/escritor*, in order to keep, to the extent possible, the "same" lexical items from NOMLEX into NomLex-BR. Our methodology provided for a fast and reliable creation of a lexical resource for Portuguese, which hereafter can work as a basis to discuss the behavior of nominalizations in general. In English, for example, many of the nominalizations with eventive readings cannot be pluralized, *confusion* and *abandonment*, e.g., lack plurals. This does not occur in Brazilian Portuguese with *confusão/confusões* and *abandono/abandonos*. Using a lexical resource that covers the same range of words as a previously existing English one, insightful comparisons, as the inter-language relation of the nominalizer morphemes and the syntactic behavior of those nominals, can be observed more easily.

However, for comparative studies a simply text file is not very easy to use. We thus finally embedded NomLex-BR into a lexical-semantic resource called OpenWordnet-PT (de Paiva et al., 2012a), greatly facilitating search and experiments.

## 2 NomLex-BR

The original NOMLEX is a lexicon of English nominalizations developed at New York University over many years. It relates the arguments of a nominalization to the predicate argument structure of its associated verb, without requiring exactly the same structure for the nominal and the verbal lexical items. It also records details of the syntactic realization of the arguments, including prepositions associated with the arguments.

Unfortunately, lexical resources for languages other than English are notoriously difficult to come by. We are involved with the creation of a Portuguese WordNet freely available for download and modification by anyone OpenWordnet-PT (de Paiva et al., 2012b). To follow the traditional pipeline for natural language understanding systems, e.g. the one described by the Bridge system of PARC (Bobrow et al., 2007), we need a collection of lexical resources as well as (much as possible) off-the-shelf systems. Ideally we would want to have a broad coverage, deep processing LFG grammar of Portuguese and while we are pursuing leads in this direction (de Alencar, 2013), this may take a while, as hand-crafted large coverage grammars are very labor-intensive. In the meantime, it seemed sensible to construct some of the resources that we are most familiar with, and a small version of NOMLEX for Portuguese, NomLex-BR, seemed to be an ideal starting point.

Our Portuguese version keeps the original structures of the English version of NOMLEX, but apart from the translated nominal and verb, adds an extra field to capture usage examples in Portuguese.

Our initial pass of translating word pairs in NOMLEX by two linguists was enough to yield direct translations of around 90% of the original resource. This high rate of correspondence resulted not only from the words in NOMLEX being somewhat erudite, but also from the fact that the inter-language relations established by the nominalizer morphemes are quite straightforward. For example, *adjourn**ment**/adia**mento***, *benefici**ary**/benefici**ário***, *corro**sion**/ corro**são***.

The NomLex-BR lexicon has more than a thousand entries, mostly nominalizations formed by *-ção*, *-mento* and *-or*, as these are the corresponding suffixes to the ones adopted by the NOMLEX project. One next goal is to introduce nominalizations formed by *-ura*, considering the description proposed by (Real, 2008). We also aim to add nominalizations formed by the suffix *-ada*. These seem to require more analysis as *-ada* produces nominals from verbs (*cutucada*) and from nouns (*pedrada*) and the semantics of these nominalizations is far from obvious, as discussed by (de Medeiros, 2008).

## 3 Evaluation of NomLex-BR

We considered several ways of evaluating our resource and different criteria to do so. Since it is hand-constructed, via two experts, its accuracy is high enough for the nominal-verb pairs that it covers. The main challenge is its coverage and representativeness of the nominalizations in place. This was addressed by increasing the coverage and by checking the representativeness using a small corpus of biographical data. As we are working with a corpus of biographies of Brazilian historical figures (DHBB) (Abreu et al., 2010), we listed the most frequent nouns in the texts of this corpus and marked them as being nominals or not. This revealed a lack of *agentive* nominals in our inititial resource that was then corrected.

A second kind of evaluation and extension we performed was comparing our resource with Nomage (Balvet et al., 2011), a similar project for the French lexicon. The Nomage corpus covers 736 nominals and 679 verbal lexemes extracted from the French Treebank (Abeille et al., 2003). Its nominalizations, annotated syntactically and semantically, are formed by the suffixes *-ade*, *-age*, *-ance/ence*, *-ee*, *-ion*, *-ment* and *-ure*. The Nomage project and ours share a similar goal, to study the inheritance of semantic and aspectual features from the verbal bases, but the Nomage lexicon was produced combining two different methodologies – "one based on transformation tests applied on real-life sentences by naive annotators, the other based on forged sentences applied by linguistically trained annotators" (Balvet et al., 2011, p. 04). We compared all of Nomage's entries with NomLex-BR. It turned out that many of the nominalizations in Nomage had to be added to NomLex-BR, somewhat contrary to our expectations that NOMLEX and NOMAGE had a big intersection.

In the future, we would like to compare the structural descriptions on each nominalization/verb pair (for example *construction/construção*) to check in which way the linguistic relations established by nominalizations with their verb bases are the same in English and in Portuguese. This kind of evaluation requires further annotation to describe the kinds of nominalizations in Portuguese. These are interesting problems on their own and we hope to report interesting results as the project progresses.

## 4 Embedding NomLex-BR into OpenWordnet-PT

Finally, we integrated NomLex-BR into OpenWordnet-PT, a version of WordNet for Brazilian Portuguese. Its main characteristics are its open-source license, its direct correspondence with Princeton WordNet, and, given its origins in the Universal WordNet(de Melo and Weikum, 2009), both a high recall and a high precision for the more salient words in the language.

Our choice of encoding OpenWordnet-PT in RDF makes the merging of these resources very straightforward. The details of this encoding are described elsewhere in great detail (Rademaker et al., 2014). In order to incorporate NomLex-BR into this encoding, we extended the RDF-based vocabulary to additionally describe relevant parts of the NOMLEX syntax (Macleod et al., 1999). Figure 1 presents a subgraph for the nominalization entry *promover/promoção* and its connection to OpenWordnet-PT. Note that the link between NomLex-BR and OpenWordnet-PT is achieved through the properties `noun` and `verb`. Both properties have as domain an instance of `Nominalization` and as co-domain an instance of `WordSense` (from the OpenWordnet-PT vocabulary).

This embedding of NomLex-BR into the open version of a Portuguese wordnet was helpful in multiple respects. First, it solved some minor problems with handling diacriticals, as OpenWordnet-PT has a consistent treatment of these. Secondly by checking how the nominalizations from NomLex-BR were related to the corresponding verbs in the wordnet version, we realized that some synsets were missing in the OpenWordnet-PT. These are in the process of being added manually. Finally, by re-checking the original English NOMLEX connections, we hope to spot-check the consistency of OpenWordnet-PT with respect to other specific phenomena, for example, the phenomenon of diminutivization of nominals.

## 5 Preliminary Conclusions

This lexicon of deverbals is just a first step for our lexical resources. It would be useful to include nominalizations of adjectives and of other nouns, which also need a common concept mapping for knowledge representation. Examples here would be the nominals "selvageria" or "bruxaria"

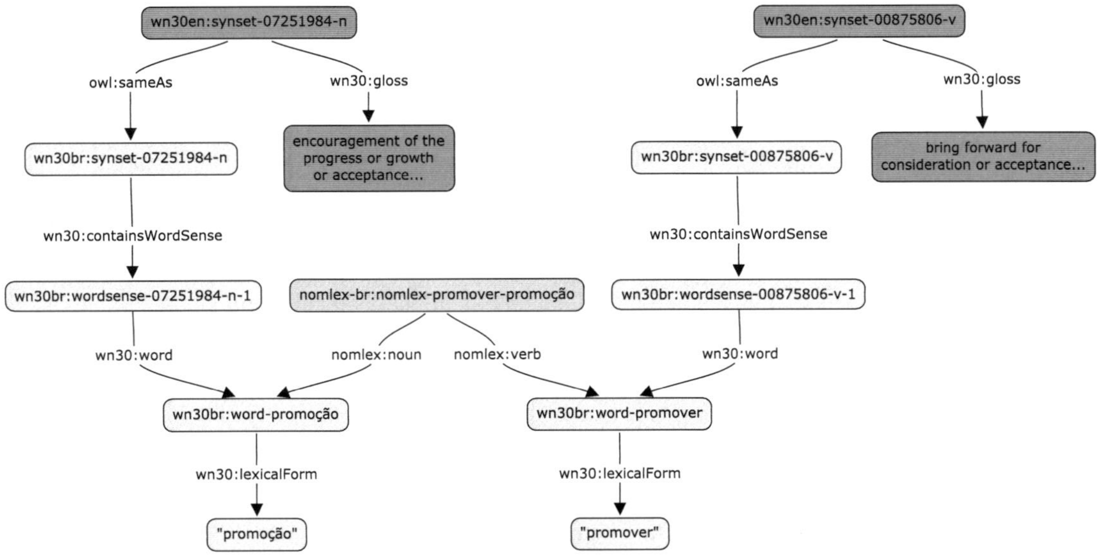


Figure 1: Entry *promover/promoção*

from the adjective "selvagem" (wild) and the noun "bruxa" (witch). Another future plan is to produce capture verb semantics and in particular verb alternations, as covered by VerbNet (Kipper et al., 2006) for English. Again, there is hope that some of the original Levin classes used for the construction of VerbNet are also valid for Portuguese.

In summary, we believe that the creation of linguistic resources requires openness of programs and of code. The only way to keep alive any resource is to make sure that people can modify it for their own purposes. If one wants the enterprise of automatic language understanding to flourish, especially in languages with fewer resources, one must make sure that the lexical resources we develop are freely available, freely modifiable and easy to use. Making our small lexicon NomLex-BR part of OpenWordnet-PT and having it downloadable, freely available from `http://github.com/arademaker/wordnet-br/` and easy to consult, we hope to make it more interesting for researchers interested in nominalizations in Portuguese.

We also wish to develop other resources for Portuguese along these same lines and we hope to work both from small hand-crafted lexica and from big machine learned ones (like OpenWordnet-PT and FreeLing-PT) to try to obtain better quality resources. Keeping these resources usable and as much as possible theory-neutral is our challange.

## References


Anne Abeille, Lionel Clément, and Francois Toussenel. 2003. Building a treebank for french. In Anne Abeille, editor, *Treebanks, Building and Using Parsed Corpora*, pages 165–187. Kluwer, Dordrecht.

Alzira Alves Abreu, Fernando Lattman-Weltman, and Christiane Jalles de Paula, editors. 2010. *Dicionário Histórico-Biográfico Brasileiro pos-1930*. CPDOC/FGV, 3 edition. `http://cpdoc.fgv.br/acervo/dhbb`.

Artemis Alexiadou. 2001. *Functional structure in nominals. Nominalization and ergativity*. John Benjamins.

Antonio Balvet, Lucie Barque, Marie-Hélène Condette, Pauline Haas, Richard Huyghe, RafaelMarín, and Aurélie Merlo. 2011. Nomage: an electronic lexicon of french deverbal nouns based on a semantically annotated corpus. In *Proceedings of the First International Workshop on Lexical Resources*, pages 8–15, Ljubljana, Slovenia.

Daniel G. Bobrow, Bob Cheslow, Cleo Condoravdi, Lauri Karttunen, Tracy H. King, Rowan Nairn, Valeria de Paiva, Charlotte Price, and Annie Zaenen. 2007. PARC's bridge and question answering system. In *Proceedings of Grammar Engineering Across Frameworks*, pages 26–45.

Noam Chomsky. 1970. Remarks on nominalization. In *Readings in English transformational grammar*. Blaisdell.

Leonel Figueiredo de Alencar. 2013. Brgram: uma gramática computacional de um fragmento do português brasileiro no formalismo da lfg. In *Proceed-*

*ings of the 9th Brazilian Symposium in Information and Human Language Technology, Sociedade Brasileira de Computação*, pages 183–188, Fortaleza, CE, Brazil.

Alessandro Boechat de Medeiros. 2008. *Tracos Morfossintáticos e Subespecificacão Morfológica na Gramática do Português: Um Estudo das Formas Participiais*. Ph.D. thesis, UFRJ.

Gerard de Melo and Gerhard Weikum. 2009. Towards a universal wordnet by learning from combined evidence. In *Proceedings of the 18th ACM Conference on Information and Knowledge Management (CIKM 2009)*, pages 513–522, New York, NY, USA. ACM. http://doi.acm.org/10.1145/1645953.1646020.

Valeria de Paiva, Alexandre Rademaker, and de Gerard Melo. 2012a. OpenWordNet-PT: An open brazilian wordnet for reasoning. In *Proceedings of the 24th International Conference on Computational Linguistics*, pages 353–360. See at http://www.coling2012-iitb.org (Demo Paper). Published also as Techreport http://hdl.handle.net/10438/10274.

Valeria de Paiva, Alexandre Rademaker, and Gerard de Melo. 2012b. Openwordnet-pt: an openbrazilian wordnet for reasoning. Technical report, FGV - EMAp.

Jane Grimshaw. 1990. *Argument structure*. The MIT Press.

Olga Gurevich, Richard Crouch, Tracy Holloway King, and Valeria de Paiva. 2006. Deverbal nouns in knowledge representation. In *Proceedings of the 19th International Florida AI Research Society Conference (FLAIRS'06)*, pages 670–675, Melbourne Beach, FL, May. AAAI Press.

Fritz Hamm and Hans Kamp. 2009. Ontology and inference: The case of german ung–nominals. *Disambiguation and Reambiguation*, 6:1–67.

Karin Kipper, Anna Korhonen, Neville Ryant, and Martha Palmer. 2006. Extending verbnet with novel verb classes. In *Proceedings of Fifth International Conference on Language Resources and Evaluation (LREC 2006)*, pages 1027–1032, Genoa, Italy, June.

Catherine Macleod, Ralph Grishman, Adam Meyers, Leslie Barret, and Ruth Reeves. 1998. Nomlex: A lexicon of nominalizations. In *Proceedings of Euralex 1998*, pages 187–193, Liege, Belgium.

Catherine Macleod, Ralph Grishman, Adam Meyers, Leslie Barret, and Ruth Reeves, 1999. *Manual of NOMLEX: The Regularized Version*.

John Maxwell and Ron Kaplan. 1996. An efficient parser for LFG. In *Proceedings of the First LFG Conference*, CSLI Publications.

Adam Meyers, Ruth Reeves, Catherine Macleod, Rachel Szekeley, Veronkia Zielinska, and Brian Young. 2004. The cross-breeding of dictionaries. In *Proceedings of LREC-2004*, Lisbon, Portugal.

Alexandre Rademaker, Valeria de Paiva, Gerard de Melo, Livy Real, and Maira Gatti. 2014. OpenWordNet-PT: A project report. In *Proceedings of the 7th Global WordNet Conference*, Tartu, Estonia, jan. to appear.

Livy Real and Christian Retoré. 2013. A generative montagovian lexicon for polysemous deverbal nouns. In *Handbook of the 4th World Congress and School on Universal Logic*.

Livy Real. 2008. Uma análise do sufixo -ura com base na morfologia categorial. *Revista InterteXto*, 1.

# OpenWordNet-PT: A Project Report

**Alexandre Rademaker**
IBM Research Brazil / FGV/EMAp
Rio de Janeiro, Brazil
alexrad@br.ibm.com

**Valeria de Paiva**
Nunance Communications
Sunnyvale, CA, USA
valeria.depaiva@gmail.com

**Gerard de Melo**
Tsinghua University
Beijing, China
gdm@demelo.org

**Livy Maria Real Coelho**
Univ. Federal do Paraná
Curitiba, Brazil
livyreal@gmail.com

**Maira Gatti**
IBM Research Brazil
Rio de Janeiro, Brazil
mairacg@br.ibm.com

**Abstract**

This paper presents OpenWordNet-PT, a freely available open-source wordnet for Portuguese, with its latest developments and practical uses. We provide a detailed description of the RDF representation developed for OpenWordnet-PT. We highlight our efforts to extend the coverage of our resource and add nominalization relations connecting nouns and verbs. Finally, we present several real-world applications where OpenWordnet-PT was put to use, including a large-scale high-throughput sentiment analysis system.

## 1 Introduction

Semantic relationships between words are crucial in many forms of natural language processing. Computational systems are not aware of the fact that *carro* and *automóvel* both refer to cars, or that *caminhão* (truck) is related to these words as well in that they all share a common more general hypernym.

OpenWordnet-PT (or OpenWN-PT for short) is a lexical-semantic resource describing (Brazilian) Portuguese words and their relationships. It is modelled after and fully interoperable with the original Princeton WordNet for English (Fellbaum, 1998), relying on the same identifiers as WordNet 3.0. This means that one can easily find Portuguese equivalents for specific English word senses and vice versa. This also means that OpenWN-PT is part of a large ecosystem of compatible resources, including domain identifiers (Magnini and Cavaglia, 2000) and mappings to Wikipedia (de Melo and Weikum, 2010).

In this paper, we specify the RDF-based representation chosen for OpenWN-PT (Section 2) and describe our recent efforts to extend this resource (Sections 3 to 5), most notably with nominalization relations connecting nouns and verbs (Section 4). We also highlight several important applications of OpenWN-PT (Section 6).

## 2 RDF Representation

Wordnets have been distributed in a wide range of different incompatible data formats. An increasingly popular way of addressing the issue of interoperability is to rely on Linked Data and Semantic Web standards such as RDF (Cyganiak and Wood, 2003) and OWL (Hitzler et al., 2012), which have led to the emergence of a number of Linked Data projects for lexical resources (de Melo and Weikum, 2008; Chiarcos et al., 2012).

We believe that OpenWN-PT should best be encoded and distributed in RDF/OWL. Not only do these standards allow us to publish both the data model and the actual data in the same format. They also provide for instant compatibility with a vast range of existing data processing tools, including databases (so-called "triple stores") providing SQL-like query interfaces based on the SPARQL standard (Harris and Seaborne, 2013).

Some years ago, a task force of the Semantic Web Best Practices Working Group proposed a standard encoding of WordNet in RDF (van Assem et al., 2006). This effort made WordNet directly accessible to Semantic Web applications. The proposed conversion aimed to be as complete as possible. The suggested representation also stayed as close to the original source as possible, that is, it reflects the original WordNet data model without interpretation. Comparing with previous RDF translations of WordNet, the main features of this version are: (1) It does not model the hyponym hierarchy as a subclass hierarchy. (2) It represents words and word senses as separate entities with their own URI which makes it possible to refer to them directly. (3) It contains all relations that are present in Princeton WordNet. (4) It provides OWL semantics in the form of inverse properties, definition of property characteristics and property restrictions on classes that can be used by both the RDFS and OWL infrastructures.

The schema of the conversion has three main classes: `Synset`, `Word` and `WordSense`. There are three kinds of properties in the schema. A first set of properties connects instances of the main classes together. The class `Synset` is linked to its `WordSenses` with the property `containsWordSense`, and `WordSense` to its `Word` with the property `word`. A second set of properties represents the WordNet relations such as hyponymy and meronymy, including those that relate two `Synsets` to each other (e.g. `hyponymOf`), those that relate two `WordSenses` to each other (e.g. `antonymOf`), and a miscellaneous set containing `gloss` and `frame`. Finally, a third set of properties provides additional information about entities using literals. Examples are `synsetId`, which records the original ID given in Princeton WordNet to a synset, and the `tagCount` of a `WordSense`. The actual lexical form of a `Word` is recorded with the property `lexicalForm`. Each synset has an `rdfs:label` that is filled with the lexical form of the first word sense in the synset.

OpenWN-PT is completely aligned to Princeton WordNet. This means that each OpenWN-PT synset is a translation of an original Princeton WordNet synset, with no additional synsets or relations so far. Given this direct relation, we decided that our RDF representation does not require a full redundant modeling of all relations and information in Princeton WordNet. Instead, we chose to model our RDF as an add-on to WordNet 3.0 that extends it with information about the Portuguese language. For this, we simply add new `Synset` and `WordSense` instances that are linked to the English WordNet.

OpenWN-PT's RDF will thus only be useful together with an RDF version of Princeton WordNet. While there is a previous RDF version of WordNet 3.0 online, [1] we wanted to ensure that all information in the WordNet 3.0 distribution was transformed to RDF. To this end, we wrote our own Common Lisp code to translate the WordNet 3.0 data files to RDF, following the W3C model (van Assem et al., 2006) with a few modifications as follows.

1. We add two more classes named `BaseConcept` and `CoreConcept` to identify the synsets that are base concepts (Vossen, 2002) or core concepts (Boyd-Graber et al., 2006), respectively.
2. We have added properties to capture information from WordNet 3.0 not available in the Prolog distribution nor in the "database files only" distribution. To this end, we have parsed and read the files *sents.vrb*, *sent-idx.vrb* and *lexnames*. A `WordSense` can have a `lexFile`, `lexId`, `senseKey`, and an example sentence (for a `WordSense` of a `VerbSynset`). A synset can have a `lexicographerFile` and a `frame` (in the case of a `VerbSynset`).
3. We omitted redundant subclasses of `WordSense` like `NounWordSense`, as the part-of-speech can be derived from the corresponding synset. A subclass of `Word` called `Collocation` is also omitted, as the lexical form of `Word` instances can easily be examined to check for collocations.
4. We have adopted a different schema for naming the resources identifiers (URIs).

In Figure 1, we show the synset 00001740-n encoded in RDF in its more readable N3 notation variant (Berners-Lee and Connolly, 2011). `Word` instances are blank resources, that is, resources without a URI or unnamed resources. In Figure 2, we present the same synset in a graphical way, additionally showing its connection with the corresponding synset in the Princeton WordNet, including relevant semantic relations. Our code for this RDF version of WordNet 3.0 is freely available. [2]

[1] See `http://bit.ly/1cVExvj`.

[2] See `http://bit.ly/1ctbGSL`. The code requires AllegroGraph and Allegro Common Lisp. Both are commercial tools but free editions can be obtained on the Franz Inc. website at `http://www.franz.com`.

```
@prefix rdf: <http://www.w3.org/1999/02/22-rdf-syntax-ns#> .
@prefix wn30: <http://arademaker.github.com/wn30/schema/> .
@prefix wn30en: <http://arademaker.github.com/wn30-en/instances/> .
@prefix wn30br: <http://arademaker.github.com/wn30-br/instances/> .

wn30br:synset-00001740-n wn30:synsetId "00001740" ;
    rdf:type wn30:NounSynset ; rdf:type wn30:BaseConcept ;
    owl:sameAs wn30en:synset-00001740-n ;
    wn30:containsWordSense wn30br:wordsense-00001740-n-1 ;
    wn30:containsWordSense wn30br:wordsense-00001740-n-3 ;
    wn30:gloss "o que é percebido, conhecido ou inferido como
    tendo existência própria (vivente ou não vivente)" .

wn30br:wordsense-00001740-n-1 wn30:wordNumber "1" ;
                              rdfs:label "ser" ;
                              rdf:type wn30:WordSense ;
                              wn30:word _:anon642 .

wn30br:wordsense-00001740-n-3 rdfs:label "entidade" ;
                              wn30:wordNumber "3" ;
                              rdf:type wn30:WordSense ;
                              wn30:word _:anon24777 .

_:anon24777 wn30:lexicalForm "entidade" ; rdf:type wn30:Word .
_:anon642 wn30:lexicalForm "ser" ; rdf:type wn30:Word .
```

Figure 1: The synset 00001740-n in N3 notation

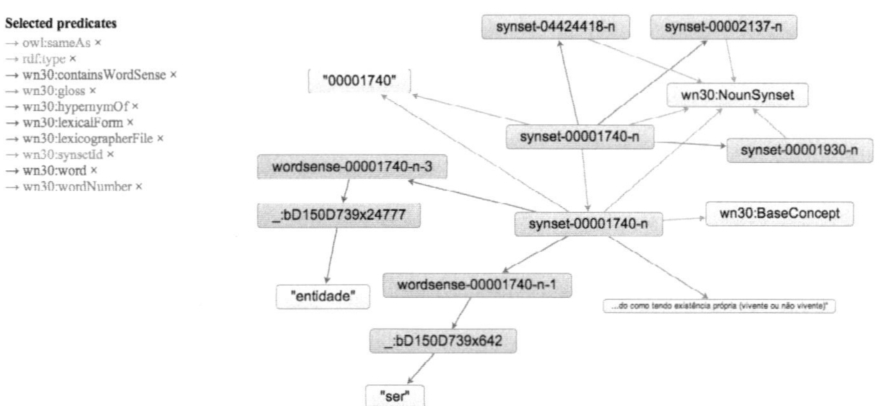


Figure 2: Synset 00001740-n and its neighbors in Princeton WordNet and OpenWordNet-PT

## 3 Extending the Coverage

The first version of OpenWN-PT was created using a semi-automated process drawing on UWN (de Melo and Weikum, 2009) and on manual revisions and gloss translations (Rademaker et al., 2012). Table 1 summarizes how OpenWN-PT has increased over the last two years. The number of synsets should be understood as the number of synsets with at least one Portuguese word. The sources of the new data were (Bond and Foster, 2013) and some manual addition of entries while working on projects that make use of the resource. These use cases are described later in Section 6.

| | 2011 | 2013 | increase |
|---|---|---|---|
| synsets | 41,810 | 43,895 | 5% |
| words | 52,220 | 54,125 | 3% |
| senses | 68,285 | 74,054 | 8% |

Table 1: OpenWN-PT's coverage development

Among resources that we can use to expand OpenWN-PT, we are considering (Dias-Da-Silva and de Moraes, 2003) and (Gonçalo Oliveira, 2013). Both projects are also concerned with the construction of a WordNet-like lexical resource for Portuguese. The former is more limited, offering around 19,888 synsets without any links to the Princeton WordNet and no relations between synsets, other than synonymy. The latter has already incorporated OpenWN-PT and is also encoded in RDF following the same vocabulary of (van Assem et al., 2006). This means that it should be straightfoward to obtain data from Onto.PT.

Besides the continuous work on increasing the number of translated synsets, we have also invested some time to expand the relations. All semantic relations in Princeton WordNet 3.0 are included in our RDF export. Figure 2 shows how one can navigate from a OpenWN-PT synset in the graph to the Princeton WordNet synset. Most semantic relations also apply to the Portuguese words. However, since the first version of OpenWN-PT came from the UWN, which does not have word sense-specific relations, we do not have any generic way to map the lexical relations (relations between word senses) from Princeton WordNet to specific words in OpenWN-PT.

Mainly because of the sentiment analysis project described later in Section 6, we focused in particular on antonomy relationships. Studying the plot in Figure 3, which shows the distribution of the number of senses per synset in both wordnets, it is clear that we could take advantage of the fact that the majority of synsets in both wordnets have only one sense to propagate the antonoym pairs in Princeton WordNet to the senses in OpenWN-PT with also only one sense. We search for synsets $A$ in Princeton WordNet with only one sense, where this specific sense is related to another sense that is also unique in its synset in Princeton WordNet, say $B$. We can propagate this antonymy relation to OpenWN-PT if synset $A$ and $B$ in OpenWN-PT also have only one sense each. Using this idea, we were able to add 707 antonymy relation instances to OpenWN-PT (only about 10% of the number of pairs in the antonym relation of Princeton WordNet 3.0). In the future, we plan to additionally use common prefixes like "des", "in" to match senses.

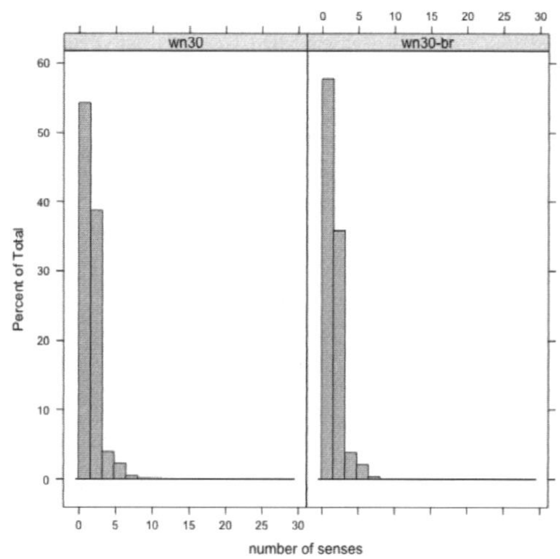


Figure 3: distribution of senses per synset

## 4 Nominalizations and NomLex-BR

Another extension of OpenWN-PT aims at incorporating links to connect deverbal nouns with their corresponding verbs. A sentence like "Alexander destroyed the city in 332 BC" can easily be parsed to obtain its semantic arguments, such as the agent (Alexander), the object destroyed (the city), and the time of the destruction (332 BC). In contrast, a sentence like "Alexander's destruction of the city happened in 332 BC" is typically much harder to interpret correctly. The latter sentence describes the same event with the same semantic arguments, but these arguments are usually much harder to obtain automatically from a syntactic parser, given that the event is described in terms of its nominalization *destruction* instead of its verbal form *destroy*. A proper handling of nominalizations (we are especially interested here in nominalizations of verbs, also called deverbal nouns) is important in numerous natural language understanding and inference tasks (Gurevich et al., 2008).

For English, NOMLEX (Macleod et al., 1998) has provided extensive descriptions of nominalizations. The original NOMLEX was constructed starting out with nominalizations with the suffixes *-ion*, *-ment* and *-er*, relying on frequent words in a corpus. NOMLEX sought not only to describe the possible complements for a nominalization, but also to relate the nominal complements to the arguments of the corresponding verb.

Our NomLex-BR project (Coelho et al., 2014) started with a manual translation of NOMLEX to Brazilian Portuguese, as NOMLEX is relatively small but still covers the most salient vocabulary. Many cases were very straightforward, due to the morphology of the words with similar nominalizer morphemes in both languages, e.g. pairs like *adjourn**ment**/adia**mento***, *benefic**iary**/benefici**ário***, *corro**sion**/ corro**são***.

Overall, we have created over 1,000 entries. These have been integrated into OpenWN-PT, which we hope will facilitate their use for linguistic research of the traditional kind. For now, most of the words from NomLex-BR are linked to `Word` instances of OpenWN-PT. Eventually, we would like to have entries of NomLex-BR linked to specific `WordSense` instances of OpenWN-PT to the extent possible. We are currently also devising strategies to create entries and model phenomena specific to Portuguese.

Incorporating NomLex-BR data into OpenWN-PT has shown itself useful in pinpointing some issues with the coherence and richness of OpenWN-PT. In particular, it seems that 20% of words in NomLex-BR (which were manually chosen) are missing in OpenWN-PT. For instance, the word *abasement* corresponds in NOMLEX to the verb *abase*, and thus we would like a similar correspondence between the Portuguese noun *aviltamento* and the verb *aviltar* (our suggested translations). However, while *abasement* in English is present in two synsets with Portuguese equivalents, the synsets for the verb *abase* have a repetition in Portuguese. OpenWN-PT simply has two synsets *humilhar*, *abaixar* and *humilhar*, *rebaixar*. The more common verb *humilhar* is repeated, while the uncommon *aviltar* was left out. Thus by verifying that verb-noun pairs in English are mapped to verb-noun pairs in Portuguese, we help ensure that the richness of synonyms in Portuguese is not lost in OpenWN-PT, which, being automatically derived from connectivity graphs, often gives preference to more commonly used words.

Other useful kinds of relationships between parts of speech (say the connections between adjectives and adverbs) are likely to also help to improve the accuracy and richness of our automatically derived resource. Altogether we reckon that by examining at random relationships that we know hold in the English WordNet in its translated Portuguese version, we should be able to both check the accuracy of OpenWordNet-PT and simultaneously investigate the parallelism between the two languages. From this perspective, one of the more interesting relationships, as far as knowledge representation is concerned, is the relationship of *entailment* between synsets. We have a goal of checking some 200 random English relationships in their translated forms as a way of measuring accuracy of the OpenWN-PT in the very immediate future.

## 5 Accuracy

Following the ideas of (Cruse, 1986), both (Vossen, 2002) and (Marrafa, 2002) used diagnostic templates of sentences to verify relations between synsets. We started a similar exercise. We choose six relations: `hypernymOf`, `memberHolonymOf`, `instanceOf`, `substanceHolonymOf`, `entails` and `causes`. For each of these relations, we randomly chose 30 pairs of synsets and then random words from each synset. Note that we had to keep drawing random synset relationships until both synsets included at least one Portuguese word. We ended up with 180 random sentences that we submitted to a linguist for manual verification (a single linguist to begin with). The linguist had to mark each sentence as being "correct", "wrong" or "dubious". As a result, we obtained 150 sentences marked as correct (83% of the sentences), 17 marked as wrong (one of the two words used to fill the template is probably placed in a wrong synset), and 13 marked as dubious (the linguist was not sure about the semantics of the sentence). In some cases, the linguist was able to give detailed feedback like indicating misspelt words or providing a more specific reason for why the sentence was considered wrong. There were also trivial pairs in which the same word was chosen from both synsets. We hope to improve our tests in these cases.

Finally, some data mining could also help us to improve the accuracy of OpenWN-PT. For instance, synsets with an uncommonly high number of senses or words with an unexpected number of senses should be reviewed.

## 6 Usage Reports

### 6.1 Word Sense Disambiguation

OpenWN-PT has been incorporated into Freeling (Padró and Stanilovsky, 2012), a well-known suite of NLP tools. With OpenWN-PT's data and Freeling's word sense disambiguation framework, a given Portuguese text can automatically be annotated with word senses, and we can use these annotations in the projects below.

### 6.2 Sentiment Analysis

We have been investigating the OpenWN-PT usage in one of our projects at IBM Research-Brazil. In this project the main concern is to gather the sentiment of microblogging posts about football matches in Portuguese in *real-time*. The most famous microblogging online social network is Twitter[3]. As of 2013, there are more than 550 million active registered users and 58 million tweets are posted per day on average. These tweets are short messages that people send to provide updates on their activities, observations, or other interesting content, directly or indirectly to others. In sports, for instance, a lot of sentiment is expressed during a game match. Recently there have been several approaches that tackle the problem of classifying tweet sentiments using supervised or semi-supervised machine learning approaches (Celikyilmaz et al., 2010; Bakliwal et al., 2012) or lexicon-based methods, which are mostly unsupervised approaches (Li et al., 2011; Hogenboom et al., 2013).

As people react to events and generate a large Twitter stream of data, it is impossible to manually process and analyze all these data during the event's lifespan. There are several challenges related to analyzing all this data as quickly as possible. First, the system must be reliable: no information should be lost. This means that a highly available system is called for, with redundancy and active fault tolerance mechanisms. Second, it must have a high throughput, which leads us to an infrastructure that allows parallelism. Thirdly, sentiment classifiers should be able to work with limited resources in both time and space. The training phase should handle an unbalanced distribution of sentiments and in real time, it should be adaptive.

OpenWN-PT, Princeton WordNet, and SentiWordNet (Baccianella et al., 2010) were used with the goal of assessing a Machine Learning-based sentiment analysis component integrated into the IBM InfoSphere Streams (ISS) platform. ISS was used to address the problem of handling large streaming Twitter data with availability and scalability in real-time. One main advantage of using OpenWN-PT and SentiWordNet during the development of the Machine Learning-based classifier was that we could start experimenting without training data. The experiment was possible because OpenWN-PT synsets are linked to Princeton WordNet synsets which, in turn, have their sentiment scores in SentiWordNet. In order to train the classifiers for sentiment analysis, we have built a training corpus comprising data posted on Twitter during four friendly matches of the Brazilian team in 2013. About 1 million tweets have been gathered from these games. We built an online interface for a collaborative labeling of the tweets with respect to seven different classes: Certainly Negative (CN), Negative (N), Maybe Negative (MN), Neutral (N), Maybe Positive (MP), Positive (P), and Certainly Positive (CP). Here, we divided both negative and positive sentiment into three more specific classes in order to capture the degree of confidence for which the user is able to associate that tweet with one of these two main sentiment classes. Another class, Don't Know (D), represents tweets for which the sentiment could not be identified by the user. We used this annotated corpus to train a Naïve Bayes classifier. OpenWN-PT and SentiWordNet were used to check the consistency of the annotations and to provide insights during the entire course of the project. Unfortunately, given the real-time characteristic of project we were not able to run both classifiers on all collected data. As future work, we plan to use OpenWN-PT to expand the training corpus. For instance, from the manually annotated tweets we

[3]See `http://twitter.com`

can produce others tweets with synonym words which are likely to retain the same semantics and thus also the same sentiment with high probability.

### 6.3 Historical Biographic Dictionary

The second project we used OpenWN-PT for is related to the digitalization of a dictionary of historical biographies. The Getulio Vargas Foundation (FGV) maintains the Brazilian Dictionary of Historical Biographies (DHBB), a resource with 7,000 entries, the majority of which are biographical entries about politicians in Brazil's recent history. The FGV would like to transform this static collection of entries into new methods of learning, teaching, acquiring, storing, and using information. Thus we decided that this knowledge would be more actionable if we could operate on it with semantic tools.

We used Freeling to automatically process this data by performing tokenization, sentence splitting, part-of-speech tagging, and finally word sense disambiguation with respect to OpenWN-PT. The DHBB corpus has a vocabulary size of 247,063 words. Table 2 shows the most frequent synsets in the corpus. The first line refers to the number of tokens without any associated synset. For instance, synset `00024720-n` refers to "the way something is with respect to its main attributes" and synset `08050678-n` is about "the organization that is the governing authority of a political unit" which, in OpenWN-PT, contains the word "governo". Note that synset `10467395-n` is about " the person who holds the office of head of state of the United States government", for which OpenWN-PT contains the word "presidente" (president) as one of its words.

| Var1 | Freq |
|---|---|
| - | 7343611 |
| 01835496-v | 76589 |
| 02604760-v | 47854 |
| 00047534-r | 30351 |
| 00065639-v | 28571 |
| 15202634-n | 27294 |
| 08050678-n | 26527 |
| 10467395-n | 23238 |
| 00024720-n | 23026 |
| 00118531-r | 20434 |

Table 2: Frequent synsets in DHBB entries

Table 3 presents some of the most frequent tokens (after lemmatization) that could not be found in OpenWN-PT. The entries are not very surprising, as our efforts have not focused on domain-specific vocabulary from the political/historical domain.[4] The exercise of running FreeLing on the DHBB entries gave us good insights about the coverage of OpenWN-PT and we plan to extend the translations of synsets from the most frequent missing words in OpenWN-PT to the less frequent ones.

| Token | Freq |
|---|---|
| [??:??/1/??:??.??:??] | 15294 |
| partido | 15292 |
| durante | 10962 |
| contra | 10180 |
| tornar | 9991 |
| militar | 9906 |
| outro | 9739 |
| segundo | 9577 |
| são_paulo | 8803 |
| estadual | 8727 |
| voto | 8287 |
| pmdb | 6615 |
| câm | 6271 |
| direito | 6170 |
| câmara_dos_deputados | 5849 |

Table 3: Frequent tokens without synset

## 7 Conclusion

We have discussed the implementation and some applications of OpenWordNet-PT, an open WordNet for Brazilian Portuguese. Recent improvements include better coverage and nominalization links connecting nouns and verbs. The resource has been used in developing a high-throughput commercial system as well as in a cultural heritage project, and we anticipate that numerous further applications will follow. The data is freely available from `http://github.com/arademaker/wordnet-br/` and via a SPARQL endpoint[5]. We are also grateful to Francis Bond for providing an online interface via the Open Multilingual Wordnet website[6].

[4] The first entry is the January encoded as a date template.

[5] See `http://logics.emap.fgv.br:10035`

[6] See `http://bit.ly/1aN0Xxd`

## References


Stefano Baccianella, Andrea Esuli, and Fabrizio Sebastiani. 2010. Sentiwordnet 3.0: An enhanced lexical resource for sentiment analysis and opinion mining. In *LREC*, volume 10, pages 2200–2204.

Akshat Bakliwal, Piyush Arora, Senthil Madhappan, Nikhil Kapre, Mukesh Singh, and Vasudeva Varma. 2012. Mining sentiments from tweets. In *Proc. of the 3rd Workshop in Computational Approaches to Subjectivity and Sentiment Analysis*, pages 11–18.

Tim Berners-Lee and Dan Connolly. 2011. Notation3 (N3): A readable RDF syntax. `http://bit.ly/1bYAs8y`.

Francis Bond and Ryan Foster. 2013. Linking and extending an open multilingual wordnet. In *Proc. of ACL 2013*, pages 1352–1362, Bulgaria. ACL.

Jordan Boyd-Graber, Christiane Fellbaum, Daniel Osherson, and Robert Schapire. 2006. Adding dense, weighted connections to wordnet. In *Proc. of the 3th Global WordNet Conf.*, pages 29–36, Jeju Island, Korea, January.

Asli Celikyilmaz, Dilek Hakkani-Tur, and Junlan Feng. 2010. Probabilistic model-based sentiment analysis of twitter messages. In *IEEE Spoken Language Technology Workshop (SLT)*, pages 79–84.

Christian Chiarcos, Sebastian Nordhoff, and Sebastian Hellmann. 2012. *Linked data in linguistics: Representing and connecting language data and language metadata*. Springer.

Livy Maria Real Coelho, Alexandre Rademaker, Valeria De Paiva, and Gerard de Melo. 2014. Embedding NomLex-BR nominalizations into OpenWordnet-PT. In *Proc. of Global WordNet Conf. 2014*. to appear.

Alan Cruse. 1986. *Lexical semantics*. Cambridge University Press.

Richard Cyganiak and David Wood. 2003. RDF 1.1 concepts and abstract syntax. Technical Report Draft 23 July 2013, W3C.

Gerard de Melo and Gerhard Weikum. 2008. Language as a foundation of the Semantic Web. In *Proc. of ISWC 2008*, volume 401.

Gerard de Melo and Gerhard Weikum. 2009. Towards a universal wordnet by learning from combined evidence. In *Proc. of CIKM 2009*, pages 513–522, New York, USA. ACM.

Gerard de Melo and Gerhard Weikum. 2010. MENTA: inducing multilingual taxonomies from Wikipedia. In *Proc. of CIKM 2010*, pages 1099–1108. ACM.

Bento Carlos Dias-Da-Silva and Helio Roberto de Moraes. 2003. A construçao de um thesaurus eletrônico para o português do brasil. *ALFA: Revista de Linguística*, 47(2).

Christiane Fellbaum. 1998. *WordNet: An electronic lexical database*. The MIT press.

Hugo Gonçalo Oliveira. 2013. *Onto.PT: Towards the Automatic Construction of a Lexical Ontology for Portuguese*. Ph.D. thesis, University of Coimbra.

Olga Gurevich, Richard Crouch, Tracy Holloway King, and Valeria de Paiva. 2008. Deverbal nouns in knowledge representation. *J. Log. and Comput.*, 18(3):385–404.

Steve Harris and Andy Seaborne. 2013. SPARQL 1.1 query language. Technical Report W3C Recommendation 21 March 2013, W3C.

Pascal Hitzler, Markus Krotzsch, Bijan Parsia, Peter F. Patel-Schneider, and Sebastian Rudolph. 2012. OWL 2 web ontology language primer. Technical Report W3C Rec 11 Dec 2012, W3C.

Alexander Hogenboom, Daniella Bal, Flavius Frasincar, Malissa Bal, Franciska de Jong, and Uzay Kaymak. 2013. Exploiting emoticons in sentiment analysis. In *Proc. of the ACM Symposium on Applied Computing*, pages 703–710, New York, NY, USA. ACM.

Lin Li, Yunqing Xia, and Pengzhou Zhang. 2011. An unsupervised approach to sentiment word extraction in complex sentiment analysis. *International Journal of Knowledge and Language Processing*, 2(1).

Catherine Macleod, Ralph Grishman, Adam Meyers, Leslie Barret, and Ruth Reeves. 1998. Nomlex: A lexicon of nominalizations. In *Proc. of Euralex 1998*, pages 187–193, Liege, Belgium.

Bernardo Magnini and Gabriela Cavaglia. 2000. Integrating subject field codes into WordNet. In *Proc. of LREC*, pages 1413–1418.

Palmira Marrafa. 2002. Portuguese wordnet: general architecture and internal semantic relations. *DELTA: Documentação de Estudos em Lingüística Teórica e Aplicada*, 18(SPE):131–146.

Lluís Padró and Evgeny Stanilovsky. 2012. Freeling 3.0: Towards wider multilinguality. In *Proc. of the 8th Intern. Conf. on Language Resources and Evaluation (LREC'12)*, pages 23–25, Istanbul, Turkey, may.

Alexandre Rademaker, Valeria De Paiva, and Gerard de Melo. 2012. Openwordnet-pt: An open brazilian wordnet for reasoning. In *Proc. of COLING 2012*, pages 353–360, Mumbai.

Mark van Assem, Aldo Gangemi, and Guus Schreiber. 2006. RDF/OWL representation of WordNet. Technical Report W3C Working Draft 19 June 2006, W3C. `http://bit.ly/1jtGsA8`.

Piek Vossen. 2002. EuroWordNet general document. Technical Report Version 3 Final July 1, University of Amsterdam.

# Issues in building English-Chinese parallel corpora with WordNets

**Francis Bond** and **Shan Wang**

Linguistics and Multilingual Studies,
**Nanyang Technological University**
bond@ieee.org,wangshanstar@gmail.com

## Abstract

We discuss some of the issues in producing sense-tagged parallel corpora: including pre-processing, adding new entries and linking. We have preliminary results for three genres: stories, essays and tourism web pages, in both Chinese and English.

## 1 Introduction

Since the first release of the Princeton WordNet (PWN) (Fellbaum, 1998) there has been a great increase in the size and number of wordnets created (Bond and Paik, 2012). Further, there has been an empirical revolution in natural language processing (Vanderwende and Menezes, 2005), with machine learning based on annotated corpora dominating the field. Given this, we would expect to see a flowering of sense annotated corpora. However, they are still relatively rare and small in size compared to part-of-speech and tree banked corpora (Petrolito and Bond, 2014).

In this paper we describe ongoing work to sense annotate data in two languages (English and Chinese), using texts provided by the *Nanyang Technological University Multilingual Corpus* (NTU-MC: Tan and Bond, 2012). We discuss some of the problems involved with pre-processing (Section 3), monolingual sense tagging (Section 4) and multi-lingually linking the data (Section 5). We then discuss some ideas to improve the annotation process (Section 6) and conclude.

## 2 Related Research

Sense-tagged parallel corpora are an important resource for NLP, contrastive linguistics and bilingual lexicography. However, there are few multilingual sense tagged corpora. One notable exception is the MultiSemCor (Pianta et al., 2002). Taking the English SemCor (Landes et al., 1998) as a source, first Italian, then Romanian and Japanese translations have been made. The leading project was the Italian SemCor with 268,905 Italian tokens and 258,499 English tokens (Pianta et al., 2002). This was followed by the Romanian SemCor with 175,603 tokens in Romanian matched with 178,499 English tokens (Lupu et al., 2005). Finally, the Japanese SemCor has senses projected across from English. Of the 150,555 content words, 58,265 are sense tagged either as monosemous words or by projecting from the English annotation (Bond et al., 2012).

Some universities have devoted efforts to construct Chinese-English parallel corpora, such as Peking University, Tsinghua University and Chinese Academy of Sciences (Chang et al., 2003; Chang, 2004), Xiamen University (Chen et al., 2005, 2006), Beijing Foreign Studies University (Wang, 2012). However, none of them are sensed tagged or aligned at word level. Chinese-English word aligned corpora are available as part of many statistical machine translation projects, but we wanted to work with a multilingual corpus, not just two languages.

Rather than translate new data, we took advantage of an existing multilingual corpus containing eight languages: English (eng), Mandarin Chinese (cmn), Japanese (jpn), Indonesian (ind), Korean, Arabic, Vietnamese and Thai (Tan and Bond, 2012). Parallel data in English, Chinese, Japanese, and Indonesian are selected for further annotation, which is composed of three genres: short stories, essays and tourism.

The Princeton Wordnet is an important resource in natural language processing, psychology, and language studies. It was developed from 1985 at Princeton University. Nouns, verbs, adjective and adverbs were grouped into synsets and linked through semantic relation (Fellbaum, 1998). We used Southeast University's Chinese Wordnet to tag the Chinese part (SEW: Xu et al., 2008),[1] and are now in the process of switching to the Chinese Open Wordnet (COW: Wang and Bond, 2013).[2]

## 3 Pre-processing the Corpus

In this paper we talk only about the Chinese and English text from the short story, essay and tourism genres of the NTU-MC, although we are also cooperating with other work on tagging Indonesian and Japanese (Bond et al., 2013). The short stories are two Sherlock Holmes' Adventures (*The Adventure of the Dancing Men* and *The Adventure of the Speckled Band*), the essay is *The Cathedral and the Bazaar* (Raymond, 1999) and the tourism data is from the Singapore tourist board's web pages (Singapore Tourist Board, 2012). The corpus sizes are shown in Table 1. We show the number of sentences, words and concepts (open class words taggable with synsets).

### 3.1 Pre-processing with NLP Tools

For English, Freeling (Padró et al., 2010) was run with number processing, name recognition, multi-words, dates and quantities all turned off. Turning them on gave quite aggressive lemmatization: for example *a bit* in *a bit of honest money* was lemmatized to *IF_bit:1* "one bit of information". We did very minimal preprocessing: for example rewriting three hyphens --- to mdash —. We had some problems with lemmatization of hyphenated expressions and mdashes: *white-counterpaned* which we would like to treat as two lemmas (*white* and *counterpane*) and *not—because* which should be treated as *not* and *because*. We ended up correcting many of these by hand.

For Chinese, we segmented and tagged with the Stanford NLP tools (Chang et al., 2008).[3] We did some post-processing: many punctuation marks were not recognized (such as: ［〔"()--®{"’), these we corrected with a script after the initial POS tagging. We also lemmatized plural-marked nouns, such as 学生+们 *xuéshēng+men* "student+s" to 学生 *xuéshēng* "student". This only occurs for 18 words.[4] The only other lemmatization we did for Chinese was for reduplicated words, where the lemma is the un-duplicated form.

Finally, we preprocess the Chinese wordnet by running it through the same segmenter, and storing the segmented forms as well.

| | POS | English | Chinese |
|---|---|---|---|
| n | noun | billiard | 台球 *táiqiú* |
| v | verb | convey | 传达 *chuándá* |
| a | adjective | curious | 奇特 *qítè* |
| r | adverb | finally | 最后 *zuìhòu* |

Table 2: Parts of Speech

### 3.2 Identifying Concepts

We add potential concepts as a separate layer, linked to the words (like terms in KAF: Bosma et al., 2009).

We identify concepts in two ways: words or multi-word expressions (MWEs) that are in wordnet or any single open class words not yet matched (these are tagged as **unknown**).

A word may potentially be part of multiple concepts (single and multi-word). For example *distribution* in *Gaussian or Poisson distributions* is marked as being part of ***Gaussian distribution***, ***Poisson distribution*** and ***distribution***. Concepts can be discontinuous (like *Gaussian distribution* above), we allow up to three extra words to intervene. After preliminary trials, we decided to ignore POS tags when matching words to concepts (see Section 3.4 for more discussion).

Our concepts comprise of single content words and MWE. Words fall into four major categories: n, v, a, r, following the standard wordnet structure. We show examples in Table 2.

Various heuristics were employed to make the matching flexible. For single word entries in wordnet, we match on lemmas, not using the wordnet form variants. If we can find no match for the lemma, then we try to match the surface form. All matching is done with lower-cased entries. For English, we further process entries with hyphens to produce extra forms without the hyphen: ***data-base*** will also match ***database*** and ***data base***.

For multiword expressions, we index them by the first token. If that matches either lemma or

[1] At the beginning of our project we tested a small sample of Chinese words by looking them up in both SEW and the Sinica Bilingual Ontological Wordnet (Huang et al., 2004) and found SEW had slightly better coverage.

[2] COW is available at `http://compling.hss.ntu.edu.sg/cow/`.

[3] We compared several free Chinese morphological analyzers and found this the most consistent.

[4] In some segmentation standards these would be two tokens, the Chinese Penn Treebank consistently treats these as one token (Xia, 2000).

| Genre | English | | | Chinese | | |
|---|---|---|---|---|---|---|
| | Sents | Words | Concepts | Sents | Words | Concepts |
| Essay | 769 | 18,693 | 10,435 | 816 | 18,216 | 11,365 |
| Story | 1,198 | 22,818 | 11,340 | 1,226 | 23,758 | 12,630 |
| Tourism | 2,988 | 74,332 | 40,844 | 3,280 | 63,905 | 43,164 |

Table 1: Size of the Corpora

surface form we then continue to match the remaining tokens, allowing up to three intervening tokens. We must check both surface and lemmas to deal with cases such as ***programming language*** which is lemmatized to $program_{VV}$ $language_{NN}$. Other wordnet taggers we tested have missed many MWEs, for example, Freeling will not recognize ***look up*** in *look the word up*.

Sag et al. (2002) classified MWE into lexicalized phrases and institutionalized phrases. The former can be grouped into fixed expressions, semi-fixed expressions and syntactically-flexible expressions; the latter includes anti-collocations and collocations. All of these types are found in our corpus, as shown in Table 3.

Our matching is still imperfect. It is too loose for fixed expressions: for example, there will never be anything (except for expletives, which can also come within words) between *ad* and *hoc* (or *for* and *example*). It therefore matches many MWEs which the annotators need to discard. It is too rigid for syntactically-flexible expressions, which can have their order changed (e.g. by passivization) and thus misses some entries.

### 3.3 Distribution of Concepts

Table 4 shows the number of concepts in the three genres of essay, story and tourism for both Chinese and English. In each of the three subcorpora, Chinese has more concepts than English, possibly because our tagging of unknown words is less precise. We show how many are found in the wordnets (in WN: PWN for English, SEW for Chinese): the remainder are unknown open class words. The coverage is best for the stories and slightly worse for the essay (which has many technical terms, such as *developer* "one who programs computers or designs software"). It is much worse for the Singapore tourist data, which introduces many new concepts, such as *ikan bilis* "an Indonesian dish made with fried anchovies and peanuts", *mooncake* "a kind of Chinese cake eaten around the Autumn festival", *Merlion* "the statue that symbolizes Singapore" and many more. The coverage is worse for Chinese, as the wordnet is not as well developed. In addition, there are many words lexicalized in Chinese but not in English, for example, 去年 *qùnián* 'last year'. Further, there are many English foreign words in the tourism corpus, which makes the coverage even worse. Finally we show the number of concepts for which the annotators chose a single wordnet sense. Not all untagged words should be tagged however: they may be mis-identified as MWEs or open class words, named entities, mis-tokenizations or concepts not currently in wordnet.

### 3.4 Part of Speech Issues

For our tagging interface, we looked up wordnet using the lemma of a word. This caused problems when the word was mis-tagged giving the wrong lemma. The well-known problematic cases of present and past-participles. For example, *drawing* in *"Have you that fresh drawing?"* was tagged as VBG with lemma ***draw*** although it should have been ***drawing*** (NN). In this case, the annotators have the option of specifying the noun synset, but the first version of our tool currently did not allow them to fix the POS and lemma.[5] In general, the annotators found distinguishing between gerunds, adjective and participles hard. For example in *dancing men* (referring to pictures of little men that look as though they are dancing): should this be the noun $\textbf{\textit{dancing}}_{n:1}$ "making a series of rhythmical steps (and movements) in time to music" or the verb $\textbf{\textit{dance}}_{v:2}$ "move in a pattern; usually to musical accompaniment"? These are linked by a derivational link, so are clearly related. We decided on a general strategy and tried to make the decision process as clear as possible in the tagging guidelines, revising them with more examples. The annotators should first check if the context makes the word clearly an adjective, verb or noun, and if so pick the appropriate sense based on this. If the word is ambiguous in context, first pre-

[5]The tool now allows the annotators to change the lemma.

| | MWE | English | Chinese |
|---|---|---|---|
| lexicalized | fixed | point of view | 不容置疑 bùróng zhìyí 'unquestionable' |
| | semi-fixed | New York police bureau | 乡村医生 xiāngcūn yīshēng 'country doctor' |
| | syntactically-flexible | make sense | 打电报 dǎ diànbào 'send a telegram' |
| institutionalized | collocations | power-making | 白发苍苍 bái fà cāngcāng 'white-haired' |

Table 3: Multi-word expression types

| Genre | English | | | | | Chinese | | | | |
|---|---|---|---|---|---|---|---|---|---|---|
| | Concepts | in WN | % | Tagged | % | Concepts | in WN | % | Tagged | % |
| Essay | 10,435 | 9,588 | 91.9 | 8,607 | 82.5 | 11,365 | 8,620 | 75.8 | 8,773 | 77.2 |
| Story | 11,340 | 10,761 | 94.9 | 9,550 | 84.2 | 12,630 | 9,521 | 75.4 | 8,737 | 69.2 |
| Tourism | 40,844 | 35,979 | 88.1 | 32,990 | 80.8 | 43,164 | 23,699 | 54.9 | 18,663 | 43.2 |

Table 4: Distribution of Concepts and Tags

| tag \ pos | n | v | a | r | x |
|---|---|---|---|---|---|
| n | 12,426 | 970 | 140 | 129 | 93 |
| v | 709 | 7,950 | 14 | 77 | 19 |
| a | 1,750 | 2,092 | 1,206 | 836 | 453 |
| r | 315 | 390 | 98 | 4,504 | 191 |

Table 5: Confusion Matrix: POS vs Tag (Chinese)

| tag \ pos | n | v | a | r | x |
|---|---|---|---|---|---|
| n | 20,763 | 903 | 481 | 151 | 249 |
| v | 538 | 11,686 | 58 | 12 | 20 |
| a | 1,085 | 481 | 7,427 | 312 | 424 |
| r | 75 | 17 | 357 | 4,171 | 347 |

Table 6: Confusion Matrix: POS vs Tag (English)

fer an adjective if it exists, then verb, then noun. Similar guidelines were written for other confusing cases.

We show the confusion matrices of wordnet part of speech versus lemmatizer tag (simplified to the four wordnet parts of speech and other (**x**) for Chinese and English (for single word lemmas) in Tables 5 and 6 respectively. A common error was NN in English tagged as **a**: this included examples such as ***Chinese***, ***open-source*** and ***last***.

In general, the POS tagger could not be relied on. The annotators picked a different tag from the system 24.1% of the time for Chinese and 11.1% of the time for English. This shows how poorly POS taggers perform outside the domains they are trained on: real-world accuracy is between 80 and 90%.

## 4 Monolingual Sense Tagging

Our annotators (for both the monolingual and cross-lingual sense tagging) were undergraduate students (and recent graduates) from the linguistics and multilingual studies division at Nanyang Technological University. All were bilingual Chinese-English speakers and several had good command of Japanese. Most had experience tagging as part of the core semantics class, where a tagging exercise is used to teach about lexical semantics.

The annotators chose between existing wordnet senses based on the lemma senses or a number of meta-tags: **e, s, m, p, u**. The expectation was that after the tagging, there would be a round of wordnet extension, and then the words with new wordnet entries would be tagged once more.

Their meaning is explained below, and their distribution is given in Table 7.

- Problems in the pre-processing:

  **p** POS that should not be tagged (article, modal, preposition, ...)

  **e** error in tokenization
  今 日*jīn rì* should be 今日*jīnrì* "today"
  *three-toed* should be *three - toed*

- Problems with wordnet:

  **s** missing sense (not in wordnet)
  *I program in python* "the computer language"
  COMMENT: add link to existing synset <06898352-n "programming language"

  **u** lemma not in wordnet but POS open class (tagged automatically)
  COMMENT: add or link to existing synset

**m** Multiword
(i) if the lemma is a multiword, this tag means it is not appropriate;
(ii) if the lemma is single-word, this tag means it should be part of a multiword.

The first two errors are those where the system has wrongly offered a word to be tagged, or the morphological processing has failed in some way. Because the annotators had no training in part of speech tagging, they were instructed to note the error (with a comment is possible) and these would be fixed and then re-tagged later. We have not done a full analysis, but a preliminary investigation suggests that modal auxiliaries and prepositions were the most common **p** and **e** tags. In general the annotators found it hard to distinguish between **p** and **e**: we are trying to make the guidelines clearer. The distinguishing criteria should be **e** means that the annotation should be fixed in some way, while **p** just means there is no need to annotate: the annotators had trouble making this distinction. The annotators often marked existential *there* and exclamatives (like *ah!*) as **s** "should add to wordnet", we have updated the tagging guidelines to make this clearer. Although the Penn treebank tag set does distinguish between existential and referential *there*, we check both anyway as the pos tagging is unreliable. However, to speed up tagging, because existential *there* and preposition *in* are so often **p** we pre-mark these entries as **p** before annotation. Further, although the tags do not distinguish between auxiliaries and main verbs, we found it fairly easy to identify them with simple patterns: such as, V:[***have***|***be***] V:VBG|VBN. We used these patterns to also pre-mark these entries as **p**.

Those marked with **s** and **u** are missed cases in either PWN or SEW. We can see from Table 7 that the Chinese wordnet (SEW) has many more missed senses and lemmas compared to PWN. This is one reason that we are switching to the Chinese Open Wordnet (COW) which has better accuracy and coverage (Wang and Bond, 2013).

One goal of the annotation is to improve the wordnets by adding the new words and senses, and we are working on this in parallel with the annotation. Anything tagged **s** or **u** is thus a possible new addition to wordnet. There were 1,375 such tags for English and 24,594 for Chinese. However, if we look at the distinct lemmas, then there are far fewer: 799 for English and 7,691 for Chinese. This gives us a rough estimate of how many new entries need to be created.

| Tag | % | Type (Example) |
|---|---|---|
| p | 38 | Shouldn't be tagged (***ah***) |
| m | 10 | Part of known multiword (***send for***) |
| e | 6 | Wrong tokenization/lemmatization ***uptimes*** → ***uptime*** |
| tag | 14 | Existing sense is ok (***idea***$_{n:1}$) |
| u | 16 | New lemma (***matter***$_{n:1}$) |
| s | 16 | New synset and lemma (***catlike***$_{n:1}$) |

Table 8: Real Distribution of New Candidates

We looked at a random sample of 50 entries (tokens) marked **s** or **u** and found the situation encouraging, only 30% really required new entries. We summarize the results in Table 8, giving the correct tag, percentage, explanation and example.

As discussed above, some exclamatives, existentials and other things that should not be tagged were marked with **s**. More problematically, the annotators often marked *Watson* (Sherlock Holmes's companion) with *s*, although they had been instructed to mark proper names with **p**. Here, although technically an error, we are sympathetic: ***Sherlock Holmes*** is in wordnet, and ***John Watson*** seems prominent enough to add.

In some cases, even where they had correctly marked the multiword, they marked the single words as **s** not **m**. This is just an error. For example in (1), ***send for***$_{v:1}$ was correctly annotated, and *send* should be marked as **m** "part of multiword" rather than **s**.

(1) *They had at once sent for the doctor and for the constable.*

In some cases the lemmatizer had incorrectly lemmatized the word: *uptimes* in (2) should be lemmatized as ***uptime***, which is in wordnet "period of time when something (as a machine or factory) is functioning and available for use". This should have been tagged with **e** and the correct lemma and tag given in the comments.

(2) *[...] its continuous uptimes spanning months or even years.*

In a few cases (tag), we judged that an existing sense could be used. For example, in (3), the annotator wanted to tag it with ***concept***$_{n:1}$ "abstract or general idea inferred or derived from specific instances", but we judged that it was Ok as the hypernym ***idea***$_{n:1}$ "the content of cognition; the main

| Genre | English | | | | | Chinese | | | | |
|---|---|---|---|---|---|---|---|---|---|---|
| | p | e | s | u | m | p | e | s | u | m |
| Essay | 552 | 354 | 258 | 189 | 418 | 202 | 40 | 178 | 1,846 | 167 |
| Story | 825 | 186 | 185 | 12 | 495 | 459 | 300 | 1,263 | 1,041 | 524 |
| Tourism | 1,630 | 954 | 286 | 445 | 2,278 | 937 | 431 | 2,769 | 17,497 | 494 |

Table 7: Distribution of Meta-Tags

thing you are thinking about" which has as its example: *it was not a good idea*. In some cases, we thought that the definition should be made clearer (often less dogmatic) in order to make the scope of the sense wider. For example in (4), wordnet has ***backer***$_{n:1}$ "invests in a theatrical production", as a hyponym of ***patron***$_{n:1}$. We feel this could be expanded to "a person who invests in something, such as a theatrical production", avoiding the construction of a new sense.

(3) *Though fetchpop had some good original ideas in it (such as its background-daemon mode)*

(4) *[. . . ] the open-source idea has scored successes and found backers elsewhere.*

Finally, there were some genuinely new senses. *The Cathedral and the Bazaar* made many references to *developers* and *co-developers*. ***developer*** is almost certainly derived from ***develop***$_{v:1}$ "make something new, such as a product or a mental or artistic creation" and ***co-developer*** from there. Some were rare uses of existing words as in (5), where *matter* meaning ***measure***$_{n:1}$ "how much there is or how many there are of something that you can quantify" is an established if old-fashioned use, some were common extensions of existing entries, as in (6), where *toolkit* refers to the skills a person possesses rather than the physical ***tool kit***$_{n:1}$ "a set of carpenter's tools", and should be a synonym for ***bag of tricks***$_{n:1}$ "supply of ways of accomplishing something".

(5) *[. . . ] my people have been at Riding Thorpe for a matter of five centuries [. . . ]*

(6) *[. . . ] it increases the probability that someone's toolkit will be matched to the problem [. . . ]*

## 5 Cross-lingual Annotation

For the second round of annotation, instead of going over the monolingual texts again, we decided to look at the sense annotation in the translation context.

For each sentence, we automatically linked words with either: the same concept (=); if still unlinked then a matching hypernym or hyponym (<, >); if still unlinked then the same lemma (this was useful even between English and Chinese as technical terms (such as ***Linux***) were often left in the Latin alphabet). We did not use word-to-word tags in the tagging because (i) they were unavailable and (ii) we already had the monolingual tags on each side, so we did not need to project the tags. In future work, we would like to investigate the use of word-links (following the lead of Bentivogli and Pianta (2005)).

The annotators then went through sentence-pair by sentence-pair and (i) checked existing links then (ii) tried to link unlinked concepts. They categorized links into the six types shown in Table 9. The annotators were instructed not to overthink the decision as to link-type: we can recalculate the distinctions using the wordnet structure.

This annotation has only been completed for the Essay and Story genres, we show the numbers of links, and the total number of taggable concepts, in Table 10. The proportion of things linked is very low: 61% for the stories and 39% for the essay. We have automatically calculated the types of links: if the tag is exactly the same, then =; hyponyms and hypernyms are shown with < and >; derivationally related forms and pertainyms found in wordnet with **d**; other linked tags with different parts-of-speech with **D**; holonyms with **m**; meronyms with **M**; antonyms found in wordnet with **!**; those the annotator marked as antonyms but we could not find in wordnet with # and everything else with ∼. The large number of part-of-speech mismatches suggests that we still do not have all the cross part-of-speech links in wordnet that we should.

An example of why things remain unlinked is shown in (7): concepts are marked with subscripts, linked concepts have the same subscript and are upper case. ***way*** and ***question*** can be linked, but ***put*** and ***answer*** can not, even though the transla-

| Symbol | Explanation | English | Chinese |
|---|---|---|---|
| = | same synset | about | 大约 *dàyuē* "about" |
| < | hyponym | armchair | 椅子 *yǐzi* "chair" |
| > | hypernym | body | 遗体 *yítǐ* "remains" |
| ∼ | lexically linked | absorb | 全神贯注 *quánshénguànzhù* "with breathless interest" |
| ≈ | pragmatically linked | absurdly | 太 *tài* "excessively" |
| ! | antonym | easy | 难 *nán* "difficult" |
| # | weak antonym | miss | 打中 *dǎ zhòng* "hit" |

Table 9: Link Types with Examples

| Link | Story | | Essay | |
|---|---|---|---|---|
| | # | % | # | % |
| = | 2,642 | 41.7 | 2,155 | 48.9 |
| < | 107 | 1.7 | 31 | 0.7 |
| > | 205 | 3.2 | 123 | 2.8 |
| ∼ | 2184 | 34.5 | 1464 | 33.2 |
| d | 166 | 2.6 | 72 | 1.6 |
| D | 1,149 | 18.1 | 624 | 14.2 |
| m | 16 | 0.3 | 1 | 0.0 |
| M | 15 | 0.2 | 5 | 0.1 |
| ! | 2 | 0.0 | 0 | 0.0 |
| # | 23 | 0.4 | 7 | 0.2 |
| Total | 6,336 | 100.0 | 4,407 | 100.0 |
| Concepts | 10,435 | | 11,340 | |

Table 10: Number of Links

tion clearly has the same meaning. In general *The Cathedral and the Bazaar* had more complicated prose than the stories, and the translations were less well aligned. Arguably, ***put*** could be linked to wèn with ≈ but the annotator did not do so.

(7) $\text{Put}_a$ that way,$_B$ the $\text{question}_c$ $\text{answers}_D$ itself.

这样$_B$ 一 问$_e$， 答案$_D$ 自明$_f$。
zhèyàng yī wèn, dá'àn zìmíng.
like this one ask, answer self-evident

"Asking like this, the answer is self-evident."

Often, there were differences in lexicalization that made the question of what to link difficult. For example in (8), 前额 *qián'é* "forehead" is lexicalized, and it matches to a unit that is not in PWN, "the front of ones brain". This is almost certainly not lexicalized in English. So we end up linking *qián'é* to ***brain*** with ≈ and then ***front*** has nothing to link to. We need to be able to link words to phrases without necessarily adding the phrases to the wordnets.

(8) The bullet had passed through the front of her brain.

子弹 是 从 她的 前额 打 进去
Zǐdàn shì cóng tāde qián'é dǎ jìnqù
bullet is from her forehead shoot enter
的。
de.

"The bullet was shot in from her forehead"

## 6 Discussion and Further Work

We have been gradually improving the tagging guidelines as we continue with the annotation, and will make these available online along with the corpus.[6] In particular, we are adding more examples for each case. We benefited from the cheat sheet and guidelines produced for the Gloss Corpus (Fellbaum pc.) and hope our guidelines can help other people. With this in mind, we are trying to keep separate, as far as possible, tool-specific procedures and general tagging guidelines.

Many of the unknown words, especially for our first attempt, were in fact words that are in wordnet with minor typographical variations: for example *tool kit* in wordnet as ***toolkit***.[7] We have added various heuristics to improve the look up within wordnet. We also started to work on improving the tokenization, but decided this was too large a task. Instead, we are looking at exploiting a more semantically aware tokenizer (Dridan and Oepen, 2012). Similarly for Chinese, we are comparing a wider variety of tokenizers. One reviewer suggested that there are more accurate proprietary pos taggers and segmenters available for Chinese. Unfortunately, the fact that they are not freely available means that we cannot test them to see if they are better. Our experience with English,

[6]The corpus and guidelines are available at `http://compling.hss.ntu.edu.sg/ntumc/`.

[7]Although not with the desired sense.

where we have more experience with state-of-the-art systems is that (i) they do not do well with out-of-domain data (a well-known failing) and (ii) they often do not mark distinctions important for the sense tagging (for example, the difference between main and auxiliary verbs). We therefore prefer to work with open-source systems that we can evaluate and potentially improve.

In this paper, we mainly discuss a breadth first approach, where we are trying to increase the coverage uniformly to cover all words. We do not report on the inter-annotator agreement, as the first rounds of tagging (which we report on here) are not the final annotation: all tags are checked once more as we do the cross-lingual annotation, and it is too expensive to do this multiple times.

We are also using the corpora as a test-bed to look at individual phenomena of interest in detail, including the use of Chinese traditional idiomatic expressions (成语 *chéngyǔ*), English possessive idioms (*X looses X's head*) and the differences in pronoun distribution across languages.

## 7 Conclusions

This paper presents preliminary results from an ongoing project to construct large-scale sense-tagged parallel corpora. The annotation scheme is divided into two phrases: monolingual sense annotation and multilingual concept alignment. We look at some of the issues raised for Chinese and English annotation of text in three genres. All annotated corpora will be made freely available, in addition, the changes made to the wordnets will be released through the individual wordnet projects.

### Acknowledgments

This research was supported in part by the MOE Tier 1 grant *Shifted in Translation — An Empirical Study of Meaning Change across Languages*. We would like to thank our annotators: En Jia Chee, Eshley Gao, Jeanette Tan, Hui Ting, Wanxuan Wang, and Hazel Wen. Finally, would like to thank Huizhen Wang for her many helpful discussions.

## References

Luisa Bentivogli and Emanuele Pianta. 2005. Exploiting parallel texts in the creation of multilingual semantically annotated resources: the multisemcor corpus. *Natural Language Engineering*, 11(3):247–261.

Francis Bond, Timothy Baldwin, Richard Fothergill, and Kiyotaka Uchimoto. 2012. Japanese SemCor: A sense-tagged corpus of Japanese. In *Proceedings of the 6th Global WordNet Conference (GWC 2012)*, pages 56–63. Matsue.

Francis Bond and Kyonghee Paik. 2012. A survey of wordnets and their licenses. In *Proceedings of the 6th Global WordNet Conference (GWC 2012)*. Matsue. 64–71.

Francis Bond, Shan Wang, Eshley Huini Gao, Hazel Shuwen Mok, and Jeanette Yiwen Tan. 2013. Developing parallel sense-tagged corpora with wordnets. In *Proceedings of the 7th Linguistic Annotation Workshop and Interoperability with Discourse (LAW 2013)*, pages 149–158. Sofia. URL `http://www.aclweb.org/anthology/W13-2319`.

Wauter Bosma, Piek Vossen, Aitor Soroa, German Rigau, Maurizio Tesconi, Andrea Marchetti, Monica Monachini, and Carlo Aliprandi. 2009. KAF: a generic semantic annotation format. In *Proceedings of the 5th International Conference on Generative Approaches to the Lexicon (GL 2009)*. Pisa.

Baobao Chang. 2004. Chinese-English parallel corpus construction and its application. In *Proceedings of The 18th Pacific Asia Conference on Language, Information and Computation*, pages 283–290. Waseda University, Tokyo.

Baobao Chang, Weidong Zhan, and huarui Zhang. 2003. The construction and management of a bilingual corpus used for Chinese-English machine translation (面向汉英机器翻译的双语语料库的建设及其管理). *Terminology Standardization & Information Technology (术语标准化与信息技术)*, (1):28–31.

Pi-Chuan Chang, Michel Galley, and Christopher D. Manning. 2008. Optimizing Chinese word segmentation for machine translation performance. In *ACL Third Workshop on Statistical Machine Translation*.

Yidong Chen, Xiaodong Shi, and Changle Zhou. 2006. Research on filtering parallel corpus: A ranking model (平行语料库处理初探:一种排序模型). *Journal Of Chinese Information Processing*, 20(z1).

Yidong Chen, Xiaodong Shi, Changle Zhou, and Qing-Yang Hong. 2005. A model for ranking sentence pairs in parallel corpora. In *Machine Learning and Cybernetics, 2005. Proceedings of 2005 International Conference on*, volume 6, pages 3820–3823. IEEE.

Rebecca Dridan and Stephan Oepen. 2012. Tokenization: Returning to a long solved problem: A survey, contrastive experiment, recommendations, and toolkit. In *Proceedings of the 50th Annual Meeting of the Association for Computational Linguistics (Volume 2: Short Papers)*, pages 378–382. Association for Computational Linguistics, Jeju Island, Korea. URL `http://www.aclweb.org/anthology/P12-2074`.

Christine Fellbaum, editor. 1998. *WordNet: An Electronic Lexical Database*. MIT Press.

Chu-Ren Huang, RU-Yng Chang, and Shiang-Bin Lee. 2004. Sinica BOW: integrating bilingual WordNet and SUMO ontology. In *Proceedings of the Fourth International Language Resources and Evaluation (LREC 2004)*, pages 1553–1556.

Shari Landes, Claudia Leacock, and Christiane Fellbaum. 1998. Building semantic concordances. In Fellbaum (1998), chapter 8, pages 199–216.

Monica Lupu, Diana Trandabat, and Maria Husarciuc. 2005. A Romanian semcor aligned to the English and Italian multisemcor. In *Proceedings 1st ROMANCE FrameNet Workshop at EUROLAN 2005 Summer School*, pages 20–27. EUROLAN, Cluj-Napoca, Romania.

Lluís Padró, Miquel Collado, Samuel Reese, Marina Lloberes, and Irene Castellón. 2010. Freeling 2.1: Five years of open-source language processing tools. In *Proceedings of 7th Language Resources and Evaluation Conference (LREC 2010)*. La Valletta. URL `http://nlp.lsi.upc.edu/freeling`.

Tommaso Petrolito and Francis Bond. 2014. A survey of wordnet annotated corpora. In *Proceedings of the 7th Global WordNet Conference (GWC 2014)*. Tartu. (this volume).

Emanuele Pianta, Luisa Bentivogli, and Christian Girardi. 2002. Multiwordnet: Developing an aligned multilingual database. In *In Proceedings of the First International Conference on Global WordNet*, pages 293–302. Mysore, India.

Eric S. Raymond. 1999. *The Cathedral & the Bazaar*. O'Reilly.

Ivan Sag, Timothy Baldwin, Francis Bond, Ann Copestake, and Dan Flickinger. 2002. Multiword expressions: A pain in the neck for NLP. In Alexander Gelbuk, editor, *Computational Linguistics and Intelligent Text Processing: Third International Conference: CICLing-2002*, pages 1–15. Springer-Verlag, Hiedelberg/Berlin.

Singapore Tourist Board. 2012. Your Singapore. Online: `http://www.yoursingapore.com`. [Accessed 2012].

Liling Tan and Francis Bond. 2012. Building and annotating the linguistically diverse NTU-MC (NTU-multilingual corpus). *International Journal of Asian Language Processing*, 22(4):161–174.

Lucy Vanderwende and Aral Menezes. 2005. The empirical revolution in natural language processing. In *4th International Conference on Natural Language Processing (ICON 2005)*, pages 7–8. (Invited Talk).

Kefei Wang. 2012. On the design and construction of the super-large-scale China English-Chinese parallel corpus (CECPC) (中国英汉平行语料库的设计与研制). *Foreign Languages in China (中国外语)*, pages 23–27.

Shan Wang and Francis Bond. 2013. Building a Chinese wordnet: Starting from core synsets. In *Proceedings of the 11th Workshop on Asian Language Resources*. Nagoya.

Fei Xia. 2000. The segmentation guidelines for the Penn Chinese Treebank (3.0). Technical Report IRCS-00-06, University of Pennsylvania Institute for Research in Cognitive Science.

Renjie Xu, Zhiqiang Gao, Yuzhong Qu, and Zhisheng Huang. 2008. An integrated approach for automatic construction of bilingual Chinese-English WordNet. In *3rd Asian Semantic Web Conference (ASWC 2008)*, pages 302–341.

# "PolNet - Polish WordNet" project: PolNet 2.0 - a short description of the release

**Zygmunt Vetulani**
Adam Mickiewicz University
Poznań, Poland
vetulani@amu.edu.pl

**Bartłomiej Kochanowski**
Adam Mickiewicz University
Poznań, Poland
bartlomiej.kochanowski@amu.edu.pl

## Abstract

In December 2011/January 2012 we have released the main deliverable of the project "PolNet - Polish WordNet". It was first presented and distributed (as PolNet 1.0) at the 5th Language and Technology Conference in Poznań (2011) and (informally, with kind permission of the organizers) distributed during the Global Wordnet Conference in Matsue, Japan, in January 2012. We intend to present to the participants of the GWC 2014 the characteristics of the new, extended release of PolNet.

## 1 Introduction

In 1985 G. Miller with collaborators at the Princeton University initiated a novel method of systematizing semantic grammatical knowledge on the basis of the concepts of synonymy and hyperonymy. He proposed to organize a lexicon in the form of a lexical database (WordNet): a hierarchical network of a set of synonyms. The project appeared to be *generic* and inspired many followers working for various languages. Its practical value was recognized by language industries and practical computer science. In particular, lexical bases similar to Princeton WordNet (PWN) were used as ontologies useful in the AI oriented research.

## 2 Lexicon-grammar, VerbNet, FrameNet

The initial WordNet was organized as a set of equivalence classes with respect to the synonymy relation. For these classes, called *synsets*, other relations were considered, like hypernymy, meronymy, holonymy etc. Within the initial approach focusing on the meaning of words, only root forms of words were stored with no morphological or morphosyntactical information. Bringing this kind of information to wordnet is an idea which has as its forerunner the *lexicon-grammar* approach developed since the early 1970s (until late 1990s) by Maurice Gross (Gross, 1994) inspired by the works of Zellig S. Harris. Gross considered *elementary sentence* as a "minimal unit of sense" and the sense of a word as determined by the minimal sentences containing this word. This led to the concept of syntactic lexicon where grammatical information (syntactic) is contained in the lexical entries (in form of syntactic and semantic requirements /valences/ of predicative words). At about the same period (1980-1992), the similar ideas of Polański led to the monumental description of Polish verbs ("Syntactic-generative Dictionary of Polish Verbs" (Polański, 1992)). These works preceded (and perhaps even inspired) the future works in the FrameNet (Fillmore et al., 2002) and VerbNet (Palmer, 2009) projects which ware natural extensions of the initial WordNet. Independently from Polański, but following the same lines and applying refined Levis' verb classes, Martha Palmers from the University of Colorado Boulder defined a lexical database where verbs were grouped according shared meaning and similar syntactic behavior (Palmer et al., 2005). These verb classes are "completely described by thematic roles, selectional restrictions on the arguments, and frames consisting of a syntactic description and semantic predicates with a temporal function". VerbNet is sometimes compared to FrameNet, a kind of dictionary of word senses with annotated examples that show the meaning and usage. This project was initiated By Charles J. Fillmore in Berkeley (1997) and based on its concepts of frame semantics and semantic roles. Both VerbNet and FrameNet were applied in Artificial Intelligence (AI) projects concerning semantic processing of texts or machine question answering.

## 3 "PolNet - Polish WordNet" project

The project "PolNet - Polish WordNet" started in 2006. It was conceived in order to fill the technological gap consisting in the lack of a digital lexical database for the Polish.[1] The development algorithm (Vetulani et al., 2007) was based on several traditional dictionaries of the Polish language (in particular (Szymczak, 1978) and (Dubisz 2006)) and a general wordnet development tool which was the DEBVisDic platform (Pala et al, 2007).

The methodology we have applied to the development of PolNet followed the so called "merge model". PolNet was built from scratch involving intensive and large scale manual lexicographers' work. At the early stage of development we decided to abstain from any automatic synset generation and to reuse the existing knowledge about Polish accumulated by the past generations of linguists and lexicographers in lexicons, dictionaries and grammars.

The team - formed of computer scientists and lexicographers familiar with computer technologies explored first of all traditional resources (dictionaries). This work was inspired by and benefited from the methodology and tools of the EuroWordNet and Balkanet projects. In particular, production of synsets was supported by the VisDic and DEBVisDic systems generously made accessible for PolNet development by Karel Pala from the Masaryk University in Brno (Czech Rep.). PolNet 1.0 was made public available in November 2011. This first completed distribution was reduced to nouns and simple verbs (Vetulani and Obrębski, 2010).

The PolNet 1.0 release consisted of nominal and verbal synsets. Both the nominal and verbal parts were set up on the basis of frequency observed in the corpus (the IPI PAN corpus was used; cf. (Przepiórkowski, 2004)). The only systematic exception from this rule was made in order to be able to test PolNet in a real-scale application. This was the POLINT-112-SMS system, an application in the field of public security and PolNet, in which the latter one served as the ontology. It appeared necessary to extend the lexical coverage in the way to make PolNet complete with respect to the *a priori* chosen domain of public security at football stadiums. In the present development we continue on the ground of the frequent-concepts-first rule.

The noun part of the PolNet 1.0 consisted of the noun synsets partially ordered by the hyponymy/hyperonymy relation and the verb part was organized by the predicate-argument relationship connecting the verb synsets with the noun synsets. In the present extension (from PolNet 1.0 to PolNet 2.0) we will continue to apply this organization.

The main statistics of the PolNet 1.0 were as follows:

- Nouns: 11,700 synsets (12,000 nouns, 20,300 word+meaning pairs)
- Verbs: 1,500 synsets (900 verbs, 2,900 word+meaning pairs)

## 4 Extension motivations, reasons and policy

Although the usefulness of PolNet 1.0 as lexical ontology was confirmed through practical applications, we concluded the necessity of further extensions and improvements. The most fundamental decision was to consider as priority the development of the verbal component, before enlargement *ad infinitum* of the noun part. This decision was motivated by the practical needs of high quality, linguistically sound tools for advanced NLP, including text understanding, useful in Question Answering (QA), Machine Translation (MT) and other AI applications involving language competence modeling. We consider the extension to PolNet 2.0 described here as an important step towards a lexicon-grammar of Polish directly useful in systems development.

## 5 From PolNet 1.0 to PolNet 2.0

The present stage of the "PolNet - Polish WordNet" project consists of development from PolNet 1.0 to PolNet 2.0. The main task of this stage is to extend substantially the verbal component with the inclusion of concepts (synsets) represented (in many cases uniquely) by compound construction in form of verb-noun collocations (by verb-noun collocations we mean compound verbal structures made of a support verb and a predicative noun). This extension brought (until now) to PolNet some 1200 new

[1] PolNet shouldn't be confused with another wordnet for Polish (plWordNet) developed by Piasecki and others within a totally different methodology whose conception is based on automatic acquisition of synsets and relations.

verb synsets corresponding to 600 predicative nouns, some of those synsets being closely related to the already existing verb synsets of the PolNet 1.0.

The verb-noun collocation imported to PolNet come from the "Syntactic dictionary of verb-noun collocations in Polish" compiled by Grażyna Vetulani (Vetulani, G. 2000 and 2012).[2] See the Example 1 in Table 1 below.

| |
|---|
| Example 1. A fragment of the entry describing the predicative noun "pomoc" (compiled from a traditional dictionary):<br><br>pomoc, f/ *[help]*<br>udzielać(Gen)/N1(Dat),<br>*"udzielać komuś pomocy" [to help](imperfective)*<br>udzielić(Gen)/N1(Dat),<br>*"udzielić komuś pomocy" [to help](perfective)*<br>pospieszyć na(Acc)/N1(Dat)<br>*"pospieszyć komuś na pomoc"*<br>pospieszyć z(Instr)/N1(Dat)<br>*"pospieszyć z pomocą ofierze wypadku"*<br>*[to help a victim]*<br>przyjść z(Instr)/N1(Dat)<br>*"przyjść z pomocą choremu"*<br>*[to help sb who is ill]*<br>przyjść na(Acc)/N1(Dat)<br>*"przyjść na pomoc oblężonemu miastu"*<br>*[to bring help to a surrounded town]*<br><br>(N1(Dat) – complement in the dative case) |

**Table 1.** Dictionary of verb-noun collocations (fragment)

Adding collocations to PolNet was not trivial because of specific syntactic phenomena related with collocations in Polish (systematic, although not general, change of syntactic requirements between the compound verb (verb-noun collocation) and its one-word synonym is required).

In PolNet, as in other wordnets, lexical units are grouped into synsets on the basis of the relation of synonymy. In opposition to nouns, where the interest is mainly in the hierarchical relations (hyperonymy/hyponymy) between concepts (represented by synsets) - for verbs the main interest is in relating verbal synsets (representing predicative concepts) to noun synsets (representing general concepts) in order to show what are the semantic connectivity constraints corresponding to the particular argument positions. Inclusion of this information (combined with morphosyntactic constraints) gives PolNet the status of a lexicon grammar. This approach imposes granularity restrictions on verbal synsets and more exactly on the synonymy relation.

Synonymous are solely such verb+meaning pairs in which the same semantic roles take as value the same concepts (this condition is necessary but not sufficient). In particular, the valency structure of a verb is one of the formal indices of the meaning (it is so that all members of a given sysnset share the valency structure). This permits to formal encoding of valency structure as a property of a synset.

Semantic roles as relations connecting noun synsets to verb synsets allow the extended PolNet to be considered as a situational semantics network of concepts.

Indeed, as it is often admitted, verb synsets may be considered as representing situations (events, states), whereas semantic roles (Agent, Patient, Beneficent,...) provide information on the ontological nature of various actors participating, actively or passively, in this situation (event, state). Abstract roles (Manner, Time,...) refer to concepts which position the situation (event, state) in time, space and possibly also with respect to some abstract, qualitative landmarks.

Formally, the semantic roles are functions (in mathematical sense) associated to the argument positions in the syntactic pattern(s) corresponding to synsets. The values of these functions are ontology concepts (here in form of noun synsets). For many verbs, the semantic role BENEFICENT takes as its value the concept representing the set of all humans (which are then considered as potential addresses of the situation effects).

In the project we use a well described set of semantic roles, adapted from works of Fillmore and later of Palmer (Fillmore 1977, Palmer 2009).

In the Example 2 in Table 2 below we may observe several inter-synsets relations which are used to express semantic requirements of the predicate (verb).

For example the "Semantic_role: [Action]" which connects the noun synset "{czynność:1}" *[activity]* to the verb synset "{pomóc:1, pomagać:1, udzielić pomocy:1, udzielać pomocy:1}" *[to help]*.tell us that the verb opens

[2] Over 14,300 collocations are described (and published) until now but this work is in progress.

an argument which must be filled by a term referring to some activity. Similarly, the relation "Semantic role [Benef]" indicates what kinds of entities may benefit of somebody's assistance.

Example 2. DEBVisDic presentation of a PolNet synset containing both simple verbs and collocations(simplified):

POS: v ID: 3441

Synonyms: {pomóc:1, pomagać:1, **udzielić pomocy**:1, **udzielać pomocy:1**} *(to help)*

Definition: "wziąć (brać) udział w pracy jakiejś osoby (zwykle razem z nią), aby ułatwić jej tę pracę"
*("to participate in sb's work in order to help him/her")*

VALENCY:
- Agent(N)_Benef(D)
- Agent(N)_Benef(D) Action('w'+NA(L))
- Agent(N)_Benef(D) Manner
- Agent(N)_Benef(D) Action('w'+NA(L)) Manner

Usage: Agent(N)_Benef(D); "Pomogłam jej." *(I helped her)*
Usage: Agent(N)_Benef(D) Action('w'+NA(L)); "Pomogłam jej w robieniu lekcji." *(I helped her in doing homework)*
Usage: Agent(N)_Benef(D) Manner Action('w'+NA(L)); "Chętnie udzieliłąm jej pomocy w lekcjach." *(I helped her willingly doing her homework)*
Usage: Agent(N)_Benef(D) Manner; "Chętnie jej pomagałam." *(I used to help her willingly)*

Semantic_role: [Agent] {człek:1, człowiek:1, homo sapiens:1, istota ludzka:1, zwierzę:2, jednostka:1, łepek:3, łebek:3, łeb:5, głowa:8, osoba:1, twarz:2, umysł:2, dusza:3} *({man:1,...,animal:2,...})*
Semantic_role: [Benef] {człek:1, człowiek:1, homo sapiens:1, istota ludzka:1, zwierzę:2, jednostka:1, łepek:3, łebek:3, łeb:5, głowa:8, osoba:1, twarz:2, umysł:2, dusza:3} *({man:1,...,animal:2,...})*
Semantic_role: [Action] {czynność:1} *({activity:1})*
Semantic_role: [Manner] {CECHA_ADVERB_JAKOŚĆ:1} *(qualitative adverbial)*

**Table 2.** A PolNet 2.0 synset

## 6 Problems

In the case of Polish, our decision to make wordnet a type of lexicon-grammar through the inclusion of possibly all relevant grammatical information, appeared to be challenging in case of verb-noun collocations. This is because the traditional relation of synonymy is not invariant with respect to the syntactic requirements of predicative words. For example the simple word "nakarmić" and its synonym in form of the collocation "dać jeść" both correspond to the English "to feed". At the same time they do not have the same syntactic requirements, as "nakarmić" requires a complement in the accusative, whereas "dać jeść" - in the dative. Therefore, they should be put into different synsets of PolNet. This is because the synset of PolNet are intended to contain complete syntactic and semantic information about words, the same for all synset members.

In PolNet 2.0 we have applied the solution, which seems optimal from the practical (language engineering) point of view - to store them in separate synsets related by the transformational relation OBJECT_TRANS (ACC,DAT) which describes the difference of their syntactic properties.

## 7 Further research plans

"PolNet - Polish WordNet" project is in progress, and it will continue to be for the foreseeable future. The total number of verb-noun collocations is estimated to be largely more than 20 000 items. The set of 14,341 described until now was considered in order to select the most frequently used in texts and to include them in the first step of enlargement. We intend to continue this extension at least through 2014. In parallel to our present main priority, we continue work on further steps of the PolNet project in particular its alignment to the upper ontology SUMO, as well as on the extension of the net to more basic terms: nouns, verbs and collocations. The long term plan is to transform PolNet into a complete lexicon grammar of Polish integrating all grammatical information necessary (and sufficient) for AI and Language Engineering (LE) applications.

## Acknowledgements

This work was done within the National Program for Humanities (grant 0022/FNiTP/H11/80/2011 managed by Grażyna Vetulani).

## References

Stanisław Dubisz (ed.), 2006. *Uniwersalny słownik języka polskiego PWN, (Universal dictionary of Polish,* in Polish), 2nd edition, Wydawnictwo Naukowe PWN. Warszawa, Poland.

Maurice Gross, 1994. Constructing Lexicon-Grammars. In: Beryl T. Sue Atkins, Antonio Zampolli (eds.) *Computational Approaches to the Lexicon*, Oxford University Press. Oxford, UK, pp. 213–263.

Charles J. Fillmore, Collin F. Baker, Hiroaki Sato, 2002. The FrameNet Database and Software Tools. In: *Proceedings of the Third International Conference on Language Resources and Evaluation.* Vol. IV. LREC: Las Palmas.

Charles J. Fillmore, 1977. *The need for a frame semantics in linguistics. Statistical Methods in Linguistics*. Ed. Hans Karlgren. Scriptor

George A. Miller, 1995. WordNet: A Lexical Database for English. *Communications of the ACM* Vol. 38, (No. 11): 39–41.

Karel Pala, Ales Horák, Adam Rambousek, Zygmunt Vetulani, Paweł Konieczka, Jacek Marciniak, Tomasz Obrębski, Paweł Rzepecki , Justyna Walkowska, 2007. DEB Platform tools for effective development of WordNets in application to PolNet. In: Zygmunt Vetulani (ed.) *Proceedings of the 3rd Language and Technology Conference: Human Language Technologies as a Challenge for Computer Science and Linguistics*, October 5-7, 2007, Wyd. Poznańskie. Poznań, Poland, pp. 514–518.

Martha Palmer, Paul Kingsbury, Dan Gildea, 2005. The Proposition Bank: An Annotated Corpus of Semantic Roles. *Computational Linguistics* 31 (1): 71–106.

Martha Palmer, 2009. Semlink: Linking PropBank, VerbNet and FrameNet. In ***Proceedings of the*** *Generative Lexicon Conference.* Sept. 2009. GenLex: Pisa, Italy.

Kazimierz Polański (ed.), 1992. *Słownik syntaktyczno - generatywny czasowników polskich* vol. I-IV, Ossolineum, Wrocław,1980-1990, vol. V, Kraków: Instytut Języka Polskiego PAN.

Adam Przepiórkowski, 2004. *Korpus IPI PAN. Wersja wstępna (The IPI PAN CORPUS: Preliminary version).* IPI PAN, Warszawa, Poland.

Mieczysław Szymczak (ed.), 1978. *Słownik języka polskiego.* PWN (Dictionary of Polish Language; in Polish).

Grażyna Vetulani, 2000. *Rzeczowniki predykatywne języka polskiego. W kierunku syntaktycznego słownika rzeczowników predykatywnych. (In Polish).* Wyd. Nauk. UAM. Poznań, Poland.

Grażyna Vetulani, 2012. *Kolokacje werbo-nominalne jako samodzielne jednostki języka. Syntaktyczny słownik kolokacji werbo-nominalnych języka polskiego na potrzeby zastosowań informatycznych. Część I.* (In Polish). Wyd. Nauk. UAM. Poznań, Poland.

Zygmunt Vetulani, 2012. Wordnet Based Lexicon Grammar for Polish. In *Proceedings of the Eith International Conference on Language Resources and Evaluation (LREC 2012),* May 23-25, 2012. Istanbul, Turkey, (Proceedings), ELRA: Paris, France, pp. 1645–1649.

Zygmunt Vetulani, Tomasz Obrębski, 2010. Resources for Extending the PolNet-Polish WordNet with a Verbal Component. In: Bhattacharyya, Pushpak, Fellbaum, Christiane, Vossen, Piek (eds.) *Principles, Construction and Application of Multilingual Wordnets. Proceedings of the 5th Global Wordnet Conference.* Narosa Publishing House: New Delhi, Chennai, Mumbai, Kolkata, pp. 325–330.

Zygmunt Vetulani, Grażyna Vetulani (in print): Through Wordnet to Lexicon Grammar. In: Fryni Kakoyianni Doa (Ed.). *Penser le lexique-grammaire : perspectives actuelles*, Editions Honoré Champion. Paris, France.

Zygmunt Vetulani, Justyna Walkowska, Tomasz Obrębski, Paweł Konieczka, Paweł Rzepecki, Jacek Marciniak, 2007. PolNet - Polish WordNet project algorithm, in: Z. Vetulani (ed.) *Proceedings of the 3rd Language and Technology Conference: Human Language Technologies as a Challenge for Computer Science and Linguistics, October 5-7, 2005,* Wyd. Poznańskie, Poznań, Poland, pp. 172–176.

## Keyword Index

# Author Index